THE SALT OF COMMON LIFE

THE SALT OF COMMON LIFE

INDIVIDUALITY AND CHOICE IN THE MEDIEVAL TOWN, COUNTRYSIDE, AND CHURCH

ESSAYS PRESENTED TO J. AMBROSE RAFTIS

Edited by

Edwin Brezette DeWindt

SMC XXXVI

Medieval Institute Publications

WESTERN MICHIGAN UNIVERSITY

Kalamazoo, Michigan—1995

Library of Congress Cataloging-in-Publication Data

The Salt of common life : individuality and choice in the medieval town, countryside, and church : essays presented to J. Ambrose Raftis / edited by Edwin Brezette DeWindt.

p. cm. -- (Studies in medieval culture ; 36)
Includes bibliographical references.
ISBN 1-879288-46-X (casebound : alk. paper). -- ISBN 1-879288-47-8 (softbound : alk. paper)
1. England--Rural conditions. 2. England--Economic conditions--1066-1485. 3. England--Social conditions--1066-1485. I. Raftis, J. A. (James Ambrose), 1922- . II. DeWindt, Edwin Brezette. III. Series.
CB351.S83 vol. 36
[HN398.E5]
307.72'0942--dc20 95-30224
CIP

Printed in the United States of America

Cover design by Linda K. Judy

“Individuality is the salt of common life.”

—*Henry van Dyke*

CONTENTS

INTRODUCTION

The essays in this volume have been produced to honor J. Ambrose Raftis on the occasion of his seventieth birthday. For over 35 years, as both a teacher and scholar at the Pontifical Institute of Mediaeval Studies, Toronto, Ambrose Raftis has exercised a profound influence on the shape and direction of the social and economic history of the medieval English countryside. Initially trained in the social sciences—particularly political science and economics, which culminated in 1951 in a doctorate in social sciences from Laval University—in 1954 he obtained a Ph.D. in history from Cambridge University, publishing his thesis in 1957 as *The Estates of Ramsey Abbey.*[1] It was a book whose subtitle—*A Study in Economic Growth and Organization*—served as a reminder of its author's first career and which drew upon that background by employing insights and concepts from modern economic theory to examine the changing economic fortunes of the abbey's estates from the tenth to the sixteenth centuries. It was also the beginning of what was to become an ongoing identification and involvement with the economy and society of the Middle Ages.

In 1964 a second book was published: *Tenure and Mobility.*[2] Again, the subtitle was significant: *Studies in the Social History of the Mediaeval English Village.* From the world of landlords and estate management, the focus of attention had shifted to the

---

[1]*The Estates of Ramsey Abbey: A Study in Economic Growth and Organization* (Toronto, 1957).

[2]*Tenure and Mobility: Studies in the Social History of the Mediaeval English Village* (Toronto, 1964).

dimly-perceived world of the medieval English peasant. Inspired by the pioneering labors of Frederic William Maitland[3] and George Caspar Homans,[4] and stimulated by the researches of modern and contemporary social and cultural anthropologists[5] and historians,[6] Ambrose Raftis examined the relationship of the peasant family to the customary tenement as well as the place of migration in the medieval English countryside, basing his inquiries on the village court roll. In subsequent years a court roll-focused body of studies would take shape, resulting in further publications by Raftis and a growing body of his students, emphasizing the ubiquity and centrality of the smallhold in peasant life, the problems of intravillage violence, the realities of a peasant land market, the behavior and activities of peasant elites, the role of women in village society, local and regional markets and marketing, village governmental structures, and even the place of the peasantry in the royal justice system.[7] It

---

[3]See, e.g., Maitland, ed., *Select Pleas in Manorial and Other Seignorial Courts*, Selden Society, vol. 2 (1888), and F. W. Maitland and W. Paley Baildon, eds., *The Court Baron, Being Precedents for Use in Seignorial and Other Local Courts, Together with Select Pleas from the Bishop of Ely's Court of Littleport*, Selden Society, vol. 4 (1891).

[4]See Homans, *English Villagers of the Thirteenth Century* (Cambridge, Mass., 1941; repr. New York, 1960).

[5]See, e.g., A. R. Radcliffe-Brown, *Structure and Function in Primitive Society: Essays and Addresses* (Chicago, 1958); Robert Redfield, *The Little Community* and *Peasant Society and Culture* (Chicago, 1960); Ruth Benedict, *Patterns of Culture* (New York, 1934); Walter Firey, *Man, Mind, and Land: A Theory of Resource Use* (Glencoe, Ill., 1960); Robert K. Merton, *Social Theory and Social Structure*, rev. and enl. ed. (Glencoe, Ill., 1957).

[6]Such as (and in no particular order), Marc Bloch, Rodney H. Hilton, Sylvia L. Thrupp, Michael M. Postan, Georges Duby, Josiah Cox Russell, Joan Thirsk, Joan Wake, Helen Cam.

[7]See, for e.g., J. Ambrose Raftis, "Peasant Mobility and Freedom in Medieval England," *Canadian Historical Association Report* (1965); idem, "Social Structures in Five East Midland Villages," *Economic History Review*, 2nd ser., 18 (1965); idem, "The Concentration of Responsibility in Five Villages," *Mediaeval Studies* 28 (1966); idem, "Changes in an English Village after the Black Death," *Mediaeval Studies* 29 (1967); idem, *Warboys: Two Hundred Years in the Life of*

is an ongoing corpus of scholarly inquiry that ranges widely over the medieval English historical landscape, and it deliberately defies neat categorization, despite persistent efforts on the part

---

an English Mediaeval Village (Toronto, 1974); idem, *Assart Data and Land Values: Two Studies in the East Midlands, 1200–1350* (Toronto, 1974); J. Ambrose Raftis and Mary Patricia Hogan, eds., *Early Huntingdonshire Lay Subsidy Rolls* (Toronto, 1967); Edwin B. DeWindt, *Land and People in Holywell-cum-Needingworth: Structures of Tenure and Patterns of Social Organization in an East Midlands Village, 1252–1457* (Toronto, 1972); idem, *The Liber Gersumarum of Ramsey Abbey: A Calendar and Index of B.L. Harley MS 445* (Toronto, 1976); idem, ed. and trans., *The Court Rolls of Ramsey, Hepmangrove, and Bury, 1268–1600* (Toronto, 1990); Anne R. DeWindt and Edwin B. DeWindt, eds., *Royal Justice and the Mediaeval English Countryside: The Huntingdonshire Eyre of 1286, the Ramsey Abbey Banlieu Court of 1287, and the Assizes of 1287–88*, 2 vols. (Toronto, 1981); Anne Reiber DeWindt, "Peasant Power Structures in Fourteenth-Century King's Ripton," *Mediaeval Studies* 38 (1976); eadem, "A Peasant Land Market and Its Participants: King's Ripton 1280–1400," *Midland History* 4/3–4 (1978); eadem, "Redefining the Peasant Community in Medieval England: The Regional Perspective," *Journal of British Studies* 26/2 (Apr. 1987); eadem, "Local Government in a Small Town: A Medieval Leet Jury and Its Constituents," *Albion* 23/4 (Winter 1991); Edward Britton, *The Community of the Vill: A Study in the History of the Family and Village Life in Fourteenth-Century England* (Toronto, 1977); Mary Patricia Hogan, "Medieval Villany: A Study in the Meaning and Control of Crime in an English Village," *Studies in Medieval and Renaissance History* 17 (1981); eadem, "The Labor of Their Days: Work in the Medieval Village," *Studies in Medieval and Renaissance History*, n.s., 8 (1986); Judith M. Bennett, "Spouses, Siblings and Surnames: Reconstructing Families from Medieval Village Court Rolls," *Journal of British Studies* 23 (1983); eadem, *Women in the Medieval English Countryside: Gender and Household in Brigstock before the Plague* (Oxford, 1987); eadem, "The Village Ale-Wife: Women and Brewing in Fourteenth-Century England," in Barbara A. Hanawalt, ed., *Women and Work in Preindustrial Europe* (Bloomington, 1986); eadem, "Public Power and Authority in the Medieval English Countryside," in Mary Erler and Maryanne Kowaleski, eds., *Women and Power in the Middle Ages* (Athens, Ga., 1988); eadem, "Conviviality and Charity in Medieval and Early Modern England," *Past and Present* 134 (Feb. 1992); eadem, "Medieval Women, Modern Women: Across the Great Divide," in David Aers, ed., *Culture and History, 1350–1600: Essays on English Communities, Identities, and Writing* (London, 1992); Sherri Olson, "Jurors of the Village Court: Local Leadership before and after the Plague in Ellington, Huntingdonshire," *Journal of British Studies* 30 (July 1991); Maryanne Kowaleski, "Women's Work in a Market Town: Exeter in the Late Fourteenth Century," in Hanawalt, ed., *Women and Work in Preindustrial Europe*; Ellen Wedemeyer Moore, *The Fairs of Medieval England: An Introductory Study* (Toronto, 1985).

of some to label it "the Toronto School."[8]

Although initially directed towards the study of the medieval village community, very few of the men and women who received professional training under Professor Raftis's direction have remained wedded to that original orientation. If anything unites them at all, it is a fundamental respect for their documentary sources and a conviction that the court roll occupies a significant place in any attempt to penetrate into the realities of everyday life in the past. That is what we have all inherited from Ambrose Raftis: not *agenda*, but an attitude, coupled with a conviction that our work—whatever its object or direction—is worth doing. Beyond that simple, shared commitment, the historians trained under Ambrose Raftis have gone off in a number of directions: to the study of the town (both big and small), to issues of gender, both past and present, and to questions of historiography. Even Ambrose Raftis himself has not felt constrained to stay on the same path of research. The decade of the 1980s—during which he served as President of the Pontifical Institute of Mediaeval Studies—saw his attention turn to the urban community and the persistent, nagging problem of change, which resulted in two books on the town of Godmanchester.[9] And, as this volume is being prepared, he is already embarked on a re-examination of the problem of capital in the medieval English countryside.

---

[8]The appellation was first coined by Prof. Zvi Razi of Tel Aviv and has subsequently taken on a life of its own that seems impervious even to silver bullets and garlic. See Razi, "The Toronto School's Reconstitution of Medieval Peasant Society: A Critical View," *Past and Present* 85 (1979); see also the same author's "Family, Land and Village Community in Later Medieval England," *Past and Present* 93 (1981), and *Life, Marriage, and Death in a Medieval Parish: Economy, Society, and Demography in Halesowen, 1270–1400* (Cambridge, 1980) for extended, critical discussion of the work of Raftis and his colleagues.

[9]*A Small Town in Late Medieval England: Godmanchester, 1278–1400* (Toronto, 1982) and *Early Tudor Godmanchester: Survivals and New Arrivals* (Toronto, 1989).

The essays collected in this volume, therefore, not only pay tribute to a man and his work; in the variety of authors—half of them former students, the other half colleagues from both sides of the Atlantic—and in their own wide-ranging objects and perspectives, they illustrate the multiplicity of interests that has marked the academic career of Ambrose Raftis since his days as an undergraduate and his subsequent ordination as a priest in the Congregation of Saint Basil in 1948. If he has not concentrated on one topic during all those years, there is no reason for a collection of essays in his honor to do so. Nevertheless, despite the broad spectrum of subjects covered in the following pages, there are some uniting elements, however unconscious. First of all, and obviously, they all address the Middle Ages, with Dr. Kathleen Biddick being perhaps the most "Raftisian" of all the contributors, by challenging us to reconsider the very terms and concepts we—and the culture we share—so blithely employ on a regular basis. Some of the authors enter onto paths long traveled but uncover further extensions or unsuspected forks in the road. Thus, Dr. Ian Blanchard takes up the question of post-plague changes in village society and, in the context of one community in the sixteenth century, is able not only to document significant social change but also give it more precise definition, at the same time he suggests a new perspective on the very nature of a community at the end of the Middle Ages. Dr. Maryanne Kowaleski, in her examination of the local Exeter grain trade, provides a profile of the participants in the feeding of that city and emphasizes the substantial role played by the peasant producer. Dr. Bruce M. S. Campbell, although he focuses attention on the county of Norfolk, provides a powerful and challenging demonstration of the importance of pastoral husbandry in the medieval English economy as a whole. Dr. Anne Reiber DeWindt, in exploring the question of economic development in the small market town of Ramsey from the thirteenth to the sixteenth century, compels us to examine seriously the extent to which the very nature of the sources over time colors and affects our framing of questions and hypotheses, at the same time calling into doubt the assumption that occupational diversity and specialization are necessarily signs of economic advancement. Dr. Sherri Olson, building upon earlier attempts at family reconstruction, emphasizes the extent to which individual variety is a hallmark of village family histories, providing concrete examples of differing types of family groups in Ellington over the late Middle Ages.

Other contributors direct their attention to paths less well known. Dr. Ellen Wedemeyer Moore demonstrates that the meaning of the term *poverty* in the medieval court roll is far from obvious. Dr. James Masschaele, working with the records of the royal exchequer, throws open a window onto the multi-faceted world of the London merchant and at the same time raises provocative questions about that society's understanding of the term *capital*. David N. Hall, temporarily setting aside his long-term involvement with establishing the patterns of open-field agriculture in the Midlands, supplies specific details on the forging of modest lay estate complexes in two Northamptonshire manors. Dr. Judith M. Bennett provides an exhaustive and at the same time sobering examination of the London Brewers' gild and especially of the place of women in it in the fifteenth century. Drs. Robert Tittler and Alexandra F. Johnston give us a dazzling introduction to the London criminal underworld at the beginning of the seventeenth century, and Dr. Richard C. Hoffmann not only reminds us of the importance of fish and fishing in the life of the countryside but, just as important, also establishes clearly that it was not only in England that ordinary men and women had lives capable of being recaptured by the historian. Finally, two scholars travel down a road only hinted at in the work of Ambrose Raftis: the clergy. Dr. Denis Brearley gives us a short but tantalizing picture of a rural vicar in the early sixteenth century, while Dr. F. Donald Logan brings us back to the place where it all began—Ramsey Abbey—with a detailed and moving account of the Dissolution and subsequent fates of the monks.

As mentioned earlier, although disparate in content and approaches, the essays in this volume are united, and by more than their simply being devoted to medieval subjects. Throughout the career of Ambrose Raftis two themes or convictions have been in evidence: a belief in the fundamental individuality of medieval English men and women, and a belief in their ability to make choices. However much environment, custom, social structure, even biology, might constrain or otherwise affect personal behavior, the men and women who appear in the often laconic entries of medieval court rolls were distinctive, one-of-a-kind persons, and their actions—their deeds and their misdeeds, their triumphs and their failures, their fortunes and their follies—were often the result of choices they had made. In this, the essays of this volume are united. The pastoral farmers of Norfolk, the included and restricted women of the London Brewers' gild, the feeders of Exeter, the paupers of St. Ives, the craftsmen and jurors of Ramsey, the merchants of London, the criminals of the capital and their pursuers, the families of Ellington, the families and affinities of Chewton, the knights of Northamptonshire, the fishermen of Tegernsee, the vicar of Fillongley, the ex-monks of Ramsey, and even the men and women who still dream about Robin Hood—all are distinctive men and women, knowable and known, who made choices.

That is the medieval world of J. Ambrose Raftis, and it is that world, and that vision, that this book honors.

Edwin Brezette DeWindt
The Feast of St. Hillary, 1993

THE GRAIN TRADE IN FOURTEENTH-CENTURY EXETER[1]

Maryanne Kowaleski

Grain was the most vital element of the human diet in the Middle Ages, when it constituted roughly 60 per cent to 75 per cent of the average English adult's caloric intake.[2] Consumed largely in the form of ale, bread, and pottage, grain was also an important source of animal fodder (usually oats). Because of grain's central role in the human and animal diet, the trade that carried this essential foodstuff from producer to consumer was particularly sensitive to changes in the size and wealth of the population; demand more than supply dictated developments

---

[1]Unless noted otherwise, all manuscripts cited here are in the Devon Record Office. The following abbreviations are employed: MCR = Exeter Mayor's Court Rolls; MT = Exeter Mayor's Tourn (market court) (NQ = North Quarter Tourn; SQ = South Quarter Tourn; EQ = East Quarter Tourn; WQ = West Quarter Tourn); PCA = Exeter Local Port Customs Accounts; PCR = Exeter Provosts' Court Rolls; BL = British Library; ECL = Exeter Cathedral Library, D&C = Dean and Chapter; PRO = Public Record Office; *CFR* = *Calendar of Fine Rolls*, 22 vols. (London, 1911–63); *CCR* = *Calendar of Close Rolls*, 47 vols. (London, 1892–63); *CPR* = *Calendar of Patent Rolls*, 48 vols. (London, 1894–1916); *TDA* = *Transactions of the Devonshire Association*. The author would like to thank Judith Bennett, Harold Fox, Derek Keene, and Richard Unger for their comments on earlier versions of this paper.

[2]Bruce M. S. Campbell, James A. Galloway, Derek Keene, and Margaret Murphy, *A Medieval Capital and Its Grain Supply: Agrarian Production and Distribution in the London Region, c. 1300* (London, 1993), p. 33 (hereafter, *Medieval Capital*). For the importance of grain in the medieval diet see also Christopher Dyer, *Standards of Living in the Later Middle Ages: Social Change in England c. 1200–1520* (Cambridge, 1989), pp. 55–58, 151–60.

in this trade. The biggest changes occurred after the Black Death in 1348–49, when population fell dramatically,[3] although wartime disruptions of trade routes during the Hundred Years War also had some effect. This essay examines developments in the grain trade over the course of the fourteenth century by focusing on the provincial town of Exeter in Devon. Particularly noticeable were changes in the maritime commerce in grain, a transformation that can be studied in some detail thanks to the survival of an excellent series of local port customs accounts for Exeter.[4] Developments in the retail trade were less marked and are here discussed mainly for the late fourteenth century, when prosopographical analysis facilitates identification of buyers and sellers of grain. This analysis, combined with evidence found in the large number of surviving court rolls for medieval Exeter, sheds light on the status, gender, occupation, geographic residence, and commercial interests of those involved in the grain trade.

Although small by some standards, Exeter was the largest borough in the four counties of southwestern England. In 1377 its population was around 3,100; before the Black Death it was certainly larger, reaching a population of perhaps 4,000 or 5,000 around 1300.[5] Exeter's prominence was reflected in its

---

[3]Most historians believe that the Black Death reduced the population of medieval England by one-third to one-half; see John Hatcher, *Plague, Population, and the English Economy, 1348–1530* (London, 1977).

[4]Annual local port customs accounts for Exeter survive for almost 70 per cent of the fourteenth century and represent the finest series of extant local customs for medieval England. Unlike most local accounts, the Exeter accounts list all incoming coastal and overseas cargoes and their owners, whether customed or not. The earlier accounts are printed in Maryanne Kowaleski, ed., *The Local Customs Accounts of the Port of Exeter, 1266–1321*, Devon and Cornwall Record Society, n.s., vol. 36 (1993); the remaining accounts (PCA) are in manuscript.

[5]For this and the following see Maryanne Kowaleski, *Local Markets and Regional Trade in Medieval Exeter* (Cambridge, 1995); the population in 1377 (based on the poll-tax return and reinforced by a murage tax of the same year) is discussed in App. 3; for the larger population of the early fourteenth century see pp. 82–87.

position as the seat of a bishopric encompassing all of Devon and Cornwall, and as the region's chief administrative center; it hosted eyre, assize, and gaol delivery courts at its royal castle and served as a staple town and the headport of the largest national customs jurisdiction in England. Its commercial hinterland was extensive, encompassing all of east Devon, much of west Somerset, and reaching well into mid-Devon. Located about 10 miles from the open sea at the head of an estuary, Exeter lay within relatively easy reach of inland residents in mid-Devon, east Devon, and west Somerset. Exeter's own access to maritime routes lay through its outport of Topsham, about four miles down the Exe River. While Exeter, like other medieval towns, drew most of its grain supplies from the surrounding agricultural hinterland, Exeter's proximity to the sea also enabled the town to meet some of its cereal needs by means of grain imported from elsewhere.

Cereal imports at Exeter were much more substantial in the first half of the fourteenth century; imports before the Black Death averaged 1,110 quarters each year, compared to only 225 quarters in the second half of the century (see Table 1 below). Similarly, the grain cargoes carried on each ship and the amounts imported by individual merchants in the first half of the century were roughly three times larger than they were after 1350. These marked differences stemmed from the greater demand for grain in the first half of the fourteenth century, when population levels were much higher than after the plagues of the mid- and late fourteenth century. The early fourteenth-century figures were also particularly high because they included grain imported during the Great Famine of 1315–22, when a series of bad harvests caused want and starvation throughout medieval Europe.[6] Indeed, almost half of

---

[6]Ian Kershaw, "The Great Famine and Agrarian Crisis in England 1315–1322," *Past and Present* 59 (1973): 3–50, repr. in *Peasants, Knights, and Heretics: Studies*

the recorded Exeter grain imports before 1350 arrived in this six-year period (Table 1). Although Devon was generally insulated from the worst consequences of overpopulation and bad harvests that affected many other areas of early fourteenth-century England, the phenomenal rise in grain exports in such years as 1319–21 and 1331–32 (Fig. 1) indicate that the county did not altogether escape these problems.[7]

The seasonal pattern of imports also points to the greater demand for grain in the first half of the century (Table 1). Before 1350, 69 per cent of the grain imports arrived at Exeter in the four months from March to June, a time when prices were at their highest and demand greatest because the previous year's supplies were running low and the new harvest was not yet in. After 1350, however, only 55 per cent of the grain arrived during these crucial months. Instead, 31 per cent arrived in the months immediately after the harvest; this implies that cereal imports were made more in response to surplus grain elsewhere than to particularly high demand at home. The low profile of shipmasters as grain importers before 1350 also points to the greater importance of cereal imports in the first half of the century, since they generally brought in grain cargoes as ballast that could bring a small but certain profit. That the percentage of shipmasters importing grain more than doubled after 1350 is a sign that grain had become a less valuable cargo than it had been in the first part of the century.

---

in Medieval English Social History, ed. R. H. Hilton (Cambridge, 1976), pp. 85–132; Henry S. Lucas, "The Great European Famine of 1315, 1316, and 1317," *Speculum* 5 (1930): 343–77.

[7]For Devon agriculture and the lack of any "Malthusian" crisis in Devon during this period, see John Hatcher, "South-Western England," in *The Agrarian History of England and Wales*, 2: *1042–1350*, ed. H. E. Hallam (Cambridge, 1988), pp. 242–45, 383–98, 675–85.

TABLE 1
GRAIN IMPORTS AT EXETER IN THE FOURTEENTH CENTURY

Category	1300/01–1349/50	1316/17–1320/21[a]	1350/51–1399/1400
Extant accounts	36	5	35
Imports (quarters)	39,966	18,768	7,866
Annual average (quarters)	1,110	3,754	225
No. of ships carrying grain	308	101	179
Grain cargo per ship (quarters)	130	186	44
No. of grain importers[b]	435	155	221
Annual cargo per importer (quarters)	92	121	36
% arriving March–June	69	70	55
% arriving July–December	16	12	31
% wheat of known imports[c]	75	76	77
(No.) % grain importers = shipmasters	(86) 20	(27) 17	(96) 43
(No.) % grain importers from Exeter[d]		(37) 24	(20) 9
% grain imported by Exeter residents		23	17
Grain cargo per Exeter importer (quarters)		116	68

Source: Exeter PCA 1300/01–1399/1400; see Table 2, below. The earliest accounts are printed in Kowaleski, *Local Customs Accounts*. Grain imports are rounded to the nearest quarter.

[a]The years of the Great Famine are usually given as 1315–22, but there were no grain imports in 1315/16 and no account survives for 1321/22.
[b]Each grain importer was counted once each year. Grain importers identified only as "mariners" or *socii* were counted as one importer; this practice especially decreases the actual number of grain importers noted for the post-1350 period when more shipmasters and their *socii* imported grain.
[c]Percentage of wheat after "corn" and mixed cargoes were subtracted from totals; see Table 2.
[d]Exeter grain importers identified through prosopographical analysis; information of greatest use was found in the Exeter Mayor's Court Rolls (which include the annual election returns and freedom entries) and the Exeter Mayor's Tourns.

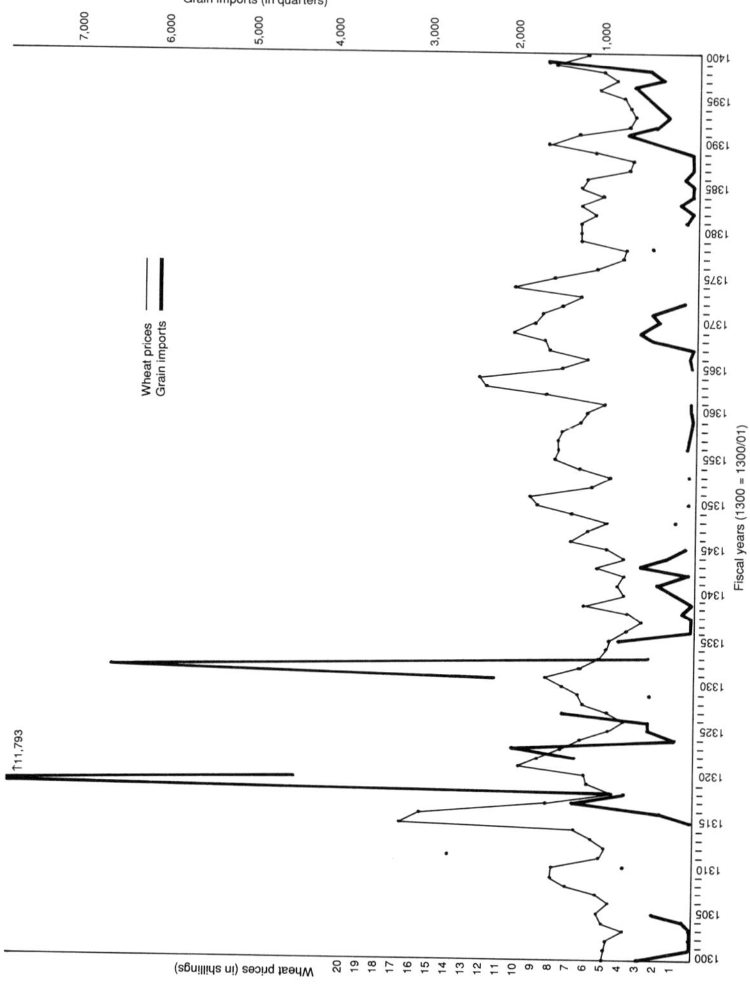

Figure 1. Grain imports in fourteenth-century Exeter

The quantity of grain imported was clearly related to fluctuations in wheat prices, an unsurprising correlation given the dominance of wheat among grain cargoes (Table 1).[8] But the exact chronological correlation between wheat prices and grain cargoes was not always as neat as might be expected (Fig. 1). The highest wheat prices, for example, occurred in 1315/16 and 1316/17,[9] years when grain imports at Exeter were actually relatively low (343 quarters). The low level of imports may have been partly due to Devon's concentration on the production of oats, a crop less affected by the rainy weather that provoked the extremely poor wheat harvests of the Great Famine.[10] It is also possible, of course, that the great scarcity of grain elsewhere may have limited grain imports to Exeter in these years.[11] Indeed, when wheat prices everywhere began to fall in 1317, grain imports at Exeter then rose to almost 1,400 quarters; perhaps this is a reflection of the greater availability of grain on the market. Both wheat prices and imports fell in

---

[8]The figures presented in Table 1 represent only minimum wheat cargoes since wheat constituted the bulk of the "corn" or mixed grain imports; see Table 2 for a breakdown of the types of grain imported.

[9]Of course these trends depend on the accuracy of Beveridge's wheat price series for Exeter (see Table 2) (William H. Beveridge, "A Statistical Crime of the Seventeenth Century," *Journal of Economic and Business History* 1 [1929]: 503–33). There is no reason to doubt his figures, however, and they have been generally accepted without question by scholars. Beveridge used wheat prices listed in the Exeter Mayor's Court Rolls when the assize of bread was taken. The MCR survive for almost every year of the century and are dated, like the customs accounts, from Michaelmas to Michaelmas; Beveridge presumably averaged all assize prices over the 12-month period. Since the Exeter bushel was about 25 per cent larger than the Winchester bushel, he also reduced the Exeter prices recorded in the assize to reflect the standard Winchester quarter used in other price series.

[10]For the relatively better position of the oats crop during these years see David L. Farmer, "Prices and Wages," *Agrarian History* 2: 790–91; for the better situation in the West Country see Kershaw, "Great Famine and Agrarian Crisis," pp. 90–91, 99, and below, pp. 10–11, 17.

[11]Wheat prices in Exeter were lower (15.42*s.* per quarter) than elsewhere in England (16.49*s.*) in 1316/17, but in 1317/18 the Exeter prices were a little higher; see Table 2.

the following year, but then the two factors markedly diverged. In 1319/20 wheat prices increased somewhat, but grain imports skyrocketed to almost 12,000 quarters, a truly extraordinary figure. Although the price of wheat in Exeter changed hardly at all the next year, imports dropped to about one-third of that imported in the preceding year.

There are several possible explanations for this anomaly whereby grain imports shot up so dramatically in a year (1319/20) when prices were not particularly high compared to other years.[12] One explanation focuses on the mercantile response to price differentials that arose when wheat was more plentiful and therefore cheaper in one region than another. In 1319/20, for example, the difference between the price of wheat in Exeter and the national price average was greater (1.55*s.* more per quarter) than in any other year of the first half of the fourteenth century, which meant that merchants would have been more willing to take on the burden of importing large amounts of grain to the city that year.[13] By encouraging exports to places like Exeter where wheat could fetch a price high enough to justify extra transport costs, these price differentials may have prompted grain imports from elsewhere in England and the Continent, which had comparatively lower wheat prices.[14] Such an explanation implies that the international grain market was highly sensitive to price differentials and that merchants were sophisticated enough to respond quickly

---

[12]Similar occurrences of falling wheat prices but rising grain imports appeared in 1323/24, 1332/33, and 1391/92; see Table 2.

[13]The two other years before 1350 with the highest differentials were 1323/24 (1.19*s.*) and 1332/33 (.84*s.*), when grain imports to the city were again especially high (see n. 12 above); see Table 2. The price differential in 1349/50 was .87*s.*, but no customs accounts survive for that year.

[14]In 1319/20 London wheat prices ranged from 4*s.* to 5.33*s.* per quarter, both lower than the 5.98*s.* average price in Exeter. For the national average (4.43*s.*) see Table 2. Regional price variations elsewhere, especially on the Continent, await further research.

and efficiently to regional price variations. Evidence from a recent study of the grain market in medieval London supports this view: high wheat prices in London expanded the distance from which the city drew upon grain supplies because merchants found it profitable to shoulder the extra transport costs associated with more extensive networks of supply.[15]

Although price differentials probably triggered the enormous grain imports of 1319/20, they do not wholly explain why imports that year were so much larger than in other years when wheat prices were higher but imports significantly lower. One explanation is that the grain imports in 1319/20 were so enormous that they simply flooded the Exeter market and lowered grain prices to levels lower than they might otherwise have been that year, a scenario that implies that the mercantile response overestimated consumer demand. Although estimates of grain consumption are hazardous at best—since they need to take into account the varying amounts and extraction rates of grain used in bread, ale, and pottage, as well as the differing patterns of consumption among rich and poor, urban and rural, young and old—some recent efforts in that direction by scholars investigating the London grain trade have suggested that roughly 1.65 quarters of grain were consumed by each urban resident ca. 1300.[16] Thus if 4,500 people lived in Exeter in 1319/20, their cereal needs that year could have been met by 7,425 quarters of grain, an amount still about 4,000 quarters less than the grain shipped into Exeter that same year.[17] Obviously, grain imports to Exeter in 1319/20 were far in excess of local demand and may in fact have been substantial

---

[15]Campbell et al., *Medieval Capital*, pp. 69–71.

[16]This includes grain used for food, drink, and animal fodder; see the extended discussion in Campbell et al., *Medieval Capital*, pp. 31–36.

[17]It should be stressed that the figure of 4,500 is only a guess based on a back projection of the poll-tax population in 1377. If the population had been 5,000 people, the grain required would have been 8,250 quarters.

enough to lower the price of wheat that year. These calculations also strongly suggest that much of the grain imported to Exeter was destined to supply the hinterland as well as the city itself. Some surplus grain may also have been shipped by coast elsewhere, but it is unlikely that much of the grain registered in the Exeter accounts was transshipped, given the important redistributive functions played by neighboring ports and the scope of the customs accounts, which would not have recorded most transshipments.[18]

Another explanation for the anomaly of 1319/20 and other years when imports rose but wheat prices fell posits that local shortages in oats more than in wheat prompted Exeter's enormous grain imports in these years. Oats, which accounted for more than half the acreage sown in Devon during the pre-plague period, was so prevalent in the county that it probably surpassed barley as the grain most often used to brew ale there.[19] A failure of the oats crop may well have been behind the over-50 per cent decline in the number of ale brewers in Exeter between 1331 and 1333, a time when wheat prices in

---

[18]Such coastal shipments may have been behind the sale of 200 quarters of wheat by an Amiens burgess to a Bristol burgess at Exeter (MCR 1300/01, m. 28). Note that transshipped grain would not have paid custom or appeared in the customs accounts unless it was first unloaded, partly sold, then reloaded—an unlikely occurrence. For the greater redistributive role of neighboring ports such as Southampton, Dartmouth, and Plymouth compared to Exeter, see Maryanne Kowaleski, "The Port Towns of Fourteenth-Century Devon," in *The New Maritime History of Devon*, 1: *From Early Times to the Late Eighteenth Century*, ed. Michael Duffy, Stephen Fisher, Basil Greenhill, David J. Starkey, and Joyce Youings (Exeter, 1992), pp. 66–69, and Kowaleski, *Local Markets and Regional Trade*, pp. 226, 233, 236, 256.

[19]For the dependence on oats in Devon see Hatcher, "South-Western England," pp. 390–94; H. P. R. Finberg, *Tavistock Abbey: A Study in the Social and Economic History of Devon*, 2nd ed. (Newton Abbot, 1969), pp. 95–115; H. S. A. Fox, "Devon and Cornwall," in *The Agrarian History of England and Wales*, 3: *1348–1500*, ed. Edward Miller (Cambridge, 1991), pp. 303–06; K. Ugawa, "The Economic Development of Some Devon Manors in the Thirteenth Century," *TDA* 44 (1962): 635–44, 665–67, 679–80. For oat malt used in brewing at Exeter see MCR Roll 1, m. 27; 1290/91, m. 37d; 1373/74, m. 18; PCR 1–23 Ric. II, m. 14.

Exeter were, surprisingly, actually falling but imports were higher than for any period but the Great Famine.[20] The county's dependence on oats could also have been behind the mild impact of high wheat prices in the first two years of the Great Famine (1315–16), when wheat prices shot up but grain imports at Exeter were very low (Fig. 1 and Table 2). The rainy weather of the early years of the Famine would have had less impact on oats, a spring-sown crop that did well in wet conditions; similarly, the weather in 1319/20 may have been extremely dry—conditions that would have adversely affected the oats crop and prompted Exeter grain imports to soar.

It is also possible that the severe cattle murrain that we know predominated in the last years of the Great Famine (1319–22) may have more negatively influenced Devon agriculture because of the county's dependence on cattle husbandry.[21] High cattle mortality would obviously have affected the supply of draught animals and thus the harvest of grain.

Unfortunately, information about the impact of murrain, or weather conditions, or even the Devon harvests in the Famine years is not readily available, so the extent to which a severe failure in the oats crop prompted the extraordinary grain imports of 1319/20 and other years is not possible to assess with any real accuracy.[22] It is worth noting, however, that the

---

[20]The brewers were listed in the annual Exeter Mayor's Tourns held every autumn; there were 197 brewers in 1331, 159 in 1332, 114 in 1333. For imports see Table 2.

[21]For the cattle murrain see Kershaw, "Great Famine and Agrarian Crisis," pp. 106–08. For Devon's reliance on livestock husbandry see Hatcher, "South-Western England," pp. 388–89, 395–98; Fox, "Devon and Cornwall," pp. 154–59, 313–21.

[22]Partial or missing accounts for the years in question do not allow us to specify the weather conditions or harvests in Devon (information courtesy of H. S. A. Fox). The evidence collected by J. Z. Titow ("Evidence of Weather in the Account Rolls of the Bishopric of Winchester 1209–1350," *Economic History Review*, 2nd ser., 2 [1960]: 387–88) for west Somerset also sheds no light on weather conditions or harvests in those years because of missing data.

TABLE 2

EXETER GRAIN PRICES AND IMPORTS

Year[a]	Exeter Price	Nat'l Price	Total Impts	Grain Types[b]	Wheat	Rye	Barley	Mixed Grain	Beans & Peas	Oats	Malt	Ships[c]	Imptrs[d]	Ship-masters[e]
1295/96	na	9.21	438	+	69	139	—	—	231	—	—	9	10	0
1296/97	na	4.84	0	+	—	—	—	—	—	—	—	0	0	0
1297/98	na	6.36	0	+	—	—	—	—	—	—	—	0	0	0
1298/99	na	5.34	3	+	—	—	3	—	—	—	—	1	1	0
1299/00	na	5.34	0	+	—	—	—	—	—	—	—	0	0	0
1300/01	na	4.99	300	WBP	—	—	—	300	—	—	—	1	1	0
1301/02	na	4.89	0	+	—	—	—	—	—	—	—	0	0	0
1302/03	na	4.63	0	—	—	—	—	—	—	—	—	0	0	0
1303/04	na	3.66	0	—	—	—	—	—	—	—	—	0	0	0
1304/05	na	4.99	46	WRB	—	—	—	46	—	—	—	1	3	0
1305/06	na	5.24	456	WX	2	60	9	384	1	—	—	6	8	1
1306/07	na	4.53	na	—	—	—	—	—	—	—	—	—	—	—
1307/08	na	5.29	na	—	—	—	—	—	—	—	—	—	—	—
1308/09	na	7.02	na	—	—	—	—	—	—	—	—	—	—	—
1309/10	na	7.99	na	—	—	—	—	—	—	—	—	—	—	—
1310/11	na	7.94	742	WBX	290	—	139	135	173	5	—	11	17	4
1311/12	na	5.04	na	—	—	—	—	—	—	—	—	—	—	—
1312/13	na	4.89	1,345	WFX	1,050	—	61	200	—	34	—	13	15	4
1313/14	na	5.55	na	—	—	—	—	—	—	—	—	—	—	—
1314/15	na	6.57	na	—	—	—	—	—	—	—	—	—	—	—
1315/16	na	16.64	0	—	—	—	—	—	—	—	—	0	0	0

1316/17	15.42	16.49	343	—	220	13	101	—	6	3	—	9	11	4
1317/18	8.11	7.94	1,369	WRB	810	—	50	408	21	80	—	12	20	6
1318/19	4.17	3.97	758	F	387	—	260	105	6	—	—	9	9	1
1319/20	5.98	4.43	11,793	WRBX	4,091	645	33	6,944	72	8	—	46	68	12
1320/21	6.00	6.26	4,505	—	306	517	—	3,652	30	—	—	25	47	4
1321/22	9.90	13.23	na	—	—	—	—	—	—	—	—	—	—	—
1322/23	8.75	8.60	1,305	—	181	—	1	1,122	1	—	—	11	11	3
1323/24	7.35	6.16	2,029	WRbPX	878	—	197	924	23	7	—	25	30	9
1324/25	6.36	7.94	199	—	—	149	—	40	—	10	—	3	6	1
1325/26	4.56	5.14	460	—	44	—	116	300	—	—	—	5	6	2
1326/27	3.87	3.87	499	WR	195	—	20	100	—	184	—	6	7	4
1327/28	4.75	4.63	1,451	WR+	350	356	25	716	4	—	—	12	20	6
1328/29	6.13	6.67	na	—	—	—	—	—	—	—	—	—	—	—
1329/30	6.42	6.51	459	WRX	205	—	17	237	—	—	—	7	12	4
1330/31	7.30	7.38	na	—	—	—	—	—	—	—	—	—	—	—
1331/32	8.25	8.09	2,242	WRBbX	665	407	—	1,020	150	—	—	22	33	4
1332/33	6.39	5.55	6,512	WRBbX	1,965	200	60	4,179	—	—	108	44	58	7
1333/34	5.11	4.38	475	WRO	275	—	—	200	—	—	—	4	4	1
1334/35	4.78	4.43	na	—	—	—	—	—	—	—	—	—	—	—
1335/36	4.60	4.99	810	WR	450	142	—	205	13	—	—	6	8	3
1336/37	3.64	4.53	0	—	—	—	—	—	—	—	—	0	0	0
1337/38	2.92	3.41	0	—	—	—	—	—	—	—	—	0	0	0
1338/39	na	3.61	100	—	100	—	—	—	—	—	—	1	2	0
1339/40	na	6.05	0	—	—	—	—	—	—	—	—	0	0	0
1340/41	3.81	4.02	174	—	174	—	—	—	—	—	—	4	4	0
1341/42	4.17	4.38	352	WB	167	7	—	130	40	8	—	9	10	1
1342/43	3.67	4.43	27	Bb	—	3	—	24	—	—	—	2	2	1

TABLE 2—*Continued*

Year[a]	Exeter Price	Nat'l Price	Total Impts	Grain Types[b]	Wheat	Rye	Barley	Mixed Grain	Beans & Peas	Oats	Malt	Ships[c]	Imptrs[d]	Ship-masters[e]
1343/44	5.42	5.85	664	Wb+	594	—	12	52	—	6	—	7	15	2
1344/45	3.70	4.07	284	—	280	—	4	—	—	—	—	3	4	0
1345/46	4.82	4.22	68	RB	8	—	—	40	—	—	20	2	2	1
1346/47	6.96	7.23	na	—	—	—	—	—	—	—	—	—	—	—
1347/48	5.82	6.87	na	—	—	—	—	—	—	—	—	—	—	—
1348/49	4.72	4.58	199	—	199	—	—	—	—	—	—	2	2	1
1349/50	6.92	6.05	na	—	—	—	—	—	—	—	—	—	—	—
1350/51	8.78	8.75	36	WBb	3	14	—	19	—	—	—	4	4	1
1351/52	9.25	11.80	na	—	—	—	—	—	—	—	—	—	—	—
1352/53	5.59	5.45	na	—	—	—	—	—	—	—	—	—	—	—
1353/54	4.55	4.58	14	—	10	1	—	—	1	2	—	2	2	0
1354/55	6.42	6.31	na	—	—	—	—	—	—	—	—	—	—	—
1355/56	7.92	6.20	na	—	—	—	—	—	—	—	—	—	—	—
1356/57	7.52	6.97	36	—	2	—	22	9	3	—	—	3	3	2
1357/58	7.52	7.18	26	—	16	—	10	—	—	—	—	1	1	0
1358/59	7.47	6.36	9	—	—	—	—	6	3	—	—	2	2	2
1359/60	6.37	6.82	0	—	—	—	—	—	—	—	—	0	0	0
1360/61	6.00	6.97	0	—	—	—	—	—	—	—	—	0	0	0
1361/62	4.92	5.40	0	—	—	—	—	—	—	—	—	0	0	0
1362/63	8.28	7.38	na	—	—	—	—	—	—	—	—	—	—	—
1363/64	11.62	10.13	na	—	—	—	—	—	—	—	—	—	—	—
1364/65	12.09	7.38	na	—	—	—	—	—	—	—	—	—	—	—

1365/66	7.48	6.06	0	—	—	—	—	—	—	—	—	0	0	0
1366/67	5.80	5.80	15	BPb	—	—	—	15	—	—	—	1	2	1
1367/68	8.02	7.79	0	—	—	—	—	—	—	—	—	0	0	0
1368/69	8.42	7.58	412	WRBPb	186	12	33	177	4	—	—	9	11	7
1369/70	10.12	17.10	583	—	325	58	138	—	55	7	—	10	11	8
1370/71	8.92	8.04	376	WBb	125	—	3	240	2	6	—	6	10	4
1371/72	8.52	6.77	442	—	408	—	24	—	10	—	—	9	10	4
1372/73	7.42	8.30	92	RBPb	61	—	—	31	—	—	—	2	3	1
1373/74	6.25	6.00	na	—	—	—	—	—	—	—	—	—	—	—
1374/75	10.02	9.67	na	—	—	—	—	—	—	—	—	—	—	—
1375/76	7.75	9.11	na	—	—	—	—	—	—	—	—	—	—	—
1376/77	5.32	4.78	na	—	—	—	—	—	—	—	—	—	—	—
1377/78	3.92	4.17	na	—	—	—	—	—	—	—	—	—	—	—
1378/79	3.75	4.07	na	—	—	—	—	—	—	—	—	—	—	—
1379/80	6.42	5.75	na	—	—	—	—	—	—	—	—	—	—	—
1380/81	6.42	6.72	na	—	—	—	—	—	—	—	—	—	—	—
1381/82	6.42	5.96	46	—	46	—	—	—	—	—	—	2	2	2
1382/83	5.50	5.60	0	—	—	—	—	—	—	—	—	0	0	0
1383/84	6.40	5.19	125	—	68	—	—	—	27	30	—	3	3	0
1384/85	5.00	4.53	0	—	—	—	—	—	—	—	—	0	0	0
1385/86	6.40	5.40	0	—	—	—	—	—	—	—	—	0	0	0
1386/87	6.00	4.78	42	—	40	—	—	—	2	—	—	1	2	1
1387/88	3.50	3.87	0	—	—	—	—	—	—	—	—	0	0	0
1388/89	3.42	3.66	0	—	—	—	—	—	—	—	—	0	0	0
1389/90	5.50	6.72	0	—	—	—	—	—	—	—	—	0	0	0
1390/91	8.25	9.57	323	—	204	22	65	—	32	—	—	8	9	3
1391/92	6.50	5.40	726	—	555	6	122	—	9	—	34	12	15	5

TABLE 2—*Continued*

Year[a]	Exeter Price	Nat'l Price	Total Impts	Grain Types[b]	Wheat	Rye	Barley	Mixed Grain	Beans & Peas	Oats	Malt	Ships[c]	Imptrs[d]	Ship-masters[e]
1392/93	3.50	3.36	370	WBOM	145	—	—	49	32	—	144	6	8	3
1393/94	3.25	4.02	278	—	244	—	—	—	21	3	10	8	12	5
1394/95	3.50	4.02	330	Wb+	175	12	27	18	96	—	2	12	16	5
1395/96	3.80	4.73	498	—	317	20	48	—	111	2	—	12	16	7
1396/97	5.25	6.57	615	F	598	—	—	4	13	—	—	15	21	7
1397/98	4.30	5.34	387	—	288	90	—	—	8	—	—	9	11	9
1398/99	5.03	5.34	472	Bb	381	59	14	1	17	—	—	12	13	6
1399/00[f]	8.00	6.11	1,613	WR	1,177	20	27	350	39	—	—	30	34	13

Sources: Exeter grain prices from Beveridge, "Statistical Crime," p. 531. National price averages from Farmer, "Prices and Wages," *Agrarian History* 2: 790–91, and idem, "Prices and Wages, 1350–1500," *Agrarian History* 3: 502–03. All prices represent shillings per quarter. Import figures from Kowaleski, *Local Customs Accounts*, and PCA 1322/23–1399/1400. Note that the accounts of 1295/96–1301/02 were enrolled on the Exeter Mayor's Court Rolls and may not be complete. Na = no account survives.

[a]Fiscal year, 29 Sept.–29 Sept.

[b]Indicates type of grain specified in mixed cargoes: B = barley; b = beans; F = flour; M = malt; O = oats; P = peas; R = rye; W = wheat; X = maslin; + indicates that there may be additional grain cargoes in illegible or missing portions of the account.

[c]Number of ships carrying grain that docked at the port.

[d]Number of individual grain importers; each importer counted only once each year. "Mariners" or *socii* counted as one importer.

[e]Number of shipmasters who imported grain; each shipmaster counted only once.

[f]The account lacks a dating clause in the heading; it could be for one year later, 1400/01.

relative national price averages of oats and barley were actually higher than for wheat in 1319/20, although both were well within normal range.[23] The only oat prices available for Exeter in this period come from fodder purchases made by the warden of the Exeter cathedral works, although he paid sums far lower than the national average perhaps because he "purchased" most of the oats in bulk from the bishop's own manor of Cheriton Bishop. In 1319/20, the year of the very high grain imports, the price he paid for oats was higher than for the year before (1318/19) and the year after (1320/21) but less than in 1316–18, when grain imports at Exeter were rising but nowhere near the level they reached in 1319/20.[24] While this evidence does not support the hypothesis that a severe failure of the Devon oats crop precipitated the huge grain imports of 1319/20, we need to assemble a greater range of oat prices for Devon before entirely discounting this hypothesis. Certainly we know that the harvests of particular grains varied widely from region to region and in this instance could have been at least partly responsible for the different pattern of response to shortages exhibited in the Exeter grain-import figures.[25]

---

[23]Farmer, "Prices and Wages," p. 791. Note also that grain imports increased by over 4,000 quarters from 1331 to 1333, even though Exeter wheat prices fell 1.86*s.* per quarter in these two years. Oat prices also fell, but only by .47*s.* per quarter; it is possible that oat prices in Devon fell even less, which would indicate a greater shortage of oats compared to wheat.

[24]Audrey M. Erskine, ed., *The Accounts of the Fabric of Exeter Cathedral, 1279–1353*, pt. 1: *1279–1326*, Devon and Cornwall Record Society, n.s., vol. 24 (1981); the annual account of the warden of the works listed quarterly purchases of oats for 8–11 horses. The prices were low (1.5–1.9*s.* in 1316/17, 1.87*s.* in 1317/18, 1.06–1.32*s.* in 1318/19, 1.16–1.80*s.* in 1319/20, 1.07–1.5*s.* in 1320/21, compared to a range of 1.98–5.56*s.* in the national average at this time [Farmer, "Prices and Wages," p. 791]) because purchases were made in bulk, from one of the bishop's own manors (this suggests that some may have been "fictional" sales for the sake of accounting) and in Devon, a county where arable production concentrated on oats.

[25]See esp. Kershaw, "Great Famine and Agrarian Crisis," pp. 97–102, for these regional variations.

Except for 1319/20 and a few other years, grain imports generally moved in the same direction as fluctuations in the price of wheat (Fig. 1). The degree of response, however, was not always the same, particularly in the second half of the century when relatively high wheat prices did not evoke the substantial imports witnessed before 1350. Differentials between the price of wheat in Exeter and the national average were actually much greater in the post-plague period than before the Black Death, but these did not prompt the same type of response as was seen in the first part of the century, when grain supplies and consumer demand were more precariously balanced.[26] The lower imports at the end of the century primarily reflected the relaxed demand for grain by the reduced population of the late fourteenth century.

Other factors, such as the disruption of trade routes during the Hundred Years War, also affected the pattern of grain imports.[27] In the periods 1337–40 and 1345–47 flare-ups of fighting in French grain-exporting regions probably lay behind the almost complete absence of grain imports at Exeter in these years, although grain prices were not particularly high during these periods, so the effect of war on local supplies was probably muted. In 1339 the impact was more noticeable, since Picardy, Exeter's main source of foreign grain (Fig. 2), was devastated by Edward III's troops during harvest season;

---

[26]Exeter wheat prices were higher than the national average in almost 38 per cent of the years before 1350 (12 of 32 years with available price data) but 54 per cent (27 of 50) of the years after 1350. Before 1350 only 19 per cent (six of 32) of the years witnessed differentials of more than 1*s*., with the highest differential being –3.33*s*. in 1321/22; after 1350, 36 per cent (18 of 50) of the years experienced a price differential of more than 1*s*.; two years (1364/65 and 1369/70) had differentials over 4*s*.; see Table 2.

[27]Demographic disasters such as the Black Death also affected the pattern of grain imports; note the low imports of 1350/51 despite the high wheat prices of 1348–51 (Fig. 1 and Table 2).

Exeter imported no grain that year, even though the price of wheat was higher than it had been for many years.[28] After 1350 wartime disruptions of grain-trade routes were even more obvious. In the strife-torn 1380s, for example, annual grain imports averaged only 21 quarters but reached 561 quarters in the following decade, when long periods of truce opened up trade routes and made all types of maritime commerce safer and less expensive.[29] Since Exeter wheat prices in the 1380s were actually slightly higher than in the 1390s (although two of the years of the latter decade did see particularly high prices), it seems that changes in the transport and sources of grain supplies may have had a bigger impact on imports than did demand from Exeter and its hinterland.

The disruptions in grain imports created by the long conflict of the Hundred Years War also point to Exeter's reliance on overseas supplies of grain. Because the local Exeter port customs accounts used in this study recorded all incoming trade, whether coastal or overseas, they offer an unusual opportunity to distinguish between imports arriving by coastal craft and those reaching Exeter directly from foreign sources of supply. A comparison of extant local and national accounts for a 14-month period in 1323–24 shows that 42 per cent of the imported grain was owned by foreign merchants.[30] This figure, however,

---

[28]See Table 2. No Exeter wheat prices are available for 1338–39, but it is not unreasonable to assume that Exeter prices at least moved in the same direction as the national averages. For the interruption of grain exports see Alain Derville, "Le grenier des Pays-Bas médiévaux," *Revue du Nord* 69 (1987): 269.

[29]Overseas imports of other foreign goods reacted in a similar fashion; see Margery K. James, *Studies in the Medieval Wine Trade*, ed. Elspeth M. Veale (Oxford, 1971), pp. 28–30, 38–41; Kowaleski, *Local Markets and Regional Trade*, ch. 6. Note that if the 1399/1400 account was for 1400/01 (see Table 2, n. f), the 1390s average would be 444 quarters.

[30]PRO E122/40/7A/3 records all alien overseas imports and exports 3 Feb. 1323–10 Apr. 1324. The accounts identify grain cargoes in terms of value rather than exact amounts, but the correspondence of dates and the names of the importers

clearly underestimates the proportion of foreign grain imported, since it does not take into account the foreign grain shipped to Exeter by English merchants. Typical of such shipments was the 82 quarters of wheat that William de Chagford of Exeter imported on an Abbeville vessel that also carried woad and weld, dyestuffs commonly exported from Picardy.[31]

The home ports of grain ships at Exeter hint at the origin of some of this foreign grain. Ships registered at ports in Picardy (Abbeville, St. Valéry-sur-Somme), Artois (Boulogne, Calais), Normandy (Barfleur, Cabourg, Caen, Harfleur, Port-en-Bessein, Wissant, Waban), Brittany (Le Vivier, St. Malo), Gascony (Bayonne, Bordeaux), and Spain (Bermeo) all carried grain to Exeter before 1350, although Picardy and then Normandy were always the major suppliers (Fig. 2). Shipmasters and mariners from these ports also imported grain to Exeter, as did merchants who resided in Abbeville, Amiens, Bordeaux, and Caen; Picard merchants from Amiens were particularly active at Exeter.[32]

The surnames of cereal importers such as Lawrence de Lysshebon, Rogrigo de Bermeo, Astorici de Serynole, and Tussard de Espayn also suggest that some grain may have arrived from the Mediterranean, while wheat imports by Richard Makepeys of Cork and Robert de Cruwes of Drogheda imply that Irish grain also formed part of the cargoes at Exeter.[33]

---

make comparison with the data in PCA 1322/23–1323/24 simple; the alien importers brought in 967 of the total 2,327.5 quarters of grain imported during this period. It is highly unlikely, given the nature of the customs duties, that these foreign importers were shipping English grain.

[31]PCA 1319/20.

[32]For example, John le Engleys (PCA 1326/27) and John Capel (1331/32) of Abbeville; Peter le Monier (1312/13–1323/24), John Petit (1319/20), Bernard de Fenes (1332/33), and Walter Flemyng (1332/33) of Amiens; Gerard de Caprespynes (1319/20, 1320/21) of Bordeaux; and Michael Bassewych of Caen (1319/20).

[33]PCA 1317/18, 1322/23, 1344/45; for the Irish merchants see PCA 1320/21, 1322/23, 1343/44; PRO E122/40/7. For Portuguese imports in 1391 see below, n. 39.

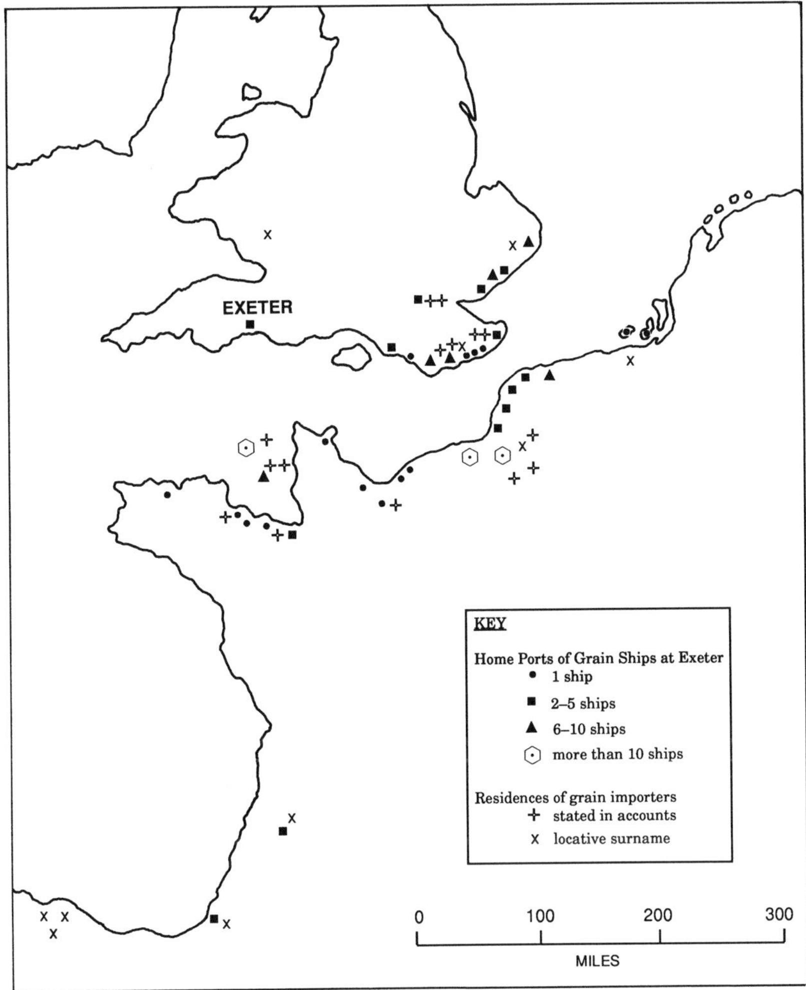

Figure 2. Origin of grain ships and importers at Exeter, 1300–49 (excluding ports west of Sussex)

Continental grain cargoes were on average larger than those owned by English merchants and in years of high demand cargoes became larger still, thus increasing the contribution of continental sources of supply, an indication of the flexibility reliance on foreign grain could furnish (albeit at a cost).[34] It is thus hardly surprising that the single largest grain shipment to Exeter (1,023 quarters) came during the year of highest imports, 1319/20, and was made by an Amiens merchant, Peter le Monier, who was the most important foreign importer of woad at Exeter for almost two decades.[35]

Foreign grain remained a significant source of imports in the second half of the fourteenth century, although the generally low level of grain imports meant that it played a less crucial role in the provisioning of the town. Despite the reduced shipments of the late fourteenth century, however, foreign grain still accounted for the bulk of cereal imports to Exeter. A comparison of the local and national port customs accounts for several years during the last two decades of the century shows that roughly 67 per cent of Exeter grain imports arrived from overseas.[36] Unfortunately, the source of this foreign grain is difficult to discern because so much was carried by Channel Island shippers who easily moved between England and France during periods of war. Brittany (allied with England for most of this time) was probably one source of supply, as is indicated by the more frequent appearance of Breton ships in the grain

---

[34]For such imports during the Famine (1315–22) see *CPR 1313–1317*, pp. 450, 466–67, 501–02, 571–72; *CCR 1313–1318*, pp. 318–19; *CCR 1318–1333*, p. 591. Note also the dates of foreign imports in nn. 31–32 above.

[35]MCR 1319/20, m. 36d. He frequently imported woad at Exeter and may have been related to the Peter le Monier of Amiens who had settled in Wells by 1340; see A. J. Scrase, "A French Merchant in Fourteenth-Century Wells," *Somerset Archaeology and Natural History* 133 (1989): 131–40.

[36]Percentage derived by comparing amount of grain (257 quarters) imported in the overseas accounts (PRO E122/102/14, 40/26, 40/16, 40/18, 40/23) with that imported (386.5 quarters) in the corresponding local accounts (PCA 1383/84, 1390/91–1392/93, 1398/99), which registered both local and overseas imports. Note that this comparison differs from that noted for 1323–24 in that it focuses not on the nationality of the importers but on the origin of the grain.

import trade.[37] During periods of truce Artois and Norman grain was also shipped to Exeter—if we can assume that grain ships from Calais, Harfleur, Honfleur, Port-Bail, Réville, and Ravenoville were carrying local products.[38] In June 1390/91, a year when grain at Exeter was so expensive that the city forgave a large part of the sum owed by the farmer of the brewing and baking tolls, a large shipment of grain owned by Portuguese merchants even appeared at the port.[39] Exeter merchants also went to Gascony to purchase corn, although they may have been responding more to the needs of royal troops and garrisons than to consumer demand at home.[40]

English grain shipped by coast from East Anglia, Kent, Sussex, and Hampshire made up the balance (probably averaging ca. 30–40 per cent) of grain imports at Exeter.[41] There is no way to tell what proportion of grain arrived from each of these places, although the large number of grain ships before 1350 from such eastern ports as Boston, Yarmouth, Ipswich, Colchester, Sandwich, Dover, Romney, Hastings, and Winchelsea certainly suggests that eastern England provided the bulk of English grain imports to Exeter. Cereal imports to Exeter by merchants from Sandwich (Henry Crowe, Walter Tabernar,

---

[37]PCA, passim. For the Breton role in this trade and Breton sources of supply see Henri Touchard, *Le commerce maritime breton à la fin du moyen âge* (Paris, 1967), pp. 82–83, 93, 136.

[38]PCA 1390/91, 1391/92, 1394/95, 1396/97, 1397/98, 1399/1400.

[39]They landed and sold 192 quarters of wheat and beans ca. 3 June 1391 (MCR 1390/91, m. 42d). For the reduction in the farmer's lease and comments on the dearness of grain that year, see Exeter City Receiver's Accounts 1390/91 and Exeter Exe Bridge Wardens' Accounts 1390/91.

[40]*CPR 1350–1354*, p. 359.

[41]The origin of the small cargoes of grain shipped from Dorset to Devon is unclear but was probably Hampshire; see *Calendar of Inquisitions Miscellaneous*, 3: *1348–1377* (London, 1937), p. 372. Grain ships from Hampshire ports (particularly Hook, Hamble, and Lymington) were also regular visitors to Exeter, although the source of the grain they carried was not explicitly stated.

William de Haukeshill), Winchelsea (Walter Launde, Raymond Noldekyn, Roger Waterman), Chichester (John Blake), and Norfolk (Roger de Norfolk), as well as by shipmasters from other eastern ports, also hint at the origin of the grain shipped to Exeter.[42] By the second half of the century, however, references to grain imports from eastern England were rare, and English grain as a whole seems to have figured even less prominently in Exeter imports than in the pre-plague period.

There are several reasons why foreign grain imports were always more important than English imports at Exeter. The cost of shipping grain from eastern English ports was probably not significantly lower than the freightage charged on cargoes from Exeter's traditional trading partners along the French coast. Sailing from eastern England to Devon was slow because it meant going against the prevailing winds, while coming across from Normandy or Brittany meant sailing with the wind, which made the voyage faster and reduced transport costs. The supposed cost advantages held by English importers may also have been infrequently realized, given the long-standing commercial connections between Exeter and its French trading partners in the Somme, Picardy, Normandy, and Brittany. The market provided in Exeter and its region for French dyestuffs, canvas, and linen cloth (items that often accompanied grain cargoes) made it worthwhile and relatively easy for foreign merchants regularly doing business there (such as Peter le Monier of Amiens) to transport grain as well as these other goods. In turn, the cloth, hides, and tin exported from Devon probably found a better market overseas than they did in eastern England.[43] Nor were customs duties always more of a

---

[42]MCR Roll 1, m. 4; 1295/96, m. 24d; PCA 1332/33, 1320/21, 1322/23, 1332/33, 1391/92, 1305/06. For 200 quarters of wheat purchased in Cambridgeshire and Norfolk to be shipped to Devon, see *CPR 1364–1367*, p. 113.

[43]For a longer discussion of these Exeter trading links see Kowaleski, *Local Markets and Regional Trade*, pp. 232–45.

liability for foreign importers than native merchants; at Exeter, custom was owed by all importers unless they belonged to one of the exempt jurisdictions such as the Cinque Ports. Since port customs duties (both national and local) on grain imports were often relaxed by the authorities, foreign grain importers also commanded a more even playing field than foreign importers of other goods enjoyed.[44]

Another difference between the early and late fourteenth-century maritime trade in grain was the greater control exercised by Exeter merchants over corn imports in the first half of the century. During the Famine years, for example, Exeter merchants represented 24 per cent of all grain importers and were responsible for 23 per cent of all grain cargoes coming into the port (Table 1). Note that these figures underestimate the true participation of Exeter merchants in the grain trade, since they do not indicate their role as distributors of grain brought in by others. Foreign and nonresident grain importers such as Walter Launde of Winchelsea, who sold over £40 worth of wheat and rye to the Exeter merchant/skinner Nicholas de Lydeford soon after he landed his cargo of 200 quarters of wheat and 100 quarters of rye, often sought local wholesale buyers who then handled the distribution or retailing of the grain in the city and further inland.[45] Indeed, the control of Exeter merchants over grain prompted vociferous complaints in Devon during the 1330s and 1340s that their unfair commercial practices led to excessively high prices for corn and other victuals.[46] In

[44]For example, *CCR 1389–1392*, p. 388. From about the 1340s, Exeter stopped charging local customs on grain imports.

[45]The grain ship arrived 12 Mar. 1321 (PCA 1320/21) and the sale was recorded in a recognizance within a week or so (MCR 1320/21, m. 26d). Lydeford's own importing activities were restricted to herring from Yarmouth.

[46]*CPR 1334–1338*, p. 445; *CPR 1338–1340*, p. 64; *CPR 1345–1348*, p. 320. Similar complaints were made in *CFR 1307–1319*, p. 139, although corn was not specifically mentioned.

contrast, long periods of nil or very low imports in the late fourteenth century meant that grain imports never figured as prominently in the commercial interests of Exeter merchants active after 1350. Exeter men imported no grain at all in the 1360s and 1380s and very little in the 1350s.[47] Over the course of the late fourteenth century their share of the grain imports did not drop as much as their representation among grain importers, a development due mostly to the replacement of the large cargoes of foreign merchant-importers by the smaller cargoes of shipmaster-importers (Table 1).

Although the relative control of grain imports by Exeter merchants changed during the course of the century, the status and commercial interests of the importers did not. Almost all of the Exeter merchants who imported grain were wealthy members of the town's ruling oligarchy, although on occasion substantial bakers also imported grain. The merchant oligarchy's commercial privileges, connections, and knowledge of both overseas suppliers and the local market clearly gave them an immense advantage in the acquisition, sale, and distribution of imported grain.[48] Their attention to the state of the market was especially evident during periods of grain shortages, when their grain-importing activities increased significantly. During the Great Famine, for instance, Philip Lovecok (who served as mayor 10 times and paid the highest lay subsidy in 1332

[47]The only grain import by an Exeter merchant during these years (23 years with extant accounts) was the one *jybbe* of rye imported by Robert Wilford in PCA 1353/54; see also Table 2. Although the Exeter importers were not identified as such in the accounts, the extensive prosopographical analysis conducted on the late fourteenth-century importers means that all have been identified; see Kowaleski, *Local Markets and Regional Trade*, App. 1, for a description of this analysis.

[48]For a more detailed discussion of these advantages see Kowaleski, *Local Markets and Regional Trade*, pp. 95–119, 250–54, 270–73.

Exeter) alone imported 505 quarters of corn.[49] In the 1370s, when wheat prices were also high, Exeter merchants were responsible for 30 per cent of cereal imports, in contrast to the 17 per cent they normally controlled in the period after 1350 (Table 1).[50] As in the earlier period, a small group of men handled the bulk of the Exeter-owned grain imports in the late fourteenth century, although the size of their cargoes was smaller. In the 1370s, for example, Robert Wilford of Exeter (the town's wealthiest merchant, who served as mayor an unprecedented 13 times) owned 63 per cent of all the Exeter grain cargoes, although his total imports came to only 171 quarters, a reflection of the lower demand for grain after the Black Death. Nonetheless, the higher grain-importing profile of Exeter merchants, when demand rose in both the first and second halves of the century shows that Exeter merchants could respond quickly to the potential for profit by exploiting their commercial contacts to acquire and ship grain to the city during periods of shortage.

Few, if any, of the late fourteenth-century merchants of the Exeter oligarchy regularly participated in the land-based trade in grain; most restricted their grain-trading activities to the sphere of imports.[51] Evidence for the early fourteenth-century

---

[49]*The Devonshire Lay Subsidy of 1332*, ed. Audrey M. Erskine, Devon and Cornwall Record Society, n.s., vol. 14 (1969): 50, 110, 127; MCR election returns. The next biggest importer was Walter Hugheton, who brought in 388 quarters; Walter was less wealthy (he paid a subsidy of 40*d.* in 1332) and never served as mayor, but he did regularly hold the highest oligarchic offices of steward, councilor, and elector for over 20 years.

[50]Note that only three accounts survive from the 1370s. The Exeter merchants' share of other imports was higher; in 1381/82–1390/91 they were responsible for 44 per cent of the wine, 51 per cent of the iron, 67 per cent of the woad, 39 per cent of the madder, and 38 per cent of the herring imported to Exeter (by volume); see Kowaleski, *Local Markets and Regional Trade*, Table 6.6.

[51]Only Thomas Smythesheghes, a merchant/smith who never appears as a grain importer in the surviving accounts, seems to have participated in the retail or

Exeter merchants is less plentiful, although the higher value of the trade in the earlier period suggests that they may have been more involved in trading grain from the hinterland than were their late fourteenth-century counterparts. The land-based grain trade cannot be quantified as precisely as the maritime trade, although it must have provided the bulk of Exeter's grain needs. The extent of Exeter's grain hinterland is also difficult to discern with any accuracy and can be only sketched by relying on anecdotal information regarding carrying services and grain sales made by outsiders in Exeter. For example, carting services owed by tenants on the bishop of Winchester's manors in Taunton, almost 30 miles away, suggest that the bishop's grain was regularly carted to Exeter and its outport of Topsham, although this practice was probably more common in the thirteenth and early fourteenth centuries.[52] Yet the late fourteenth-century villeins of Porlock, almost 35 miles north of Exeter near the coast of Somerset, were also expected to carry rye from their demesne to Exeter, presumably to be sold at the market there.[53] The dean and chapter's customary tenants at Branscombe, about 20 miles away on the east Devon coast, were also expected to cart demense grain to Exeter.[54]

The residences of grain sellers in Exeter also give us some idea of the scope of this hinterland in the last three decades of the fourteenth century; similar evidence for the period before 1350 is, unfortunately, not available, although from its larger

---

land-based side of the grain trade; see MCR 1386/87, mm. 38, 39, for his sale of about six quarters of barley to an Exeter hosteler.

[52]T. J. Hunt, *The Medieval Customs of the Manors of Taunton and Bradford on Tone*, Somerset Record Society, vol. 66 (1962).

[53]C. E. H. Chadwyck-Healey, *The History of the Part of West Somerset Comprising the Parishes of Luccombe, Selworthy, Stoke Pero, Porlock, Culbone and Oare* (London, 1901), p. 410.

[54]ECL D&C 3683, fol. 8, notes carrying duties from the demesne to the Exe River, making Exeter the obvious destination.

population and greater demand for cereals we can surmise that the city's grain hinterland may have extended farther in the earlier period. Yet the late fourteenth-century grain hinterland of Exeter was surprisingly large and diverse, stretching well into south Devon, the most arable-intensive region in the county.[55] Court cases concerning grain sales in the late fourteenth century show that at least two malt sellers came from Kingskerswell, about 17 miles away in south Devon.[56] Both of these men disposed of malted wheat, while another south Devon man from Newton Abbot (13 miles away) marketed over one quarter of barley malt.[57] Yet another malt seller came from Chudleigh, located just north of Newton Abbot near the borders of Dartmoor.[58] Malt and barley were also sold in Exeter by men from east Devon parishes such as Bampton (almost 20 miles north up the Exe Valley), Newton St. Cyres and Crediton (both within seven miles in the part of east Devon bordering mid-Devon), Cullompton (12 miles to the east of Exeter), and the nearby manors of Clist Gerard, Alphington, Stoke Canon, and Heavitree.[59] Oats vendors came from Alphington and Stoke Canon, as well as from Witheridge, 15 miles away in the heart of the oats-producing region of mid-Devon.[60] Rye was sold by residents of Crediton and Honiton (17 miles to

---

[55]For south Devon agriculture see Fox, "Devon and Cornwall," pp. 305–07. For a map of the city's grain hinterland at this time see Kowaleski, *Local Markets and Regional Trade*, Fig. 7.1.

[56]MCR 1370/71, m. 41d; PCR 1–23 Ric. II, m. 49.

[57]WQMT 1400.

[58]MCR 1391/92, m. 47.

[59]PCR 1–23 Ric. II, mm. 14 (Reginald Croppe was from Stoke Canon), 25, 49, 60; MCR 1373/74, m. 18; 1375/76, m. 5; 1386/87, m. 6; 1389/90, m. 22 (William Radeclyf, from Clist Gerard); 1390/91, m. 16 (Giles de Esse, from Knowle in Crediton); WQMT 1400.

[60]PCR 1–23 Ric. II, m. 14; MCR 1386/87, m. 7; WQMT 1403. Malted oats also came from Newton St. Cyres (MCR 1373/74, m. 18).

the east),[61] while wheat was marketed in Exeter by men from Martock, over 38 miles away in Somerset.[62]

The locations of manorial demesnes that carted grain to Exeter to provision the lord's household or supply others there also offer some clues about the city's hinterland for grain. In 1391/92 the reeve of Sherford Manor, situated well over 30 miles to the south of Exeter near the Kingsbridge estuary, "sold to the granary at Exeter" about 16 quarters of wheat, 17 quarters of barley, and one quarter of oats.[63] Closer to town (within eight miles) was the manor of Hele, whose reeve delivered over eight quarters of oats to Exeter for the horses of the lord and his steward and an additional 1.5 quarters to a man who had loaned him oats at Exeter.[64] Demense and tithe grain from the estates of the dean and chapter of the cathedral was also carted to Exeter, most from the manors closest to Exeter. From their coastal manor of Dawlish 11 miles to the south came a variety of produce, including oats that had already been milled.[65] Tithe grain from Stoke Canon, just north of the city, was usually collected in the manorial barn for the use of the canons; in some years tithe grain from nearby Ide, Littleham, Dawlish, and even Culmstock, some 17 miles away in east Devon, was similarly treated.[66] When combined with the evidence from customary carrying services and the court cases, these data, although hardly systematic, suggest that Exeter's grain hinterland extended furthest (about 30 miles to the south and east) for the most expensive grains (wheat,

---

[61]MCR 1390/91, m. 16.

[62]MCR 1392/93, m. 21.

[63]BL Add. Roll 13091; Sherford was owned by the Benedictine priory of St. Nicholas in Exeter.

[64]Somerset Record Office, DD/CN/Box 3/14, mm. 9, 17.

[65]ECL D&C 5030.

[66]ECL D&C 3777, mm. 47d, 48d, 50–50d; 5031, 5232, 5234, 5238.

malted barley, and malted wheat) and that it reflected the regional specializations that agricultural historians have previously noted for medieval Devon.[67]

This same evidence can tell us something about who sold grain in towns like Exeter during the fourteenth century. Such large estate owners as the dean and chapter were obviously important sellers of grain in medieval Devon, but their sales have left little trace in the extant records. In the late thirteenth and early fourteenth centuries such sales were sometimes recorded as formal recognizances in the borough court rolls. In the 1290s, for example, two Exeter men made a recognizance to purchase 21 marks' worth of corn at the hamlet of Coddiford in Crediton, while four others promised to pay for part of the demesne wheat and one-half of the oats tithes of Woodbury Manor for £15.[68] In 1286, Henry de la Forde made a similar recognizance for corn he purchased at Littleham for over 9 marks from the treasurer of Exeter Cathedral; repayment was to be made at Exeter in two equal installments.[69] Such recognizances were also employed by the dean and chapter in the late fourteenth and early fifteenth centuries, to market their tithe and demesne grain. Unfortunately for us, these recognizances became so formulaic by the second half of the fourteenth century that they noted only the parties to the debt and the amount owed rather than offering the detail available in the earlier recognizances.[70]

---

[67]On this last point see esp. Fox, "Devon and Cornwall," pp. 303–09, and idem, "Peasant Farmers, Patterns of Settlement and *Pays*: Transformations in the Landscapes of Devon and Cornwall during the Later Middle Ages," in *Landscape and Townscape in the South West*, ed. Robert Higham (Exeter, 1989), pp. 57–64 and Fig. 12.

[68]MCR 1291/92, m. 28d; 1299/1300, m. 15.

[69]MCR 1285/86, m. 8.

[70]Thus when suing for unpaid sums on these recognizances they noted the amount of the debt or the existence of a written obligation but never the reason for the

The grain marketing activities of substantial landlords elsewhere has been discussed at length in several recent studies. Manors disposed of surplus grain in a variety of ways; some was sold directly to consumers (usually local tenants) and some was purchased by corn dealers and merchants, while roughly one-third probably went to markets for sale.[71] Few of these markets were more than 10 miles from the manor, although more distant markets could be targeted when prices were higher. Once at these markets, the grain might be sold directly to consumers or bought up by cornmongers for sale elsewhere or at a later date. From the Exeter evidence, it seems that much of this grain was sold in smaller lots to a variety of consumers, once it reached the market.

Lay lords with smaller holdings may have followed a different path. The Devon landowner Giles de Esse, for example, sold almost four quarters of malt in 1391 to John Shephurde (probably the Exeter baker and innkeeper of that name).[72] He apparently made the sale in two lots, of 13 bushels and 16 bushels, without the intervention of a middleman, reeve, or bailiff.[73] That three years earlier Esse had been sued by John Shephurde for breaking an agreement is perhaps an indication of a long-standing arrangement between the two men.[74] Esse

---

debt; see their debt suits in MCR 1387/88, mm. 28, 31d, 41, 42, against the tithe farmers of St. Sidwell, as noted in ECL D&C 2707, m. 2d; 2708.

[71]For this and the following see David L. Farmer, "Two Wiltshire Manors and Their Markets," *Agricultural History Review* 37 (1989): 1–11; idem, "Marketing the Produce of the Countryside, 1200–1500," *Agrarian History* 3: 358–67; Campbell et al., *Medieval Capital*.

[72]MCR 1390/91, m. 16; there were two John Shephurdes (brothers) at this time; one was a baker, one a butcher. John Shephurde baker was also a brewer (WQMT 1387–93), an activity that depended on malt.

[73]Note that the sergeant, not the lord, made grain sales for the small lay manor in Essex studied by Richard Britnell, "Production for the Market on a Small Fourteenth-Century Estate," *Economic History Review*, 2nd ser., 19 (1966): 380–87.

[74]MCR 1387/88, m. 28.

owned £35 worth of land in Devon, including small manors in east Devon and scattered properties in Exeter and Crediton.[75] He lived at Great Ash (about 12 miles to the northwest in the parish of Crediton) but owned property in Exeter and paid rent for a house there.[76] His property interests in Exeter are an indication of his strong connections in the town, in large part because his first wife was Alice Rede, the extremely wealthy widow of the Exeter oligarch John Rede.[77] Before his marriage to Alice, Esse also had mercantile interests, on one occasion importing steel at Exeter and on another purchasing over £105 worth of merchandise at Bristol with four other men.[78] After his marriage to the wealthy Alice he seems to have limited his commercial interests and settled down to the life of a country squire, serving on two occasions as a county tax collector.[79] His past mercantile experience may in part explain why he appears to have handled the grain sale himself, or it may be that smaller lay lords commonly handled marketing arrangements such as this, particularly if they had strong social and economic ties to one market community.

---

[75]PRO E159/169 Hilary recorda, m. 16. In 1412 his properties were worth £40 (*Inquisitions and Assessments Relating to Feudal Aids*, 1: *Bedford to Devon*, ed. A. S. Maskelyne [London, 1899], p. 418). He was also known as Giles Aisshe.

[76]*CPR 1381–1385*, p. 504; *The Register of Edmund Stafford (A. D. 1395–1419): An Index and Abstract of Its Contents*, ed. F. C. Hingeston-Randolph (London, 1886), pp. 93, 274, 504; MCR 1390/91, m. 28; T. W. Venn, "Crediton alias Critton alias Kirton and Hereabouts," unpub. typescript deposited in the West Country Studies Library (Exeter, 1955): 159–60.

[77]*The Register of Thomas de Brantyngham, Bishop of Exeter (A.D. 1370–1394)*, ed. F. C. Hingeston-Randolph, 2 vols. (London, 1901–06), 2: 451 (Rede's estate was valued at £717); PCR 1–23 Ric. II, m. 56; MCR 1390/91, m. 17.

[78]PCA 1381/82; PRO C241/166/78 (where he is identified only as a "merchant of Devon," but his unusual name and association in this deal with a man called Andrew Deicestre—Andrew of Exeter—strongly suggest that this was the same Giles de Esse noted here).

[79]*CFR 1377–1383*, p. 338; *CFR 1391–1399*, p. 78.

Reeves and bailiffs also visited Exeter to market manorial corn or other produce. A reeve's duties, as the custumal of Branscombe made clear, included doing business for the lord at local markets, fairs, and towns.[80] The reeve at Dawlish was rewarded with a special cash payment for selling the manor's grain tithes and conducting other business for his lord.[81] As the biggest market town in medieval Devon, Exeter must have served as a magnet for manorial officials who were seeking purchasers for surplus demesne grain. Such officials included men like Walter Colman, the reeve of Langford Manor, some eight miles up the Culm Valley, who made several trips to Exeter one year on the lord's business, probably to market the rye produced on the demense.[82] Many other reeves were drawn to Exeter because of its role as an administrative center. Reeves and bailiffs for the manors of the dean and chapter, for example, regularly showed up in person at the latter's exchequer to make payments on rents, arrears, and other items.[83] These visits could easily have accommodated marketing activities on the lord's, or even on their own, behalf. Appearances in Exeter courts by men such as Henry Godale, a reeve of Thorverton, to answer a complaint of debt by the farmer of the manor, the Exeter canon William Feriby, suggest that Godale's business there might have been related to manorial affairs.[84] John Denebaud, the bailiff of St. Sidwell's fee and manor outside the East Gate, grew peas and other crops there, farmed almost £3 worth of tithes one year, and also made grain sales of two

---

[80]ECL D&C 3683, fol. 8d; see also Farmer, "Marketing the Produce," pp. 363–67, for marketing by reeves.

[81]He received 1 mark (ECL D&C 5032).

[82]Corpus Christi College, Oxford, Kn. 3/1.

[83]ECL D&C 2706–08; 2713; 3777, passim.

[84]MCR 1385/86, m. 26; 1388/89, m. 4; ECL D&C 2708; 3777, fol. 4; see also PRO CP40/480, m. 89d; CP40/484, m. 370d.

quarters of barley and about seven bushels of malted barley to local residents.[85]

Tithe farmers were also major grain sellers, marketing corn both in gross and at retail. Their ranks included Richard Lucas of Heavitree, a rural parish of about 3,500 acres only one mile from Exeter. Lucas farmed the tithes of Heavitree for at least four years in the 1380s, normally paying £20 or more each year.[86] This put him in a good position to supply grain to nearby Exeter residents, as is indicated by the fact that he always appeared as a creditor and never as a debtor in the borough courts. His sales included 5*s.* worth of grain to an Exeter skinner and 24*s.* of malt to an Exeter hosteler.[87] On one occasion Lucas's grain-marketing activities seem to have extended to the importation of 40 quarters of wheat and two quarters of malt.[88] Other tithe farmers also expanded their grain marketing over some distance. John Hytteway of Sidbury, one of three tithe farmers who paid £28 for the great tithes of Sidbury (15 miles to the east) was called a "cornmonger" in his dealings with the Exeter hosteler Thomas Coblegh, an appellation he had also received many years earlier in transactions in the small town of Sidmouth.[89] Hytteway had a fair-sized holding at Sand Barton in Sidbury, consisting of a messuage

---

[85]MCR 1382/83, m. 7; 1391/92, m. 32; PCR 1–23 Ric. II, mm. 38, 70; ECL D&C 2708, 4859 (25 Oct. 1391).

[86]ECL D&C 5233–35, 5238. The tithes may have come from only the vicarage lands; see Ethel Lega-Weekes, "The History of St Katherine's Priory, Polsloe. Part IV. Polsloe Tithes," *TDA* 70 (1938): 424.

[87]PCR 1–23 Ric. II, mm. 60, 85.

[88]PCA 1394/95; his name appears without a residential designation (itself an indication that he was probably well-known in Exeter), but it was probably the same man. This was the sole appearance by a man of this name in the local port customs, he was the only importer on this ship, and he also paid custom, for which he would have been liable as a resident of Heavitree.

[89]ECL D&C 2708, 5238; PCR 11 Edw. III–1 Ric. II, m. 77d; BL Add. Charter 27284.

and eight ferlings (roughly 180 acres), so he himself may also have produced grain for the market.[90] Other tithe farmers controlled even larger acreages. John Wonard of Clist St. George, a lawyer of the minor gentry who had extensive holdings in several rural manors and who purchased the tithes of Clist Honiton for over £7, frequently appeared in the Exeter borough courts as a creditor.[91]

Exeter residents were also tithe farmers, usually buying up the valuable tithes of the suburban manors outside the North and East gates. John Burnard, an Exeter hosteler who farmed wheat and barley in the eastern suburb, purchased the tithes of Polslo, St. Sidwell's, and St. David's (the latter two were suburban manors of Exeter) for at least three years in a row, once with John Sturre, another hosteler/farmer, and once with William Lange, a butcher/farmer, paying over £27 one year.[92] Only one of his grain sales was recorded (12*s.* worth of corn to an Exeter fisher), but his dealings with three different bakers suggest that he may have sold some of his grain to them.[93] Another tithe farmer was John Scarlet, a brewer who bought the St. Sidwell tithes with two others for over £26 and also purchased more than £13 worth of "diverse grains" from the dean and chapter with Robert Plomere, a fellow landholder in St.

---

[90]ECL D&C 2945; PRO JUST3/15/7, m. 2. The acreage is an average since ferlings in Devon ranged from 15 to 30 acres (Finberg, *Tavistock Abbey*, pp. 39–40).

[91]PRO CP40/472, m. 120d; CP40/490, mm. 151, 180, 226d; ECL D&C 2945, 5232, 5234; *Calendar of Inquisitions Miscellaneous*, 7: *1399–1422* (London, 1969), p. 121; he also served as an MP for Exeter and other Devon towns (J. J. Alexander, "Exeter Members of Parliament. Part II. 1377 to 1537," *TDA* 60 [1928]: 203). He appeared as a creditor five times and a debtor twice in MCR and PCR debt cases, 1378–88; as a creditor 11 times (for amounts over £2) in PRO CP40/472, mm. 120d, 199; CP40/490, m. 151; PRO C241/151/24, 155/87.

[92]ECL D&C 5232, 5233, 5235, 4857 (12 Oct. 1379), 2708, 2713. For the marketing of tithes by York artisans see Heather Swanson, *Medieval Artisans: An Urban Class in Late Medieval England* (Oxford, 1989), p. 136.

[93]PCR 1–23 Ric. II, mm. 60 (Moses and Hugh Baker), 73 (Alexander Baker), 78.

Sidwell's.[94] The only recorded sales by Scarlet are for very small amounts of wheat and beans, so it may be that he intended to use most of his grain purchases in his brewing business, which was probably the largest in Exeter at this time.[95] His fellow purchaser, Robert Plomere, was also a major brewer who sent considerable sums of grain to local mills; several times he accused millers of taking portions of the grain he sent to be milled, citing totals of two quarters of oat malt, six bushels of barley malt, two bushels of malt, and another 40*d.* worth of malt.[96] The extent to which he himself consumed or marketed this grain is unclear.

The tithes and manors controlled by individual members of the clergy also made them important sellers of grain in both the first and second halves of the fourteenth century. Entrepreneurial Exeter canons such as John Cheyne and Hugh Bridham paid large sums to purchase the tithes of such nearby manors as Heavitree and St. Sidwell; Bridham and other canons (e.g., William Feriby and Robert Vaggescombe) also farmed manors owned by the dean and chapter (Ide, Norton, and Thorverton) or properties owned by other ecclesiastical institutions (e.g., Totnes Priory's lands in Broadclyst).[97] Vicars all over Devon also bought up the tithes of the rural parishes they served. The vicar of Morthoe annually paid at least £13 for the tithes of his parish, the vicar of Colyton paid over £32, and the vicar of Culmstock, £9.[98] Since it was unlikely that all this surplus

---

[94]ECL D&C 2707; MCR 1388/89, mm. 6, 7.

[95]ECL D&C 4857 (9 Nov. 1379). He was the only man ever termed "brewer" in the records and was frequently involved in debts concerning sales of ale.

[96]MCR 1378/79, mm. 46, 47; 1379/80, mm. 5, 10; EQMT 1384.

[97]ECL D&C 2706, m. 1; 2857; 3550, fol. 67; 3777, m. 4; 5232; PRO CP40/480, m. 392. For other examples see ECL D&C 2713; PRO SC6/1102/1.

[98]ECL D&C 3777, fols. 47d, 48d, 50d; 5234, 5238; for other examples see ECL D&C 2706–08, 2713.

grain was destined for the clerics' own households, much of this tithe grain, as well as grain from the demesnes farmed by individual clerics, must have been put on the market for sale. Grain marketing by clerics in Exeter is evident in the sale of over 10*s.* worth of wheat and beans by the archdeacon of Exeter to Alexander Cole, a villager of Woodbury, located eight miles south of the city; in the one quarter of malted oats sold by the servant of the vicar of Newton St. Cyres to an Exeter resident; and in the substantial debt that at least one Exeter baker owed to the canon William Feriby, who farmed several manors.[99] Clerics also sold locally, as when the bailiff of the parson of Powderham, a small coastal village just south of Exeter, sold two bushels of barley to one of his parishioners.[100]

Among the more active grain sellers were the cornmongers and (especially in Devon) oatmongers, who often served as middlemen between producers and consumers. Since the civic authorities believed that their enterprises raised prices and reduced town customs, the circumstances surrounding their appearance in the Exeter records were usually negative. Cornmongers came to Exeter both to buy and sell grain, although the only specific references to their carrying grain out of the city for sale elsewhere occurred in the early fourteenth century when grain shortages were more common.[101] In the late fourteenth century they were mainly criticized for buying up grain before it went on sale in the market or purchasing grain in order to resell it later at a higher price. When grain prices were low such activities were sometimes tolerated, but when prices rose, so did the chance that any intermediaries in the grain

---

[99]MCR Roll 1, m. 8d (1286); 1373/74, mm. 5, 18; PCR 1–23 Ric. II, m. 71.

[100]MCR 1305/06, m. 4.

[101]MCR 1315/16, m. 23d; 1322/23, m. 4d.

trade would be hauled into court and fined. Such court presentments were especially numerous in 1390–91, 1396, and 1399–1400, for example, years when prices of particular grains were extremely high.[102]

Although sales and especially purchases by cornmongers could take place at unsanctioned locations, most nonresident grain traders clearly centered their activities on the town's marketplace.[103] Some idea of the amounts they marketed can be gained from the presentments against them in the court rolls, although such sums were obviously estimates. While individual sales ranged from two bushels to three quarters, annual sales of 20, 40, and even 100 quarters were noted.[104] In the late fourteenth century these corn dealers often came from east Devon (Crediton, Honiton, Sidbury) and west Somerset (Martock), but the grain they sold in Exeter could have come from elsewhere, since they traveled the countryside, buying up supplies for sale.[105] Many were engaged in other activities as well. John Hytteway, the cornmonger from Sidbury, also bought up wool from local manors and farmed about 180 acres of land.[106] Two Somerset men, John Belchere and William Yonge, sold wheat to two Exeter bakers but also regularly traded for fish, as did John Cokyll of Somerset, who sold beans and peas, and John Everard of Cullompton, from whom a sack

---

[102]MCR 1390/91, m. 16; NQMT 1390, 1391; SQMT 1391, 1396, 1400; WQMT 1396. For prices see Table 2 and David L. Farmer, "Prices and Wages, 1350–1500," in *Agrarian History*, 3: 503. For a similar situation elsewhere see Derek Keene, *Survey of Medieval Winchester*, 2 vols. (Oxford, 1985), 1: 252–53.

[103]MT, passim; see also MCR 1391/92, m. 52; 1391/92, m. 2.

[104]SQMT 1396; WQMT 1400, 1405–06, 1410–11, 1413.

[105]PCR 47 Edw. III–1 Ric. II, m. 77d; MCR 1390/91, m. 16; 1392/93, m. 21. For cornmongers' forays outside urban markets see MCR 1322/23, m. 4d; PRO JUST1/195, mm. 2, 8d; PRO CP40/509, m. 289d; Farmer, "Marketing the Produce," pp. 363–75.

[106]ECL D&C 2713 and above, n. 90.

of malted wheat was stolen.[107] Whether these men specialized in corn or fish or both is difficult to determine.

Most of the individual grain sellers, whether small lay lords, tithe farmers, clerics, reeves, bailiffs, or cornmongers, sold at retail as well as in gross. An analysis of 80 sales of grain made in Exeter between 1378 and 1393 reveals something of the nature of this trade, particularly the retailing end.[108] While the recorded transactions were for amounts ranging from one bushel to about 70 quarters, the average amount sold was 13 bushels, and sales of more than five quarters were rare. Over 90 per cent of the grain sales were for sums less than £1, which indicates the predominance of retail transactions between individual consumers and dealers. The average debt for grain was just over 7*s.*; in the 1380s, when grain prices were generally low, this sum could buy 10.25 bushels of wheat, at a

[107]WQMT 1403; SQMT 1372, 1384–93; MCR 1375/76, m. 5; 1392/93, m. 21.

[108]The sample was selected from debt cases concerning grain in the Exeter courts; 43 were drawn from an analysis of all debts (4,526) in the Exeter borough courts (MCR and PCR) from 1378–88; this analysis is discussed in more detail in Kowaleski, *Local Markets and Regional Trade*, pp. 347–49. The remainder were randomly selected from MCR 1370/71–1376/77, 1388/89–1392/93; MT 1375–96; and the St. Sidwell Court Rolls 1379/80 and 1391–93 (ECL D&C 4857–58). When only the sum of the debt was known the amount of grain actually transferred was calculated using the prices in Farmer, "Prices and Wages, 1350–1500," pp. 502–03. Amounts of malt were estimated by adding 1.5*d.* per bushel to the price of the grain specified; this differential was derived by calculating the average difference in price between barley and first-grade malt as noted in J. E. Thorold Rogers, *A History of Agriculture and Prices in England from the Year after the Oxford Parliament (1259) to the Commencement of the Continental War (1793)*, vol. 2 (Oxford, 1884), pp. 234–35 for 1377–93. For the 31 cases involving unspecified "malt," it was assumed that the malt was made of barley. While this assumption could deflate the amount of cereal calculated if the malt was made from lower-priced oats (often the case in medieval Devon), the use of Farmer's wholesale prices serves as a counter-balance, since the retail prices represented in these debt cases were almost certainly higher than the wholesale prices Farmer derived mainly from manorial accounts. The difference between retail and wholesale prices is confirmed in those debt cases where the price, amount, and type of grain were noted; retail prices ranged from 2.6*d.* to 9.4*d.* more per bushel than wholesale prices, with the greatest differences being registered for wheat and barley.

time when eight bushels was enough to make some 250 loaves of bread weighing about two pounds each or to brew roughly 60 gallons of strong ale.[109] Over the span of a year an adult probably consumed about 12 bushels of bread grains and perhaps 16 bushels of malted grains for ale.[110] Those who kept horses had larger requirements, since cart horses needed almost seven quarters of oats per year.[111] Thus purchases of one quarter of grain (eight bushels) would have to be made almost monthly to feed a family of four and even more frequently if horses were kept.

For the grain sales occurring in the marketplace, the Exeter authorities, like officials in other towns, specified certain locations for the sale of oats and wheat.[112] City officials were anxious to channel all sales to the central marketplace, where they could more easily regulate and tax transactions; yet vendors often risked the heavy fines that could be assessed and made bargains outside the sanctioned locations: in other streets, in houses, next to the West Gate, on the roads coming into the city.[113] One of the biggest problems concerned the

---

[109]Average price based on data from 60 cases (n. 108, above). For Exeter wheat prices see Beveridge, "Statistical Crime," p. 531. For the bread and ale figures, which probably represent a fairly high standard of living, see Dyer, *Standards of Living*, pp. 57–58.

[110]Dyer, *Standards of Living*, pp. 152–53; these estimates are based on peasant maintenance agreements, since few figures are available for urban dwellers. Dyer's figures may be a little large, even for the late fourteenth century when living standards were higher than around 1300, when Campbell et al. (*Medieval Capital*, pp. 33–35) think that *per caput* consumption in London was only about 13.5 bushels (1.65 quarters) of grain—a figure that includes livestock consumption.

[111]John Langdon, "The Economics of Horses and Oxen in Medieval England," *Agricultural History Review* 30 (1982): 33.

[112]Kowaleski, *Local Markets and Regional Trade*, pp. 181–83.

[113]For example, MCR 1324/25, m. 2d; 1374/75, m. 17; 1390/91, m. 16; SQMT 1372, 1391. Concern for these practices surfaced most often in times of shortage or high prices.

sale of flour and meal in private houses and in nonstandardized measures, since individual sales of these items were usually for very small amounts. This trade was largely in the hands of women, some of whom forestalled the market by purchasing flour from people leaving the city's mills in the northern suburb of Duryard and then resold it at a higher cost in the town marketplace.[114] Grain deals must also have been made in private, particularly for bulk transactions, but there is little trace of this in the records. The prominence of hostelers as grain sellers and the presence of rural grain sellers at Exeter inns, however, suggest perhaps one locale where such bargains could have been struck.[115]

Sales of malted grains were mentioned much more frequently than any other variety, accounting for 65 per cent of the Exeter grain sales in the last decades of the fourteenth century.[116] While malted barley was increasing in popularity during the late fourteenth century, oat malt remained common in many parts of Devon; the Exeter sources mention both, along with malted wheat.[117] The frequent references to malt reflect the high levels of urban ale consumption; ale brewing and consumption expanded in Exeter and other English towns during the late fourteenth and early fifteenth centuries, as is indicated by the substantial increase in the number of urban brewers.[118] Malt imports also became more common during this

---

[114]MCR 1324/25, m. 15d; 1376/77, m. 6; 1390/91, m. 16. The flour custom was the only city custom regularly farmed by women (Exeter City Receivers' Accounts 1368/69, 1372/73–1374/75, 1384/85, 1385/86).

[115]For hostelers in the grain trade see below, pp. 47–48. For nonresident grain dealers at Exeter inns see MCR 1375/76, m. 5.

[116]They accounted for 52 of the 80 sales; wheat, eight; barley, oats, and beans and peas, five each; rye, two. The remainder were unidentified by type.

[117]Malted barley was noted six times; oat malt, five times; wheat malt, three times; the other references did not specify the type of malt.

[118]For this expansion in Exeter see Kowaleski, *Local Markets and Regional Trade*, ch. 3, esp. Table 3.2. For the expansion elsewhere see Keene, *Medieval Winchester*

period (Table 2). Commercial brewers, particularly hostelers, probably represented the single biggest group of malt buyers. They could stockpile fairly large amounts of malt; one of the wealthier hosteler/merchants, William Rok, at one time had at least six quarters of malt stored in his establishment.[119] But it was the individual households that brewed commercially who together constituted the greatest urban malt consumers. Joan and Matthew Ekesbonere (a spurrier), for example, were substantial brewers who made individual malt purchases of 3*s.*, 3*s.* 1*d.*, and 18*s.* and also paid 5*s.* for six bushels of barley and 18*s.* 4*d.* for 12 bushels of malted wheat, amounts sufficient to brew roughly 400 gallons of ale.[120]

Specific sales of other types of grain were noted less frequently than bargains made for malt. The small number of retail transactions for wheat and rye largely reflects the dependence of urban residents on bakers for bread. In Exeter as in other English towns, most bread was produced in the establishments of bakers rather than in domestic ovens.[121] Few grain purchases of bakers were noted, however, perhaps because they tended to make bulk purchases under a recognizance. Their purchases were clearly larger than those of most Exeter buyers. The baker William Shildon, for example, purchased about 50 bushels of rye, while his fellow baker John Shephurde was prosecuted for diverting 13 quarters of wheat to a mill not owned by the city.[122] On occasion, substantial bakers also imported grain; John Dollying imported wheat once

1: 267–69; R. H. Britnell, *Growth and Decline in Colchester, 1300–1525* (Cambridge, 1986), pp. 88–93, 144, 269.

[119]MCR 1385/86, m. 20.

[120]PCR 1–23 Ric. II, mm. 38, 43, 49, 61, 62; MCR 1380/81, m. 12.

[121]Keene, *Medieval Winchester* 1: 254–55.

[122]PCR 1–23 Ric. II, m. 73; EQMT 1384.

in 1320 in partnership with two wealthy Exeter merchants, and William Gardiner imported five cargoes of wheat and rye in 1399/1400.[123] Most of the Exeter bakers seem to have concentrated their efforts on wheaten bread, since the Duryard mills, which all the city bakers were compelled to use, sold off eight times as much wheat as rye from the multure collected at the mill.[124] At the Crikelpit mills near Exe Bridge, which were employed mainly by individual consumers, profits came primarily from malted grains, with "tolcorn" a distant second, followed by wheat.

Peasant producers must have provided much of the grain consumed by Exeter residents. It is likely that most of this grain arrived in small lots that peasants or the dealers who purchased supplies from them then sold in the marketplace. The amounts peasants carried to market were probably limited by the reliance upon pack horses in medieval Devon; while a cart could haul up to four quarters of grain, pack horses could carry only about four bushels or less.[125] Even some Devon manorial lords seem to have envisioned carriage by pack horse for their customary carrying services. The custumal of Branscombe, a manor situated almost 20 miles to the east of Exeter, specified one load as either four bushels of wheat, barley, rye, beans, or peas or six bushels of oats; two such carriages were required annually of each tenant, either between the demesne and the Exe River (Exeter being the obvious destination) or the

---

[123]Kowaleski, *Local Customs Accounts*, p. 181; PCA 1399/1400. For their activities as bakers see WQMT 1309; MCR 1328/29, m. 34d; 1332/33, m. 2d; 1397/98, mm. 7d, 19d, 21d, 30d.

[124]Duryard Receiver's Accounts 1370/71–1389/90. For the following see Exe Bridge Wardens' Accounts, passim.

[125]Based on figures given in John Langdon, "Horse Hauling: A Revolution in Vehicle Transport in Twelfth- and Thirteenth-Century England?" *Past and Present* 103 (1984): 59. For the difficulties of transport in Devon see Kowaleski, *Local Markets and Regional Trade*, pp. 48–49.

demesne and the Axe River.[126] In the 1380s and 1390s four bushels of wheat sold wholesale for about 2.8*s.*, four bushels of oats for 1.2*s.*[127] Malted grains fetched slightly higher prices: four bushels of malted wheat went for about 3.2*s.*, malted barley, about 2.4*s.*, and malted oats, about 1.7*s.* Yet even if peasants came to town with two or three pack horses loaded with grain, they were unlikely to collect more than 10*s.* in any one trip, even considering the greater profits they might have accrued through smaller retail sales. This sum is very close to the average 9*s.* debt of non-Exeter grain sellers in the borough courts in 1378–88. With a cartload of wheat they could do better, taking home a little over £1, while a cartload of oats would fetch 9–10*s.*

The average sale of nonresident grain vendors in late fourteenth-century Exeter was just over 14 bushels, a little higher than the average of 13 bushels for all sellers.[128] Nonetheless, about 44 per cent of the non-Exeter vendors sold eight bushels or less, roughly the amount that could be carried on two pack horses. The sack of malted wheat containing four bushels that was stolen from John Everard of Cullompton at the inn of Thomas Coblegh may well have constituted the sum total of the grain he had brought with him on that trip.[129] Yet the bushel of oats that John Pitman of Witheridge sold for 14*d.* may have represented only one sale out of several that he had made in the marketplace.[130] Others traded larger

---

[126]ECL D&C 3683, fol. 8 (dated 1339).

[127]Prices based on average of those in 1380–99 as stated in Farmer, "Prices and Wages, 1350–1500," p. 444; for the derivation of the prices of malted grains see above, n. 108.

[128]Amounts or prices known for 41 sales by nonresidents in the sample; see above, n. 108.

[129]MCR 1375/76, m. 5.

[130]MCR 1387/88, m. 6.

amounts, particularly to bakers, hostelers, and commercial brewers. John Frigge sold seven quarters of rye to John Brendon, an Exeter baker/hosteler; William Growbe transferred about 6.25 quarters of rye to the baker William Shildon; and Richard Lucas of Heavitree sold over three quarters of malt to the hosteler Walter London.[131] Given the larger amounts these vendors sold, it is possible that they struck private bargains with purchasers in advance of delivery, perhaps based on samples they had brought with them on earlier trips. Complaints against vendors who "detained" grain, such as those made by the merchant John Grey against Martin Fishacre for two quarters of wheat or by Thomas Houghe against Walter Clerk for 12 bushels of beans, 26 bushels of beans, and 12 bushels of wheat, point to this form of sale.[132]

Exeter residents also acted as intermediaries in the grain trade, although their activities were largely restricted to the city and its suburbs in the late fourteenth century. Much of the trade in flour and meal was in the hands of poorer women and men, sometimes identified only with the surname "Melmanger" and obviously dealing on a purely retail basis.[133] Malt was frequently retailed by brewers, particularly female brewers, who probably dominated the retail trade in malt as they did the brewing industry. Most malt sellers brewed frequently, and, unlike the flour- and mealmongers, they more often enjoyed high status. Of four women accused in 1364 of being common regrators of malt *in foro*, one (Heloise Noble) was the widow of an ex-mayor, one (Isabel Troubrigg) was married to an oligarch,

---

[131]PCR 1–23 Ric. II, mm. 24, 60, 73.

[132]PCR 1–23 Ric. II, mm. 85, 86; MCR 1381/82, mm. 48, 49.

[133]SQMT 1339 and MT, passim, esp. for presentments on selling oats, salt, or flour in their houses or in false measures; and see above, n. 114. Imports of flour were few; see Table 2 under "Grain Types."

and another (Claricia Plente) was the mother of a mayor.[134] With their financial resources, these women were obviously in a position to buy up malt and retail what they did not use in their own businesses; given their regular dealing in malt, we may suppose them also to have been maltsters. Women were a highly visible presence in the malt trade; it is striking, for example, to see how wives automatically appeared with their husbands in debt cases concerning malt, when they were normally omitted from all other commercial disputes involving their spouses.[135]

Because brewers, bakers, and hostelers were the biggest buyers of grain in the city, they also had an opportunity to sell some of their purchases. Most of their recorded transactions were retail sales, as is indicated by the charges brought against them of regrating grain or selling oats in semi-filled or improper measures. In contrast to the situation that seems to have existed in such towns as Winchester, bakers in Exeter did not play much of a part in selling grain.[136] Hostelers enjoyed a more substantial role, as is indicated by their more frequent appearance as tithe farmers and payers of fines for improperly selling oats in their inns. Such Exeter hostelers as John Burnard, John Sturre, and John Splot purchased tithes in the suburban manors for large sums and also sold grain.[137] Their grain-trading enterprises were probably limited by their own

---

[134]SQMT 1364. Heloise sometimes appeared under her husbands' names (Robert Noble, Thomas Webber) and Isabel, under hers (Peter); Clarice was the mother of Roger Plente and widow of the oligarchic merchant Walter Plente (NQMT 1360–76; EQMT 1360–69).

[135]The five purchases made by Matthew and Joan Ekesbonere are a good example; see above, n. 120.

[136]Keene, *Medieval Winchester* 1: 254; nor did Exeter bakers lease any grain mills in this period, as bakers did in Winchester.

[137]ECL D&C 2707, m. 2d; 2708; 5232–33, 5235; 3550, fol. 67; 3777, fol. 50. For Burnard and Sturre see also above, p. 36.

tremendous need for oats (for stabled horses) and malted grains (for ale) in their inns. With the possible exception of the merchant importers of grain (who may have augmented their activities with bulk grain purchases from the surrounding countryside), Exeter people generally restricted their grain sales to the retailing of relatively small amounts, leaving the supply of grain and bulk transactions largely in the hands of non-Exeter residents.

The retail trade in grain changed less than the wholesale and import trade during the fourteenth century. In both the first and second halves of the century nonresidents (especially peasant producers) were probably responsible for most grain sales; women always played an important role, particularly in the sale of malt, flour, and meal; and most retail transactions occurred in the marketplace, usually in a location set aside for the sale of grain. But even in grain retailing there were notable differences in the conduct of trade in the first and second halves of the century. Before 1350 the town more closely regulated the grain trade; most of the annual Mayor's Tourns commenced with lists of grain forestallers and regrators, and there are many more direct references to how such practices contributed to the impoverishment of the people and famine in times of shortage.[138] Grain shortages may have encouraged those who could to stockpile as much grain as possible, thus affecting buying patterns in the marketplace.[139] Residents of Exeter were also more directly involved in grain production

---

[138]For example, MCR 1313/14, m. 28; 1315/16, m. 23d; MT, passim.

[139]Grain assessed for taxation in the early lay subsidies could have represented grain stockpiled in anticipation of the needs of the household and local shortages; James F. Willard (*Parliamentary Taxes on Personal Property, 1290 to 1334: A Study in Mediaeval English Financial Administration* [Cambridge, Mass., 1934], pp. 84–85) believes that this grain was meant to be marketed rather than stockpiled.

before 1350; references to the cultivation of wheat, barley, peas, and especially beans by both artisans and merchants in the suburbs outside the East and North gates are far more frequent in the earlier period.[140] After the Black Death rising standards of living also promoted greater use of malt in ale brewing, so that malt tended to dominate retail sales in the urban marketplace.

Although more changes occurred in the wholesale trade of grain, some features of the bulk trade remained relatively stable during the century. Estate sales of cereal crops always furnished large amounts of grain to Exeter and other towns, while small estate owners and the clergy, in their role as tithe owners, vicarage holders, and manorial farmers, also regularly marketed grain. Tithe marketing by small landowners, the clergy, and such urban residents as hostelers and other artisans was a regular feature of the late fourteenth-century trade and probably of the earlier trade, although the records to show this are not extant for Exeter. It is possible that individual members of the clergy played a more active role in grain marketing in the later period, as demesne leasing by ecclesiastical institutions intensified; certainly this was the pattern followed by the Exeter canons, whose commercial activities as farmers of the manors of the dean and chapter increased in the late Middle Ages. In contrast, the role played by cornmongers in the grain trade declined markedly in the late fourteenth century; evidence from both London and Exeter indicates that they considerably scaled back their activities.[141]

Changes probably also occurred in the size of the hinterland for grain upon which Exeter drew, but these are more difficult

---

[140]For example, MCR 1289/90, m. 33d; 1298/99, mm. 19, 24; 1301/02, m. 33d; 1309/10, m. 31d; 1312/13, m. 5d; 1317/18, mm. 43d, 45d; 1318/19, m. 49d.

[141]Farmer, "Marketing the Produce," pp. 370–74; see also Campbell et al., *Medieval Capital*, on this point.

to trace. The larger demand for grain in the early fourteenth century must have enlarged the area from which the city drew supplies, although the grain hinterland was still fairly large in the late fourteenth century. In the first half of the century the city itself also served a more central role in the regional marketing of grain, acting as a bulking center for grain that could be distributed (usually by overland routes) elsewhere in the region.[142] Sales at Exeter to such nonresident bakers as William de Bynedon in 1336 show that wholesale buyers came to Exeter seeking large quantities of grain.[143] Certainly the larger cereal imports of the early fourteenth century must have promoted Exeter's role in the distribution of grain to its hinterland. Evidence that Exeter performed this function to the same extent in the late fourteenth century is less forthcoming.

The most dramatic changes in the grain trade occurred in the seaborne trade, which witnessed marked differences in the amounts, average cargoes, and personnel involved in the first and second halves of the fourteenth century. Demand for grain in the early fourteenth century, especially during the Great Famine of 1315–22, was much greater and often rooted in shortages, as the seasonality of imports makes clear. Greater demand made for larger profits, which pushed the richer oligarchic merchants of Exeter into the grain import trade in greater numbers before 1350; their participation generally declined after this period as reduced demand and the lower scale of the

[142]There are far more references in debt cases to nonresident grain buyers at Exeter before the Black Death than later in the century. For references to corn being carried out of the city to other markets see MCR 1315/16, m. 23d; 1322/23, m. 4d. For grain imports to Exeter shipped elsewhere see above, n. 18. See also Kathleen Biddick, "Missing Links: Taxable Wealth, Markets, and Stratification among Medieval English Peasants," *Journal of Interdisciplinary History* 18 (1987): 277–98, on the role towns played as grain bulking centers in this period.

[143]He purchased 28*s*. worth of corn from Robert White of Plymouth (MCR 1335/36, m. 27d).

trade made substantial profits less likely. In the second half of the century their place and that of foreign merchant-importers was increasingly supplanted by shipmaster-importers, who expected less profit. Despite these changes in personnel, foreign sources of grain supplies were always more important at Exeter than grain shipped by coast from eastern England. Only disruptions of the traditional trade routes for grain during the conflicts of the Hundred Years War altered the carriers of grain shipments to Exeter, and probably sources of supply as well. In the early fourteenth century Exeter overseas trade focused largely on Picardy and Normandy, which supplied not only grain but also woad, a valuable blue dye; as the war heated up, Breton and Channel Island shippers became more prominent, and Picardy in particular declined in importance as a grain exporter to Exeter.

Grain imports generally followed the trend of wheat prices, although in some years, particularly in 1319/20, when imports reached the astronomical level of almost 12,000 quarters, high imports lagged one year behind a particular rise in wheat prices. These lags, along with the low level of imports during the first two years of the Great Famine, point to the commercial impact of regional price variations, which in Exeter's case might have been partly due to the dependence on oats in Devon. Regional price differentials were actually greater in the second half of the century than in the first, but the reduced demand for grain after 1350 altered mercantile response to these differentials. When prices rose enough to threaten shortages, however, Exeter importers were quicker to step up their importing activities, as is evident in the early 1370s and in 1399/1400, when they captured a larger share of imports.[144]

---

[144]In the early 1370s their imports accounted for 30 per cent of imports and in 1399/1400, 28.5 per cent, compared to the 17 per cent share they enjoyed for the second half of the century as a whole; see Table 1 and Table 2.

Their response, as well as that of foreign and shipmaster-importers to fluctuations in demand at Exeter, also indicates the highly commercial nature of the seaborne grain trade and its international connections. Such imports provided coastal communities greater flexibility in meeting their fundamental need for grain, especially in the early fourteenth century, when the balance between local consumer demand and local supply was more precarious. In illustrating the different marketing patterns for cereals during the fourteenth century, the Exeter evidence thus gives us a better understanding of how urban demand and the vagaries of arable agriculture helped determine patterns of local, regional, and international trade.

THE TOWN OF RAMSEY: THE QUESTION OF ECONOMIC DEVELOPMENT, 1290–1523[1]

Anne Reiber DeWindt

The monastic town of Ramsey, perched on the edge of the Huntingdonshire fens, might claim kinship with hundreds of small market towns throughout medieval England. What distinguishes Ramsey from many others is its relatively large collection of sources, which begins in the late thirteenth century and carries forward through the sixteenth century. It is this abundance of primary source material that encourages questions about change and allows the historian to wonder how life during the reign of Edward I was different from life at the time of Henry VIII.

Such musings soon raise the thorny issue of "economic development" at a time when some historians are challenging the relevance of such a concept to societies such as late medieval England. Towns such as Ramsey may have made pragmatic shifts back and forth among a variety of social and economic organizational structures until long after both the medieval and the early modern periods.[2] Profound transformations in the

---

[1]I thank Kathleen Biddick, Richard Britnell, Judith Bennett, and Sarah Gravelle for helpful comments on earlier versions of this essay. I also received stimulating comments from participants at the Fourth Anglo-American Seminar on the Medieval Economy and Society (Leicester, 17–20 July 1992).

[2]Note Derek Keene's introduction to Penelope J. Corfield and Derek Keene, eds., *Work in Towns, 850–1850* (Leicester, 1990), "Continuity and Development in Urban Trades: Problems of Concepts and the Evidence."

scale of agrarian and industrial production, as seen in the eighteenth and nineteenth centuries, are not immediately relevant to discussions of medieval and early modern towns and villages.[3] This means that the task of the historian—constructing a narrative of change over time—can be redirected and does not have to shoulder the responsibility of tracing the presumably progressive stages that "culminated" in a single climactic agricultural and industrial revolution.[4]

Economic historians and historical geographers have recently revealed the remarkable growth in the number of markets in England during the course of the twelfth century and, as they disappeared from smaller communities, the subsequent concentration of markets in the larger towns.[5] Ramsey was granted a Wednesday market charter in 1200 and from 1267 was the site of an annual fair, which was held until at least the mid-fourteenth century.[6] Such links with regional and national trade networks are undoubtedly crucial to a full understanding of change in that town. With an increase in the number of taxpayers from 169 in 1290 to 247 in 1523, Ramsey, in at least one

---

[3]One study of a village community would date significant change in community life to as late as 1900. B. J. Davey, *Ashwell, 1830–1914: The Decline of a Village Community* (Leicester, 1980).

[4]See Mark Overton, "Agricultural Revolution? England, 1540–1850," in Anne Digby and C. H. Feinstein, eds., *New Directions in Economic and Social History*, vol. 1 (Basingstoke, 1989): "This research shows that the process of agricultural change is too continuous and too varied to enable any one episode in a long history of development to be identified as *the* agricultural revolution" (p. 9).

[5]For example, Tim Unwin, "Towns and Trade 1066–1500," in R. A. Dodgshon and R. A. Butlin, eds., *An Historical Geography of England and Wales*, 2nd ed. (London, 1990), pp. 123–49; R. H. Britnell, "The Proliferation of Markets in England, 1200–1349," *Economic History Review*, 2nd ser., 34 (1981): 209–21. See also James Masschaele, "A Regional Economy in Medieval England," unpub. Ph.D. thesis (Univ. of Toronto, 1990).

[6]*Victoria County History: Huntingdonshire*, vol. 2 (Folkestone, 1974 [repr. of 1932 ed.]), p. 188 (hereafter, *VCH Hunts*). In the surviving monastic accounts the last reference to the fair is in 1353; see BL Add. MS. 33445, fol. 57v.

sense, must have benefited from the shifting patterns of the concentration of market activity in Huntingdonshire.[7]

This essay will focus on the micro level, in an effort to discover the role of individual Ramsey residents as agents in these larger, national, processes. Decisions made at the local level must always be respected as part of the complex pattern of cross-regional economic activity. Decisions about what to produce, which services to provide, and which markets to seek for those products and services always involve very personal, and necessarily local, conditions.

John Patten has suggested that economic change, prior to the modern industrial revolution, was the cumulative effect of innumerable individual decisions: "The individual was at the root of the urban [and, I might add, the agrarian] geography of the time to a much greater extent than now."[8]

The medievalist's challenge, therefore, would be to trace the twisting paths of those decisions. As is always the case, the historian must face the hard fact that source survival shapes any impressions regarding the nature and extent of change. Ramsey's sources are fairly typical of the kinds of sources surviving from many well-documented medieval villages and towns, so discussion of the nature of those documents and questions raised about changes over time in those documents as texts should be relevant.

The documents that survive from late thirteenth-century Ramsey are texts of a very different kind from those of the 1520s. This simple, unavoidable fact raises an inevitable

---

[7]The 1290 figure includes Bury and Hepmangrove. J. Ambrose Raftis and Mary Patricia Hogan, *Early Huntingdonshire Lay Subsidy Rolls* [Toronto, 1976], pp. 42–56 (hereafter, *Early Hunts. Lay Subsidy Rolls*). For the 1523 lay subsidy see PRO E179/122/91.

[8]"Urban Occupations in Pre-industrial England," *Transactions of the Institute of British Geographers*, n.s., vol. 2 (1977): 296.

question: Did the town of Ramsey experience substantive economic or social change over that time period, or is it simply the *messager* that takes on a different "personality"? Does our historical narrative shift direction because the actors in the drama have changed their behavior or because a new group of storytellers has replaced the old? In Ramsey's case, the extent of economic change can easily be overestimated, and the significance of those changes that are apparent will be missed, unless it is noted that each decade of Ramsey's history provides its own unique combination of primary sources.

Ramsey's sources can be divided into two general types, those that reveal vertical relationships among townspeople and their social superiors and those that reveal horizontal relationships among the townspeople themselves. Obedientiary accounts (Ramsey was part of the wealthy Benedictine abbey's *banlieu*) and royal subsidies filter out horizontal relationships among the townspeople themselves and highlight those between tenants and their monastic lord, or among the king's subjects and his royal bureaucrats. Charters, wills, and the earlier town court rolls filter out vertical relationships and highlight those among neighbors and family members. In general, the sources that reveal horizontal relationships tend to be those initiated from within the town itself, whereas the other sources are the results of royal or monastic initiatives that elicited responses, often reluctant ones, from the townspeople.[9]

The fact that one type of source dominated the earlier period of Ramsey's history and another type of source dominated the later period poses a challenging paradox (see Tables 1 and 2).

---

[9]This oversimplification obscures the fact that when the abbey offered tenancies, initiatives may have come from tenants eager to withdraw from a tenement or to campaign aggressively for an opportunity to take one up.

TABLE 1
RAMSEY'S VERTICAL SOURCES (NUMBER OF DOCUMENTS) 1250–1620

Decades	Abbey Accounts (Post-1540: Cromwell Accounts)	*Liber Gersumarum* (Number of Ramsey Entries)	Lay Subsidies	Churchwardens' Accounts	Parish Registers (Ramsey and Bury)
1250					
1260	1				
1270					
1280	2				
1290	1		2		
1300					
1310	4				
1320	3		1		
1330	2		1		
1340					
1350	8				

TABLE 1—*Continued*

Decades	Abbey Accounts (Post-1540: Cromwell Accounts)	*Liber Gersumarum* (Number of Ramsey Entries)	Lay Subsidies	Churchwardens' Accounts	Parish Registers (Ramsey and Bury)
1360	3				
1370					
1380	9				
1390	39	5			
1400	27	12			
1410	33	16			
1420	19	23	1		
1430	32	35	1		
1440	74	45			
1450	32	15	1		
1460	13				
1470	20				

1480	36				
1490	6				
1500	18				
1510	23			11	
1520	49		3	7	
1530	5			4	
1540	4		3	6	
1550	17		2	1	1
1560	7		1		19
1570	2				20
1580	2				20
1590			1		20
1600					19
1610					19

TABLE 2
RAMSEY'S HORIZONTAL SOURCES (NUMBER OF DOCUMENTS) 1250–1620

Decades	Town Court Rolls	Wills or Administrations	Charters	Feet of Fines
1250			11	
1260	1		2	
1270			2	
1280	3		14	
1290	4		19	
1300	9		27	
1310	5		41	
1320	8		43	
1330	5		57	1
1340	4	1	46	
1350	9		47	4
1360	7		18	2

1370	5		10	2
1380	13		15	
1390	10		20	
1400	3		19	2
1410	4		16	
1420	6		15	1
1430	5		16	6
1440	2	1	9	
1450	5	2	11	
1460	6	1	10	
1470	1	1	2	
1480		1	5	3
1490	1		3	

TABLE 2—*Continued*

Decades	Town Court Rolls	Wills or Administrations	Charters	Feet of Fines
1500	1		1	4
1510	2	1	3	3
1520		3	2	
1530	8	2	1	
1540	11	1	1	3
1550	15	25	2	5
1560	11	25		2
1570	14	10	1	2
1580	24	32	16	2
1590	9	53	2	2
1600	3	46		
1610		15		

Horizontal relationships appear to provide scope for a greater number of economic decisions, simply because a man or woman has many more neighbors than kings or overlords, so that when the earlier Ramsey records provide more detail about horizontal relationships they reflect a vital, flexible economy with varied opportunities for investment and growth. For example, in the leet courts and charters of the early fourteenth century a townsman may appear in a debt plea, as ale brewer and tanner, as a pledge for the future behavior of a neighbor or family member, and as the grantor or grantee of a messuage or plot of arable land and meadow. The text of a horizontal source presents Ramsey individuals embedded in a web of complex social and economic relationships with their neighbors.

Because vertical relationships appear to isolate the individual from his fellows and lift him out from apparent constraints of communal life or familial obligations into a larger world of monastic estates, county, and king, it is tempting to herald this later change in the sources as the emergence of some "liberated" *homo economicus*. Vertical sources provide lists of these disengaged individuals, filed by orders from the landlord, Parliament, or, later, Thomas Cromwell, into categories such as rent payer, taxpayer, or the baptized or buried. For example, a tenant listed in the midst of a string of others in an almoner's account held on to one tenement for several years and then later appeared as tenant of another plot belonging to the treasurer. Years later he held a tenement from yet another obedientiary, from whom he withheld part of his rent and paid a reduced rate.[10] These "vertical" texts thrust the subject onto a bare

[10]To illustrate: Richard Hert held a tenement of the almoner in 1509 (BL Add. MS. 33449, fol. 34r). By 1512 he held a tenement from the treasurer, from whom he withheld part of his rent (BL Add. MS. 33449, fol. 41d). In 1536 he appears in the accounts of the chamberlain who received rent from the warden of the chapel of Blessed Mary for a tenement held by Richard Hert (BL Add. Roll 34606).

stage, stripped of his network of extended family and neighbors, "liberated" from both his rivals and his support systems.[11]

The search for the individual decisions that shaped Ramsey's economic history therefore must be undertaken in two very different source environments. The key question, of course, remains: Do these changes in the sources signify substantive changes in lifestyle or world-view on the part of Ramsey's inhabitants?

At first glance the two documents that would appear to provide anchors for a study of economic change in Ramsey would be the two royal subsidies of 1290 and 1523. They offer seemingly consistent material for a comparison of late thirteenth-century Ramsey with the early sixteenth-century town because they appear to be similarly "vertical" documents, in the sense that they both were initiated from Westminster and both pluck individual Ramsey inhabitants out of their neighborhood networks to respond to orders from their king. Differences between the two documents are profound, however, and give the 1290 subsidy many of the characteristics of horizontal sources such as leet court rolls or charters (see Table 3). It is much easier to associate the taxpayer of 1290 into a network of economically interdependent neighbors and family members than it is to do the same thing in 1523, when most

---

[11]What price these "liberated" men and women paid for their presumed release from neighborhood networks remains an important question. There is no doubt that the historian pays a price—best illustrated by contrasting the amount of detailed information available in the 1290 lay subsidy with that in the 1523 subsidy. Paul Glennie appreciates the problems raised by the changing nature of available sources, but his categorization of the earlier sources as "feudal" implies that they were primarily vertical. I have not described the earlier Ramsey sources in the same terms. See Glennie, "In Search of Agrarian Capitalism, c. 1450 to c. 1560," *Continuity and Change* 3, pt. 1 (May 1988): "So it is perhaps understandable that the transition from medieval society, visible largely through feudal eyes, to early modern society with its very different array of documentary sources, has come to be associated with major qualitative changes in economic and social life" (p. 13).

individuals are categorized into formulaic niches of a class hierarchy, niches that result from a bureaucratic desire for order originating from royal officials and that obscure the rich variety of individual responses to economic opportunity.

Both subsidies produced lists of individual names along with assessments created through the machinery of an experienced local leadership, but the 1523 subsidy categorized taxable wealth only as "goods and chattels," "wages," or "land" (see Table 4). Over one-third of the names listed in 1523 are lumped together under the category of £1 worth of goods or wages, and most of the other assessments fall into standardized units of £2, £3, or £4. A class stratification scheme has replaced the gradual spectrum of various assessments that appear in the detailed document of 1290, when the town leaders left behind descriptions of an individual's assets such as wheat or barley, carts, eels, and fodder, and when very few people were assessed at exactly the same amount as a neighbor. Women were directly represented less than half as often in the 1523 subsidy as in the 1290 subsidy.[12] In other words, a greater variety of individual decisions is revealed in the 1290 document than in the later subsidy.[13] Excerpts from each subsidy roll illustrate some of these crucial differences (see Tables 3 and 4).

---

[12]Fourteen per cent (24) of the 169 individuals from 1290 were women. Five per cent (13) of the 249 individuals from 1523 were women. In 1523 all but one of the women mentioned were widows. The 1290 subsidy for Ramsey with Bury and Hepmangrove has been edited by Raftis and Hogan, *Early Hunts. Lay Subsidy Rolls*, pp. 42ff. For the 1523 subsidy see PRO E179/122/91.

[13]The collectors of the 1290 lay subsidy penetrated a little further into the family economy, revealing more about the division of labor and investments among individual family members. Single representatives of a surname group are a little more likely to "represent" untaxed relatives in the later period: in 1523, 37 per cent of the taxpayers shared a surname with at least one other taxpayer; in 1290, 45 per cent of the taxpayers shared a surname with another taxpayer.

Table 3

Excerpts from the Ramsey Lay Subsidy of 1290

(See Raftis and Hogan, *Early Hunts. Lay Subsidy Rolls*, p. 49.)

Robert Clere:	1 qr. wheat, 2 qr. drage, 3 cows, 2 calves (present year), 1 pig, 3 piglets, 400 of thatch. *Sum*: 26*s*.2*d*. *Thence* 15th: 21*d*.
Benedict Clere:	4 cows, 4 two-year old mares, 4 calves (present year), 5 pigs, fish in pond 2s., 100 of fodder. *Sum*: 33*s*.4*d*. *Thence* 15th: 2*s*.2*d*.*ob*.*q*.
Emma Clere:	1 cow, 2 two-year old bullocks, 1 calf (present year), 200 of fodder. *Sum*: 9*s*.2*d*. *Thence* 15th: 7*d*.*q*. *Additional*: 1*d*.*ob*.
Margaret Herveus:	3 cows. *Sum*: 12*s*. *Thence* 15th: 9*d*.*ob*. *Additional*: 1*d*.*ob*.
John de Smalwode:	6 bu. wheat, 3 qr. drage, 3 qr. beans and peas, 3 cartloads of hay, 1 mare, 1 three-year old foal, 1 foal (present year), 1 cow, 2 two-year old bullocks, 3 yearling bullocks, 1 calf (present year), 4 pigs, 3 sows. *Sum*: 45*s*.9*d*. *Thence* 15th: 3*s*.*ob*. *Additional*: 1*d*.*ob*.
Peter la Lanender [*sic*]:	5 qr. grout, 3 qr. malt, 6 cows, 2 two-year old mares, 2 yearling calves, pigs, retained fish 16*s*., reeds worth 2*s*.6*d*. *Sum*: £4 20*d*. *Thence* 15th: 5*s*.5*d*.*q*. *Additional*: 1*d*.*q*.
Robert Chaceden:	3 cows, 3 three-year old mares, 4 calves (present year), 6 pigs, 500 of fodder. *Sum*: 29*s*.8*d*. *Thence* 15th: 23*d*.*ob*.*q*.

TABLE 4
EXCERPTS FROM THE RAMSEY LAY SUBSIDY OF 1523/24
(PRO E179/122/91)
(Bury cum Hepmangrove: Names of persons taxed and the value of their grant towards the subsidy of the lord king.*)

	Goods/Chattels	Subsidy
John Andrew sr.	£9 (g)	4*s*.6*d*.
John Andrew jr.	20*s*. (g)	4*d*.
John Goslyn	100*s*.	2*s*.6*d*.
William Samwell	60*s*.	18*d*.
William Darley	40*s*.	12*d*.
John Robyns, his servant	20*s*.	4*d*.
Thomas Edward	£10 (g/c)	5*s*.
William Tailor	20*s*.	4*d*.
Richard Halley	£4	2*s*.
Richard Thompson	40*s*.	12*d*.
Thomas Caster	20*s*.	4*d*.
Robert Brothe	60*s*.	18*d*.
Richard Goreser	20*s*.	4*d*.
John Clerke	20*s*.	4*d*.
William Campion, in wages	20*s*.	4*d*.
William Halley	£7 (g/c)	3*s*.
Thomas Stone	20*s*. (g)	4*d*.
Robert Parisseye	20*s*.	4*d*.
Thomas Wright, laborer	40*s*.	12*d*.
John Lane	£4	2*s*.
William Wilderove, laborer	20*s*.	4*d*.
William Bentley	£7 (g/c)	3*s*.6*d*.
William Wright	60*s*. (g)	18*d*.
William Wilson	£4 (g)	2*s*.
Margaret Baker	£8 (g)	4*s*.
Thomas Dymylby	£15 (g)	7*s*.6*d*.
Richard Fenell	40*s*. (g)	12*d*.
Blase Roresyng	40*s*. (g)	12*d*.
William Sewer	100*s*. (g)	2*s*.6*d*.
John Ridmayn	£19 (g/c)	9*s*.6*d*.
" "	in lands and free tenements per year: 100*s*.	

*These are the first 30 names in the subsidy list, in the order in which they appear in the manuscript.

The 1523 subsidy presents a picture of a "stylized" town more fragmented than that of 1290. The spread between the highest and lowest assessments is much greater in 1523 than in 1290, and class labels such as "laborer," "yeoman," and "gentleman" are new to the later period.[14] How should we interpret these textual differences? They can easily mislead us into an exaggerated contrast between the two eras. Even though the term "laborer" does not appear in 1290, wage earners certainly were present in great numbers in late thirteenth-century Ramsey, judging from the number of fines in the court rolls for receiving outsiders and from the fact that in other Ramsey sources 150 contemporary surnames appear, representing individuals who apparently failed to accumulate the minimum wealth to qualify for appearance in the subsidy list.[15] It may be true that the assessors were dipping further down into the poorer strata of Ramsey inhabitants in 1523 than in 1290,[16]

---

[14]The titles "widow" and "laborer" appear in the 1523 subsidy. The other class titles appear in such contemporary sources as wills or court rolls. The highest assessment in the 1290 roll, which includes Ramsey, Bury, and Hepmangrove, was £16 17*s*.6*d*.; the lowest 1290 assessment was 80*d*., a spread of £16 10*s*.10*d*. The highest assessment in the 1523 roll (for goods and chattels only), which also included Ramsey, Bury, and Hepmangrove, was £133 6*s*.8*d*.; the lowest 1523 assessment was £1, a spread of £132 6*s*.8*d*.

[15]L. R. Poos noticed (in Essex) a high level of wage dependence in 1524, i.e., taxpayers assessed on wages and on goods worth less than 40*s*. (43 per cent in three central hundreds); see idem, *A Rural Society after the Black Death: Essex, 1350–1525* (Cambridge, 1991), pp. 30–31. He notes "a very pronounced imbalance of landed resources and wage dependency" and a "remarkable continuity of landholding profiles throughout the period of this study" (1350–1525); reliance on wage earnings in Essex dates at least as early as 1381. Poos continues, "the poll-tax data and the tenurial patterns are . . . strikingly consistent. No more than one-quarter, and in practice probably rather fewer, of the families in north-central Essex derived their livelihoods from agriculture on their own properties to such a degree that their contemporaries regarded them primarily in these terms" (pp. 23–24).

[16]All "household stuff" was assessed in 1523, whereas there were exemptions in 1290. "And of every person borne under the kynges obeysaunce yerely duryng the said twoo first yeres for every pounde in coyne and the value of every pounde that

but the lowest assessments in 1290 certainly also included many individuals who earned wages, judging from the number of individuals on the monastery's payroll at that time, and judging from the fact that 13 individuals (8 per cent) in 1290 were assessed for neither livestock nor crops and 63 individuals were assessed for livestock only.[17] Men and women labored in exchange for wages in the thirteenth century as well as in the sixteenth, and it seems unlikely that all of those earlier wage earners could have escaped royal taxation. Nonetheless, the label "laborer" is a sixteenth-century phenomenon.[18]

The contrast between the 1290 document and the 1523 document now becomes clearer. It appears that by 1523 personality and individuality have been sacrificed for the sake of a

---

any suche person hath of his owne in plate, stocke of marchaundise, all manner of cornes and blades severed from the grounde, houshold stuffe and of all other goodes and catell moveable as well withyn this realme as without . . ." (*The Statutes of the Realm* [London, 1810–28; repr. 1963], 3: 231). Even though the peasant's household goods and food in the larder were not explicitly exempted in 1290, they were left unvalued. "Such goods as a man needed for his life work, whatever that might be, were not assessed for the levy of taxes." (James F. Willard, *Parliamentary Taxes on Personal Property, 1290 to 1334: A Study in Mediaeval English Financial Administration* [Cambridge, Mass., 1934; repr. New York, 1970], pp. 79–80).

[17]With only one exception there are no records of assessments for crops from the poorest third of the individuals assessed in both 1290 and 1295; this would indicate that they may not have held any land beyond an urban tenement. In a 1264 list of 22 named abbey servants (*garcones*) most stipends were ca. 2*s*. (see BL Cotton Galba E.X., fol. 8). The Ramsey cartulary includes a late thirteenth-century list of monastic servants with payments in bread or landed allotments in various Ramsey vills. Twenty-three of those job descriptions coincide with Ramsey surnames; see W. H. Hart and P. A. Lyons, *Cartularium Monasterii de Rameseia*, 3 vols. (London, 1884–93; repr. Weisbaden, 1965), 3: 236–41.

[18]For example, Godfrey Andrew was fined as early as 1280 for receiving a mower. See Edwin B. DeWindt, ed., *The Court Rolls of Ramsey, Hepmangrove, and Bury, 1268–1600* [Toronto, 1990], **1280**, entry no. 97 (henceforth, *Court Rolls*). (All subsequent references to the Ramsey court rolls are from this edition; entry dates are printed in bold type.) The earliest use of "laborer" occurs in the court rolls in **1392** (no. 55) when a group of men was fined for being outside tithing; one man was described as a "laborer," along with mention of a couple of tailors and several servants.

systematic vision of class hierarchy. In fact, the context or frame supporting individual identity has shifted. From the assessors' point of view individual identity hung on the nature of the taxpayer's investments in 1290, but in 1523 identity hung on association with others who shared a similar level of wage income or a similar quantity of capital goods.

Therefore, in spite of the fact that both subsidies are "vertical" documents, the survival from 1290 of uniquely individual assessments allows the historian to appreciate the networks of interdependence among neighbors and even among individual family members.[19] Some investments were in livestock only and others were in various combinations of crops and livestock.[20] The fact that individuals specialized in certain kinds of assets indicates a reliance on networks of exchange. For example, 1 per cent of the 1290 taxpayers were assessed only for crops; 38 per cent were assessed only for livestock; and 8 per cent had neither crops nor livestock among their assessed goods. Twenty-two per cent of the taxpayers were assessed for fish, eels, nets, or boats, yet most of those assessed for eels did not have fish included in their assessments.

The 1290 subsidy roll reveals patterns of specialization even among members of the same surname group. For example, there are 26 individuals bearing the surname Chaceden in the Ramsey sources between 1287 and 1340. Three male Chacedens paid tax in 1290. All three had livestock, yet only one was assessed for fodder. All three wives were brewers, but only one

---

[19]See Raftis and Hogan, *Early Hunts. Lay Subsidy Rolls*, pp. 15–17.

[20]Were there any question about the role of the market in such cases, the presence of Adam Fulham, a citizen of London in the 1290 lay subsidy who was assessed for fish, should dispel any such doubts. Also see Kathleen Biddick's study of the Bedfordshire lay subsidy for further investigations of peasant specialization ("Medieval English Peasants and Market Involvement," *Journal of Economic History* 45/4 [Dec. 1985]: 823–31).

of the men was assessed for malt, or, indeed, for any crop at all. The largest assessment was assigned to the oldest man, and one male relative was not assessed at all.[21] This specialization within a family "corporation" allowed several Chacedens over the course of two generations to pursue the perhaps not-incompatible professions of ale brewer and clerk.

The Ramsey taxpayer in 1290 raised sheep or pigs, cultivated barley or wheat or oats, or was a fisherman with boats and nets. In 1523 the taxpayer was defined simply as a wage earner, or as a member of a group associated with a specific level of capital ownership. *Capital* in the earlier period could be identified with a variety of named goods. In 1523 *capital* takes on an abstract numerical value. Is this abstraction an accident of record survival? Certainly many 1290 subsidy rolls do not include the detailed descriptions left behind by the Ramsey assessors, so it is unclear whether the difference between the two Ramsey subsidies reflects a change in attitude toward wealth, or capital, by 1523.[22]

These important differences between the two subsidies are typical of the differences between the entire collection of sources available for the study of Ramsey prior to the Black Death and most of those from the early sixteenth century. The later sources that survive in the greatest number lift townspeople out of any clearly visible network of horizontal, or peer,

---

[21]For two Robert Chacedens' assessments see Raftis and Hogan, *Early Hunts. Lay Subsidy Rolls*, pp. 49, 56. Of the three Chacedens assessed in 1290, Robert Chaceden "cook" is the first to appear in the records. He appears on the 1264 list of monastic servants and received a 2*s.* stipend (BL Cotton Galba MS. E.X., fol. 8). Richard and Thomas Chaceden appear as witnesses in several mid- to late-thirteenth-century Ramsey charters but do not appear in the 1290 lay subsidy (see BL Add. Charters 33406, 33632, 33708, 33709, 33710, 33711, 33713, and 33704, 33705).

[22]Jim Masschaele's study in the present volume demonstrates that two fourteenth-century London merchants conceptualized *capital* not in the abstract but as meaning material, physical goods.

relationships and isolate them in their relationships with both the abbot who collected rent from them or paid them wages and the king who collected taxes from them.

Not only do monastic accounts begin to survive in significant numbers only after the 1380s and '90s[23] but also by the sixteenth century the later town court rolls have changed dramatically, revealing fewer of the networks of interpersonal relationships that characterized the late thirteenth-century debt pleas, pledging relationships, and fines for receiving outsiders into town illegally and trespassing against neighbors' properties.

The sixteenth-century court appears less frequently as an institution available for the negotiation of interpersonal disputes or exchanges (plaints disappear at the end of the fifteenth century), more and more as an institution for the publication and enforcement of ordinances and the regulation of trades and agriculture by town officials.[24] Weavers are listed in the court rolls in 1397, fullers by 1422, dyers by 1519, and collar-makers by 1542. Perhaps mediation of interpersonal disputes[25] was still entrusted to the town jury, whose activities in that arena are no longer reflected in the later court rolls. It is also possible that the increasing number of officials chosen by the court and listed in the court roll—new officers such as fen reeves, hay-

---

[23]An unclassified central account dates from 1331/32. BL Add. Roll 34517.

[24]There is one final, brief section of plaints in the 1501 Ramsey court roll. In the 1530s a spate of assault cases appears. A similar pattern appears in Havering records, where the number of personal suits opened in court dropped sharply between 1405 and the 1440s but increased again after 1460. Marjorie K. McIntosh, *Autonomy and Community: The Royal Manor of Havering, 1200–1500* (Cambridge, 1986), tables, pp. 193, 199. Similar patterns in other leet courts are cited (p. 199, n. 49) by McIntosh from the work of Elaine Clark and Christopher Dyer.

[25]In the Havering court records McIntosh found reference to private compromises among disputants made "through the counsel or intervention of their friends or neighbours" (*Autonomy and Community*, p. 191).

wards, and inspectors of meat and fish—may also have provided leadership in settling disputes outside of court.[26]

Earlier court rolls recorded transfers of property among town inhabitants. There are 15 entries in the pre-Black Death courts recording such "horizontal" transactions.[27] The fifteenth- and early sixteenth-century rolls have no such entries. In the 1530s, after the cellarer's court ceased to record land transfers, grants from the abbot began to be recorded in the court rolls. Thus large sections of these later court rolls take on the appearance of a monastic account, and this format almost transforms these court rolls into vertical sources.[28]

Finally, charters were used by some townsmen and -women to sanction exchanges of town properties, so they provide an excellent source of information about individual investment decisions. In conformity with the pattern that has been emerging so far, the greater number of these charters survive from the period before 1400. Charters were probably chosen as the technology of transfer during this time because they provided a tool for a detailed description of property transferred with the support of witnesses in extra-traditional exchanges involving women, clerics, and foreigners not "covered" by customary transfers. In any case, if survival is a reliable indicator this particular tool was less highly valued in the fifteenth century,

---

[26]Constables are mentioned much more frequently after the Black Death than before. Over time the number of village offices and corresponding titles grew in number; e.g., the court roll of 1459 notes the election and swearing in of one constable, two ale tasters, two keepers of the marsh, and one capital pledge. Later, tasters of meat and fish appear (**1473**, no. 49). The hayward appears after the Black Death, and the fen reeve in the early fifteenth century. A number of new offices are mentioned for the first time in the sixteenth century, including such titles as supervisor of the cow path, overseers of Muchwood, fen and field; hog reeve; and wardens of the free warren.

[27]Most of these are orders to show charters. See E. DeWindt, *Court Rolls*: **1297[1]**, no. 21; **1309[2]**, nos. 4, 5; **1317**, nos. 89–106; **1321**, nos. 33, 34.

[28]Note the series of grants from the abbot to tenants in the court rolls 1535–42.

and transfers were later sanctioned in ways that did not leave traces for later study.[29]

Given the preponderance of vertical sources during the latter period of this study, we must acknowledge the kinds of individual decisions thrust to the forefront during that time period, that would thus shape the historian's image of Ramsey's economy. How might those decisions differ from those revealed by the greater frequency of horizontal documents during the pre-Black Death period?[30]

Vertical documents give us the impression that we can assess the relative success of individuals presumably in competition for monastic tenements or for the material wealth that would attract the interest of tax collectors. Decisions about which type of tenement to acquire from the abbot, how many of these to invest in, whether to invest in opportunities such as an inn, a waterway ferry,[31] or a fishpond;[32] whether or not to seek employment from the abbot for such tasks as administration or maintenance and repair work, and decisions about how much time should be invested in the holding of town offices—these are areas open to historians of the fifteenth and early sixteenth centuries.

---

[29]See Table 2.

[30]Yet another combination of sources characterizes the period after 1530. Much of our information about early sixteenth-century townspeople comes from sources such as monastic accounts bearing barren formal entries without hint of subletting arrangements and very sparse descriptions of the nature of the property holdings, royal subsidies with no individualized information about investment strategies, or court rolls in which fewer and fewer networks of individual interactions are apparent; but the sixteenth century also saw the appearance of the individual will, in which bequests reveal ties within and outside the family. Parish registers survive from mid-century and provide the first real opportunity to trace marriage alliances among the town families.

[31]BL Add. Charter 33447 (dated 1397) records a grant of all profits from a certain ferry at Paddock. Rent from an inn called the Crown appears in the sacristan's accounts from 1535 (BL Add. Roll 34755).

[32]For example, BL Add. Roll 34608 from 1406.

The horizontal documents, that is, the charters and court rolls of the early fourteenth century, combined with the detailed assessments of the 1290 lay subsidy, bring different kinds of individual decisions to the fore. Ramsey's inhabitants were deciding whether or not to lend and borrow capital from each other,[33] whether or not to purchase, sell, or sublet messuages or fractions of messuages among themselves. They decided whether or not to sanction the exchanges taking place among their neighbors by either agreeing or refusing to act as witnesses to those transactions. They were deciding how to apportion their time and capital among livestock such as cattle, bulls, oxen, and sheep and landed property such as arable, meadow, or pasture. Should arable be devoted to malt, wheat, or oats? Should capital be directed toward the accumulation of urban messuages, the purchase and repair of such equipment as carts, weirs, hedges, walls, and fences? Would the assumption of responsibility for the behavior of a neighbor be beneficial or too time-consuming and intrusive? I doubt that economic decisions were radically distinct from such social decisions, especially if Ramsey's social and political networks helped define one's economic opportunities in what was certainly a society based on a complex exchange of "favors" and services.

It does not seem reasonable to assume that the category of decisions revealed by horizontal sources ceased to be relevant to Ramsey's economy at the same time that those sources ceased to reign supreme in the archives. For that reason, it is difficult to abandon the attempt to find a consistent medium that can be used across the centuries to monitor "real" changes in economic decision-making. Because the court rolls cover this entire

---

[33]Debt pleas no longer appear in the court rolls after 1460. The amounts of debts run from 4*d*. to 21*s*. A £20 debt plea involving a Ramsey resident appeared before Common Pleas in 1392 (PRO CP40/525, m. 321r).

period, 1290–1520, perhaps they offer such a tool, despite the fact that they too change over this period. These evolving court documents do reveal one institution that persisted over that entire period, and, even though it also was subject to change,[34] the leet court jury does provide material for a comparison of some economic decisions made by town leaders in 1290 with those made in 1523. Because an individual's identification with a trade or craft does not rely completely on consistency of source material, it is useful to trace the trades associated with successive generations of juries. Certainly the types of trades engaged in by jurors reveal the occupations that provided the kind of economic base and/or status required for leadership in the town courts.

From the earliest court rolls to the end of the sixteenth century at least, the town court was regulating the practice of certain, select, trades. When this information was combined with the descriptive titles associated with some individuals and with surname evidence from the earlier period when surnames and occupations were most likely to coincide, a study of the jurors' trades was found to be possible.[35]

The data for the initial stages of this study are based on a sample of Ramsey town court jurors from four decades, 1280–97, 1383–93, 1426–36, and 1530–40. These 176 men provide the focus for an examination of individual decision-making within the context of occupations and trades.

---

[34]See Anne Reiber DeWindt, "Local Government in a Small Town: A Medieval Leet Jury and Its Constituents," *Albion* 23/4 (1991): 627–54.

[35]The use of the prefix *le* before many of the surnames in pre-Black Death Ramsey encourages the assumption that surnames were still associated with trades. The surname Tanner appears in the 1290 lay subsidy in connection with the assessment of a tannery. For one discussion of the nature of surname evidence see Zvi Razi, *Life, Marriage, and Death in a Medieval Parish: Economy, Society, and Demography in Halesowen, 1270–1400* (Cambridge, 1980): "In the post-plague era surnames stabilized and only a small number of villages had aliases" (p. 3).

These Ramsey jurors, as a group, practiced a total of 33 different trades, not counting yeoman and husbandman, during this entire period.[36] Eleven of those 33 trades were associated with the processing and/or selling of foods and beverages, and these are the trades most often mentioned in the court rolls.[37] Between 1280 and 1321 jurors were cited in such occupations as brewer, vintner, and baker. By the end of the fourteenth century jurors appear as butchers, a spicer, victualers, bakers of horse bread and white bread, and tanners.[38]

The first evidence that jurors were "branching out" into other kinds of trades comes in 1422 with mention of tailors and fullers; in 1440 cobblers are listed. By 1473 drapers and a "common craftsman with a window onto the road" join the group.

A later generation of jurors also broke new ground in the 1530s and '40s: the records now show that jurors were barbers, mercers, shopkeepers, a tallow handler, a lamp seller,[39] and a seller of herring. Milling appears to be specifically associated with these sample jurors for the first time in 1568.

---

[36]John Patten considers from 18 to 27 trades to be the dividing line between rural and urban centers ("Village and Town: An Occupational Study," *Agricultural History Review* 20/1 [1972]: 11). Marjorie McIntosh noted for Havering that for each half century before 1450 there were ca. 30 nonagricultural occupations mentioned, or approximately 18 per decade (*Autonomy and Community*, p. 152). A similar number was noted by Hilton for another small market town (R. H. Hilton, "The Small Town and Urbanisation—Evesham in the Middle Ages," *Midland History* 7 [1982]: 2). In Ramsey 40 to 50 people can be demonstrated to have been engaged in crafts and trades 1380–1410; that number rose to 85 by the 1440s.

[37]Ramsey's pattern is similar to that of Havering (see McIntosh, *Autonomy and Community*, pp. 152ff). The largest occupation group in Havering among the craft, trade, and service sectors was engaged in the production and sale of food and drink. There were five to six butchers, and references to leather working exist from the early thirteenth century on. As in Ramsey, tanners had large establishments with sizeable capital investments by 1350.

[38]Tanning is not specifically cited in a court roll in association with a juror until the late fourteenth century, but there was a large and prosperous family in Ramsey named Tanner who regularly appear on jury lists of the late thirteenth century. Relatives of these jurors were assessed for tanneries in the 1290 lay subsidy.

[39]The lamp seller appears in the 1551 court roll.

All of the trades mentioned so far have been identified through the regulatory function of the town court. Other trades are evident from the chance references in a variety of sources to men's identifying titles. In 1295 one juror was called "carter" (not a surname), and in 1372 another was referred to as a mason (*cementarius*). Fifteenth-century sources identify several jurors as smiths and carpenters, and in the sixteenth century jurors were labeled steward, fishmonger, clothmaker, and fisherman.

Of the 176 jurors about one-third (57) appear in the records associated with an occupation other than that of husbandman or yeoman. Almost half of these (at least 26) can be associated with more than one trade or occupation. Investment decisions were flexible and able to change readily as new opportunities presented themselves or old ones proved disappointing. For example, John Wright (1462) was described as a tailor and draper, but he also was fined as victualer and retailer of ale. William Eynesworth (1502) was described as "fishermonger" but was fined as mercer and retailer of ale and wine. Thomas Mease described himself as a tanner in his will and was licensed as such several times throughout the 1530s, but he also paid a fine as a draper in mid-decade. William Smith (first appearance, 1514) was described as "fisherman" but also was fined as a cobbler.

Thus it is clear that these men sometimes engaged in related trades, such as brewing, baking, and the sale of victuals, but at other times their occupations seem to have borne no direct relation to one another. Oliver Sylcok was both a weaver and a barber in the 1530s, and John Ynge somehow either combined the making and selling of shoes with baking bread or changed occupations in mid-career. John Asheton appears to have been a brewer, baker, and mercer simultaneously. Richard Beres was a tanner, barber, and retailer of ale and victuals during the same period that he was paid by the churchwardens for making wax.[40]

One more juror's dossier will underscore the impressive diversity of individual investments and occupational involvements found among these men. Robert Burrow was an early sixteenth-century Ramsey yeoman who was also a brewer, baker, and victualer. His property included at least two messuages, a cottage with a fishpond, gardens, orchard, meadow, and small pieces of arable land and pasture. Other investments included bullocks, calves, and horses, as well as draw nets.

These Ramsey jurors were certainly not "specialists." They preferred not to invest all their energy and capital in any single enterprise.[41] These strategies reflect either a wisely cautious policy of "risk management" or simply a response to limited or changing market conditions.

Of course, the appearance of wives in the court records sometimes helps explain the seeming versatility of these enterprising males. Martin Meadow was a baker and a brewer, but his wife was also fined for brewing. William Goslowe, baker, brewer, and cobbler, had a wife who was fined for baking and brewing, which fact suggests the possibility that fines may at times have been imposed on men whose wives or other family members were in fact performing the relevant tasks.[42]

---

[40]Ramsey churchwardens' accounts, Huntingdon Record Office (HRO) 2449/25, fol. 34v.

[41]Marjorie McIntosh found patterns in medieval Havering similar to those of Ramsey; in Havering "commerce, like capital, was distributed among many people." *Autonomy and Community*, pp. 159–60.

[42]In this sample of 26 men with more than one trade half of the biographies come from the sixteenth century, because the town court licensed a greater variety of trades in the later period. Only one example comes from the late thirteenth century; three, from the fourteenth; eight, from the fifteenth century. See James Masschaele's study in the present volume on the London merchants described as vintner and fishmonger who dealt in a wide variety of goods, from wool and hides to handmills.

The monastic accounts of Ramsey Abbey and the churchwardens' accounts reveal that many of the 176 jurors studied here took advantage of the parish's and the monks' need for laborers, skilled workmen, and civil servants. At least 43 of the 176 jurors earned cash from the obedientiaries or the churchwardens for a wide variety of tasks between 1264 and the late sixteenth century. In various monastic and churchwardens' accounts there survive more than 250 entries referring to jobs performed by Ramsey jurors between 1264 and 1552.[43]

Some may have earned wages while they were young men, in order to set themselves up in business later on. John Asplond collected a stipend from one of the obedientiaries in 1441 for making fences and "other labors" 14 years before he was first cited as a baker and victualer. John Brown was paid for working with tiles and bricks in 1526, a decade prior to his appearance as brewer and tenant of the Crown Inn in Ramsey. Martin Meadow received payment from the churchwardens for the "making and felling of willows" in 1517, two years before he first was fined for baking bread against the assize.[44] Jurors were paid for carpentry, thatching, roofing, and carting. Others provided services (e.g., fishermen, smiths, foresters) or were servants (e.g., cooks or simply "valets"). Often they collected stipends from monastic obedientiaries for unspecified jobs.

John Gritford traveled to London and Canterbury for the abbot during the 1350s, delivering letters and money. Twenty-five jurors filled administrative offices for the monastery (e.g., bailiff, rent collector, "doorkeeper" or janitor, "granarius,"

---

[43]The churchwardens' accounts for Ramsey (HRO 2449/25, fols. 1r–46r) include most years between 1513 and 1552.

[44]The 1441 subcellarer's account: BL Add. Roll 34625. 1526 account of the master of works: BL Add. MS. 33449, fol. 169d. 1517 churchwardens' account: HRO 2449/25, fol. 19r.

collector of court estreats). These duties are referred to throughout the period under study, from the late thirteenth century until the Dissolution.

One juror in particular owed much to the opportunities for employment offered by the abbey in whose shadow he probably spent most of his life. Edmund Goslow collected payment from the monks for carpentry and repair work on various tenements at least 52 times between 1485 and 1526, and he was paid for carting services at least 33 times. Over and above these jobs, Goslow also received payments for serving as bailiff of the almoner in 1517 and 1520. From those jobs he collected a total of £12 19*s.*5*d*. Goslow would have derived still further remuneration for his posts of rent collector for the almoner (1524) and warden of the shrine of St. Ives (1523).[45]

It was not unusual for a Ramsey juror associated with one of the trades to leave evidence of arable holdings.[46] Ramsey may have been a market center with ample customers for wine, ale, bread, leather, and cloth, but it was also a fen-edge agricultural community of farmers and fishermen. It would be very difficult to prove that any of the well-to-do inhabitants made their livings without any involvement in mixed husbandry. In the 1290 subsidy list the bottom third of taxpayers is distinguished from the rest by the fact that this group shows no crops included in the assessments. It seems very likely that the "tenements" recorded in the fifteenth- and sixteenth-century

[45]BL Add. Rolls 34705, 34743, 34707, 34696, 34708, 34720; BL Add. MS. 33449: fols. 14d, 18r, 26v, 27r, 53v, 67r, 74r, 76v, 80r, 82r, 104v, 90v, 91r, 93r, 119r, 124v, 130r, 139v, 156v; HRO 2449/25: fols. 9r, 9v, 10r, 11r, 19r, 19v, 24v. Paul Glennie points out the opportunities for capital accumulation by administrators employed by the Duchy of Lancaster: "Thus the relationships between the agrarian and non-agricultural sectors even in agriculture-dominated communities require explicit attention" ("In Search of Agrarian Capitalism," pp. 23, 27).

[46]Twelve of the sample jurors in this study left evidence of a nonagricultural occupation as well as tenure of arable property during the course of their careers.

obedientiary accounts and attributed to most of the later jurors of this study included some arable land.[47]

Ramsey thus provides us with another reminder that in the Middle Ages involvement in trades and "urban-like" occupations did not necessarily isolate a family from agrarian involvements.[48] The appearance of tighter court regulation of trades by the fifteenth century, along with the mention in the court rolls of more specialized crafts such as fulling, weaving, lamp selling, shoemaking, and barbering, lends to Ramsey the appearance of urbanization. Indeed, the distribution of wealth within Ramsey by the 1520s may reflect an urban rather than rural model. Notice that the distribution of wealth in Ramsey in 1523 seems to conform more closely to the urban patterns of Chelmesford, Sudbury, and Towcester than to the arable regions of Norfolk and Berkshire[49] (see Figs. 1 and 2).

It is not possible to credit specialization with bringing about any developing urbanization process during the period between 1290 and 1523. If one of the important hallmarks of a developed economy is urbanization, and if urbanization is measured by the number of specialized trades supported by a community, problems still remain in any attempt to apply a model of economic progress to patterns of change in Ramsey. The late thirteenth century also left behind its own distinctive evidence of a variety of trades and occupations even more numerous, and at least as "specialized," as those recorded in fifteenth- and sixteenth-century court rolls. Well over 100 surnames from the

---

[47]The court rolls refer periodically to Mill Furlong, Ramsey Field, and North Field.

[48]For instance, John Patten suggests that the presence in early sixteenth-century Suffolk parishes of barbers or bakers "is a good indicator of a near-urban society" ("Village and Town," p. 14); Ramsey had both.

[49]J. C. K. Cornwall, *Wealth and Society in Early Sixteenth Century England* (London, 1988); Sudbury figures, p. 53; the arable regions of Norfolk and Berks., p. 33; Towcester, p. 269; Chelmsford, p. 268.

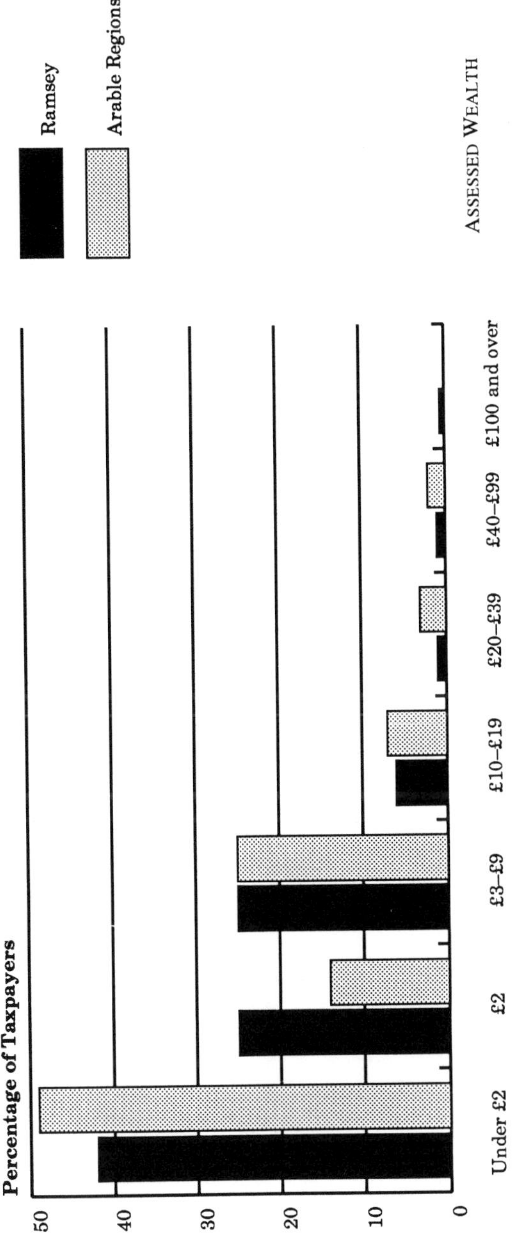

Figure 1. Distribution of wealth: 1520s lay subsidies: arable regions (Arable figures for Norfolk and Berks. from J. C. K. Cornwall [Ramsey taxpayers: 247; arable regions: 9,515])

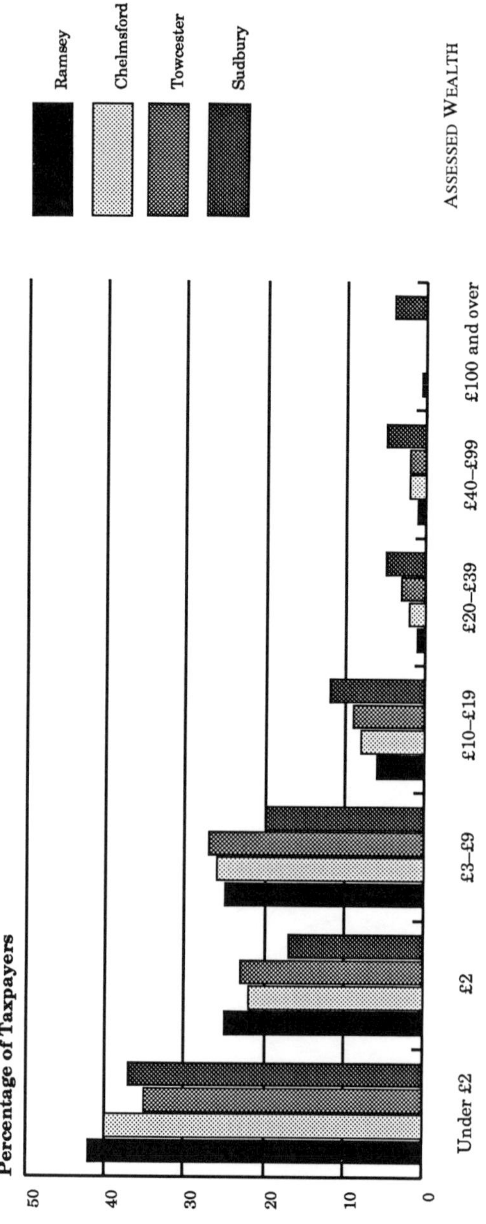

Figure 2. Distribution of wealth: 1520s lay subsidies: small towns (Ramsey taxpayers: 247; Chelmsford: 883; Towcester: 278; Sudbury: 221 [figures from Cornwall, *Wealth and Society*])

surviving Ramsey records from 1264 to 1350 refer to a wide variety of trades and occupations totaling well over 70 (see Appendix below). For John Patten the Suffolk Muster rolls from 1522 yielded a grand total of only 66 occupations.[50]

Several of these early Ramsey surnames, such as Goldsmith,[51] Hanepermaker,[52] Quilter,[53] Silksewester,[54] and Tredgold, reflect luxury crafts.[55] Others indicate specialties within the textile and leather trades (e.g., Pellipar, Webster, and Gaunter).[56] Several reflect merchant activity in names such as Monger.[57] Other surnames such as Wright, Tiler,[58] Roper, Sawyer, Plomer, Parmenter (tailor), Dauber, Cooper, and Braider (le Breyder)[59] point to the kind of specialization John Patten argues distinguished the Suffolk town of Sudbury from most other communities in its hundred (Babergh), where he

---

[50]"Village and Town," p. 14.

[51]Simon Aurifaber appears in the 1260s in a deed in re the grant of a messuage in Ramsey (*A Descriptive Catalogue of Ancient Deeds in the Public Record Office*, 6 vols. [London, 1890–1915], vol. 1, no. A5098).

[52]Walter le Hanepermaker was the victim of assault and appears in the Ramsey court roll of **1312[2]**, no. 101.

[53]PRO CP40/325 in re messuage and land in Ramsey.

[54]Ramsey court roll: **1312[2]**, no. 75: "Le Silkesewester" was the victim of assault.

[55]Ramsey court roll, **1287**, no. 117: William Tredegeld's house in Ramsey was mentioned in a theft case.

[56]Thomas Le Pelletier, clerk. See *Ancient Deeds* 1: 152, no. A1349, from 1318. Several men with the surname Pellipar appeared in the Ramsey courts of 1280, 1289, 1304. John le Webster appears in the Ramsey court rolls of **1309[1]**, **1312[1]**, **1312[2]**, **1317**, **1327**, and **1329**. Walter le Gaunter appears in the **1287** court roll, when he was received into town with his wife and children. Note also the surnames Sherman, Woolmonger, Girdler, Whittawer, Sutor, and Tanner in the index to the edited Ramsey court rolls.

[57]Also note the names Mercator, Pedder, and Strykemarchaunt in the index to the edited Ramsey court rolls.

[58]Matilda le Tyler appears in the Ramsey lay subsidy of 1290 (Raftis and Hogan, *Early Hunts. Lay Subsidy Rolls*, p. 48). The surname also appears in Ancient Deed no. B3021 of ca. 1268 (*Ancient Deeds* 1: 358) and in PRO CP40/47 and 54.

[59]These names appear in the Ramsey court roll index in entries prior to 1350.

ranked settlements on the basis of the distribution among them of 32 different occupations, including husbandman and laborer.[60]

Services required by the monastery complex resulted in names such as Provost, Rydman, Scriptor, Squiller, Vine, Winyard.[61] Names such as Butler (Boteler), Cater, Chanter, Gardener, Hawker, Cook, de Kitchen (Coquina), Lavender, Lumenor, Messenger, Peynter, Pantry (le Paneter), and Porter must also have arisen from the community of monastic servants and officials.

The fen environment produced such surnames as Botewright, Fyshher, Flote, Heryngmonger, Seman,[62] Shipwright and Stearman,[63] Fenner, Venur, and Turber. Abundant pasture and meadowlands bred such names as Cowherd, Horseman, Nethirde, Porcarius, Schepherde (Bercar), and Sweyn.

It is hard to believe that the economic diversity reflected in these early names represented a more "backward" economy than that of the sixteenth century.[64] In fact, Ramsey proved

---

[60]"Village and Town," p. 12. I thank participants in the 1992 Anglo-American Seminar at Leicester for pointing out the hazards of using surnames as evidence of occupation. The fact that so many of these names are preceded by the article *le*, and the fact that I cite such names only to associate occupations with Ramsey's economy rather than to identify precisely an individual with a specific trade, encouraged me to use surname evidence as I have in this essay. I have refrained from making such use of any surname evidence after 1350, by which time the use of surnames as family identifiers rather than occupational titles had become a tradition with a longer history and thus further removed from occupational activity.

[61]Names appear in the Ramsey court roll index. Note also: Priest, Prior, Chaplain.

[62]The surname Seman appears in BL Add. Charters 33783, 33784, 33830. All other surnames cited can be found in the index to the edited Ramsey court rolls.

[63]Ramsey court roll **1287**, no. 96. Stearman escaped the index.

[64]Margaret Bonney also found the list of occupations for early fourteenth-century Durham "much more extensive" than any compiled for the later Middle Ages. She lists 54 nonagricultural trades and crafts for the period prior to 1300: "Using three main sources . . . by c. 1400 a very approximate total of 38 different occupations can be collected, revealing fewer specialists and traders in luxury items; and this total was reduced even further, to 19, by 1500." Bonney adds one cautionary note:

more profitable to the tax collectors in 1290 than it did in 1523.[65] If the increase in assessed wealth between 1290 and 1523 is taken at face value (£563 5*s*.*ob*. to £1076 4*s*.8*d*.) and evidence in and of itself of some kind of economic development, then the tantalizing question of how to interpret the nature of this "development" remains.[66] The later assessment is only 1.9 times larger than the early one, and it may have included a larger percentage of the population because wages as well as chattels were taxed.[67]

Important clues point to sociological or political changes rather than economic development per se. First, some occupations and trades, even though they were present in the town throughout the period under study, are not associated with the town jury until the later period. For example, a tailor is mentioned in the earliest court roll of 1268, but the trade cannot definitely be associated with a member of the jury until 1425.[68] The fact that in the records tailors and cobblers begin

---

"This reduction in numbers does, of course, conceal the fact that many closely related crafts were probably operating under an umbrella organization . . ." (*Lordship and the Urban Community: Durham and Its Overlords 1250–1540* [Cambridge, 1990], pp. 148–49, and tables on pp. 269–71).

[65]Bury and Hepmangrove are included in each instance; £37 15*s*.1*d*.3*q*. was collected in 1290 (computed by Raftis and Hogan, *Early Hunts. Lay Subsidy Rolls*, Table 1A), and a total of £31 15*s*. was entered in the roll for 1523 (PRO E179/122/91). The tax of 1290 was one-fifteenth, and the rate in 1523 varied according to the wealth of the taxpayer (see Cornwall, *Wealth and Society*, pp. 3–4).

[66]We have been warned not to evaluate the strength of the economy on the basis of accumulating material wealth—"The unfavorable turn of England's position in the twelfth-century world economy cautions against interpreting the proliferation of forms of material culture as unambiguous evidence of economic growth" (Kathleen Biddick, "Power in Early English Development," *Comparative Studies in Society and History* 32/1 [Jan. 1990]: 16).

[67]There were 169 taxpayers in 1290, 48 in 1327, 39 in 1332, and 247 in 1523 (Ramsey, Bury, and Hepmangrove are all included). Monastic properties such as tanneries, dairies, and granges were also included in the 1290 assessment.

[68]John Hosyer was juror in 1425. A Thomas le Taillor was on the jury in 1384 and may be the same man cited in the court roll of 1414 as practicing the trade his name implies.

to appear on the jury by the fifteenth century could signify any number of possibilities. Had those particular occupations become more prosperous during the course of the late fourteenth century, their practitioners could have had the opportunity to serve on the jury; but other nonagricultural occupations had provided sufficient economic base for participation on juries as early as the thirteenth century. In fact, a look at the surnames of all the jurors who served between 1268 and 1350 reveals that many were probably engaged in nonagrarian pursuits. Tanners, a variety of victualers, a weaver, a fisherman, a boatman, and smiths, as well as members of service trades, such as lavender and carter, and estate offices, such as chamberlain, woodward, messor, and rideman, are all represented among the surnames of the earliest Ramsey jurors.[69]

One reason certain occupations took longer to appear on the jury lists may be that some of the earlier tradesmen were less committed to the political life of the town. Many of the pre-Black Death trades surnames appear only once or twice in the records; they seem to have failed to establish long-term connections with the town. Of 126 such surnames, 50 appear only from one to three times in the Ramsey records (see Appendix). As year-round shops became more important to Ramsey's commercial activity and competed with weekly markets or annual fairs, such tradesmen as tailors and cobblers did more and more of their business in one place and therefore must have developed a greater interest in the power politics of local town government.[70]

---

[69]The following surnames appear in the jury lists 1268–1350: le Akatur, del Bakkous, Barker, le Baxster, le Brasur, le Carter, Chamberleyn, Cook, Faber, le Fannere, le Ferrour, le Flanner, Flote, Forestarius, Hayward, le Lavender, Manger, Messor, Pistor, de Pistrino, le Plomer, Poleter, le Porter, Provost, le Rideman, le Tanner, le Teler, Tixtor, de Vinea, le Webester, le Wodeward. See the Appendix below for a list of all Ramsey occupation names 1250–1350.

[70]The earliest mention of a shop in the Ramsey records is in the 1389 court roll, in association with John Heymys, fined for failing to clear the gutter in front of his

Furthermore, the sources that provide clues to a juror's occupation changed over time. Later, family surnames gave way to court regulations as evidence of the very presence of nonagricultural occupations. For example, the Tanner family in Ramsey, called "le Tanner" during this earlier period, produced several jurors between 1268 and 1312: Richard, Alan, Alan junior, Simon, John, and Adam. The name Tanner is associated directly with the occupation in the 1290 lay subsidy, where two men with that name were assessed for tanneries. The institution of the family, in this case, has provided the enabling context and the support for the development of the skills necessary to pursue a trade.

For the later period it is the town court implementing the statutes of Edward III and Richard II that brings occupations to the notice of the historian.[71] The family no longer appears

---

shop. The first juror so associated was Thomas Coke "bocher" (1452); in 1446 Thomas and his wife took up the tenancy of "one plot recently held by Elena Mody, with one shop recently held by John Ryvenale, lying in Bridge Street next to the big bridge at the eastern end . . ." (Edwin B. DeWindt, ed., *The Liber Gersumarum of Ramsey Abbey: A Calendar and Index of B. L. Harley MS 445* [Toronto, 1976], p. 313, no. 3758). The local court licensed shopkeepers by the sixteenth century (**1537**, no. 21: "Tailors - 1*d.* each from Robert Emotte, Martin Nellsone, William Parkyn, Robert Lyvvet, John Thomas and Christopher Thomas, common storekeepers"). The appearance of the village shop during the late fifteenth century was noted by Christopher Dyer and interpreted as a sign of the sophistication of the late medieval economy (*Lords and Peasants in a Changing Society: The Estates of the Bishopric of Worcester, 680–1540* [Cambridge, 1980], p. 349.) Kathleen Biddick demonstrated the importance of commercialization among the thirteenth-century Bedfordshire peasantry and suggested that over the course of the later Middle Ages "the changing role of merchants and the development of local shops are of central importance" ("Missing Links: Taxable Wealth, Markets, and Stratification among Medieval English Peasants," *Journal of Interdisciplinary History* 18/2 [Autumn 1987]: 297 n. 22); Biddick cites the discussions of this issue by Rodney Hilton ("Medieval Market Towns and Simple Commodity Production," *Past and Present* 109 [1985]: 3–23) and Charles Phythian-Adams (*Desolation of a City: Coventry and the Urban Crisis of the Late Middle Ages* [Cambridge, 1979], pp. 1–30).

[71]*Statutes of the Realm*, 23–42 Edw. III (1: 308ff.). See also 13 Ric. II (ibid. 2: 63ff.). Fifteenth-century Havering court rolls reflect a similar increase in regulation of trades; see McIntosh, *Autonomy and Community*, pp. 152ff.

to wield the dominant influence over choice of trade and its practice. National statutes regulated artificers and victualers and resulted in entries in the town court rolls such as the following:

> 3*d*. from John Wolston for practicing the art of the tanner and cobbler contrary to the Statute. (**1414**, no. 33)
>
> 12*d*. from John Brabon, 6*d*. from Richard Webster, 2*d*. from Thomas Snellyng, 3*d*. from William Conyngton and 2*d*. from John Hance, weavers, for charging too much for weaving. (**1425**, no. 40)
>
> 6*d*. from Thomas Fuller and 3*d*. from Thomas Munne, fullers, for charging too much for fulling cloth. (**1425**, no. 41)

The Ramsey court rolls thus provide many more specific references to the trades associated with leather, wool, and cloth and to miscellaneous "other" trades after the beginning of the fifteenth century than they do during the earlier period.[72]

The predominance of vertical sources during the fifteenth and sixteenth centuries therefore betrays significant underlying changes with both political and economic implications. The vertical sources of the later period did emerge from broader institutions with wide geographic scope. The leet court regulations of trade by the fifteenth century and the 1523 subsidy resulted from initiatives taken in Westminster. The pledging networks, debt relationships, and charter subleases from the earlier horizontal sources were all "home grown." Decisions about which trades to pursue or whether to take up a trade at all must have been influenced more and more by the tax policies and regulations of outsiders as time progressed. In that sense we might see Ramsey as a town being colonized—a process

---

[72]See E. DeWindt, *Court Rolls*, Table 2, pp. 32ff.

made possible by the co-operation of local officials who were eager to use national institutions in order to increase their own influence over the town's economy. It looks as if Westminster had intended that justices in sessions would wield the power of regulation, and yet the Ramsey court rolls indicate that local town juries were usurping that role.[73]

It is not certain how this "interest from above," in the form of statutory regulations, actually affected the practice or the prosperity of these trades. The judgments made by local jurors who implemented these regulations must have affected individual decision-making about which trade to pursue, or whether to pursue a trade at all.

When town jurors acquired the power to fine a greater number of tradesmen, perhaps this power to regulate was used to allocate jobs among the families and individuals seen as best suited to the task, or perhaps it was seen simply as a means to create patronage networks. Perhaps the regulations were used to encourage or discourage economic activity considered valuable or superfluous by local leaders.[74]

In any case, it seems likely that neighbors, family members, and even the monks were not as influential in the shaping of an individual's economic decisions in the later period as they had been earlier. The fact that so many early trade surnames were

---

[73]"The Justices of Peace in every County, in [two of] their Sessions . . . shall make Proclamation . . . how much every mason, carpenter, tiler and other craftsmen, workmen and other labourers by the day . . . shall take by the day. . . . And in the right of victuallers, It is accorded, that they shall have reasonable gains, according to the discretion and limitation of the said Justices. . . ." (*Statutes of the Realm*, 13 Ric. II [2: 63]).

[74]The question of why local juries took an interest in these statutory regulations is an important one, considering that the statutes ordered the JPs to supervise enforcement. Note that the Ramsey jurors at times threatened to report local transgressors to the Justices. See E. DeWindt, *Court Rolls*, p. 24 n. 128. The jurors apparently used this threat to transfer the real power of enforcement into their own hands.

associated with monastic or estate service indicates that the economic base or motivating market for many trades was originally the community of monks associated with the town. Thirty-one of the occupation names from late thirteenth-century Ramsey can be explicitly associated with monastic offices or service (see Appendix). Many individuals were acquiring family names based on a close dependence on the monastery for their livelihoods.

By the late fifteenth century the town appears to have been much less dependent on the abbey for jobs. Even though several jurors in the later period continued to hold offices and find employment with the abbey, many workers paid by the abbey were sporadic employees, and many of them were apparently not resident townsmen.[75] It appears that the town and the abbey were pulling apart as the town forged its own independent institutional and economic foundations. In any case, economic independence from the abbey would have had to exist, to explain the fact that Ramsey was the most populous community in Huntingdonshire at the time of the 1666 hearth tax, more than a century after the Dissolution, and it had already been ranked second in the Elizabethan survey of households.[76]

Whether the town of Ramsey measured itself against its neighbors in terms of population or by the measure of the royal tax assessments, Ramsey's status was much higher in the sixteenth century than in the fourteenth, and the town maintained that high rank into the late seventeenth century, when the great abbey had become but a dim memory.

---

[75]Edwin DeWindt has found that 44 per cent of the workers hired by the abbot and his obedientiaries in the fifteenth century left no other trace in the Ramsey records and were therefore probably not from local families (figure cited in a paper delivered at the Anglo-American Seminar at Leicester, July 1992).

[76]Ramsey is the largest parish in Hunts., with 16,696 acres, most of it fenland. The drainage of Middle Level was completed by the 1660s. See *VCH Hunts.* 2: 187 and vol. 3 (1974), pp. 249ff.

In 1327, for population density Ramsey tied (with Alconbury) for the rank of twenty-seventh out of 81 Huntingdonshire vills. In 1523 Ramsey had displaced all but perhaps one of her "superiors," to rank at the top of the county in number of assessments.[77] An Elizabethan census ranked Ramsey second after Godmanchester in number of households, and the hearth tax of 1666 found Ramsey parish (including Bury and surrounding fenland) to have more taxpayers than any other Huntingdonshire town or vill (see Table 5).

If economic status is measured in terms of taxable wealth, Ramsey's "progress" seems a little less dramatic than its growth in population share but still provides an impressive success story. Ranked by the 1327 tax assessors at twenty-second among 81 vills and towns, Ramsey rose to the status of fourth in 1523. By 1666, when the monarchy raised money by taxing hearths, Ramsey's material investment in buildings per family was not as impressive as that of St. Ives or Huntingdon, but Ramsey did tie with Godmanchester for third place in number of hearths, while it ranked first in population (see Table 6).

---

[77]The population count for the town of Huntingdon is incomplete for 1523 because parts of the roll are illegible.

TABLE 5
RAMSEY'S RANK AMONG 34 HUNTINGDONSHIRE TOWNS AND VILLS—POPULATION*

1327 Number of Taxpayers	1520s Number of Taxpayers**	Elizabethan Period Number of Families	1666 Number of Taxpayers
St. Ives with Slepe cum Soke 146	**Ramsey cum Bury and Hepmangrove 247**	Godmanchester 170	**Ramsey with Bury and fen 321**
Fen Stanton cum Hilton 124	St. Neots 193	**Ramsey cum Bury and Hepmangrove 154**	St. Ives 316
Kimbolton cum Soke 109	Godmanchester 187	St. Neots 140	Godman-chester 314
Spaldwick 109	Yaxley 132	St. Ives 125 *(Slepe and Soke are not listed separately)*	Huntingdon 238
St. Neots 106	Fen Stanton and Hilton 131	Huntingdon 119	St. Neots 209

Sources: 1327: Hogan and Raftis, *Early Hunts. Lay Subsidy Rolls*, pp. 156–216; 1523: PRO E179/122/91, 99, 100, 109, 111 (dates range from 14–16 Hen. VIII); Elizabethan census: BL Harl. MS. 618; 1666 Hearth Tax: PRO E179/249/1

*Some parishes have been combined and composite totals used, so that counts are comparable from source to source.

**The list of legible names for the borough of Huntingdon in 1523 is incomplete.

TABLE 5—*Continued*

1327 Number of Taxpayers	1520s Number of Taxpayers**	Elizabethan Period Number of Families	1666 Number of Taxpayers
Godmanchester 94	Buckden 109	Yaxley 99	Alconbury, Alconbury Weston, and Weston 170
Upwood with Great and Little Raveley 87	Somersham 94	Fen Stanton with Hilton 98	Yaxley 164
Huntingdon 86	Catworth 92 *(approximate)*	Brampton 97	Stanground and Farcet 163
Great Staughton with Dillington cum Beachampsted 85	Great Staughton 92	Somersham 91	Kimbolton 162
Yaxley 79	Stanground and Farcet 82	Great Staughton 90	Brampton 137
Leighton cum Salene 78	Holywell cum Needingworth 76	Orton Longueville with Botolphbridge 85	Somersham 134
Old Weston 77	Warboys 76	Holywell cum Needingworth 81	Buckden 132

TABLE 5—*Continued*

1327 Number of Taxpayers	1520s Number of Taxpayers**	Elizabethan Period Number of Families	1666 Number of Taxpayers
Elton 73	Eynesbury 75	Alconbury cum Weston 80	Great Staughton 132
Somersham cum Soke 70	Alconbury cum Weston 70+ *(incomplete)*	Stanground cum Farcet 74	Fen Stanton and Hilton 129
Abbots Ripton 69	Glatton 69	Kimbolton 70	Warboys 122
Eynesbury 67	Sawtry (Beaumes Judith and Moyne) 68	Warboys 70	Elton 113
Buckden 65	Elton 68	Elton 69	Holywell cum Needing-worth 110
Great Gransden 65	Great Gransden 65	Eynesbury 68	Old Weston with Brington and Bythorn 110
Abbotsley 64	Earith 64	Pidley 60 *(Fenton is not listed separately)*	Earith 109

TABLE 5—*Continued*

1327 Number of Taxpayers	1520s Number of Taxpayers**	Elizabethan Period Number of Families	1666 Number of Taxpayers
Glatton 64	Upwood with Great and Little Raveley 64	Earith 58	Upwood with Great and Little Raveley 101
Keyston 59	Hemingford Grey 63	Buckden 56	Holme 93
Warboys 57	Hemingford Abbots 61	Sawtry 54	Bluntisham 91
Buckworth 53	Abbots Ripton cum Wennington 61	Glatton 53	Sawtry (Beaumes and St. Judith) 87
Ellington 53	Stonely and Wornditch 58 *(approximate)*	Ellington 51	Eynesbury 80
Great Gidding 52	Hail Weston 56	Colne 50	Hemingford Grey 79
Broughton 51	Old Weston with Brington and Bythorn 56 *(approximate)*	Leighton 50	Colne 70

TABLE 5—*Continued*

1327 Number of Taxpayers	1520s Number of Taxpayers**	Elizabethan Period Number of Families	1666 Number of Taxpayers
Sawtry 50	Holme 52	Abbots Ripton 50	Great Gransden 70
Alconbury cum Weston 48	Great Gidding 51	Bluntisham 49	Great Stukeley 70
Ramsey cum Bury and Hepmangrove 48	Conington 49	Stow and Capella 49	Southoe 69
Hemingford Abbots 47	Orton Longueville with Botolphbridge 49	Great Gransden 48	Glatton 68
Holywell cum Needingworth 47	Little Stukeley 46	Upwood and Raveley 47	Pidley cum Fenton 66
Little Stukeley 47	Hamerton 45	Hemingford Grey 46	Orton Longueville cum Botolph-bridge 64
Brampton 46	*[Illegible name]* 45	Spaldwick 45	Hemingford Abbots 60
Stanground and Farcet 45	Great Paxton 45	Woodhurst 45	Houghton 57

TABLE 6

RAMSEY'S RANK AMONG 34 HUNTINGDONSHIRE TOWNS AND VILLS—TAXATION†

1327 Lay Subsidy	1520s Lay Subsidy	1666 Hearth Tax (Number of Hearths)
St. Ives and Slepe £11 10*s*.3*d*.	Huntingdon £46 16*s*.4*d*.	St. Ives 635
Yaxley £10 1*s*.6*d*.	Godmanchester £35 11*s*.6*d*.	Huntingdon 621
St. Neots £9 1*s*.7*d*.	St. Neots £34 8*s*.5*d*.	Godmanchester 581
Great Gransden £8 15*s*.10*d*.	**Ramsey cum Bury and Hepmangrove £32 2*s*.2*d*.**	**Ramsey cum Bury and Hepmangrove 581**
Stanground and Farcet £7 8*s*.	Fenstanton and Hilton £27 11*s*.3*d*.	St. Neots 470
Great Staughton with Dillington cum Beauchampsted £7 7*s*.11*d*.	Great Staughton with hamlet £21 4*s*.7*d*.	Buckden 340
Kimbolton cum Soke £6 15*s*.2*d*.	Yaxley £20 5*s*.11*d*.	Kimbolton 339
Fenstanton cum Hilton £6 13*s*.7*d*.	Elton £19 4*s*.10*d*.	Alconbury Weston and Alconbury 326

†See Table 5 for sources. In those cases where different assessments appear in two different documents, the larger assessment is cited. The monetary figures represent the amount of tax collected.

TABLE 6—*Continued*

1327 Lay Subsidy	1520s Lay Subsidy	1666 Hearth Tax (Number of Hearths)
Godmanchester £6 9*s.*7*d.*	Eynesbury £16 11*s.*4*d.*	Brampton 292
Upwood with Great and Little Raveley £6 5*s.*9*d.*	Buckden £15 5*s.*4*d.*	Fenstanton and Hilton 291
Eynesbury £6 2*s.*4*d.*	Wooley £14 18*s.*2*d.*	Yaxley 277
Leighton cum Salene £6 2*s.*	Glatton £14 7*s.*8*d.*	Stanground and Farcet 268
Old Weston £6 1*s.*3*d.*	Somersham £14 6*s.*2*d.*	Great Staughton 260
Elton £6 1*s.*2*d.*	Upwood with Great and Little Raveley £13 1*s.*5*d.*	Somersham 245
Huntingdon £6 3*d.*	Stanground and Farcet £13 2*d.*	Elton 198
Glatton £5 13*s.*5*d.*	Catworth £12 11*s.*	Warboys 198
Somersham cum Soke £5 11*s.*	Little Stukeley £11 12*s.*10*d.*	Old Weston and Brington, Bythorn 192
Buckworth £5 1*d.*	Holywell cum Needingworth £11 4*s.*1*d.*	Holywell cum Needingworth 191

TABLE 6—*Continued*

1327 Lay Subsidy	1520s Lay Subsidy	1666 Hearth Tax (Number of Hearths)
Conington £4 14*s*.8*d*.	Sawtry (Beaumes Judith and Moyne) £10 15*s*.4*d*.	Earith 180
Spaldwick £4 14*s*.	Southoe £10 14*s*.2*d*.	Upwood with Great and Little Raveley 171
Great Stukeley £4 11*s*.6*d*.	Grafham £10 11*s*.4*d*.	Eynesbury 165
Ramsey cum Bury and Hepmangrove £4 10s.	Warboys £10 10*s*.	Stilton Collerton 159
Water Newton £4 8*s*.9*d*.	Hail Weston £10 5*s*.6*d*.	Sawtry (Beaumes and St. Judith) 156
Orton Waterville £4 8*s*.5*d*.	Everton cum Tetworth £9 17*s*.8*d*.	Bluntisham 146
Sawtry £4 4*s*.7*d*.	Great Gransden £9 7*s*.4*d*.	Hemingford Grey 146
Abbotsley £4 4*d*.	Abbots Ripton cum Wennington £8 17*s*.2*d*.	Great Stukeley 139
Great Gidding £3 17*s*.8*d*.	Hemingford Grey £8 14*s*.7*d*.	Holme 133
Hamerton £3 17*s*.5*d*.	Hamerton £8 12*s*.4*d*.	Great Gransden 131

TABLE 6—*Continued*

1327 Lay Subsidy	1520s Lay Subsidy	1666 Hearth Tax (Number of Hearths)
Keyston £3 17*s*.5*d*.	Conington £8 5*s*.8*d*.	Orton Longueville with Botolphbridge 128
Buckden £3 17*s*.1*d*.	Colne £8 3*s*.7*d*.	Glatton 123
Brampton £3 15*s*.	Hemingford Abbots £8 1*s*.8*d*.	Hemingford Abbots 122
Warboys £3 13*s*.8*d*.	Diddington £7 7*s*.8*d*.	Southoe 121
Abbots Ripton £3 10*s*.8*d*.	Offord Darcy £7 4*s*.10*d*.	Spaldwick cum Upthorp 121
Ellington £3 9*s*.	Earith £6 2*s*.2*d*.	Colne 115

Looking at the tax records from another perspective, we find that the contribution of Ramsey's two rural suburbs to its overall tax assessments shrank over the centuries; this gives the impression that Ramsey's urban wealth became more important to that community.[78] Furthermore, a comparison of the percentage increase of assessed wealth in Ramsey between

[78]In 1290 the taxable wealth in Ramsey, Bury, and Hepmangrove was assessed at £563 5*s*.*ob*.; Bury and Hepmangrove's contribution to that total was £191 14*s*.5*d*. In 1523 the total assessed wealth from Ramsey, Bury, and Hepmangrove was £1079 4*s*.8*d*.; Bury and Hepmangrove contributed £145. Ramsey's assessed wealth increased between 1290 and 1523 from £371 10*s*.7*d*. to £935 4*s*.8*d*; Bury and Hepmangrove dropped their combined assessments from £191 14*s*.5*d*. to £145 during that same period. (Such abbey properties as tanneries, dairies, and granges are included in the 1290 assessment totals.)

1327 and 1523 reflects a greater rate of growth than has been found by Julian Cornwall for many sixteenth-century towns.[79] In other words, there seem to be several signs (for the historian looking for them) that Ramsey's economy was somehow more "developed" (i.e., urbanized) in 1523 than in 1327.

After the depredations of Henry VIII the town of Ramsey did not pine away for its monastic partner of 600 years. On the contrary, the loss of the monastery brought a kind of liberation. So successful was the town in creating its own lay economy, that the disappearance of the abbey coincided with a period of improved ranking for Ramsey in its competition for Huntingdonshire wealth and population. The monastery's dual role as employer/consumer and landlord in time condensed to that of simple landlord—a role easily filled by the abbey's successor, Richard Cromwell. It may well be that the presence of the monastery helped encourage growth between 1327 and 1523, but the fact remains that the town's status in Huntingdonshire did not decline after the monks left. By 1549 the abbey had successfully raised a child no longer dependent on its parent.

Chris Husbands has noted significant regional relocations of taxable population and taxable wealth during the course of the sixteenth and seventeenth centuries. Ramsey data suggest that those processes reached back at least into the fourteenth century—"The urban hierarchy was itself in flux."[80]

---

[79]Between 1327 and 1523 Ramsey's increase in assessed value (including Bury and Hepmangrove) compares very favorably with the best growth rates found by Cornwall in Bucks. and Sussex towns (*Wealth and Society*, pp. 248, 250). Ramsey, Bury, and Hepmangrove showed an increase from £90 in 1327 (Table 1A, Raftis and Hogan, *Early Hunts. Lay Subsidy Rolls*) to £1079 4*s*.8*d*. in 1523, compared to 922 per cent and 1,100 per cent increases for the best rates in Bucks. and Sussex.

[80]"Regional Change in a Pre-industrial Economy: Wealth and Population in England in the Sixteenth and Seventeenth Centuries," *Journal of Historical Geography* 13/4 (1987): 357. For a similar study from the earlier period see Tim Unwin, "Rural Marketing in Medieval Nottinghamshire," *Journal of Historical Geography* 7/3 (1981): 231–51.

To conclude, Ramsey's improved status in the ranking of Huntingdonshire vills cannot be explained simply in terms of specialization. Ramsey's inhabitants did not necessarily have a greater array of occupational choices available in the 1520s than they had had in 1290; there does not appear to be a more specialized economy in the sixteenth century than in the late thirteenth. Rather than looking to increased specialization as the engine of change, we should look instead to changes in the institutions that influenced economic decisions. These changes may in part have involved a shift in the commercial dominance of markets and fairs to year-round shops, but we must look at other institutional changes as well. By the fifteenth century the individual job-seeker in Ramsey was influenced not only by family, neighborhood, and monastery but also by a hierarchy of local and national officials who were attempting to regulate and control the town economy in new ways that took advantage of royal statutes regulating wages and prices.

As horizontal sources give way to vertical ones, that is, as locally produced court records and charters cede to tax records and monastic tenurial accounts initiated by outsiders, we see the family and a broadly based local jury give way to new cliques of town officials wielding power handed down in statutes from Westminster. A power struggle between local and national institutions was under way. Horizontal documents represent waning institutions that had provided one distinct context for individual economic decisions. Later, new institutions encroached upon their territory. By the sixteenth century men and women were looking beyond their neighborhood networks for validation. Royal taxation, trade regulations issued from Westminster, and monastic tenurial accounts all brought the king and the abbot's accountants into the household from the outside. In all of these situations the family and neighbors, while hardly irrelevant, became weaker influences. When the later court rolls no longer reveal pledging relationships and show fewer debt and trespass pleas, they no longer portray the individual enmeshed in a context primarily of the neighborhood. The Ramsey court no longer provided the same institutional support for the social and economic relationships that resulted in debt and trespass pleas or in the responsibilities of suretyship.

The willingness on the part of at least some of Ramsey's inhabitants to accept national regulations and a royal tax burden can further be understood in the context of presumed benefits coming from participation in a broader regional economy. As the number of markets in England declined between 1300 and 1500, commercial activity concentrated in fewer towns, creating shifting patterns in county urban hierarchies. In some cases, an influx of capital from London accelerated these developments.[81] Ramsey's rise toward the top of the Huntingdonshire urban hierarchy suggests that similar factors affected that small town.[82]

Only a look at the documents coming out of Ramsey itself can help us determine how and why townsmen developed the institutions that enabled them to plug into these national networks. Local responses to national institutions intruding into a local culture can only be measured from inside the town itself.

The historical questions opened up by institutional changes, then, focus on the reasons behind the seeming willingness to abandon the old arrangements for the new.[83] The relation-

---

[81]J. Ambrose Raftis, *Early Tudor Godmanchester: Survivals and New Arrivals* (Toronto, 1990), pp. 74–75, 162ff. McIntosh, *Autonomy and Community*, pp. 125, 133.

[82]For discussion of the shifting patterns of trade and summary of the debates on questions of late medieval urbanization, see R. H. Britnell, *The Commercialisation of English Society 1000–1500* (Cambridge, 1993), pp. 155ff.

[83]Paul Glennie, in his study of Lea Valley tenants, suggested interesting ways to view the relationship between individual choice and the individual's cultural and institutional framework. When he found individual tenants in the sixteenth

ships between individual decisions, on one hand, and social and political institutions, on the other, encourages investigations of historical developments from the inside out—from the viewpoint of an individual responding to an array of opportunities—rather than from the outside in—from the viewpoint of a foreign enforcer manipulating compliance from afar.[84]

---

century accumulating unusually large tenements and holding them longer than had been the earlier pattern, he noted that those same tenants still "joined with poorer tenants on matters such as the maintenance of common rights and the regulation of stints on the common pasture and waste," even though their withdrawal from popular culture became quite clear by the seventeenth century. As was true in Ramsey, individual decisions to support social and political institutions are an important part of individual expression—or "individualism." Questions can then focus on the reasons behind the seeming willingness to abandon old arrangements for new. Opportunities for significant choices exist during all historical periods but operate within different institutional frameworks. Note Glennie's useful summary of the position of "structuration theorists": "In highlighting the potential creativity of individuals, they focus empirical attention on two types of interactions between society and individual agents, operating simultaneously in different 'directions'. The first interaction is the way in which social structures, both material and symbolic, constrain and enable the exercise of individuals' creativity. The second is the acknowledgement that the continued existence of institutions, discourses, and other social structures occurs not . . . by default, but through the continuing actions (intended or otherwise) of active human subjects. Thus it becomes impossible to explain the stability or changing character of social structures purely in terms of themselves or their relationships with other structures" ("In Search of Agrarian Capitalism," p. 35).

[84]Some historians see the opportunity for decision-making as subject to change over time. Note the following observations by Marjorie McIntosh: "By the mid-fourteenth century the manor's residents appear to have been making rational decisions with the aim of improving their economic condition. They sought profit and advancement rather than the satisfaction of minimal or short-term needs" (*Autonomy and Community*, p. 176). McIntosh suggests that certain prerequisites set the stage for decision-making: "Havering's experience suggests that in trying to understand the processes by which early modern patterns developed, we need to concentrate upon those factors which at any time within the medieval or Tudor periods contributed to geographical mobility, freedom of landholding, opportunities for commerce and the power of local people to control the activities of their own community" (ibid., p. 262). Prof. Raftis contrasts the royal manors of Havering and Godmanchester and emphasizes "the decisions of the town." *Early Tudor Godmanchester*, pp. 206–07.

Appendix

OCCUPATION SURNAMES IN RAMSEY[†] 1250–1350

Ramsey Surnames	Occupation Type	Occupation Description	Number of Appearances in Sources
Dycher	Agricultural laborer	ditch digger, or lives by dike	3
Stedman	Agricultural laborer	farm worker, or horse tender	4
Turber le	Agricultural laborer	peat cutter	6
Veyne Wynhard del	Agricultural laborer	servant or worker in vineyard	20
Wheker le	Agricultural laborer	servant or dairy farm dweller	2
Trituratur	Agricultural laborer	thresher	4
Fannere Vannator	Agricultural laborer	winnower	28
Thurner	Agricultural laborer?	turver or turner?	1

[†]The following surname dictionaries were consulted: B. O. Eilert Ekwall, *Studies on the Population of Medieval London* (Stockholm, 1956); Gustav Fransson, *Middle English Surnames of Occupation, 1100–1350, with an Excursus on Toponymical Surnames* (Lund, 1935); Bertil Thuresson, *Middle English Occupational Terms* (Lund, 1950); Ingrid Hjertstedt, *Middle English Nicknames in the Lay Subsidy Rolls for Warwickshire* (Uppsala, 1987); P. H. Reaney, *A Dictionary of British Surnames*, 2nd rev. ed., corr. R. M. Wilson (London, 1977).

Ramsey Surnames	Occupation Type	Occupation Description	Number of Appearances in Sources
Tresser le	Agricultural laborer?	thresher or plait maker?	1
Tyler	Building trades	maker of tiles	14
Peyntor Pictor	Building trades	painter	10
Tector	Building trades	plasterer	2
Dawbour	Building trades	plasterer or whitewasher	3
Segerre	Building trades	reed cutter or thatcher	5
Coopertor	Building trades	roofer	2
Girdelere le	Clothing	maker of girdles	1
Gaunter le	Clothing	maker of gloves	4
Sutor	Clothing	maker of shoes	25
Parmenter	Clothing	tailor	1
Cissor	Clothing	tailor	18
Sewer	Clothing	tailor	1
Silksewester	Clothing (luxury)	tailor of silk fabric	1
Fenner le	Fens	hunter	8

APPENDIX—*Continued*

Ramsey Surnames	Occupation Type	Occupation Description	Number of Appearances in Sources
Venur Venatur	Fens	hunter or fen dweller	3
Skinner	Leather	skinner	13
Pellipar	Leather	skinner or pelterer	3
Barker	Leather	tanner	160
Tannator	Leather	tanner	219
Whittawer	Leather	white leather dresser	2
Schechere	Leather?	maker of sheaths	3
Biker	Livestock	beekeeper	38
Cowherd	Livestock	herder of cows	11
Nethirde	Livestock	herder of oxen or cows	1
Schepherde	Livestock	herder of sheep	11
Porcarius	Livestock	herder of swine	11
Sweyn	Livestock	herder of swine or servant	30
Mercer le	Mercantile	dealer in costly textiles	1
Wllemonger	Mercantile	dealer in wool	3
Chapman	Mercantile	dealer, merchant	2

APPENDIX—*Continued*

Ramsey Surnames	Occupation Type	Occupation Description	Number of Appearances in Sources
Manger	Mercantile	dealer, merchant	14
Marchaunt	Mercantile	merchant	6
Stryke-marchaunt	Mercantile	merchant of calves, heifers	1
Pedder	Mercantile	peddler	2
Draper	Mercantile	seller or maker of wool cloth	5
Ladeler	Metal	maker of ladles	14
Pannier le	Metal	maker of pans or hawker?	1
Syveker le	Metal	maker of sieves	1
Lokyeṛe	Metal	maker of or dealer in locks	2
Haneper-maker	Metal	maker or seller of goblets	1
Tynker	Metal	mender of pots	3
Plomer	Metal	plumber or dealer in feathers?	9
Ferror	Metal	smith	112
Smyth Faber	Metal	smith	168
Goldsmith Orfrasere	Metal (luxury)	goldsmith	4

Ramsey Surnames	Occupation Type	Occupation Description	Number of Appearances in Sources
Chauntor	Monastic office	chorister	4
Chamberleyn	Monastic office	servant in charge of chamber	69
Hayward Messor	Monastic office	keeper of the meadow	45
Hostiarius	Monastic office	doorkeeper	2
Pondre	Monastic office	keeper of the pound or pond?	11
Parker	Monastic office	keeper or servant of the park	25
Provost	Monastic office	officer of the manor	42
Reeve	Monastic office	officer of the manor	10
Rydman	Monastic office	messenger	225
Rider le	Monastic office	mounted rider	2
Porter Janitor	Monastic office	servant or officer of the doorway	120
Stabler le	Monastic office	stable keeper or hostler	7

Ramsey Surnames	Occupation Type	Occupation Description	Number of Appearances in Sources
Colhop	Monastic servant	cook, house-keeper	22
Rener or Revere	Monastic servant	runner, messenger or robber?	6
Revesman	Monastic servant	servant of the reeve	8
Priorisman	Monastic servant	servant of the prior	1
Squiller	Monastic servant	servant of the scullery or dishmaker	3
Gardner Gardyn	Monastic servant	servant of the garden	23
Fower	Monastic servant	servant of the hearth	20
Kechene de	Monastic servant	servant of the kitchen	2
Page	Monastic servant	servant or page	11
Lavender	Monastic servant	washer or launderer	91
Woodward	Monastic servant or officer	forester	202
Messenger	Monastic servant or officer	messenger	83

Ramsey Surnames	Occupation Type	Occupation Description	Number of Appearances in Sources
Lymnour	Monastic servant or officer	manuscript illuminator	2
Butler	Monastic servant or officer	servant in wine cellar	25
Horseman	Monastic servant or officer	servant or keeper of horses	1
Emptor Cator	Monastic servant or officer	servant to purchase provisions	23
Pantry	Monastic servant or officer	servant or officer of the pantry	8
Knyt	Monastic servant or officer	servant or soldier	4
Hauker le	Monastic servant?	falconer?	1
Scryven Scriptor	Scribe	writer, scribe, copier	18
Clerk	Scribe or cleric	scribe or cleric	185
Breyder	Textiles	maker of cord or net	1

Ramsey Surnames	Occupation Type	Occupation Description	Number of Appearances in Sources
Quilter	Textiles	maker of mattresses or quilts	1
Roper	Textiles	maker of rope	3
Flexmonger	Textiles	seller of flax	1
Flexman	Textiles	seller or dresser of flax	1
Scherman	Textiles	shearer of woolen cloth	3
Webster	Textiles	weaver	35
Tredgolde	Textiles (luxury)	embroiderer	4
Carter	Transport	driver of carts	57
Dryver	Transport	driver of vehicle or animals	1
Stearman	Transport	pilot or herder of bullocks	4
Hevere le	Transport	porter, carrier?	1
Flote	Transport	sailor	37
Seman	Transport	seaman	12
Bakhouse de Pistrina	Victuals	baker	68
Baxter	Victuals	baker	3
Pistor	Victuals	baker	43

Ramsey Surnames	Occupation Type	Occupation Description	Number of Appearances in Sources
Swetebryd	Victuals	baker of unleavened bread	11
Braciator	Victuals	brewer	55
Bracino de	Victuals	brewer	9
Brasur	Victuals	brewer	1
Butcher	Victuals	butcher	28
Cook	Victuals	cook	109
Pykeler	Victuals	cook, sauce-maker	1
Herberourer le	Victuals	dealer in herbs or collector of herbs	1
Heryng	Victuals	dealer in herring	21
Poulter	Victuals	dealer in poultry	27
Fyshher Piscator	Victuals	fisherman	10
Flanner le	Victuals	maker of custards or pancakes	11
Heryng-monger	Victuals	merchant of herring	4
Miller	Victuals	miller	51

APPENDIX—*Continued*

Ramsey Surnames	Occupation Type	Occupation Description	Number of Appearances in Sources
Bacon	Victuals	pork butcher	4
Boltere	Victuals	sifter of meal or bolt maker	1
Carpenter	Wood	carpenter	17
Wright le	Wood	carpenter, joiner	2
Botewright	Wood	maker of boats	1
Couper le	Wood	maker of casks, buckets	44
Shipwright	Wood	maker of ships	1
Waynman	Wood	maker of wagons	18
Sawyere	Wood	timber sawyer	1
Turnor	Wood?	turner	23

ASPECTS OF POVERTY
IN A SMALL MEDIEVAL TOWN

Ellen Wedemeyer Moore[1]

We know a great deal about poverty in the Middle Ages, and yet at the same time we know very little about it. Because it was a religious ideal for many who strove to imitate Christ, poverty inspired a wide range of writings as well as the creation of such durable institutions as monasteries, friaries, hospitals, and almshouses. Many studies have helped us better understand both of the basic groupings of medieval paupers: those who chose poverty voluntarily as a way of knowing God more fully, and those who experienced it involuntarily and thus became recipients of institutionalized charity.[2]

---

[1]I should like to thank the Quebec government for a grant under the *fonds pour la formation de chercheurs et l'aide à la recherche*, which provided me with enough time to begin this study in the proper fashion.

[2]The most useful recent studies on medieval poverty in general are Michel Mollat, *Les pauvres au moyen-âge: étude sociale* (Paris, 1978), the collection of shorter pieces edited by Mollat in *Etudes sur l'histoire de la pauvreté [Moyen-âge—XVI siècle]*, 2 vols. (Paris, 1974); and Bronislaw Geremek, *La potence ou la pitié: l'Europe et les pauvres du moyen âge à nos jours*, trans. Joanna Arnold-Moricet (Paris, 1987), ch. 1. Specific works on poverty as a religious ideal include Brian Tierney, *Medieval Poor Law: A Sketch of Canonical Theory and Its Application in England* (Berkeley, 1959); Réginald Grégoire, "La place de la pauvreté dans la conception et la pratique de la vie monastique médiévale latine," in *Il monachesimo e la riforma ecclesiastica (1049–1122)*: Settimana internazionale di studio Mendola, 23–29 agosto 1968 (Milan, 1971), pp. 173–92; Lester K. Little, "Evangelical Poverty, the New Money Economy and Violence," in David E. Flood, ed., *Poverty in the Middle Ages* (Werl, 1975), pp. 11–26; Marcel Pacaut, "La notion de pauvreté dans

It is the latter group, the "involuntary" paupers, who, lacking the means to record their ideas and experiences, remain the most elusive. What we do know about them comes largely through the records of their benefactors and therefore stresses much more strongly the nature of the benefits and the beneficent institutions than the lives of the paupers themselves.[3] Recently a number of serious efforts have been made to investigate poverty in the lives of ordinary people—those neither so destitute as to be inmates of charitable institutions nor so spiritually driven as to join the Franciscans, Waldensians, or other groups extolling the redemptive virtues of poverty: in short, the working poor. These studies have usually taken the form of general overviews exploring the connections of poverty with the manorial system (Lis and Soly, and Hilton), with the natural disasters of the later Middle Ages (Goglin), with criminal behavior (Geremek), or with the advent of the money economy (Geremek).[4] Even more recently Christopher Dyer has

la règle de saint Benoît," in *Economies et sociétés au Moyen Age: mélanges offerts à Edouard Perroy* (Paris, 1973), pp. 626–33.

[3]Much of the literature on this subject, as regards England, is summarized in Miri Rubin, *Charity and Community in Medieval Cambridge* (Cambridge, 1987), and more recently and succinctly in Christopher Dyer, *Standards of Living in the Later Middle Ages: Social Change in England c. 1200–1520* (Cambridge, 1989), ch. 9. In addition, Marjorie Keniston McIntosh, who is working on a broadly-based history of English charitable institutions, has revealed some preliminary findings in "The Foundation of Hospitals and Almshouses in Medieval and Tudor England: A Reflection of Changing Responses to the Poor" (unpub. paper delivered in Oxford, 1990). She has kindly sent me a copy of this paper.

[4]Catharina Lis and Hugo Soly, *Poverty and Capitalism in Pre-Industrial Europe* (Hassocks, Sussex, 1979), ch. 1; R. H. Hilton, "Reasons for Inequality among Medieval Peasants" and "Peasant Movements in England before 1381," both repr. in idem, *Class Conflict and the Crisis of Feudalism: Essays in Medieval Social History* (London, 1985), pp. 139–51 and 122–38, respectively; Michel Mollat, "Hospitalité et assistance au début de xiiie siècle," in Flood, *Poverty*, pp. 37–52; Jean Louis Goglin, *Les misérables dans l'Occident médiéval* (Paris, 1976); Bronislaw Geremek, *The Margins of Society in Late Medieval Paris*, trans. Jean Birrell (Cambridge, 1987 [1971]), and idem, *La potence ou la pitié*, ch. 1.

suggested that our vision of poorer peasants has perhaps been too simplistic and requires a good deal more evidence.[5]

One source of evidence with the potential to shed light on the experience of poverty in individual lives is the presence in court records of notations of remission of fines "quia pauper" or "pro pauperitate." For example:

> Robert Durand, Agnes Mulit, and Robert Durand's wife made their law [to prove] that they had not robbed Matilda, Robert Laweman's daughter, of one penny, as she had claimed against them. Therefore, [she is] amerced. She is poor. Pledge, Richard Laweman.
>
> From Margaret le Permongere for a false claim against John Moring and his wife: she is poor. Pledge, William Wygar.
>
> It is presented by the jurors of Bridge Street that Avenandus received prostitutes; therefore he is amerced; he is pardoned because he is poor.[6]

Entries like these are found infrequently but with some regularity in the court records of the later Middle Ages. They offer the possibility of contributing to our understanding of a number of persistent questions. How poor was "poor"? What were the conditions of life for someone legally labeled *pauper*? What was the attitude of society towards poverty?

References to "pauperes" in thirteenth-century court rolls have not gone unnoticed by historians: Michael T. Clanchy and Doris M. Stenton, working with royal records; and Frederic W.

---

[5] *Standards of Living*, pp. 184–87.

[6] The texts cited come from the court rolls for the Ramsey Abbey market/fair town of St. Ives, Hunts.: Public Record Office (PRO) Land Revenue (LR)11/78/904 (1279); SC2/178/100 (26 May 1300); SC2/178/96 (30 Apr. 1287). In the last extract the word for "poor" is "elemosinarius," a rare usage in Ramsey records. All other cases referred to in this study, and others I have seen thus far, use "pauper."

Maitland and George C. Homans, with manorial records.[7] The meaning of these references, however, has never really been explored, at least in part because, like much court roll material, these references to poverty yield their secrets only when placed in the broader context of other evidence from the same society.

The methodologies developed by J. Ambrose Raftis, R. H. Hilton, and others have begun to unlock some of these secrets.[8] In the hands of Professor Raftis, the Ramsey Abbey collection, in particular, has proven well suited to sociological analysis. This essay focuses on St. Ives, one of the manors in the Ramsey estates. A small town with a population of about 175 families around the turn of the thirteenth century, St. Ives provides not only a good demographic base but also one that has sufficient documentation for analysis, especially for the late thirteenth and early fourteenth centuries.[9] This is precisely the period of

---

[7]M. T. Clanchy, *Civil Pleas of the Wiltshire Eyre, 1249*, Wiltshire Record Society, vol. 26 (1971): 18 (hereafter, *Wiltshire Eyre*); Doris M. Stenton, ed., *Rolls of the Justices in Eyre: Being the Rolls of Pleas and Assizes for Lincolnshire 1218–9 and Worcestershire 1221*, Selden Society, vol. 53 (1934): lxiii–lxvi (hereafter, *Justices in Eyre*); George C. Homans, *English Villagers of the Thirteenth Century* (New York, 1960 [1941]), p. 202 (hereafter, *English Villagers*); Frederic W. Maitland, *Select Pleas in Manorial and Other Seignorial Courts*, Selden Society, vol. 2 (1889): 42. See also Paul R. Hyams, *Kings, Lords, and Peasants in Medieval England: The Common Law of Villeinage in the Twelfth and Thirteenth Centuries* (Oxford, 1980), p. 76.

[8]See, e.g., Rodney H. Hilton, "Freedom and Villeinage in England," *Past and Present* 31 (1965), and *The English Peasantry in the Later Middle Ages: The Ford Lectures for 1973 and Related Studies* (Oxford, 1975); Raftis, "Social Structures in Five East Midland Villages," *Economic History Review*, 2nd ser., 18 (1965): 83–100, and "The Concentration of Responsibility in Five Villages," *Mediaeval Studies* 28 (1966): 92–118. For good descriptions of the method and range of information derived from it see Zvi Razi, *Life, Marriage, and Death in a Medieval Parish: Economy, Society, and Demography in Halesowen, 1270–1400* (Cambridge, 1980), pp. 2–5 (hereafter, *Life, Marriage, and Death*), and Edward J. Britton, *The Community of the Vill: A Study in the History of the Family and Village Life in Fourteenth-Century England* (Toronto, 1977), pp. 1–7.

[9]**Town Court Records:** PRO LR11/78/904 (1279), SC2/179/7 (1291), BL Add. Rolls 34339 (1292), 39597 (1294), PRO SC2/179/9 (1296), 179/10 (1299), 179/11 (1301), BL Add. Roll 34774 (1305), PRO SC2/179/12 (1306), 179/15 (1308), BL Add. Rolls

time regarded by many historians as one of widespread impoverishment in the medieval population, although there is no consensus on the reasons for the economic crisis.[10] On the other hand, as a community within the East Midlands region St. Ives may well have been unusually prosperous, both in terms of soil productivity and in terms of the average size of agricultural holdings.[11] Therefore, like any detailed study of a local population, this one cannot claim to provide sweeping answers for all of England or beyond. It can provide a detailed analysis of the *pauperes* of one community, complementing the disparate references found elsewhere.

The practice of remitting court fines because of poverty is of some considerable interest. At the very least it indicates a remarkable accessibility to the judicial system for the weak and vulnerable in society. For the townsfolk of St. Ives, fines were

---

34775 (1309), 34776 (1310), PRO SC2/179/16 (1311), 176/17 (1313), 179/18 (1318). **Fair Court Records:** PRO SC2/178/93–106 (1270, 1275, 1287, 1288, 1291, 1293, 1295, 1300, 1302, 1311, 1312, 1315, 1316, 1324); and BL Add. Roll 34785 (1317). **Account Records: stallage accounts of the fair**: BL Add. Roll 34783 (1278); PRO SC11/315 (1284), 11/316 (1286); BL Add. Roll 34784 (1287); accounts of the manor: BL Add. Rolls 39736 (1290–92), 34773 (1298); PRO SC6/884/1–4 (1307, 1311, 1313, 1313), 883/1 (1314), 884/5 (1314), 884/6 (1318), 884/7 (1318), 883/2 (1318). **Landholding Records:** PRO SC2/178/94 (hundred roll of 1279), SC2/178/95 (entry fine roll, 1262–1358); BL Add. Roll 39693 (entry fine roll, 1310–11); PRO SC11/322 (tallage roll, undated, 1290–1340), E179/122/4, 10, and 7 (subsidy rolls, 1327, 1327, 1337). N.B.: When a note in this study refers solely to a year, the *town* court roll is the source; when a note refers to a day and a year, the records of the *fair* court are the source. All other references are specified by a manuscript number.

[10]A. N. May, "An Index of Thirteenth-Century Peasant Impoverishment? Manor Court Fines," *Economic History Review*, 2nd ser., 26/3 (1973): 399, identifies the first decade of the fourteenth century as the "absolute low" point in the fortunes of the English medieval peasantry. A good, short summary of the important secondary literature surrounding the "Postan Thesis" of the crisis of this period is in J. Z. Titow, *English Rural Society, 1200–1350* (London, 1969), ch. 3. Razi (*Life, Marriage, and Death*, pp. 38, 40) gives detailed evidence for focusing on 1293–95 and 1316–19 as the specific moments of greatest overall rural poverty.

[11]See Herbert E. Hallam, *Rural England, 1066–1348* (Brighton, 1981), pp. 16, 73, 119, 122.

remitted *quia pauper* in the courts of both the manor, which met semiannually, and the international fair, an annual event of about six weeks' duration.[12] Although the records of the St. Ives town courts extend through the sixteenth century, the remission of fines in them is confined to the late thirteenth and early fourteenth centuries. In all, the fines of 40 St. Ives townspersons were remitted on account of poverty in 43 instances—20 in the fair court and 23 in the town court—between 1275 and 1318 (a series of 29 court rolls). The chronological distribution of the instances over the period was heaviest in the 1290s, but little can be deduced from a quantitative analysis at this stage because, among other considerations, the number of extant court rolls for St. Ives is also quite large for the 1290s (see Table 1).

TABLE 1
INSTANCES OF "POVERTY" AND NUMBERS OF COURT RECORDS 1270–1320

Period	Number of Cases of "Poverty"	Number of Court Records
1270s	11	3
1280s	4	2
1290s	15	8
1300s	10	7
1310s	3	9

Given the uncertainties and controversies over medieval demographics, it is extremely difficult to estimate what percentage of the population of St. Ives was included in this appellation

[12]See Ellen Wedemeyer Moore, *The Fairs of Medieval England: An Introductory Study* (Toronto, 1985) (hereafter, *Fairs*), for discussion of both the fair and the town of St. Ives.

of *pauper*. A very rough estimate, using Krause's multiplier of 4.5 on the 175 families in the community, could suggest that between 2 per cent and 4 per cent of a population of around 800 was functioning as *pauper* at any given time. One of the many reasons why this estimate is probably too low is the generally acknowledged fact that many desperately poor people never appeared in court records.[13] In any case, the figures suggest that among the "visible" segment of the population the label *pauper* was used quite sparingly. Thirteen of the *pauperes* were women and 27 were men. Three individuals, all men, appear as *pauperes* in two separate situations each, and for two of these men the incidents were spaced over a period of years, four and 22, respectively.[14] The St. Ives jurors did not lightly remit fines for poverty, but they did allow for a "second chance" on occasion.

There was no connection between the type of action in court and the remission. The variety of actions connected with remitted fines was almost as great as the entire scope of actions in the respective courts, from unjust detention of goods or money, fraud, and slander to serving as surety for a defaulting suitor, buying a license to settle out of court, or lodging a false claim (see Table 2). Yet the notation "condonatur quia pauper" was not simply a device to clear the books of bad debts. Particularly

---

[13]See John T. Krause, "The Medieval Household: Large of Small?" *Economic History Review*, 2nd ser., 9 (1956–57): 420–32. Discussions of the problems of estimating medieval populations appear in Titow, *English Rural Society*, pp. 66–73, and Britton, *Community*, pp. 134–38. Britton lists some 11 people in Broughton whose fines were remitted for poverty 1288–1329 and estimates that these "represent less than 2% of the people who appeared in the court of Broughton between 1280 and 1380" (p. 157). By way of comparison Nicole Gonthier, using evidence of the tax lists of the fourteenth and fifteenth centuries, estimates that ca. 40 per cent of the population of Lyon lived a precarious existence and that 10 per cent of that same population lived almost exclusively from alms; see *Lyon et ses pauvres au Moyen Age (1350–1500)* (Lyon, 1978), p. 239.

[14]Ba twice, 1287; Wodereve, 1275 and 1279; Wygar, 1279 and 1301.

in the St. Ives fair court, many explanations were given for not collecting fines. Probably the most common of these was intervention by a monastic official, usually to help influential outsiders, such as the cloth dealers Robert of St. Leonard and Ralph de la Pole, who lost their case simply because of a technicality in pleading. Sometimes the fair steward remitted the fine of a perfectly ordinary person such as the St. Ives resident Peter of Tooting for reasons not revealed in the records. Some reasons are obvious: "condonatur quia imprisonatus," or "nichil quia est homo prioris," or "condonatur quia non culpabilis." Even when no explanation is given, the scribes and steward were at least avoiding false attributions.[15]

In financial terms, few of the fines remitted would have exceeded 12*d.* had they been levied, since really serious offenses transcended the jurisdiction of the local courts.[16] Even so, this humanitarian practice on behalf of the residents of St. Ives cost Ramsey Abbey anywhere from 6*d.* to 4*s.* per year in lost revenues; indeed, the total for the 43 offenses was 27*s.*6*d.* With some two dozen manors, Ramsey Abbey must have sustained losses from this practice that were certainly not negligible, even in the context of gross annual receipts of around £1,400 ca. 1300.[17]

---

[15]St. Leonard and de la Pole, 6 May 1287; Tooting, 6 May 1287; other explanations for fine remissions: 22 May 1287, Thomas de Vinea; 1279, Reginald Newman; 14 May 1291, William of Stanton; 22 May 1287, Hugh Cut; 20 May 1287, Agnes la Cartere.

[16]See *Royal Justice and the Medieval English Countryside: The Huntingdonshire Eyre of 1286, the Ramsey Abbey Banlieu Court of 1287, and the Assizes of 1287–88*, ed. and trans. Anne Reiber DeWindt and Edwin B. DeWindt, 2 vols. (Toronto, 1981), vol. 1, chs. 2, 3, 5 (hereafter, *Royal Justice*). A perusal of the court records for all Ramsey Abbey manors reveals that fine remissions for poverty occurred on all of them around the turn of the fourteenth century, but time has not permitted a full comparative analysis.

[17]J. A. Raftis, *The Estates of Ramsey Abbey: A Study in Economic Growth and Organization* (Toronto, 1957), p. 122 (Table 27).

Since the practice was not only specifically noted in the records but also entailed monetary sacrifice, it must have had a purpose or at least a reason. Was it Christian charity? Canon law, notably the Decretals of Gregory IX, stipulated that poor persons should be exempt from court fees and also from the expenses of summoning witnesses in a trial.[18] A specifically English juridical precept may have been more relevant. Many researchers have noted that Magna Carta, clause 20, prohibits the fining of any freeman so heavily that he would be thereby deprived of his livelihood, according to the assessment of a local jury.[19] Certainly the Ramsey Abbey evidence suggests that magnates who imposed Magna Carta on the king were putting this clause into practice, at least for the benefit of their own manorial tenants. In addition, if the secular tradition connected with Magna Carta can be considered relevant to manorial court practice, then we can assume that it was the local jurors who determined who was *pauper* in a given instance.

Whatever the motivation behind the practice, an examination of all available information relating to the St. Ives paupers produces two clear observations, the subjects of the rest of this paper. First, while some of these paupers were probably destitute, most were not; they were living on the threshold of poverty. Second, the remission of fines might have helped them move back from the threshold, however temporarily. This may have constituted a policy of charitable activity, an adherence to traditional jurisprudence, or simply good estate management on the part of the landlord.

Who were the paupers of St. Ives? How did they earn their livings? What caused their economic problems? What were their

[18]Quoted by Tierney, *Medieval Poor Law*, pp. 13–14.

[19]Clanchy, *Wiltshire Eyre*, p. 18; Stenton, *Justices in Eyre*, p. lxvi; May, "Index," p. 398.

positions in the town? While complete answers to these questions will never be possible, many of the available answers lie in an analysis of court situations in which these men and women were declared too poor to pay an amercement. These situations were essentially connected with four types of activity: the operations of the court itself, overtly anti-social or criminal acts, landholding, and trade (see Table 2).

TABLE 2
TYPES OF ACTIVITY CONNECTED WITH POVERTY IN COURT RECORDS

Operations of the Court	*13*		
Failure to prosecute	2	Wm. Cokeston	1301
		Wm. of Mattishall	1291
False claim	3	Matilda Laweman	1279
		Marg. le Permongere	1300
		John of Yarmouth	1295
Out of court settlement	2	Simon Pund	1292
		Wm. Wygar & wife	1301
Pledging for defaulting principal	6	Wm. Beadle	1301
		Benedict Gere	1296
		Richard Hayward	1291
		Robert Marshall	1291
		John Medicus	1301
		John Reeve	1279
Violent or Antisocial Acts	*4*		
Slander	2	Matilda Redeknave	1306
		Hugo Sterne	1279
Assault or burglary	1	Henry servant of Thomas Catworth	1306
Fraud	1	Thomas le Tayllur	1275

TABLE 2—*Continued*

Infractions Related to Landholding	*14*		
Failure to keep watch	6	Walfrid of Ba	1287
		Wm. of Dunstable	1275
		Walfrid Reeve	1275
		Alice Saleman	1275
		Ralph Scot	1275
		Simon Wodereve	1275
Receiving unacceptable persons	3	Agnes le Baker	1301
		Agnes of Deene	1299
		Simon Wodereve	1279
Receiving prostitutes	3	Wm. Avenandus	1287
		Agnes le Baker	1300
		Wm. le Redeknave	1287
Default on work obligations	1	Wm. Wygar	1279
Default on taxes	1	John le Swappere	1301
Activities Related to Commerce	*12*		
Distraint of goods	1	Walfrid of Ba	1287
Debt	2	Roger Barman	1293
		Hugo Toth	1295
Contract	1	Robert Wygar	1296
Brewing/Sale of ale	6	Matilda Bracino	1313
		Agnes Ledman	1294
		Agnes Spygot	1318
		Agnes Steyk (wife)	1291
		Agnes Steyk (daughter)	1292
		Nich. Sturdy's wife	1299
Other	2	Simon Bateman	1311
		Godfrey Steyk	1291

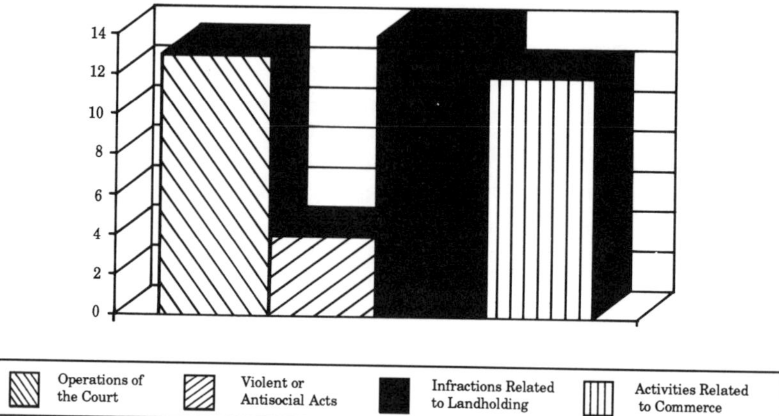

Figure 1. Types of activity connected with poverty in court records

The "operations of the court" comprise some activities that were not specifically pursued by the litigants or not sufficiently recorded by the court scribe to permit analysis. They include withdrawing a suit without license, settling a case outside of court, lodging a false plea, and acting as surety or pledge for a suitor who subsequently failed to appear in court, thus causing an amercement to be levied on the surety.[20] The nature of the plea and other specifics are missing from the account. Information from these kinds of records usually is useful for analysis only if the name of one or more of the participants is traceable to other actions or records.

If we go beyond the context in which an individual was labeled *pauper* and look at all his or her recorded activities, we can find a number of court-related situations that reveal a great deal about the position of poor people in their society. One of these is pledging. Pledging was to the manorial court what bail is to most modern courts: it was meant to assure conformity on

[20]Fuller discussions of these and other actions in manorial courts appear in Homans, *English Villagers*, ch. 20; see also Clanchy, *Wiltshire Eyre*, pp. 10–12.

the part of the pledgee (or bailee) with some court order or procedure. A personal pledge or surety therefore had to be regarded by court officials as sufficiently respectable to assure the desired behavior on the part of the principal, or to accept responsibility in case of default.[21] Many students of the rural legal system have come to regard court acceptance of a given individual as pledge as an indication of his good standing in the community. Even stronger indications of community approval are provided when an individual is named in the court rolls as juror, constable, or ale taster. These offices in the town government entailed year-round responsibility for transmitting correct information and acting in the best interests of the community.[22] The major limitation on what we can learn from the ways in which the "poor" related to these various court functions is that women (and children) were virtually never allowed to serve in any of them, and so this gauge of acceptability works fully for only about one-third of the population.[23]

Male-dominated though it was, the society that produced the St. Ives court rolls did not equate solvency with respectability; far from it. Only four of the 40 *pauperes* were without personal sureties at the time of their financial problems, and it is not purely coincidental that three of the four seem to have

---

[21]Pledges faced fines—usually 3*d.* or 6*d.*—if the principal failed to conform to the court-ordered behavior. See, e.g., William of Broughton (1306), Laurence Frauncecys and Nicholas Reeve (1308). See also 30 Apr. 1275: Thomas of Northampton acknowledging in court a debt of 6*s.* to John Faukes of Hulme for a loan, and a further 20*d.* for "damage as a result of pledging" by Thomas against a certain Richard of Barton.

[22]See J. A. Raftis, *Tenure and Mobility: Studies in the Social History of the Mediaeval English Village* (Toronto, 1964), ch. 4; William A. Morris, *The Frankpledge System* (New York, 1910).

[23]See Judith M. Bennett, "Public Power and Authority in the Medieval English Countryside," in Mary Carpenter Erler and Maryanne Kowaleski, eds., *Women and Power in the Middle Ages* (Athens, Ga., 1988), pp. 18–36. See also Shulamith Shahar, *The Fourth Estate: A History of Women in the Middle Ages*, trans. Chaya Galai (London, 1983), pp. 220–34.

left town or died shortly thereafter.[24] More significantly, no fewer than 16 of the 27 males labeled *pauper* actually served as pledge, juror, ale taster, or constable at some point: six of these did so in the same year as their financial difficulty, and 10 did so in subsequent years. Apparently no one was ostracized or barred from even the highest office of rural government for being poor. Richard Messor, Ralph Scot, Hugo Sterne, Godfrey Steyk, and William Wygar all served as jurors during or after their inability to pay court fines. In addition, in 1291, the same year in which his name appears as *pauper*, Godfrey Steyk was chosen by court officials as one of four townsmen entrusted with two rayed cloths worth 10 marks, which were being kept to ensure the appearance of a certain defendant in court the following year.[25]

Some of the pledging can be seen as a function of occupational confraternities, probably of an informal nature.[26] Thus Agnes ad Fontem found as pledge the baker Roger Multon when she had to pay a baking fine of 12*d.*; and Roger le Barman, baker, served as pledge for Robert Baker of Lincoln and for Johanna of Walmesford selling halfpenny loaves, both in 1291, and was pledged by Thomas of Cley, another baker, in 1293. Nicholas Sturdy, a tanner, pledged twice for Ralph Raven, a dealer in horsehides (1275). Alewives generally had their husbands to stand as surety for them.[27] In fact, only three

---

[24]Henry the servant of Thomas Catworth, Agnes of Deene, and Benedict Gere. The fourth, William of Mattishall, whose poverty was noted in 1291, was pledging for his wife, Elena, 1306–08. It must also be noted that personal sureties are never mentioned in connection with fines for failure to provide a night watchman.

[25]1291: Andrew Chaplain of Hemmingford.

[26]For further discussion of occupational pledging groups see Ellen Wedemeyer (Moore), "Social Groupings at the Fair of St. Ives (1275–1302)," *Mediaeval Studies* 32 (1970): 27–59.

[27]Avenandus's wife (1291); Bateman's wife (1308, 1310, 1311); Matilda Bracino (1306, 1310, 1311); Ledman (1291, but not 1294); Mattishall's wife (1306, 1308);

times do we encounter a husband who did not pledge for his brewing wife, and in two of those cases the husband may well have been dead (Ledman and Spigot), while in the third the husband was surely having grave financial difficulties of his own (Steyk).

Aside from this conjugal support, families showed relatively little solidarity through pledging. Aside from John le Swappere and William Beadle, each of the *pauperes* had family—nuclear or extended—yet only three had recorded pledging connections with any of those members.[28] Most of the other pledging support was neighborly. To judge from the wide-ranging pledging network, St. Ives around the beginning of the fourteenth century was a community whose members knew and generally respected one another, and financial problems do not seem to have deeply affected the patterns of that respect. The "poor" do not seem to have been a separate community, dependent solely upon each other for support. While there was considerable interpledging within this "group" of 40 persons, there was much more pledging for and by a larger group of townspersons.[29]

The network of pledging and poverty in the career of William Wygar will serve to illustrate a number of the points just made. Unable to pay a fine in 1279 for reneging on his

---

Medicus's wife (1294, 1299, 1301, town); Agnes Spygot (1313, but not 1318); Sterne's wife (1291 and even 1299, when she was too poor to pay the ale fine); Juliana Wygar (1291, 1292).

[28]Richard Laweman for Matilda, daughter of Robert Laweman (1279); William Ledman for Agnes, wife of Thomas (1294); William Wygar, John Wygar, and Jamota Wygar, in separate cases in 1312.

[29]Mary Patricia Hogan, studying the treatment of wrongdoers in the rural East Midlands, describes a situation quite similar to that of the *pauperes* of St. Ives: "In effect, the community had no intention of freezing the troublesome villager in a position of irresponsibility, but rather encouraged his lawabidingness by engaging him in pertinent judicial responsibilities" ("Medieval Villany: A Study in the Meaning and Control of Crime in an English Village," *Studies in Medieval and Renaissance History* 17 [1981]: 213).

obligation to reap in the lord's fields, William nevertheless served as a juror for the Bridge Street community in that year, and also later, in 1287, 1291, and 1293. Sometime between 1284 and 1287 he acquired a house and a shop, from which the abbot derived 8*s*. in rent during the fair alone, yet in 1288 his wife had to give a tunic to the lord as payment for a 6*d*. debt. In 1291 all William's goods were ordered seized into the lord's hand until he paid his license fee to operate as a tanner, but he was able to pledge for his wife's payment of 2*s*. for brewing ale that same year. He served as a pledge for three separate individuals between 1292 and 1300, but in 1301 he and his wife were unable to pay for a court settlement with a certain Margaret of Raveley, and poverty was again given as the reason. The Wygars were supported in this case by Thomas Baker, who also supported them in another case that same year. By 1306 William was again serving as pledge for various of his neighbors and was paying fines, primarily for disregarding rules relating to his Bridge Street property. He does not disappear from the records until 1312, at which time he would have been over 50 years old, if we assume that jury service was not normally assigned to anyone under the age of 20.[30]

In comparison with positions of responsibility, the connection between poverty and "criminal" activity is remarkably faint in the St. Ives court records. Consider first the small range and volume of criminal situations that were specifically connected

---

[30]All dates refer to town or fair court rolls except 1284 and 1287, which are stallage lists for rentals during the fair. The unpaid debt of 1288 is noted in a list of such debts at the end of the fair court record of 1291. William's pledgees were Juliana Gere (1300, town) and her daughter Margery (1306, town), Margaret le Permongere (1300, fair), Henry Canne of Huntingdon, John Wygar, and Jamota Wygar (all 1312, fair). This portrait of a St. Ives pauper differs markedly from that drawn by Zvi Razi for Halesowen at the same period: "never elected to public office in the village and only rarely accepted by the court as pledges" (*Life, Marriage, and Death*, p. 78).

with an inability to pay the amercement: four of 43 situations, specifically one act of slander, one case of fraud, and two actions that caused a hue and cry to be raised, probably for assault. But the range remains equally small when we examine all the available information about the 40 persons involved in this study. Only one tried to perpetrate a fraud; only two were accused of assault, although Simon Bateman was so accused and convicted twice (1311 and 1313). Bateman is also the only person fined for burglary (in 1311), and he is one of only two against whom the hue was justly raised.[31]

Part of the explanation undoubtedly lies in the nature of the records. The scope of really "criminal" behavior included in the jurisdiction of a manorial or even a piepowder court was not great. Criminal court records, such as gaol delivery rolls or the records of the Châtelet in Paris, may lend themselves much more readily to an understanding of the range of criminal activities to which poverty might drive or entice a person.[32] Even so, the "poor" of St. Ives are remarkable for their lack of involvement with the relatively small incidence of socially injurious behavior discernible in the available records. By way of comparison, the entire town court records of 1279, 1291, 1294, and 1308 yield the names of, respectively, five, two, eight, and 23 persons convicted of assault. The fair court record for 1291 yields a total of 18 names, and for 1301, 20 names, of

---

[31]Fraud: Thomas le Tayllur (1275: theft of a coat worth 20*d.* that he took on pretense of being a bailiff); assault: William Avenandus (1287) and Simon Bateman (1311, 1313). The hue was justly raised upon Simon Bateman and William the servant of Thomas Catworth, both in 1306.

[32]See Barbara A. Hanawalt, "Community Conflict and Social Control: Crime and Justice in the Ramsey Abbey Villages," *Mediaeval Studies* 39 (1977): 402–23, and eadem, "Economic Influences on the Pattern of Crime in England, 1300–1348," *American Journal of Legal History* 18 (1974): 281–97; Geremek, *Margins of Society*, chs. 1–3. See also Jacqueline Misraki, "Criminalité et pauvreté en France a l'époque de la guerre de Cent Ans," in Mollat, *Etudes*, pp. 535–46.

assaulters.[33] In addition, it should be noted that, for whatever reason, the poor of St. Ives managed to avoid involvement in the more serious, royally-adjudicated crimes, at least in the late thirteenth century.[34]

None of this is to say that these individuals were necessarily models of civic behavior, but they were more often the victims of crime than its perpetrators. Agnes le Baker (1292), Simon Bateman (1308), William Cokeston (1313), William Wygar (1313), and John son of Adam of Yarmouth (1295) all fell prey to assaults, for example. When these *pauperes* did fall afoul of the law they were much more frequently violating the rules of land tenure or commerce.

Landholding entails obligations in any class and any society. Some of these obligations are more onerous than others, and the 16 paupers of St. Ives who can be specifically identified as property holders had difficulty with each of them: work obligations on the lord's demesne, taxes, the need to respect neighbors' rights to common land, and the need to preserve the integrity of the village community by taking responsibility for any problems created by outsiders "received" in one's house.[35]

Because St. Ives had a market center (Bridge Street) as well as a more agrarian area (the Green), many properties had additional obligations. One of these was high rent. The properties of

---

[33]See also the extensive investigation of Warboys, a village near St. Ives, where assaults were much more common, in Hogan, "Medieval Villany."

[34]*Royal Justice* (DeWindt and DeWindt) contains the Huntingdon Eyre of 1286. None of the 40 individuals included in this present study was brought before royal justices in these courts, although certainly other residents of St. Ives were mentioned in them, e.g., William of Bontingford (1: 424, no. 364).

[35]Work obligations: William Wygar, reaping (1279), William Avendandus, making hay (1279); taxes: John le Swappere (1301); rights to common land: Simon Bateman (1311), Godfrey Steyk (1291); receiving outsiders: Agnes le Baker (1301), Simon Bateman (1313), Agnes of Deene (1299), John le Swappere (1313), Simon Wodereve (1279).

three of the *pauperes* appear in a collection of rental contracts kept by the abbots of Ramsey precisely for the St. Ives holdings, and there one rented at 22*s*. annually, with an additional entry of a half-mark, one rented at 18*s*. annually, and one rented at 16*s*. plus a 2*s*. entry fine.[36] On the average, between about 1275 and 1325 a landholder on Bridge Street paid as much in annual rent to the abbot of Ramsey as did the most affluent 30 per cent of his rural tenants, the virgaters. In order to pay that rent the tenant was primarily dependent upon market forces of various sorts (since the holdings were too small for agrarian purposes). Surely tenants were specifically affected by the gradual decline of the international fair of St. Ives and the crisis in certain industries, such as that of English and Flemish luxury cloths, which reduced the number of fairgoers requiring foodstuffs, beverages, shops, and lodging. All of these developments were clearly evident by the late thirteenth century.[37]

The true cost of these properties cannot be measured simply in terms of rental figures. The contract on Simon Bateman's property specified that

> he will maintain the houses of the aforesaid row *at his own expense* in as good condition as, or better than, that in which he receives them; and he shall do for the tallage and for the other customs as the others on Bridge Street do. And he shall find a man to perform the autumn boon-work. (italics mine)

The "other customs," as clarified by fines in the court records, included specific regulations on renting during the fair, most prominent of which was the restriction against renting out the

---

[36]PRO SC2/178/95: Agnes le Baker (1300), Godfrey Steyk (1298), and Simon Bateman (1305). The first two names are those of former tenants; Simon Bateman was just beginning his tenancy in 1305.

[37]See Moore, *Fairs*, p. 238 and ch. 5.

(most lucrative) front rooms, a privilege generally reserved to the abbot of Ramsey. That meant that the "selling" part of the properties was unavailable to the St. Ives resident just during the most profitable period of the year. He or she could rent out the back rooms as lodging and/or warehouse space, on the stipulation that prostitutes and other undesirables were excluded and that a watchman was provided for the property every night of the fair. In order to discharge the latter obligation property holders would have to find a family member to stay awake each night or pay someone to do so, with fees running around 1*d.* per day in the late thirteenth century and fines for failure to supply a watchman running around 6*d.* a day.[38]

The court records suggest that these regulations contributed significantly to poverty in individual cases. Simon Wodereve, whose frontage brought the abbot 4*s.* in 1287, was driven to renting to prostitutes in order to get rental income for himself from the back location of his property; in 1275 he paid a 6*d.* fine for the practice, while in 1287 the prostitute herself, Alice of Lincoln, paid the 6*d.* fine. The houses of William Redeknave and Alice Saleman were also serving as brothels around the turn of the century. The properties of four townspeople—Wodereve, Dunstable, Reeve, and Saleman—failed to produce watchmen on a Thursday during the fair of 1275, and each was prevented by poverty from paying the 6*d.* fine levied on many neighbors for the same offense. In 1288 Robert Marshall experienced the same difficulty.[39]

John Reeve, whose property brought between 3*s.* and 4*s.* 6*d.* to the abbot during the fair in the late 1280s, was found

---

[38]Bateman (PRO SC2/178/95 [1305]). For rental regulations during the fair see Moore, *Fairs*, p. 189.

[39]Redeknave, 1287; Saleman, 1300; Wodereve, Dunstable, Reeve, and Saleman, 10 May 1275; Marshall, 22 Apr. 1288.

renting to someone selling woolfells illegally from his front room in 1288. Hugo Sterne's frontage was rented to a man accused (falsely, as it turned out) of receiving prostitutes. Hugo was also convicted in court of obtaining a half-acre plot of land illegally, and after his death his widow, Matilda, was fined in the fair court for failing to provide a watchman for the property.[40] William Wygar in 1306 was fined for receiving undesirable outsiders and for reneging on a contract to sublet a house to another townsman at farm and for failing to provide a watchman on Monday after the Ascension in 1312. Godfrey Steyk, who owed the abbot 18*s.* each year for his St. Ives property, tried to rent sales places to two separate individuals in 1293 (a seller of woolfells, a seller of furs, both selling illegally). A "little ditch of water" running near the house of John le Swappere was found to be "outside the proper course," so he was fined and ordered to correct the problem at his own expense. Simon Bateman, who had to pay 16*s.* each year for his property, was found trying to sublet illegally for three years to William of Queye in 1311 and illegally receiving an outsider in 1313. Agnes le Baker ran afoul of the fair authorities in 1300 for renting to prostitutes, and the notice in the town court records for 1301 cited her for "having been presented in the last court for receiving outsiders against the rules" and repeated the explanation of "condonatur quia pauper" in dealing with the amercement.[41]

The "receiving" of outsiders could in theory refer to a gesture of love as well as of money, but it would seem that many such incidents were rentals of spare (or not so spare) rooms to

[40]Reeve, PRO SC11/315, BL Add. Roll 34784, and 22 Apr. 1288; Sterne, 25 May 1291, 1301, and 9 May 1312.

[41]Steyk, 30 Apr. 1293 (both rentals); Swappere, 1309; Bateman, 1311 (town court), receiving Thomas le Thatcher, 1313; Baker, 12 May 1300.

anyone willing to produce (or at least promise) cash, regardless of his/her qualifications. In an incident from 1291 a certain Cecilia of York, with only her faith as surety, sued St. Ives resident William Wodereve for unjust detention of a tapet of Rheims and a linen sheet belonging to her, to a total value of 10*d.* In the pleading that followed it became clear that Cecilia had rented a house for 14*d.* from William, that on 21 May he had seized those items because she had not paid the rent, and that on the thirty-first day of the fair (1 June) Cecilia was still in such financial straits that she continued to owe 6*d.* on the rent and was excused from her fine as a pauper, leaving William with the rather vague comfort of knowing that "she should satisfy him." Although William Wodereve was never reduced to the status of *pauper* in any of the records still extant, his dilemma, like that of those who received prostitutes or otherwise broke rental regulations, attests to the difficulties of holding expensive rental properties, particularly during the straitened economic circumstances of the late thirteenth and early fourteenth centuries.

Commercial activity was an equally common characteristic of local paupers, involving at least 17 of the 40. Craftsmen were perhaps the most obvious traders. William Wygar and Nicholas Sturdy were tanners as well as commercial property holders. Simon Bateman, carpenter, Roger Barman, baker, and Agnes ad Fontem le Baker appear numerous times in the court and account records in connection with their crafts. These five individuals constituted a good percentage of the specialized craftsmen living in St. Ives between 1270 and 1325; the records suggest a total of about six tanners, 10 bakers, and three carpenters. Another career connected with poverty in St. Ives is that of Robert Marshall, who, in accordance with the implications of his name, seems to have kept a stable. He was sued in 1287 over a contract he had made to put new shoes on three hooves and remove the shoe from the fourth on a horse belonging to John son of Alan of Colne, and he also served as pledge for a man suing another over custody of a horse.[42]

The practice of these crafts was by no means unrelated to the economic difficulties that beset the craftsmen. When William Wygar declared in court that he was not willing to pay the lord anything for the right to operate as a tanner, his goods were ordered seized until such time as he changed his mind, and a similar fate befell Nicholas Sturdy.[43] Agnes ad Fontem and Roger le Barman both seem to have functioned perfectly well as retailers for a number of bakers in the St. Ives fair, but both found that baking their own bread and selling it through retailers was more difficult. In 1300 Agnes fell victim to poverty from which we do not see her emerge. Roger le Barman was sued for a debt of 3*s.*2*d.* and was unable to pay the fine for settling out of court in 1293, the same year in which he first appeared as a baker on his own. He may actually have been having problems as early as 1291—the abbot's account rolls record him as owing 6*d.* from that time, but Roger eventually did recover financially.[44]

Simon Bateman's declaration of poverty came in connection with a fine for having a big beam or large pole ("magnum lignum") jutting into the main street. Either he was building a house or (more likely) he had erected a signpost to identify his services, much like a barber's pole. (Another man was fined

[42]Wygar and Sturdy were tanners in 1291. (Most St. Ives tanners held commercial property, since tanning is a pursuit requiring a specialized workplace near running water.) Bateman, 1311 (account), 1313 (account, three times), 26 Apr. 1312, 14 and 18 May 1317; Barman, 20 May 1287, 28 May 1291; Fontem, 1291 (town), 14 May 1293 (twice), 16 May 1300. Other St. Ives craftsmen appear in Moore, *Fairs*, App. 6.

[43]May 1287, and 5 June 1291.

[44]Wygar and Sturdy, 1291 (town); Fontem and Barman, retailed 1293–1300 and 1287–93, respectively; Fontem baking, 16 May 1300; Barman baking, 14 May 1293, debt 1292.

18*d.* for a similar offense.) Simon also came into the fair court on seven other occasions between 1311 and 1317, to sue or be sued in pleas of unjust distraint, debt, or contract. Some pleas were settled out of court, with no details given, but even the shreds of evidence are very suggestive: plaintiff against William le Turnour for unjust distraint of 12*d.*; plaintiff against John le Chapman for unjust distraint of a window; plaintiff against Roger of Moulton to collect 4*s.*11*d.* for carpentry on his house; defendant against the same Roger of Moulton on the grounds that the contract between them stipulated that Simon was to build a house using no old wood.[45] Simon collected his payment through the court, plus 6*d.* damages for late payment, but he had to turn around and pay out 2*s.* in damages for cheating (or misunderstanding) on the quality of the wood. Simon's career also illustrates the difficulties encountered by any provider of goods or services in extracting payment from insolvent customers. In 1311 Simon appeared as plaintiff against Agnes Drynkewater for a debt of 3*s.*3*d.* plus damages of a half-mark. Judgment had already been rendered in favor of Simon, but Agnes had been unable to produce the cash and so the court handed over to him, in partial payment, four basins worth 2*s.* plus two linen sheets and three towels collectively worth 8*d.* that it had been able to seize from Agnes. From the sale of those items Agnes's 6*d.* fine to the court had to be deducted before Simon's share would be reckoned![46]

Brewing was also connected with poverty on occasion. Six St. Ives residents were specifically declared "poor" at the time they were required to pay fees in connection with the brewing and selling of ale. Another six paupers were clearly dependent

---

[45]1318 (town): pole in street; Bateman, 11 May 1311, town 1313, 26 Apr. 1312, 14 May 1317. See also PRO SC6/884/4 (account 1313, twice), 8 May and 9 May 1315.

[46]18 May 1317, 28 May 1311.

upon the craft for at least part of their livelihoods.[47] Although brewing was certainly a much more common occupation in rural towns and villages than any of the other crafts mentioned above, in several ways it was a deceptively easy commercial endeavor. Requiring relatively little skill or time, it was an activity that could be carried on by a woman despite her many other obligations, while the man of the family engaged in other pursuits. Most brewers were not only female but also wives, a fact that at least one historian attributes to the "complex and costly" nature of the craft.[48] The equipment required was not negligible: large vats, scrupulously standard selling vessels (pint, quart, and gallon), and the raw material, usually malted barley, to which various flavorings and/or yeast might be added. The real problem for the neophyte or the unwary lay in the "assize of ale." This nationally-applied rule required any brewer who was selling ale to send for the ale taster of the community, to have it tested (literally, tasted) for sufficient fermentation of the grain and for proper pricing, and especially to verify the conformity of the brewer's sales vessels to those of the national standard. Fines for "breaking the assize" were unusually high, with a St. Ives mean of 18*d.* and on occasion reaching 4*s.*[49] Brewers were fined so regularly that many historians have surmised the fines to be more like license fees for offering various quantities of ale for sale. In any case, an investment in equipment could take very long indeed to be amortized, let alone lead to a profit.

---

[47]Matilda Bracino, 1313; Agnes Spigot, 1318; Walfrid Steyk's wife, 1291, and daughter, 1292; Agnes Ledman, 1292, and Nicholas Sturdy's wife, 1299 (all town records). Also Avenandus, Bateman, Mattishall, Medicus, Sterne, and Wygar were dependent on brewing.

[48]Judith M. Bennett, "The Village Ale-Wife: Women and Brewing in Fourteenth-Century England," in Barbara A. Hanawalt, ed., *Women and Work in Preindustrial Europe* (Bloomington, 1986), p. 25.

[49]Matilda the wife of Hugo Sterne, in 1313, for example.

Two brewing families, those of Godfrey Steyk and William Wygar, can actually be seen hurtling themselves into economic ruin by contracting large debts for purchases of malt: 7*s.* 10*d.* and 22*s.*, respectively. Unable to pay immediately, Wygar undertook an elaborate scheme to discharge the outstanding debt over a period of three years, with four personal pledges to guarantee execution. Neither family seems to have recovered fully from the economic burden of these debts, since both were declared pauper subsequently.[50]

Godfrey Steyk did not restrict his commercial activities to the ale trade. We have already observed that he was also a landlord of commercial properties, and his renters specialized in the wool and fur trades.[51] He went to some lengths to press an advantage over a business rival (e.g., his obstruction of the road permitting access to the house that John Cook rented from Godfrey's neighbor John Mariot in 1291). William Cookston was another resident who derived at least some of his livelihood from commerce. He appears several times in the St. Ives fair court records in connection with detention of goods or money, but the exact nature of the transactions is not made clear. John Medicus, William's pledge in a suit that he did not pursue, also seems to have experimented with credit. He can be observed suing a certain Robert Baldewine for 17*d.* owed to him and serving as pledge in a number of debt suits. William Wygar and his wife, Juliana, were sued for debt twice in the fair court of 1295. Hugo Toth was sued for a debt of 16*d.* for books and worked out a scheme to pay 8*d.* of the total within four months and the rest later.[52]

---

[50]Debts: Steyk, 1279, Wygar, 14 May 1295; poverty: Steyk, 24 May 1291 and 1292, Wygar, 1301.

[51]30 Apr. 1293. See also above, p. 137.

[52]Steyk, 24 May 1291; Cookston, 13 May 1312 (twice), 2 May, 1317; Medicus pledging, 1301, suing, 1313, pledging in debt suits, 6 May 1295, for Walter Gris,

Partnerships constituted another commercial technique known to at least some of these paupers. Simon Bateman and a certain John of Bytham did carpentry work together and pledged for one another from at least 1311 until 1317, and Simon also worked with Thomas Aunprun, trimming spars for the abbot of Ramsey. In both cases the two men were paid one lump sum for work and supposedly divided the payment between themselves. Some of the long-term relationships, like that between William Wygar and the troubled Gere family, might signal a form of partnership and may have contributed to the financial problems of certain individuals.[53] In all, some 23 of the "poor" (58 per cent) had some sort of clear economic asset, in the form of income-producing property or commercial skill or a combination of the two (see Table 3).

In all, looked at from the reverse perspective, this same information reveals that a wide variety of rural crafts and/or responsibility for the obligations of land tenure could be part of a pattern of economic hardship. Here, for example, are exceptions to the general observations that brewing was often a pursuit of the wives of some of the wealthiest villeins in a rural community, and, at the other end of the financial spectrum, that partnerships and credit arrangements were helping to create the considerable fortunes of English international merchants of the thirteenth century.[54]

While economic security was surely elusive for many, poverty did not necessarily entail destitution (see Fig. 2). The poor

---

23 May 1300, for William of Deste, 27 May 1300, and for custody of 21*d.* for Richard Trot; Wygar, 14 May 1295; Toth, 25 May 1295.

[53]Bateman and Bytham, PRO SC6/884/2: 1311 (account), 14 May 1317, 18 May 1317; Bateman and Aunprun, PRO SC6/884/4: 1313 (account); Wygar and Gere, 14 May 1295, 1300, 1306, 4 Apr. 1312.

[54]On brewing see Bennett, "Village Ale-Wife," p. 24, and Moore, *Fairs*, pp. 256–62. On merchants, credit, and partnerships see Michael M. Postan, *Medieval Trade and Finance* (Cambridge, 1973), chs. 1 and 3.

of St. Ives comprise two dominant subgroups: those whose stay in the town was very brief (one to three years), and those who, whether faring poorly or well, remained in the town much longer (11 to 36 years). The genuinely destitute were actually a minority in the group of rural poor. They include at most some 15 individuals,[55] whose extremely brief appearances in the St. Ives records suggest a short life, a transient lifestyle characteristic of the poorest levels of rural society,[56] or at least the need or desire to go elsewhere to lead a viable life. Within this group were surely at least a few landless vagabonds, who were probably losing the battle for survival as autonomous and productive men or women.

Particularly grim is the information concerning Henry the servant (*garco*) of Thomas of Catworth. We are told only that the hue and cry was raised justly upon him by a woman in 1306 and "therefore he is amerced. He is poor." His employer, Thomas, a prominent baker who appeared often in the courts of both town and fair to pledge for many another person,[57] neither paid Henry's amercement nor stood surety for him in court. Perhaps Thomas had dismissed him by then. In any case, Henry had no surety. We never see his name again. He sinks into an obscurity that is full of implications about the isolation and helplessness of the very poor.

---

[55]Ba, Beadle, Catworth, Deene, Gere, Hayward, Laweman, Ledman, Permongere, Pund, Walfrid Reeve, Saleman, Steyk, Tayllur, and Yarmouth.

[56]See Mollat, *Les pauvres*, pp. 299–302; Razi, *Life, Marriage, and Death*, p. 97.

[57]Thomas's career spans the period 1299–1317; he was also a juror and a landholder.

TABLE 3
CAREER SPAN AND POVERTY IN ST. IVES

Name	Entire Recorded Career in St. Ives (Years in Town*)		Year Recorded as Pauper	Assets**
Wm. Avenandus	1287–91	(5)	1287	p
Walfrid Ba	1287	(1)	1287	—
Roger le Barman	1287–1302	(16)	1293	t
Simon Bateman	1299–1317	(18)	1311	p & t
Wm. Beadle	1299–1313	(3)	1301	—
Matilda Bracino	1306–13	(8)	1313	t
Henry servant of Thomas Catworth	1306	(1)	1306	?
Wm. Cokeston	1301–28	(28)	1301	t
Agnes of Deene	1299	(1)	1299	—
Wm. of Dunstable	1275–87	(13)	1275	p
Agnes ad Fontem le Baker	1291–1300	(10)	1300	p & t
Benedict Gere	1296	(1)	1296	—
Richard Hayward (Messor)	1291	(1)	1291	—
Matilda Laweman	1279	(1)	1279	—
Agnes Ledman	1294	(1)	1294	t
Robert Marshall	1287–91	(5)	1291	p & t
Wm. of Mattishall	1291–1308	(14)	1291	t
John Medicus	1288–1302	(15)	1301	t
Margaret le Permongere	1300	(1)	1300	—
Simon Pund	1292–94	(3)	1292	—
Matilda le Redeknave	1301–06	(7)	1306	—
Wm. le Redeknave	1287–1316	(20)	1287	—
John Reeve (Prepositus)	1279–1314	(36)	1279	p
Walfrid Reeve (Prepositus)	1275	(1)	1275	—

*In calculating the total I have counted both the first and the last years, since the individual's presence was specifically recorded in St. Ives during both years.
**p = real property, land; t = trading experience or craft skills.

TABLE 3—*Continued*

Name	Entire Recorded Career in St. Ives	(Years in Town*)	Year Recorded as Pauper	Assets**
Alice Saleman	1275	(1)	1275	p & t
Ralph Scot	1275–93	(19)	1275	p
Agnes Spygot	1301–18	(18)	1318	t
Hugo Sterne	1279–1311	(33)	1279	p & t
Godfrey Steyk	1279–98	(24)	1291	p & t
Agnes Steyk Godfrey's wife	1275–91	(17)	1291	t
Agnes Steyk Godfrey's daughter	1292	(1)	1292	t
Nicholas Sturdy's wife	1275–99	(25)	1299	t
John le Swappere	1301–13	(13)	1301	—
Thomas le Tayllur	1275	(1)	1275	—
Hugo Toth	1295–1306	(12)	1295	—
Simon Wodereve	1275–87	(13)	1275, 1279	p & t
Robert Wygar	1287–96	(10)	1296	—
Wm. Wygar	1279–1312	(34)	1279, 1301	p & t
Juliana Wygar Wm.'s wife	1288–1301	(14)	1301	t
John son of Adam of Yarmouth	1295	(1)	1295	—

Even within the group of the very poor, however, Henry was unusual in his total lack of support. Virtually no one else was as helpless as he. All the others were at least part of the network of neighborly support that enveloped nearly everyone involved in this study and included even the most rootless.[58]

---

[58]Walfrid Ba, labeled *pauper* twice in 1287, managed to find Walfrid of Hilton as pledge in one of those instances (9 May 1287); the other instance involved a failure to provide a watchman at night, and pledges were not called for in connection with that offense. Benedict Gere, another "rootless" individual, was himself pledging for Robert Eveline in 1296. When Richard Hayward was declared pauper he had as his pledge William in the Croft (25 May 1292). Simon Pund had John Medicus in

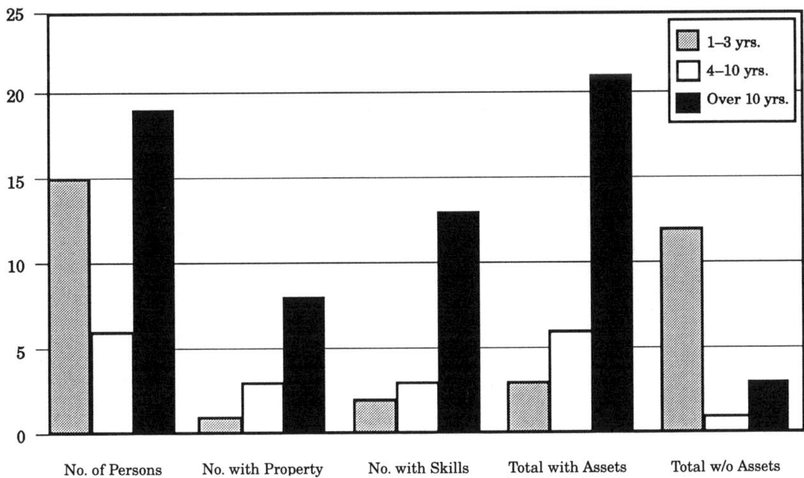

Figure 2. Assets, career span, and poverty in St. Ives

These transient paupers were not cut off from the community, but few of them left a record of a connection with a marketable skill or property. This is true at least for the men who were unable to find more than a toehold in the community before being obliged to move along.

The destitute women made up a much less homogeneous group. Three of them were ale brewers.[59] For them, the pitfalls of commercial life had become chasms, and the network of community support did not manage to keep them functioning in town for any length of time. At this point we must observe that the women who appear as bit players in the drama of poverty were not necessarily destitute. Their disappearance from the records may constitute nothing more than marriage

---

an analogous situation in 1292. Thomas le Tayllur had Henry Cissor of Houghton, and then Elias Hundredor, a bailiff of the fair, in various stages of his suit on 7 and 8 May 1275. John of Yarmouth found as pledge Thomas of Wistow plus his own body on 11 May 1295. See also Mollat, *Les pauvres*, pp. 218–19.

[59]Agnes Ledman, Alice Saleman, and Agnes Steyk, daughter.

and a change of surname, although, as many manorial tenants' marriages were recorded in court or on landholding documents, it is somewhat surprising that we do not see this evidence for any of these female paupers. Death seems more likely than marriage in the case of Agnes Ledman, who was both married and sick at the time of her poverty; she does not reappear in the St. Ives records, although her husband, Thomas, functioned as ale taster two years later.[60] At least two women of brief appearance in the records seem to have been widows, and two others were probably quite young, still maidens.[61] Perhaps some of these women eventually improved their economic situations through marriage, but perhaps not—the lot of most medieval wives, as well as of most *femes soles* who lacked support from family, is still largely unknown.[62]

Those paupers who remained in the St. Ives records for more than three years constituted the majority (25 of the total 40), and many spent over 10 adult years in the town. In general, there was a correlation between length of stay and control of either property or commercial skill, or both. Of the longer-term resident poor, only four (Ralph Scot, John le Swappere, Hugo Toth, and Robert Wygar) persevered year after

---

[60]1294, 1296.

[61]Widows: Agnes of Deene, whose only entry records that she was illegally receiving her son William in 1299, and Agnes Spygot, whose husband was active 1301–13 but who had no husband to pledge for her to pay her brewing fine in 1318. Young women: Matilda Laweman and Agnes Steyk, both identified only as daughters in the records (1279 and 1292, respectively).

[62]Margaret le Permongere, 26 May 1300; Alice Saleman, 10 May 1275. Conversely, Matilda le Redeknave (1306) had a family that actively added to her problems, judging from the violent career of William le Redeknave (1287–1316): receiving prostitutes and others illegally, false claims in court, stealing oaks from the abbot's wood. For a general survey of the kinds of information available thus far on women "outside the family," see Bonnie S. Anderson and Judith P. Zinsser, *A History of Their Own: Women in Europe from Prehistory to the Present*, 2 vols. (New York, 1988), 1: 140–45.

year in the town without visible means of support. Three individuals (all women: Agnes Ledman, Agnes Saleman, and Agnes Spygot) who did have some economic resources did not manage for long to continue the struggle for existence. Despite these exceptions, and despite the many pitfalls of economic activity in the late thirteenth century, most individuals who managed to remain in the same town for most of their lives were those equipped with at least some economic resource. This relative economic stability may well have been related to the fact that assets were not severely endangered by lack of liquidity when it was time to pay court fees.[63] Thus, although the economic currents of the time were undeniably recessionary, the definition of *pauper* in the manorial courts was not limited to the most severely deprived.

We have seen that most paupers who had some skills or assets suitable to life in a rural town managed to maintain a longer residence in St. Ives than those who did not. Was the remission of court fines another significant help in the struggle to survive? It is impossible really to answer the question, and it is doubtful in any case that a policy this simplistic could make a major difference. Certainly it made no difference at all for the very poor, who appear only once or twice in the records. But for those whose careers were longer and more varied, the chronological moment of poverty in the career can be informative. A situation in which someone reached an official declaration of poverty at the end of a long series of actions is quite different from one in which that declaration occurs early in the series: in the latter case one could reasonably assume an economic recovery,

---

[63]Certainly the inability to pay on demand did not entail bankruptcy in the peculiarly devastating sense that befell members of Italian banking families, for example. See Richard W. Kaeuper, *Bankers to the Crown: The Riccardi of Lucca and Edward I* (Princeton, 1973), ch. 5, esp. p. 213.

depending to some extent on the nature of the actions and the length of time involved. The complete range of court records and the years of fine remission appear in Table 4. On the basis of this information, we can reach some observations about how the poor of St. Ives were coping with poverty and/or overcoming it.

Most individuals were not able to transcend their poverty. The majority (25 of the 40) ended their recorded careers on a note of distress. It is probably not coincidental that all the women fall into this category. We have already observed that many of the women were single or widows, members of groups that traditionally have found life most difficult. Matilda the wife of Thomas Bracino may well have been typical of a married woman in distressed circumstances. Probably the most revealing piece of information about her family comes from the fair court of 1300, where Thomas, ordered to pay 40*d.* damages to his successful opponent in a lawsuit, has not appeared to do so, and his two pledges are being distrained by a rayed coat and 17*d.*, respectively, to respond for Thomas in the next fair. Thomas's actions are unaccounted for over the next few years, but by 1306 he was pledging for his wife's brewing fine of 2*s.* Perhaps she was never able to pay the full sum; in the abbatial account roll for 1307 a sum of 6*d.* had been relaxed to her name. Matilda brewed rather often, incurring fines of 2*s.* in 1310 and 1311 and being pledged by her husband on both occasions. By 1313 she was unable to pay her fine, and although her husband was still accepted as her surety, he did not pay it, either.[64] Their names never reappear in the records of St. Ives.

This pattern of struggles, moments of helplessness, minor victories, and final defeat had many variants and was not restricted to any particular decade, trade, or economic pursuit

---

[64]22 May 1300; account roll (PRO SC6/884/1), 1307. All other references are to town court records.

TABLE 4
ASSETS, CAREER SPAN, AND POVERTY IN ST. IVES

Total Recorded Career in St. Ives: years	1–3	4–10	Over 10	Total (% of 40)
Number of Persons (% of 40)	15 (37.5%)	6 (15%)	19 (47.5%)	40 (100%)
Number of Persons with Real Property (% of group)	1 (6.5%)	3 (50%)	8 (42%)	12 (30%)
Number of Persons with Commercial Skills (% of group)	2 (13%)	3 (50%)	13 (68%)	18 (45%)
Total Number of Persons with Assets* (% of group)*	3 (20%)	6 (100%)	21 (111%)	30 (75%)
Total Number of Persons with No Recorded Assets (% of 40)	12 (80%)	1 (16.5%)	3 (16%)	16 (40%)

*Some individuals have record of both commercial skills and real property; they are counted twice in this category and in the percentages.

around the turn of the fourteenth century. The remission of a fine, even a large one in the range of 2*s.*, was not sufficient to prevent the hardships of life from causing either death or a need to seek survival elsewhere.

Somewhat more positive is the information concerning paupers like Godfrey Steyk. A juror of Bridge Street in 1275, he also stood as personal surety for three persons in the fair that year. In all three cases he was one of two pledges—perhaps an early indication of some economic weakness on his part, should the principal default; usually only one personal surety was necessary, unless the principal was mistrusted by the court. However, all three cases may well have required a double surety on their own grounds. One of the principals was an outsider, and he was being pledged to pay a rather steep sum for damages in a slander suit. The other two pledgees were local residents, but one, William of Eltisley, an otherwise unexceptionable tanner and property holder, was also being pledged to pay relatively large sums: 5*s.* 1*d.* 3*q.* owed for a purchase of oats, plus 12*d.* damages, and an additional 12*d.* court amercement. The other, Simon Wodereve, had already been declared *pauper* earlier in the same court.[65]

The Steyk family had a prosperous connection with brewing at the time, since Godfrey's wife, Agnes, was one of 14 local women named as ale weighers in the fair. In 1279 Godfrey was once again a juror, and his wife was fined 12*d.* for brewing (a blot on the roll makes it impossible to verify that the fine was actually paid). By then Godfrey's business dealings seem to have expanded. He and his wife had contracted a debt of 7*s.* 10*d.* for ale, which they formally acknowledged in court, with John of Morden as surety. Since they were buying ale as well as brewing it, they were probably running an ale house, and indeed Godfrey's house appears on rental lists for the St. Ives fair from 1284 through 1287, commanding rents of between 16*d.* and 40*d.* for the abbot during the fair. By 1291, however, Godfrey encountered problems, perhaps related to his business. He was not only found guilty of obstructing entrance to John Mariot's house in St. Ives during the fair but he also was unable to pay the amercement. Moreover, in the same year his

[65]Juror, 24 Apr. 1275, pledge, 15 May 1275, 16 May 1275 (twice). The outsider was John of Beeston of Nottingham. Wodereve was declared *pauper* 10 May 1275.

wife, Agnes, and the following year his daughter, Agnes, were unable to pay for brewing ale.[66]

Despite the family's obvious short-term financial problems, they retained their row of houses on Bridge Street undisturbed. It changed hands only in 1298, when it was taken over by Nicholas Tanner and his wife. The family also maintained its good standing in the community. In 1291, amidst all the declarations of poverty, Godfrey was one of four local residents given custody of goods worth 10 marks and taken as distraint by the fair court, to be kept in the town in order to encourage a certain defendant to appear to answer charges in the fair court the following year. His fellow-custodians—William of Houghton, John of Queye, and Thomas of Stow—were relatively prosperous and definitely respectable jurors and property holders.[67] The court officials were far from connecting poverty with lack of reliability.

The last we hear of Godfrey and his family is the notice that their house was passing into the hands of the Tanners. Godfrey had tried to extract maximum income from his property, to the point of renting out rear rooms illegally as selling places, twice in 1293. Both times the renter was fined and ordered to leave. At least one of them, Robert Persun, who was selling furs, was a prominent London skinner and may well have brought a tidy sum to Godfrey's coffers.

It may well be that the remission of three fines in the difficult years 1291–92 made a significant difference for the Steyks, enabling them to retain possession of their commercial

---

[66]Agnes as ale weigher, 24 Apr. 1275; Godfrey unable to pay his fine for obstruction, 24 May 1291; wife Agnes unable to pay fine for brewing, 4 June 1291. All other references are to town court records.

[67]Houghton pledging, 1279, 1291 (town courts), and also 27 Apr., 1 May, and 6 May 1275.

property and use it to economic advantage. In any case, the family was not obliged to leave town at its moment of greatest difficulty, although we cannot be confident that its economic condition had improved, either.

Few paupers managed to emerge from their difficulties as thoroughly as Hugo Sterne. Convicted of slander against William Avenandus in 1279, Hugo's earliest surviving act was his inability to pay the requisite fine, on grounds of poverty. But from that moment on his career appears to have been almost completely untroubled. From 1284 he held at least one house in town, in a prime location next to the Stone Hall and commanding a rent of 40*s.* for the abbot during the fair for the front room and thus presumably a comparable rent for Hugo and his family at other times. He was accused in 1291 of renting space to a brothel-keeper, but the charge was dismissed. He functioned as constable in the fair of 1291 and as a juror and constable in 1293 and 1300. Between 1291 and 1310 he pledged almost annually for the brewing fines of his wife, Matilda. These fines, ranging between 12*d.* and 3*s.*, attest to a good volume of activity and thus, presumably, of profit; in any case, she was never unable to pay them. He also served as surety for a variety of other people over the years, and a hint about his professional orientation is provided by the fact that the court chose him as one of six evaluators of a collection of pots taken in distraint from a defendant in 1302. In 1310 it was recorded that he was a serf and had not paid the *merchet* owing to the landlord at the marriage of his daughter, Juliana. Possibly he was unable to pay, but more likely he was merely unwilling: many *nativi* ignored the fine, and Hugo or Matilda did manage to pay a 3*s.* amercement for brewing that same year. Even after his death (sometime after 1310), Hugo's wife continued to reside in town and continued to brew, paying the high fines accruing to that activity (e.g., 4*s.* in 1313).[68]

We might surmise that the upturn in Hugo Stern's life was occasioned at least in part by the humane treatment of his financial distress in 1279. It is true that only eight of the 40, or 20 per cent, can be seen to have thoroughly recovered from poverty by the time of their deaths or departures from St. Ives. Other factors were undoubtedly at work as well. The economic climate of the 1280s was healthier than either of the two subsequent decades, particularly for townsfolk. Yet Roger le Barman and William of Mattishall recovered during the 1290s, and William Cokeston and John le Swappere did so during the first decade of the fourteenth century. In addition, the feebler but not insignificant periods of recovery experienced by William Avenandus, Simon Bateman, William of Dunstable, John Medicus, Godfrey Steyk, Hugo Toth, and William Wygar enabled many of them to remain in St. Ives for a full lifetime and usually with a family, although with some serious difficulties. Their average stay in the town (17.3 adult years) was significantly longer than that of the 25 persons whose careers ended in poverty (5.6 adult years), and that greater length may be attributable to the community attitude of support towards members in financial difficulty, expressed in part through fine remissions.

These residents of St. Ives, whose neighbors, acting as members of the local jury, assessed them as too poor to pay a small court fine at some point between 1275 and 1320, made up a varied group of individuals who defy an attempt to categorize and clarify patterns of behavior. Some of their stories are bright

---

[68]Property: PRO SC11/315; rental, 23 May 1291; constable, 1 May 1291, 30 Apr. 1293, 7 May 1300; juror, 30 Apr. 1293, 7 May 1300; pledging in town court, 1291, 1294, 1300, 1301, 1306, 1308, 1310; evaluator, 31 May 1302; serf, 1310 (town court); wife brewing, 1312, 1313 (town court).

and full of actions in which they had control; others are dark, with little indication of comfort from family, job, or property. The correlation of these stories leads to several conclusions. First, whatever their relative economic conditions, virtually all of the poor in St. Ives were enveloped by a social network of support, expressed in court through pledging and more generally through the fact that the legal label *pauper* did not entail an impediment on any activity discernable in the court records. Second, the majority of the "poor" were not destitute but in fact had resources that were specifically being protected by the remission of their fines. Clearly, then, a precept expressed in Magna Carta for the benefit of freemen was being applied, by some landlords at least, to all tenants. And the jurors producing an assessment of "too poor to pay" had a definition of poverty perhaps more flexible than those we usually use, but one that did identify individuals who were truly struggling with many economic problems. The remission of fines *quia pauper* was part of a community attitude towards financial distress which tried to minimize the isolation and helplessness of poverty.

THE TRIALS OF PARTNERSHIP IN MEDIEVAL ENGLAND: A CASE HISTORY, 1304

James Masschaele

On 1 May 1304 two prominent London merchants, John Chigwell and William de Flete, entered into a formal partnership.[1] To ratify their intentions, the two drew up an indenture spelling out the terms of their association: each man agreed to invest £40 in the venture for one calendar year. In this indenture Chigwell specified that his share of the capital was to come from certain goods held in Picardy, while de Flete stipulated that he would contribute goods held in London, specifically, wine, beans, and salt. Profits from the partnership were to be split evenly between the two entrepreneurs. These details can be reconstructed from a pair of extraordinary accounts surviving in the Accounts Various classification of the Exchequer documents in the Public Record Office, London (PRO E.101). Using these accounts, we can reconstruct in considerable detail the trading activities of the two men over a period of several months, activities that led them from London to Scotland to Artois and ultimately into acrimonious disagreement.

We have no way of knowing what brought Chigwell and de Flete together. Partnership was becoming a fashionable business

[1]Unless otherwise specified, details of the partnership are based on PRO E.101/506/1 (see Appendix below). These documents are also described in Gwyn A. Williams, *Medieval London, from Commune to Capital* (London, 1963), pp. 122–23.

arrangement in the reign of Edward I, perhaps, as Maitland suggested, a consequence of Italian mercantile influence.[2] English merchants never developed the formal contractual basis for partnership that characterized southern Europe, but there is no shortage of examples showing that they emulated the techniques of their continental counterparts.[3] The advantages of partnership were the same in England as they were on the Continent, the same in the early fourteenth century as they are today—to foster capital initiatives with returns to scale greater than those available to the isolated investor. Chigwell and de Flete were natural partners. Both were members of the headstrong merchant community of London, both, indeed, from leading families of that community. Two years after he signed the partnership agreement, de Flete was appointed by Edward I to represent the English merchant community in negotiations with the French king over commercial damages incurred as a result of the recent war between the two kings.[4] In later years he would be chosen to represent London in Parliament.[5] Chigwell was cut from the same cloth. He served in the household of Walter Langton, Lord Treasurer, one of the most powerful men in the country.[6] He also owned multiple properties in the city, enough to stand as collateral for a debt of £110 in 1302.[7] He

---

[2]Frederick Pollock and F. W. Maitland, *The History of English Law before the Time of Edward I*, 2nd. ed., 2 vols. (Cambridge, 1898), 2: 221–22.

[3]M. M. Postan, "Partnership in English Medieval Commerce," in idem, *Medieval Trade and Finance* (Cambridge, 1973), pp. 65–91.

[4]*Calendar of Patent Rolls, Edw. I*, 4: *1301–1307* (London, 1898), p. 427.

[5]*Calendar of Letter-Books Preserved among the Archives of the Corporation of the City of London at the Guildhall*, Books A–L, ed. R. R. Sharpe, 12 vols. (London, 1899–1912), *Letter Book E* (London, 1903), pp. 58, 104.

[6]*Select Cases in the Exchequer of Pleas*, ed. Hilary Jenkinson and Beryl E. R. Formoy, Selden Society, vol. 48 (1932): 211–12.

[7]*Cal. Letter-Books: Letter Book B*, ed. R. R. Sharpe (London, 1900), pp. 121–22. That he owned multiple properties can be surmised from the number of entries for

may also have been related to Hamo de Chigwell, Lord Mayor of the city for a number of years.[8] There is no conclusive proof of this, but Chigwell was not a common name.

That day in May 1304 was not the first to see Chigwell and de Flete joined together in a commercial enterprise. A few years earlier the two men, along with four others, had bound themselves to a Spanish merchant for a collective debt.[9] Indeed, there was a history of co-operation between the families of the two men, stretching back to the London revolt of 1263.[10] Nor, in spite of its unhappy outcome, was the 1304 partnership to represent the last contact between the two men. Years after the dust from their dispute had settled, we find one of Chigwell's associates employing de Flete's assistant, Thomas de Barrow, as a commercial factor.[11] Chigwell dealt with de Barrow several times in the course of his partnership with de Flete, and it is likely that personal acquaintance was responsible for de Barrow's subsequent appointment.

Both partners actually contributed more to the venture than the £40 for which each was bound. Chigwell's goods in Picardy were valued, by Chigwell, at £55, and de Flete's goods in London were worth £68 13*s.*4*d.* Their agreement was that profit or loss would be apportioned evenly for the first £80 of trading activity, and thereafter that each party would receive the entire profit or loss on the surplus of capital invested. The fact that each man invested chattels rather than cash should not surprise us. Such investment was the norm in England, as much among the peasantry as among the great merchants. Cash was

---

him in R. Sharpe's index of the Hustings Rolls, deposited in the Corporation of London Record Office (CLRO).

[8]On Hamo de Chigwell see Williams, *Medieval London*, pp. 285–303.

[9]Sharpe, *Letter Book B*, pp. 121–22.

[10]Williams, *Medieval London*, p. 123.

[11]Williams, *Medieval London*, p. 123.

sterile, not only in the arguments of theologians and canon lawyers but also in daily life: only when it was translated into land or chattels did it present opportunity for financial gain. The principal form of taxation at the time, the lay subsidy, was, after all, a tax on chattels.

The partnership began on what seemed a promising note. De Flete sent his goods to Scotland with two servants to oversee the voyage. The goods comprised 18 barrels of wine, 120 quarters of beans, and 20 weys (*pise*) of salt. The servants sold their master's goods in Stirling and Berwick, most likely to the English garrisons there: Edward I was comfortably ensconced before Stirling Castle at the time, making a show of one of his new siege engines as he mopped up the vestiges of his Scottish opposition.[12] After paying 26*s*.8*d*. in wages to the crew of the transport ship, de Flete's servants were able to hand £74 14*s*. over to Chigwell as the gross sales receipts. A further £9 16*s*.8*d*. was credited to Chigwell in the king's Wardrobe account for two barrels of wine and 10 quarters of beans that were purveyed from de Flete's servants. By de Flete's reckoning, his goods, valued in London at £68 13*s*.4*d*., brought in a gross of £85 17*s*.4*d*., whence he calculated that the profit was £17 4*s*. in total, or 5*s*. on the pound—a profit of 25 per cent. The risk associated with shipping goods into a recent war zone undoubtedly helped the partners' profit margin.

De Flete further reckoned that at the rate of 5*s*. on the pound, the profit generated by his investment of £40 in the partnership was £10. As the two men agreed, profit was to be split down the middle, so Chigwell's share came to £5. According to de Flete, this amount could be deducted from the money his servants had turned over to Chigwell, leaving Chigwell in

---

[12]F. Maurice Powicke, *The Thirteenth Century, 1216–1307*, 2nd ed. (Oxford, 1991), pp. 710–12.

possession of £69 14*s.* of de Flete's money. Chigwell claimed at this point that he had "made satisfaction" to de Flete for half of the Wardrobe debt (£4 18*s.*4*d.*), exactly how is not explained, and accordingly that he had only £64 15*s.*8*d.* of de Flete's money at this stage of the enterprise. This disagreement was an omen of things to come.

Disposing of de Flete's merchandise in Scotland took a little over a month. The partnership was scheduled to run for an entire year, and Chigwell began to cast about for new business. He was not disappointed. Around the middle of June the Scottish magnate John Comyn requested that Chigwell visit him. Comyn, an erstwhile foe of Edward I, had recently been reconciled with the English king and regained possession of his private estates.[13] The Scottish magnate sent a retinue of four knights and four servants to meet Chigwell in Stirling, to escort him to his castle of Lochindarb in Badenoch, where he had merchandise that he thought might interest the London merchant. Comyn was probably an old hand at this sort of thing; he was careful to invite an Italian merchant, William Person, to view the merchandise at the same time, presumably to encourage a little healthy bidding on what he was about to show them. Person sent a partner, Cambinus Fulberti, to represent him before Comyn.

While Comyn did not have the riches of the Orient to show the two merchants, he did have merchandise that was sure to interest a Londoner and an Italian: wool, hides, and woolfells—45 sacks of wool, eight lasts of hides, and 1,200 woolfells, to be exact. He even had a couple of barrels of ointment to throw into the bargain.[14] Chigwell and Fulberti decided that they were

---

[13]*Calendar of Close Rolls, Edw. I*, 5: *1302–1307* (London, 1908), p. 130.

[14]This may represent a backlog from his estates built up while he was in opposition to Edward I, which could now be cleared because of his political

better off pooling their resources in order to acquire the material, and they formed a partnership on the spot, Chigwell and de Flete having one share in the partnership and Fulberti and Person, the other. As partners the two men reached agreement with Comyn to buy the merchandise for £220.

The merchandise was quickly packed up and shipped to St.-Omer in Artois. Shipping expenses amounted to £125, raising the total invested in the enterprise to £345. Displaying healthy suspicion, Chigwell and Fulberti both went with the goods to St.-Omer and worked together to dispose of them. They did this with some success, selling the wool, woolfells, and ointment for just over £267, four lasts of hides for £69, and the other four lasts of hides for £60 2*s.*2*d.* Total revenue in the transactions amounted to £396 3*s.*6.5*d.* Deducting incidental expenses, this yielded a total profit of £51 3*s.*6.5*d.*, or just under 25 per cent of the initial cost of the goods in Scotland. Profit had to be split between the "Lombards" and the Londoners, so the Chigwell–de Flete share amounted to £25 11*s.*9.25*d.* Split down the middle again, each man gained £12 15*s.*10.5*d.* from the deal.

While Chigwell was in St.-Omer, de Flete began to have suspicions about Chigwell's role in their partnership. The £40 that Chigwell had agreed to put into the partnership when it was formed, supposedly tied up in Picardy, never materialized, and de Flete began to feel that he had been duped. He began an "action" against Chigwell while the latter was disposing of the goods purchased from Comyn. According to Chigwell, this action forced him to sell the final four lasts of hides short, receiving almost £9 less for them than for the first four sold under more opportune circumstances. The two men now disagreed over how to apportion the shares of the profit from the St.-Omer venture.

---

reconciliation. If so, it raises interesting questions about the economic sanctions applicable in a medieval war zone.

Chigwell's tack was that de Flete only had £40 in the partnership and therefore did not deserve a full share of the profit made in Artois. He calculated—on grounds not fully explained—that de Flete's share of the profits pertaining to his investment of £40 was £7 6*s.*8*d.* The total capital in the venture was substantially higher than this figure, but, Chigwell maintained, de Flete was only in for the sum that he had invested in the partnership. Chigwell maintained further that as de Flete's partner he was entitled to half of this profit emanating from the investment of £40, or £3 13*s.*4*d.* To show his good faith while these complicated affairs were being sorted out, Chigwell handed over £63 3*s.* to the servants of de Flete. But he also entered a new claim against his partner, stating that the £40 he had invested in the partnership in the form of goods in Picardy had been totally lost by hazard, and that as his partner de Flete should shoulder half of the loss, or (in other words) compensate him in the amount of £20.

It is worth reflecting on what this method of accounting reveals about Chigwell's concept of how the partnership worked. Ostensibly, the agreement was that each party had a share of £40 invested in the joint concern. But there was no abstract sense of capital involved here. Each man's £40 consisted of tangible chattels. The trading in Scotland and St.-Omer was based wholly on de Flete's capital: it was his merchandise that was sold in Stirling and Berwick, and it was the revenue from this merchandise that was turned over into the wool, woolfells, and hides purchased from Comyn. Through all of this Chigwell's capital remained in Picardy, eventually to be lost by hazard, at least according to Chigwell. There is no abstract sense of "capital," of "shares" based on invested money. The shares are very tangible—Chigwell's goods and de Flete's goods. Even when the sum of capital invested in an enterprise such as the St.-Omer venture was large enough that the £40 of each partner should have been involved, they still conceived of the venture as involving only de Flete's money, because Chigwell's money was in his goods in Picardy. The capital in Scotland was de Flete's capital, based on the sale of de Flete's goods. Thus, when it came time to account for the profit of the venture, the accounting was for £40 of de Flete's money. Likewise, when it came time to apportion the loss for Chigwell's goods, each man lost £20. In effect, the partnership meant that each party swapped £20 worth of merchandise with the other. The difference between this and outright purchase was that each agreed to exert himself on the other's behalf to obtain the highest yield for these swapped goods. In short, capital only existed *in re*; it was not an abstract concept in the minds of these two prominent London merchants.

Chigwell claimed that his work in St.-Omer was interrupted by a legal process begun by his partner. What exactly was this *actio* pressed by de Flete, the one that led Chigwell to liquidate the remaining hides? The accounts are silent on this point, but we can reconstruct the process from analogous contemporary situations. De Flete had several options open to him, once his suspicions were aroused, all based on his legal right to coerce a formal accounting. The law dealt with an active commercial partner as though he were a bailiff and gave remedy to the sitting partner, just as it did to the lord seeking an account from his bailiff.[15]

Outside of the boroughs and other franchises an action of account was heard in the county court. As a citizen of London, though, de Flete had other options open to him. The simplest option he could have chosen was to lodge a plaint in the mayor's court of London.[16] A very similar case was heard

---

[15] T. F. T. Plucknett, *The Mediaeval Bailiff* (London, 1954), pp. 23, 30.

[16] *Calendar of Early Mayor's Court Rolls Preserved among the Archives of the Corporation of the City of London at the Guildhall*, A.D. *1298–1307*, ed. A. H. Thomas (Cambridge, 1924), p. xxii.

there in 1302.[17] A more formal process would have been to take out a writ to begin the action, in which event the case would have gone to the Hustings.[18] Given that the sum involved in the partnership was fairly substantial, we may guess that de Flete might have viewed this as the preferable route to take.

If he wished to take the case to the Hustings, de Flete would still have had several decisions to make. The choice of writ always had a tremendous impact on the outcome of a case. The common writ in an action of account was a standard *Justicies*. In matters of partnership the *Justicies* was issued in one of two forms, *Justicies de computo* or *Justicies inter mercatores*.[19] The former variant permitted the defendant to answer the charge by wager of law, a feature that most plaintiffs wished to avoid. The latter variant allowed the case to be heard according to the Law Merchant. This was a desirable procedure in the eyes of most merchants because it avoided the normal essoins permitted by the common law and thus allowed a quicker recovery of outstanding monies. A case heard according to the Law Merchant would be heard quickly, and it would be heard by fellow merchants.

Pleading in an action of account often began with the plaintiff offering a deed or other form of proof to substantiate his claim that a partnership did exist.[20] If we imagine de

---

[17]S. F. C. Milsom, "Account Stated in the Action of Debt," *Law Quarterly Review* 82 (1966): 537.

[18]Thomas, *Early Mayor's Court Rolls*, p. xxii. The *Liber albus* states that these cases belonged in the London sheriff's court, but this was a procedural innovation introduced in 1337 (ibid., p. 105n.) See *Munimenta Gildhallae Londoniensis: Liber albus, Liber custumarum, et Liber Horn*, ed. H. T. Riley, Rolls Series, 12, vol. 1 (London, 1859), pp. 216–19.

[19]Thomas, *Early Mayor's Court Rolls*, p. xxii.

[20]This account of procedure in a plea of account is based on Edmund Belshaim, "The Old Action of Account," *Harvard Law Review* 45 (1931–32): 493–99.

Flete opting for this procedure, we can picture him bringing the indenture of agreement between him and Chigwell to the court. The defendant was then asked to answer the charge. If he admitted the charge, he agreed to render an account before auditors. If he denied the charge—either on the basis that there was never an obligation to account or that a satisfactory account had already been made—issue was joined. If the court found for the defendant, the case was over. If, however, the court found for the plaintiff, a writ of *capias ad computandum* was issued. Barring any recalcitrance on the part of the defendant, the account would then be made, usually before three auditors appointed from clerks of the court. As a rule both parties, bearing tallies and other supporting documents, were present at the audit. A disagreement over the validity of evidence submitted would be tested by inquest jury. The end result of the account was that a sum total of outstanding liabilities would be declared and judgment issued accordingly. Few cases went beyond this point, but if the defendant was found owing and refused to pay, the plaintiff could now bring an action of debt against him. The action of account did no more than compel the defendant to account; it did not compel him to pay the amount due.[21]

In the case of Chigwell and de Flete much of this was academic. At some point in the proceedings the case was brought before the Barons of the Exchequer. This was an unusual though not a unique move. According to the Statute of Westminster II, c.11, a bailiff defending in an action of account had the right to appeal to the Exchequer.[22] There was a twist, however, in this particular instance. Chigwell did not neces-

---

[21] R. M. Jackson, *The History of Quasi-Contract in English Law* (Cambridge, 1936), p. 9.

[22] *The Statutes of the Realm* (London, 1810–28; repr. 1963), 1: 80.

sarily need to rely on his legal standing as a bailiff, to have his private business affairs brought before the Barons. As mentioned above, Chigwell was associated with the household of the treasurer, Walter Langton. One of the legitimate purposes of the court of the Exchequer was to adjudicate matters touching the financial interests of royal officials. Chigwell stretched the jurisdiction of this tribunal to include the household of a royal official. A precedent for this had been set in 1301, when Chigwell brought a certain Robert, son of Roger, into the Exchequer on a plea of debt.[23] Robert's attorney argued that the case did not belong there because Chigwell was not an officer of the Exchequer. Langton lent his support to Chigwell's claim, though, and the Barons found that it was appropriate for Chigwell to haul his debtor before them. The Barons also found in favor of Chigwell, and they awarded him not only the initial debt of 120 marks but also a further 100*s*. in damages. Obviously, Chigwell could hope for a favorable hearing in a court intimately connected with his own private patron.

Chigwell did not contest the fact that he was obliged to render an account to de Flete; his hope was that the Barons would agree with his figures. Two auditors sat in judgment on the account, and the complicated affairs of the partnership were rehearsed before them. Chigwell probably brought an account with him. The document finally deposited in the Exchequer as a result of this hearing consists of three parts. One is a membrane recording the information detailed above. The other two were probably drawn up in the Exchequer. One is a rough copy of the accounting there, the other a fair copy that essentially duplicates the rough copy. It is entirely possible that the initial account was derived from the *actio* that de Flete initiated against Chigwell. Both parties were probably present when the

[23]Jenkinson and Formoy, *Select Cases, Pleas*, pp. 211–12.

Exchequer auditors drew up their version of the financial liabilities between them; certainly de Flete's side of the matter comes through more forcefully than in the earlier account.

The first item in the Exchequer account is a recognizance by Chigwell for the cash he received from de Flete's servants in Scotland, the receipts from the sale of de Flete's merchandise. Then we get William's side of the St.-Omer venture: he claims that Chigwell invested £50 of his (de Flete's) money in the enterprise and that this translated into a profit of £14 10*s.*, which Chigwell now owed to him. According to de Flete, Chigwell also used the money he received in Scotland to dabble in other business opportunities there, which yielded a total of £7 2*s.*6*d.* in profit. De Flete claimed that these profits belonged to him because it was his money that was invested. For good measure, de Flete also asserted that he gave Chigwell 46*s.*3*d.* in cash and nine handmills worth 9*s.*, for which he expected reimbursement. He concluded by acknowledging that de Flete had already given £56 8*s.* to his servant in St.-Omer and a further £6 15*s.* to him personally in London. Allowing 5*s.*2*d.* for unexplained expenses, de Flete reckoned that Chigwell still owed him £35 4*s.*7*d.*

Chigwell wished to dispute de Flete's calculations, and much of the remainder of the account consists of claims and counter-claims as to what should and should not be reckoned into the account. First Chigwell sought a deduction of 72*s.*10*d.* as half the profit of the wine, peas, and salt sold in Scotland. De Flete countered by saying that these were his own private goods, sold by his servant, and that Chigwell had no claim to any profit. This runs contrary to the spirit of the partnership and to de Flete's own word as spelled out in the first account. De Flete apparently decided to adopt a completely new approach to the partnership in front of the Exchequer Barons. His reasons for doing so will soon become apparent.

Chigwell's second claim for a deduction from the sum owed de Flete was for the goods that King Edward had purveyed in Scotland. De Flete countered that the debt for these goods had been enrolled in the Wardrobe under Chigwell's name and thus should not be deducted from what he owed de Flete, a legitimate if not entirely charitable response. Chigwell proceeded to seek deductions for his share of the profit from the St.-Omer venture and to contest de Flete's claim that he did some extra trading on the side using de Flete's money. De Flete, in turn, contested both of these claims. Regarding the additional cash and the pepper mills, Chigwell contended that he had received them before the partnership officially began and therefore did not need to include them in the account. The law would have backed him up on this point, and de Flete could not hope for much gain from this quarter. The statement further corroborates that the two men had had dealings with each other before the partnership began.

Up to this point the differences between the two men were undoubtedly ones that trusting partners could have resolved in private. The problem was that de Flete and Chigwell were no longer trusting partners, and the cause of their mistrust came fully into view in the last stage of the accounting. Chigwell entered a claim for a deduction of £20 from the amount he owed de Flete. He based this claim on the misfortune that overtook his goods in Picardy, the goods that made up his share of the capital invested in the partnership. Chigwell stated that his £40 consisted of 10 barrels of woad. His servant, Simon de Henleie, had the woad carried to St.-Valery-en-Caux (Dép. Seine Maritime) some time in the month of May, shortly after the partnership was formalized. This woad Chigwell "believes to have perished insofar as he has not heard tell anything further about Simon or his goods." Chigwell maintained that de Flete should share this loss, hence the claim for a deduction of

£20 from the amount owing. One can see that de Flete might have found this unpalatable, but partners are partners in loss as well as in gain.

De Flete had another story, however. He told the auditors that the goods which Chigwell pretended represented his share of the partnership "never came before the gaze of any man," that is, Chigwell did not have any goods in Picardy and thus had entered the partnership under false pretenses. The record continues:

> On account of this John [Chigwell] traded with William[de Flete]'s goods and invested nothing of his own and now seeks allowance for half of the £40 that he ought to have put into the partnership. He invested nothing and lies when he says he lost his goods.

Even filtered through an Exchequer scribe and translated into Latin, the hostility de Flete now felt toward Chigwell comes across. De Flete plainly felt that Chigwell had pulled a fast one on him and that a pound of flesh was now due.

The auditors asked Chigwell if he had any evidence to substantiate his claim about the woad, specifically, corroborating letters from the bailiffs of St.-Valery-en-Caux that his servant had put the goods into the sea there. Chigwell replied that he did not, but said that he was willing to prove his statement by the verdict of lawful merchants. In other words, he was ready to wage his law on this point, as he was allowed to do under the Law Merchant. In the end, a wager of law was not necessary. Chigwell and de Flete came to an agreement: Chigwell would give de Flete £20 to settle the matter, half to be paid on the following 24 June and the other half on 8 September. One presumes that Chigwell did honor his word and that the two men thenceforth went their separate ways.

What do we learn from this vignette of merchant life in the early fourteenth century? First of all, we must be careful not to exaggerate its peculiarity. The evidence we have for this partnership is exceptionally rich because of the Exchequer's involvement as arbitrator, but the partnership itself was not exceptional. We see, for example, how easily Chigwell formed a second partnership with Cambinus Fulberti, to dispose of Comyn's materials. We might also note that the two London merchants had been part of a larger association of merchants several years earlier.[24] Any lingering doubts on this score can be satisfied by perusing the London debt recognizance rolls, where joint debts are almost a daily occurrence.[25] Chigwell himself occurs twice in these rolls in this guise, in 1293 and again in 1300.[26] During the reign of Edward I partnership was already a common business arrangement.

In retrospect, we can also see where some of the shortcomings of partnership lay during this period. The concept of capital was still limited to tangible goods and would remain so in England for some time to come. This undoubtedly put a strait-jacket on capital investment in the period. Furthermore, the common law was ill-equipped to deal with issues of commerce such as partnership. Remedies were available, but they were cumbersome grafts onto what remained a system of law rooted in landed property. The Law Merchant was a more fruitful source of law in this respect. This is not the place to explore the elusive workings of the Law Merchant, except to say that it must not have fully satisfied the needs of the merchant community. When the Equity jurisdiction of the Chancery began to accept cases of fractured partnerships later in the fourteenth century, litigants were quick to take advantage of

---

[24]Sharpe, *Letter Book B*, pp. 121–23.

[25]CLRO, Recognizance Rolls. Postan makes this same point in "Partnership," pp. 83–84.

[26]CLRO, Recognizance Rolls, Roll 3, m. 4; Roll 5, m. 4.

the new opportunity.[27] As a matter of course in these proceedings, plaintiffs lamented their inability to find justice from any source other than the Chancellor.[28] This was particularly true of parole contracts—which de Flete wisely chose to eschew in his relationship with Chigwell—but extended to written contracts in numerous situations as well. The remedies available at common law did not hamper commercial development in England as much as writers of a previous generation have contended, but it is equally true that they were not propitious for such development, either.[29]

Finally, the affairs of de Flete and Chigwell remind us of the entrepreneurial spirit that characterized the medieval merchant. De Flete was ostensibly a vintner and Chigwell, a fishmonger, but in their partnership we see two men looking for profit wherever it could be found.[30] In the few months described in the surviving accounts we see them dealing in beans, salt, wine, wool, woolfells, hides, woad (at least in Chigwell's version), even handmills. We also get a flavor of the international milieu of these entrepreneurs: within these same few months Chigwell's world extended from London to Scotland, Picardy and Artois, and included a co-operative venture with a "Lombard." One would like to know what Chigwell thought of

---

[27]W. T. Barbour, *The History of Contract in Early English Equity* (Oxford, 1914), pp. 128–30 and passim.

[28]Barbour, *Contract*, p. 56, n. 1.

[29]Postan attempted to exculpate the common law on the grounds that the law of trusts obviated the need for a more expeditious law of partnership: an active partner could be said to hold the goods of a sleeping partner in trust rather than in the Roman law terms of *commenda* or *societas*. Remedy for a broken partnership would thus be a branch of the law of trusts rather than standard commercial law. The Chancellors sitting in Equity in the fifteenth century, hearing time and again about the difficulties of litigating fractured partnerships at common law, would certainly not have subscribed to this point of view.

[30]Williams, *Medieval London*, p. 122; Sharpe, *Letter-Book B*, p. 179.

the places he went, what foods he ate, what languages he spoke. We must settle for what the Exchequer officials decided to record and preserve; for this, however, we can be grateful.

Appendix

THE ACCOUNTS OF A TRADING PARTNERSHIP, 1304–05 (PRO E.101/506/1)

The document consists of three membranes rolled up together, in an excellent state of preservation. I have not transcribed the rough copy of the accounting, which duplicates the information on the fair copy. The original order of the membranes transcribed here can no longer be determined with certainty; I assume that the description of Chigwell's activities was compiled before the accounting and final agreement was reached. Uncertain readings are indicated by pointed brackets, editorial comments or additions are italicized within square brackets. Monetary sums printed as underlined correspond to the underlining done by the auditors as they examined the document. Marginal notes indicating Chigwell's agreement or disagreement with the accounting have been excluded because their alignment with the text would be misleading and confusing, and because they duplicate information that is readily grasped by the paragraph and entry structure. Common abbreviations have been expanded, except for those dealing with units of currency, place names, or personal names other than those of the two principals.

Anno regni regis Edwardi filii Regis Henrici .xxxii°. primo die Maii convenit inter Johannem de Chigewell' ex parte una et Willelmum de Flete ex altera quod simul mercandizarent per unum annum proximum sequentem de quadam summa peccunie quam ad commune proficuum posuerunt prout in quadam indentura inter eos confecta plenius continetur et inferius annotatur videlicet per manus valletorum suorum etc.

[Chigewell] In primis Johannes de Chigwell posuit ad eandem societatem .xl. li'. sterlingorum per manus Simonis de Henle valleti sui pro communi proficuo In Pikardia. Et alia catalla ad valentium xv. li'. etc. extra societatem predictam etc.

[Flete] Item Willelmus de Flete posuit ad eandem societatem ad commune proficuum catalla subscripta per manus Thome de Barewe et

Johannis Gourder valletorum suorum videlicet — x. dolia vini precium .xxiii. li'. vi.s. viii.d. precium dolii xlvi.s. viii.d. Item viii.^{to} dolia vini precium .xxi. li'. vi.s. viii.d. precium dolii Liii.s. iiii.d. Item Cxx quarterie fabarum precium .xv. li'. precium quarterie ii.s. vid. Item .xx^{ti} pise salis precium .ix. li'. precium pise ix.s.

> Summa catallarum ipsius Willelmi .Lxviii. li'. xiii.s. iiii.d. — unde xl. li'. sunt participantes ad commune proficuum etc. prout patet in indentura societatis predicte etc.

Exitus dicti catalli predicti Willelmi factus [*fuit*] apud Strivelyn et Berewicum per manus dictorum garcionum suorum unde denarii subscripti pervenerunt ad manus Johannis de Chigwell videlicet — per manus Thome de Barewe idem Johannes de Chigwell recepit .Lvi. li'. viii.s. — Item per manus J. Gourder .vi. li'. xv.s. — Item de sale vendita — xi. li'. xi.s. — Item iidem garciones solverunt marinariis .xxvis. viii.d. quos dictus Willelmus ab eo mutuavit Lond' — Item dominus Rex caperi fecit .x. quarterias fabarum et ii. dolia vini in manibus dictorum valletorum suorum precium .ix. li'. xvi.s. viii.d. quas dicti garciones scriberi fecerunt super Johannem de Chigwell in Garderoba Regis.

> Summa exitus bonorum dicti Willelmi ascendit in universo ad .iiii^{xx}.v. li'. xvii.s. iiii.d. — unde Lucrum ascendit ad .xvii. li'. iiii.s. videlicet de qualibet libra .v.s — Et sic est lucrum participium de xl. li'. in communi proficuo positis .x. li'. — unde pars dicti Johannis de Chigwell C.s. secundum conventionem indenturatum qui C.s. debent subtrahi de totali exitu. Debent etiam subtrahi xxvi.s. viii.d. pro <custibus?> marinariorum ut supra. Debent etiam subtrahi .ix. li'. xvi.s. viii.d. de prisa domini Regis superius notata. etc. Et sic remanent in manibus dicti Johannis de catallis dicti Willelmi .Lxix. li'. xiiii.s. unde idem Johannes calumpnit .iiii. li'. xviii.s. iiii.d. de medietate prise dicti domini Regis desicut

dicto Willelmo plenarie est satisfactum etc. Et sic remanent in manibus dicti Johannis de claro — Lxiiii.li'. xv.s. viiid.

Postea per xv.^{cim} dies ante festum Nativitatis beati Johannis baptiste anno predicto quadam mercandiza intimata dicto Johanne de Chigwell et cuidam W. persone lumbard' de domino J. Comyn de Badenough' idem Johannes de Chigwell cum garcione suo et iiii^{or} equitibus cum .iiii. garcionibus suis de familia dicti domini J. Comyn perexierunt de Strivelyn usque Lougherdoron castellum dicti domini .J. Comyn in Badenough' prope mourez in Scocia ad videndum mercandizam predictam si eis placeret. Et habito visu predicte mercandise Eadem mercandisa comparata fuit pro CC.xx. li'. sterlingorum. Quorum custagium ascenduit in universo de Scocia usque sanctum Omerum prout inter dictum Johannem de Chigwell pro se et socio suo Willelmo de Flete ex una parte et Kambinum Fulberti socium predicti Willelmi personis ex altera parte fuerat computatum. — Cxxv. li'. Et fuit mercandisa .xlv. sacce lane. viii. lasti coreorum . MCC pelles lanuti et duobus[*sic*] dolia sepi. etc.

Summa tam empcionis quam expense usque sanctum Omerum de Scocia .CCC.xlv. li'. sterlingorum prout computabatur inter dictos Kambinum et Johanem etc. apud sanctum Omerum. etc.

De qua mercandisa empta de predicto domino J. Comyn exitus factus fuit apud sanctum Omerum in presencia dictorum Cambini et Johannis videlicet de lana pellibus et cepi ad .CC.lxvii. li'. xvi.d. ob'. et de .iiii. lastis coreorum lxix.li'. sterlingorum. Et de iiii. lastis coreorum Lxix. li'. sterlingorum — Et de iiii. lastis coreorum residuis Lx. li'. ii.s. ii.d. Et non plus vendebant ultimos iiii^{or} lastos coreorum pro accione facto super dictum Johannem per Willelmum de Flete socium suum prout declarabat etc.

Summa tocius exitus .CCC.iiii^{xx}. xvi. li'. iii.s. vi.d. ob'. — Inde debent subtrahi — CC.xx. li'. de prima empcione — Et Cxxv. li'. pro expensis de Scocia usque sanctum Omerum etc. Et sic remanent .Li. li'. iii.s. vi.d. ob'. de Lucro — unde Cambinus predictus recepit medietatem videlicet xxv. li'. xi.s. ix.d. q[a]. Et alia medietas remanet cum predicto Johanne de Chigwell pro se et Willelmo de Flete sociis contra predictum Cambinum. unde medietas medietatis predicti lucri xii. li'. xv.s. x.d. ob'. Et Inde petit Johannes de Chigwell medietatem lucri pertinentem ad xl. li'. positas in societate predicta per dictum Willelmum secundum formam conventionis inter eos habite et indenturate. quod lucrum ascendit ad vii. li'. vi.s. viii.d. videlicet pertinens ad .xl. li'. Inde medietas .Lxxiii.s. iiii.d. quos dictus Johannes calumpnit. — Et idem Johannes calumpnit .xliii.s. positos in expensis pro predicto Willelmo sicut ostendere poterit.

Item Idem Johannes de Chigwell liberavit Thome et Johanni valletis predicti Willelmi de Flete socii sui .Lxiii. li'. .iii.s.

Idem Johannes de Chigwell sibi allocat .xx. li'. de .xl. li'. in societate predicta per ipsum positis. Et perditis a casu. etc.

M. 2

Compotus Johannis de Chiggewell' socii et Receptoris Willelmi de Flete barber a primo die maii anno regni Regis Edwardi xxxii. usque ad consimilem diem anno revoluto.

In primis dictus Johannes onerat se de .Lvi. li. viii.s. receptis de eodem Willelmo per manus Thome de Barowe apud Stryvelin. Et de vi. li'. xv.s. receptis de eodem Willelmo per manus Johannis valleti sui apud Berwicum. Et de .xi. li'. xi.s. receptis de eodem Willelmo per manus eiusdem Johannis ibidem — Summa Receptarum .lxxiiii. li'. xiiii.s. de recognicione ipsius Johannis.
Item idem Willelmus onerat ipsum Johannem de .xiiii. li'. x.s. de medietate .xxix. li. proveniencium de quodam Lucro quorumdam

Lanarum et coreorum emptorum de Johanne Comyn in Scocia pro .L. li'. de denariis superius oneratis et postea venditorum apud sanctum Omerum.
Item idem Willelmus onerat dictum Johannem de Lviii.s. iiii.d. de lucro ipsum contingente de xxxv. Dacris coreorum emptorum de W. de Bedewynd de denariis superius oneratis. Et de iiii. li'. iiii.s. ii.d. de Lucro ipsum contingente de uno lasto coreorum uno sacco et quarta parte unius sacci Lane et MCC pellibus lanutis emptis de residuo denariorum superius oneratorum.
Item idem Willelmus onerat ipsum Johannem de .xxiii.s. eidem liberatis apud London'. Et de xiiii.s. iii.d. similiter eidem Johanni liberatis . Et de ix. molis manualibus penes ipsum Johannem remanentibus precium ix.s. — Summa .xxiii. li'. xviii.s. ix. d. — Summa totalis .iiii^{xx}.xviii. li'. xii.s. ix.d. — De quibus idem Johannes liberavit predicto Willelmo per manus Thome de Barwe valleti ipsius Willellmi apud sanctum Omerum. Lvi. li'. viii.s. Et eidem Willelmo .vi. li'. xv.s. per manus suas proprias. Et pro expensis ipsius Willelmi et valleti sui — v.s. ii.d. — Summa. Lxiii. li'. viii. s. ii.d. Et remanent — xxxv. li'. iiii.s. vii.d — De quibus predictus Johannes petit sibi allocari — lxxii.s. x.d. de medietate lucri provenientis de vinis fabis et sale emptis London' et missis apud Strivelyn in Scocia et ibidem venditis per vadletum dicti Willelmi.
Item petit sibi allocari .Lxxiii.s. iiii.d. de medietate lucri provenientis de Lanis et coreis emptis in Scocia et venditis apud Sanctum omerum.
Item petit allocacionem de ix. li'. xvi.s. viiid. de precio .ii. doliorum vini. x. quarteriarum fabarum ipsorum Johannis et Willelmi captorum ad opus Regis in Scocia unde satisfactum est eidem Willelmo.
Item petit exonerari de Lviii.s. iiii.d. et de iiii. li. iiii.s. ii.d. de quibus oneratur supra de Lucro proveniente de coreis lanis et pellibus lanutis eo quod eidem corei lane et pelles non fuerunt empti de denariis ipsius Willelmi sed tantummodo de denariis ipsius Johannis qui fuerunt extra societate.
Item idem Johannes dicit quod non debet in compoto isto onerari de predictis .xxiii.s. nec de xiiii.s. iii.d. nec de ix. s. de precio molarum de quibus oneratur supra quia denarios illos recepit diu ante tempus societatis predicte.
Item petit allocacionem de — xx.li'. de quadam summa — xl. li'. quam

posuit in societate predicta et quam Simon de Henleie valectus euisdem Johannis habuit apud Amyas in .x. doliis Wysde implicatis versus London' et cariatis apud sanctum Waleric' infra mensem post primum diem Maii. anno xxxii. que credit perichtari eo quod numquam inposterum audivit rumores de predicto Simone nec de bonis suis.
Et predictus Willelmus dicit quod de predictis .Lxxii.s. x.d. quos clamat de medietate Lucri provenientis de bonis misis apud Strivelyn non debet sibi allocacio fieri quia dicit quod ipsemet Willelmus emerat bona predicta in London' et ea misit usque Scocia per valectum suum proprium sub periculo ipsius Willelmi qui quidem valectus ea vendidit ibidem et tota catalla et Lucrum quod inde proveniebat liberavit predicto Johanni.
Item idem Willelmus dicit quod de Lxxiii.s. iiii.d. quos idem Johannes dicit provenire de medietate lucri de Lanis et coreis emptis in Scocia et venditis apud sanctum Omerum etc. non debet sibi allocacio fieri quia dicit quod nec de catallis nec de lucro aliquid recepit set si huiusmodi empcio vel vendiciones facte fuerint totum quod inde proveniebat remansit in manibus ipsius Johannis.
Item quo ad predictas .ix. li'. xvi.s. viii.d. de precio .ii. doliorum vini et .x. quarteriarum fabarum captorum ad opus Regis dicit quod nulla sibi fieri debet allocacio quia dicit quod dicta captio irrotulata est in Garderoba Regis sub nomine ipsius Johannis et non sub nomine ipsius Willelmi et tamen non oneratur inde superius nec dictus Willelmus aliquid inde clamat.
(*dorse*) Et quo ad .Lviii.s. iiii.d. et iiii. li'. iiii.s. ii.d. provenientes de Lucro de coreis lanis et pellibus lanutis quos idem Johannes dicit se emisse de denariis suis propriis extra predictam societatem existentibus non debet sibi allocacio fieri quia dicit quod eedem summe continentur in summa receptarum superius nominate de — Lxxiiii.li'. xiiii.s.
Item quo ad .xxiii.s. et xiiii.s. et ix.s. de precio molarum de quibus dictus Johannes dicit se non debere onerari quia eos recepit ante tempus quo socii devenerunt petit iudicium ex quo dictam receptam cognovit si debeat inde exonerari.
Et quo ad hoc quod dictus Johannes petit allocacionem de .xx. li'. de predictis xl. libratis quas dicit se perdidisse per servientem suum proprium dicit quod nullam allocacionem inde habere debet quia dicit

quod quando ipsi inierunt societatem statutum fuit inter eos quod uterque ipsorum apponeret .xl. li'. ad mercandizandum unde ipsemet Willelmus posuit .xl. li'. et dictus Johnannes verbo tenus apposuit alias xl. li'. de bonis suis que dixit se habuisse in partibus transmarinis que numquam devenerunt in visu alicuius hominis et ex quo dictus Johannes mercandizavit de propriis bonis dicti Willelmi et nichil apposuit de suo et modo petit allocacionem de medietate xl. li'. quas apposuisse debuit in societate ubi nichil apposuit sed sub dissimulacione dicit se ea perdidisse. Et petit iudicium et similiter petit ut dictus Johannes sibi respondeat de toto Lucro catalli sui de quo dictus Johannes mercandizavit — Requisitus predictus Johannes per auditores si habeat aliquas litteras testimoniales de Ballivis sancti Vallerici quod bona sua per dictum Simonem servientem suum deposita fuerunt ibidem in mari qui[*sic*] dicit quod non set dicit quod paratus est hoc verificare per legales mercatores

Concordati sunt sic. Johannes dabit Willelmo .xx.li'. medietas ad festum Nativitatis sancti Johannis et alia medietas ad festum Nativitatis beate Marie.

Magister J. de Bukluet et Magister Henricus de Bleanlick

WOMEN AND MEN

IN THE BREWERS' GILD OF LONDON, CA. 1420

Judith M. Bennett[1]

In the countryside of medieval England, brewing was largely a female trade. Women worked in brewing as both producers and sellers of ale, and in many villages they essentially controlled the market. Female control reflected the informal nature of the rural trade in ale; in most villages, ale was supplied by local wives who sold to their neighbors excess from brewings intended primarily for domestic use. This trade was not entirely informal (especially since commercial ale sales were supervised by manorial officers), but most commerce in ale was haphazard and casual. The rural ale market was small and localized; alewives were numerous, and brewing was a by-trade, not a profitable profession. As a result, brewing suited the multiple responsibilities of rural wives, and in many early fourteenth-century villages—from Kent to Cambridgeshire to Lincolnshire to Yorkshire—women dominated the trade in ale.[2]

---

[1]I could not have undertaken this study without the extensive advice about London history and London sources generously offered to me by Ian Archer, Caroline Barron, Vanessa Harding, Derek Keene, and Steve Rappaport. I also thank Maryanne Kowaleski and Cynthia Herrup for their critical readings of early drafts of this essay, and Tim Wales for checking some archival citations. In the form in which it appears here, this essay was completed in September 1992.

[2]Judith M. Bennett, "The Village Ale-Wife: Women and Brewing in Fourteenth-Century England," in Barbara A. Hanawalt, ed., *Women and Work in Preindustrial*

As the ale market changed, women's involvement in brewing also changed. In the countryside, women's control of brewing began to slip at the very end of the fourteenth century, but the trend was a slow and uneven one. Even in the seventeenth century, some villages—such as Ottery St. Mary in Devon—still boasted female brewers. In towns, change was quicker and more dramatic. Even before the mid-fourteenth-century Black Death, the organized and profitable urban trade in ale attracted male brewers, some of whom were active enough in the trade to claim brewing as their main occupation. In London between 1309 and 1312, 34 men who entered the freedom of the City stated that they were brewers. In York men also entered the freedom as brewers, albeit in smaller numbers: one male brewer before 1349, and seven between 1350 and 1399. In Oxford 26 men in the poll tax of 1380–81 identified their main occupation as brewing. Women were still active in the brewing trades of fourteenth-century towns (e.g., four women in the Oxford poll tax identified themselves as brewers), but they worked in a more complex market than did rural brewers and they worked alongside men. Moreover, women's involvement steadily waned; by the seventeenth century urban brewing was almost exclusively a male trade.[3]

Europe (Bloomington, 1986), pp. 20–36. I discuss patterns of brewing in the medieval countryside more fully in my forthcoming book on *Ale, Beer and Brewsters in England: Women's Work in a Changing World, 1300–1600.*

[3]For Ottery St. Mary see Univ. of London, Fuller MS. 34/1. For entries to the freedom of London 1309–12 see R. R. Sharpe, ed., *Calendar of Letter-Books of the City of London* (*CLB*), vol. D (London, 1902), pp. 35–179; I cite the *CLB*, and other calendared sources for London, *unless* additional pertinent information is found in the original, in which cases I refer readers to both the appropriate calendar and the original. For entries to the freedom of York see Francis Collins, ed., *Register of the Freemen of the City of York, from the City Records . . . 1272–1759*, Surtees Society, 2 vols., vols. 96, 102 (1897, 1900). For the Oxford poll tax see J. E. Thorold Rogers, ed., *Oxford City Documents 1268–1665*, Oxford Historical Society, vol. 18 (1891): 3–45.

In the later Middle Ages, however, male dominance of the urban brewing trade was still in the future, and women and men together shared the profits to be made in towns from producing and marketing ale and (by the fifteenth century in some places) beer.[4] Their market was closely regulated, for mayors and city councilors were anxious to ensure that urban populations had ready access to affordable, good-quality ale, an essential foodstuff in the medieval diet. Their market was also quite profitable, for the density of medieval towns ensured a large market within a small space. In this regulated and profitable trade, how did women and men work together? And what determined the divisions by sex that emerged in their trade? These questions are particularly pertinent to the brewing trade of late medieval towns, for the trade itself was in transition, perched betwixt the contemporary reality of female dominance of brewing in the countryside and the future prospect of male dominance of brewing in early modern towns (and eventually villages, as well). As women and men sorted out their respective places in the brewing trades of such late medieval towns as London, York, and Oxford, they were both accommodating to change in their own time and determining how change might proceed in the future.

---

[4]The first mention I have found of beer (made with hops, as opposed to the more traditional unhopped ale) in London is 1372, but beer was not an important commercial product in the City until the mid-fifteenth century. Although a few members of the Brewers' gild ca. 1420 were beerbrewers (e.g., William Claisson and his wife, Isabella), most brewed ale. Hence, I have throughout this paper referred to ale alone as the primary product of brewers at this time. For the 1372 mention see A. H. Thomas, ed., *Calendar of Plea and Memoranda Rolls* (*CPMR*), 2: *A.D. 1364–1381* (Cambridge, 1929), p. 147. In addition to enjoying a large cadre of potential customers located within a small space, urban brewers also benefited from the decline of domestic brewing in towns and cities. Due to space limitations and city ordinances about the physical condition of brewhouses (see an example for London in 1212, discussed below), urban dwellers were much more likely than rural dwellers to rely exclusively upon purchased ale.

In this essay I examine how women and men worked together in the brewing industry of the emerging metropolis of London, a city three to five times as large as any other English town in the later Middle Ages.[5] London provides not only the starkest contrast to the circumstances of rural brewers but also unusually detailed information about its brewers. In February 1418, William Porlond was appointed clerk of the Brewers' gild of London, and he began immediately to record information about the gild in a special book that he kept from his initial appointment until his death in 1438/39. In this book he recorded not only miscellaneous petitions, arguments, and accounts but also information about the personnel of the gild: he made careful lists of those who paid the annual dues or quarterage; he noted those who attended the yearly breakfasts and dinners of the gild; he recorded all those who wore the gild liveries of either hood or gown; and he copied out the accounts of the gild's various officers (accounts that included lists of not only new members but also persons newly admitted to the freedom). As if particularly eager to fill his new post well, Porlond kept especially careful records in the early years of his tenure. For the first seven years of his book (1418–25), we have complete lists of members, and for 1420/21 in particular we know not only who was in the gild but also who attended the gild breakfast, who wore what liveries, who feasted at the gild

[5]Population estimates for late medieval cities are notoriously difficult, but London had perhaps as many as 80,000 inhabitants ca. 1300 and 40,000 ca. 1380. These figures were proposed in lectures given by Derek Keene and Caroline Barron at the Univ. of London (spring 1990), but they are only rough estimates. Keene has also suggested that for London ca. 1300 estimates as high as 100,000 residents or as low as 50,000 residents are both plausible; see his "A New Study of London before the Great Fire," *Urban History Yearbook* (1984): 11–21, esp. p. 20. In ca. 1311 the population of Norwich (the second largest city in the realm) was perhaps as high as 17,000. See Elizabeth Rutledge, "Immigration and Population Growth in Early Fourteenth-Century Norwich: Evidence from the Tithing Roll," *Urban History Yearbook* (1988): 15–30.

dinner, who joined the gild as new members, and who acquired the freedom of the City via the gild. Porlond's careful records during the early years of his clerkship are especially useful because two additional sets of information about brewers during this time were generated by a bitter dispute in 1419–20 between brewers and the mayor (Richard Whittington): a census-like list of brewers compiled by the City (found in Letter Book I), and a special collection among brewers to raise funds for their fight against the City (carefully recorded as a *taxacio voluntaria* in Porlond's book).[6] For early fifteenth-century London, then, we have an exceptionally early and exceptionally full "snapshot" of a brewers' gild—a gild of both men and women—in day-to-day operation.

By the time William Porlond began to keep the Brewers' records in 1418, commercial brewing in London was already a highly developed and organized trade. Many London brewers managed quite substantial physical plants, far removed in terms of equipment, size, and expense from the household operations of most rural alewives. Even in the early thirteenth century, brewhouses in London began to take on industrial characteristics that distinguished them from ordinary dwellings; after the fire of 1212 the City ordered bakers and brewers, in the interest of both sanitation and fire prevention, to have their premises whitewashed and plastered. Two centuries later brewhouses

[6]Guildhall Library (GL), MS. 5440. On fol. 1 Porlond noted that he took up his position in Feb. 1418. In the masters' accounts for 1438/39 a pension for Porlond's widow is noted, as well as the fees of a new clerk for three-quarters of the year (see fol. 324). In the Appendix I have described these various sources in greater detail and have therefore not repeated these citations in the notes. After the accounts for 1424/25 Porlond's records suffer a gap of five years, resuming only in 1429/30. The analyses presented here therefore focus solely on the early years covered by Porlond's records. As I plan to undertake a full study of all the years covered by Porlond's books, this investigation should be considered a preliminary report of work in progress.

were often large, complex, and well-equipped establishments. In 1407 the brewhouse of Stephen Hamme included not only a large number of movable items (vats, tubs, barrels, and the like) but also built-in equipment which could not be moved from the tenement (including leaden tubs, leaden taps, mashtons, quernes, and millstones). In addition, Hamme, like most other London brewers, still retailed ale in his brewhouse, and his equipment included tables and benches to accommodate his drinking clientele. Probably few brewhouses in early fifteenth-century London were purpose-built, but establishments like those of Stephen Hamme had been substantially modified for the production and sale of ale. They could also be quite expensive to equip and maintain. No valuation is appended to our description of Hamme's brewhouse in 1407, but in 1486 a brewhouse committed to William Robinson contained equipment worth more than £22.[7]

Nevertheless, most brewers were not very rich, at least not by the standards of early fifteenth-century London. In 1412 a list of Londoners holding freehold or leasehold property was compiled for tax purposes, naming some 1,200 property-holders in the City. Brewers appeared rarely in this list, and only for small properties. Only 18 brewers (of the 187 households in the quarterage list of the Brewers' gild in 1419/20) appeared in this valuation, and most held little property. Property values for brewers ranged from as low as 6*s.*8*d.* to as high as £19 10*s.*, but all brewers were assessed far below the £25 considered "sufficient and substantial" but not "outstandingly large" by con-

---

[7]For the order of 1212 see H. T. Riley, ed., *Munimenta Gildhallae Londoniensis*, vol. 2, pt. 1: *Liber custumarum*, Rolls Ser., no. 12 (London, 1860), pp. 86–87. For Stephen Hamme's brewhouse see Helena M. Chew and William Kellaway, eds., *The London Assize of Nuisance, 1301–1431: A Calendar*, London Record Society, vol. 10 (1973), item 646. For William Robinson's brewhouse see *CLB* L, p. 232, and Corporation of London Record Office (CLRO), Letter Book L, fols. 217v–218.

temporary standards. Even allowing as much leeway as possible for deaths, departures, and other slippages of personnel between 1412 and 1419, the data suggest that few brewers—even among those successful enough to seek gild membership—held substantial property in the City.[8]

Wealth aside, brewers also lacked social cachet. The brewing trade had long been associated with disreputable and disorderly persons; in the late thirteenth century, for example, sumptuary legislation grouped brewers (in this case, noted as female brewers only) with nurses, servants, and women of ill fame. Over time, this association of brewers with misconduct shifted away from brewers and onto retailers of ale; by 1382, City orders about the sale of ale singled out hucksters as responsible for enticing whores, thieves, priests, and apprentices into drunkenness and evil-doing. Nevertheless, brewing per se remained a suspect trade, even in the fifteenth century. Although hucksters were increasingly blamed for drunkenness and disorder, brewers remained culpable, in the public eye, of serious trade violations. Public suspicion of brewers seems to have been well grounded, for the City records are full of complaints about them; brewers refused to sell at the prices set by

---

[8]J. C. L. Stahlschmidt, ed., "Lay Subsidy, temp. Henry IV," *Archaeological Journal* 44 (1887): 56–82 (a transcript of Public Record Office [PRO] E179/144/20). I am grateful to Vanessa Harding for bringing this source to my attention. In order to assess the social status of brewers in London from this listing, I searched by name in the subsidy list for each person listed on the quarterage payments for 1419/20 (and have excluded from my count of 18 brewers a few persons not in the gild in 1419/20 who were noted in the 1412 listing as brewers). The comments about the relative value of a £25 assessment are taken from Caroline M. Barron, "Richard Whittington: The Man behind the Myth," in *Studies in London History Presented to Philip Edmund Jones*, ed. A. E. J. Hollaender and William Kellaway (London, 1969), p. 227. Brewers were also relatively poor (and unprofessionalized) in the early fourteenth century. In the lay subsidy of 1332 only 15 brewers were named, and all were assessed under 10s. (see Margaret Curtis, "The London Lay Subsidy of 1332," in George Unwin, ed., *Finance and Trade under Edward III* [Manchester, 1918], pp. 35–92).

the City; they threatened and bribed officers; they used false measures; they brewed insufficient quantities of cheap ale for the poor. In 1383 the City tried to prevent any brewers (or ale-sellers) from holding office, and in 1406, when the City allowed the mystery of brewers to supervise the ale trade, it stipulated rather insultingly that the mystery would lose its new privileges if it abused them. In early fifteenth-century London, then, brewers were neither very rich nor very respected.[9]

Distinctions among brewers, however, were perhaps as important as distinctions between brewers and other Londoners. Not all brewers managed operations as large as those of Stephen Hamme and William Robinson, and, as a result, clear divisions developed between greater and lesser brewers. In 1379 the City decided that fines levied upon brewers should vary according to the extent of their trade; those who brewed five quarters of malt a week or less were liable for fines of 40*d.*, and those brewing more than five quarters of malt were liable for fines of 6*s.* 8*d.* This ordinance might never have been put into effect, but it suggests, first, that distinctions in the brewing trade were hardening and, second, that even more humble brewers could run large concerns. Brewing at the cut-off level of five quarters of malt, a lesser brewer would have made about 300 gallons, which sold for between 25*s.* and 37*s.* 6*d.*—not bad for a weekly gross income.[10] Many brewers, of course, might have brewed

---

[9]For the late thirteenth-century ordinance see *CLB* A, p. 220. For the 1382 ordinance see *CLB* H, p. 184, and CLRO, Letter Book H, fol. 144v. For some examples of the false trading practices of brewers see CLRO, Plea and Memoranda Roll A7 (brewers cited for excessive prices, 1355); *CPMR* 2: 210 (brewer and hosteler imprisoned for refusing to sell at set prices, 1375); *CPMR* 2: 6 (brewer threatening an officer, 1364); *CLB* D, pp. 201–02 (fourteenth-century aletasters' oath that includes injunction against bribery); *CLB* F, p. 245 (false measures, 1352); *CLB* H, pp. 107, 183 (insufficient brewing of cheap ale, 1379, 1382). For the 1383 ordinance about officeholding see *CLB* H, pp. 209–10. For the 1406 agreement between City and gild see *CLB* I, pp. 50–51.

[10]In making this estimate I have assumed that a bushel of malt produced about 7½ gallons of ale, roughly the yield reported for most of the brewings made for the

much less than five quarters.

Brewers were also distinguished from each other by the nature of their trade. Some brewers sold in only small measures to customers who either consumed ale in the brewhouse or carried it home in buckets. This retail trade had been closely regulated by the City for centuries. In 1392, for example, aldermen were ordered to see that all brewers in their wards used sealed measures of gallon, pottle, and quart, giving their customers hanaps (drinking vessels measuring about a pint) into which the ale could be poured once it had been properly measured in sealed vessels. Other brewers traded in larger quantities. As early as 1277, the City was regulating the measurement of not only gallons, pottles, and quarts for the retail trade but also ale tuns (containing 150 gallons) for the wholesale market. At least some ale sold in tuns was shipped abroad, but most was probably sold to large households or hostelries in the City. By 1408 the wholesale trade had expanded enough to prompt the City to issue new orders about new measures—barrels and kilderkins. The order noted specifically that the brewers' trade "en groos" supplied not only hostelers and hucksters but also the households of lords and gentry.[11]

The actual working conditions of brewers also varied considerably from brewhouse to brewhouse. Some brewhouses were by-

---

Clare household, 1334–35: see PRO E101/92/1. I am grateful to Caroline Barron for calling my attention to this source. Christopher Dyer has estimated the same yield in his "English Diet in the Later Middle Ages," in T. H. Aston, ed., *Social Relations and Ideas: Essays in Honour of R. H. Hilton* (Cambridge, 1983), pp. 202–03. Of course commercial brewers had strong incentives to extract as much from each brewing as possible, so their yields might have been higher than those reported in domestic accounts. In making this estimate I have also relied upon information about prices in 1377: in July the City set the price of ale at 1½*d*. for a gallon of best ale and 1*d*. for a gallon of other ale; see CLRO, Letter Book H, fol. 71v.

[11]For the 1392 order see *CLB* H, p. 373, and CLRO, Letter Book H, fol. 265v. For the 1277 order see *CLB* A, p. 216. For an example of ale exported from London in 1364 see *Calendar of Patent Rolls* (*CPR*), *38 Edw. III*, ser. 4, 13: 33. For the 1408 order see *CLB* I, p. 63, and CLRO, Letter Book I, fols. 65v–66.

trades, demanding the attention of servants or wives but not constituting the main source of household income. Brewing as a by-trade had a long and enduring place in medieval London. Sometimes a servant ran the trade; in 1276, for example, a woman named Lucy, a servant of Maunsell the Tailor, was brewing and selling ale out of his household (with the help of some accomplices, she beat to death a woman who was attracting away her customers). More often, the trade was managed by a wife, perhaps assisted by children or servants. In 1325, for example, a fracas at a brewhouse of Gilbert de Mordone involved his wife, his son, and a servant, but he was nowhere about. Since he was a stockfishmonger, his wife probably managed the brewhouse as a trade ancillary to his. In 1444, for another example, Katerina the wife of Edward Frank worked independently in brewing ("sola marcandisat in arte de Brewers"). As in the countryside, Londoners who pursued brewing or ale-selling as by-trades occasionally merged their commercial and domestic duties. Hence, in 1355 several women accused of regrating ale were able to claim (some successfully) that the large quantities of ale found in their houses were for family consumption, not sale.[12]

Yet brewing as a by-trade was not necessarily synonymous with small-scale operations. Of the brewhouses that served the king in 1356, perhaps as many as one-third were managed as by-trades (since husbands worked as barbers, goldsmiths, cordwainers, and in a variety of other trades). A decade later Maud

---

[12]For the case involving Lucy the servant of Maunsell the Tailor, see Martin Weinbaum, ed., *The London Eyre of 1276*, London Record Society, vol. 12 (1976): 26 (item 89). For the 1325 fight at the brewhouse of Gilbert de Mordone see R. R. Sharpe, ed., *Calendar of Coroners' Rolls of the City of London, A.D. 1300–1378* (London, 1913), p. 115. For the 1444 case see CLRO, Mayors' Court Bills, MC1/3, item 210. I am grateful to Caroline Barron for directing me to the mayors' court bills. For claims in 1335 that ale was for domestic, not commercial, use see CLRO, Plea and Memoranda Roll A7.

Martyn (wife of William Martyn, a cook who was overseas) was confident enough about her skills as a brewer to rent a brewhouse for the very large sum of 11 marks per year; she intended to manage it on her own with the help of servants. Brewing as a by-trade also did not quickly fade away. In the early fifteenth century several wives—including Johanna Amwell the wife of John Amwell, skinner—were successful enough in brewing to maintain independent memberships in the Brewers' gild. Indeed, of the brewhouses associated with the gild during Johanna Amwell's time, at least 15 per cent probably still produced and sold ale as a by-trade.[13]

In contrast to these by-trade brewhouses, other brewhouses—like those run by Stephen Hamme and William Robinson—were major operations, employing not only a husband, wife, and children but also numerous servants. Servants were integral to the brewing trade. As the examples of both Maunsell the Tailor and Gilbert de Mordone show, servants worked even in the smallest brewhouses, but they were especially essential in the running of large enterprises. By the late fourteenth century, some brewhouses employed numerous servants, and the trade had a growing "servant problem." In the wake of the labor

---

[13]For the 1356 listing of royal brewers see *CLB* G, p. 76. In tracing these 30 brewers in other sources I have found 11 identified as involved in other trades; eight identified as brewers; one identified as a huckster. For Maud Martyn in 1368 see CLRO, Mayors' Court Bills MC1/1, item 56. Johanna Amwell paid quarterage to the Brewers' gild in 1422/23, 1423/24, and 1424/25. Of the 488 households that I have identified from City and gild lists as involved in brewing 1418–25, men in 71 were named—like John Amwell, skinner—as pursuing other trades. The resulting estimate that 15 per cent of brewhouses were worked as a by-trade must be qualified in two ways. First, trade identifications in London did not always correspond to trade activity, since some men belonged to gilds other than the gilds of their actual trades (in the early fifteenth century this practice was still relatively rare). Second, since trade identifications were noted by Porlond and other clerks only sporadically, many more than 71 men might have been involved in trades other than brewing. I only know the stated trades of men in 116 households, or only about one-quarter of all households (45 households had men identified as brewers).

shortages that followed the Black Death, brewers' servants—like laborers in other trades—began to agitate for better pay. In 1350, Adam le Brewere, servant of John de Oxonia, skinner, was imprisoned for maligning his master and others, and for threatening to convince other servants in brewing to agree to work only by the day, and then only for the exorbitant wage of 12*d.* per day. Few servants were as obstreperous as Adam le Brewere, but others did take excessive wages, depart early from service, claim an expertise in brewing that they lacked, or attempt to play one master against another. In the early years of the fifteenth century, brewers' servants—by then called journeymen—won their battle for a daily wage rate, obtaining either 3*d.* or 4*d.* per day (depending on the season). A few decades later, journeymen constituted a distinct and powerful group within the brewing trade. In 1427/28, when the gild prepared a set of regulations about servants, they were differentiated by skill ("chief brewers" receiving 53*s.*4*d.* a year and "second brewers" getting no more than 40*s.*); they were able to marry and live away from their masters' households; and they were numerous enough to threaten their masters with a confederacy. Servants were, quite simply, essential to many brewers. In 1438, when the members of the Brewers' gild, armed with a new royal charter of incorporation, sought to restrict brewing to themselves alone, they tried to cut off non-gild brewers by eliminating two crucial resources, water and servants.[14]

---

[14]For the rebellious behavior of Adam le Brewere see *CPMR* 1: 235. His behavior was not unusual in the decades that followed the Black Death, when servants and journeymen in other trades also agitated for better working conditions. See, e.g., the quarrel between the fusters and saddlers reported in *CPMR* 1: 239. For servants taking excessive wages in 1372 see *CPMR* 2: 148. For a brewer's servant departing early from service in 1388 see *Calendar of Close Rolls* 40: 658. For servants claiming an expertise they lacked in 1375 see *CPMR* 2: 204. For brewers competing for servants in the late fourteenth century see CLRO, Mayors' Court Bills, MC1/2A, item 20. For wages of servants in the early fifteenth century see

The brewing trade in London was also, by the 1420s, shared among several distinct occupations: brewers, to be sure, but also hostelers, cooks, piebakers, and hucksters. Some hostelers bought ale from brewers to sell to their guests (in which case, they could only sell ale to be consumed on their premises); other hostelers themselves brewed ale (which they were allowed to sell both to guests drinking on the premises and—like brewers—to those who took ale away to be consumed elsewhere). Cooks, piebakers, and hucksters sometimes produced their own ale, but they usually regrated ale—that is, they bought ale from brewers, which they then hawked throughout the City for a profit. Cooks and piebakers sold ale along with other foodstuffs; hucksters often specialized in retailing ale alone. As in most medieval towns, regrating of any commodity—because it inflated prices—was vigorously opposed by London's governors, but as in most medieval towns, regrating in London was never eradicated. In 1406 the City agreed that the mystery of brewers could supervise all persons working in the ale trade—brewers, brewsters, hostelers, cooks, piebakers, and hucksters—in order to ensure that they sold good ale in lawful measures at proper prices.[15]

Among all these various aspects of the brewing trade, three seem to have been largely associated with only one sex. Hucksters were usually women—as suggested not only by the suffix of the English term but also by both the Law French *regrateress*

CLB I, pp. 50–51, and CLRO, Letter Book I, fols. 51v–52v. For gild legislation about servants (and the threat posed by a "confedereseye" of brewers' servants), see William Porlond's various notes on the subject in GL MS. 5440, esp. fols. 22v, 38–41v, and 130–130v. See also CLRO, Journal 7, fol. 95v. For the attempt to impose a monopoly by restricting access of non-gild brewers to trained servants see Porlond's notes, fol. 292v, and CLRO, Journal 3, fols. 176/162 and 169/166.

[15]For the 1406 agreement see *CLB* I, pp. 50–51, CLRO, Letter Book I, fols. 51–52v. For a 1382 statement of the terms under which hostelers could retail ale see *CLB* H, p. 184, and CLRO, Letter Book H, fol. 144v.

and the Latin *retalliatrices*.[16] Although men were presented for huckstering ale, their presentments might have been a legal fiction (that is, husbands might have been presented for the huckstering of their wives), and men were, in any case, quite outnumbered by women. In 1355, 19 women and seven men were convicted of huckstering; in 1370, 10 women and only one man were named as hucksters; in 1372, 11 women and three men were cited as hucksters; and in 1421, 19 female and seven male hucksters were listed.[17] Hucksters often had close business relationships with brewers, and in at least some instances, brewers seem to have employed servants who worked for them in huckstering ale. In 1372, for example, Emma atte Grene claimed that her master, Robert Bryan, was detaining money from her wages without cause; she was supposed to sell ale at 5*s*. to the barrel, but he was now demanding an extra 6*d*. per barrel from her. Between Michaelmas and Easter, she had sold 48 barrels of ale in Bryan's employ.[18] Emma atte Grene lost her case, and her quarrel with her master illustrates just one of the many difficulties faced by hucksters. As has been

---

[16]In 1348, e.g., a royal order about the retailing of ale during parliament referred to alesellers exclusively as "retalliatrices." See *CLB* F, p. 178, and CLRO, Letter Book F, fol. 150v. In 1362, when especially low fines were set for female brewers and hucksters, the sole term for aleseller was "regrateresse" (*CLB* G, p. 150, and CLRO, Letter Book G, fol. 107v). On other occasions, however, terminology suggests that men as well as women regrated ale; e.g., in 1356 an order by the City about the sale of ale referred to "regratour" as well as "regrateresse." See *CLB* G, p. 52, and CLRO, Letter Book G, fol. 41v.

[17]These are partial lists of hucksters in the City, so the total numbers cited do not represent the number of hucksters active in London; they also represent only some of the extant lists of hucksters in the City. For 1335 see CLRO, Plea and Memoranda Roll A7. For 1370 see CLRO, Letter Book G, fol. 258v. For 1372 see CLRO, Plea and Memoranda Roll A17 (presentments for 10 June). For 1421 see *CPMR* 4: 140.

[18]For Emma atte Grene's suit see *CPMR* 2: 145–46 and CLRO, Plea and Memoranda Roll A17. The City objected to relationships of this sort between brewers and alesellers; see, e.g., orders in 1368 (*CLB* G, p. 226, and CLRO, Letter Book G, fol. 207), and 1382–83 (*CLB* H, pp. 184, 215; CLRO, Letter Book H, fols. 144v, 164v).

mentioned, hucksters were especially likely to be blamed for disorderly houses and disruptive clients. They also were quite poor; in 1362 their fines (and those of female brewers) were set at especially low levels. And they were perhaps particularly vulnerable to exploitation; in 1375 an impostor was able to extract bribes from several hucksters who thought—simply because he was carrying counters (*tabulae*)—that he was an officer sent to confiscate their ale.[19]

Yet, hucksters' greatest difficulties came from the City itself. About two decades after the Black Death, the City began to try to eliminate the hucksters' trade altogether. In 1368 brewers were ordered not to sell any ale that was later to be resold and neither to maintain nor to encourage hucksters—orders much repeated in the following years. In 1377, the City additionally proclaimed that there should be no hucksters at all working within the liberty. Then in 1382, the City began an offensive against hucksters that almost eliminated its supply of good ale. In May of that year, the City reiterated—in a piece of general legislation about the brewing trade—that no huckster could buy ale to resell at a profit. This order, which seems to have been seldom enforced in the past, was put into effect the following April, when a woman named Juliana atte Vane was punished for huckstering (she had bought 30 gallons of ale from Benedicta Bracciatrice in order to resell it at 2*d.* a gallon). She was forced to forfeit her ale and punished on the "thewe." Hucksters seem to have reacted quickly and en masse to the punishment of Juliana atte Vane—they withdrew from the City and plied their trade from the safer jurisdictions of Westminster and Southwark. Since brewers continued to sell their best ale to these hucksters, the City's ale supply came under threat, and the City

[19]For the 1362 case see *CLB* G, p. 150, and CLRO, Letter Book G, fol. 107v. For the 1375 incident see *CLB* H, pp. 18–19, and CLRO, Letter Book H, fol. 26v.

responded a month later by trying to prevent ale from being transported out of its jurisdiction. The eventual end of this story cannot be traced, but the City certainly lost in the long run. In the fifteenth century, as in the fourteenth century, hucksters remained essential to the marketing of ale in the City. Finally, in 1431, the City abandoned its efforts to eliminate huckstering and began instead to try to regulate it in a systematic fashion, stipulating that hucksters be limited in number, free of the City, well-behaved, and backed up by sureties.[20]

In contrast to the large numbers of women involved in huckstering, two brewing occupations were largely male. First, most hostelers were male. A list of innkeepers compiled in 1384 reported only 10 women among 183 men (many of these men, of course, probably were assisted in their businesses by their wives).[21] Second, servants, aside from servants working as hucksters, were exclusively male. I have found numerous references to brewers' servants and journeymen in London, but none that suggests the employment of women, except as hucksters. Servants who worked as chief brewers or second brewers in the actual manufacture of ale seem to have been exclusively male.[22] The preponderance of males as brewers' servants was not peculiar to London; in Oxford in 1381, most brewers' servants were male, and at least some female servants worked in huckstery, not in manufacture.[23] Curiously enough, references

---

[20]For 1368 see *CLB* G, p. 226, and *CPMR* 2: 124 (for enforcement). For 1377 see *CPMR* 2: 235. For 1382/83 problems see *CLB* H, p. 184, and CLRO, Letter Book H, fol. 144v; CLRO, Letter Book H, fol. 164; *CLB* H, p. 215, and CLRO, Letter Book H, fol. 164v. For 1431 see *CLB* K, p. 132, and CLRO, Letter Book K, fol. 95v.

[21]CLRO, Roll A27. I am grateful to Caroline Barron for bringing this list to my attention.

[22]See, e.g., the servants presented in Oct. 1372, in *CPMR* 2: 148.

[23]See the edition of the Oxford poll tax for 1380–81 ed. Rogers, *Oxford City Documents*, pp. 3–45. I counted 28 male servants and 18 female servants among brewers in this listing (one female servant was noted as a tapster). My count

to apprentices in the brewing trade of London (and elsewhere) are rare before the sixteenth century, for reasons that are unclear. On the one hand, since references to brewing apprenticeships are so uncommon in late medieval towns, brewing—a domestic skill in origin and a trade that required perhaps more regulation of its market than training for its production—might have developed formal training schemes quite late. On the other hand, brewers' servants were clearly skilled, and it is quite likely that brewing, like other trades in the City, accommodated "a class of workmen who had not been apprenticed."[24] In any case, service (informal training, formalized apprenticeship, or skilled journeywork) was an important route to success for aspiring male brewers in fifteenth-century London. Many servants were included among the men who achieved freedom of the gild (and hence, of the City) in the 1420s and 1430s, and some of these men eventually ran their own brewhouses. Some, however, did not, but worked instead for others throughout their lives.[25]

By the time of William Porlond, a brewers' gild was perched at the top of this complex and diverse brewing trade. Brewers had acted together to advance their collective interests as early as the late thirteenth century, and in this sense of informal association there had been a mystery of brewers in the City throughout the fourteenth century. In 1376, for example, the brewers, acting as a mystery, returned four members to serve

---

includes corrections made to Rogers's text, esp. regarding the household of Walter Wycombe: see PRO E179/161/47.

[24]George Unwin, *The Gilds and Companies of London*, 2nd ed. (London, 1925), p. 91. For the importance of skill among brewers' servants see *CPMR* 2: 204. None of the 34 male brewers who entered the freedom of the City between 1309 and 1312 entered via apprenticeship.

[25]As Steve L. Rappaport has noted, brewers' servants in the sixteenth century had very slight chances of advancement (*Worlds within Worlds: Structures of Life in Sixteenth-Century London* [Cambridge, 1989], pp. 329–40).

on the Common Council. By this time, however, a more formal organization of brewers was evolving under the aegis of a religious fraternity. This fraternity traced its origins to 1342, when seven men had formed a fraternity to repair the church of All Saints, London Wall. When only one of these men, a brewer named John Enfield, survived the plague, he began to gather into it "other good men among the brewers of London and others of the City." By 1388, when the fraternity had to answer a royal inquiry about its history and constitution, it was combining religious and social functions with trade regulation.[26]

During the early fifteenth century the Brewers' gild emerged as a powerful corporation of tradespeople in the City. In 1406 the City approved a mystery of brewers and granted it broad regulatory powers over the trade, but the gild remained firmly subordinated to civic authority; the agreement was reached on the explicit understanding that if the Brewers' gild failed to regulate the market properly, the mayor would resume his customary oversight. In 1438 the gild obtained—at the great cost of more than £141—a royal grant of incorporation. This incorporation gave the gild not only an existence independent of the City but also a perpetual existence (since it was allowed to hold lands worth 10 marks per annum in mortmain). In addition to stipulating the gild's method of self-governance, the charter gave the gild the right to supervise all sales of malt liquor ("licoris cuiuscumque de brasio") in London and its suburbs. Although the City reacted to this new charter by seeking a promise of obedience from the Brewers (which they gave), the balance of

[26]The use of a fraternity to mask economic association was not uncommon in London. See esp. Elspeth M. Veale, "Craftsmen and the Economy of London in the Fourteenth Century," in Hollaender and Kellaway, *London History*, pp. 133–55. For 1376 see *CLB* H, p. 43. For the 1388 return (which relates the early history of the fraternity and contains, in Law French, the phrase quoted), see PRO C47/42/206 and C47/46/471.

power between City and gild was permanently altered. After 1438 the City and the gild acted as more or less equal partners in negotiating the terms of the market in ale and beer—prices, supervision, quality, measures, and the like. Nevertheless, the Brewers' gild was not among the most distinguished gilds in the urban hierarchy—perhaps not ranked at all before 1400, it placed only twenty-sixth of 65 gilds in 1487.[27]

Not all brewers belonged to this gild. Given the great diversity of those associated with the trade, many who brewed as a by-trade only—perhaps many wives, certainly many hostelers and cooks—avoided gild membership. Hucksters and servants were regulated by the gild but were not always part of it.[28] As a result, many persons involved in London's ale market evaded full involvement in the gild—not paying quarterage, not wearing livery, or eschewing both. When the City compiled its list of brewers in 1419/20, it named 290 persons; of these only

---

[27]For the 1406 agreement see *CLB* I, pp. 50–51, and CLRO, Letter Book I, fols. 51–52v. For 1438 see *CPR 1436–1441*, p. 142, and PRO C66/441, m. 1. For the costs of the charter see GL MS. 5440, fol. 290–290v. For the City's reaction see CLRO, Journal 3, fol. 11v. For the precedence of the Brewers' gild among the gilds of London I have relied upon the 1487–88 list ed. Charles Welch, *History of the Worshipful Company of Pewterers of the City of London*, 2 vols. (London, 1902), 1: 66–67. In general, the ranking of the Brewers in 1487–88 was fairly typical of precedence lists in the fifteenth and sixteenth centuries: the Brewers tended to be found at the bottom of the top third of companies. In 1422 they were ranked eleventh of 31 companies; in 1532, twenty-second of 60; in 1545, fourteenth of 28. For 1422 see *CLB* K, p. 3; for 1532, see John Stow, *A Survey of London*, ed. Charles L. Kingsford, vol. 2 (Oxford, 1908), pp. 190–92. For 1545 see William Herbert, *The History of the Twelve Great Livery Companies of London*, 2 vols. (London, 1834–37), 1: 135.

[28]In the sixteenth century a "custom of London" allowed a freeman of the City to practice any trade whatsoever, regardless of the gild to which he belonged (Rappaport, *Worlds*, p. 91). In the early fifteenth century, however, the Brewers' gild actively sought to include *all* free brewers in its membership. On the one hand, the Brewers' gild regularly admitted men of other crafts, e.g., in 1421–23 new brethren included a draper, a goldsmith, a tiler, a vintner, a smith, two tailors, several maltmen, and several members of the clergy. See GL MS. 5440, fols. 85–86v and 108v–109. On the other hand, the Brewers also tried to force non-gild brewers out of the trade by denying them access to both servants and water (see above).

about two-thirds (185) had any association with the gild.[29] The gild, in short, represented the upper crust of the brewing trade, and its membership excluded many humble brewers, many part-time brewers, and most alesellers.

In early fifteenth-century London, about 40,000 people—most of whom relied exclusively upon ale for their daily drink—created a large and ready market for ale. Their needs were supplied by a complex network of brewers, hucksters, hostelers, piebakers, and cooks who produced ale and marketed it throughout the City. And their interests were protected, insofar as possible, by a City government committed to ensuring a steady, cheap, and high-quality supply of ale for its citizens and visitors. Working with (and sometimes against) the City in this effort was a trade organization—the fraternity and craft of brewers, which represented the most powerful of those involved in the production and marketing of ale in the City. About one-third of the members of this gild were women.

The number of women in the Brewers' gild has been consistently under-reported since William Herbert in 1834 counted 39 women among the livery-wearers of the Brewers in 5 Henry V.[30]

---

[29]In comparing these lists I have adjusted for the fact that these sources often described a particular brewhouse differently—the City list often cited *husbands* for a brewing business that was identified in gild lists by either a *wife's* name or the names of a *married couple*. Hence, I have compared households, not individuals. Of those households named in the City list, 135 paid quarterage to the gild in 1419/20, three paid late quarterage, and 47 contributed to the *taxacio voluntaria*. Over time, many of the brewing households found only in the City list of 1419/20 did associate with the gild, but nearly two-thirds had still not formed any links with the gild by 1425. It is worth noting that the City's coverage was perhaps just as poor as the gild's. Of the 187 households that paid quarterage to the gild in 1419/20, only 135 (73 per cent) were picked up in the City's survey.

[30]Herbert, *Livery Companies* 1: 62. For repetitions of this count see Unwin, *Gilds and Companies*, p. 191; Mia Ball, *The Worshipful Company of Brewers: A Short History* (London, 1977), p. 62; Kay E. Lacey, "Women and Work in Fourteenth and Fifteenth-Century London," in Lorna Duffin and Lindsey Charles, eds., *Women and*

I have been unable to replicate Herbert's count, but it is wrong; the quarterage lists from 1418 to 1424 show between 78 and 152 women each year paying quarterage (accounting for between 31 per cent and 42 per cent of all quarterages).[31] I think the main difference between my figures and those of Herbert (and the many modern historians who have followed him in this regard) is that I counted the *wives*. Although many men and women paid quarterage as independent brewers (usually paying

---

Work in Pre-Industrial England (London, 1985), p. 51; Caroline Barron, "The 'Golden Age' of Women in Medieval London," *Reading Medieval Studies* 15 (1989): 47.

[31]The total cost of livery given by Herbert (£185 4*s*.10*d*.) matches the total given on fol. 9 for the livery disbursements of 1418/19. I believe that Herbert misdated this account (he dated it as 1417/18) and mistranscribed (and hence misunderstood) the heading at the top of fol. 9v (this folio contains the names of brothers and sisters who had paid quarterage to the gild but did not wear livery: "ount payez lour quarterages et navoient drap' de notre liverie en ceste an"). In any case, I have been unable to replicate Herbert's count of 39 women. One woman (Agnes Bugge) appears in the livery list proper; 20 women are listed among those who paid quarterage but did not wear livery; 42 women appear in a listing (fol. 10v) of those who were counted as members of the gild but had failed to pay quarterage. Folios 105–107 of Porlond's book, cited by Barron in her discussion of this count of 39 female members of the gild, describe a dinner held in 1423, not the membership of 1418. In 1916, Herbert's calculations received apparent verification from another source when Annie Abram noted that the City census of brewers in 1419/20 tabulated about 300 brewers, of whom fewer than 20 were women. Abram's estimate has been repeated, with some minor variations, by Sylvia Thrupp, Kay Lacey, and John Butt. I have been able to replicate Abram's count roughly (I found 21 women of 290 brewers), but her source is also flawed, since it—by reporting heads of brewing households rather than brewers per se—underreports the extent of female participation in the trade ("Women Traders in Medieval London," *Economic Journal* 26 [1916]: 279). See also repetitions of this figure in Sylvia L. Thrupp, *The Merchant Class of Medieval London, 1300–1500* (Ann Arbor, 1948), p. 42; Lacey, "Women," p. 51; John Joseph Butt, "The Transition of Privilege in Medieval Urban Society: A Study of English Brewers," diss. (Rutgers Univ., 1982): 97. To avoid future confusion, let me specify the women found in the City list of 1419/20 (the spelling of names has been modernized): Beatrice Tye, Margaret Leonard alias Pyle, Margaret Nightingale, Agnes Riche, Juliana Heterset, Katherine Roche, Alice Gayton, Matilda Rolf, Alice Gildsborough, Margaret Stoket, Agnes West, Christina Bekeswelle, Elena Darling, Lucy Streetman, Constance Hosard, Millicent Burgh, Johanna Scot, Katherine Pinchbeck, Alice Drayton, Margaret Settingborn, Cecilia Raff. The City list is printed in *CLB* I, pp. 233–37 (in a printed edition that accurately renders the original).

12*d.* a year), most people paid as married couples, jointly rendering 24*d.* each year. Hence, some women (some widows, some never-married women, and some wives) belonged to the gild independently in the early 1420s, but dozens of other women participated in the gild together with their husbands and paid, just like their husbands and just like independent brewers, 12*d.* dues each year. In other words, Porlond's quarterage lists provide us with two sorts of information: they tell us how each household attached itself to the gild (whether through a man, a woman, or a married couple), and they also tell us about the actual constitution of the personal membership of the gild.[32]

As Table 1 shows, a fair number of women independently paid dues to the gild between 1418 and 1425; thus, roughly 10 per cent of the businesses represented in the gild were run primarily by women.[33]

---

[32]As is suggested by its name, quarterage was once paid on a quarterly basis. In 1388/89 the Brewers' fraternity of All Hallows noted that its members paid 12*d.* on four occasions through the year, for a total annual dues of 4*s.* Sisters paid as much as brothers, although married women ("soers qe sount desouth coverture de Baroun") paid only 12*d.* per year (and nothing, if they did not attend the annual feast). See PRO C47/42/206. By the fifteenth century annual dues were lower, wives paid the same amount as husbands, and, as far as I can tell, dues were paid on an annual basis.

[33]This figure compares reasonably closely with the 7 per cent of households headed by females in the 1419/20 City list of brewers. The lower proportion of independent female brewers in this latter list reflects the focus of the City list upon heads of households (as opposed to heads of businesses). For the City list differs from the quarterage lists in one important respect: the compiler of the City list, concerned about legal liability, named women as independent brewers only if they were widowed or never-married, but Porlond, concerned about gild income, sought to name and to extract quarterage from every woman primarily responsible for a brewing concern, *regardless of her marital status.* As a result, several wives paid independent quarterage to the gild in 1418/19, although their husbands were noted as legally responsible in the City list of 1419/20 (see Idonia Hatton, wife of Roger Swanfield and Agnes Bugge, wife of Stephen Bugge). Hence, the quarterage lists, by naming wives who ran independent brewhouses, give a more accurate gauge of the actual extent to which brewhouses were run independently by women.

TABLE 1
HOUSEHOLDS REPRESENTED BY QUARTERAGE PAYMENTS

Year	Membership of Male Alone		Membership of Female Alone		Membership of Married Couple		Total Households
	No.	%	No.	%	No.	%	No.
1418/19	81	51	17	11	61	38	159
1419/20	110	59	18	9½	59	31½	187
1420/21	84	53	18	11	58	36	160
1421/22	83	46	17	9	82	45	182
1422/23	68	34	18	9	113	57	199
1423/24	75	34	23	11	121	55	219
1424/25	88	37	22	9	130	54	240

Marital status alone does not explain why some women paid quarterage independently, for not only widows and spinsters but also wives did so. Of the 17 women who paid independent quarterage in 1418/19, half (nine) were probably widowed, and some were widows of brewers. Some of these women might have been managing brewhouses that had been and continued to be the main economic resources of their households. Other widows might have been managing brewhouses that, once only a by-trade to the main occupations of their husbands, had taken on new economic importance in widowhood. The predominance of widows among independent female brewers increased over the seven years covered by Porlond's early lists. In the quarterage of 1424/25 more than two-thirds of women paying separate quarterage were widows.[34]

[34]Confirmed as certain widows: Alice Hore (widow of John Hore, citizen and brewer, d. by 1413); Johanna Horold (widow of John Horold alias Turmyn, d. 1418/19); Constance Hosard (widow of Robert, d. 1410); Agnes Stratton (widow of Nicholas, master of the Brewers' gild in 1406, d. 1413); Juliana Heterset (widow of Richard, citizen and brewer, d. 1419). The following were probably widows in

Never-married women also joined the Brewers' gild as independent members—perhaps as many as four in 1418 and two in 1425. For such women, brewing seems to have been a particularly profitable trade. John de Dachet certainly thought this was true when in 1300 he left his daughter Agnes a brewhouse that she was to use for eight years in order to establish herself in business. And Robert de Huttokeshatre probably thought the same when he, dying of the plague, left a brewhouse to Johanna the daughter of Henry Wyght for one year (after which it was to be sold). Both men assumed that never-married women could run brewhouses—and run them at a good profit.[35] Indeed, brewing, more than most trades, seems to have possessed a special suitability for households headed by females, since a single woman—never-married, abandoned, or widowed—could earn a fair living at it.[36] In early fourteenth-century Oxford, for example, single women accounted for about one-fifth of brewers in the town. In York at the same time, single women perhaps accounted for one

---

1418/19, since they were so cited in the more complete listing of 1419/20: Milicent Burgh (widow of Adam); Dionisia Barthorp (widow of John, citizen and brewer); Katherine Roche; Johanna Oretarde (widow of Peter Morle). The full count for 1424/25 is as follows: 15 widows, two wives, three women of unknown status (who were probably either unmarried or widowed), two more women of unknown status (probably either married or widowed).

[35]Never-married women were not identified as such in the quarterage lists, but the marital statuses of many wives and widows were denoted by William Porlond (and I have been able to determine the marital status of others through wills and other sources). Since never-marrying generates an *absence* of information about marital status (no statement of status by Porlond, no will of a dead husband, no livery worn by a husband, etc.), it can be surmised but not proven. Hence, I have no information on the marital statuses of four women in 1418/19 and two women in 1424/25; some of these women (if not all) were probably unmarried. For John de Dachet's will see R. R. Sharpe, ed., *Calendar of Wills Proved and Enrolled in the Court of Husting, London,* A.D. *1258–*A.D. *1688*, 2 vols. (London, 1889–90), 1: 45–46 (hereafter, *Hustings Wills*). For Robert de Huttokeshatre's will see *Hustings Wills* 1: 577.

[36]The term *single woman* in this study designates women who lived without a male household head—including never-married women, wives without husbands in residence, and widows.

of every six commercial brewers. Single women brewed because they gained exceptionally good incomes from the trade—at least by the low standards of what a single woman might hope to earn. Most single women worked as servants or spinsters, occupations that offered only meager support; in comparison, brewing was a very profitable option. The Oxford poll tax of 1380–81 illustrates this well. In that tax the 190 single women identified as servants or spinsters usually paid the minimum sum required—*4d.* The taxes paid by single women named as brewers were much higher: 10*s.*, 4*s.*, and 3*s.* Hence, perhaps more important than the sheer numbers of single women in the trade is the importance of the trade to single women as a group; brewing was one of the most desirable economic options for single women in the late Middle Ages.[37]

Wives also sometimes maintained gild membership independently of their husbands, and in the 1418/19 quarterage list four wives did so. In most cases it is likely that these wives were running brewhouses as by-trades, as concerns separate from the occupations of their husbands. Agnes Bugge, the wife of the draper Stephen Bugge, for example, independently paid dues to the gild throughout the 1420s. When Stephen Bugge died in

---

[37]Oxford presentments of brewers and alesellers in the early fourteenth century cite householders; women accounted for the following proportions of those cited: 21 per cent in 1311, 19 per cent in 1324, 17 per cent in 1335 and 1344, 15 per cent in 1351. See H. E. Salter, *Mediaeval Archives of the University of Oxford*, vol. 2, Oxford Historical Society, vol. 73 (1921): 129–265. In the list for York in 1304, 21 women are named of 70 brewers; 10 of these women were identified as married. See Michael Prestwich, ed., *York Civic Ordinances, 1301* (York, 1976), pp. 25–26. For the Oxford poll tax returns see Rogers, *Oxford City Documents*, pp. 3–45. In the Southwark poll tax of 1380–81 the three women named as brewers also paid slightly higher taxes than most women: one paid 4*d.* (the minimum) and two paid 12*d.* (See PRO E179/184/30.) Women did work in other victualing trades in medieval towns, but they tended to work as low-status retailers, not higher-status producers. Only in brewing did women work in large numbers both as brewers per se and as retailers of ale. See, e.g., Maryanne Kowaleski, "Women's Work in a Market Town: Exeter in the Late Fourteenth Century," in Hanawalt, *Women and Work*, pp. 145–64.

1429, he bequeathed what he called *his* brewhouse ("totum tenementum meum bracineum") to Agnes, and deeds indicate that he was, in fact, the legal owner of the property. Yet his failure to join the gild and his clear involvement in the drapery trade suggest that Agnes was the primary manager of the brewhouse.[38] In other cases, wives who independently paid quarterage might have been representing the primary occupation of their households, not by-trades ancillary to their husbands' occupations. For example, Idonia Hatton, wife of Roger Swanfield, was the sole member of her household paying quarterage for the five years between 1418 and 1423. During these years, however, her husband seems to have been actively involved in the brewhouse, and in 1424 he also joined the gild as a full member.[39] Why a wife such as Idonia Hatton would maintain independent gild membership for so long is unclear, but it is likely that Roger Swanfield (and other husbands involved in brewing) eventually joined under pressure to regularize their relationship to the trade (and its gild).

Similar pressure was exerted upon wives whose husbands initially paid independent quarterage to the gild. Probably most of the men who paid independent quarterage were married and representing—via their single quarterage payments—co-operative household enterprises. Over time, many of these men brought their wives into the gild. At the end of the 1418/19 quarterage, Porlond noted that considerable numbers of persons

[38]For Stephen Bugge's will see GL, Commissary Wills, Register 3, fol. 218. For the deed see CLRO, Husting Roll 145, items 37–39. For Stephen Bugge's economic activity as a draper see *CLB* I, p. 42.

[39]Swanfield's involvement in the brewhouse for many years before he formally joined the gild is suggested by first, his wearing of the gild livery; second, his naming as a creditor of the Crown in the lists of royal ale debts compiled by William Porlond in 1420–22; third, his identification as a "brewer" in a 1420 entry (see CLRO, Journal 1, fol. 72v). When Swanfield wrote his will in 1439 he styled himself a citizen and brewer (see GL, Commissary Wills, Reg. 4, fol. 35v).

were evading quarterage and that more rigorous accounting would be undertaken in the future. The main result of this greater rigor seems to have been the compelling of married men to bring their wives into the gild; of the 81 men who paid quarterage alone in 1418/19, 37 had brought their wives into the gild by 1424/25—hence, the relationship in the quarterage lists as shown in Table 1 between declining proportions of independent male quarterage-payers and rising numbers of quarterages paid by married couples. Nevertheless, at least some married men persisted in paying single quarterage; perhaps their wives worked in other by-trades, or perhaps they simply resisted pressure to bring their wives into the gild. In any case, although the number of independent male members of the gild who were either unmarried or widowed is impossible to determine, it is likely that most men who joined the gild independently were, in fact, married.[40]

Insofar as quarterage payments can suggest the actual nature of brewing in early fifteenth-century London, the data in Table 1 suggest that although some brewhouses were managed by individuals—widows, never-married women, some married men and married women in dual-trade households, and perhaps some bachelors—most brewhouses in London were managed

---

[40]Of the remaining 44 men who maintained independent membership, at least six were married. Given the difficulty of tracing the marital statuses of men, there is no basis for assuming that the remaining 38 were bachelors. Of course, some of the 37 men who brought their wives into the gild might have married for the first time between 1418 and 1425, but it is highly unlikely, given premodern rates of marriage, that the transition from bachelorhood to married status accounts for the bulk of this shift away from independent male quarterages and towards married quarterages. It is also likely that widowerhood was a very temporary state for most men, perhaps especially men involved in the brewing trade. Three men (John Philip, Henry Trebolaus, and John Wightmore) remarried immediately after the deaths of their wives, bringing their second wives into the gild without any interruption of membership. A fourth man (John Quinton) dropped out of the gild briefly after his wife's death, then began to pay quarterage again (just for himself), and finally brought his second wife into the gild.

jointly by husbands and wives. Over the years covered by Porlond's early quarterage lists, the gild was increasingly able to profit from this fact; by 1422 more than half of the brewhouses represented in the gild paid double quarterage, for both husband and wife. We cannot know why some brewhouses were represented in the gild by husbands only and others by wives only, and still others by both husbands and wives, but we do know that most of the most profitable brewhouses in London (i.e., those that joined the gild) demanded the attention of a married couple. Although single women brewed in significant numbers and some wives brewed as a by-trade, most commercial brewing in London was a family affair.

Table 2 examines the same data found in these quarterage lists from another perspective, by breaking down married couples into individuals and examining the number of persons who actually paid dues to the gild. It shows that women constituted roughly one-third of the gild's members, a proportion that rose slightly over the years, as the gild successfully encouraged more married men to bring their wives into the membership.

These figures are not an historical artifact. Although many of the women counted in this list paid quarterage as wives with their husbands, they were—at least fiscally—full members of the gild. They were usually identified by name in Porlond's list, and, just like their husbands and just like independent members, they paid 12*d.* dues each year.[41] In accepting quarterage payments from large numbers of widows, never-married women, and wives, the Brewers' gild of early fifteenth-century London was quite exceptional. Most other London gilds tolerated no female members at all; this was true of the Grocers in 1373, the

---

[41]The only exception is the first quarterage list (1418/19), in which William Porlond did not specifically give the names of wives.

TABLE 2
INDIVIDUALS REPRESENTED IN QUARTERAGE PAYMENTS

Year	Males		Females		Total
	No.	%	No.	%	No.
1418/19	142	65	78	35	220
1419/20	169	69	77	31	246
1420/21	142	65	76	35	218
1421/22	165	62½	99	37½	264
1422/23	181	58	131	42	312
1423/24	196	58	144	42	340
1424/25	218	59	152	41	370

Coopers in 1439/40, and the Weavers in 1456.[42] The Brewers' gild would have been exceptional, then, in accommodating *any* female members even in only small numbers; but among the Brewers one woman was numbered in the gild for every two men. In this most unusual of circumstances, how did women

[42]Quarterage lists are quite common for the sixteenth-century London gilds, but they are rare for the late medieval City (hence the particular importance of Porlond's book). I have sought comparable data in both printed and manuscript sources. For the Grocers see John A. Kingdon, *Facsimile of the First Volume of the Ms. Archives of the Worshipful Company of Grocers of the City of London, A.D. 1345–1463* (London, 1886), pp. 45–47. For the Coopers see GL MS. 5614a. For the Weavers see Frances Consitt, *The London Weavers' Company*, vol. 1 (Oxford, 1933), p. 90. Jean M. Imray has noted that one woman gained the freedom of the Mercers' Company (via the unusual route of redemption): see " 'Les bones gentes de la Mercerye de Londres': A Study of the Membership of the Medieval Mercers' Company," in Hollaender and Kellaway, *London History*, p. 163n. Elspeth M. Veale has noted a few instances of widows carrying on as skinners but concludes that women did not learn the trade in any numbers: see *The English Fur Trade in the Later Middle Ages* (Oxford, 1966), p. 100. The first Bakers' records—perhaps the gild most comparable to the Brewers—date from the early sixteenth century. At that time only a few widows were in the company (see GL MS. 5179/1). For the minimal involvement of women in London gilds in the sixteenth century see Rappaport, *Worlds*, pp. 36–42. It is interesting to note that although few women in sixteenth-century London presented apprentices, female brewers presented proportionally more than women in other trades (see Rappaport, ibid., p. 41n).

and men together share the responsibilities and opportunities of gild membership?

Although large numbers of women paid quarterage, they did not partake fully with men in the associational life of the gild. For a young man embarking on a career as a brewer the gild offered a set of very clear and hierarchical opportunities. After proving himself in service he could expect to become free of the gild, paying usually 6*s*.8*d*. to gain thereby not only civic enfranchisement but also the right to wear the livery of the Brewers. Yet, after gaining his freedom, he often would continue to work for others, and it was not until he was able to establish his own brewhouse (if at all) that he might move to the next stage of the gild hierarchy.[43] At that time he could acquire (usually for a fee of 3*s*.4*d*.) entry to the fraternity of Brewers. With entry to the fraternity came the obligation of paying annual quarterage and the right to join others in the gild's annual feast. In time, a very successful man might expect to advance still further, attaining invitations to the special meals held for the "more noble" of the craft and being chosen to serve in gild offices. Essentially, then, a young male brewer faced a gild of three tiers: (1) those free of the gild and in livery; (2) those admitted to the fraternity; and (3) those selected for participation in the governance of the gild.[44]

For a young woman the situation looked very different, and, in essence, only the second tier was open to her (and only partly

---

[43]Some men simultaneously paid to become free of the gild and to enter the fraternity.

[44]This career sequence for the Brewers' gild seems to have been very distinctive. At this time at least one other gild, the Mercers, restricted livery to only an elite few members. (See Imray, " 'Les bones gentes'.") By the sixteenth century all gilds limited livery to only a very exclusive group of gild members. But among the Brewers of William Porlond's time, livery was worn by all men who had become free of the gild (including nonhouseholders and servants).

open, at that). With very few exceptions, the first tier was closed to women, probably because freedom and livery were so closely associated with civic life, ceremony, and politics. The gild was never a route to civic enfranchisement for women. Of the 24 persons who acquired the freedom between 1419 and 1421, not one was a woman; and the same absolute exclusion of women from the freedom recurs throughout Porlond's book. Although one female brewer styled herself a "freewoman" of the City in her will, her status came from her widowhood, not from the gild.[45]

Similarly, the public declaration of association that came through wearing the livery of the gild—either the hood worn by lesser brewers or the gown worn by greater brewers—was also rarely undertaken by women. By wearing livery, members publicly expressed gild association and solidarity; livery was worn at funerals of gild brothers and sisters, at gild functions (both within the Brewers' Hall and also outside it), and on civic occasions (when all gilds would gather in their liveries). The wearing of livery was so important and so frequent that it was replaced every two years—a quite rapid turnover, considering the expense involved. Indeed, the biennial costs of the livery speak eloquently to its critical importance as a public expression of gild unity. In 1420/21 the gild spent more than £135 on livery; individual members usually paid 6*s*. (for the cloth for

[45]The new freemen are listed in the masters' accounts for 1419–21 in GL MS. 5440, fol. 60. Margaret Cruse, widow of John Spenser, brewer, styled herself a freewoman (and claimed that she achieved this status on 30 May 1449) in a will enrolled in Oct. 1451. (See *Hustings Wills* 2: 520.) According to London custom, a freeman's widow could claim free status, as long as she remained unmarried. (See Barron, " 'Golden Age'," esp. pp. 44–45.) For lists of new freemen in Porlond's book see GL MS. 5440, fols. 1 and 17v (1418/19), 37v and 60 (1419–21), 84–85 and 108–108v (1421–23), 149–150 and 153v–154 (1423–25), 162 (1429/30), 187 (1430/31), 199 (1431/32), 223v (1432/33), 233 (1433/34), 253 (1434/35), 265 (1435/36), 288 (1436/37), 303 (1437/38) and 319v (1438/39).

a hood) or about 20*s*. (for the cloth for a gown). Livery had originally been associated with the fraternity of the Brewers, but by the time of William Porlond most men donned livery once they had entered the freedom of the craft (and before they, as householders, paid to enter the fraternity). Yet the rules about who did and did not wear livery were by no means clear; at the end of his main livery list for 1418/19, William Porlond appended several other lists of anomalous cases: those who were brothers and sisters of the fraternity and had paid quarterage but had no livery; those who had entered the fraternity and had livery but had paid neither for entry nor for quarterage; those who had livery but had not paid quarterage; those who had livery but were not in the fraternity.[46] The situation clearly was somewhat chaotic, but as a rule only men wore livery, and they wore it from the time that they gained the freedom of the craft.

In its report to the Crown in 1388, the Brewers' fraternity—although it consisted of both brothers and sisters—spoke only of a livery for its brothers.[47] This notion that livery (and its public expression of solidarity) was for men only seems to have survived fairly intact into the fifteenth century. Although William Porlond's records occasionally noted women wearing livery, few women did so. Six women took livery in 1418/19; no women, in 1420/21; three women, in 1422/23; and in most subsequent years, a mere handful of women (if any) purchased or received livery. With only one exception, all of these women took material for wearing the lesser livery of the hood.[48] Who were

---

[46]See GL MS. 5440, fols. 9–11.

[47]PRO C47/42/206.

[48]The one exception was William Porlond's wife, who in 1436/37 was noted as receiving cloth for a gown. Since I have not found a clear administrative distinction between brewers who wore hoods and gowns (e.g., brewers who entered the fraternity did not automatically advance to the gown livery), I think it is likely that

these few women who every other year were listed among the literally hundreds of men who received livery cloth? In many cases they wore livery because of the status of their husbands; masters' wives often received livery cloth, as occasionally did William Porlond's wife and female servant. Indeed, in 1418/19 enough cloth was given without charge to the masters to provide liveries for both themselves and their wives (in later years, masters actually had to pay for their wives' liveries). Yet in many other cases the women who wore livery appear to have been completely unexceptional—ordinary women who, usually with their husbands, paid quarterage to the gild.[49] Nothing, in short, explains why *they* wore livery when most women did not.

In any case, the wearing of livery by these few women was clearly exceptional. Unlike most men who regularly purchased livery cloth every two years, most women who received livery cloth took it on only one occasion. Perhaps these women wore their livery so seldom that they did not need to replace it; perhaps they thought it too expensive to replace; perhaps they found that having livery was an unnecessary extravagance. And

---

individuals wore the livery they could afford—cheaper hoods or more expensive gowns. If this surmise that the hood/gown distinction was primarily an economic distinction is correct, then it is scarcely surprising that most women wore the lesser hood. It also explains why one woman wore a gown livery: William Porlond (who received some cloth free from the gild in 1436/37) was apparently willing to spend an additional 11*s.* 6*d.* to purchase extra material for a gown for his wife.

[49]In a very few cases the women who wore livery were exceptional—either boasting long-standing attachments to the gild or paying for their own entry into the fraternity (a payment that was rare for women). Both Agnes Bugge (a married woman who received livery in 1418/19) and Emma Canon (a probably unmarried woman who took livery in 1422/23) paid independent quarterage to the gild over many years. Katrina Wygeyn entered the fraternity alone in 1421–23 and received livery in 1422/23. Juliana Scot entered the fraternity alone in 1429/30 and received livery cloth in 1432/33. Given the overall patterns of livery-wearing by women, I think that these exceptional women wore livery not because their long dues' payments or entry into the fraternity made them *eligible* for livery but because they chose to wear it as part of their exceptionally close association with the gild.

unlike most men, most women never wore livery at all. When Emma Canon, Katrina Wygeyn, and William Porlond's servant Rosa took livery cloth in 1422/23, they were among 224 men who did so. To put it another way, in the livery distribution of 1420/21, none of the women who paid quarterage had donned the livery of the gild, but nine of every 10 men had.[50] In practice, women were the only group in the gild who regularly failed to wear livery.

Nevertheless, it must be emphasized that the general absence of women in livery lists appears to have been more practical than philosophical. Women could wear livery; there simply was little reason for them to do so. Livery for men came with freedom (something unattainable for women), and livery was worn on many civic and gild occasions from which unenfranchised women were excluded. Hence, livery was generally superfluous for women. Yet if it suited gild honor to put women in livery (as in the case of masters' wives) or if individual women wished to obtain livery, they were not, it seems, refused.

The position of women in the second tier of the gild progression for men—entering the fraternity, paying quarterage, and attending the annual feast—was certainly better, although somewhat awkward. Most women entered the fraternity by virtue of their husbands' entry (and the standard entry fee of 3*s*.4*d*. remained unchanged for both married couples and individuals).[51] Hence, women rarely paid separately for entry to

---

[50]For livery lists see GL MS. 5440, fols. 4v–11 (1418/19), 53–56 (1420/21), 74–77 (1422/23), 123–129v (1424/25), 173–180 (1430/31), 208–215v (1432/33), 237–244v (1434/35), 272–279v (1436/37), 307–314 (1438/39).

[51]In some entry lists wives are explicitly noted as entering the fraternity with their husbands, but such notations were not always made (see, e.g., the lists for 1421–23). Men who married after having entered the fraternity brought their wives into the fraternity with apparently no extra charge (see, e.g., a 1421/22 list of such men and their wives, fol. 69).

the fraternity, but they could do so; Johanna Amwell and Katrina Wygeyn entered the fraternity in 1421–23, Juliana Scot entered in 1429/30, and Johanna Sturmyn did the same in 1430/31. These patterns suggest that entry involved not individuals as much as households; entry to the fraternity registered the establishment of a new brewhouse, and the names associated with such entries suggest that these new brewing concerns were run by unmarried men, married couples, and, occasionally, independent female brewers.[52] It seems clear that the women who entered the fraternity alone managed independent brewhouses. Johanna Amwell's husband was a skinner and Johanna Sturmyn's husband was a tailor; both men seem to have been completely uninvolved in the commercial brewing of their wives. Juliana Scot was probably unmarried. Katrina Wygeyn was actually married to a brewer (William Termeday), but they were kept so separate in gild records that they probably managed two brewhouses.

Yet Johanna Amwell, Johanna Sturmyn, Juliana Scot, and Katrina Wygeyn were not the only women who managed separate brewhouses. Why did not all the other women who paid independent quarterage to the gild also formally enter the fraternity? The answer is twofold. First, some women who appear in Porlond's list as independent brewers were widows who would have entered the fraternity with their husbands long before. Second, never-married women might have been too poor for the gild to extract an entry fee from them. Since never-married

---

[52]It is impossible to separate unmarried men from married couples. Porlond usually listed entry to the fraternity only in his annual accounts, and since entry fees did not vary by marital status, he often failed to note wives of married men. Compare, e.g., the list of new brethren, fols. 149–151, and the report of the same in the accounts for that year on fol. 154–154v. In other words, because most entry lists occur in accounts, they usually list only one person for each household, regardless of whether or not that person was married.

female brewers were exceptionally poor and disadvantaged (compared to other brewers), the gild might have taken quarterage from them without insisting upon entry fines because quarterage was the best the gild could get. In short, it seems that women running independent brewhouses could be liable for entry fines to the fraternity but rarely were. In any case, most women entered the fraternity in tandem with their husbands.[53]

The obligation to pay quarterage accompanied, of course, entry to the fraternity, and whether or not women formally entered the gild, they were liable for quarterage payments. As we have seen, women paid quarterage to the gild in large numbers. Roughly one-third of all quarterage payers—and hence, I would argue, one-third of all members of the gild—were female. With entry to the fraternity and payment of quarterage, gild members also acquired the right to attend the annual feast of the gild; this right extended to women as well as men. In 1421, 155 persons attended the annual dinner, including 36 wives who came with their husbands and six women who attended alone. This annual dinner, called "Our Feast" in the accounts, usually entailed substantial feasting (the opulent menu included such foods as swans and capons), good entertainment (minstrels and players were paid for their work), and some transacting of gild business. Masters' accounts were sometimes settled at these dinners (sometimes at the breakfasts), and the feast probably also included politicking—possibly gild elections (this was certainly true in later years) and possibly discussions about gild policy and governance. Women probably participated either not at all or only infor-

[53]For information on persons entering the fraternity see GL MS. 5440, fols. 1v and 17v (1418/19), 38 and 60v (1419–21), 85–86v and 108v–109 (1421–23), 149–151 and 154–154v (1423–25), 162–162v (1429/30), 187–187v (1430/31), 199v (1431/32), 223v–224 (1432/33), 233 (1433/34), 253–253v (1434/35), 265–265v (1435/36), 288 (1436/37), 303 (1437/38), 319v (1438/39).

mally in the political aspects of the annual dinner; since women could neither serve in gild office nor gain civic enfranchisement through the gild, it is unlikely that they participated in electoral processes. It is even possible that women and men sat in different rooms at these dinners (as was done in some gilds).[54]

In any case, women, although present at these dinners, did not attend as regularly as men. In 1421, women accounted for one in three members of the gild but only one in four persons at the annual dinner. Moreover, although nearly half of the households in the gild sent persons to the dinner, very few of the women who belonged to the gild independently did so (only three of 18, or 17 per cent). Costs might partially explain the comparatively low attendance of women. The dinner was not free to members, and women, interestingly enough, paid lower charges than men: most men alone paid 16*d.*; most married couples paid 2*s.*; and most women alone paid 12*d.* This lower charge might reflect the gild's expectation that women would consume less food than men, but since some men also paid 12*d.*, it seems probable that the lower charges reflect a qualitative decision about ability to pay.[55] Certainly, many poorer members of the gild—and perhaps especially, therefore, single women—might have eschewed the dinner because, despite the reduced charge, they were unable (or unwilling) to pay. Whether they were excluded by policy or poverty, single women were

---

[54]For the expenses of the dinner in 1420/21 see GL MS. 5440, fols. 57v–58v. In 1431 Porlond's notes suggest that the dinner was held on the day of annual accounting (see fol. 173v). In the sixteenth century the Brewers regularly held their elections at an annual dinner (see Rappaport, *Worlds*, pp. 228–29). For seating in different rooms see Unwin, *Gilds and Companies*, p. 196.

[55]Two women were nonpaying guests; one woman had her payment pardoned; one woman paid with her husband 16*d.*; two women paid 12*d.* The men who paid 12*d.* were not of especially low status within the gild; e.g., John Riche and John Serle were full quarterage-paying members of the gild, but, unlike most men, they paid only 1*s.* each for the dinner.

largely absent from this annual celebration of the gild, and wives attended in quite reduced numbers.[56]

As members of the gild, women also contributed to the exceptional tax of 1419/20, the *taxacio voluntaria* through which the gild raised money for its fight against Richard Whittington. Seven women offered sums independently and two other women paid indirectly through their husbands. Indeed, Agnes Bugge, through her husband Stephen (who was not a member of the gild), offered by far the largest sum collected in the levy (20*s.*). Nevertheless, women failed to hold their own in this special collection. First, women were much less likely than men to contribute at all to the tax. Of the 18 women who were independent members of the gild in that year, only four (22 per cent) contributed to the *taxacio voluntaria*, a rate far below the general level of participation (overall, 55 per cent of members gave additional monies to the special fund).[57] Five other women who were not members of the gild contributed to the tax, but overall female contributors to the tax were far outnumbered by men (nine women versus 146 men, or 6 per cent). Second, female contributors—with the exception of the two wives who contributed through their husbands—tended to offer much smaller sums than men. Most single women contributed less than 2*s.*; most men contributed more than 2*s.* Of the almost

[56]Of the 160 households represented in the quarterage list for 1420/21, 73 had representatives at the dinner (46 per cent). Of the 18 women who paid single quarterage in this year, two attended the dinner alone and a third attended with her husband. The other women who attended the banquet alone were two guests, one new widow, and one wife who attended without her husband. The tendency of poorer gild members to avoid the dinner can be seen by comparing the dinner list to those contributing to the *taxacio voluntaria*. Only one-third of those paying less than 3*s.* to this tax attended the dinner, whereas three-quarters of those paying 10*s.* or more attended.

[57]Among these four women, moreover, were two—Agnes Bugge and Idonia Hatton—who contributed to the fund only indirectly (via their husbands).

£32 raised in the levy, women directly offered only 24*s.*[58]

The third and final tier of gild life—participation in gild politics—seems to have been entirely closed to female members. Through most of the 1420s, the gild was governed by four masters who remained in power for two-year terms; in 1429 the term was shifted to a single year in order (among other rationales) to allow younger members to enjoy the honors and benefits of mastership. Yet, although the gild sought by this change to open office to as many able members as possible, only men were judged able; no woman ever served as a master of the gild. Moreover, women seem not to have participated in general decisions about gild life and policy. In its 1388 description of practices, the Brewers' fraternity framed ordinances in masculine terms only, that is, "the brothers agree and ordain. . . ."[59] The political disability of women in this specific case is scarcely surprising, and since gild office was generally reserved for only the most successful men, many men as well as women never achieved mastership. But men could at least aspire to gild office and know that, if they were clever, judicious, and lucky, they

[58]In 1419/20, 18 women joined the gild as independent members; three were married. The husbands of two of these women contributed to the tax; the husbands of Idonia Hatton and Agnes Bugge, although not members of the fraternity, contributed to the tax and paid unusually large sums (Hatton's husband, Roger Swanfield—quite likely an active brewer, despite his avoidance of quarterage payments—paid 6*s.*8*d.*; Stephen Bugge, a draper, contributed the largest sum collected, 20*s.*) Although these women were independent members of the gild and perhaps ran brewing businesses that were fairly separate from the concerns of their husbands, obviously neither was a single woman. Of the seven women who paid the tax directly (including two female members of the gild and five women who did not pay quarterage in 1419/20), the sums paid were 6*s.*8*d.*, 5*s.*, 5*s.*, 2*s.*, 2*s.*, 1*s.*8*d.*, and 1*s.*8*d.* Only one of these women—Alice Hercy, who contributed 5*s.*—was married. The collection as a whole was distributed as follows: 11 persons (7 per cent) paid between 10*s.* and 20*s.*, 26 persons (17 per cent) paid 6*s.*8*d.* or 8*s.*, 58 persons (37 per cent) paid between 3*s.* and 5*s.*, and 60 persons (39 per cent) paid less than 3*s.* (58 of these paid 2*s.* or less).

[59]See PRO C47/42/206.

might achieve their aspirations. Men could also at least participate in the general decisions of gild life. For women such possibilities were impossible. Women joined the gild and supported it with the same quarterages as were paid by men, but they were always part of the governed, never part of the governing.[60]

Women also did not attend the "power event" of the gild year, the annual breakfast. Porlond noted that the breakfast held on 20 May 1421 was a "jantaculum nobilioribus artis predicte," and his list of those who attended entirely bears out this description; only an elite subset of the membership attended the gild breakfast. Of the 40 men breakfasting together on 20 May (another 12 were invited but failed to attend), many were past, current, or future officers in the gild; many were involved in the lucrative ale trade with the Crown; most wore the more prestigious gowned livery; and many contributed quite substantial sums to the *taxacio voluntaria* of 1419/20. While they breakfasted, these men conducted some gild business—adjudicating quarrels, dispensing alms, reviewing accounts, appointing clerks, and the like. In return, they seem to have feasted at the expense of the gild, and feasted very well. The two-course breakfast included veal, geese, and capons, and its expenses totaled 64*s.*7*d.* Most members of the gild were excluded from this opulent and free feast, but the only group consistently excluded were women. Among men attending the breakfast in 1421 were some who wore only the lesser hood of the Brewers' livery, some who ran only modest brewhouses, and some who had not even paid quarterage in that year to the gild. In other words, some male brewers of modest status and marginal attachment to the gild attended the breakfast, but no

[60]For the general exclusion of women from political activity in the Middle Ages see Mary C. Erler and Maryanne Kowaleski, eds., *Women and Power in the Middle Ages* (Athens, Ga., 1988).

female brewer—no matter how successful in trade—joined the feast.[61] Idonia Hatton, for example, was a long-standing member of the gild and with her husband, Roger Swanfield, managed a very successful brewhouse, but she did not attend the breakfast; instead, her husband—who would not join the gild until four years later—feasted with 39 other men.

William Porlond's detailed records about gild affairs between 1419 and 1421—who gained civic enfranchisement through the gild and then wore the liveries of hood and gown; who paid quarterage to the gild, feasted at the gild dinner and contributed to the *taxacio voluntaria*; who held office and attended the elite annual breakfast—offer a remarkably clear picture of life in a late medieval gild. The place of women in the brewing trade was certainly exceptional, for, unlike other gilds, the Brewers' gild admitted women in large numbers. Yet women were not full members of the gild. In part, women seem to have been excluded from certain functions, such as admission to the freedom or feasting at the annual breakfast. In part, however, women also seem to have failed to distinguish themselves as enthusiastic members of the gild, for they attended the annual dinner less frequently than men and they responded to the special call of the *taxacio voluntaria* less readily than men. These two trends undoubtedly complemented each other, as women, offered only a partial membership in the gild, failed to support it as fully as men (a failure that probably seemed to justify their lesser status as partial members).

Women's place within the Brewers' gild of early fifteenth-century London, then, was special in two ways. On the one hand, the very presence of large numbers of female members marks the Brewers' gild as an exceptional organization among

[61]At some later breakfasts or dinners of this sort, masters' wives were included in the guest list—clearly an honorific exception to the general exclusion of women.

the many gilds of late medieval London. On the other hand, women's activities in the gild were quite different from those of most men: women were excluded from some aspects of gild life, and they participated in reduced numbers in others. In terms of the day-to-day life of the gild, women were in the gild but not full participants. This ambivalent place for women within the Brewers' gild of early fifteenth-century London seems to reflect the general place of women in the brewing trade of the City. Women had once so dominated brewing in London that civic ordinances—from the thirteenth century through the mid-fourteenth century—sometimes specified brewers using exclusively feminine terms.[62] By the early fifteenth century, however, the brewing trade was thoroughly mixed, pursued by men as well as women. In many cases, as is suggested by the prevalence of joint gild memberships by married couples, men and women shared the trade within a conjugal household, with a husband and wife together managing a brewhouse. In other cases, men and women who were not married to one another either worked together or competed outright in the ale market. Some women worked as hucksters for male brewers, and some female brewers competed for customers with brewhouses run either by men or by married couples. Yet, whether they were working in the trade as married women or single women, women worked under certain disadvantages.

For married women the disadvantage was less economic than perceptual. Married women, either working with their husbands or working at brewing as a by-trade, often reaped considerable profits from the ale market. The economic clout of

---

[62]For examples see *CLB* A, p. 216, and CLRO, Letter Book A, fol. 129v (1277); Riley, *Munimenta Gildhallae Londoniensis*, 1: *Liber albus* (1859), p. 355 (1283); *CLB* F, p. 178, and CLRO, Letter Book F, fol. 150v (1348); *CLB* G, p. 4, and CLRO, Letter Book G, fol. 2v (ca. 1352).

married women in the brewing trade is particularly evident in their contributions to the *taxacio voluntaria*. Of the three wives noted as paying independent quarterage in 1419/20, two contributed to this levy (albeit through their husbands, at least as rendered by Porlond in his listing), and they contributed quite large sums. Stephen Bugge, the husband of gild member Agnes Bugge, offered the largest contribution of all (20*s.*), and Roger Swanfield, husband of gild member Idonia Hatton, paid a quite respectable 6*s.*8*d.* Of the 59 married couples in the gild, an exceptionally high number (39, or 66 per cent) contributed to the tax, and they offered exceptionally generous sums. These patterns of contribution to the *taxacio voluntaria* indicate that married women—pursuing brewing as a by-trade or brewing in co-operation with their husbands—were often quite successful at their work. Indeed, some were so successful that they were able to break into the profitable trade in ale with the Crown; wives were actively involved in brewing in at least 19 of the 24 brewing concerns to which the Crown owed money in 1420–22.[63] In other words, at least about four of every five brewhouses involved in the lucrative royal trade in ale were managed, at least in part, by a married woman.

What is especially striking about the success of married women in the brewing trade is that many of them seem to have worked quite independently of their husbands. Their success, in other words, might have been enhanced by the financial and

---

[63]Although only about one-quarter of contributors to the *taxacio voluntaria* offered 6*s.*8*d.* or more, half of all married couples did so. In the lists of creditors of the Crown only men are named, but 19 of these 24 men had wives who were members of the gild. It is, of course, quite possible that wives of the other five men were also involved in brewing, despite their failure to join the gild. Thirty-two debts by the Crown are noted overall, but eight men appear in both years; hence, 24 households. Married couples were also particularly prominent among the handful of brewers wealthy enough to be assessed in the 1412 subsidy of property-holders in the City (12 of 18).

social assistance of their husbands, but it was not necessarily a result of the direct day-by-day involvement of husbands in the trade. Agnes Bugge's husband, Stephen, might have contributed on her behalf to the *taxacio voluntaria*, but he worked in another trade altogether—he was a draper. Their arrangement was not unusual; men in at least 15 per cent of the households covered by this analysis were involved in other trades, and many of the women in these households must have been primarily responsible for the brewing undertaken therein.[64]

Yet, although married women were often quite successful in brewing, their public presence as brewers was somewhat restricted. To be sure, married women enjoyed a public presence in brewing—as members of the gild—that was itself quite unusual, but in other aspects of brewing, husbands often acted alone on behalf of themselves and their wives (or even on behalf of their wives alone). Hence, only men are noted as creditors of the Crown in the lists of 1420/21 and 1421/22, despite the fact that most of these men belonged to the gild jointly with their wives. Even Roger Swanfield (who was not a member of the gild in these years) is noted as a creditor of the Crown instead of his wife, Idonia Hatton (who was in the gild). Hence, both Roger Swanfield and Stephen Bugge—not their wives—contributed to the *taxacio voluntaria* of 1419/20. Hence, the City list of brewers compiled in that year apparently ignored all wives, assigning to their husbands (including, again, Roger Swanfield and Stephen Bugge) public liability for the conformity to City rules of their family brewhouses (or brewhouses run by their wives as a by-trade). Hence, husbands alone participated in gild breakfasts and wore gild livery—both extremely important public expressions of corporate solidarity. Indeed, some men *not*

[64]For Stephen Bugge's work as a draper see n. 38 above. For an explanation of the 15 per cent figure see n. 13 above.

members of the gild participated in these activities: in 1420/21, Idonia Hatton paid quarterage on her own, but it was her husband who attended the gild breakfast and gild dinner, and her husband who wore the livery of the gild. In short, the trend was towards a sort of "shadow economy" within the brewing industry; married women increasingly worked in the shadow of the public presence of their husbands, who—whether they worked in the trade or not—personified in public the brewer in the household.

This tendency to subsume the wife's brewing into the person of her husband can be explained by legal and practical considerations. Because the City, in compiling its list in 1419/20, sought to make brewers liable for future infractions, it focused upon the responsible person under the law—the husband. Because the gild sought to enhance its place within civic hierarchies, it celebrated its male membership in public displays and public processions. And because both City and gild blamed the disruptions that were an inevitable offshoot of the drink trade upon women (who were seen as encouraging—in an Eve-like fashion—drunkenness, vice, and gaming), both perhaps sought a brewing trade controlled solely by well-organized, somber men.[65] Nevertheless, this tendency to privatize brewing by wives would become even stronger over the course of the fifteenth century. By 1500/01 wives had become so much a part of the shadows of the brewing industry that they had even ceased to belong to the gild; in that year only 13 women (most, perhaps all, widows) joined the gild—out of a total membership of 191.[66] Yet wives continued to brew. As late as 1544, Richard

---

[65]I have elaborated more fully upon this point in "Misogyny, Popular Culture, and Women's Work," *History Workshop Journal* 31 (1991): 166–88. For a London example of the tendency to associate disorder in the trade with women see the orders of 1382 in *CLB* H, p. 184, and CLRO, Letter Book H, fol. 144v.

[66]GL MS. 5442, vol. 1 (see accounts rendered in Mar. 1501/02).

Pickering, a member of the Brewers' Company, told the mayor and aldermen that he could not answer their inquiry about the yields of brewing because "he commytteth the hole charge therof to his wyfe." His wife was not a member of the gild.[67]

For single women the disadvantage was less perceptual than economic. Single women did not work in the shadows of husbands' public personification of "the brewer," but they seem to have profited considerably less from brewing than did most people in the trade. Unlike married women (and male members of the gild), only a few single women contributed to the *taxacio voluntaria*, and they usually contributed only a few shillings. Unlike married women (and male members of the gild), single women did not profit from the lucrative ale trade with the Crown. And unlike married women (and male members of the gild), single women remained in the gild for quite short periods of time—often only a year or two. Of the 13 single women who paid their own quarterage in 1418/19, only five (38 per cent) were still members of the gild in 1425; almost two-thirds of the men were still members. The dropout rate was particularly high for never-married women. Of the four such women in the 1418/19 quarterage, only one (Emma Canon) remained in the gild seven years later. William Porlond's careful records of the Brewers' gild ca. 1420 show quite clearly that single women in brewing—never-married, widowed, or abandoned—often worked on the very margins of the trade.[68]

---

[67]CLRO, Repertory 11, fols. 120–121. After Richard Pickering's death his widow paid quarterage for one year to the gild (GL MS. 5445/1).

[68]Only one woman of the 17 (Margaret Settingborn) is known to have died between 1418 and 1425. For the best possible comparison I looked only at the dropout rate of men who had independent memberships in 1418/19: 54 of these 81 men were still in the gild seven years later (67 per cent). The rate was somewhat lower but still relatively high for those independent male members in 1418/19 who did *not* bring their wives into the gild by 1425; 25 of 44 were still active at that time (57 per cent).

Porlond's records, moreover, only tell us about those single women who were among the most successful of their kind—that is, single women who joined the gild. Many women worked in the brewing trade, as either brewers of ale or sellers of ale (or both), at levels that escaped both gild and civic supervision. Some single women who worked as brewers avoided gild membership. For example, in the City list of brewers compiled in 1419/20, most women named therein had no known contact with the gild.[69] For another example, five of the seven women who independently contributed small sums to the *taxacio voluntaria* had no formal association with the gild.[70] Both of these sources suggest that large numbers of women brewed (and, hence, either were listed by the City or found it in their interest to contribute to the *taxacio voluntaria*) but somehow eschewed (or possibly were denied) association with the gild. Other single women (and some wives, as well) huckstered ale, suffering gild supervision but ineligible for gild membership. For example, in a list of those fined by the gild for selling ale by false measures in 1420/21, nearly half were women. Most seem to have been unmarried or widowed, and none was associated with the gild.[71] We can, of course, catch only glimpses of these women in our records (since so much of our information was generated by precisely the sorts of supervision these women evaded). But the glimpses are quite telling. As part of another sort of "shadow economy" of brewing, these women

[69]Of the 21 women in the City list of brewers, nine (43 per cent) had some connection to the gild (e.g., paid quarterage, attended dinner, contributed to the *taxacio voluntaria*). Of 268 men, 202 (75 per cent) had such gild connections.

[70]Of the 148 men who contributed to the *taxacio voluntaria* only 48 had no other known contact with the gild.

[71]Of the 58 persons listed, the sex of 56 is clear. Of these 56, 26 were women (46 per cent). Of these 26 women, eight were named as wives, two as widows. None of the women paid quarterage to the gild or had other known connections. Of the 30 men listed for false measures, 10 had further connections with the gild.

worked in the humblest parts of the industry; they largely escaped supervision and its expenses, but their operations were necessarily small and their profits probably were low.[72]

In early fifteenth-century London, brewing still offered women unusual opportunities. Unlike other trades, brewing was regulated by a gild that included women as well as men. And unlike other trades, brewing offered women, especially single women, a particularly good opportunity for independent work. But brewing was becoming much like other trades in its treatment of women. In terms of the gild, women were excluded from crucial gild activities and marginalized in others. In terms of the ale market, the work of wives was largely subsumed into the public personalities of their husbands, and the work of widows and spinsters was largely pushed to the least profitable margins of the trade. Women and men often worked together in the brewing trade, but insofar as they competed, they competed on unequal terms.

The story of women in the brewing trade of late medieval London offers important cautions about the interpretation of women's work in the Middle Ages. At first glance, William Porlond's book offers a very "upbeat" tale about women in the brewing trade, for his quarterage lists tell us that one of every three members of the Brewers' gild was a woman. Yet in this case, membership did not have its privileges: women were in the gild but not a full part of it. And since the Brewers' gild

[72]Although single women seem to have worked at the very bottom of the brewing trade in late medieval London, their relatively humble place in the ale market was an important economic resource. Within the context of the economic opportunities available to women in medieval London, commercial brewing—even at its lowest levels—was an important resource for women. We must not forget that of the dozens of London gilds in this period, only the Brewers' gild accommodated women in large numbers, much less admitted single women as independent members. Single women who ran brewhouses might have been among the most modest members of the gild, but at least they were in a gild.

represents a *best* case—a case in which women were present in a gild and its trade in large numbers—the place of women in other gilds must only have been worse. The full tale told by William Porlond's book suggests that gilds even in the Middle Ages were fundamentally associations of men.[73]

At first glance, the story of women in London's brewing trade also seems to be a tale of decline, as women slowly lost control of the ale market to men. Yet this is really more a story of change in the brewing trade than of decline in women's work status. In 1300, when women's control of the ale market was more secure, the brewing trade was relatively undistinguished, unprofitable, and unprofessionalized. At that time female brewers worked in a low-status, unprofessionalized, and low-profit trade. By 1400, when men were more active in the trade, it was much more respected, more profitable, and more professionalized. Women, however, still worked in the sectors of the trade that were lowest in status, profit, and professionalization. Between 1300 and 1400 women did not lose their control over a high-status occupation. Instead, the trade slowly gained in status—more to the profit of men than to the profit of women.

[73]Hence, this case study provides detailed evidence to confirm the marginality of women in medieval gilds, as argued in Maryanne Kowaleski and Judith Bennett, "Crafts, Gilds, and Women in the Middle Ages: Fifty Years after Marian K. Dale," *Signs: A Journal of Women in Culture and Society* 14/2 (1989): 474–88.

Appendix

THE MAIN SOURCES

1. Quarterage Lists. These lists identify all persons who paid annual dues or quarterage in a given year. At the end of some quarterage lists, William Porlond included additional lists naming those who paid late, those in arrears, those who died during the year, etc. For example, the quarterage information for 1420/21 begins with a list of 160 persons or married couples paying quarterage. This main list is followed by lists of (a) eight persons who died during the year and did not pay quarterage, (b) two persons who did not pay quarterage because of poverty, (c) three persons or married couples who did not pay "causa denillacionis," (d) eight persons who refused to pay quarterage, (e) 10 persons who paid quarterage late, (f) 12 spouses who entered the gild during the year, (g) three persons who paid arrears on past quarterages, and (h) two persons who owed arrears for past quarterages. I have used the data included in these additional lists in reconstructing the personal histories of gild members, but for two reasons, I have *not* included the persons named in these additional lists in my quarterage counts for each year. First, all quarterage lists did not include these additional lists; hence, including the information for some years and not others would have skewed secular trends. Second, most of the persons named as current gild members in the additional lists also appear in the main quarterage lists (e.g., most of the spouses named in the additional lists as newly entering the gild were also named as quarterage payers in the main list). In other words, most of the information about current members contained in these additional lists is redundant.

The quarterage lists are as follows:

1418/19 (fols. 2–4)
1419/20 (fols. 47–49v)
1420/21 (fols. 63v–64v)
1421/22 (fols. 67v–69)
1422/23 (fols. 82–83v)
1423/24 (fols. 115v–117v)
1424/25 (fols. 131–133)

2. *Taxacio Voluntaria, 1419/20.* This list appears on fols. 25–26. A short opening paragraph explains that it lists those who contributed money towards an effort to modify the orders of the Common Council made against the brewers during the mayoralty of Richard Whittington.

3. *Gild Breakfast, 1421.* On fol. 51, William Porlond began to note details of a breakfast held on 20 May in the mayoralty of William Cambridge. He noted the menu and various expenses, and on fol. 51v he listed names of (a) 38 brewers attending the breakfast, (b) 12 persons invited to the breakfast who did not come, and (c) two persons who came to the breakfast uninvited. I have included all these persons in my count of 52 persons attending or invited to the breakfast.

4. *Gild Dinner, 1421.* On fol. 59–59v, William Porlond listed those involved in the dinner held in "anno ix" (1420/21). He gave three lists, as follows: (a) a long list of "brothers and sisters" attending the dinner and sums paid by them (101 persons or married couples), (b) a list of 18 persons or married couples who attended without contributing to the dinner, and (c) a list of 14 persons "de vestitu Braciatorum & non de fraternitate" who attended the dinner (these 14 persons appear with payments appended in the first, longer list).

5. *Livery List, 1420/21.* On fols. 53–56, William Porlond listed expenses incurred in securing liveries for the gild during the mayoralty of William Cambridge. On fol. 53 he related the costs of large purchases of cloth, and beginning on fol. 53v he detailed the disbursement of these cloths (for either "gownes" or "chaperons") to individual members and the sums they paid.

6. *Royal Brewers, 1420/21 and 1421/22.* On fols. 27–27v and 46–46v, William Porlond copied out the accounts of men responsible for receiving from the Exchequer monies to pay debts owed to London brewers in 8 and 9 Henry V. The accounts specify gross sums collected and disbursed, as well as the individual accounts of specific brewers (i.e., total value of ale sold, total value of sums received to date, total value of sums still outstanding).

7. Masters' Accounts, 1419–21. On fols. 60–61v appear the accounts of Thomas Grene, Robert Hylton, John Piken, and Robert Carpenter, masters of the Brewers' gild for two full years from All Saints Day, 7 Henry V. The accounts include receipts from men who paid for admission "ad libertatem" and for entry into the fraternity.

8. City List of Brewers, 1419/20. This list was compiled during the mayoralty of Richard Whittington and appended to an order reviving an old ordinance about brewers' vessels and setting new prices for ale in the city. The severity of the new order is suggested by a statement that the ordinance might be amended in the future if it proved too rigorous. I have relied upon the listing accurately edited by Sharpe in *CLB* I, pp. 233–37.

"TO CATCH A THIEF" IN JACOBEAN LONDON

Alexandra F. Johnston

Robert Tittler[1]

Thanks to the vast, rich, and familiar literature on the subject, the metropolis of London has long been known as a haven for criminals and others who came from elsewhere to escape some aspects of their earlier lives. In the succinct description of the late Professor F. J. Fisher, it was "the obvious Mecca for the ambitious and the footloose, . . . by far the most promising milieu for the thief, the prostitute and the professional beggar,"[2] and when the Privy Council wrote in 1598 to the Justices of the Peace of Middlesex, urging them to deal with people in their suburban jurisdiction who let rooms to "base people, and to lewd persons that do keep evil rule, and harbour thieves, rogues and vagabonds," its members were merely voicing the conventional sentiments of the "better sort" of the day.[3] The very size of the metropolis did much to facilitate this problematical social function. At roughly 200,000 people at the turn of the seventeenth century and continuing to

---

[1]We are grateful for the research assistance of Mr. Tim Wales.

[2]"The Growth of London," orig. pub. in E. W. Ives, ed., *The English Revolution, 1600–1660* (London, 1968), repr. in F. J. Fisher, *London and the English Economy, 1500–1700*, ed. P. J. Corfield and N. B. Harte (London, 1990), p. 175. See also Fisher, "London as an 'Engine of Economic Growth'," repr. in ibid., pp. 185–98.

[3]Quoted in A. L. Beier, "Social Problems of Elizabethan London," *Journal of Interdisciplinary History* 9/2 (1978): 209.

grow at an astonishing rate, London was by far the largest urban area in the British Isles and close to the top of the population scale of the European continent.[4]

Despite this vivid reputation for harboring the footloose, the ambitious, and the undesirable, revisionist views of London society have come to emphasize the fundamental stability of the metropolis and the efficacy of its governing authorities in dealing with social problems. The work of Valerie Pearl, Steve Rappaport, and Ian Archer has described the extent to which the jurisdiction of those authorities reached right down to the level of the parish and ward. Indeed, they convey the distinct impression that officials responsible for maintaining law and order were so numerous, widespread, and vigilant in neighborhoods in which they themselves resided, that any untoward behavior must quickly have come to their attention.[5] Though dealing only with London within the walls, Rappaport, for example, extended his description of the forces of law and order to include the livery companies, whose jurisdiction over both their members and that proportion of London males who dwelt within the walls seemed to him to have a powerfully positive effect on maintaining law and order.[6]

---

[4]Roger Finlay and Beatrice R. Shearer, "Population Growth and Suburban Expansion," in A. L. Beier and Roger Finlay, eds., *London 1500–1700: The Making of the Metropolis* (London, 1986), p. 49, Table 5, and Beier and Finlay's "Introduction," ibid., Fig. 1, p. 3. Only Naples, Paris, and Constantinople were more populous at that time.

[5]See esp. Pearl, "Change and Stability in Seventeenth-Century London," *London Journal* 5/1 (May 1979): 3–34, and eadem, "Social Policy in Early Modern London," in Hugh Lloyd-Jones, V. Pearl, and Blair Worden, eds., *History & Imagination: Essays in Honour of H. R. Trevor-Roper* (London, 1981); Rappaport, "Social Structure and Mobility in Sixteenth-Century London," pt. 1, *London Journal* 9/2 (1983): 107–35, and pt. 2, *London Journal* 10/2 (1984): 107–34; idem, *Worlds within Worlds: Structures of Life in Sixteenth-Century London* (Cambridge, 1989), passim; Archer, *The Pursuit of Stability: Social Relations in Elizabethan London* (Cambridge, 1991).

[6]Rappaport, *Worlds*, esp. chs. 6–7.

However eloquently and thoroughly this revisionist case has been stated, controversy remains regarding the stability of London society and the efficacy of its administrative provisions for maintaining law and order. Some effort has already been made to document the extent of riot and disorder during this same period. Building on the work of Keith Lindley, Roger B. Manning in particular has counted 96 instances of insurrection, riot, and unlawful assembly in London between Evil May Day, 1517, and the calling of the Long Parliament, 35 of those disorders coming in the last two decades of Elizabeth's reign. This pattern seems to have continued thereafter, for Lindley counted 24 Shrove Tuesday riots alone between 1603 and 1641, most of them in the suburbs.[7] All of this considered, it will take a good deal more work on particular cases before we can be sure of the somewhat theoretical model put forth by Pearl and Rappaport.

One small step in this direction may be represented by a consideration of the adventures of Raphe Handes,[8] the agent of Sir Thomas Temple,[9] of Burton Dasset, Warwickshire, sent by

---

[7]Lindley, "Riot Prevention and Control in Early Stuart London," *Transactions of the Royal Historical Society*, 5th ser., 33 (1983): 109–26; Manning, *Village Revolts: Social Protest and Popular Disturbances in England, 1509–1640* (Oxford, 1988), ch. 8.

[8]Handes served as both notary and steward to the Temple family from at least 1597 until ca. 1628. He was probably related to Edward Handes of Yardley, Worcs., whose wife, Mary, was the daughter of John Woodward of Avon Dassett, next to Temple's seat at Burton Dassett. He is likely to have been of yeoman or minor gentry stock from the West Midlands (Temple Papers, Huntingdon Library MS. STTF, Boxes 4–10, passim; John Fetherston, ed., *The Visitation of the County of Warwick in the Year 1619*, Harleian Society, vol. 12 [1877]: 227).

[9]Temple (1567–1637), son of John Temple of Burton Dassett, Warwicks., came from an old Warwicks. family. He was educated at Oxford and Lincoln's Inn and married Hester, daughter of Miles Sandys of Latimer, Bucks., who seems to have secured for Temple a seat in Parliament for Andover, Hants., in 1589. Knighted in 1603, he would be made baronet in 1611 and serve as sheriff of Oxfordshire in 1606–07, Bucks. in 1616–17, and Warwicks., 1620–21 (P. W. Hasler, ed., *The House of Commons, 1558–1603*, vol. 3, History of Parliament Trust [London, 1981], p. 481).

his master in December 1605 to track down three forgers and cozeners who hoped to find refuge in the size and anonymity of London. Let it be said at once that the activities of forgers and cozeners are not what most scholars who have written on order and disorder in London have had in mind. Pearl, Rappaport, Archer, Manning, and the rest have been much more concerned with large-scale and socially or economically derived unrest, riot, and the like than the more traditional and even relatively genteel forms of criminal behavior. But the difficulties of dealing with crime, as we hope to show, seem also to exemplify the difficulties of dealing with social and political unrest. Thus, they provide some justification for proceeding with the picaresque tale at hand.

This colorful story has come to light among the Temple Papers now in the Stowe Collection held at the Henry E. Huntington Library: "R. H. His accompt to his m[aste]r S[ir] Tho[mas] Temple, knight."[10] As its title would imply, this is a detailed expense account submitted by Handes to Temple, covering the approximate period of 10 weeks in which the former undertook to track down his quarry. The text seems so richly detailed with names, places, and circumstances that it has seemed desirable to publish it in an Appendix, below.

Our first objective in the pages that follow will be to present Handes's quest as a commentary on the difficulties of apprehending criminal suspects in the vastness and density of greater London, and some of the means that were employed in that task. This is especially interesting in the London setting, for

---

[10]Henry E. Huntington Library, STTF, Box 6 (1605–06), unnumbered. Three separate paper accounts prepared by Handes for Temple are in this box. The first covers 29 Nov. 1605 to Handes's departure for London on 29 Dec. The second is the account of his adventures that serves as the basis of this study and is reproduced in the Appendix below. The third, covering the same period, is the regular estate account plus a summary statement of the expenses incurred "in pursuite of Coseners."

what little of scholarly worth that has been written about apprehension has derived either from the experience of particular village or parish communities in the countryside or from London at a later time.[11] In that rather more intimate former milieu, the knowledge of the suspect by the community seems to have been an important factor in the willingness of the general population, and even of the law enforcement officials themselves, to help in his apprehension. In London, obviously far less intimate and not in the usual sense of the term a single community at all, such considerations may not have applied to the same extent.

Second, the case affords us an understanding of two distinct criminal types, both undoubtedly typical of that time and locale, who were most likely to slip through the netting of gild or other administrative structures so well described by, for instance, Pearl, Rappaport, and Archer. Both types help to justify the judgment of Fisher and others on one of the more dubious roles of the great metropolis.

Third, the details of Handes's chase itself, full of references to places and people connected with the shadier parts of London society, add both color and detail to the functions of sheltering the ne'er-do-wells of Fisher's verdict.

---

[11]See, e.g., Joan R. Kent, *The English Village Constable, 1580–1642: A Social and Administrative Study* (Oxford, 1986), esp. chs. 6, 7; Keith Wrightson, "Two Concepts of Order: Justices, Constables and Jurymen in Seventeenth-Century England," in John Brewer and John A. Styles, eds., *An Ungovernable People: The English and Their Law in the Seventeenth and Eighteenth Centuries* (New Brunswick, N.J., 1980), pp. 21–46; Cynthia B. Herrup, *The Common Peace: Participation and the Criminal Law in Seventeenth-Century England* (Cambridge, 1987), esp. pp. 73–78. For a slightly later period the literature on both England generally and London in particular is somewhat more complete: cf. J. M. Beattie, *Crime and the Courts in England, 1660–1800* (Princeton, 1986), esp. ch. 2; Douglas Hay and Francis G. Snyder, eds., *Policing and Prosecution in Britain, 1750–1850* (Oxford, 1989); and Robert B. Shoemaker, *Prosecution and Punishment: Petty Crime and the Law in London and Rural Middlesex, c. 1660–1725* (Cambridge, 1991).

The men who had bilked Temple and had thus become the objects of Handes's chase were Robert Swaddon (also known as Captain Roberts, Captain Swanne, and Webb),[12] John Selman (also known as Selby),[13] and William Matthews (also known as Wright and John Jones).[14] This trio had conspired to forge Temple's signature and seal in a ruse to extract money from a Master Thomas Farrington, a master vintner and prominent merchant of Broad Street, London.[15] Farrington had long been a business associate of Temple's, a fact evidently well known to the forgers.

The plot was rather complex. In order to get a copy of Temple's handwriting and seal, the plotters first forged a letter to Temple from his friend Sir Henry Baynton of "Bremble,"

---

[12]For Swaddon see below, pp. 248–51.

[13]It has been impossible to identify John Selman with certainty.

[14]It has also been difficult to identify Matthews for certain because of the multiplicity of namesakes, but a man by that name is otherwise identified with Robert Swaddon as a co-defendant in a Star Chamber case brought on the complaint of John Pettus, merchant and alderman of Norwich, in 1604 (see PRO STAC 8/228/4 and STAC 8/5/6). In the second of these cases Matthews is said to have used the aliases Jones and Wright (see the bill of complaint of 3 James I).

[15]Thomas Farrington (ca. 1550–1611), a merchant and vintner of Broad St., London, came up through the ranks of the Vintners' Company as freeman by apprenticeship (1575), warden (1598), and master (1605–06), the latter post being held at the time of the case at hand. He was also a Common Councillor of London for Broad St. (1596), a member of the Spanish Company, and a governor of Christ's Hospital (1599–1601). At his death he left his wife, Alice, and five children, two of whom had come to their majority. His estate was substantial, including assets of £1,019 8*s.ob.* against debts of £744 1*s.*10*d.* but with an additional £2,382 16*s.*3*d.* in debts owed to him, much of which sum was received by his estate within ca. three years of his death (R. M. Benbow, "Index to London Citizens, c. 1550–1603," unpub. typescript held at the Corporation of London Record Office (CLRO), p. 239 and n. 392); Anne Crawford, *A History of the Vintners' Company* (London, 1977), p. 286; Frank F. Foster, *The Politics of Stability: A Portrait of the Rulers in Elizabethan London*, Royal Historical Society (1977): 169; J. Pauline Croft, ed., *The Spanish Company*, London Record Society, vol. 9 (1973): p. 20 and n. 136; Testamentary Records, Parish of St. Peter le Poer, Guildhall Library (GL) MS no. 9168/16, fols. 126v, 329r, 414r.

Wiltshire,[16] and retrieved Temple's reply, suitably signed and sealed. They used this reply as a model from which to forge an obligation in Temple's name for money to be borrowed from Farrington. On the feast day of St. Thomas the Apostle, 21 December 1605, Farrington released what he took to be a "loan" of £120 to the forgers, obviously posing as Temple's associates.

It cannot have taken Temple long to uncover the ruse, for he sent Handes off to find the three forgers but eight days later. Thus began a chase of some two-and-a-half months from Warwickshire to London and its environs, through the worst of winter weather. As the document attests, it took Handes through the run of London's inns, alehouses, stables, bowling alleys, gaming houses, and tenements; it brought him into contact with the shadier parts of London and with the officials of city and nation. His experiences are both colorful and instructive.

The usual means of instigating a prosecution of a suspected criminal was for the victim to swear out a written warrant before a JP, who would then mandate the constable to engage in the chase. Yet, in reality, the constable's role seems largely to have been relegated to searching for missing goods within the jurisdiction of his parish or to bringing in an apprehended suspect for questioning. The real business of apprehending the alleged perpetrator still fell almost wholly on the shoulders of the victim. At least in the countryside, a great deal depended as well on the co-operation of members of the community, who

---

[16]Sir Henry Baynton, of "Bremble" (probably Bromham, near Calne, though possibly Bremhill, near Chippenham), Wilts., ca. 1571–1616, second son of Edward Baynton, attended Lincoln's Inn (1588–), married Lucy, daughter of Sir John Danvers of Dauntsey, and had one son and one daughter. He served as MP for Chippenham (1589), possibly for Devizes (1593, 1604), and as Knight of the Shire for Wilts. (1597). He was knighted in 1601, served as JP for Wilts. by 1594, as sheriff in 1601–02. He owned property in Calne, Devizes, and Chippenham and remained active in Wiltshire affairs all his life.

were expected to come forth with information and even actively to help in the chase and apprehension: though thought of as a medieval system, remnants of the "hue and cry" persisted well into the period at hand. Yet this worked far less effectively in the great metropolis of London, where ties among neighbors and the sense of community itself were (to say the least) far less vivid, and it worked hardly at all in London's suburbs.[17]

The difficulty of applying this rurally conceived model to the case of Handes's trio of suspects is that they were thought to have moved around continually in the large and very populous environs of the metropolis, continually leaving and entering different jurisdictions and neighborhoods. In this they may have been typical even of the majority of London's population, and certainly of those who were poor and/or newly arrived. Not only did this make it very difficult to know where warrants might best be sued but also it undermined much of the expectation of community support. Though, as we will see, Handes did follow the prescribed method of sueing warrants before JPs and did receive some help from constables and similar petty officials as well as from some members of the numerous communities involved, the very nature of the metropolis made his quest that much more difficult. From the felon's perspective, of course, that was the whole idea.

As his expense account makes clear,[18] Handes began his quest from Temple's seat in Warwickshire, hoping at first to find those who had brought Sir Henry Baynton's letter to Temple. He received news of Selman—whose role in the ruse seems to have been outside London—as having passed through the village of Farnborough, in Warwickshire, and tracked him

---

[17]Herrup, *Common Peace*, pp. 69–70; Kent, *English Village Constable*, pp. 205–11; Beattie, *Crime and the Courts*, pp. 36–37.

[18]See Appendix below.

through there and then into Oxfordshire. He stayed over at Woodstock, riding through the snow to get there, and then to Oxford, where he had reason to believe Selman had stayed as well. From there the trail led east again, into the Buckinghamshire Chilterns, where criminals might make good time through the beech forest, by way of High Wycombe, and then by the first of January to Uxbridge in Middlesex and thence to London itself.

Proceeding like a true detective, Handes sought first to find stables where he might locate the horse that Selman used—"a white flea bitten jade with a short mane"—and also to canvas the seal makers to locate the craftsman who would have forged seals of Bainton and Temple. Along the way he received useful bits of information from an innkeeper and a hostler at The Bell on St. John Street, a carman on the Strand, and a number of other people.

One interesting but ultimately costly lead was the suggestion that a certain "Captain Pierson" may have been one of those for whom Handes was looking.[19] Shortly after the emergence of this suggestion and the subplot that it introduces, Handes was joined by a man called Pulman,[20] who appeared to remain steadfast in Handes's support even to his own peril. With Pulman as his guide through the labyrinthine world (and underworld) of London, Handes began to track down Pierson as well as the original trio. Additional tips and other co-operation came from Brookes, the oldest underkeeper of Newgate, the beadle of St. Sepulchre's Ward, diverse constables in specific

---

[19]"Captain" Thomas Pierson appears to have resided in St. James, Clerkenwell, in or near Cow Cross and to have been described variously (possibly illegitimately) as tailor, yeoman, or especially as a victualer, though as we will see below he was engaged in far more than these respectable occupations would suggest.

[20]"Pulman" proved to have been John Pulman, described below, n. 24 and pp. 245–48.

parishes and wards, and Israel, Lord Treasurer Sir Thomas Sackville's bailiff.

Although Handes stayed first at The Unicorn and eventually at other inns, he often took meals with Master Farrington, whose money had been deceitfully taken on the pretense of the loan to Temple. For his part, Farrington seems to have been entirely sympathetic with Temple, though he could simply have demanded repayment according to the terms of the forged obligation. This may suggest that when men of substance were bilked they closed ranks in the effort to locate the perpetrator, as well as taking steps to recover the sums involved. It may also have derived from the deference that a merchant, even a London merchant, still bore towards a knight. Thus Farrington, a man of wealth and influence in the City, also seems to have been supportive of the effort to catch the forgers, and we may presume that he used that influence in support of Handes's efforts.

To little avail. Handes remained remarkably steadfast throughout, making sorties during January and February to Islington, Tottenham, Ratliffe, Hounslow, Smithfield, Uxbridge, to the Black Bear in Holborn ("where divers gallants and captains came at midnight"), Westminster, Knightsbridge, Bermondsey (where he thought the suspects might have gone to the theater), down to Newington in Surrey, and back to Bishopsgate Street in London, where he himself spent time in The Green Dragon. Most of these areas, of course, were in the suburbs; they did not come under the jurisdiction of the City magistrates or Companies to the same extent as the City, and they were precisely the sort of places where criminals could be expected to thrive during this period.

Not only did Handes sue at several points in his chase for warrants from several Middlesex JPs (including Sir Henry Drewry and Sir Francis Goodwin) but also he sued for a warrant from the "Chief Justice" (presumably of the King's

Bench),[21] and, as already noted, he received further help from the bailiff of Lord Treasurer Sackville.

In time, Matthews was found and apprehended in Islington with the help of three constables there. He was then brought to arraignment before Justice Fowler and eventually taken to make his confession before the Recorder of London.

Handes and his men eventually found and took Pierson at Uxbridge, but not without cost: a battle ensued in which Pulman was apparently wounded and required the services of a surgeon. When Pierson surrendered, it seems to have been to Handes rather than to anyone in an official position, and it was Handes personally who kept him under guard at The Red Lion in Holborn while the Lord Chief Justice could be roused. Why Pierson was not handed over to a constable or to an official of the King's Bench, or placed in some lock-up or cell, remains uncertain. It is possible that after so vigorous a chase Handes feared the sly Pierson might have escaped anyone else's grasp but his own, or possibly Handes was unwilling to pay the fees that would almost certainly have been involved in arranging such custody.

The chase for Selman in London and for Swaddon, who seems to have been sought in Buckingham on Handes's way back to Warwickshire, takes up the last pages of the manuscript. There is nothing here to suggest that either one was captured. Despite the help of a Mr. Isard, bailiff of Middlesex, a woman described as Selman's "hostess," another, a Mistress Bradley, described as Swaddon's paramour, and a close watch on the home of a Mrs. Woodhouse, where Selman was thought to be a frequent visitor, he seems to have escaped Handes's grasp. As for Swaddon, Handes seems to have determined that

[21]The Chief Justice of the King's Bench at that time was Sir John Popham, who served until his death shortly thereafter.

he had fled again outside of London. When Handes left London for Warwickshire in mid-March, close to three months after he had begun his chase, he left a warrant for Swaddon's arrest with a Raphe Barnaby, presumably a constable or similar official, at Buckingham.

This, then, ends the story of Ralph Handes's chase of those who had bilked his master, as well as of the interesting Captain Pierson, who seems somehow to have gotten mixed up on the wrong end of the chase and who was the only major figure captured. From Handes's perspective it is not a story of success. And yet there was something more to the story than Handes recognized, and his adventures, witting and unwitting, prove interesting to us for a number of reasons that will become more apparent.

At this point, we pick up the story in the records of the Middlesex Sessions and other contemporary sources that shed more light on the characters involved. When we look further in this manner, three figures jump out at us as having considerable importance to our understanding not only of the events themselves and the whole issue of apprehension but especially of the types of men whom Handes sought to apprehend. These figures are Pulman and Pierson, fascinating representatives of the London underworld of the day, and Swaddon, a bigger fish by far.

As is well documented in the court records of Middlesex, Thomas Pierson was deeply involved in the world of petty criminals in and around Clerkenwell and appears to have worked with roughly equal frequency on both sides of the law. His name often appears in the Sessions Rolls for Middlesex, where he frequently stood as a surety for petty criminals of his acquaintance: those accused of being cutpurses, prostitutes, pickpockets, and small-time thieves. On at least one occasion he seems to have helped in the apprehension of one such suspect, "leading" him to gaol. On the other side of the law, he himself was variously accused of victualing without a license, petty theft, harboring rogues, burglary, housebreaking, and the like.[22] It is not at all impossible that he exacted a fee or some other compensation for standing surety to those whom he appeared to help, and his apparent apprehension of one petty miscreant may well have resulted from the refusal of the latter to extend such a gift. Practices such as these are well documented for the eighteenth century in London,[23] and there is considerable reason to think that Pierson may have been an early practitioner of such "arts."

Pulman appears to have engaged in similar activities, also on both sides of the law, but we find him in a much more prominent position on the side of the victims of crime and the authorities who prosecuted it. Indeed, it is clear that Pulman had the local reputation of being what was known more familiarly in the eighteenth century as a "thief-taker." This seems to have been how he came to the attention of Handes, and indeed we may infer from Handes's account that Pulman came well recommended for such skills. Handes requested from his master, Temple, funds for paying Pulman for his services, and thus obviously he was willing to reward Pulman for his help.

Handes's patronage aside, contemporary court records show Pulman's frequent involvement in bringing suspects before the authorities, along with such other activities as standing surety for still other suspects and himself being accused of a variety of petty crimes and misdemeanors.[24] Indeed, in a case before the

---

[22]Greater London Record Office (GLRO), William Le Hardy, ed., "Calendars of Sessions Rolls, Gaol Delivery and Sessions Registers" (typescript), vol. 1 (1607–08), pp. 58, 257, 279; vol. 2 (1608–09), pp. 13, 46, 134, 209; vol. 3 (1609–10), p. 219; vol. 4 (1610), p. 3.

[23]Beattie, *Crime and the Courts*, pp. 55–57.

[24]A total of 67 references to "John Pulman" have been found to date in the records of the Middlesex Sessions 1606–16, of which only 15 may conceivably refer to a namesake instead. He is described most often as John Pulman of St. Sepulchre's (or Newgate, St. Sepulchre's, or Cock Lane of the same parish), yeoman and/or

Middlesex Sessions in May 1609 he and a colleague, William Elder, are actually described as "Theifetakers" in the record.[25] This is an important indication that the professional thieftaker was already on the scene at the turn of the seventeenth century, well before he has been observed in most scholarly literature.[26] This is quite possibly the earliest recorded use of the term in English, as opposed to Scottish, records.

Pulman holds one more point of interest for us, and it certainly would have been of interest to Handes as well. In fact, the record repeatedly suggests that Pulman and Pierson were not to remain, *and perhaps never had been*, the adversaries of Handes's account. Instead, they prove to have been sometime neighbors in Clerkenwell and mutually supportive associates over a period extending from at least 1609 to 1611, a few years after Pulman was allegedly injured at Handes's side in the confrontation with Pierson and his men but possibly during that time as well.

On two occasions in that time span Pulman and Pierson stood together as sureties for third parties accused of petty

---

sometimes "horse corser," or as John Pulman of St. James, Clerkenwell, yeoman. But as the John Pulman references at both the St. Sepulchre's and Clerkenwell locations show him to have associated with the same figures, we must assume that this was indeed the same person, with two different residences. Among the fuller references are: Le Hardy, "Calendars" 1 (1607–08): 18 (Pulman is indicted), 138, 143, 176, 197, 230, 267; 2 (1608–09): 46, 58, 61–62; 3 (1609–10): 29, 64, 186, 190–91; 4 (1610): 2–3; 5 (1610–11): 73, 76–77, etc.

[25]CLRO MS. SF 27 (Sessions of the Peace and Gaol Delivery Records), recognizance of 19 May 1609, noting that Elizabeth and Thomas Laurence of St. Sepulchre's without Newgate are bound over to appear at the next Gaol Delivery with "Johi Pullman et Willma Elder de poai pred Theiftakers" as their sureties.

[26]Beattie discussed them as characteristic of the early and mid-eighteenth century, without denying, per se, that they could have operated earlier. The earliest reference cited in the *Oxford English Dictionary* is 1535, but the reference is Scottish, not English. (Beattie, *Crime and the Courts*, pp. 55–59; *OED*, *vide* "thieftaker." We thank Dr. Beattie for his advice on this matter.) See also Ruth Paley, "Thief-Takers in London in the Age of the McDaniel Gang, c. 1745–54," in Hay and Snyder, *Policing and Prosecution*, pp. 301–42, and Gerald Howson, *Thief-Taker General: The Rise and Fall of Jonathan Wild* (London, 1970).

crimes,[27] and in March of 1609 Pierson stood as a surety for Pulman.[28] We know that the two lived near each other at least some of the time. While Pierson is almost always described as living in St. James, Clerkenwell (and often at nearby Cow Cross in the same parish) throughout the period, Pulman is also described as residing there on several occasions between 1610 and 1616,[29] and even in Cow Cross itself three times between 1608 and 1612,[30] possibly having given Pierson's address as his own. Several other people seem to have been associated with both Pulman and Pierson during this period, of whom the most interesting is William Elder, whom the sessions clerk described as a "thieftaker" along with Pulman.[31]

At this point it is worth noting again the geographic element in these activities. Clerkenwell and the northern suburbs running east all the way to Shoreditch had become especially difficult areas for the authorities of the day. Relatively recently settled and built up, crowded with theaters, taverns, brothels, and cheap housing, they had become focal points not only for a good deal of criminal activity but also for the civil disorders that such scholars as Lindley and Manning have discussed. Lindley identified 22 riots in these areas between 1606 and 1623; Margaret Pelling has identified Clerkenwell itself as a haven for unlicensed medical practitioners and prostitutes.[32]

---

[27]GLRO, Le Hardy, "Calendars" 4 (1610): 2–3; 7/1 (1611): 79.

[28]GLRO, Le Hardy, "Calendars" 2 (1608–09): 46, in which Pierson and others stood surety for Pulman.

[29]GLRO, Le Hardy, "Calendars" 4 (1610): 2–3; 7/1 (1611): 79; W. H. C. Le Hardy, *Middlesex Sessions Records: Calendar to the Sessions Records*, n.s., vol. 1, 1612–14 (London, 1935), pp. 26, 268; ibid., vol. 4, 1616–18 (London, 1941), p. 73.

[30]GLRO, Le Hardy, "Calendars" 1 (1607–08): 176; 7/1 (1611): 52–53.

[31]See n. 24 above.

[32]Lindley, "Riot Prevention and Control," pp. 110, 126; Manning, *Village Revolts*, pp. 211–12; Pelling, "Appearance and Reality: Barber-Surgeons, the Body and Disease," in Beier and Finlay, *London 1500–1700*, p. 88.

The association of Pulman and Pierson opens a number of possibilities. It seems very likely that Pulman was playing a double game with Handes, appearing to help him in the chase for Pierson but in fact keeping him away until such time as an ambush could be laid, not for Pierson but for Handes. It may well be that the confrontation between the two sides was such a plan gone awry, resulting not in the demise of Handes but in Pulman's injury and Pierson's capture. This is, of course, mere speculation, anachronistic at that, based on the well-documented and very close association between Pulman and Pierson just a few years thereafter. But if this was not the case, then the rapprochement between Pulman and Pierson so soon afterwards was little short of remarkable, considering the events of that dramatic encounter.

In any event, it is clear that Pulman and Pierson, along with their associates who crop up in both Handes's account and the records of the Middlesex Sessions, were of a kind, lingering in and around the petty criminals of their parts of London, taking opportunity wherever they found it and on whichever side of the law seemed most convenient. They came directly under no gild regulations or jurisdiction, and although they frequently used the administrative network of local government in London and Middlesex, they seem not to have been hindered thereby for very long in their chosen "occupations."

Robert Swaddon operated on an entirely different level, and we must now turn to this last—and most fascinating—major player in this story. If Pulman and Pierson were but petty figures who preyed in one way or another on the unwary for their livelihoods, Swaddon had seen far better and entirely legitimate opportunities, and he appears to have followed a life of crime much more out of choice than necessity.

To begin with, there is absolutely no doubt that Swaddon followed his chosen path as a swindler or cozener from at least

1603 to 1612 and that he made of it a full-time and lucrative occupation. We first hear of his wrongdoing in a letter between former associates, to whom we will return, who remarked on his being imprisoned in March 1604/05 for counterfeiting bills of exchange. The same letter hints broadly at wrongdoing along similar lines among the merchant community of Middlesburg.[33] With that reference, we recognize that Swaddon's activities were by no means even confined to England, much less to London itself, and we begin to realize that he operated at least much of the time on a much higher level than did Pierson and Pulman.

Swaddon's incarceration of 1604/05 seems to have followed from his having swindled a Mr. John Pettus, merchant, alderman, and future mayor of Norwich, out of £100 in the spring of 1603 and then, a short while later, out of £200 more. In both cases Swaddon used a forgery of the same Sir Henry Baynton's signature, just as he would later do to swindle Temple and Farrington. It is interesting that he was accused by Pettus on that occasion along with two other accomplices, one of whom was the same William Matthews who assisted Swaddon in the Temple-Farrington ruse.[34] Obviously, Swaddon worked with Matthews, and probably with Pierson and Pulman, over a long period of time.

Swaddon appears to have served in the Wood Street Compter from 28 January to 13 June 1605 (new style) and then to have escaped, allegedly with the help of several of the gaolers,

---

[33]9 Mar. 1604/05, letter from "Ottley" in Middlesburg to Lionel Cranfield in London, both obviously engaged in large-scale cloth trade with continental connections (HMC, *Calendar of the Manuscripts of the Right Honourable Lord Sackville of Knole, Sevenoaks, Kent*, 2: *Letters Relating to Lionel Cranfield's Business Overseas, 1597–1612*, ed. F. J. Fisher [London, 1966], p. 158).

[34]Bill of complaint by Pettus of 17 Mar., 1 James I, PRO STAC 8/5/6, and another bill of complaint by Pettus, dated 21 Nov., 3 James I. Both bills are against Thomas Llewellyn, Robert Swaddon, and William Matthews; both concern the same case.

by sawing through a window bar and letting himself down with a torn towel.[35] He appears to have fled abroad immediately thereafter.

We next hear of him in the context of a letter that he sent from Cologne, attempting to blackmail his long-term landlord and alleged associate, William George, a Southwark innholder, in 1610. In the course of the investigations of this case, brought against Swaddon by George in the Star Chamber, several others testified as to how Swaddon (under one or the other of several assumed names) had swindled them, by means of forged bills of exchange and for sums of up to £200 at a time.[36] Clearly, the paper trail of Swaddon's crimes and misdemeanors between ca. 1603 and 1612 against victims in London, Cambridge, Bury St. Edmunds, and Newcastle is very rich indeed.

Who, then, was this Robert Swaddon, so easily trusted by merchants of considerable standing and well known to cloth merchants in the continental trade as well? How did he get involved in this dubious profession?

Swaddon seems to have been the fourth son of a substantial Wiltshire clothier, William Swaddon, who was sufficiently prominent in his own time to have sat for Calne in the Parliament of 1604.[37] By 1595, presumably using his connections to the London merchant William Cranfield, and to have done so at the same time that Cranfield's nephew Lionel, the future earl of Middlesex, served his uncle.[38] In the following year Swaddon

---

[35]PRO STAC 8/5/6, second bill of complaint brought by John Pettus of Norwich against Swaddon and seven alleged accomplices, including William Matthews.

[36]PRO STAC 8/155/1, STAC 8/92/13. See esp. George's bill and the depositions of Nathanial Craddock, mercer (Cambridge) and Francis Martin, citizen and draper (London).

[37]William Swaddon's will, PRO PROB 11/109, fols. 245v–246r, dated 16 Apr. 1602.

[38]Reference of 7 Dec. 1595, HMC, *Calendar of the Manuscripts of Major-General Lord Sackville*, 1: *Cranfield Papers, 1551–1612*, ed. A. P. Newton (1940), pp. 10–11. Confusingly enough, Swaddon described himself in this document (a

figures, somewhat prophetically, in a letter from the elder Cranfield to his nephew: "As yet we have heard nothing of Swadon [*sic*]," suggesting that Swaddon, like Lionel Cranfield, was in William Cranfield's employ in what was clearly the international cloth trade.[39] Three years later, in a letter of 1600 from John Sheppard to Lionel Cranfield, Swaddon is identified as a dealer in pack clothes.[40]

It cannot have been long after this that Swaddon began to show signs of straying from the straight and narrow, for when his father came to write his will in 1602 he bequeathed decidedly less to Robert than to his other sons, and he did so with the sour note that Robert should receive but £10 (as compared to houses for two of his brothers) and even that only "accordinge to the discretion of my Executor."[41]

In addition to leaving Robert with far less than he might have anticipated, thus possibly contributing to the temptation of crime, the will of the elder Swaddon gives one more hint at the origins of Robert's evil ways. In leaving small sums to his grandchildren, William singled out his granddaughter Jane, to whom he referred as Jane Segar, alias Parsons. She may have been the wife or daughter of Robert Seager, a servant to Sir Henry Baynton of Bremble, also a substantial figure in Swaddon's town of Calne and elsewhere in Wiltshire. Baynton left a Robert Seager £5 in his own will[42]—hence the likely connection between Swaddon and Baynton, the man whose signature he forged on at least two occasions for his own gain.

bond) as "servant to Richard Sheppard, Grocer" but also refers to "my master, William Cranfield." Lionel Cranfield himself was present on this occasion; he, Swaddon, and a third party signed the document.

[39]HMC, *Cranfield Papers*, pp. 18–19.

[40]HMC, *Cranfield Papers*, p. 16.

[41]PRO PROB 11/109, fol. 245v.

[42]PRO PROB 11/128, fol. 399v.

What may we conclude from this picaresque tale? First of all, even discounting some exaggeration that (understandably) may have crept into his account for expenses submitted to his master, Handes worked long and earnestly on the case. Though he sought out and received help from Thomas Farrington, a number of petty officials, JPs, and even representatives of the Lord Chief Justice, the Lord Treasurer, and the Recorder of London, and though he received such support over a period of some two months, such help was still not particularly effective. Handes succeeded in capturing but one of the three original suspects in a space of 10 or 12 weeks, and it appears that he did it more or less on his own.

It also appears that Handes had to pay, officially or otherwise, for at least some of this aid, which a poorer victim could ill have afforded. Members of the community, that other important component at the grassroots of the contemporary justice system, were sometimes willing to help and were occasionally even effectively helpful. Yet the very size of the area, the diversity of its neighborhoods, and the ease with which the suspected felons could move from one area of the metropolis to another rendered such help far less valuable than, presumably, it would have been in the rural environment. In addition, the theoretical obligation of householders to take their turns in the watch and ward seems by this time to have given way to the hiring of stand-ins to perform those duties, a sort of privatization of a traditional public responsibility, which may have resulted in less effective performance.[43]

As for the role of the livery companies in maintaining law and order in London, much emphasized in recent scholarship, there is no sign whatever of it in this case, nor should we expect there to be in a situation of this sort, however common. Some of

---

[43]Lindley, "Riot Prevention and Control," p. 119.

the reason for this lay with the difficulties of maintaining effective administration or criminal jurisdiction in those suburbs of London where the events took place: not only Clerkenwell, where Pulman, Pierson, and Matthews lived and operated but also the other suburban areas in which they led Handes his merry chase.

Much of the explanation also lay with the type of figures Handes pursued. Pierson and Pulman, essentially London figures as adults wherever they may have been born, remained well outside the grasp of livery companies' authority and seem to have had no difficulty in plying their dubious trades in the London area. Judging by the evidence of Sessions Rolls, they found the court system of the day as much of an aid as an obstacle to their livelihoods. In addition, Pulman at least seems to have moved his place of residence easily enough from one area of the metropolis to another, thus perhaps avoiding the extended scrutiny of officials in his parish or ward. For his part, though Pierson retained residence for several years in the same place, he seems to have had no particular difficulty with the officials in that area. Both men, of course, seem on several occasions to have been accused of crimes or misdemeanors, but neither seems to have had difficulty avoiding serious penalties. They seem to have been constantly at large and fairly free to go about their affairs during an extended period of time. These were by no means isolated instances of evasion. Eight months after a Privy Council warrant had been issued for the arrest of 20 known perpetrators of a serious riot in Holborn in 1638, only eight had been caught.[44]

Second, in the course of his quest Handes came upon several others who had been bilked in a similar manner—a Mr. Parkehurst and a Mr. Barnes, both of whom had also been

[44]Lindley, "Riot Prevention and Control," p. 124 n. 74.

cozened by Matthews, and Sir James Harrington, who had been cozened out of plate and linen by one "Thornton" and a Mr. Rowbotham—as well as a host of men who were either accomplices of the cozeners and/or who had been labeled as cozeners themselves. In short, Handes's adventures once again reveal the frequency and success with which such crimes were perpetrated in and around London at this time. More than that, they attest to the vulnerability to fraud and deceit of merchants throughout the realm.

The third point is raised by the third criminal figure of note, Robert Swaddon: London provided opportunities to the grand thief along with the petty. Only a true metropolis could have harbored a figure operating on his scale or could have afforded him the wide contacts in the community of prominent merchants on whom he preyed. Though Swaddon does appear to have wound up in gaol more often than Pierson and Pulman, probably because his sort of victim was more likely to have had the resources to pursue him, he did not find it difficult to escape incarceration, to flee abroad, or to wander up and down the countryside—particularly in eastern regions that were farthest from his home turf—while he was at large in England. Yet throughout his sundry wanderings and despite his brief incarcerations, London seems to have remained his home base. It not only afforded him the camouflage of numbers in which to hide but it also sustained opportunities to engage in his activities and to garner the assistance of others of like mind in those efforts. Once again we have one of a type, though undoubtedly a smaller and more specialized type, and once again, a type that proved resilient to the normative institutions and agencies responsible for the maintenance of law and order in the London of his time.

To be sure, there seems little in what Selman, Swaddon, and Matthews were accused of doing that would cause the fabric of London society to come unravelled, or—save for the confrontation at the end of the chase—that would provoke violence in the streets. In that sense, there is nothing here that would subvert social stability in the metropolis, and thus nothing that contravenes the essential thesis of Pearl, Rappaport, Archer, and others.

Yet one must assume that a most substantial share of the lawless and criminal activity in and around London consisted of such ruses as we have discussed here. After all, everything we know about crime in England at this time suggests that it focused more on violations of property than on crimes of violence.[45] It is also likely that a great many of those who committed their crimes elsewhere would have found their way to London and disappeared therein with similar success.

In sum, we can only conclude that the recent tendency to emphasize the lawfulness and stability of Tudor and Stuart London ought not to be taken to extremes. The matrix of law enforcement and civil administration that has of late been so well documented may have worked effectively in regard to the City's resident freemanry, especially within at least some of the geographic boundaries of gild and livery company jurisdiction. Yet its effect on those passing through and moving around, and on those who were not freemen, cannot have been as substantial. The siren appeal of London continued to attract those in the mold of not only Dick Whittington but also of Dick Turpin.

---

[45]See, e.g., J. S. Cockburn, "The Nature and Incidence of Crime in England, 1559–1625," in J. S. Cockburn, ed., *Crime in England, 1550–1800* (Princeton, 1977), and J. A. Sharpe, *Crime in Early Modern England, 1550–1750* (London, 1984), passim.

APPENDIX

I have used throughout the transcription policy of the REED (Records of Early English Drama) project of the University of Toronto. This preserves the original spelling and capitalization; indicates all expansions with italics; indicates all marks of punctuation including the virgule (/) used as a punctus in the period; includes the dittography where it occurs, and indicates a cancellation by the use of square brackets rather than over-striking a line through the cancelled letters. I have also preserved the MS lineation. For a more complete explanation of editorial principles used in the REED project, see Alexandra F. Johnston and Margaret Rogerson, eds., York, *Records of Early English Drama, 1 (Toronto, 1979), Introduction.*

Raphe Handes
dat*us* & deliberat*us*
12o Maij 1606

R. H. His accompt to his m*aster* S*i*r
Tho*mas* Temple knight/

A perticuler Accompt of expences & chardges
expended & Laid out by Raphe Hand*es* in searchinge
& fyndinge out those (viz Robert Swaddon alias Captaine
Robert*es* al*ias* Captaine Swanne alias Webb/ Iohn Selman
al*ias* Selby & Will*iam* Matthewes al*ias* Wright) who
did faigne a L*ett*re from S*i*r Henry Baynton [kni]
of Bremble in the Countye of Wilt*shire* knight [directed]
And did direct the same l*ett*re to S*i*r Thomas Temple
of Byrton Dassett in the Countie of War*wickshire* knight,
thereby to gett A l*ett*re fro*m* the said S*i*r Thomas Temple
By w*hi*ch they might (and did) see his writinge &
Counterfaict his hand and Seale/W*hi*ch said said
Letter obtayned, they did frame & forge A l*ett*re
& an obligacion in the name of the said S*i*r Thomas
Temple and did carry the same to M*aster* M*aster* Thomas
ffarrington of Broadstreett in London Marchaunt
And dyd Cosen hym the said M*aster* ffarington of
the so*m*me of Cxx li, vppon the feast daie
of St Thomas Thapp*os*t*l*e beinge the [2i] 2ith of decemb*r*e
1605/ Anno regni Rex Iacobi Tertio

Anno 1605/
Decemb*er*
29: In pr*im*is Spent at ffarnborrough enquiringe for hym that brought S*ir* Henry Baintons L*ett*re (as he said) to Dassett viz. Iohn Selman, who did Leave his horse at the alehouse there & did Lye there/ And framinge there A discription of his p*er*son clothes & horse by the help of those that did see hym there iij d

Item Sp*en*t at Adderbury enquiringe for one Bellowes there, who did Lye w*ith* Selman at ffarnborrough/ and geven to one that did goe to seeke hym a myle of vj d

It*em* my Supper & Breakefast at Woodstock where I was enforced to Lodge because my mare was tyred & Yt snowed fast & was night & not able to trauaile furth*er* xiiij d

It*em* my Mares meate there xij d

It*em* fyre that nyght beinge very wett ij d

It*em* thostler & Chamb*er*laine there ij d

30 It*em* my expences that daie in oxon. searchinge & enquiringe in all houses of receipt for Selmans Lodginge there, vj d my dyn*ner* Supp*er* & breakfast there—xvij d my mares meate there all that daie & all night—xviij d, frostinge my mares there ij d fyre there beinge wett w*ith* goinge vp & downe the towne ij d, the Chamb*er*laine & hostler ij d iij s x d

3i It*em* Sp*ent* enquiringe for hym at Stoken Church on my mare beinge beinge tired & on myself &c vj d

It*em* my Supp*er* & br*eakfast* at Wicombe xiiij d, my mare then— xiiij d & Sp*ent* at the katherine Wheele, where I heard that such a man did Lodge iust at the tyme I enquired of discribing

hym in all ij d geven thostler
& chamberlaine ij d ij s viij d

Item fire that night & morninge to dry my clothes &c yt
hauinge Rayned extreamely all that daie iiij d

pag: 1
00.10.07 Summa pagine x s vij d

Ianuary Item Spent at vxbridge enquiringe at all the Innes there
— ij d & bayte my mare iiij d vj d

London Item when I came to London that night beinge wett againe
& weary with goinge on foote my mare beine Tyred againe
for fyre iiij d

2 Item Spent that daie enquiringe amonge the seale makers,
& takinge directions of them to fynd out hym that made
the Seale which was made like my master Sir Thomas Temple
his seale, hauinge vj or viij of them to geather xvij d

3 Item Spent that daie searchinge dyvers stables in
Southwark & after in Smytthfield & coming ouer the
water vj d

5 Item Spent that daie enquiringe amongest dyvers viz Iohn
Wright, of the Bell in Saint Iohns strett where I found
A White fflea:Bytten Iade with a shorne mane, And with ij
that I brought thyther with me to beare wittnes what was
spokken & with others, At which tyme both the Master &
Hostler confessed that, that Iade had A iourney at the
tyme I enquired of And that A man iust of the Discription
I declared had that horse xiij d

Item Spent that aftirnone at Master Iacobes in the
Strande enquireinge out A carr man one Peare who wright

said gaue Credit for the Retourne of that horse that Iorney, in the company of M*aste*r Iacob, M*aste*r Durk & others then makeing merry there [vij d] vj d

It*em* Sp*ent* w*ith* one M*aste*r Shepheard & others who first told me that Captaine Pierson was A man like vnto my discription & everlyvid by Coseninge & Cheating trick*es* vij d

I had thought to haue taken Thornton was disswaded & then he & both the other ran away that daye

It*em* Spent in the Company of Pullman at the first meeting after I was directed to but then hym in the Company of ij the knight Marshall*es* men & one Thornton, who was one that had [Cosened] Counterfaicted S*ir* Iames Harringtons L*ettr*e, One Rowbotham al*ias* higgenbothom who hath also an other name was his companyon/ they Cosened hym of a Chest [of] or trunk of Plate & lynnen xj d

It*em* Sp*ent* on the chamb*er*laine hostler & maid of the Vnicorne bringing twise to se one M*aste*r Counstable when I brought him to the Sessions & to the Recorders house vj d

pag: 2
10.06.09

Su*m*ma pag*ine* vj s ix d

It*em* Sp*ent* w*ith* Brook*es* the auncientest vunder kep*er* of Newgat vnto whome I went by the p*ers*wasyon of dyvers hoping he could &c who told me then of many but not the Right M*aste*r Sheapheard being in his company vj d

It*em* Sp*ent* w*ith* Pullman at sondry tymes in company because I would see as many knowne villaines as I could to see & heare &c in their meeting*es* xx d

Item S[tt]p*ent* w*ith* the Beadle of S*ain*t Sepulchres ward Pulman & others when we Searched one Warrall*es* house & one other: where we hoped to haue tak*en* Capt*ain* Pierson [Barth*olomew*] Hopkins & Io*hn* Hopkins & Bussh [at one Worralls] iij s whereof I p*ai*d [xij d] xviij d

Item Sp*ent* w*ith* Pullman searching dyvers houses for Sellman*n*, on the Constables & others that assisted vs in Dyvers plac*es* & at seu*er*all tymes xviij d

Item Sp*ent* an oth*er* tyme in like mann*er* vj d

I sawe not Bussh — Item Sp*ent* an oth*er* tyme when I went to meete & see Iohn Hopkins Barth Hopkins Rich Bussh & worrall xij d

his name is cheese one M*aste*r Broneleyes ma*n* of the Temple — Item to M*aste*r Thomas Swayne wh*om* he paid for the ffee of the Lo*rd* Thre*asure*rs Bailiffe for aresting hym that was said to be hym that talked w*ith* my fellow Tho*mas* Swayne xv d

Item Sp*ent* w*ith* [Iskeall] Israell the Lo*rd* Thre*asure*rs Bailiff going thrise w*ith* me to westm*inster* &c to see yf wee could fynd hym againe after he had lett hym goe vj d

Item to hym*m* for going three daies w*ith* me to c*er*taine gameing houses & Bowling alleys to se yf wee could fynd that, Cheese iij s

Item my Mares haie from the first Daie of Ianuarie vuntill the xxiijth being the first daie of Hillarie terme viz xxviij night*es* at vv d the night xv s iiij d

Item provander that 23 night*es* vij s vj d

Item Sp*ent* againe with Brook*es* the vnderkeper of newgat & ij others searchinge & enquiring &c vj d

It*em* my owne comons for those 23 daies, and for vij daies more, (at w*hi*ch tyme yo*u*r wor*ship* came to the towne) viz. for xxx Daies xl s of w*hi*ch I had some xv or xvj meales wi*th* m*aste*r ffarrington and so aske alloweanc*e* only for xxiiij daies [<n.1.>] not out viij d the meale xxx s

pag. 3
3:04:9 Su*m*ma pag*ine* iij li iiij s ix d

M*emorandum* yo*u*r wor*ship* came to L*ondon* the— xxxth Daie of Ianuarie and tarryid there vntill the— i4th of ffebr*uary* in w*hi*ch tyme I was wholly wi*th* yo*u*r wor*ship*, and therefore aske no allowaunc for meales in this accompt because yt p*er*tyneth not to this busynes

It*em* paid for A Bottle & Vsquebaugh in my sicknes viz the bottle viij d the Vsq*ue*baugh vj d xiiij d

It*em* Sp*ent* sondrie tymes goinge to Shordich both by night & daie about Captain Pierson & to see & to heare of the horse I found there &c viij d

It*em* geven one that was sometyme M*aste*r Tho*mas* ffoxe his man, whoe watched night by night for pierson & told vs of hym,/ to watch still And that yf Persons wife were sent for he might hire one to goe with her & so finde the whole Crewe ij s vj d

It*em* p*ai*d the Lord Chieff Iustic*es* man M*aste*r Michell for my Lord*es* warraunt vij s vj d

It*em* Sp*ent* wi*th* M*aste*r ffoxe ij d

It*em* my mares Haye for the xxiijth of Ianuarie, vntill the —xxth of ffeb*ruary* beinge 28 night*es* at 8d the night xviij d vij d feb. 20 It*em* Pullmans & myne owne expens*es* then Ridinge to knight*es* bridge to enquire out Capt*ain* Pierson Phillipp Striker & Rich*ard* Bussh & others their companyons, viz. o*u*r dynners —xj d o*u*r mares iiij d xv d

It*em* to the Smytth then for settinge on my mares shooes againe & for paring & letting her bloud in the feete before vj d

Md I did this daie dep*ar*t fro*m* lodging at the Vnicorne and paid in the house there viz. for ffyve dyvers night*es* Coming wett in and for Beere & to the hostler & Chamberlaine ij s vj d

20 feb: It*em* my mares meat that night at the greene Dragon in Bisshop*es* gate strett xiiij d

It*em* my owne & Pullmans meat the 2j of ffeb*ruary* at Tottnam where wee waighted all daie for Capt*ain* Pierson & his Company but they came not till night & then ou*er* Rode vs xij d

It*em* my mare then iiij d Sp*ent* then besides iij d vij d

pag: 4
02:04:02. Su*m*ma pag*ine* ij li iiij s ij d

1605

2jo feb: It*em* my supp*er* that night w*ith* Pullman & oth*er*s beinge Sat*er*daie the 2jth of ffeb*ruary* viij d

It*em* expenc*es* that night & on the sondaie morninge w*ith* three Counstables & others of Islington &c afterward that daie, searchinge all Islington & other plac*es* nere at w*hi*ch tyme wee found Will*ia*m Matthewes al*ia*s Wright xij d

It*em* Sp*ent* more then w*ith* the Counstable that Did app*re*hend the said Matthewes & w*ith* others & had hym before Iustice ffowler iiij d

It*em* Sp*ent* more w*ith* Matthewes & Pullman at Pullmans house where I vnderstood that he had ben a doer before by one that knew him there iij d

It*em* my Mares haie that Sat*er*daie night & all on the morrowe at Islington x d

It*em* for p*ro*vander there vj d

It*em* geven thostler there for helping to make me cleane my mare haueing fallen w*ith* me in the myre &c iij d

It*em* Sp*ent* w*ith* Pullman & old Bromley &c sondrie tymes enquiring out matter against W*illia*m Matthewes & his fellowes xij d

It*em* geuen old Bromley for his travaile & inteeligenc*es* of matter against Matthewes &c xij d

It*em* Sp*ent* on Shroue tuesdaie at night at Pullmans, and at Ratliffe vppon the const*able* and 8 or i0, who did assist hym & vs to app*re*hend Iohn Clerke one of Piersons Crewe and on two that went w*ith* me thyther, in Drincke fire &c, where we stayid from —xj of the clock in the night till v. of the clock in the morninge xviij d

It*em* Sp*ent* w*ith* Pullman Clerke &c that morning at Breakefast vij d

It*em* Sp*ent* at twise w*ith* the Carryer of Winchest*er* to enquire matt*er* against matthewes conc*er*ning thet Coseninge of M*aste*r Barnes, & Parkehurst &c xij d

Item *paid* more w*hi*ch Pullman Sp*ent* at Islington Dogging after Selmans wife there, whilest I did dogg one to London & Returned iij d

Page [5]
5 — 00 09 03 Su*m*ma pag*ine* ix s iij d

Item Sp*ent* w*ith* old Bromley who procured me A woman to get Sellmans hostes to to talke w*ith* me, A Sp*ent* w*ith* those women xx d

Item my Mares hay from the 22th of ffeb*ruary* vntill the vjt of March beinge xij night*es* vij s

Item her p*ro*vand*er* then for that tyme iij s

Item Sp*ent* the vijth of March Pullmans Dynn*er* & myne &c goinge then forward to Apprehend Captayne Pyerson & that Crewe of Coseners vpon hownslow Rode xij d

Item my Mares standing therewhile in Smithfield ij d

Item Sp*ent* at Hounslowe enquiringe for them — ij d, at vxbridge Myssinge them there — before Supp*er* in Beere iiij d in bread j d vij d

March: 7 Item Supp*er* that night thoughe Pullman Did eate nothinge xvj d

Item o*ur* mares meate that night ij s ij d

Item thostler there ij d

8 Item for S*ir* Henry Drewry his Warraunt to app*re*hend captain Pierson Phillipp Striker & Richard Busshe vij d

It*e*m Pullmans Breakfast & myne at Beaconsfield xij d

It*e*m o*u*r mares bait there [xij d] vj d

It*e*m to the Chirurgian at vxbridge for dressing Pullmans wound*es* being hurst by Captaine Pierson iij s

9 It*e*m o*u*r horsmeat then ij s ij d

Sp*ent* more in drink then iiij d

It*e*m to thostler & chamb*er*laine then iiij d

It*e*m Sp*ent* by the waie homeward ij d

It*e*m Sp*ent* at the Redd Lyon in Holborne where Capt*ain* Pierson & I rested whilest I enquired yf the Lo*rd* chieffe Iustice were at leasure iiij d

It*e*m Sp*ent* that night w*ith* Pullman ij d

pag: 6
01—08.07 Su*m*ma pag*ine* xxviij s vij d

It*e*m Sp*ent* againe W*ith* Pullman Bromeley Pullmans Chiurgi*an* Sellmans Hostes (M*istriss* Will*ia*ms) &c enquiring further of Matthwes Rob*ertes* &c xij d

It*e*m Spent more at Westm*inster* againe of M*ist*riss Will*iams* M*ist*riss Haynes M*ist*riss Bradley (Swaddins paramo*u*r) M*aste*r will*ia*ms &c ij s iiij d

It*e*m Sp*ent* more at sondrie tymes w*ith* the said Bromley M*ist*riss Haynes &c for the Causes a foresaid xiij d

Item Sp*ent* goeinge thrise to the Myneryes to see & enquire of an other fleabitten horse I heard was there vij d

Item Sp*ent* with Pullman & oth*er*s at sondrie tymes by j d ij d & iij d at atyme iij s

Item my ferry thrise ou*er* the Water to see the Cominge out of people from the play*es* iij d

Item Spent thrise at those playes w*ith* Pullman beinge there to see yf wee could espie Sellman or Rob*ertes* vj d

Item Sp*ent* [g.] at twise at the blacke Beare in Holborne where I heard diu*er*s gallant*es* & Captaines came in at mydnight vj d

Item Sp*ent* w*ith* one Hand*es* who enquired out for me where one Iones, an old acquaintaunce of Matthewes Did Dwelle w*ith* whome Matthewes kept his christmas vj d

Item Sp*ent* on the company of one M*aste*r Isard a Bayliffe of Midd*lesex*, borne at Banbury who told me he saw Selman when he came home & did knowe one that was in his Company &c [Spent there seu*er*all tymes] xij d

Item Sp*ent* more enquiring out Ione[.]s his house at Westm*inster* iij d

Item Sp*ent* w*ith* M*aste*r White who did help me to one haies an especiall companyon of Selmans Isard spent w*ith* them enquiring xiiij d

pag: 7
00 i2i02 Su*m*ma pag*ine* xij s ij d

Item Sp*ent* W*ith* Matthewes and his keper when he went to make his confession before m*aste*r Recorder, beinge very Sicke xij d

Item Sp*ent* goeinge to Neweington w*ith* Iames Haies, enquiring in sondry plac*es* there for Sellman, And on one M*ist*riss Woodhouse, vnto whose house Selma*n* often Resorted, viz. on hym & my self xvj d

Item for iij Linck*es* Burnt in the night*es* wee went Searchinge &c xij d

Item for 4 newe shoes at my coming home for my Mare xvj d

Item for wasshinge my mare w*ith* sope twise for the Lyce vj d and for Syming her onc*e* in the thames ij d viij d

Item my Mares haie from the 8th of March vntill the — 18th daie of Aprill beinge—xlj night*es* at — viij d the night xxviij s

Item Provander then for that tyme ix s

Item *delivered* Pullman at Sondry tymes viz. first Lent hym v s then Lent hym ij s then geven hym by M*aste*r ffaringtons Consent v s then let hym to redeeme his hatband v s Su*m*ma xvij s

Item my Comons at London for oio7 daies & di*midium*, whereof I haue askid allowaunce in this accompte for xxiij daies and in my accompte to yo*u*r wor*ship* of other busynes — vij daies & di*midium* viz. for xv meales, And then Remayneth of daies iij xx xvj [& di*midium*], Of w*hi*ch number I require allowaunce onely for xv daies the Rest I hadd w*ith* M*aste*r ffarington &c being — iij xxj daies & di*midium*, so I aske nowe onely xx s

Item geven thostlers & chamberlaine at the greene dragon in Bishopes gate streett viij d

Pag: 8
03—18.08.1 Summa pagine iij li xix s iiij d

Item geven Master ffarmers man who hope me to Dresse my Mare &c at Cookham iij d

Item Baytid my Mare homeward at Aylesbury & Spent my selfe there vj d

Item geven Sir ffraunces Goodwines man for helpinge me to his masteres hand to my warrauntes xij d

Item Spent with Raphe Barneby at Buckingham with whome I Leafte warraunt for Swadden I saie at twise vj d

I hope your worship will not thinck this which ensueth to much (or much) considering the daungers, hazards, travaile & paynes night & day sustaynde in the colde [nightes] and amonge daungerous people but will in your compassion regard my willinges trauvaile & endeuour in so desperatt & hopeles^⌈a⌉ busynes: with somewhat els]
Item Spent in necessary thinges vppon my selfe Duringe the tyme of my beinges in London about the foresaid busynes the which I should not haue spent yf I had ben At home as followeth viz:

Item for iij paire of Shooes ix s
Item for ij paire of Stockinges v s vj d
Item for mending a pair of Shooes iij d
for Soaling ij pair of Shooes ij s
Item for mendinge A pair of Shooes iiij d
Item for an old dublett & a pair of old hose to Shafte me with all xij s iiij d

It*e*m for mending Buttonholing setting on Buttons on my dublett & hose	xij d
It*e*m for vj dozen of haire Buttons	ix d
It*e*m for A *quar*terne of oz of Silk to Buttonhole &c my dublettes &c	vj d
It*e*m for setting on three Doz*en* of Buttons vppon my other dublett	vj d
It*e*m for mending & footing ij p*ai*r of Stocking*es* sondrie tymes	xvj d
It*e*m for Nailes & Nayling my shooes	ij d
It*e*m for a Shirt hauing quite worne out — ij shirt*es*	iiij s
It*e*m for j p*ai*r of gloues & mending others	ix d
It*e*m for a *yar*ed of ffustian & for the Lyning & mending my Breeches	xviij d

Pag—9
2.3.4 Su*m*ma pag*ine* xliij s iiij d

It*e*m for mending [my] shooes	iiij d
It*e*m for soaling an other p*ai*r of shooes	xij d
It*e*m for dressing & mending ij hatt*es*	ij s
It*e*m for mending my shooes	vj d
It*e*m my wasshing viz eu*er*y weeke a shirt ij band*es* & ij handkerchiff*es*— at—iiij d the weeke — xv week*es*	v s

8.10 Su*m*ma pag*ine* viij s x d

Su*m*ma to*ta*lis of this accompt in [p*re*] pursuit of the Coseners
xv li vij s ix d/

THE LIVESTOCK OF CHAUCER'S REEVE: FACT OR FICTION?[1]

Bruce M. S. Campbell

> *The REVE was a sclendre colerik man. . . . Wel koude he kepe a gerner and a binne; Ther was noon auditour koude on him winne. Wel wiste he by the droghte and by the reyn The yeldinge of his seed and of his greyn. His lordes sheep, his neet, his dayerie, His swyn, his hors, his stoor, and his pultrie Was hoolly in this Reves governinge, . . . Of Northfolk was this Reve of which I telle, Biside a toun men clepen Baldeswelle.*[2]

Few aspects of the *Canterbury Tales* have escaped the attention of Chaucerian scholars, but Chaucer's description of the husbandry—and particularly the pastoral husbandry—practiced by Oswald, the reeve of Bawdeswell in Norfolk, appears to be one. Oswald had in his charge his lord's horse, his dairy, neat and store cattle, his sheep, his swine, and his poultry[3]—ostensibly the range and combination of animals and

---

[1]I am grateful to Malcolm Andrew for advice on Chaucer's reeve, to John Langdon for providing data, to John Power and Jenitha Orr for research assistance, and to Gill Alexander for drawing the maps. Earlier versions of this paper were presented at seminars in the Dept. of English Local History, Univ. of Leicester, and Dept. of History, Univ. of Alberta; I am grateful to their participants for comments. Part of the research upon which this paper is based was undertaken whilst in the tenure of an ESRC research fellowship.

[2]Geoffrey Chaucer, *The General Prologue to the Canterbury Tales*, ed. James Winny (Cambridge, 1966), pp. 69–70.

[3]Chaucer, *CT, Gen. Prol.*, p. 69, lines 599–601.

poultry that might be found on almost any demesne in any part of the country in an age when, as R. H. Hilton observed in 1954, "everyone had to produce (on the whole) the same type of crop and tend the same sort of domesticated animals for meat, wool, and pulling power."[4] But was medieval agriculture so undifferentiated? Could it be instead that Chaucer's account is here more factual than fictional and that in characterizing the reeve, his dwelling, and his husbandry Chaucer had in mind a specific landscape and rural economy recognizable by repute to many in his audience? Such a view would certainly accord with the mounting body of evidence which shows that by the fourteenth century the countryside was deeply penetrated by commercial forces, with the result that farmers were increasingly specializing in what they produced and how they produced it.[5] In fact, Norfolk had already emerged as one of the most distinctive farming regions in England.[6]

Bawdeswell is situated in the Wensum Valley in the very heart of Norfolk, 14 miles northeast of Norwich. Soils in the area range from moderately heavy clays to light and free-draining sands; Faden's map of Norfolk shows that the latter, in accordance with Chaucer's description, gave rise to several extensive areas of heath.[7] The manor of which Oswald was

---

[4]"Medieval Agrarian History," in *Victoria County History: Leicestershire*, vol. 2 (London, 1954), p. 145.

[5]For a pioneering study of market specialization see Kathleen Biddick, "Medieval English Peasants and Market Involvement," *Journal of Economic History* 45/4 (1985): 823–31; eadem, "Missing Links: Taxable Wealth, Markets, and Stratification among Medieval English Peasants," *Journal of Interdisciplinary History* 18/2 (1987): 277–98.

[6]John P. Power and Bruce M. S. Campbell, "Cluster Analysis and the Classification of Medieval Demesne-Farming Systems," *Transactions of the Institute of British Geographers*, n.s., 17 (1992): 232–41; Bruce M. S. Campbell, Kenneth C. Bartley, and John P. Power, "The Demesne-Farming Systems of Post Black Death England: A Classification," *Agricultural History Review* 44/2 (1996).

[7]William Faden, *Faden's Map of Norfolk*, intro. J. C. Barringer (Dereham, 1989), sheet 15.

reeve was evidently in lay hands and "biside" rather than in Bawdeswell itself.[8] Manors in the neighboring townships of Bintree, Billingford, Foulsham, Sparham, and Themelthorpe could all fit Chaucer's description, although, if John Matthews Manly is to be believed, the prime candidate is the de Hastings manor in the immediately adjoining township of Foxley.[9] It is to this manor that a solitary manorial account of 1305/06 probably relates. At Michaelmas 1306 the stock enumerated in this account comprised five cart horses and stots, three mares, three young horses and foals, 10 oxen, 32 cows, 18 head of young cattle, 12 ducks, 13 capons, and eight hens.[10] Apart from the absence of sheep and swine, this range of livestock corresponds closely with that described by Chaucer on possibly the same manor at the end of the fourteenth century. Moreover, the payment of wages to a shepherd and swineherd and the receipt of mutton and pork by the lord's larder testify that sheep and swine must both have been present in the locality. Tallying even more closely with Chaucer's description is the stock maintained at Michaelmas 1348 on John de Gyney's manor of Guton Hall in Brandiston, five miles to the east. Here were 14 horses of varying ages, two bulls, nine oxen, five steers, five heifers, 19 cows, six calves, 67 sheep, 32 lambs, 55 swine of various ages, three swans, 19 geese, 46 capons, nine ducks, and 13 hens.[11] On this mixed-farming demesne horses and oxen evidently satisfied the draught requirements of arable husbandry, a substantial breeding and dairying herd was maintained, and sheep, swine, and assorted poultry were kept. The

---

[8]Chaucer, *CT, Gen. Prol.*, p. 70, line 622.

[9]*Some New Light on Chaucer: Lectures Delivered at the Lowell Institute* (London, 1926), pp. 84–94.

[10]PRO SC6/935/19.

[11]Magdalen College Oxford, Estate Records 166/7.

only significant departure from the list of stock enumerated by Chaucer is the presence of oxen to provide draught power. Thirty years later, however, at the time that Chaucer was writing, most demesnes in this locality (like the peasantry before them) were well advanced in the changeover to all-horse ploughing and were actively disposing of their oxen.[12]

Analysis of a national sample of 787 demesnes recorded between 1250 and 1449 helps to put the pastoral profiles of Foxley and Guton Hall into perspective: whereas 45 per cent of all Norfolk demesnes carried as wide a range of livestock, nationally less than a third of all lowland demesnes did so.[13]

For Norfolk there are over 2,000 extant manorial accounts representing more than 200 different demesnes, both lay and ecclesiastical.[14] The detailed listings of the stock remaining each Michaelmas that these provide may be analyzed statistically to reveal the range and distribution of pastoral types that existed within the county. This is most effectively undertaken by means of the technique known as cluster analysis. This is a statistically consistent method of classifying data into groups on the basis of differences between cases (i.e., individual

---

[12]Bruce M. S. Campbell, "Towards an Agricultural Geography of Medieval England," *Agricultural History Review* 36/1 (1988): 91–93.

[13]The latter proportion falls to 35 per cent during the final quarter of the fourteenth century, of which Chaucer was writing. John Langdon supplied the national sample of manorial accounts on which these figures are based.

[14]These are preserved among the following public and private archives: PRO (London), Norfolk Record Office (NRO), North Yorkshire Record Office, Nottinghamshire Record Office, West Suffolk Record Office, Bodleian Library (Oxford), British Library (BL), Cambridge Univ. Library, Canterbury Cathedral Library, Joseph Regenstein Library, Univ. of Chicago, Harvard Law Library, John Rylands Library (Manchester), Lambeth Palace Library, Nottingham Univ. Library, Eton College, Christ's College (Cambridge), King's College (Cambridge), Magdalen College (Oxford), St. George's Chapel (Windsor), Elveden Hall (Suffolk), Holkham Hall (Norfolk), Raynham Hall (Norfolk), Pomeroy and Sons (Wymondham). I am grateful to the relevant authorities for granting access to these materials. A handlist is available on request from the author.

demesnes) as measured across all the variables of which they are composed (i.e., the livestock with which they were stocked).[15] Table 1 summarizes the results of such an analysis obtained utilizing the *relocation method* as applied to the percentage of total livestock units accounted for by horses, oxen, adult cattle (cows and bulls), immature cattle, sheep, and swine.[16]

As will be noted, seven basic pastoral types are identified in the period 1250–1349 and a further seven in the period 1350–1449. The smallest of these groupings comprises a single demesne (Cluster 5, 1350–1449, distinguished by its exceptionally high proportion of swine) and the largest, a total of 35 demesnes (Cluster 1, 1250–1349). The two demesnes so far discussed—Foxley and Guton Hall in Brandiston—are placed respectively in Clusters 1 and 2 in the period 1250–1349, the difference in classification reflecting the absence of sheep and swine from Foxley and their presence at Guton Hall. As will be seen from Figure 1, other Cluster 1 demesnes occur in the immediate vicinity of Bawdeswell—at Alderford, Kerdiston, North Elmham, Gateley, and Hindolveston—while both before and after 1350 Clusters 1 and 2 form the predominant pastoral types in much of north-central and eastern Norfolk. Had Chaucer enumerated the numbers as well as the types of

---

[15]For a fuller exposition of the application of cluster analysis to data from manorial accounts see Power and Campbell, "Cluster Analysis and Classification," pp. 227–45; Bruce M. S. Campbell and John P. Power, "Mapping the Agricultural Geography of Medieval England," *Journal of Historical Geography* 15/1 (1989): 26–27.

[16]Total livestock units = (horses x 1.0) + (oxen x 1.2) + (adult cattle x 1.2) + (immature cattle x 0.8) + (sheep x 0.1) + (swine x 0.1). These weightings relate to the relative feed requirements of the various livestock and are based on those used by J. T. Coppock, *An Agricultural Atlas of England and Wales* (London, 1964), p. 213, and J. A. Yelling, "Probate Inventories and the Geography of Livestock Farming: A Study of East Worcestershire, 1540–1750," *Transactions of the Institute of British Geographers* 51 (1970): 115.

TABLE 1
NORFOLK: CLASSIFICATION OF DEMESNE PASTORAL-FARMING TYPES 1250–1349 AND 1350–1449

	Cluster	No. of Demesnes	% of Demesnes	Mean Percentage of Total Livestock Units					
				Horses	Oxen	Adult Cattle	Young Cattle	Sheep	Swine
1250–1349	1	35	27	17	10	51	17	4	2
	2	14	11	21	6	32	17	14	12
	3	31	24	15	7	30	10	37	2
	4	5	4	26	3	<1	<1	64	6
	5	32	25	19	24	26	19	10	2
	6	3	2	87	13	0	0	0	0
	7	9	7	34	58	2	1	3	2
	Overall	129	100	21	15	31	14	16	3
1350–1449	1	33	31	17	4	49	20	4	5
	2	13	12	17	13	62	5	1	2
	3	33	31	12	6	34	10	37	2
	4	12	11	10	2	4	2	81	1
	5	1	1	39	0	0	0	0	61
	6	10	9	90	1	3	4	0	3
	7	5	5	43	48	0	0	9	0
	Overall	107	100	23	7	34	11	22	3

Source: Manorial accounts
Method: Cluster analysis (relocation method), seven-cluster solution. For calculation of livestock units see n. 16 above.

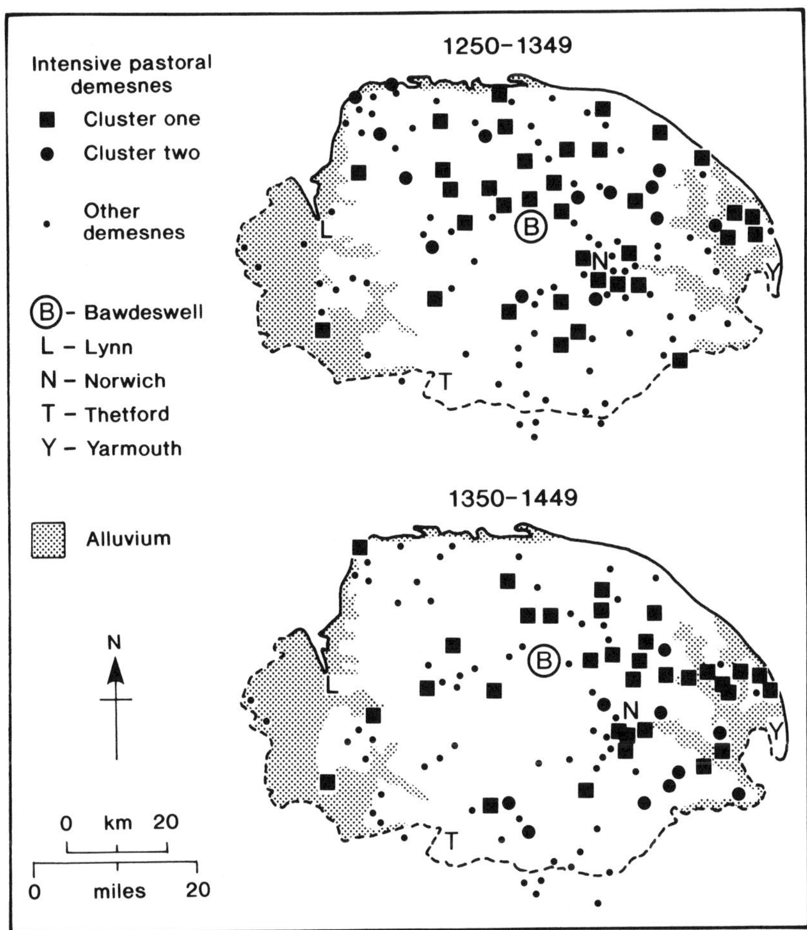

Figure 1. Norfolk: distribution of "intensive" pastoral-farming demesnes 1250–1349 and 1350–1449 (for explanation see Clusters 1 and 2, Table 1)

Oswald's livestock, and were it possible that these could have been included within the cluster analysis, it is highly likely that the Bawdeswell demesne would likewise have fallen into one or other of these two cluster groupings.

What distinguishes both these Norfolk pastoral types is their developed and intensive nature. Five features are particularly worthy of note. First, draught animals comprised barely a quarter of demesne stock, with the result that working animals were greatly outnumbered by nonworking animals. Second, within the draught sector oxen were outnumbered by horses, with a tendency for that bias to become increasingly pronounced over time as oxen were progressively replaced by horses.[17] Third, within the nonworking sector cattle predominated, accounting on average for almost half of all livestock units on Cluster 2 demesnes in the period 1250–1349 and two-thirds on Cluster 1 demesnes in the periods 1250–1349 and 1350–1449 and Cluster 2 demesnes in the period 1350–1449. Fourth, the structure of these cattle herds was demographically skewed towards adult females, so that cows and bulls outnumbered their followers by at least five to four and in many cases by more than two to one. Such ratios are indicative that dairying rather than rearing was their prime function, and this is borne out by direct evidence of butter and cheese production and the domination of butchery and sale by the disposal of decrepit adults and surplus calves. Finally, sheep, swine, and poultry occupied essentially subsidiary positions within the overall pastoral profile. This applies particularly to sheep, whose importance was, in fact, often eclipsed by swine, which were capable of more intensive forms of management.[18] The range of poultry kept was also often quite considerable: the hens, capons, geese, ducks, and swans kept on the demesne at

[17]For the diffusion of horses in Norfolk see John L. Langdon, *Horses, Oxen and Technological Innovation: The Use of Draught Animals in English Farming from 1066 to 1500* (Cambridge, 1986), pp. 50–53, 101–05; Campbell, "Towards an Agricultural Geography," pp. 91–93.

[18]Kathleen Biddick, "Pig Husbandry on the Peterborough Abbey Estate from the Twelfth to the Fourteenth Century," in Juliet Clutton-Brock and Caroline Grigson, eds., *Animals and Archaeology*, British Archaeological Reports, Internat'l. Ser., 227 (Oxford, 1985), pp. 161–77; eadem, *The Other Economy: Pastoral Husbandry on a Medieval Estate* (Berkeley, 1989), pp. 121–25.

Guton Hall in Brandiston were by no means unusual. Pigeons also were a feature of many demesnes. The merit of these lesser categories of livestock lay in their more rapid breeding cycles and their capacity to utilize resources either surplus or unsuited to the requirements of the other animals.[19] Ecologically, that meant that not even the smallest niches within the farm's food chain were left unoccupied.

The comparatively exceptional nature of these characteristics is brought out by a wider survey of demesne livestock within the country as a whole. Thus, Table 2 provides summary statistics at a county level of certain key diagnostic features of demesne pastoral husbandry during the period 1250–1349.[20] As will be seen from Column B, Norfolk was alone among lowland, arable counties in supporting such a small proportion of working animals. Its nearest rivals, also in the south and east, were Essex and Kent. During the course of the fourteenth century, as arable husbandry contracted and pastoral husbandry expanded, the ratio of working to nonworking animals fell almost everywhere: draught animals accounted for 46 per cent of demesne livestock in the mid-thirteenth century, 38 per cent in the mid-fourteenth century, and 29 per cent in the mid-fifteenth century. The same trend is detectable in Norfolk, but the proportion always remained consistently smaller—36 per cent, 23 per cent, and 20 per cent, respectively. Indeed, before 1350 it was only in the far north of the country, where opportunities for arable husbandry were environmentally circumscribed, that smaller proportions of working animals appear

[19]Martin Stephenson, "The Role of Poultry Husbandry in the Medieval Agrarian Economy, 1200–1450," *Veterinary History* 10 (1977–78): 16–24; Biddick, *Other Economy*, pp. 125–28.

[20]The data upon which this analysis is based were generously supplied by John Langdon.

TABLE 2
ENGLAND: SOME CHARACTERISTICS OF DEMESNE PASTORAL HUSBANDRY BY COUNTY, 1250–1349

COUNTY	A	B	C	D	E	F	G	H	I
Bedfordshire	10	46	24	25	6	4.5	62	15	25
Berkshire	16	43	30	25	3	4.8	112	23	50
Berwickshire	1	28	31	38	2	7.8	147	—	—
Buckinghamshire	15	46	33	17	5	2.4	93	42	34
Cambridgeshire	12	50	28	19	3	1.7	99	24	11
Cheshire	1	56	35	2	8	6.8	50	—	—
Cornwall	8	36	32	31	<1	4.8	33	40	62
Cumberland	3	23	61	16	0	9.3	59	18	21
Derbyshire	3	86	8	0	6	5.8	266	13	88
Devon	15	38	38	24	1	6.3	74	49	86
Dorset	6	45	26	27	2	6.3	156	25	53
Co. Durham	26	79	9	8	4	7.3	165	—	—
Essex	28	33	32	34	2	0.7	52	61	35
Gloucestershire	17	48	23	26	3	8.8	128	40	90
Hampshire[x]	36	47	26	25	2	4.7	84	47	44
Herefordshire	4	41	17	37	6	7.7	49	37	38
Hertfordshire	16	38	39	20	4	0.5	54	21	29
Huntingdonshire	8	50	39	14	7	1.4	158	7	38
Isle of Wight	8	52	28	19	1	10.8	113	23	18
Kent	49	34	36	23	6	1.4	72	82	29
Lancashire	6	73	26	0	0	6.4	123	—	—
Leicestershire	9	66	6	25	3	3.8	87	32	*40
Lincolnshire	31	37	40	21	2	3.5	97	48	38
Middlesex	15	38	45	15	2	1.5	53	8	50
Monmouthshire	6	73	21	6	<1	14.8	84	14	63
Norfolk	124	30	46	21	3	0.7	69	78	26
Northhamptonshire	26	44	40	12	5	1.9	138	36	36
Northumberland	4	89	10	0	1	3.5	174	19	30
Nottinghamshire	5	49	31	18	2	6.5	230	12	73
Oxfordshire	29	48	26	23	4	3.0	109	41	75
Rutland	4	48	22	25	5	2.2	127	—	+
Shropshire	2	57	38	0	5	5.1	79	46	30
Somerset	21	72	19	6	2	11.2	174	38	70
Staffordshire	9	51	21	26	2	7.7	97	14	25
Suffolk	33	37	44	17	3	1.2	111	60	37
Surrey	18	39	37	21	3	3.2	138	18	49
Sussex	22	37	24	34	5	6.9	83	42	35

TABLE 2—*Continued*

COUNTY	A	B	C	D	E	F	G	H	I
Warwickshire	20	67	23	7	4	6.3	167	21	41
Westmorland	—	—	—	—	—	—	—	—	—
Wiltshire	21	35	14	50	2	7.7	83	44	71
Worcestershire	6	47	20	30	3	3.9	53	16	43
Yorkshire E. R.	11	58	9	31	2	5.1	91	—	—
Yorkshire N. R.	6	88	6	0	6	7.5	221	25	62
Yorkshire W. R.	27	49	36	14	1	7.4	84	—	—
England	*737*	*47*	*29*	*22*	*3*	*4.6*	*91*	*1,179*	*41*

*including Rutland
+with Leicestershire
xexcluding Isle of Wight
A Number of demesnes with accounts
B Draught animals as percentage of total livestock units (from accounts)
C Cattle other than oxen as percentage of total livestock units (from accounts)
D Sheep as percentage of total livestock units (from accounts)
E Swine as percentage of total livestock units (from accounts)
F Oxen per horse (imposed maximum individual ratio of 20) (from accounts)
G Young cattle per 100 adults (from accounts)
H Number of *Inquisitiones Post Mortem*
I Pence of grassland per 100 pence of arable (from *IPM*s)

to have been supported. These were possibly the breeding areas from which non-self-sufficient lowland areas further south drew their replacement stock.[21]

Nationally, oxen remained unquestionably the single most important source of draught power throughout the period 1250–1449, consistently outnumbering horses by at least four to one. As John Langdon has shown, it was Norfolk that pioneered the application of horses to farm work, and Norfolk stands out

[21]On the strong pastoral bias to husbandry in the extreme north of England see Edward Miller, "Farming in Northern England during the Twelfth and Thirteenth Centuries," *Northern History* 11 (1975): 11–12; idem, "Farming Techniques: Northern England," in H. E. Hallam, ed., *The Agrarian History of England and Wales*, 2: *1042–1350* (Cambridge, 1988), pp. 408–11.

as the only county in which from as early as 1250 horses were consistently in the majority (Table 2, Col. F).[22] After 1350, however, it was joined by Essex and Hertfordshire, with Suffolk, Kent, and Cambridgeshire not far behind, these six counties representing a geographically contiguous block concentrated in East Anglia and the southeast.

By switching from oxen to horses these counties were relieved from the need to devote such a large share of pastoral resources to the breeding of replacement work animals, and a relative expansion in other types of pastoral enterprise became possible. Hence, the prominence of cattle other than oxen in Norfolk: these comprised no less than 46 per cent of total livestock units in the period 1250–1349, a proportion rivaled only by Middlesex and Suffolk and exceeded only by Cumberland, whose extensive pastures offered considerable scope to cattle rearing (Table 2, Col. C). The distinctiveness of this emphasis is highlighted by the fact that nationally cattle other than oxen accounted for, on average, 29 per cent of demesne livestock before 1350 and 31 per cent thereafter, by which time they accounted for almost half of all demesne livestock units in Norfolk.

Within the country at large the ratio of adult to immature cattle was only marginally in favor of the former, although the gap began to widen after 1350, as cattle herds expanded in the wake of the demographic collapse and subsequent contraction in arable cultivation.[23] Before that catastrophe Norfolk was one of only a dozen English counties in which there was a decided imbalance between adults and immatures, and of these only Cumberland, Essex, Hertfordshire, Middlesex, and Hampshire

---

[22]*Horses, Oxen and Technological Innovation*, pp. 50–53; Campbell, "Towards an Agricultural Geography," p. 93.

[23]The growing practice of farming out dairies may also mean that younger animals are increasingly masked from view.

could boast stocking densities of cattle that were as high or higher. These contrast with no less than 19 counties—the six northern counties of Berwickshire, Northumberland, Durham, Yorkshire North Riding, Lancashire, and Derbyshire prominent among them—in which immatures exceeded adults and where, therefore, the emphasis was upon rearing.[24] Indeed, if a relatively heavy emphasis upon cattle other than oxen (i.e., at least 30 per cent of total livestock units), a low proportion of oxen among cattle (i.e., less than 40 per cent of total cattle), and a low ratio of immature to adult cattle (i.e., fewer than 75 immatures per 100 adults), are taken as diagnostic features of a strong specialist interest in dairying, then only Norfolk, Middlesex, and Hertfordshire fulfill all three criteria before 1350, and only Norfolk, Suffolk, Essex, and Hertfordshire, thereafter. In the Middle Ages these were quite clearly England's premier dairying counties.

Norfolk's concentration upon cattle-based dairying (a specialism that Chaucer includes in his description of Oswald's agricultural activities) plainly eclipsed any interest that demesne lords may have taken in sheep farming, for all that it is for the latter activity that the county is most usually celebrated. This is not to deny the presence of significant numbers of sheep within the county, for their importance is confirmed by the size of Norfolk's contribution to the 1341/42 wool tax,[25]

---

[24]On commercial cattle rearing on the de Lacy estates in northern England see *Victoria County History: Lancaster*, vol. 2 (London, 1908), pp. 268–84; G. H. Tupling, *The Economic History of Rossendale*, Chetham Society, n.s., 86 (1927): 17–41; R. Cunliffe Shaw, *The Royal Forest of Lancaster* (Preston, 1956), pp. 353–91; M. A. Atkin, "Land Use and Management in the Upland Demesne of the De Lacy Estate of Blackburnshire, c1300," *Agricultural History Review* 42/1 (1994): 1–19.

[25]W. M. Ormrod, "The Crown and the English Economy, 1290–1348," pp. 149–83 in Bruce M. S. Campbell, ed., *Before the Black Death: Studies in the 'Crisis' of the Early Fourteenth Century* (Manchester, 1991), pp. 178–79.

but on the evidence of demesne stocking schedules the majority of these sheep must have been peasant owned rather than seigniorial animals. Within the demesne sector sheep tended only to assume prominence where environmental circumstances rendered cattle unsuitable: in the Broadland and fenland marshes, on the sandy soils of Breckland, and wherever soils were light and surface water scarce. On the demesne front Norfolk thus stands in the middle rank of sheep-farming counties, well behind the southern downland counties of Wiltshire and Sussex but ahead of most of central and northern England. Much the same applies to swine.[26]

Pastoral husbandry in Norfolk was therefore distinctive in almost every respect, and especially so by dint of its developed and intensive nature. The latter is the more remarkable in that as far as several grassland (i.e., grassland belonging exclusively to the demesne and excluding that held in common) was concerned, it was one of the least grassy counties in England—a point that can be readily demonstrated using the land-use information recorded in the extents attached to *Inquisitiones Post Mortem* (*IPM*s). This information relates to the estates of lay tenants-in-chief of the Crown and is available for the greater part of the country, although the consistency with which demesne resources are recorded varies according to the relative importance of the resources in question and the practices of particular groups of escheators.[27] For both sets of reasons there are grounds for believing that pastoral resources are

[26]See Table 2.

[27]Systematic use of *IPM*s to cast light on variations in land use and land values was pioneered by J. Ambrose Raftis, *Assart Data and Land Values: Two Studies in the East Midlands, 1200–1350* (Toronto, 1974). For a recent appraisal of the source and its potential see Bruce M. S. Campbell, James A. Galloway, and Margaret Murphy, "Rural Land-Use in the Metropolitan Hinterland, 1270–1339: The Evidence of *Inquisitiones Post Mortem*," *Agricultural History Review* 40/1 (1992): 1–22.

consistently under-recorded in the counties north of the River Trent. In much of the rest of the country, however, the *IPMs* provide the best available guide to the relative supply of permanent grassland. Table 2, Column I, summarizes the mean ratio of the value of arable resources to the value of pastoral resources (meadow, pasture, herbage, and other sources of forage) by county for the decade 1300–09. This decade was chosen because it probably represents the culmination of medieval demographic and economic expansion and is numerically well served by *IPMs*. The total of 1,179 extents used provides coverage of every English county, except the palatinate counties of Cheshire, Lancashire, and Durham, and for every county except Huntingdonshire and Middlesex (both small and dominated by ecclesiastical estates) the number of available extents is in double figures.

In the country as a whole the average demesne had grassland worth 40 per cent of the value of its arable. Equivalent "grassland ratios" calculated on a county basis reveal strong regional variations and highlight Norfolk's position at the most arable and least grassy end of the land-use spectrum. Norfolk lay within a block of counties concentrated in the East Midlands, East Anglia, and the extreme southeast that had grassland ratios decidedly below the national average. These ratios fell to a low of 26:100 in Norfolk, 25:100 in Bedfordshire, and a meager 11:100 in Cambridgeshire—England's least grassy county. By contrast, above-average ratios prevailed in much of the west and parts of the north of England. Thus, grassland ratios were highest of all in Derbyshire, Gloucestershire, and Devon, where they were more than three times higher than in Norfolk and the value of grassland came to within 15 per cent of the value of arable. In the neighboring counties of Nottinghamshire, Oxfordshire, Wiltshire, Somerset, and Monmouthshire, followed by Yorkshire, Cornwall, Dorset, and Berkshire, supplies of demesne grassland were also more than double those in Norfolk and worth between 50 per cent and 75 per cent of the value of the arable. Were the northern returns less defective, the same would probably be true of Northumberland, Cumberland, Staffordshire, and Shropshire, since in environmental terms they share much in common with the grassy counties of the southwest, although it is possible that more of their grassland was in common than in several ownership.

Within Norfolk, as Figure 2 shows, there was obviously some local variation in grassland supplies according to environmental circumstances and prevailing institutional arrangements. For instance, several of the demesnes on the fen-edge and in Broadland enjoyed relatively abundant supplies of rich pasturage. Demesnes on the Breck-edge in south Norfolk were also better off than most. But in much of eastern, central, and northern Norfolk several grassland was in extremely short supply and there were some quite sizeable demesnes (especially on the light soils of the northwest) that had little or no several grassland at all and were thus almost totally reliant for pasturage on the various heaths and common wastes of the locality. The situation in the immediate vicinity of Bawdeswell appears to have been only marginally less tight, and Oswald the reeve must have been grateful for the pasturage afforded by the heath beside which he lived. In 1314 an *IPM* of the demesne at Foxley of Hawise de Veer recorded 200 acres of arable worth 7*d*. an acre, six acres of meadow worth 18*d*. an acre, and eight acres of pasture worth 12*d*. an acre; 10 years later (1324) an *IPM* of the demesne, also at Foxley, of Aymer de Valence, earl of Pembroke, recorded 306 acres of arable worth 8.8*d*. an acre, 15 acres of meadow worth 24*d*. an acre, and 30 acres of pasture worth 9*d*. an acre.[28] With respective grassland ratios

[28]PRO C134/34 (7); C134/83 (99).

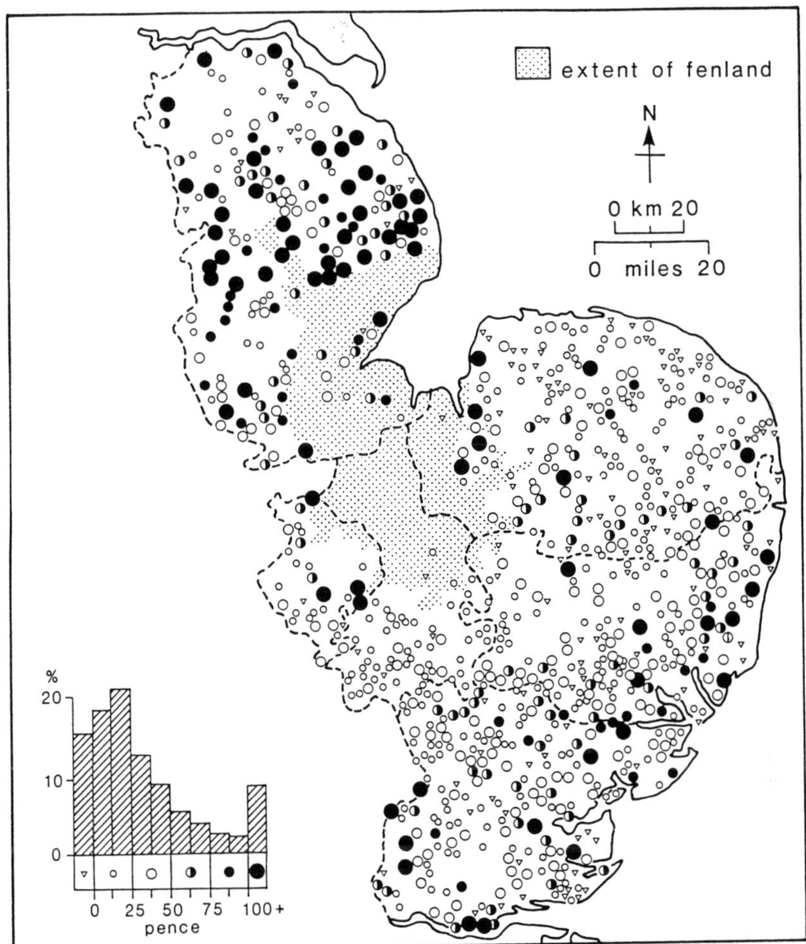

Figure 2. Eastern England: value of demesne grassland (meadow and pasture) per 100 pence of demesne arable, 1270–1349 (source: *Inquisitiones Post Mortem*)

of 15:100 and 23:100, neither of these demesnes was well provided with several grassland.

Land-use and farm enterprise thus present a striking paradox in medieval Norfolk. How was such a developed pastoral regime reconciled with such a shortage of the grassland that

M. M. Postan, for one, has argued was one of its most essential prerequisites? After all, it was his great thesis that by the end of the thirteenth and the beginning of the fourteenth centuries, "in corn-growing parts of the country taken as a whole, pasture and the animal population had been reduced to a level incompatible with the conduct of mixed farming itself."[29] For Postan, therefore, stocking densities were a direct function of the availability of permanent grassland.[30] What the Norfolk evidence shows is that this relationship was less direct than he supposed. Demesne stocking densities in medieval Norfolk were certainly by no means high, averaging 36 livestock units per 100 grain acres between 1250 and 1349 and 42 livestock units per 100 grain acres between 1350 and 1449. They were thus respectively 20 per cent and 35 per cent below the corresponding national averages of 44 and 65 livestock units per 100 grain acres, the discrepancy being greater in the later period, when livestock numbers rose significantly in many parts of the country, especially those environmentally better suited than Norfolk to convert from arable to grass. Nevertheless, Norfolk's stocking density was not disproportionately as low relative to other counties, particularly those of southern and southwestern England, as its low grassland ratio would suggest. The explanation lies in the intensity with which pastoral resources were exploited and the extent to which they were augmented by other sources of sustenance. Kathleen Biddick has recently arrived at a similar conclusion for the estates of Peterborough Abbey: "the changing composition of livestock in the herding

---

[29] *The Medieval Economy and Society: An Economic History of Britain in the Middle Ages* (London, 1972), p. 59.

[30] "We have so far assumed that it was the shortage of pasture that kept the numbers of animals down. That the assumption is right and that the shortage of pasture was great and widespread is revealed by the high and rising rents and by the prices of pastures as given in manorial surveys, custumals and similar manorial valuations of the land," Postan, *Medieval Economy and Society*, p. 59.

economy of the estate characterizes a pastoral sector of some dynamism and complexity and dispels any notion of linear relations between animal and cereal husbandry."[31] In Norfolk the careful management of meadow lands and integration of the arable and pastoral sectors via fodder cropping, the fold-course system, and convertible husbandry served to boost stocking densities.[32] The productivity of the pastoral sector further benefited from an emphasis upon those types of livestock that were most productive of draught power and food.

What recommended the horse to Norfolk farmers was that it worked faster and for longer hours than the ox and thereby allowed the size of plough teams to be reduced and the range of road transport to be extended.[33] The price of this change was higher depreciation and running costs, the former because, unlike oxen, old, worn-out horses could not be fattened and sold for meat, and the latter because horses consumed greater quantities of oats, vetches, and other legumes. The substitution of horses for oxen thus entailed a shift from natural to produced fodder. On the prior of Norwich's intensively managed demesnes of Martham and Hemsby, 51 per cent and 74 per cent, respectively, of the oats harvested between 1261 and 1335 were consumed as fodder, and 6 per cent and 10 per cent of the peas.[34] In contrast, at Sedgeford in northwest Norfolk only 47 per cent of the oats were consumed as fodder, augmented by 25

[31]*Other Economy*, p. 65.

[32]Bruce M. S. Campbell, "Agricultural Progress in Medieval England: Some Evidence from Eastern Norfolk," *Economic History Review*, 2nd ser., 36/1 (1983): 26–46; Mark Bailey, "Sand into Gold: The Evolution of the Foldcourse System in West Suffolk, 1200–1600," *Agricultural History Review* 38/1 (1990): 40–57.

[33]Langdon, *Horses, Oxen and Technological Innovation*, pp. 158–71; idem, "Horse Hauling: A Revolution in Vehicle Transport in Twelfth- and Thirteenth-Century England?" *Past and Present* 103 (1984): 37–66.

[34]NRO DCN60/15 and 23; DCN62/1–2; L'Estrange IB4/4.

per cent of the rye and 29 per cent of the peas.[35] Swine and poultry also were consumers of legumes and grain, and as converters of calories were more efficient meat producers than either sheep or cattle.[36]

Such a change from natural to produced fodder, as Ester Boserup has observed, represents a major increase in drudgery on the part of the labor force.[37] It also constitutes a change to a more intensive type of agricultural food chain. According to I. G. Simmons, within sedentary agriculture there are three main pastoral food chains. In the first, livestock are fed solely upon managed grassland and natural vegetation; in the second, they are fed upon a combination of managed grassland, natural vegetation, and tillage crops; and in the third, they are fed on tillage crops alone.[38] The substitution of horses for oxen and the management of swine in styes rather than as a forage animal thus represent a shift from the first to the second food chain and a corresponding step-up in the intensity of pastoral husbandry. This change constitutes a significant advance and presupposes a closer integration of arable and pastoral husbandry to the mutual benefit of both, as fodder crops contributed to the sustenance of the livestock and the latter contributed traction and manure to the arable. The next major change in the evolution of pastoral husbandry was not to take place until the late seventeenth and the eighteenth centuries, when mixed-farming systems in which livestock became almost wholly reliant upon an improved range of fodder crops were evolved. Norfolk again stood in the van of these developments.[39]

---

[35]NRO DCN60/33; DCN62/1–2; L'Estrange IB1/4 and 4/4.

[36]Ester Boserup, *Population and Technology* (Oxford, 1981), p. 18.

[37]*The Conditions of Agricultural Growth: The Economics of Agrarian Change under Population Pressure* (London, 1965), pp. 36–39.

[38]*The Ecology of Natural Resources* (London, 1974).

[39]Mark Overton and Bruce M. S. Campbell, "Norfolk Livestock Farming 1250–1740: A Comparative Study of Manorial Accounts and Probate Inventories,"

In the thirteenth and fourteenth centuries dairy cattle were the principal beneficiaries of these important changes. They became the recipients of the grass and hay released by the substitution of horses for oxen, while the reduced demand for replacement oxen allowed a greater concentration on dairying at the expense of rearing. This marked preference for dairy cattle derived from the fact that they are more productive of human food per unit area—in the form of milk, butter, cheese, and the meat of surplus calves and decrepit females—than any other class of livestock. On the evidence of modern agricultural statistics, David B. Grigg has shown that milk production is 180 per cent more productive per unit area of calories and protein than beef production, and four times more productive of calories and five times more productive of protein than mutton production.[40] It is also superior in productivity to egg and poultry production. For medieval farmers with scarce land resources, intensive dairying therefore offered the best food return per unit area, especially where labor was both relatively abundant and cheap.[41] By contrast, the inferior productivity of sheep meant that they tended to be relegated to those types of environment—particularly heath and marsh—where cattle did not thrive.

Journal of Historical Geography 18/4 (1992): 382–92; Bruce M. S. Campbell and Mark Overton, "A New Perspective on Medieval and Early Modern Agriculture: Six Centuries of Norfolk Farming c.1250–c.1850," *Past and Present* 141 (1993): 88–95.

[40]*The Dynamics of Agricultural Change: The Historical Experience* (London, 1982), p. 71.

[41]It was possibly these kinds of relationship that H. E. Hallam had in mind when he observed, "the progressive parts of England had large herds of dairy cattle whose milk the people drank and made into butter and cheese. On the Winchester estates the lord generally made cheese out of ewe's milk, a sign of a primitive economy, for a ewe gives only a quart of milk a day and is difficult to milk, whereas a goat gives a gallon and a cow two gallons. Eastern England and the east Midlands also used stots and affers (small horses) instead of slow oxen for ploughing and could therefore plough twice as much land in a given time" (*Rural England 1066–1348* [London, 1981], p. 14).

Implicit in these developments were higher inputs of capital and labor both per animal and per unit area. Labor was required to manage grassland, make hay, cultivate fodder crops, supervise flocks and herds, collect and spread manure, milk and calve cows, make cheeses, shoe horses, and attend to a host of minor tasks entailed in the management of animals. Capital was required in the form of the animals themselves, the seed for the fodder crops that they consumed and the tools and implements with which these were cultivated, and, most conspicuously, for specialist housing and equipment. The working horses were generally stabled, and some at least of the dairy herds were housed, thus facilitating stall-feeding and the accumulation of farmyard manure. Swine, too, were often housed in styes, and it was not uncommon for sheep cotes to be constructed to provide shelter during the most severe weather. Butter and cheese production required investment in pails, churns, vats, presses, and scales and regular purchases of salt and cheese-cloths.[42] On some of the larger demesnes, such as those of the prior of Norwich at Hemsby, Great Plumstead, and Newton, purpose-built dairy houses were provided.[43]

Such a system of pastoral husbandry was expensive and the outputs—in terms of traction generated, milk and meat produced, and breeding rates maintained—needed to be such as to justify the inputs. Yet the productivity of such a system is extremely hard to measure.[44] One index of the gross return

---

[42]Bruce M. S. Campbell, "Commercial Dairy Production on Medieval English Demesnes: The Case of Norfolk," in Annie Grant., ed., *Animals and Their Products in Trade and Exchange, Archaeozoologica (Quatrième Numéro Spécial)*, 16 (Paris, 1992), pp. 107–18.

[43]David Yaxley, *The Prior's Manor-Houses: Inventories of Eleven of the Manor-Houses of the Prior of Norwich, Made in the Year 1352 A.D.* (Dereham, 1988), pp. 5–7, 14–18.

[44]Mark Overton and Bruce M. S. Campbell, "Productivity Change in European Agricultural Development," pp. 12, 33–34, in eidem, eds., *Land, Labour and*

obtainable from dairy farming is provided by the rate at which cows were let at farm. The farming of demesne dairies was a profitable and reliable source of income and became increasingly common practice during the course of the fourteenth century. The terms on which the cows were leased varied. Usually the lessee was entitled to the milk of the cows, the calves that they produced, and, presumably, their manure. Occasionally the lessee was entitled to their milk (or lactage) only, and their issue was retained by the lord. Arrangements also sometimes were made whereby the calves were divided between the lessee and the lord. The rate of farm varied according to the terms agreed, but whatever the latter, as will be seen from Table 3, it is plain that cows potentially were an extremely lucrative asset. At a rate of 4*s.*–6*s.* per head when farmed for their milk and calves, one cow could be as profitable as several acres of prime arable. Since herds were usually farmed out en bloc, the payments made by the farmers were often quite considerable. At Foxley, for instance, the farm of 30 cows raised £6 15*s.*0*d.* in 1306.[45]

Cash payments of this order of magnitude presuppose that a significant part of the produce must have been sold for cash, and manorial accounts confirm that under direct management cattle, swine, and poultry were regular sources of income.[46] On the prior of Norwich's seven demesnes of Gnatingdon, Thornham, North Elmham, Taverham, Monks Granges, Plumstead,

---

Livestock: Historical Studies in European Agricultural Productivity (Manchester, 1991), pp. 1–50.

[45]PRO SC6/935/19.

[46]On demesnes within the hinterland of London, sales of animals and animal products contributed 14 per cent and 17 per cent, respectively, of gross agricultural sales income c.1300 (B. M. S. Campbell, "Measuring the Commercialisation of Seigneurial Agriculture c.1300," in Richard H. Britnell and Bruce M. S. Campbell, eds., *A Commercialising Economy: England 1086 to c.1300* [Manchester, 1995], pp. 148–49).

TABLE 3
NORFOLK: FARM OF COWS

Manor	Year	Rent per Cow
Burgh in Flegg	*1296–97*	*4*s.*0*d.
Hautbois	*1363*	*4*s.*0*d.
Horning	*1372*	*4*s.*0*d.
Wroxham	1342–43	3*s*.4*d*.
Hainford	1363–64	4*s*.0*d*.
Haveringland	1356–57	4*s*.0*d*.
Haveringland	1376–77	4*s*.0*d*.
Ludham	1355	4*s*.9*d*.
Foxley	1305–06	5*s*.0*d*.
Gimingham	1358–59	5*s*.0*d*.
Tunstead	1359–60	5*s*.6*d*.
Melton	1332–33	5*s*.6*d*.
Melton	1366–67	6*s*.0*d*.
Thurning	1319–20	6*s*.0*d*.
Horning	1372	6*s*.0*d*.
Gateley	1326–27	6*s*.8*d*.
Arminghall	1347–48	6*s*.8*d*.

Italics = lactage only

Sources: PRO SC6/935/19, SC6/1090/4, DL29/288/4719, 4720, 4734; NRO Diocesan Est/2, 2/15 and 17, Diocesan Est/10, NRS 2848 12 F1, DCN 60/25/1–3, DCN 62/1 and 7, NRS 2796 12E2; BL Add. Roll 26060, Add. Charter 15199–202

and Martham in the period 1326–27, 53 per cent of all cheeses produced were sold; this proportion rose to 66 per cent at Martham and 96 per cent at Thornham.[47] In the heartland of cheese production, in east-central and northeastern Norfolk, there is a clear implication that specialization in dairying was a response to market opportunities. Between 1307 and 1315 the Norwich Cathedral Priory manor at Attlebridge sold 59 per cent of its cheeses and 79 per cent of its butters; between 1305 and

[47]NRO DCN62/1.

1338 the sacristan of Norwich's manor at Bauburgh sold 63–90 per cent of its cheeses and 80 per cent of its butters; in the years 1296–97 the queen's manor at Cawston sold 93 per cent of its cheeses and 94 per cent of its butters (the remainder being paid as tithe); during the 1270s the royal manor at Costessey sold 94 per cent of its cheeses and butters; and during the same decade the Broadland manor of Acle sold its entire output of cheese and butter.[48]

Norfolk's dense network of over 120 markets must have provided a ready outlet for this dairy produce, much of which may eventually have found its way onto the Norwich food market. Costessey, for example, for which a series of detailed though damaged dairy accounts survive from the 1270s, was actively engaged in the large-scale commercial production of butter and cheese and possibly traded directly with Norwich.[49] It is situated in the valley of the River Wensum, four miles northwest of the city, and maintained a herd of 25 to 30 milking cows. This was a well-managed herd: on the three occasions for which there are legible figures of the number of cows kept and calves born, the calving rate was 100 per cent (although two out of three calves born were subsequently sold). Such a high fertility rate reflects both a favorable ratio of labor to animals—the herd was under the charge of a permanent cowman, while the dairy was staffed by a permanent dairymaid—and the careful culling of aged and sterile females. This high fertility rate was matched by similarly favorable milk yields, to judge from the quantities of cheese and butter produced and sold. One year the sale of cheese, butter, milk, and calves produced by the 25 cows kept on the demesne yielded an income of £6 8*s*.4*d*., another—

[48]NRO DCN61/11–13 and 16–19; PRO SC6/1090/4, SC6/933/13, SC6/929/1–7.

[49]PRO SC6/933/13.

this time from a herd of 26 cows—an income of £6 12*s*.0*d*. On both occasions this was equivalent to a gross income for its dairy produce alone of just over 5*s*. per cow (at least 1*s*. a head higher than the going rate at which cows were farmed for their lactage).

This intensive pastoral regime—producing butter, cheese, calves, pigs, bacon, fat lambs, poultry, and eggs for consumption and for sale—attained its fullest development during the third quarter of the fourteenth century (see Table 4), as resources were released by a contracting but still buoyant arable sector and before demand had been too seriously eroded by changing dietary preferences and prolonged population decline.[50] With the demise towards the end of the fourteenth century of the conditions of land shortage and labor surplus that had brought the system into being, this high-cost system of pastoral husbandry lost its competitive edge.

Spiraling wage rates and falling prices squeezed profit margins, and in certain markets Norfolk producers found themselves undercut by farmers whose more extensive methods meant they had lower production costs.[51] During the final quarter of the fourteenth century a trend towards more land-extensive and less labor-intensive forms of pastoralism is thus increasingly apparent in Norfolk.[52] It is at this point that

---

[50]Christopher Dyer has identified a significant decline in the amounts of dairy produce consumed by harvest workers at Sedgeford in Norfolk from the closing decades of the fourteenth century, as increasing quantities of meat were consumed: "Changes in Diet in the Late Middle Ages: The Case of Harvest Workers," *Agricultural History Review* 36/1 (1988): 25–28.

[51]For evidence of a pronounced swing from arable to pastoral production within the country at large during the fourteenth century, see Bruce M. S. Campbell, "Land, Labour, Livestock, and Productivity Trends in English Seignorial Agriculture, 1208–1450," pp. 144–82 in Campbell and Overton, *Land, Labour and Livestock*, pp. 153–59.

[52]For a parallel trend in arable production see Campbell, "Land, Labour, Livestock, and Productivity Trends," pp. 144–49.

TABLE 4
NORFOLK: TRENDS IN DEMESNE PASTORAL HUSBANDRY 1250–1449 (50-YEAR STAGGERED MEANS)

Years	Mean per Demesne							
	Livestock Units	Livestock Units per 100 Grain Acres	Percentage of Livestock Units					Oxen per Horse
			Draught Animals	Cattle other than Oxen	Young Cattle per 100 Adults	Sheep	Swine	
1250–1299	46	31	35	45	74	17	3	0.8
1275–1324	47	33	32	46	76	20	3	0.9
1300–1349	46	36	27	47	67	24	3	0.6
1325–1374	47	41	23	50	61	24	4	0.5
1350–1399	49	45	20	52	54	25	4	0.4
1375–1424	43	36	20	47	43	29	3	0.3
1400–1449	44	31	20	39	39	38	4	0.3

Source: Norfolk manorial accounts
Method: For calculation of livestock units see n. 16 above.

small, one-man plough teams began to emerge, dairy herds were frequently leased out, and sheep, with their lower unit costs and capacity to produce milk, meat, and wool at a time of uncertain markets, began to gain at the expense of cattle. In fact, when Chaucer penned his portrait of the Norfolk reeve the long-established character of pastoral husbandry in that county was on the threshold of a far-reaching transformation.[53]

It would be misleading to represent this intensive pastoral response to land shortage, labor abundance, and favorable market opportunities as unique to Norfolk, for it clearly was not. The cluster analysis of Norfolk pastoral-farming types may be matched against a corresponding cluster analysis of pastoral farming on a sample of 660 demesnes within the country as a whole during the period 1250–1349.[54] Six basic pastoral types emerge, as set out in Table 5 in descending order of intensity.

Of these six types it is the first, Cluster 1, that corresponds most closely to the intensive husbandry described in Norfolk, sharing the characteristics of a favorable ratio of nonworking to working animals, a significant contribution by horses to draught power, dominance of the nonworking sector by cattle (with some demographic bias towards adults), and the relegation of swine and especially sheep to subsidiary positions. Demesnes belonging to this cluster grouping, and therefore sharing in some measure these characteristics, were widely distributed and, as Figure 3 shows, examples may be found in most parts of the country. In part, this wide geographical scatter represents the lumping together of upland demesnes, which practiced large-scale cattle farming using extensive methods, with lowland demesnes whose cattle farming assumed a

[53]Overton and Campbell, "Norfolk Livestock Farming," pp. 383, 391, 393.

[54]Campbell and Power, "Mapping the Agricultural Geography."

TABLE 5
ENGLAND: CLASSIFICATION OF DEMESNE PASTORAL-FARMING TYPES 1250–1349

	Cluster	No. of Demesnes	% of Demesnes	Mean Percentage of Total Livestock Units					
				Horses	Oxen	Adult Cattle	Young Cattle	Sheep	Swine
1250–1349	1	100	15	11	18	34	29	6	1
	2	116	18	19	28	23	20	6	5
	3	132	20	11	21	18	14	33	3
	4	75	11	10	26	3	2	58	2
	5	40	6	25	37	6	3	12	17
	6	43	7	53	38	2	1	5	2
	7	154	23	15	79	2	2	2	1
	Overall	660	100	17	38	14	12	17	3
	*Norfolk**	*69*	*54*	*19*	*14*	*41*	*18*	*5*	*4*

*Norfolk** = mean characteristics of Cluster 1 demesnes in Norfolk

Source: National sample of manorial accounts and Norfolk manorial accounts

Method: Cluster analysis (relocation method), seven-cluster solution. For calculation of livestock units see n. 16 above.

different form and was underpinned by very intensive methods. Within such lowland contexts the distribution of these demesnes was strongly biased towards the south and east, and in certain specific localities they became the predominant pastoral type. Eastern and central Norfolk, of course, stand out, as do much of southern and eastern Suffolk, Huntingdonshire, the Soke of Peterborough, and the Lincolnshire fen-edge, east Hertfordshire, the immediate environs of London, southeast Kent, southern Hampshire, and south Somerset and east Devon. Some of these concentrations reflect the presence of environmental opportunities that were particularly advantageous for the development of pastoral husbandry—the fen-edge, the vicinity of Romney Marsh, and east Devon—but at least as important were demographic pressure, commercial opportunity, and institutional arrangements that allowed the evolution of more individualistic forms of pastoral husbandry.[55] Such factors certainly seem to have been the common denominators of the concentrations of these demesnes in East Anglia and the Home Counties.

In all of these respects the situation prevailing in Norfolk seems to have represented something of an extreme. Norfolk was fourteenth-century England's most populous county, contained England's largest provincial city, possessed a common-

---

[55]For the fen-edge see J. Ambrose Raftis, *The Estates of Ramsey Abbey: A Study in Economic Growth and Organization* (Toronto, 1957), pp. 129–58; Biddick, *Other Economy*. For Romney Marsh and east Kent see R. A. L. Smith, *Canterbury Cathedral Priory: A Study in Monastic Administration* (Cambridge, 1943), pp. 146–65, and P. F. Brandon, "Farming Techniques: South-Eastern England," pp. 312–25 in *Agrarian History*, vol. 2. For east Devon see N. W. Alcock, "An East Devon Manor in the Later Middle Ages. Part I: 1374–1420. The Manor Farm," *Report and Transactions of the Devonshire Association* 102 (1970): 141–87; K. Ugawa, "The Economic Development of Some Devon Manors in the Thirteenth Century," ibid. 94 (1962): 630–83; John Hatcher, "Farming Techniques: South-Western England," pp. 383–98 in Hallam, *Agrarian History* 2: 395–98; H. S. A. Fox, "Peasant Farmers, Patterns of Settlement and *pays*: Transformations in the Landscapes of Devon and Cornwall during the Later Middle Ages," pp. 41–73 in Robert Higham, ed., *Landscape and Townscape in the South West* (Exeter, 1989), pp. 57–64.

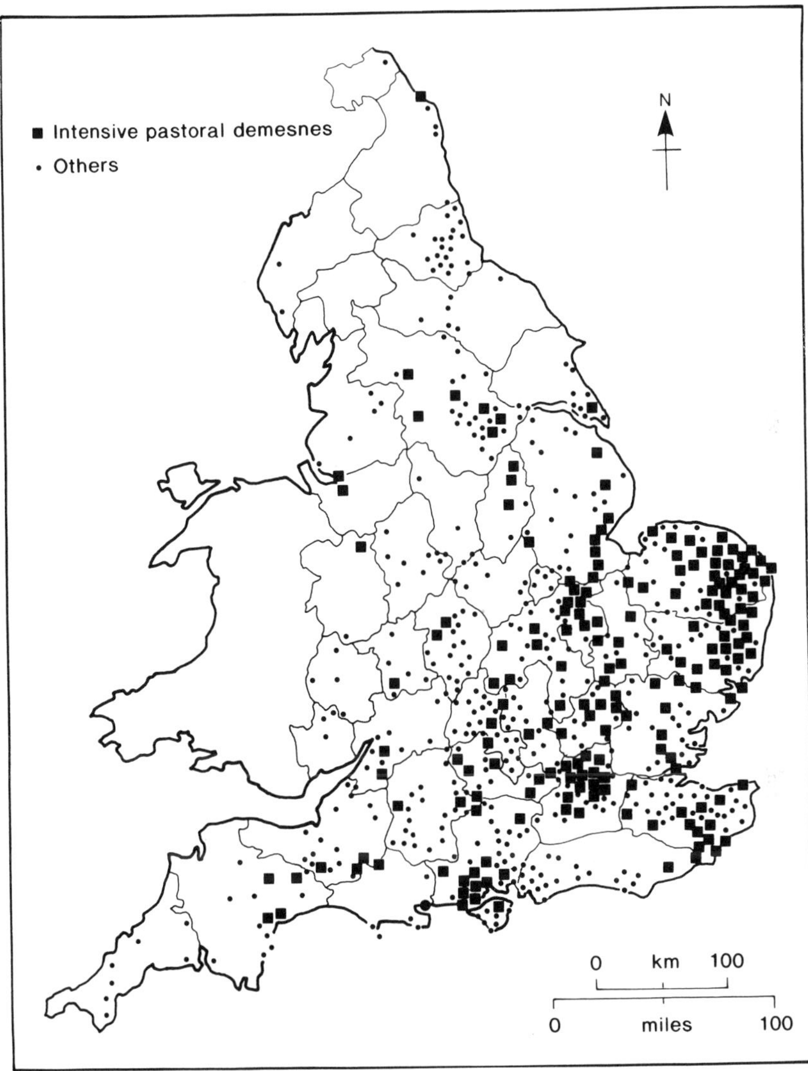

Figure 3. England: distribution of "intensive" pastoral-farming demesnes, 1250–1349 (for explanation see Cluster 1, Table 5)

field system that allowed a high degree of flexibility and freedom to the cropping of land and herding of animals, and conducted a lively trade in agricultural products both with the

Continent and other parts of the country.[56] The most progressive and productive of its arable demesnes, mostly concentrated in the east and northeast of the county, combined heavy labor inputs with the best available agricultural technology in order to obtain levels of output per unit area that were unsurpassed elsewhere in the country.[57] It can be no surprise to discover that pastoral husbandry in this area, although economically subordinate to arable production, was similarly advanced. This is borne out by a comparison of the mean characteristics of Cluster 1 demesnes in Norfolk with their mean characteristics in the country at large. As Table 5 shows, the distinctive traits of this most intensive and developed of pastoral regimes were at their most accentuated in Norfolk: here working animals comprised a smaller proportion of total livestock, horses made a greater relative contribution to draught power, and dairy cattle most eclipsed other classes of animal in their relative importance.

By medieval standards Norfolk's pastoral sector performed remarkably well. That it did so bears witness to the ability of medieval agriculture to evolve mixed-farming systems in which

---

[56]Alan R. H. Baker, "Changes in the Later Middle Ages," pp. 186–247 in H. C. Darby, ed., *A New Historical Geography of England* (Cambridge, 1973), pp. 190–92; Elizabeth Rutledge, "Immigration and Population Growth in Early Fourteenth-Century Norwich: Evidence from the Tithing Roll," *Urban History Yearbook* (1988): 15–30; Bruce M. S. Campbell, "The Regional Uniqueness of English Field Systems? Some Evidence from Eastern Norfolk," *Agricultural History Review* 29/1 (1981): 16–28; Anthony Saul, "Great Yarmouth in the Fourteenth Century: A Study in Trade, Politics and Society," unpub. D.Phil. thesis (Univ. of Oxford, 1975); R. A. Pelham, "Medieval Foreign Trade: Eastern Ports," pp. 298–329 in H. C. Darby, ed., *Historical Geography of England before 1800* (Cambridge, 1936), pp. 301; Vanessa Parker, *The Making of Kings Lynn: Secular Buildings from the 11th to the 17th Century* (London, 1971), pp. 3–16; Bruce M. S. Campbell, James A. Galloway, Derek Keene, and Margaret Murphy, *A Medieval Capital and Its Grain Supply: Agrarian Production and Distribution in the London Region c.1300*, Historical Geography Research Ser., no. 30 (1993), pp. 181–82.

[57]Campbell, "Agricultural Progress"; idem, "Arable Productivity in Medieval England: Some Evidence from Norfolk," *Journal of Economic History* 43/2 (1983): 379–404.

the arable and pastoral sectors were complementary rather than competitive.[58] It is particularly notable that this crucial development was taken furthest within a county more remarkable for its institutional and economic attributes than for any intrinsic environmental suitability to pastoralism. That it did not develop further and evolve into the sort of intensive mixed-farming system based more or less exclusively on fodder cropping, of the kind with which the county was to become inextricably associated during the so-called agricultural revolution of the eighteenth century, was a function of available technology and the level of market demand for livestock and their products, both of which were to advance significantly by the late seventeenth century.[59] As it was, arable and pastoral husbandry together attained a pitch of development in fourteenth-century Norfolk that was not to be matched in much of the rest of the country until several centuries later.

Herein may lie the explanation for Chaucer's choice of Norfolk as the county of origin of his reeve, an origin that he is at pains to reinforce by endowing Oswald with a number of additional Norfolk attributes—the stot upon which he rides, the

[58]As Biddick observes, "The simple relations between pastoral and cereal husbandry posited by Postan do not adequately account for the comparative commercialization of haulage, dairying, and wool production over the thirteenth century and the trade-offs made between producing such products and selling pastoral resources to others to produce them" (*Other Economy*, p. 130). See also Mark Bailey, *A Marginal Economy? East Anglian Breckland in the Later Middle Ages* (Cambridge, 1989), pp. 85–96.

[59]Campbell and Overton, "New Perspective," pp. 90–93, 102–03. For inadequacies in the scale of market demand as an explanation for the lack of agricultural progress in many parts of medieval England, see Bruce M. S. Campbell, "People and Land in the Middle Ages, 1066–1500," pp. 69–121 in R. A. Dodgshon and R. A. Butlin, eds., *An Historical Geography of England and Wales*, 2nd ed. (London, 1990), p. 83; Campbell, "Ecology versus Economics in Late Thirteenth- and Early Fourteenth-Century English Agriculture," in Del Sweeney, ed., *Agriculture in the Middle Ages: Technology, Practice, and Representation* (Philadelphia, 1995), pp. 76–108.

accent with which he speaks, his residence upon a heath, and, as it would now appear, the combination of livestock that he tends.[60] For as well as hailing from Norfolk, the reeve is also portrayed as a shrewd, hard-bargaining, and experienced husbandman who is fraudulent to his young master and oppressive to those socially beneath him. By associating these personal characteristics with a specific Norfolk provenance, John Matthews Manly has argued that Chaucer was alluding to an actual case of mismanagement on the estates of the earls of Pembroke (which included the manor of Foxley, in which Bawdeswell was partially situated), of which Chaucer apparently had firsthand knowledge.[61] This claim has failed to convince subsequent scholars—especially as the events in question happened almost 20 years before the General Prologue was written—and instead it is more likely that Chaucer had in mind, if not a particular person and actual events, then at least a recognizable social and regional type who would have been immediately familiar to his audience. Both Jill Mann and Alan J. Fletcher have drawn attention to a contemporary stereotype of Norfolk people as crafty, cunning, and avaricious—characteristics shared by the reeve.[62] The distinctive character of

---

[60]The stot, or work horse, was a quintessentially East Anglian animal; at this date stots were present in significant numbers only on demesnes in East Anglia and the southeast. Hamlets and isolated farms were a characteristic feature of Norfolk settlement, and during the later Middle Ages became especially associated with the edge of commons, heaths, and wastes: "The vast majority of medieval farms looked out over commons" (Tom Williamson, *The Origins of Norfolk* [Manchester, 1993], p. 167); David Dymond, *The Norfolk Landscape* (London, 1985), pp. 99–102. The reeve's tale makes deliberate use of northern dialect forms, blended with others that would have been current in East Anglia; see J. R. R. Tolkien, "Chaucer as Philologist: *The Reeve's Tale*," *Transactions of the Philological Society* (1934): 1–70, esp. pp. 6–7.

[61]*Some New Light*, pp. 84–94.

[62]Mann, *Chaucer and Medieval Estates Satire. The Literature of Social Classes and the General Prologue to the Canterbury Tales* (Cambridge, 1973), pp. 166; Fletcher, "Chaucer's Norfolk Reeve," *Medium Ævum* 52/1 (1983): 100–03.

Norfolk's medieval economy and society, to which its pastoral husbandry bears witness—more commercialized, technologically developed, competitive, and individualistic than that prevailing in much of the rest of the country—possibly explains how such a reputation came to be earned and why Norfolk people were seen to be so different.[63]

---

[63]Oswald's shrewd and hard-bargaining character was certainly shared by many of his real-life Norfolk contemporaries: Elaine Clark, "Debt Litigation in a Late Medieval English Vill," in J. Ambrose Raftis, ed., *Pathways to Medieval Peasants* (Toronto, 1981), pp. 247–79; Bruce M. S. Campbell, "Population Pressure, Inheritance and the Land Market in the Fourteenth-Century Peasant Community," in Richard M. Smith, ed., *Land, Kinship, and Life-Cycle* (Cambridge, 1984), pp. 87–134.

SOCIAL STRUCTURE

AND SOCIAL ORGANIZATION

IN AN ENGLISH VILLAGE AT THE CLOSE OF

THE MIDDLE AGES: CHEWTON, 1526

Ian Blanchard[1]

A quarter of a century has passed since Professor Raftis first revealed that new methodological approach to the use of manorial court rolls which was to revolutionize perceptions of English village life in the late thirteenth and early fourteenth centuries.[2] During subsequent years the study of medieval economic and social history gradually re-oriented from a conjunctural towards a structural analysis that investigated the organizational forms and mechanisms deployed within the economy and society and revealed the framework within which

[1]This paper has a long history. At its inception a version was presented at a seminar organized by Keith Wrightson at St. Andrews University. Many years later a more refined but still incomplete paper was given to Richard Smith's and Barbara Harvey's seminar at All Souls, Oxford. I would like to thank all who participated at these seminars for their comments. My greatest debt, however, is to successive generations of students, who participated in a course that Tony Goodman and I organized at Edinburgh University concerning "English Peasant Society, circa 1270–1700." I hope that they enjoyed our discussions of the ideas that have come to fruition here as much as I did.

[2]A methodology first outlined in two classic articles, "Social Structure in Five East Midland Villages," *Economic History Review*, 2nd ser., 18 (1965), and "The Concentration of Responsibility in Five Villages," *Medieval Studies* 28 (1966).

medieval men and women accomplished the tasks of everyday life. An important influence on these changes was the adoption and refinement of these techniques, pioneered at Toronto, by scholars of many nations who produced what was probably the most exciting corpus of contemporary research.[3] The questions posed were inspired, the results illuminating. Among a host of new topics that were investigated, the motives and methods of those operating both in and between land and labor markets were explored.[4] Familial forms and the vital characteristics of populations were defined.[5] All was flux, and as those pursuing

---

[3]For critiques of and refinements to the basic methodology see, e.g., L. R. Poos and Richard M. Smith, "Legal Windows onto Historical Populations: Recent Studies on Demography and the Manor Court in Medieval England," *Law and History Review* 2 (1984); L. R. Poos, "Life Expectancy and the 'Age of First Appearance' in Medieval Manorial Court Rolls," *Local Population Studies* 37 (1986); Zvi Razi, "The Toronto School's Reconstitution of Medieval Peasant Society: A Critical View," *Past and Present* 85 (1979); and Judith M. Bennett, "Spouses, Siblings and Surnames: Reconstructing Families from Medieval Village Court Rolls," *Journal of British Studies* 23/2 (1983).

[4]Space limits details of the rich corpus of work utilizing this methodology; the following studies merely provide the apperitif. On land markets and their participants see, e.g., Anne R. DeWindt, "A Peasant Land Market and Its Participants: King's Ripton, 1280–1400," *Midland History* 4/3–4 (1978): 142–59; Richard M. Smith, ed., *Land, Kinship, and Life-Cycle* (Cambridge, 1984), chs. 3–7; Zvi Razi, "Family, Land and the Village Community in Later Medieval England," *Past and Present* 93 (1981); Cicely Howell, *Land, Family, and Inheritance in Transition: Kibworth Harcourt, 1280–1700* (Cambridge, 1983). Migration and employment is the subject of J. Ambrose Raftis's classic *Tenure and Mobility: Studies in the Social History of the Mediaeval English Village* (Toronto, 1964) and R. K. Fielden's later essay, "Migration in the Later Middle Ages: The Case of the Hampton Lacy Villeins," *Midland History* 8 (1983). Labor market conditions are dealt with in the brilliant study of Elaine Clark, "Medieval Labor Law and the English Local Courts," *American Journal of Legal History* 27/4 (1985); other industrial employment opportunities are considered in Ian Blanchard, "The Miner and the Agricultural Community in Late Medieval England," *Agricultural History Review* 20/2 (1972), together with the reply and rejoinder, ibid. 22/1 (1974).

[5]See, e.g., Edward Britton, "The Peasant Family in the Fourteenth Century," *Peasant Studies* 5 (1976); Judith M. Bennett, "The Ties That Bind: Peasant Marriages and Families in Late Medieval England," *Journal of Interdisciplinary History* 15/1 (1984); Richard M. Smith, "Kin and Neighbours in a Thirteenth Century Suffolk Community," *Journal of Interdisciplinary History* 16 (1985); L. R.

a sectoral approach steadily widened topic horizons, others attempted total "village reconstitutions" allowing a delineation of the forms of social structure and organization in the communities studied.

Those undertaking the reconstitutions of village communities revealed the existence during the years ca. 1290–1348 of a basic land-based hierarchical structure in which a family's status was related to the size of its landholding (itself in part a function of the number of family members) and reflected in its access to public office.[6] The highest, or A-status, families enjoyed the use of extensive landed resources, and members acted on a regular basis in the capacity of juror, capital pledge, taster, reeve, or beadle, while B-status families were poorer and rarely acted in such official capacities; the lowest, C-status, families enjoyed access to neither land nor these offices. Within this hierarchical ordering families tended to establish relationships in accord with their status. Social organization thus assumed a horizontally integrated form: families of like status were conjoined in a variety of relationships with the objective of strengthening and promoting their mutual interests. The vertical ordering of social organization and the nature of interstrata relationships has remained a matter of some debate. Initially,

---

Poos, "The Rural Population of Essex in the Later Middle Ages," *Economic History Review*, 2nd ser., 38/4 (1985).

[6]Patricia M. Hogan, "Wistow: A Social and Economic Reconstitution of the Thirteenth and Fourteenth Centuries," unpub. Ph.D. thesis (Univ. of Toronto, 1971); Edwin B. DeWindt, *Land and People in Holywell-cum-Needingworth: Structures of Tenure and Patterns of Social Organization in an East Midlands Village, 1252–1457* (Toronto, 1972); Anne Reiber DeWindt, "Society and Change in a Fourteenth-Century English Village: King's Ripton, 1250–1400," unpub. Ph.D thesis (Univ. of Toronto, 1972); J. Ambrose Raftis, *Warboys: Two Hundred Years in the Life of an English Mediaeval Village* (Toronto, 1974); Edward Britton, *The Community of the Vill: A Study in the History of the Family and Village Life in Fourteenth Century England* (Toronto, 1977); Zvi Razi, *Life, Marriage, and Death in a Medieval Parish: Economy, Society, and Demography in Halesowen, 1270–1400* (Cambridge, 1980).

positions in relation to this question polarized. Interstrata relationships were seen either as being mutually dependent, bringing a certain cohesiveness to society as a whole, or as existing in a state of tension and strife, which threatened to split society asunder and render that edifice into its atomistic elements. Gradually, however, the forces of synthesis triumphed and village society came to be perceived in almost Soboulian terms: interstrata relations came to be seen as normally existing in a state of conflict that was sublimated only when, on the initiative of the village elite, these destructive forces were focused against an external agency—normally the manorial lord.[7] Such, then, is the perceived state of village society during the years ca. 1290–1348.

The fate of this edifice during the subsequent period of demographic decline from ca. 1348 to ca. 1525 has been somewhat less fully investigated. The only systematic attempt to analyze the nature of village society at this time was undertaken by Professor Raftis in his study of Warboys.[8] The picture presented by him is a gloomy one of disintegration and decay. The communal discipline that had characterized earlier village society and was represented by a system of pledging, which delineated personal relationships both within and on occasion between strata groups, is said to have disintegrated, as villagers no longer wished to support one another in this fashion. Individual families are represented as operating independently of these links, subject to the constraints imposed upon them by "manorial law," which increasingly assumed the form of a series of bylaws enforced by village officials. Yet this new regulatory system is portrayed as having never really succeeded, at least

---

[7]For examples of this externalization of tensions see Barbara A. Hanawalt, "Community Conflict and Social Control: Crime and Justice in Ramsey Abbey Villages," *Mediaeval Studies* 39 (1977).

[8]*Warboys*, pp. 216–24, 263–65.

insofar as it was capable of fully recovering the social spirit of the late thirteenth and early fourteenth centuries. Under the influence of market forces there was a marked increase in violence among villagers, and families showed an increasing disrespect for their fellows' property, both agricultural and personal. The argument as to the nature of village society at this time is thus essentially a negative one: the new form of social ordering was emphatically not that of the late thirteenth and early fourteenth centuries.

What form it did assume is unclear. Certainly the behavioral patterns of individual families had certain distinct characteristics. They were more violent than before and, in a period when agrarian systems were changing, they failed to conform to the regulatory patterns of pre-existing practice.[9] The motives and objectives of these families, who utilized force and the usurpation of others' rights to achieve their ends, remains unexplored, as does the nature of their social values or the form of the social relationships that they forged in order to attain their objectives. The negative aspects of the new social order are clear—it was not like that of the late thirteenth and early fourteenth centuries—but Professor Raftis in this study did not describe its positive attributes.

That task was left to Professor Alan Macfarlane, who proclaimed the appearance of a new "Age of Individualism."[10] An examination of his argument reveals that it rests on his

---

[9]On changing agrarian practices see Christopher Dyer, *Warwickshire Farming 1349–c.1520. Preparations for an Agricultural Revolution*, Dugdale Society Occasional Papers, no. 27 (1981), and Richard H. Britnall, "Agricultural Technology and the Margin of Cultivation in the Fourteenth Century," *Economic History Review*, 2nd ser., 30/1 (1976); each provides a picture of the increasingly irregular cultivation patterns in post-Black Death England. More questionable are the authors' attempts to link these practices to the new agrarian technologies of the sixteenth century.

[10]*The Origins of English Individualism: The Family, Property and Social Transition* (Oxford, 1978).

attachment of positive attributes to the existing negative argument. For Professor Raftis, villagers existed in a series of relationships of unknown character that could only be described as *not* being those of their early fourteenth-century counterparts. For Professor Macfarlane, unknown became nonexistent. Villagers were thus perceived as existing in an atomistic and hedonistic condition distinguished from anarchy only by the existence of an autonomously enforceable corpus of law. Such an archetype, while possessing a certain analytical usefulness, is a poor descriptive tool. The manorial court, far from being an autonomous institution, was an integral part of village society; as such, its existence provided the basis for the formation of politico-social relationships among families that, with other as yet undefined relationships, constrained the possibilities for individualistic action.[11]

It is the contention of this paper that only through an understanding of prevailing patterns of social relationships and organization can the extent of the residual opportunities for individualistic action be defined. Accordingly, such an analysis is presented in the following pages, exploring the nature of social relationships and organization in a late medieval rural community—Chewton on Mendip—and examining the opportunities that existed for individualistic behavior.

The circumstances that gave rise to the documentation for the analysis were associated with the acquisition of the Bonvillle properties in Devonshire and Somerset by Henry Gray, marquis of Dorset (later duke of Suffolk) in 1526. On this occasion and in respect of one of these properties, the manor and hundred of Chewton in Somerset, a new rental was ordered to be made.

[11]On the role of the peasantry in the operation of manorial and other courts see Barbara Hanawalt, *Crime and Conflict in English Communities, 1300–1348* (Cambridge, Mass., 1979).

The reason for the creation of this rental resided in the customary right of new lords in this hundredal manor to collect a *gressum* from all the tenants, free and unfree and of whatever degree. The document is a remarkably comprehensive one.[12] It not only provides detailed information on the amounts of each type of land (arable, meadow, pasture, etc.) held by individual tenants, its tenurial form and the rent, services, and customary fine payable for the property—but it also yields information on the land's topographical location and form (whether in the open fields or in severalty), together with an estimate of its capital value. From the perspective of this study, the data concerning the *gressum* levied at the entry of the new lord is of even greater significance, for in order to ensure payment each tenant was expected to provide two pledges, save only for the most substantial, who were allowed to self-pledge.

It is these pledges that are presented in Figure 1, to provide a representation of the rural community at Chewton in 1526. In this figure each family is accorded a pledge status. The highest, A-status, families are those given the right of self-pledging, who pledge others but are not themselves pledged. The lowest, E-status, families are those who never acted in the capacity of pledgers but were only the recipients of pledges. The intermediate groups that have been assigned status from B to D both gave and received pledges, the relative frequency of each act determining their positioning in the ranking: the more frequently they acted as pledger, the higher their status; the more frequently they were the recipient of a pledge, the lower their status.

It is information from the biographical histories discussed in the Appendix below, combined with data on pledging patterns

[12]The reader is referred to the Appendix below for details and a discussion of the sources utilized.

contained in the rental of 1526, that is presented in Figures 1, 2, and 3 and that forms the basic analytical framework for this paper. To facilitate identification of the families involved, a key to the alpha-numerical system employed in those figures is presented below:

CHEWTON FAMILIES IN 1526

"Incomers"

a. Smith, John
b. Phillips, William
c. Broke
d. Cole
   [1]John
   [2]Thomas
e. Okey
f. Hoskins alias Malette
g. Gay, John jr.
h. Magge
i. Smith, Simon Becket
j. Collier

"Traditional" Society

1. Doggat
2. Spering
3. Attwood
4. Symonds-Pococks
5. Gay, John sr.
6. Bridges
7. Samse
8. Bars-Wilcock
9. Hutchins
10. Andrews
11. Gelibron
12. Hippesley
    [1]Nicholas
    [2]John
13. Wyvean
14. Vowlys
15. Phillips
    [1]Sibella
    [2]John
16. Quick
17. Taylor
18. Plenty
19. Bathe
20. Radway
21. Baller
    [1]Henry
    [2]William
22. Dryall
23. Mallett
24. Shettil
25. Bendel
    [1]William
    [2]Thomas
26. Payne

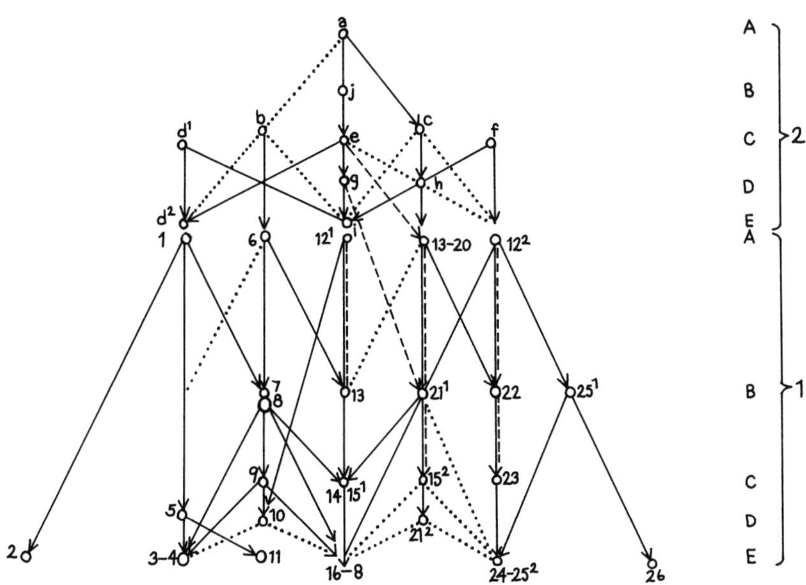

Figure 1. ———→ Pledges *within* systems 1 and 2
- - - -→ Pledges between systems 1 and 2

For one family to undertake the pledging of another in such a manner required not only considerable personal knowledge but also trust between the parties concerned, and thus the pledge relationship encapsulates a whole series of ties, of undefined character, that bound them one to the other. As an indicator of such relationships, the pledge had the advantage of being free of deterministic considerations, save insofar as the transaction involved monetary payments that were likely in part to condition its nature: the pledger of necessity was relatively richer than the pledgee. An examination of all the entries concerning the size of the *gressum* that are contained in the rental and a comparison of the sums involved with both the taxable income and capital assets of the villagers, however, reveals that the financial commitment of the individual villager involved in the act of pledging was small and encompassed only a small proportion of either his current income or his wealth. The tenant seeking pledgers, of whatever income and wealth, thus enjoyed considerable freedom in making this choice and was not constrained to approaching only the wealthiest members of village society.

Thus, on the occasion of Henry Gray's acquisition of the hundred and manor of Chewton in 1526, every tenant had to reveal something of his social relations with his contemporaries, as he was forced to seek two of his fellows to act as pledges for his payment of *gressum* to his new lord. Because of the sums involved, his freedom of action and range of choice in this matter were relatively wide. Acting under minimal constraints, therefore, the tenants' decisions concerning who should act as pledges provide an unusual insight into social relationships within the village and allow an analysis of the forms assumed by these relationships.

It should be noted that the picture presented in Figure 1 of social relationships at Chewton in 1526 is a "snapshot" of a society undergoing a process of change, and thus it encompasses both new emergent elements in that society (system 2) and long-established ones (system 1). As will be seen, families within one system did enjoy fairly intimate relationships with members of the other. Many of the "incomers" were involved in pledge relationships with "traditional" families.[13] Thus John Smith (incomer family *a*) pledged the Wyveans (traditional family 13), while John Gay junior (incomer family *g*) was similarly linked with Henry Baller (traditional family 21^1). Indeed, a consideration of the figure will show that five of the 11 families of incomers were involved in such relationships with traditional families and that the remaining six families, although they

[13]"Systems," distinquished in Fig. 1 by nos. 1 and 2 on the right of the figure, are data subsets that together encompass each family in Chewton society in 1526.

enjoyed no direct relationships with traditional families, all existed in dependency relationships with the five who maintained such links.

Turning first therefore to these five families of incomers (families *a*, d^1, *e–g*) an examination of Figure 3, in which is delineated the relationship between landholding status and income, reveals that the five, together with their partners in traditional society, constituted a deviant group from the norm (represented by functional relationship A).[14] Each of these incomers enjoyed an income higher than was normally associated with their status-landholding. Their counterparts in traditional society, in contrast, received incomes lower than that norm. As has been shown elsewhere, the transfer of the incomer's incremental income to his counterpart in traditional society ensured that both families adhered to the norms of their society. The two parties were engaged in a relationship that endowed the incomer with what has been called "successor status."[15] Existing established families who were doomed to imminent extinction and lacked sufficient manpower to work their holdings because they were aged childless individuals (Henry Baller-no. 21^1) or couples with only daughters to inherit or work their land (Wyveans-no. 13, Doggats-no. 1[16], and Radway-no. 20), and families whose future advancement in

[14]In the case of the relationship between the Doggatts (traditional family no. 1) and Coles (incomer family no. d^{1-2}) this is obscured in Figures 1 and 3 by taking place on the basis of constituent family elements. John Doggatt sr. made provision for himself, his wife, Joan, and daughter, Agneta, with John Cole in this manner. His son, John Doggatt jr., encompassed within the familial unit in terms of status and income, however, enjoyed at this time a semiautonomous existence, collaborating with his uncle, Thomas, and cousin, also named John, in various enterprises at the Priddy lead workings.

[15]On this relationship see Ian Blanchard, "Industrial Employment and the Rural Land Market, 1380–1520," in Smith, *Land, Kinship, and Life-Cycle*, pp. 241–48.

[16]See above, n. 14.

status had been assured by the acquisition of reversionary rights (Dryalls-no. 22) were prepared to sell to incomers the reversion of their holdings and the appendant rights for a cash flow that would ensure their places in contemporary society. The incomers, assured of these future rights by either marriage (Smith [family *a*], Cole [family d^{1-2}] and Okey [family *e*]) or the granting of a reversion (Hoskins alias Malette [family *f*] and Gay [family *g*]), were prepared to forgo the ephemeral pleasures associated with current income in return for the assured long-term rights associated with establishment status for themselves and their heirs.

Having secured an assured future position in village society, moreover, they could attract other incomers to form their own social groupings: each of the five successor families acted in the capacity of pledgers for the six other families of incomers (families *b–c*, d^2 and *h–j*) who had no access to pledges from families in traditional society. Members of the group of incomers thus formed an integral part of village society, but their position must be viewed not as an aspect of present reality but rather in terms of future anticipated position. As such, the two elements (systems 1 and 2), though temporally distinguished, may be considered as part of an integrated whole that can now be analyzed with respect to its structure and organization.

Structurally, the society, like its late thirteenth- and early fourteenth-century counterpart, can be described as being hierarchically ordered. As has been shown, families in their pledging ordered themselves in a strict ranking order. The highest, A-status, families are those who were given the right of self-pledging, who pledged others but were not themselves pledged. The lowest, E-status, families never acted in the capacity of pledgers but were only the recipients of pledges. The intermediate groups that have been assigned B through D status both gave and received pledges, the frequency of each act determining their relative positioning in the ranking. The more frequently they acted as pledger, the higher their status. The more frequently they were recipients of a pledge, the lower their status. The basis for the relationships underlying these pledging patterns was a relatively simple one. As will be seen from Figure 2, the A-status families, who pledged others but were not themselves pledged, all possessed holdings worth between £6 5*s*.0*d*. and £12, amounting to between about two and five virgates, predominantly in pasture and meadow that was often held in severalty on an intermanorial basis. B-status families possessed holdings worth between £4 10*s*.0*d*. and £6 5*s*.0*d*., amounting to between one and two virgates, again predominantly in pasture and meadow held in severalty within the manor. C-status families held land worth between about £2 10*s*.0*d*. and £4 10*s*.0*d*., again amounting to between one and two virgates but weighted much more heavily towards common-field arable. D-status families held land worth between about £1 10*s*.0*d*. and £2 10*s*.0*d*., amounting to between a half and one virgate in severalty. Finally, at the bottom of the ranking were the E-families, who were receivers and not givers of pledges and who possessed land worth less than about £1 10*s*.0*d*., which normally comprised less than half a virgate and at the bottom of the ranking amounted to little more than a cottage and curtilage. All families, whether members of the incomer or traditional groups, at Chewton in 1526 conformed to the normative relationship in Figure 2, their status being directly related to the size and value of their landholdings. Like its late thirteenth- and early fourteenth-century counterpart, rural society at Chewton in 1526 can be described as adhering to the form of a land-based hierarchy.

Unlike its earlier counterpart, within this hierarchical ordering at Chewton in 1526 families tended not to establish relationships in accord with their status. As an examination of

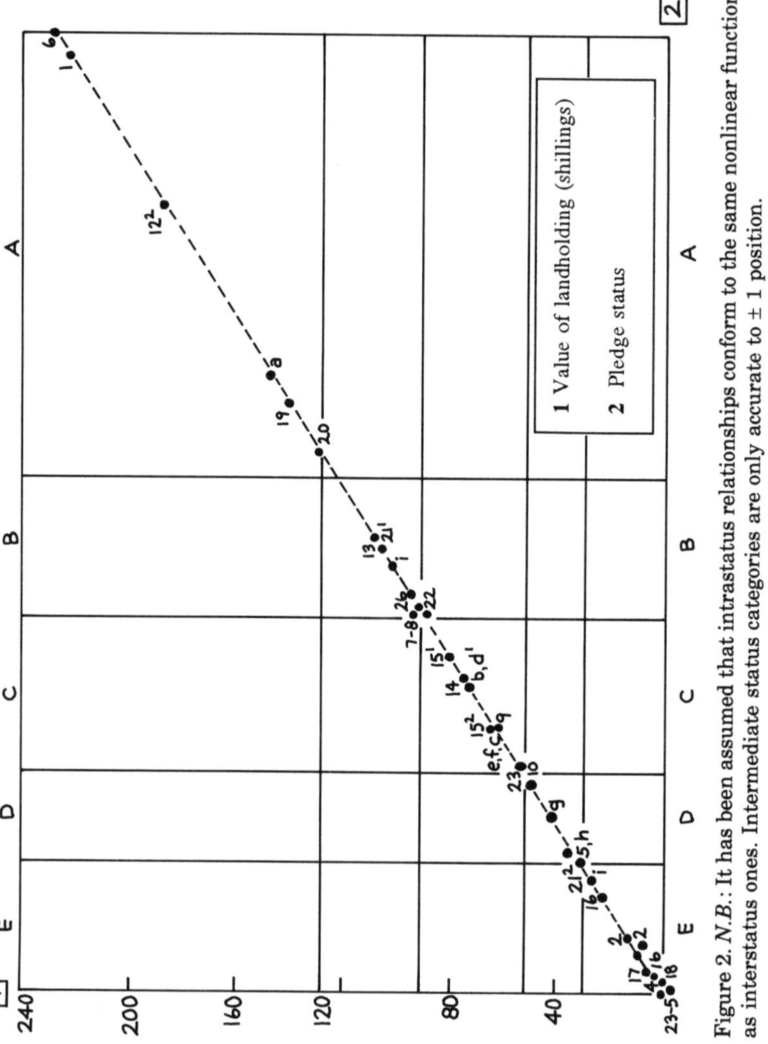

Figure 2. *N.B.*: It has been assumed that intrastatus relationships conform to the same nonlinear function as interstatus ones. Intermediate status categories are only accurate to ± 1 position.

Figure 1 reveals, social organization no longer assumed a horizontally structured form, there being a total absence of lateral pledging among families of similar status. Social structure and

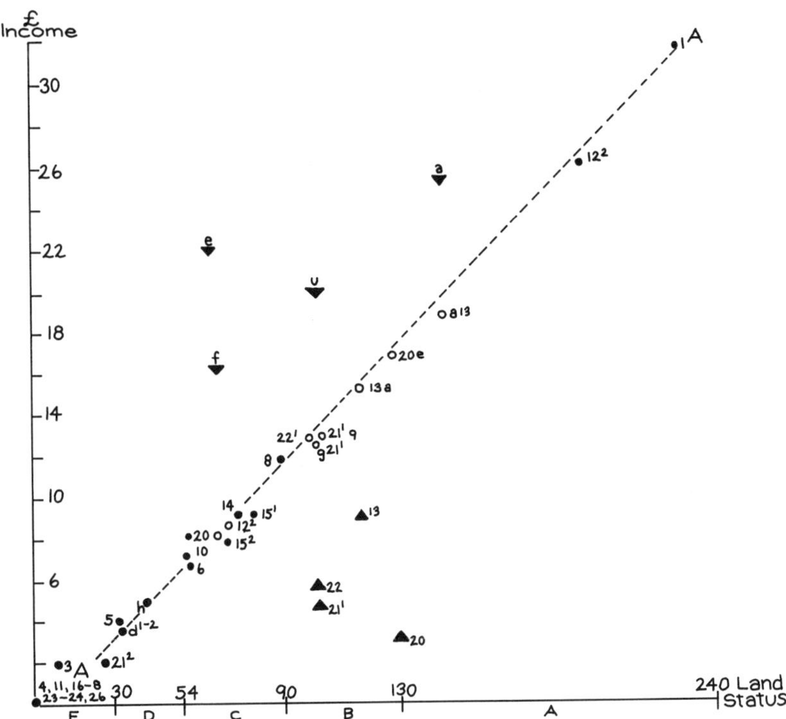

Figure 3. Income and status
• Independent families
o Mutually dependent families

organization had been split asunder. Families would recognize hierarchical status distinctions but did not form their social relationships on the basis of these distinctions. They thus conformed to the norms of what might be called a "code of behavior." Operating in accord with the tenets of such a code, a family would recognize and act upon status-based distinctions with regard to another, without of necessity maintaining any relationship to that party. In walking down the village street, for instance, an individual's acceptance of the code of behavior would determine to whom he doffed his cap or for whom he stepped aside, whether the recipient of these acts was a member of his relationship network or totally unrelated to him. Indeed, in accepting the tenets of such a hierarchically ordered code of behavior in relation to each member of the rural community a family adopted a whole series of constraints upon its actions.

The code of behavior determined how much cash income a family in 1526 was permitted to earn (Fig. 3) and how it would secure that sum (Figs. 4, 5).[17] A- and B-status families (group 1) enjoyed cash incomes of between £12 and £32, which they derived entirely from sales of the produce from their extensive pasture lands. Families of C- and D-status (group 2) earned between £4 and £12, and as incomes decreased, the proportion derived from work undertaken outside the holding (usually of an artisan character) increased. Finally, the E-status families (group 3), with incomes between £1 and £4, can be further divided into two subgroups. The first (status E^2) with land holdings normally comprising a cottage and curtilage worth up to 16*s*.0*d*., from mining, craft activity, or laboring earned between £1 and £4, most of which was spent on grain to make up for the deficiencies of their arable holding—so that their disposable income as opposed to their total earnings approximated to the £1 level. Their better-off neighbors, of E^1-status, who had holdings worth between 16*s*.0*d*. and £1 10*s*.0*d*., possessed enough landed resources both to feed themselves and generate a cash income from sales of pastoral produce, but they supplemented this with laboring in the mines or crafts, to earn a disposable income of from £1 to £4. Inhabitants of Chewton in 1526 thus earned a disposable cash income that accorded with

[17]The following analysis suggests very strongly that the subsidy of 1524 was not, like earlier subsidies, levied on the value of nonsubsistence moveables but was a true income tax. The tax categories provide an indication of the source of that income: "land" indicating land in free-hold tenure; "goods" indicating at Chewton that the individual only *legally* owned goods, not land that he or she might possess but held in copyhold tenure. "Wages" were earned by laboring activity.

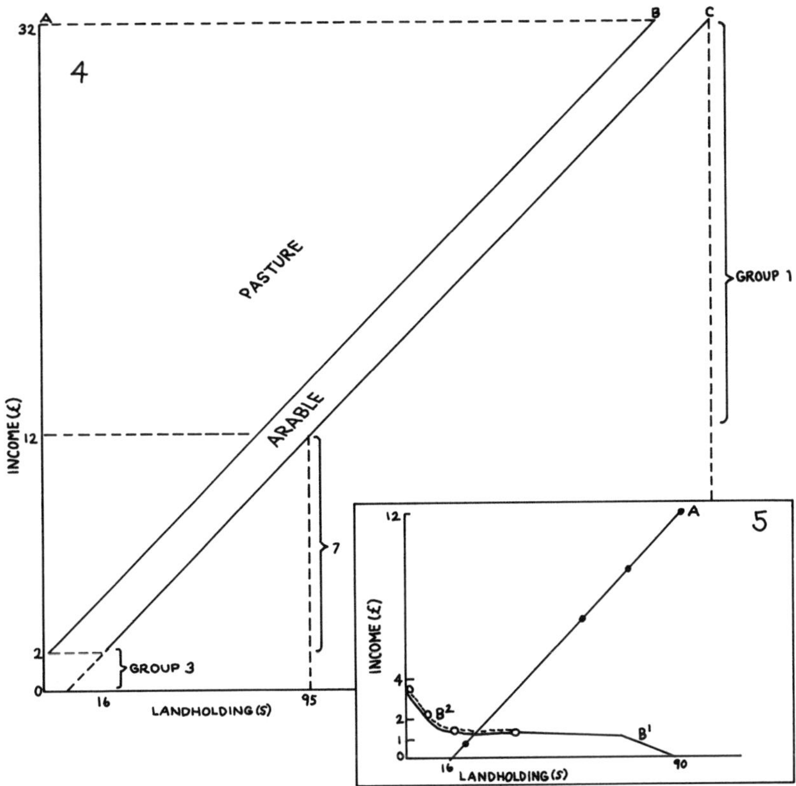

Figure 4. Work behavior: group 1: income £12 and above derived entirely from pasture lands (at 5*s*. per acre); group 2: grain obtained from holding or livery as *famulus*, per capita cash 10*s*.–14*s*. from outside work, residual from holding; group 3: dependent upon outside work for both consumption goods and sustenance

Figure 5. A: income from pasture; B^1: income from laboring; B^2: mining income

their status (Fig. 3), and the more this income was derived from activity undertaken beyond the bounds of their holdings, the lower was their status (Figs. 4, 5). As an examination of the behavioral patterns of families of C- to E-status reveals, moreover, the level of disposable income was not resource-determined but rather was a product of the conscious decisions of families as to how much work time they would expend to achieve an income that would conform to the norms of the code of behavior to which they adhered.[18]

In making these decisions as to the hierarchical ordering of their income, they also adjusted their work intensity to conform to the tenets of their code of behavior in establishing a hierarchically ordered pattern of labor and leisure. The higher a family's status, the more man days a year its members had available for "voluntary" leisure activities. B-status families with a virgate holding worth about £4 10*s.* 0*d.* enjoyed a hundred such days a year, which they could devote to voluntary leisure pursuits. In contrast, families in the upper echelons of the E-status group, who possessed a half-virgate worth about £1, enjoyed about 70 days of leisure time; and their poorer counterparts, with only a cottage and curtilage, had only about 20 days of such time. Labor and leisure time expenditure and income levels were all linked to a family's status in a hierarchically ordered code of behavior to which all members of Chewton society adhered in 1526.

An analysis of their earnings and expenditure patterns, moreover, reveals that these same hierarchical considerations also provided an ordered pattern of consumption.[19] By linking status to landholding, it placed at each family's disposal the resources that would shape the form of their consumption. Their labor ensured all, be they members of the peasant elite or

---

[18]See Blanchard, "Miner and Agricultural Community" (1972), and the reply and rejoinder (1974), and idem, "Labour Productivity and Work Psychology in the English Mining Industries, 1400–1600," *Economic History Review*, 2nd ser., 31 (1978).

[19]See Ian Blanchard, "Consumption and Hierarchy in English Peasant Society, 1400–1600," *Chicago Economic History Workshop Papers*, no. 20 (1980): 1–12, and "English Peasant Consumption: The End of an Epoch, 1580–1680," *Kwartalnik historii kultury materialnej* 30/1 (1982), which may be supplemented by reference to W. R. D. Jones, *The Tudor Commonwealth, 1529–1559: A Study of the Impact of the Social and Economic Developments of Mid-Tudor England upon Contemporary Concepts of the Nature and Duties of the Commonwealth* (London, 1970), pp. 93ff., and Felicity Heal, "The Idea of Hospitality in Early Modern England," *Past and Present* 102 (1984), for retrospective comments on hospitality.

cottars, an adequate diet. Save under the most extreme conditions, each male worker in the village was able to procure 5.5 quarters of grain, whether this grain was the produce of his holding or had been acquired by purchase. This amount provided each member of his family with what contemporaries, taking cognizance of changing worker-dependency ratios, regarded as adequate sustenance—1.2 to 1.6 bushels per month. Each member of village society (according to circumstances) had at his disposal from 14 to 20 bushels of grain a year, an amount rooted in the realities of the peasant's holding, which in its bounty yielded not only his basic diet but also (in the form of ale grain) that insurance against risk achieved by consumption allocation rather than production organization. If villagers were thus quantitatively undifferentiated in the amount of grain available to them for food and the purpose of risk alleviation, status still continued to impose qualitative distinctions in basic diet. Members of the elite and middling peasant groups were distinguished by their ability to acquire higher quality, if nutritionally inferior, panificable grains (wheat, barley, and rye), while those further down the scale were confined to the purchase of lesser grains and pulses for their almost wholly farinaceous diet. Bread was thus confined to the middling and wealthy members of peasant society, while their lesser brethren consumed gruels and porridge. Within the ranks of the *majores* the increasing consumption with status of protein foods led to a reduction of bread grains consumed and an increasing deployment of grain towards ale-making. Within peasant society, therefore, diminution in status went hand-in-hand with an increasingly farinaceous diet. Hierarchical considerations determined the form, if not the quantity, of the peasant's basic diet.

Hierarchical considerations, through the intimate connection among status, landholding, and income, also imposed a similar pattern of ordering on familial acquisitions of consumer goods. Such direct evidence as is available concerning the purchase of such goods reveals that at the bottom of the social scale families had neither the landed resources nor the monetary income, over and above that required to purchase (5.5 quarters) grain or pulses, to diversify their diet beyond the provision of a few vegetables. The scope was not much wider for the families of middling status. Their holdings yielded enough grain to provide each adult with bread (one bushel a month), ale (two-thirds of a bushel a month) and a small amount of meat (sharing in about three-quarters of a carcass), as well as cash from the sale of pastoral products that, when supplemented by earnings from outside employment, allowed them (after meeting production expenses and rent charges) to acquire a small basket of consumer goods that in 1526 cost about 9*s*. If the greater size of the holding allowed the middling group of peasants a diversified if modest consumption, the elite reveled in abundance, if not luxury. An elite family, whose basic household was extended to incorporate a live-in servant and who possessed over 60 acres in several pasture as well as the primary arable holding, had the resources to live well. With supplementary purchases to eliminate worker-consumer imbalances and irregularities in stock-killing cycles, the holding was able to provide not only an ample annual diet comprising eight animal carcasses and 8.5 quarters of grain, yielding a prodigious quantity of ale (1.33 quarters of ale grain, per capita per month) and a commensurate amount of bread (a third of a bushel per capita per month) but also some 32 yards of kersey or saye (textiles fabricated from the wool of the family flocks) and a substantial family cash income. After the deduction of rent charges and expenses this income could amount to some £8–9 to purchase consumer goods complementary to, and an extension of, the produce of the holding. Each family with its cash income thus acquired a packet of consumer goods that embellished and heightened the significance of the basic products of its holding. Consumer goods purchases were accordingly directly related to landholding and status; they provided an overt display of that status, both intrinsically in their possession and in their disposal: in conjunction with their acquisition, the common code of behavior also imposed rules concerning their disposal in accord with the precepts of "hospitality" and "good housekeeping."

Each familial unit, comprising one or more households, which formed the basic elements of rustic society, adhered to an ordered code of behavior of finely graded dependence that determined its position of superiority or inferiority in relation to its fellows, independently of its participation in particular forms of social organization. Whatever the social relationships it formed, the family acquired its sense of place and identity by accepting the dictates of a common code of behavior whose long-term existence, spanning the years ca. 1270–1520 and beyond, was independent of particular, ephemeral forms of social organization. The influence of that code of behavior, moreover, was all-pervasive, determining many aspects of the peasants' lives, including their expenditure of labor and leisure time, their income levels, and their consumption patterns.

While families thus adhered to the tenets of an enduring code of behavior that accorded them a sense of place and identity among their peers and provided a structure for their lives, the forms of social organization in which they engaged were much more ephemeral. As has been suggested, in the late thirteenth and early fourteenth centuries villagers within this structured, hierarchically ordered code of behavior formed relationships with others of like status in a horizontally structured form of social organization. At Chewton in 1526, as may be seen from Figure 1, this was not the case. Families in this late medieval rural community positively eschewed such horizontally stratified social groupings, avoiding any laterally ordered pattern of pledging and adopting new forms of social organization that, as Professor Raftis has suggested, were very different from those of the late thirteenth and early fourteenth centuries. Families in 1526 ordered their social relationships vertically in terms of six largely separate, pyramidal structures, each encompassing subgroupings of similar form. Each pyramid had at its head one of the A-status families who acted independently of the others but directly or indirectly formed relationships with a number of B- to E-status families to create an affinity.

One such affinity was headed by the Doggats (traditional family no. 1): an extended family comprising John senior, the hundredal constable, and Joan, his wife, of Compton Martin, who held in their own right rents from three free holdings at Chewton, together with some 30 acres in severalty in Priddy with their daughter Agneta, who subsequently married John Cole, the miller's son (a member of incomer family d^1); John Doggat junior, their son, who held some 52 acres of land, mainly pasture, in severalty and 50 acres, mainly arable, in the common fields of Chewton; and John's brother Thomas Doggat, an innkeeper, with some eight acres also in Priddy. There is no evidence that members of this family enjoyed any direct social relationships with other heads of affinities at this time. They did enjoy direct "patron-client" relationships with the Sperings (family no. 2), an E-status family holding 10.25 acres in Westbury; John Gay senior (family no. 5), a first-generation D-status incomer with a cottage, various closes, and half a virgate of predominantly arable land; and the B-status interlocking family grouping that included the Samse-Bars-Wilcock families (families no. 7–8).

Through these latter D- and B-status families, the Doggats exerted their influence on two distinct subaffinities. The former of these subaffinities, headed by John Gay senior, encompassed artisan families resident in Chewton village: the Attwoods (family no. 3), butchers and brewers; the Gelibrons (family no. 11), who on occasion worked in the capacity of wet-stone quarrymen, miners, bakers, and brewers; and the Symonds-Pococks (family no. 4), innkeepers through whom links were made to the other Samse-Bars-Wilcock subaffinity. At the head of this latter subaffinity was the B-status Bars family (family no. 8) whose members, utilizing the practice of "temporary alienation,"[20] formed intimate ties with others to create a tight interfamilial grouping. Robert, resident at Priddy, by such means formed close relations with the Wilcocks. His brother, the baker Richard, formed similar relationships with the Symonds-Pococks (family no. 4), another partnership of bakers who had entered into a "successor" relationship with the widow Margery Samse and her brood (family no. 7). The Bars family thus encompassed within itself the Priddy connection, which linked it to its "patron"—the Doggats—and that connection which bound its interests to those of the artisans resident in Chewton village; and it was these connections that determined the membership of its subaffinity. As has been shown, Richard's artisan connections at Chewton village linked the family with the Symonds-Pococks (family no. 4), and similar ties bound him to the closely connected Taylor-Plenty-Quick family grouping (families no. 16–18). In contrast, Robert's connections were with the Hutchins (family no. 9) and Andrews (family no. 10) families, who were substantial landholders in Priddy.

Within this affinity, as in all the others, families thus did not seek relationships with others of like status but rather sought to form such relationships with a powerful patron, directly in the case of the Sperings or indirectly in the case of members of the Gay and Bars-Wilcock subaffinities, thereby

[20]On this practice see Blanchard, "Industrial Employment and the Rural Land Market," pp. 241–48.

gaining access to the Doggats, whose extensive landed estate in Compton Martin, Priddy-Westbury, and Chewton transcended manorial boundaries and formed the basis for a regional network of contacts extending throughout western Mendip.[21] Separated from the other affinities, these families sought the realization of their ambitions not within the confines of village life but through those extended regional networks within which their patron could exert influence on their behalf.

Only at the base of each of the affinities did the artisans and laborers who inhabited Chewton village seek to participate in other organizational forms. While these poor villagers owed their primary allegiance to the patron of their particular affinity, these families formed relationships with other families also residing in Chewton who owed allegiance to other patrons, thereby creating an interlocking network of subaffinities that provided a coherent form of village society. Social disciplines of manorial and village life, very different in form from those of an earlier age, thus continued to exert an influence, but only upon those laborers and artisans who now inhabited the old-fashioned dwellings of Chewton village. The dynamic social forces that were shaping this rural community were now being played out elsewhere—in the new large farms on "the hill" that acted as the nodes of the new affinities, within which families, enjoying little scope for "individualistic" activities, sought to form relationships with a powerful patron who had access to, and influence in, an extended regional network of contacts.

---

[21]A similar situation also existed in the other affinities: the Hippesley (families no. 12^{1-2}) family's properties, extending beyond the bounds of Chewton into Enborough, formed the basis for an eastern Mendip network; the Bridges' (family no. 6) properties, which extended from Wells into Priddy in Chewton, formed the basis of a southern network; the Bathe-Radway (families no. 19–20) network extended through Litton into northern Mendip; and only the Smith-Wyvean (families *a* and no. 13) properties centered on Chewton formed the basis for a central Mendip network.

APPENDIX

The present paper is based upon materials collected for a wider study of a group of Somerset mining villages in the period ca. 1400–1600. This project involved the reconstitution of four villages on Mendip utilizing two categories of records, both of which are engrossed on documentation of manorial provenance. First there are the records of the minery courts.[22] These are preserved in two collections at the Somerset Record Office—the Chapel MSS (DD/S/HY) and the Waldgrave MSS (C924/DD/WG)—and record not only the deliberations of the minery court but also detail the lead that was due to the lord of each field as "lot" from each individual workman who worked within the mining jurisdictions. In order to extend the analysis to encompass other industrial activities as well as the villagers' agricultural pursuits, and to explore the interaction between the industrial and agrarian activities of the inhabitants, it proved necessary to utilize the second group of records—manorial records of a more conventional character. By analyzing the ministers' accounts, rentals and, above all, court rolls in the above-mentioned collections, together with documentation of a similar character from the episcopal manuscripts preserved at Lambeth Palace and Wells, the Somerset Rolls at the Bodleian, the Seymour Papers at Longleat, the Ashton Court MSS at the Bristol Record Office, and records from the central government archives, it proved possible to investigate the fortunes of every family within certain of these mining communities over specified periods of time. The oldest late-medieval mining complex—Ubley and Hinton (comprising ca. 25 families)—was studied for the whole period 1403–1553, while within the newer mining centers, Wells and Chewton (ca. 50 families each), the investigation was restricted to the years 1523–53 and 1523–1603, respectively. For other centers, such as Compton Martin and Harptree, the documents permitted only brief

[22]The nature of these jurisdictions is discussed in the present author's unpublished papers "La loi minière anglaise 1150–1850. Une étude de la loi et de son impact sur le developpement économique," 1: "Réalité. 1150–1550" and 2: "Mythe, 1550–1850," presented at seminars conducted at the École des Hautes Études en Sciences Sociales, Paris (1985).

glimpses of social structure. By juxtaposing these two reconstitutions—of mining camp and village—it proved possible to examine the interplay among mining, other industrial, and agrarian activities.

The manorial documentation relating to Chewton, the subject of this paper, during the years ca. 1523–1603 is particularly complete and reveals the high degree of administrative efficiency of officials in enforcing the rights of successive lords in both the hundred and the manor.

> Court Rolls: engrossed rolls of the hundredal, manor, and minery courts of Chewton: Somerset Record Office, Taunton. Earl Waldgrave MSS, C924/DD/WG/16/1 (1493–94, 1528–46), 2 (1534–35), 3 (1539–40), 4 (1542–43), 5 (1544–45), 6 (1547–56), 7 (1578–79), 8 (1579–80), 9 (1581–82), 10 (1584–86), 11 (1587–88), 12 (1591–92), 13 (1593–94), 15 (1596–1601), 17 (1602–05), and 15/2 (1602–28).
>
> Court book of the manors of Henry Gray, marquis of Dorset in Devon and Somerset, 1533–44: MSS of the marquis of Bath at Longleat, Seymour Papers XXI, fols. 4–226.
>
> Rentals: rental of lands of Henry Gray, marquis of Dorset, 27 August 1526: PRO E315/385, fols. 30r–39v.

It also contains the records of that extended "minery" on Mendip that encompassed all those mineral rights on the hill that had been usurped to the manor of Chewton ca. 1536. During the years prior to ca. 1536, mineral jurisdiction on Mendip, as elsewhere, had formed an aspect of the manorial court jurisdiction. Within the manor of Ubley the reeve accounted for the stock of lead within the manor and for issues of "lot" collected therein. "Lot" was the tenth levied from each unit of 5 cwt. collected at Hockday and Michaelmas.[23] Yet when records of these courts again appear after a lapse of 40 years, there is no reference to mining in the period 1537–42.[24] Similarly, at Temple

---

[23]Somerset Record Office (SRO) DD/S/HY, minister's account 9 and court roll 12.

[24]SRO DD/S/HY, court rolls 22–25.

Hydon, a Hospitaler manor, the revenues from the lead mine were received by the lessees as late as 1533,[25] but after the Dissolution, when the current holder of the lease, John Tityll, sold his rights therein to John Thorn, a Bristol merchant, there was no mention of mineral rights.[26] At Priddy a centralized, estate-orientated, administrative structure in operation in the mid-fifteenth century had by the early sixteenth century given way to the manorial organization common throughout the area. In 1503–04 the reeve accounted at the Michaelmas hallmote[27] for the stock of lead and the lot lead collected throughout the year, and this practice continued until the *Valor ecclesiasticus*, at which date the bishop still received the profit from the mining jurisdiction. Yet at some time after 1535 the production of the minery was extinguished.[28] Finally, at Chewton, when manorial court rolls first become available (1532–33), the familiar pattern is in existence. The reeve of the manor accounted at the manorial court at Michaelmas for the previous year's lot lead, collected by the lead reeves of the lord's minery *within* the manor and presented at the manorial court,[29] a practice that continued until at least 1536.[30] The court, moreover, as elsewhere, was the custodian of custom and worked by certain rules or orders "like as . . . is taken in other mynderies to the same adjoining."[31] Thus, throughout all the mining areas on Mendip, the mineral jurisdiction (at least to 1536) seems to have been appendant to the manor, and manorial officials exercised jurisdiction in all mining matters, being the arbitrators of custom and collectors of revenue.

By 1541, however, a new system had emerged out of the seeming demise of the old, by which Henry Gray, marquis of Dorset, lord of the hundredal manor of Chewton, seems to have exerted a claim to receive

[25]BL Cotton MS., Claudius E VI, fols. 27, 244v.

[26]SRO DD/S/HY, G(b) 5.

[27]SRO C795/DD/SAS/BA 3.

[28]PRO SC6/Hen. VIII/3075–76; SC6/Edw. VI/420; SC6/P&M/263.

[29]SRO C924/DD/WG, manor courts of Chewton, 25 Sept. 1532 and 2 Oct. 1533.

[30]SRO C924/DD/WG, manor court, 19 July 1536.

[31]J. W. Gough, *The Mines of Mendip* (Oxford, 1930), p. 76.

dues from lead raised on every soil upon his hill of Mendip. For some years prior to this date the Chewton lead reeves had gathered revenues from throughout the mining area on Mendip, although in the confusion of the years 1536–41 it had not been delivered to any accounting official.[32] On 10 March 1541 a minery court, perhaps the first, was held by officials of Henry, marquis of Dorset, at which the lead reeves presented the lot lead due from within every manor of Mendip in which mining occurred, manors that belonged to a variety of lords and fell within a number of hundreds: Priddy, Chewton, Enborough, Litton, East Harptree, Compton Martin, Ubley, and Hinton.[33] This lead, collected over a number of years, was subsequently presented by the lead reeves of "the mines" at the manor court held on 1 September 1541, and, as none was sold, the lot lead, said to be of this year and previous ones, was left in his custody. The minery court of the lord of Chewton seems to have risen to a place of supremacy over the entire Mendip field. It acted as arbitrator of custom;[34] its officials collected revenues from throughout the field, the lot lead being accounted for by the same lead reeves at the manorial court of Chewton at the Michaelmas term and any revenue accruing from its sale passing to the lord of Chewton.

This, then, seems to have been the practice on Mendip until Henry Gray, now duke of Suffolk, fell in 1553. Out of the turmoil of the years 1536–41 Henry Gray seems to have been able to usurp the mineral jurisdiction on Mendip. The long-established rights of manorial lords as arbitrators of mining custom and as collectors of lot lapsed with the rise to omnipotence of the minery court of Henry Gray, self-styled "lord of the hill of Mendip."[35] Yet while the annexation of revenues was carried through with a degree of ease, the assimilation of mining custom from many different sources proved much more intractable, and a source drawn up after Suffolk's fall speaks of these years in the following terms:

---

[32]SRO C924/DD/WG, manor court of Chewton, 1 Sept. 1541.

[33]SRO C924/DD/WG, minery court, 10 Mar. 1541.

[34]SRO C924/DD/WG, minery court, 30 Sept. 1544.

[35]SRO C924/DD/WG, minery court, 9 May 1553.

> For as much as the said miners and workmen upon the said mineries there before this time have claimed customs to and for their occupation in and upon the disafforested ground and amongst themselves to be kept and observed, having no ancient writing or prescription in Antiquity to be showed for the same, so that for lack thereof the said customs were altered, changed and used amongst them diverse and sundry ways whereby no little contention strife and debate hath of late been erected and moved.[36]

The solution to this problem had to await Suffolk's successor as lord of the minery, Sir Edward Waldgrave,[37] the only man who could enforce a uniform code throughout the mineries on Mendip, mineries from which he drew lot lead. The Chewton chronicler may now take up the story again: in order to allay the confusion already alluded to, the miners determined and agreed upon certain customs,

> from time whereof man hath no memory; together with certain good and laudable customs and ordinances agreed, ordained and renewed or made at the minery court of Sir Edward Waldgrave holden at his manor of Chewton, 10 July 1554 [the which customs] should from henceforth be deemed, taken, holden, reputed, judged and stand for ancient customs to the said mineryes and workmen within the said mineries to be observed and kept for ever. And for perfecting and full concluding of the same it is also concluded and agreed that the same ordinances shall remain in writing indented, whereof the one part to be in the custom and keeping of the said Sir Edward Waldgrave and his heirs and the other part to be permanent and remain in the custody of the tenants and inhabitants of Chewton to the use of the said miners and workmen for ever. . . .

This, then, was the high point of the system instituted by Henry Gray in the years 1536–41. The minery of the lords of Chewton engrossed

[36]Extract from the minery court roll of 10 July 1554 quoted, in the preamble to an early seventeenth-century copy of Chewton laws: J. W. Gough, ed., *Mendip Mining Laws and Forest Bounds*, Somerset Record Society, vol. 45 (1931): 20.

[37]It is noteworthy that in the grant of the properties to Sir Edward Waldgrave, in consideration of his service and a loan of £1,118, his mineral rights are described as "all the lead mine accruing in the common of Mendiff within the manor of Mendiff, co. Somerset, with all priviledges of digging the same."

the entire mining region of Mendip. The mining law of Mendip was that indented in the Waldgrave court, and this court was arbitrator of custom through all "the miners and workmen upon the mineries of Mendip." Moreover, at this court was collected the lot due from each mining district on Mendip, which already in 1557 had begun to assume the names recorded on the famous mining maps of Mendip.[38]

SOURCES FROM WHICH THE LORD OF CHEWTON DREW LOT LEAD[39]

1541	1557	1610
Priddy	Priddy	Priddy[40]
Ubley Compton Martin Hinton	West	West
Chewton	Chewton	Chewton
Enborough Litton Harptree	East	Harptree

As will have been seen from the previous discussion, no attempt has been made to link mineral jurisdiction with those nebulous characters the "lords royal" of Mendip, for while there is Leland's famous reference to the "chefe lords" of Mendip, no contemporary document suggests any link between mining jurisdiction and the "office" of lord royal.[41] This link, which has produced so much confusion for both contemporaries and subsequent historians, seems to

[38]SRO C924/DD/WG, minery court 26 May 1557.

[39]1541. SRO C924/DD/WG, minery court, 1 Sept. 1541; ibid., 26 May 1557. For 1610 see Gough, *Mines*, p. 153; the format of this account is identical to that of 1557.

[40]Relating at this time only to that part of Priddy within the manor of Chewton.

[41]See below for a reinterpretation, in the light of earlier arguments, of materials contained in Gough, *Mines*, ch. 4, esp. pp. 85–96.

be a product of that curious enrollment in *Scaccario dominae reginae* of two disparate documents, one the famous case heard before the lords royal concerning rights of common pasture, the other the copy of the mining laws. In the standard work on the Mendip industry Dr. Gough clearly distinguished the different provenance of the two parts, yet continued to tie mining production to the lords royal, thereby perpetuating a late sixteenth- and early seventeenth-century myth based upon that original documentary juxtapositioning.

Certainly before Elizabeth's accession to the throne no such link was considered, yet from the very beginning of that reign such a view seems to have been coming into existence (and for many, fortunate that it was)—in order to break the hegemony of Chewton. With the revival of production within the bishop's manor of Wells after 1557, this myth seemingly allowed Berkeley to reassert his right to collect lot within episcopal lands, and the returns of such lead from that part of Priddy which lay within the manor of Wells, absent from the general accounts of 1555, are again included in 1567. Further, as the myth of the lords royal gradually gained credence, it strengthened others' claims to exercise mineral jurisdiction. Thus, up to about 1625 the mining area seems to have been divided between two jurisdictions (pertaining to the lord of Chewton and the bishop of Wells). Thereafter, all sorts of claims blossomed forth. In 1633 the Newtons, lords of East Harptree, claimed a separate jurisdiction, while at about this time the lords of Hinton Charterhouse claimed their own liberty. These multiform claims found ultimate sanction in the decision (ca. 1648/49) that on

> Mendypp . . . where have been manye strifes & contentions concerning the common of pasture and herbage there, between diverse people there and chiefly about the mines, the lords royal are to keep customary courts freely at their charge . . . the poor workmen do lay out to the lords royal the tenth of their labours.

The lords royal now reigned supreme on the ruins of the Waldgrave empire and this is reflected in the latter's accounts, for no longer after ca. 1626 do they draw lot lead from a multiplicity of areas. Rather, when information again becomes available about the accounts in the '50s they seem to have only been drawing lead from Chewton while other lords were collecting the other revenues. At first these seem fairly clearly defined. To each minery was a lord: Waldgrave to Chewton; Newton to Harptree; May to West; the bishops of Bath and Wells to Priddy. Yet, as Dr. Gough has shown, the relationship between the lords royal of the 1660s and the "chefe lords" of Leland's description is remote. They held their "office" by grace and favor of Elizabethan mythology, and as time passed so vague a position became interpretable almost at will. Mining liberties proliferated, as did the number of lords royal.

Such was the nature of customary law in the sixteenth and early seventeenth centuries, a curious combination of myth and tradition; but with jurisdictional forms identified it has proven possible to undertake a "village reconstitution" of the Chewton community and to explore the interaction between the industrial and agrarian activities of the inhabitants. Using nonmanorial documentation, moreover, it was possible to extend this analysis and complete a fuller picture of the lives of Chewton's inhabitants. In 1524 the lay subsidy of that year—Lay Subsidy 1524 for Chewton and Wellow hundreds: PRO E179/169/143—provides information on taxable income at that time. For minor embellishments to family histories, establishing aspects of moral and religious practice, and providing certain demographic data, two groups of documents of ecclesiastical provenance have been utilized:

1. Archives of the Bishop of Bath and Wells, Diocesan Registry, Wells. Deposition books 1530–1606, License books, 1558–1620, and Act books or presentments in visitation, 1526–1549.

2. Calendars of books relating to the contents (now lost) of the Wells Registry covering the years 1530–1608 and wills registered at the Prerogative Court of Canterbury.

Finally, and of paramount importance, there is the relatively recently discovered parish register of Chewton for the years 1555–1619, information from which has been subjected to the now familiar process of family reconstitution, to create a data set that both provides a bridge between the two (1533–56 and 1578–1628) separate and discrete village reconstitutions created from the manorial documentation and adds new and revolutionary insights into the processes of demographic change, so poorly served by the latter technique.

These are the sources employed to recreate, by the methods of "village reconstitution" and "family reconstitution," the biographical histories of every family in Chewton during the years 1523–1603.

HEMINGTON AND BARNWELL, NORTHAMPTONSHIRE: A STUDY OF TWO MANORS

David N. Hall

This paper considers the manorial history and township structure of Hemington with some notes on Barnwell, two Northamptonshire villages lying on the northwestern fringe of the main estate of Ramsey Abbey. Half of both townships belonged to Ramsey Abbey, and a good series of records survives for both, many of them from the abbey's administration. The estates represent an intrusion by Ramsey Abbey into the southern part of the central estate of Peterborough Abbey, the neighboring parishes of Oundle with Ashton, Polebrook, Lutton, and Luddington being almost entirely Peterborough property. The other half of Hemington was shared among three knights of Peterborough Abbey, and the other half of Barnwell belonged to the Crown. The two Barnwell manors each had a church, so forming separate parishes that were administered in different hundreds. Later, Barnwell and Hemington formed the nucleus of an estate built up by the family of Montagu in the fifteenth and sixteenth centuries, thereby preserving the early estate records, which have had only one change of ownership since the monastic period.

Barnwell and Hemington lie adjacent to each other, Barnwell touching to the River Nene, at about 80 feet, and

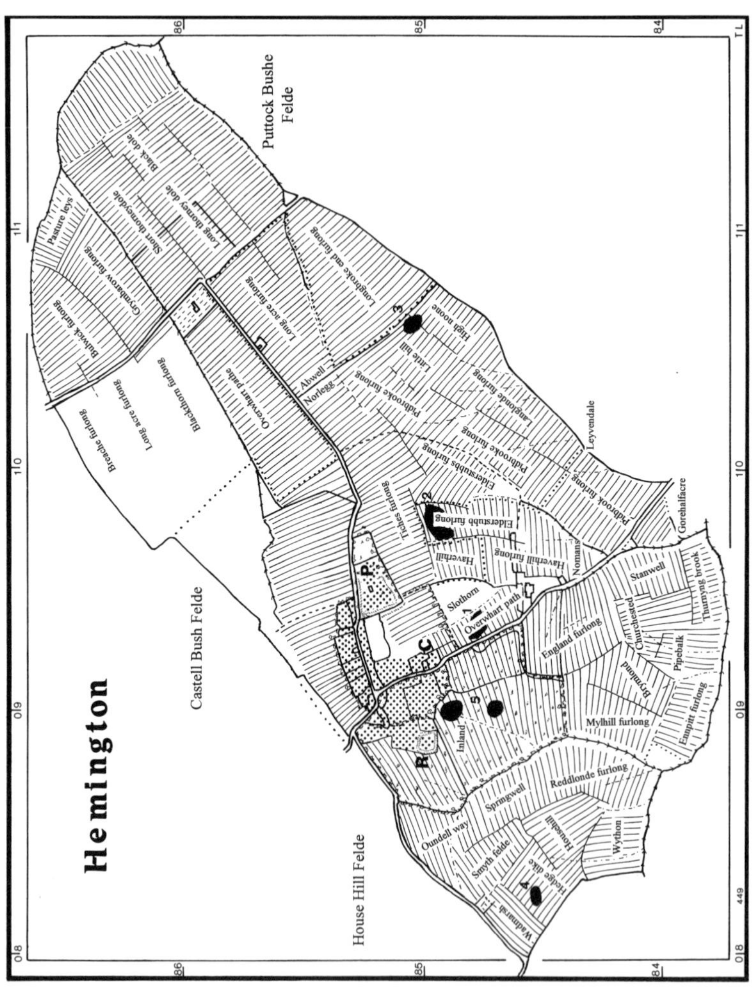

Hemington on higher ground, at ca. 230 feet, where it meets the Huntingdon county boundary. At Barnwell there are riverine meadows and exposures of limestone forming rich soil. Higher up, the terrain lies as a plateau of clayey till, formerly supporting a woodland called by the Saxons the *bruneswold*.

Techniques of archaeological fieldwork were used to provide evidence of settlement and land use before the medieval vills and their fields were established. Archaeological methods were also used to reconstruct plans of the open fields. For reasons of space this study deals with Hemington in detail and refers to Barnwell as appropriate.

Field Survey Results. Every field in both parishes was searched for archaeological remains (pottery sherds, building debris, etc.) and also for earthworks representing the sites of village tofts and crofts and the open-field furlongs. Although largely ploughed out, the remains of medieval fields survive as slight banks of soil lying on the edges of the furlongs. The techniques of reconstruction and some applications have been described previously.[1]

Hemington revealed five premedieval sites: one Iron Age and Roman (site 3), three Roman (sites 1, 2, 4), and site 5, which yields sherds of Iron Age, Roman, and Saxon date. The last lies near the village and may perhaps be considered its precursor.

Barnwell had 14 early sites in all, including one Mesolithic and one Roman site lying on low limestone. The remaining sites were all on the high boulder clay—four Iron Age, one Iron Age and Roman, six Roman, and one small Saxon site. Until sites are excavated and environmental samples taken from waterlogged deposits buried in deep features, it is impossible to be sure what activity was going on. Probably much of the area was cleared of woodland and had a pastoral use.

At the eastern part of Barnwell it is possible to identify three stages of woodland from these results and the subsequent historical evidence. The region is called the Wold and is a long

---

[1]See David N. Hall, "Fieldwork and Documentary Evidence for the Layout and Organization of Early Medieval Estates in the English Midlands," in Kathleen Biddick, ed., *Archaeological Approaches to Medieval Europe* (Kalamazoo, 1984), pp. 43–68; eadem, *Medieval Fields* (Aylesbury, Bucks., 1982), pp. 25–28.

tongue on the high ground, one of several such extensions formed by neighboring parishes. These extensions doubtless shared a block of the *bruneswold*, the Saxon woodland that spread over a wide area of the claylands, the name of which is preserved in the modern place names of Newton Bromswold, Leighton Bromswold (Hunts.), and Luddington, formerly Luddington Bromswold and Warrington Bromswold (Bucks.). The sequence of land use had three phases of woodland growth and three clearances:

1. "Primeval wood," post glaciation.

2. Clearance by the Iron Age (ca. 100 B.C., proved by the occurrence of the sites).

3. Regrowth in the early Saxon period (the *bruneswold*).

4. Clearance by the thirteenth century (after 1086; there was still woodland at Barnwell recorded in the Domesday Survey, fairly certainly in this region). The existence of ridge and furrow in the present woodland shows that it had been ploughed.

5. Wood again by the eighteenth century (after Barnwell enclosure).

6. Partial clearance in the 1970s.

The Earthworks. The medieval village plan of Barnwell is mainly linear, following a brook, and there are now some empty paddocks and a hollow way near the site of the Crown manor house at All Saints' Church (the Crown manor and church). Saint Andrew's manorial site (Ramsey) is dominated by the impressive ruins of the castle built in 1256 by Berengar le Moine, a knight in the Crusades. The later Montagu mansion stands nearby.

Hemington, too, is now apparently linear, with the church isolated on the south along a T-junction. However, there were (until recently) earthworks linking the church to the vill,[2] so making the original plan T-shaped. On the east is a moated site enclosing seven acres where the de Hemington/Montagu manor house stood. Ploughed-out earthworks, including another moated site on the west, yielded sherds of twelfth- to fifteenth-century date. The moated enclosure produced glazed pottery and stone roofing tiles, which distinguish it as a more important site, likely to be of manorial status. Since the records show that Ramsey Abbey property was concentrated on the west of the vill, the moated site can be identified as the Ramsey Abbey manor house.

Manorial History. In the Domesday Survey of 1086 Hemington was assessed at five hides, held equally by Ramsey and Peterborough abbeys. In ca. 1124 Ramsey had the same hideage and a slightly higher total was recorded for Peterborough.[3]

In 1086 Barnwell was split between the king and Ramsey Abbey. The king had 6.25 hides and the abbey had six hides, with a wood of 210 acres. In 1124 estates of the same size were in the hands of Robert de Ferrers, holding of the king, and Reginald le Moine, holding of the abbey.[4]

Ramsey Abbey. The cartulary of Ramsey Abbey outlines its possessions in Hemington and Barnwell. William I confirmed

---

[2]*Archaeological Sites in North-East Northamptonshire*, Royal Commission on Historical Monuments (London, 1975), p. 53.

[3]The distribution of hideage holdings in 1124 was as follows: Ramsey Abbey: 2.5 hides held by Berengar le Moine; Peterborough Abbey: one hide and 1.5 virgates held by Richard FitzGilbert; a half-hide and a half-virgate held by Guy Maufe; a half-hide and a half-virgate held by Reginald le Moine. The descents of these four holdings are outlined below.

[4]*Victoria County History: Northamptonshire*, vol. 1 (London, 1970 repr. of 1902 ed.), pp. 365, 367 (hereafter, *VCH Northants.*).

Hemington to the abbey in 1078.[5] Between 1133 and 1160[6] Abbot Walter granted to Berengar le Moine all the lands in Hemington for 40 marks. Hemington was granted by Abbot William to the wife of Berengar le Moine as dotage.[7] In the period 1184–89 Hemington was said to be 3.5 hides[8] and in ca. 1240 Ramsey claimed three hides, of which each hide contained seven virgates and each virgate was equal to 36 acres.[9]

In a list of fees and manors,[10] six hides at Barnwell are stated to have been the gift of Ethelric, bishop of Dorchester, and confirmed by William I in 1078.[11] Pope Alexander III confirmed Barnwell and Hemington in 1178.[12]

Barnwell. The family of le Moine was an important local family who held Ramsey Abbey land in Upwood, Wood Walton, Hemingford, Sawtry, Gidding, and Great Raveley, as well as Barnwell and Hemington, and even Shillington (Beds.). The Barnwell branch held Barnwell and Hemington possibly as early as 1091.[13] The manors were run as one estate and followed the descent of the family until Berengar le Moine III sold them back to the abbey as demesne in 1276.

The grant to Abbot William of the manor of Barnwell with Hemington, Crowthorpe, Littlethorpe, and the church of Barnwell St. Andrew for £1,606 13*s.*4*d.*[14] provides the first detailed

---

[5]*Cartularium monasterii de Rameseia*, ed. W. H. Hart and Ponsonby A. Lyons, 3 vols., Rolls Ser., no. 79 (London, 1884–93) (hereafter, *Cart. Ram.*), 2: 94.

[6]*Cart. Ram.* 2: 269.

[7]*Cart. Ram.* 1: 101.

[8]*Cart. Ram.* 3: 49.

[9]*Cart. Ram.* 3: 211.

[10]*Cart. Ram.* 1: 280.

[11]*Cart. Ram.* 2: 94.

[12]*Cart. Ram.* 2: 136–37.

[13]*VCH Northants.* 3: 73.

[14]*Cart. Ram.* 1: 107; 3: 185.

view. In the cartulary there is an extent (survey) of Barnwell taken while it was still in the hands of Berengar le Moine, in ca. 1266.[15] This can be compared with a similar extent taken by the abbey on receipt of the manor in 1276.[16]

The 1276 extent is slightly fuller than that of the cartulary and shows that there were 7.5 yardlands of freehold, 21 yardlands (held mainly as halves by villeins, who are named), and one yardland belonging to the rector, that is, 28.5 yardlands in all. There were 25 cottars holding 24 houses. It is interesting to see two villein holdings in the hands of Richard and John de Hemington, the lords of Hemington. The demesne is not quantified, but in 1417 it amounted to 450 acres.[17] The descent of the Barnwell yardlands can be followed in detail through a series of rentals and a *compotus* to 1416.

Hemington. Hemington is not detailed in the Ramsey cartulary, but from 1276 there is record of eight freeholders, holding a total of 8.5 virgates and 5.5 acres of land in Hemington and Littlethorpe for rents varying from a halfpenny to 4*d.*, a pound of cumin, a pair of gloves, and suit to court.[18]

Fifteen villein half-yardlanders paid 1 mark rent and did one day's work-service with food in the autumn; their daughters were fined for marrying outside the manor and their sons were fined if they entered the Church. There were five cottars holding six messuages with five acres (or crofts), paying rent of

[15]*Cart. Ram.* 1: 48–53.

[16]Northamptonshire Record Office (NRO) Box X387A, 18-155, C10.

[17]NRO Box X387A, 18-155, C7.

[18]NRO Box X387A, 18-155, C10. Specifically, the freeholders, with their tenements and rents, were as follows: Richard (II) son of John de Hemington (three virgates; 6*d.*, a pound of cumin); Agnes de Beaumeyse (three virgates; 4*d.*, a pair of gloves); Thomas son of Ralph (3.5 acres; 1*d.ob.*); John Scot (a half-acre; halfpenny); Thomas de Bereford (one acre; halfpenny); William son of Simon (one acre; 1*d.*); Hinchingbrook Hospital (one virgate and a half-virgate in Littlethorpe; two suits to court); abbot of Thorney (one virgate; two suits to court).

2*s.* each. In Littlethorpe seven people paid 1 mark rent (and so were probably half-yardlanders).[19] Finally, Elen de Beaumeys paid 1 mark for two tenements held in widowhood. In all, the manor embraced 19.5 yardlands, of which 8.5 (44 per cent) were held freely. Littlethorpe had five yardlands, of which 1.5 (30 per cent) were free. The manor, therefore, was not strongly feudal, having a small demesne and a low proportion of villeins, although the holdings of the other religious houses had probably originally been villein land.

Hemington was assigned to the cellarer of Ramsey in 1293,[20] although Abbot John of Ramsey leased the manor for seven years to John Mann of Little Stewkley in 1300 for £10 rent and provision of two ploughs and a cart for the use of the abbey, as well as four payments of 30*s.* (for tax) and eight oxen. The grant included buildings, walls, ditches, fishponds, a garden, and a windmill.[21]

Several account rolls survive for all the cellarer's many holdings, listing short entries for Hemington. In 1406 the rent from the tenants, who also held the demesne, was £12 5*s.*11*d.* John Hemington owed 6*d.* in arrears that had not been paid since 1389. The bailiff of Polebrook Hundred received 18*d.* and there was 2*s.* profit of one court and £3 from heriots.[22] By 1416 no court was held, no fines were collected, and John

---

[19]The villein half-yardlanders were: Henry and Richard, sons of Robert Edward, Robert de Lodington (Lutton), John and Richard, sons of the reeve, Reginald son of Robert, John Lorde, John Garlek, Matthew son of Richard Myward, Walter son of Simon de Barnwell, Robert son of Walter Reve, Walter de Peykyrk, William Godefrey, Walter son of Robert, and the widow Sabina. The cottars were: Beatrice de Peykyrk, Matilda Rolf, Henry son of Robert Edward, Simon Garlek, and William son of Richard. The seven tenants in Littlethorpe were: Adam Hannok, the wife of Hugh Poer, Adam de Weston, Thomas son of Robert Edward, Walter Hardy, Beatrice Garlek, and William de Wynewyk.

[20]*Cart. Ram.* 2: 240.

[21]NRO Box X8676, 25-1, A48.

[22]BL Add. Ch. 34608.

Hemington had still not paid;[23] this last item is entered in the rolls until 1538, when it was said to be 152 years in arrears.[24] In 1416 there was a remittance of £5 rent, as well as a payment of 6*s.*8*d.* to the collector of rents. The entries for 1424 record the same items with a breakdown of why most of the £5 rent was remitted. Ten one-sixth virgates worth 33*s.*4*d.* were in default, as well as a half-virgate called "Hertys Place" in hand worth 10*s.* Also in hand were a cottage, a toft, and other items, worth in all 78*s.*4*d.*[25]

This detail tells us that some of the half-virgates of the thirteenth century had been broken down into smaller parts, that manorial control had weakened with the Hemingtons no longer paying dues, and that there was probably reduction of population with holdings in hand. The fifteenth century seems to have been a century of depopulation in the area, partly as a result of the Black Death, which is recorded as being serious at Raunds (12 miles to the south) in 1349[26] and where there were still many properties in hand in 1464.[27]

More items of expenditure were listed in 1454, implying that much property was in hand. Fifteen acres were remitted 15*d.*, and 14 acres left waste were allowed 9*s.*4*d.* Two carts brought from Hemington to Ramsey cost a total of 2*s.* A carpenter repaired a malt kiln in the tenure of William Henderson for 16*s.*8*d.*, and John Roger of Clopton cleaned the ditch and the spring in the Inland, being provided with clothes and payment of 23*s.*6*d.* The remitted rents for lands and tenements in ruinous condition amounted to £4 16*s.* 0*d.*[28]

---

[23]BL Add. Ch. 34609.

[24]BL Add. Ch. 34617.

[25]BL Add. Ch. 34610.

[26]PRO DL49/9/7.

[27]PRO DL29/328/5366.

[28]BL Add. Ch. 34611.

In 1511 Edward Montagu, later Lord Chief Justice of England, leased the whole manor from the abbot for £7 yearly, so there were no expenses recorded for collecting the rent or making repairs.[29] He had another lease for the same rent in 1529, for 60 years, which was renewed in 1539 for another term of 60 years. Montagu was to make repairs to all the houses and property, but the abbey would provide great timber. Although the rent was probably to Montagu's advantage, the abbot drew a firm bargain, to make sure that the land belonging to the abbey was not lost to sight over the long term of the lease: he demanded that a terrier of all the lands should be prepared and sent to him every seven years. If more land belonging to the abbey was identified than that already in the hands of five named tenants, then Montagu was to pay extra for each acre. If there was to be enclosure, then the land belonging to the abbey should be clearly identified by means of markers and trenches.[30]

A terrier of the Ramsey land made in 1517 (probably one of the seven-year cycle returns following the lease of 1511) showed that six tenants held 321.25 acres in the open fields, plus another seven acres in Cross Dole furlong, and Inlands Close (72 acres); the last two items were called 79 acres of "selions," perhaps meaning leys. There were also three messuages, 10 crofts, and one cottage held by six tenants, five of them the same as held open-field land.[31]

The Manor Court. For Barnwell, court rolls survive from the years 1342–48, 1400–20, 1445, 1452, 1457, and 1482.[32] They record the names of many villagers, and the kinds of offenses

---

[29]BL Add. Ch. 34614–34615.

[30]NRO Box X8678, 25-28.

[31]NRO Box X8677, 25-29.

[32]NRO Box X388, 18-162.

recorded are typical of those found in most court rolls of this date, except that the fourteenth-century rolls still present tenants for failure to do work-service.[33] More common presentments were for debt, trespass, theft of fruit from a garden, cutting of trees and carrying them away in the dead of night, digging stone without license, and failure to use the lord's mill. Copyhold transfers of yardlands and houses also occur, as well as notices of tenants' obligations to repair ruinous properties.

Peterborough Abbey Holdings at Hemington. Much of the land of Peterborough Abbey was held by knights in 1086. Nearly all of them had complex holdings consisting of an array of fractions of manors in several villages. This was presumably to prevent, or minimize, the likelihood that the knights would claim the holdings as their own property. Three unnamed knights held the Peterborough half of Hemington in 1086; from the known descent of these three holdings it is likely that the knights were Roger Maufe, Geoffrey Suthorpe, and Viel Engaine.[34]

The *Maufe fee* included Woodford (the main holding), as well as Kingsthorpe (in Polebrook) and Hemington.[35] In 1124 the Hemington part was a half-hide held by Guy Maufe. Simon Maufe held the property in 1179. Lucas Maufe was holding the land in 1200, and William Maufe was tenant in 1212 (d. ca. 1222). His heir was Robert Maufe (d. before 1254); in 1315 the fee of Maufe in Hemington was in the hands of the abbot of Thorney.[36]

---

[33]In secular manors work-service had long been commuted to rent, e.g., the Duchy of Lancaster holdings at Raunds and Rushden *ante* 1314.

[34]See William T. Mellows, ed., *Henry of Pytchley's Book of Fees*, Northamptonshire Record Society, vol. 2 (1927): lii–liv.

[35]Mellows, *Pytchley, Book of Fees*, pp. 56, 60–61.

[36]Mellows, *Pytchley, Book of Fees*, p. 131.

The *Southorpe* or *Gunthorpe fee* included one knight's fee in Hemington and Stoke Doyle.[37] The first holder, Geoffrey, a minor in 1086, was nephew of Abbot Torold. Geoffrey de Gunthorpe was succeeded by his son Ives in 1117. Geoffrey III held the fee in 1189 and was still tenant in 1212. The last Geoffrey (IV) died in 1291 and the fee was mortgaged and then sold to Peterborough Abbey, when it was assigned to the almonry. Richard de Hemington, heir of Sir Richard de Hemington, was a named freeholder in these transactions, and Hemington was stated to be three-quarters of a fee.

The fee of *Engaine* was held by Viel Engaine in 1086, and his son William held a fee consisting of three virgates in Littlethorpe, a half-hide in Hargrave, and 1.5 hides and one virgate in Pytchley.[38] He was succeeded by his son and grandson, both called Richard. The family tree down to three heiresses in 1357 is traced by W. T. Mellows. In 1228 Viel Engaine had three quarters of a fee in the three vills. John Engaine held a third of a fee at Hemington and Littlethorpe in 1315 and Reginald le Moine, one-sixth of a fee in the same vills of the ancient feoffment of Viel Engaine. The total Hemington Peterborough fee was then 2.5 hides of the soke of Oundle.

The de Hemington Family. The de Hemington family was resident at Hemington and constituted the most important tenants there, holding Ramsey Abbey lands at Hemington and Barnwell as well as those of Peterborough Abbey. The manor followed the descent of the family to Katharine Hemington in the fifteenth century, when it was dispersed among her three daughters and eventually became the property of Thomas Montagu.

There has been much confusion among the many Richards

---

[37]Mellows, *Pytchley, Book of Fees*, pp. 61–72.

[38]Mellows, *Pytchley, Book of Fees*, pp. 130–32.

and Johns in this family,[39] but the Buccleuch charters make it possible to bring some order to the seeming chaos. Between 1248 and 1272, Richard de Hemington I acquired many small pieces of freehold land and several virgates. Twenty-five charters record these transactions.[40] Land mostly scattered on the open fields amounted to 19.5 acres; these were freeholds and acquired in parcels of one-half to two acres. The rents were usually nominal, such as a grain of wheat,[41] but two reserve a much larger rent of 40*s.* "in time of necessity," even though only 1.5 acres were involved.[42] Three virgates were acquired,[43] another was leased from the prioress of Hinchingbrook,[44] and one was bought in Kingsthorpe.[45] The Hinchingbrook land had been given by the grandparents of Berengar le Moine of Barnwell in the early thirteenth century.[46] Many of the acquisitions were from other members of the de Hemington family.

Richard de Hemington I was dead by 1272 and was succeeded by his grandson, a ward of the abbot of Thorney. In 1272 the abbot granted an estate to Thomas de Luddington for a rent of 38*s.*8*d.* It consisted of two-thirds of a yardland formerly belonging to Amice, wife of Richard I (10*s.* rent), a half-yardland held by John Colvi[lle] for a rent of 1 mark, another half-yardland held by Walter de Kingsthorpe for a rent of 1 mark, one house and a half-acre (held by?) Richard son of Agnes de

---

[39]*VCH Northants.* 3: 80–83. Using the charter evidence as a base, I have reconstructed the family tree as follows, in Appendix 1.

[40]NRO Box X8676, 25-1: A1, A5, A8, A10, A12, A13, A15, A16, A18, A20–24, A27, A29–31, A34–40.

[41]NRO Box X8676, 25-1, A13.

[42]NRO Box X8676, 25-1, A8.

[43]NRO Box X8676, 25-1, A23–24, A31.

[44]NRO Box X8676, 25-1, A24.

[45]NRO Box X8676, 25-1, A40.

[46]NRO Box X8676, 25-1, A7.

Hemington, rendering 2*s.* in rent. This property is likely to be the villein land that belonged to Hemington's manor—1.5 yardlands, with a third in dower, belonging to Amice, wife of Richard I, who had remarried, to John Colville. In 1277 the abbot granted the lands to Isabelle, widow of Walter de Colville, kt., for a rent of 10*s.*[47]

Richard de Hemington II died in 1290, and an extent of his Peterborough Abbey estate was made by Brother William de Wodeford, sacristan of Peterborough Abbey, who found that Richard II held an estate including meadow, pasture, arable, and rents, all scattered throughout several Peterborough fees.[48]

We have a view of the structure of a small manor made up of a remarkable array of small parts, of freehold and villein land in Hemington held from all three Peterborough fees. There are similarly mixed types of holdings from other fees in neighboring villages. Some of these small properties are likely to be those purchased by Richard de Hemington I. The moated manorial site called the park, seven acres in size, was already in existence.

The survey falls into distinct parts. First were the manor house and arable, worth 9*d.* an acre. Next, the (demesne) meadow at 3*s.* per acre (14 acres in all) is seen to have been made up of dispersed pieces in various other townships, but the pasture (11 acres) was all in Hemington. There then follows a list of property and land in other villages, that from Sussex possibly being a marriage portion. These amount to 76 acres of arable plus a yardland, 4.5 acres of meadow, a house in Stamford, and a rent of 28*s.* 6*d.* This property is not mentioned

[47]NRO Box X8676, A42, A43.

[48]The holdings of Richard de Hemington II are presented in Appendix 2, below, with the annual value of properties in rent given in parentheses.

again as part of the manor and may possibly have been only a short-term acquisition. A dozen Hemington freemen paid 10*s*.6*d*. for eight houses, two crofts, 1.5 yardlands, and 18.625 acres. Thirteen villeins held nine houses, 1.5 yardlands, and 3.75 acres of the Gunthorpe Peterborough Abbey fee. Another 11 villeins held of the fee of Berengar le Moine (the Engaine fee of Peterborough), and of the Maufe fee of Peterborough Abbey, there were four houses, 3.5 acres, and one yardland. Of these villein yardlands, held as five half-yardlands, only 1.5 were in Hemington, paying a rent of 13*s*.4*d*. each; these are identifiable as the 1.5 yardlands that are described as part of the Hemington manor on several occasions up to 1489.

The manor was described in 1345, when it was acquired by Richard de Hemington IV from his father, John III, as having a park, 50 acres of land, three villeins (John Wappelode, Walter Lolk, and Matilda Miller), renting three yardlands for 13*s*.4*d*. each, and two cottages, one held by William Carpenter for 5*s*. rent.[49] This seems much reduced from the description of 1290, especially the arable. The manorial property underwent a large number of transactions between 1384 and 1488. Richard de Hemington V passed it (holding during his father's [Richard IV] lifetime) to trustees in 1384 and 1394.[50] They remaindered it to Richard VI in 1415, after it was to pass to other members of the family, the widow of a cousin, and then the nephew of Richard V.[51]

A detailed terrier was made of the land in 1415. As before, the estate consisted of 50 acres and also had with it three half-yardlands, three messuages, and two cottages. The lands lay mainly in three blocks near the village and the rest in pairs

---

[49]NRO Box X8676, 25-1, A69.

[50]NRO Box X8677, 25-2, 8 Ric. II, 18 Ric. II.

[51]NRO Box X8677, 25-2, 5 Hen. V.

throughout the furlongs, made up partly of compact demesne and partly of dispersed holdings.[52]

In 1414 John Erpyngham and Katherine his wife, daughter of Richard de Hemington VI, granted the manor to trustees who included William Est of Winwick.[53] Katherine Hemington, lady of Hemington, widow of John Kirkeby, confirmed Hemington's manor to trustees in 1424 and 1427, describing the property as before.[54] There then followed numerous transactions with attorneys and trustees that show Katherine Hemington had three daughters who each inherited a third part of the manor, all of which eventually came to William Est and his son Robert.[55] An inquisition found the property equaled 20 messuages, one cottage, and 10 yardlands.[56]

In 1488 Robert Est, draper of London, son of William Est of Barnwell and Hemington, possessed five messuages, 1.5 virgates, 50 acres of arable, and 7.5 acres of meadow in Hemington, Kingsthorpe, Polebrook, Warmington, and Clopton.[57] He sold the property to Thomas Montagu of Clopton for £100. Thomas Montagu was in residence by 1494–95.[58] He was presumably "in the know" about the availability of Hemington through the Dudleys of nearby Clopton, since he was married to Anne, daughter of William Dudley.

Thomas Montagu increased his holdings in Hemington. A messuage and two closes called Wards and Garlyks and 27 acres were bought in 1493 from Thomas Henson and Thomas

---

[52]NRO Box X8677, 25-2, 2 Hen. V.

[53]NRO Box X8677, 25-2, 5 Hen. V.

[54]NRO Box X8677, 25-27, 25-28.

[55]*VCH Northants.* 3: 81; NRO Box X8677, 25-61.

[56]NRO Box X8678, 25-26.

[57]NRO Box X8677, 25-29, 29-30.

[58]NRO Box X8677, 25-36.

Davy,[59] and a messuage and virgate were obtained from William Hyson of Hemington in 1495.[60] In 1498 Thomas bought one messuage and 40 acres from Thomas Davy.[61] These were all freeholds and originally could have belonged to either Peterborough or Ramsey Abbey.

Manors and Vills after 1500. We have noted the acquisition of the Hemington family manor and other properties by Thomas Montagu. In 1512 the Montagu possessions in Hemington amounted to 19 messuages, one cottage, and 10 yardlands in Hemington and Kingsthorpe.[62] Also, in 1511, Edward Montagu, son of Thomas, took a lease of the Ramsey Abbey manor. In 1540 he obtained the Hemington land of the dissolved Ramsey Abbey from the Crown, as well as that formerly belonging to Thorney Abbey[63] and Hinchingbrook Priory. The land of Ramsey at Barnwell was acquired in the same year.[64] Edward Montagu thus owned the whole of both townships.

A rental of ca. 1588 describes Hemington as 24.25 yardlands (three in demesne), 10 houses, and 20 closes. Probably the closes were originally house plots, one for each yardland.[65] The estate is twice the size it had been in 1512, since the monastic land had come to the Montagues.

Hemington descent then followed that of the Montagu family, who moved to Boughton and received a dukedom in 1705. The Hemington manor house and park were let out, John

---

[59]NRO Box X8677, 25-2, 25 Hen. VI, 2 Hen. VII, 8 Hen. VII.

[60]NRO Box X8677, 25-37, 25-50, 25-51, 25-52.

[61]NRO Box X8677, 25-2, 18 Hen. V, 13 Hen. VII.

[62]NRO Box X8677, 25-39, 25-40.

[63]R. H. Brodie and James Gairdner, eds., *Letters and Papers, Foreign and Domestic, of the Reign of Henry VIII*, vol. 15 (London, 1896), p. 436, no. 52.

[64]Brodie and Gairdner, *Letters and Papers* 15: 733, no. 60.

[65]NRO Box X388, 18-156.

Hewlett taking an 11-year lease in 1623 for £190 annually. The estate was sold by the duke of Buccleuch in ca. 1920 to Benjamin Measures, whose family still farmed the whole parish in 1992.

The Vill Structure and the Manorial Sites. Part of Hemington was called Littlethorpe, and some of the yardlands, although dispersed with the others, related to the latter. A house and a half-yardland in Littlethorpe are mentioned in a grant to Hinchingbrook Hospital, Huntingdon, in ca. 1245; the land is listed in the Ramsey extent of 1276. (Little) Thorpe is described as "next to Hemington" in 1284[66] and 1365,[67] and thus it is clearly established as being part of Hemington. A house at Littlethorpe had the fields on its western side in ca. 1280,[68] so the actual location was the western end of the village, associated with the moated site. That this was the manor house site is clear from the archaeological evidence (above) and from reference to John *atte Hall de Thorpe* in 1371.[69]

The de Hemington seven-acre manorial site is mentioned in the 1290 extent and probably gave rise to the name *housditches* in 1260. Other topographical items mentioned are a windmill in 1300[70] and a cross in 1380.[71]

Turning to the fiscal structure, the 1276 rental of the Ramsey manor accounts for 19.5 yardlands. The demesne is not then mentioned but the Inland was 79 acres in 1511. At this date the acreage of land, said to be 10 villein yardlands, was 328.25

---

[66]NRO Box X8676, 25-1, A44.

[67]NRO Box X8676, 25-1, A80.

[68]NRO Box X8676, 25-1, A25.

[69]NRO Box X8676, 25-1, A83.

[70]NRO Box X8676, 25-1, A48.

[71]NRO Box X8677, 25-2, 4 Ric. II.

acres, that is, about 33 acres to the yardland, which agrees well enough with the 36 acres stated in 1240.[72] From this the demesne can be taken as equivalent to two yardlands, so the Ramsey manor was 21.5 yardlands in all, concording with the three hides of seven yardlands each in 1240.

For the Peterborough manor, shared between the three knights, there is no overall statement. The 1290 extent gives the Gunthorpe fee as having a half-yardland each of free and villein land. Thus the whole manor would have 1.5 yardlands of each, three in all, there being three equal fees.

Thus, the total for both manors is 24 yardlands, which agrees well with the 24.5 given for the parish in 1588. The apparent small size of the three Peterborough holdings is most surprising and does not tally with equal-sized holdings stated for both abbeys in 1086 and 1124. The matter is resolved by considering the large acreage (224 a.) that went with the de Hemington manor in 1290. Normally this would be stated as demesne and given in yardlands; at 36 acres to the yardland this is equivalent to 6.2 yardlands. If each of the three fees had the same amount, there would have been an 18.6 yardland equivalent. If this is added to the three yardlands above, the Peterborough holding was 21.5 yardlands, exactly the same as that of Ramsey Abbey.

Such a large area of unvirgated land has not been encountered by modern scholars in Northamptonshire. Presumably it was once (seigniorial) woodland or waste that had been assarted and brought into cultivation after the vill had been virgated, but before 1086.

At Barnwell the virgated land was 7.5 yardlands freehold and 21, villein. A yardland was 40 acres (from Beaumys yard-

---

[72]*Cart. Ram.* 3: 211.

land surveyed in ca. 1417),[73] so the unvirgated demesne of 450 acres was equivalent to 11 yardlands, making a notional 39.5 yardlands for the whole manor. The manor was assessed at six yardlands in 1086 and 1124, that is, close to seven yardlands to the hide, as at Hemington. Domesday Book states that the demesne was one-quarter of the total, not much different from 11/39.5 (27.8 per cent). Again there is a large area of unvirgated land, in this case stated to be the demesne.

Church and Other Monastic Properties. The church of Hemington was granted to the priory of St. Neots, Huntingdonshire, in 1149 by the de Hemington family. Several original charters concerning this grant survive;[74] the lords Richard son of Geoffrey de Gunthorpe and Alexander Maufe approved. The register of Hugh Wells (ca. 1230) records that the vicar had the alterage and the tithes of two yardlands in [Little] Thorpe.[75] There are many confirmation charters of these possessions.[76] In addition, Richard de Hemington had license from the bishop of Lincoln to have a chapel in the grounds of his house for his family in 1254, but without rights of burial, baptism, or having bells.[77]

Hinchingbrook Priory, Huntingdon, also had property, given to it by William le Moine and confirmed by his grandson Berengar III ca. 1280. It consisted of a yardland with two villein owners.[78] There was also a grant of two-thirds of the demesne tithe.[79] A rental of the fourteenth century totaling £10 17*s*.6*d*.

---

[73]NRO Box 387A, 18-155, C7.

[74]F. M. Stenton, *Facsimiles of Early Charters from Northamptonshire Collections*, Northamptonshire Record Society, vol. 4 (1930): 62–78.

[75]Alfred W. Gibbons, ed. *Liber antiquus de ordinationibus vicariarum tempore Hugonis Wells, Lincolniensis Episcopi, 1209–1235* (Lincoln, 1888), p. 32.

[76]NRO Box X8678, 25-22; photostats of Buccleuch charters B21, B1.290.

[77]NRO Box X8678, 25-14; Buccleuch charters B14, B1.289.

[78]NRO Box X8676, 25-1.

[79]Stenton, *Facsimiles*, p. 80; from original in NRO, Box X8678, 25-19.

lists tenants' names; for example, Andrew de Thorpe had a yardland for 10*s.* and paid another 6*s.* for tithe.[80]

In 1356 Prioress Anne of Hinchingbrook leased to Hugh Viel de Polebrook, vicar of Hemington, two tenements and a yardland for 20 years, at a rent of 40*s.* annually.[81] John de Hemington and Joan his wife leased for life, at a rent of 40*s.*, a messuage, two tofts, and a yardland in 1401. John Hendson of Hemington had two messuages and their tithe for 36 years in 1450. Edward Montagu leased for 20 years, in 1535, at a rent of 24*s.*, all Hinchingbrook land and tithes in the area, being one acre of land in Thurning, a messuage at Thorpe in Luddington, and three half-yardlands in Hemington.[82]

Richard Williams, alias Cromwell, acquired the Hinchingbrook monastic land at Huntingdon after the Dissolution, and he sold to Edward Montagu in 1538 all of it at Hemington, Stoke Doyle, and Luddington.[83]

Open Fields: Barnwell. The demesne of Ramsey Abbey is described in an undated terrier of the fourteenth century, hereafter referred to as 1350.[84] It consisted mainly of large pieces of furlongs spread fairly uniformly through the whole double parish. This is proved internally from the names, because there were furlongs next to all the neighboring villages: Armston, Thurning and the Wold, and (Wigs)thorpe. There were three fields called "haylondfeld," "waldfeld," and "pyrtonefeld."

In this terrier 78 furlongs are named and show the former presence of woodland, mainly in the Waldfeld, there being five furlongs with *wald* name elements and three others with

---

[80]BL Add. Ch. 34363.

[81]NRO Box X8678, 25-20.

[82]NRO Box X8678, 25-21, 25-13.

[83]NRO Box X8678, 25-24.

[84]NRO Box X387A, 18-155, C11.

"woody" names. Scandinavian influence is found in the occurrence of five *dale* (valley) and 17 *wong* name elements, that is, 30 in all, nearly 38 per cent. Another description of the demesne furlongs in 1417 described 174.75 acres, but there is no statement as to how many yardlands this represents.[85]

The presence of a single field system suggests that once (before 1066) Barnwell had one manor. Its subsequent division into two manors and two parishes has many parallels, but unique is the placing of the manors and parishes into separate hundreds. A map of the hundred boundaries would be very complex, with intermixed strips in the Barnwell fields.

Open Fields: Hemington. In Hemington the strip fields covered the whole parish apart from small areas near the brooks. Most of the furlong names are found from the thirteenth century until enclosure in the seventeenth century. It is likely that the earliest arrangement of the fields for cropping purposes was in two blocks, but none of the medieval records states this. By 1517 there were three fields: Castell Bush, Puttock Bush, and House Hill.[86] Since the first two shared furlongs of the same name, it is likely that this is a modification of an earlier two-field arrangement. The Ramsey Abbey open land consisted of 128.5 acres (House Hill), 125.5 (Puttock Bush), and 117.15 (Castell Bush), in all 371.15 acres, an equal division.

The disposition of the manorial demesne lands of the two manors is contrasting. A terrier of Hemington's manor of 1415 shows there were 50 acres that were laid in three blocks near the village, with the remainder dispersed throughout the fields. Ramsey Abbey's demesne was in a block at the end of the vill, called the Inlands.

---

[85]NRO Box X387A, 18-155, C8.

[86]NRO Box X8678, 25-59.

The land of Ramsey Abbey was surveyed in 1517, giving orientations and abuttals. This information has been combined with data from a survey of all the furlongs made by Edward Montagu in 1559, itemizing the lands and leys;[87] some orientations are given in 1528 also.[88] The 1517 terrier shows that often Thorney Abbey or Hinchingbrook Priory had lands next to Ramsey, which indicates that large parts of furlongs had been given to monasteries. Frequently the Ramsey land is at the end of a furlong (proved by abutting the next furlong), so a regular order is likely.

No Ramsey Abbey court rolls for the manor survive, but later field regulations may be deduced from the Montagu court rolls. In 1499 Thomas Coke had animals in the sown fields, and Leonard Robinson had his cows there.[89] The men of Thurning tied horses in Hemington Field in 1520.[90] In 1510 half a yardland was allowed two cows and 20 sheep (i.e., four cows and 40 sheep per whole yardland).[91] This allowance was reduced by 1556 to four beasts and 30 sheep per yardland.[92] In 1523 all tenants with a plough were to drain the furlongs after Michaelmas so that water would run out of the lands and meadows.[93] This was repeated in 1554.[94] There were to be no dunghills in the village (1535).[95] In 1554 rabbits were not to be taken from the nests in Conyez, nor any gelding to go at

[87]NRO Box X889, 25-71, no. 152.

[88]NRO Box X889, 25-71.

[89]NRO Box X889, 25-74, no. 100.

[90]NRO Box X889, 25-74, no. 106.

[91]NRO Box X889, 25-74, no. 102.

[92]NRO Box X889, 25-74, no. 112.

[93]NRO Box X889, 25-74, no. 107.

[94]NRO Box X889, 25-74, no. 111.

[95]NRO Box X889, 25-74, no. 110.

large.[96] Finally, an order list for 1556[97] states that each tenant should contribute to making a common pound, scour drains and make hedges and mounds, and make a sufficient cote for hogs and put them in the common herd. All with pigs, geese, hens, or other poultry to sell should offer them to the lord first. The wheat field was to be laid separate at Twelfth Day, and cattle were not to be put on it thereafter.[98]

Enclosed Grounds: Hemington. Hemington Inland was enclosed before 1517,[99] and in 1528 there were 430 sheep and 428 lambs in it.[100] More enclosure of the township had taken place by 1623 when the manor house was leased for 11 years as Hemington House with 200 acres called Hemington Park.[101] Samuel Bird, usurping minister, complained to Lord Montagu about having to maintain the hedge of his newly enclosed ground in 1658, so completion of enclosure was ca. 1657. In 1661 a block of 127 acres was said to abut New Field Close and a new-made ditch there.[102]

A lease of 1664 made it a condition that if any ground was ploughed up that had not been cultivated for more than three years (1661), there was to be an increase in rent of £3 per acre. Tithes were payable on the grounds. In 1692 a farm of 240 acres was let for £62 rent. The same restrictions on ploughing

---

[96]NRO Box X889, 25-74, no. 111.

[97]NRO Box X889, 25-74, no. 112.

[98]This list was repeated in successive years and other items were added to it: in 1560 no steer over three years old was to be with the common herd; in 1562 the meadow in Longbrook was not to be cut without common consent (NRO Box X889, 25-74, nos. 112, 114); in 1576 those who had set willows should cut them (NRO Box X889, 25-74, no. 126).

[99]NRO Box X8678, 25-59.

[100]NRO Box X889, 25-73.

[101]NRO Box X8678, 25-66.

[102]NRO Box X8676, 25-70.

were made in 1749 (£5 extra rent per acre). These very high rents for arable were doubtless to discourage any reversion of pasture to arable.

Some Conclusions. In surveying the surviving documentary material for the two manors of Hemington and Barnwell, it can be noted that the charters and other deeds of the Hemington manor from 1250 to 1415 are comparable to the secular cartularies of Wollaston[103] and Clopton,[104] but in the Hemington case the original deeds survive and were not formed into a cartulary. All three contain early charters of acquisitions and have a terrier of the demesne. Hemington and Wollaston manors had a large number of fictitious suits and leases to ecclesiastics and other trustees, presumably to strengthen the title. It is probable that many secular manors where the lord was resident once had such records.

The Hemington records surviving in the Montagu Collection are also important because of the information about the Peterborough monastic manor. Although many detailed records survive for the demesne manors of the abbey, there is very little material in the cartularies of the manors undertenanted by knights that throws any light on the manorial structure.

Hemington had two manorial sites, one for each monastic holding. At the west end the manorial site belonging to Ramsey Abbey was in the part of the vill called Littlethorpe. This name presumably represents a Norse settlement added to Hemington in the ninth century, which probably is the cause of the formation of two manors. Much of the land of the eastern, Peterborough, manor was unvirgated, so perhaps the Saxons were left with land that contained waste or woodland.

---

[103]Leicestershire Record Office, ID50/xii/28.

[104]E. J. King, ed., *A Northamptonshire Miscellany*, Northamptonshire Record Society, vol. 32 (1983): 1–58.

The division of the Peterborough manor among three knights appears to have been administrative only. There is no suggestion from either the physical or historical evidence that there were three Peterborough manorial sites. None of the knights lived at Hemington, and the view of the manor given in 1290 shows that the de Hemingtons held property from all three fees. This was probably always the case, with a single manor undertenanted by the resident local family paying dues to three knightly families, themselves undertenants of Peterborough Abbey.

The tenurial structure of Hemington and Barnwell St. Andrew's has been noted above. Both vills had unvirgated demesne, but the discovery that nearly half of Hemington township was unvirgated is so far without parallel. It presumably reflects the nature of the terrain, where arable land had been reclaimed from woodland in the late Saxon period, after the land had been virgated.

The fragmented Peterborough manorial state at Hemington must have contributed to a weakening of manorial custom that survived elsewhere, especially in places having a single central manor belonging to an estate that maintained its authority as a bureaucracy, following the custom of the manor. Examples of long-lived manorial custom occur at the Ramsey Abbey manor of Barnwell until the Dissolution, and similarly at Badby and Newnham, belonging to Evesham Abbey. Even longer central control can be found at the Duchy of Lancaster manors of Raunds and Rushden, which had copyhold tenure enforced until 1922, rents remaining unchanged at the medieval values.

At Hemington we see a fragmented estate, and by the fifteenth century no manorial or feudal dues were recorded in property transactions, which seem to have been freehold. In 1488 came Thomas Montagu, probably with the intention of building up an estate, buying up all land possible, beginning with the main manor and adding freehold. None of his purchases was accompanied by copyhold restrictions or other dues. He was able to extinguish any manorial rights without fuss from the residents (who were probably few by that date, in a small village) and establish leasehold on his own terms. A survey of the manor made in 1512 is at pains to explain that all the property was held at the will of Thomas Montagu.[105] The acquisition of the lands of Ramsey Abbey and the priory of Hinchingbrook, and the tithes from St. Neots Priory, enabled Thomas's son to complete the purchase of the whole of Hemington, after which he ran the estate as he saw fit.

---

[105]NRO Box X8677, 25-39.

APPENDIX 1

THE DE HEMINGTON FAMILY TREE
(Reconstruction from charter evidence)

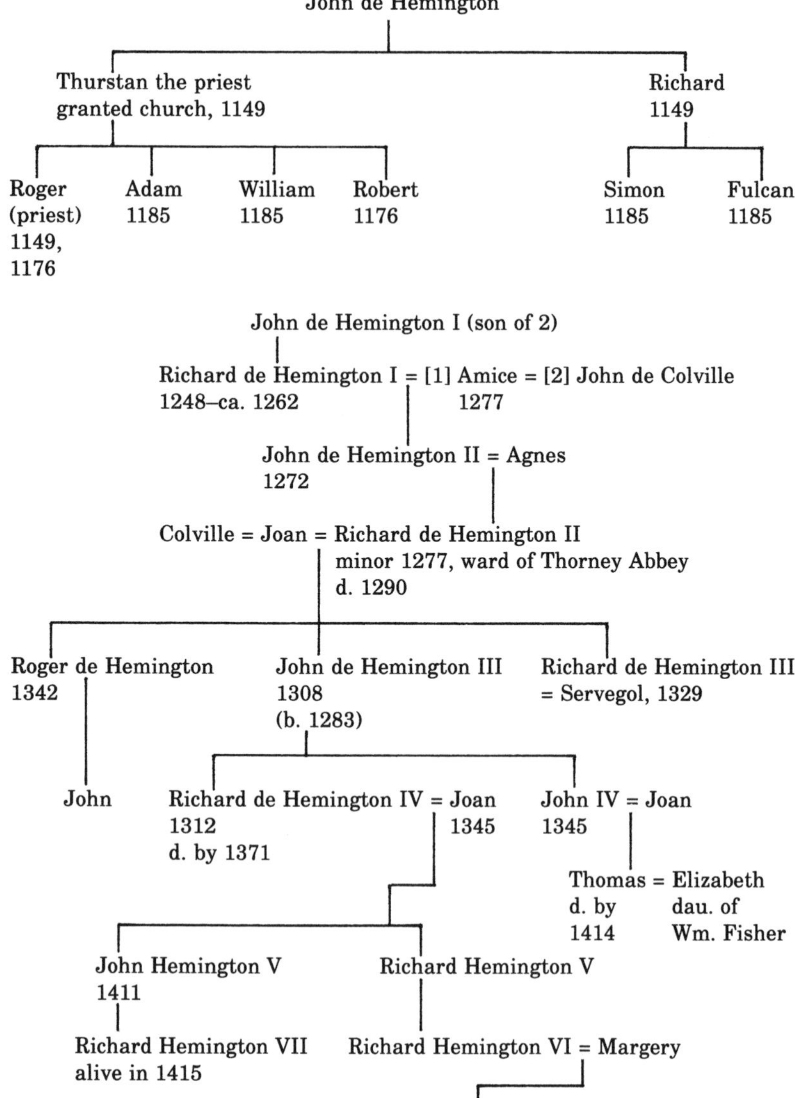

John de Hemington
Thurstan the priest
granted church, 1149
Richard
1149
Roger
(priest)
1149,
1176
Adam
1185
William
1185
Robert
1176
Simon
1185
Fulcan
1185
John de Hemington I (son of 2)
Richard de Hemington I = [1] Amice = [2] John de Colville
1248–ca. 1262
1277
John de Hemington II = Agnes
1272
Colville = Joan = Richard de Hemington II
minor 1277, ward of Thorney Abbey
d. 1290
Roger de Hemington
1342
John de Hemington III
1308
(b. 1283)
Richard de Hemington III
= Servegol, 1329
John
Richard de Hemington IV = Joan
1312
d. by 1371
1345
John IV = Joan
1345
Thomas = Elizabeth
d. by
1414
dau. of
Wm. Fisher
John Hemington V
1411
Richard Hemington V
Richard Hemington VII
alive in 1415
Richard Hemington VI = Margery
John Erpyngham = Katherine Hemington = John Kirkeby

Appendix 2

THE HOLDINGS OF RICHARD DE HEMINGTON II
(Annual value of properties in rent in parentheses)

The Fee of Southorpe

A house in Hemington and 224 acres of land (£8 18*s*.0*d*.)

Meadow

Dabbholme, of the fee of William de Tyndale: 3 a. (9*s*.)
In Warmington, of the fee of John Papple: 7.5 a. (22*s*.6*d*.)
Pynhowe, of the fee of John Knyvet: 1 a. (3*s*.)
In Barnwell, of the fee of Berengar le Moine: 2 a. (6*s*.)
In Cosynisholme, of the fee of Cosyn de Southwick: .5 a. (1*s*.6*d*.)

Total: 14 acres (42*s*.)

Pasture

Thirthe Medwe: 2 a.
In the park: 7 a.
In Grescroft: 2 a.

Total: 11 acres (10*s*.)

Properties Elsewhere

Daniel le Wallerie, fee of Ct. Warwick in Stamford: 1 messuage (10*s*.)
Stibbington, fee of Ranulph de Stantone: 1 yardland, rent at Hemington (2 marks)
Roger Miller of Southwick, fee of Costyn: 2 a. (2*s*., 2 capons)
William de Hilling, Hunts.: rent of 30*s*.
Stilton, of the fee of Ct. Glover: 50 a. (45*s*.)
Yarwell, of the fee of Thomas de Yarwell: 14 a. land, 4.5 a. meadow, rents (42*s*.4*d*.*ob*., 6 capons)
Cadeham, Sussex: 1 messuage, 10 a., 80 a. (38*s*.8*d*.)

Assize Rents

12 tenants, holding 8 messuages, 2 crofts and 1.5 yardlands (16*s*.3*d*., 10 capons, 1 pair of spurs)

Rents from Villeins (Gunthorpe fee)

13 villeins, holding 1.5 yardlands (67*s*., 1 hen, 2 chickens)

Other Peterborough Fees

12 villeins, holding 4 messuages and 1 yardland, 6 a. (£2 2*s*.2*d*.)

FISHERS IN LATE MEDIEVAL RURAL SOCIETY AROUND TEGERNSEE, BAVARIA: A PRELIMINARY SKETCH

Richard C. Hoffmann[1]

How do we grasp ordinary lives in the past? Martin Vörchel (ca. 1450–1518) probably went no further from his home in Egern on the Tegernsee at the edge of the Bavarian Alps than occasional 50-kilometer trips to Munich for his lord and chief employer, the Benedictine abbey just across the bay (see Fig. 1). In 1471 young Martin was helping his father, Hans Vörchel, a long-time tenant and mason for the monks. Then in 1474 he took the tenure called "in der Gassen" not far from Hans and by the latter's death (1492) had himself become a master mason. Later that decade a census of abbey serfs found Martin's six surviving siblings still in their father's house. Martin and his wife, Barbara, had at home only their son Oswald, whose brothers Ulrich and Sebastian had gone south to the mines at Schwaz in Tirol and Freisach in Carinthia. From 1474 to 1518,

[1]This essay reports part of a larger investigation into the economic, social, and environmental history of medieval freshwater fisheries. I am grateful for support from the Social Sciences and Humanities Council of Canada, York University, and the American Philosophical Association and for the advice and help of Helmut Irle, Pierre Reynard, Bela Bodo, the Cartographic Drafting Office at York University, and the staffs of the Bayerische Hauptstaatsarchiv (BHSA) and Bayerische Staatsbibliothek (BSB), Munich.

each year, Martin paid 15 pounds money rent and symbolic dues of two chickens and 32 eggs for the farm and an additional 1 pound 15 pfennig for two extra parcels of land. Besides working for the abbey as a mason—142 "long" and 12 "short" days at 10δ the day in 1518, for example—he pursued other economic interests, including a loan he and Hans made in a village 12 kilometers away and repeated sales of fishing equipment (a boat, nets, hooks) to the abbey. In April 1518 Martin gave the Egern parish church an annuity on property in a village near Munich to fund perpetual memorial masses and contributed 3½ florins to the local confraternity. The next year Oswald Vörchel held the tenure "in der Gassen" and the livestock, mason's tools, and silver later inventoried there.[2]

Martin's dossier confirms that not only English Benedictines kept records with remarkably detailed raw materials for study of medieval peasant life. Eighth-century Franco-Bavarian nobles tucked their abbey of St. Quirinus into the secluded Alpine fringe at Tegernsee, but they endowed it with rich estates on the upper Bavarian plain and further down the

[2]Wilhelm Koch scanned BHSA Klosterliteralien Tegernsee (KL Teg) 99–104 and 184–186 for references to Martin Vörchel and listed results in his "Die Geschichte der Binnenfischerei von Mitteleuropa," in Reinhard Demoll et al., eds., *Handbuch der Binnenfischerei Mitteleuropas*, vol. 4 (Stuttgart, 1925), pp. 25–26, and Wilhelm Koch, *Festschrift zum 100jährigen Fischereijubiläum in Bayern, Allgemeine Fischerei-Zeitung*, no. 81/16 (München, 1956), pp. 313–15. See also Johannes N. Kisslinger, *Chronik der Pfarrei Egern am Tegernsee*, Oberbayerisches Archiv, vol. 53, no. 8 (München, 1907), p. 29. Familial relationships and wealth are recorded in KL Teg 21, fol. 9r; KL Teg 22, fol. 15v; and KL Teg 105 1/2, fol. 17r. Like others in late medieval southern Bavaria, Tirol, and Austria, the Tegernsee abbey accounts use the "long" schilling (ß) of 30 pfennig (δ), so 8ß made 1 pound (*£b*) of 240δ. Until the early 1500s the *£b* was there treated as roughly equal to the coined florin or gulden (fl) and to 60 of the heavy pennies called "kreutzer" (xer). In 1516 Bavarian authorities in Munich stopped official use of the *£b* and set the following ratios: 1fl = 7ß = 210δ = 60xer. But *£b* remains common in the Tegernsee accounts well into the 1530s.

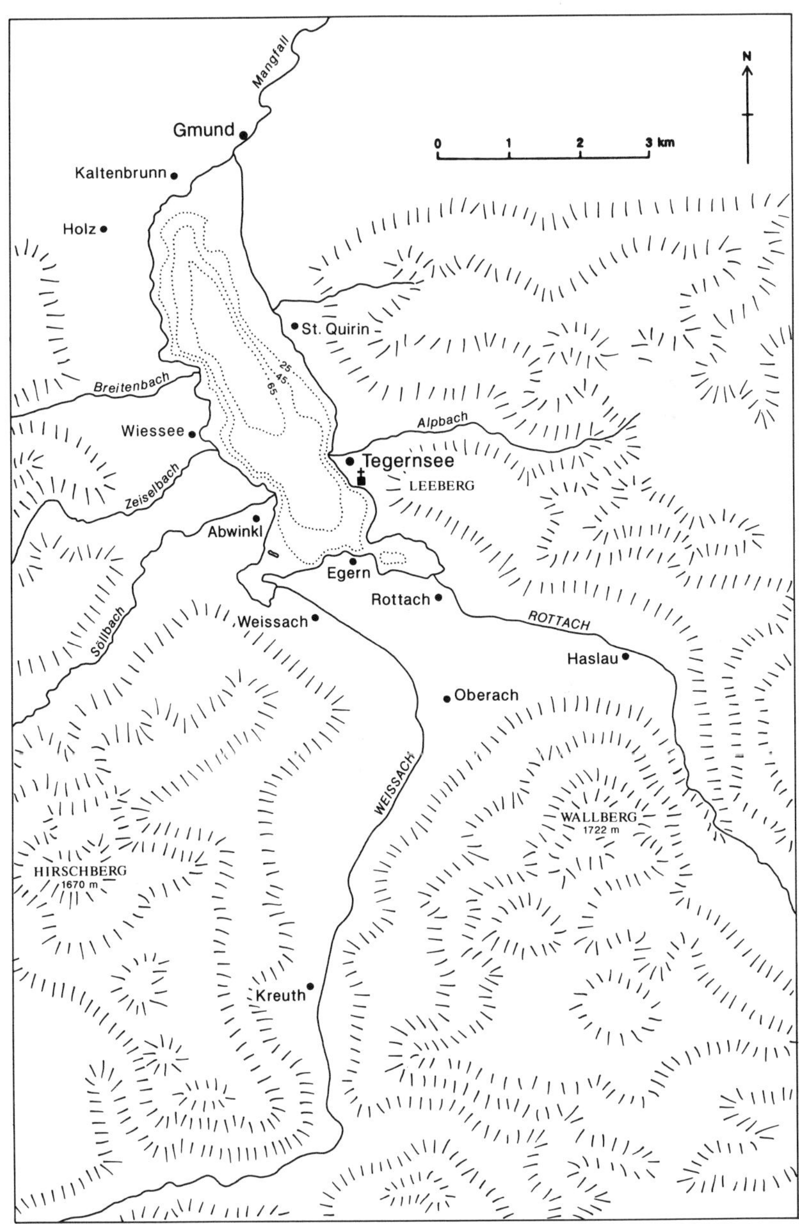

Figure 1. Tegernsee

Danube.[3] Traces still survive of the economic stewardship that sustained the eleventh- and twelfth-century political influence and cultural achievements of this house, and then 200 more years of rivalries with nearby lords.[4] Long communal decay ended in 1426, when Tegernsee accepted internal reforms pioneered at Austrian Melk. A dynamic young abbot, Kaspar Aindorffer (1426–61), and his successors restored Tegernsee to leadership of a purified Bavarian monasticism able to sustain momentum into the Baroque Age.

Reform in practice included impeccably close and ever-expanding supervision and written record of the lordship's resources in the hands of grain-growers on the flat lands and of hill people around the abbey itself.[5] Administrators began (in 1427) a new *Saalbuch*, to register tenurial changes in the 16 administrative districts (*Ämter*) of the abbey's estate and new *Stiftsbücher* for annual records of what each tenant owed and

---

[3]For what follows see A. Wessinger, "Kaspar Aindorffer, Abt in Tegernsee 1426–1461," *Oberbayerisches Archiv für vaterländischen Geschichte* 42 (1885): 196–260; Virgil Redlich, *Tegernsee und die deutsche Geistesgeschichte im 15. Jahrhundert* (München, 1931; repr. Aalen, 1974); Michael Hartig, *Die Benediktinerabtei Tegernsee 746–1803* (München, 1946); Joachim F. Angerer, *Die Bräuche der Abtei Tegernsee unter Abt Kaspar Ayndorffer (1426–1461), verbunden mit einer textkritischen Edition der Consuetudines Tegernseenses* (Ottobeuren, 1968); Josef Hemmerle, "Tegernsee," pp. 297–304 in *Germania Benedictina*, 2: *Die Benediktinerkloster in Bayern* (Ottobeuren, 1970).

[4]BSB, Clm 18181, fol. 118v, is an economic inventory of the cellarer's office done in 1023 on parchment used later that century to bind a codex of grammatical and rhetorical works. BHSA KL Teg 1–5 are *Urbare*, and KL Teg 7, 7a, and 8, cartularies originating from the eleventh century up to the Black Death. Compare J. Sturm, "Die chronologische Reihenfolge der Tegernseer Urbare des 13. Jahrhunderts," *Studien und Mitteilungen zur Geschichte des Benediktinerordens und seiner Zweige* 47 (1929): 103–05.

[5]Max Edelmann, *Die Almen im Tegernseeer Tal: Zur Rechts- und Wirtschaftsgeschichte des ehemaligen Klostergerichts Tegernsee* (München, 1966), described the pastoral economy of alpine meadows and Georg Breu, "Der Tegernsee, eine limnologische Studie," *Mitteilungen der geographischen Gesellschaft in München* 2 (1907): 184–92, its overwhelming economic dominance even in the early twentieth century.

paid. One series covered the outer *Ämter* and another what they called the "Winkel" or "Angulo," the narrow valley reaching southward from Gmund along the lake past the abbey and then up its feeder streams into the looming crags. There above the bridge at Gmund only the abbot was lord, and the entire district was in the charge of the abbey's chief economic officer, the cellarer. The new inventory of abbey properties (*Urbar*) compiled in 1436 listed 286 farms in the Winkel. By 1526 there were 380 households with close to 2,500 people, most of whom, especially the men, were repeatedly and differently enrolled in dozens of successive volumes of administrative records.[6] Official diligence continued, the forms of records multiplied, and the files and volumes accumulated—until in 1803, when Bavaria secularized its monasteries, everything moveable at Tegernsee Abbey was carted off to Munich.

Five centuries later the traces of Martin Vörchel and thousands of his contemporaries still rest in property surveys, rental books, serf lists, tax assessments, tithe returns, income and expenditure accounts, and court books kept by Tegernsee's administrators, officials, and clerks. Until now few other of their trails have been traced, even for genealogical ends. Certainly none has been handled with the disciplined system required to make larger sense of the details of Martin's life. But why, indeed, should Martin Vörchel matter at all?

Martin is the visible thread leading into a hitherto unsuspected web of late medieval human and ecological relationships.

---

[6]KL Teg 9, 9a, 10, 11, 12, and 12a are fifteenth-century *Saalbücher* averaging 200 large folios. Twenty-eight still larger volumes of *Stiftsbücher* cover the outer *Ämter* and 11 more (KL Teg 96–106), the Tegernseer Winkel from the 1430s to 1550s. KL Teg 6, the 1436 *Urbar*, includes 21 topographic headings in 173 leaves with 35 leaves for the three parishes of the Winkel. Of course, as anyone exposed to medieval prosopography knows too well, the job of linking the highly variable spellings and forms of names in real medieval records is both complex and time-consuming. See note a to the Appendix below.

He is the one person named in an anonymous manuscript tract on fishing that was written at Tegernsee about 1500. What I call "Tegernsee Fishing Advice" is the earliest such text known from the Alpine region, and it is among the oldest from the entire European continent. Further, through Martin—to whom the text attributes a semimagical bait recipe—this is the only early writing on fishing with demonstrable connections to a particular local society and its natural surroundings.[7] Part-time mason, part-time pastoralist, sometime fisher, Martin uniquely links late medieval writing about a widespread economic activity, freshwater fishing, with its practice by real members of society. The peculiar interests and diligence of the Tegernsee record keepers, and the fortuitous survival of their labors, allow the practitioners and their society to be reconstructed using historical methods modeled on those J. Ambrose Raftis pioneered to elicit social and economic sense from huge and repetitive sources of medieval English rural history.

Martin Vörchel was an occasional fisher, not a specialist, and medieval sources of various kinds everywhere reveal others of that sort—from elite sportsmen such as Martin's contemporary Emperor Maximilian I or the twelfth-century canon Gui de Bazoches to such seekers after subsistence as four peasants who poached the lord's pike at Wakefield, Yorkshire, in 1314 or

[7]I call "Tegernsee Fishing Advice" the untitled fish-catching instructions on fols. 97r–109v of BSB Cgm 8137, a handbook-sized codex written at the Tegernsee cellarer's office in several stages, 1450s–1530s. Folio 104r warrants sure success for fish traps baited with a dried paste of human blood, woman's milk, and barley powder credited "a Martino Vörchel." The one published edition, neither dependable nor complete, was Anton Birlinger, "Tegernseer Angel- und Fischbüchlein," *Zeitschrift für deutsches Altertum* 14 (1869): 162–79, and the most recent scholarly introduction, Gerhard Eis, "Nachträge zum Verfasserlexikon, Tegernseer Angel- und Fischbüchlein," *Beiträge zur Geschichte der deutschen Sprache und Literatur* 83 (1961): 217–18. A first complete edition from the manuscript, with an English translation and full interpretive commentary, appears in my forthcoming book *Fisher's Craft and Lettered Art at the Close of the Middle Ages*.

the seventh-century Irish hermit St. Gall.[8] But the peculiar economic demands of monastic life at Tegernsee, where the monks maintained total abstinence from "animal" meat (i.e., that of quadrupeds) deep into the sixteenth century,[9] and the special resources of the subalpine lake at its front door, gave Tegernsee an unusual focus on the freshwater fishery. To meet abbey needs and to gain from its authority over fishing rights in the Winkel, the abbey gave steady work to fishers more specialized than Martin. They, too, had counterparts across medieval Europe. One of them speaks in Aelfric of Eynsham's tenth-century *Colloquy*. Seven of 33 tenures at late-thirteenth-century Kotowice on the Odra River in Silesia owed fishes every few days to the nuns at Trzebnica convent. Two similar professionals, John Boys and his son, settled in 1420 at Godmanchester, Huntingdonshire.[10] The craft of fishing was widespread despite its glancing mention in most medieval writings and modern scholarship. The sources from Tegernsee are unusual for their identification of individual practitioners within a broadly-recoverable social setting.

---

[8]Many medieval recreational fishers are treated in Richard C. Hoffmann, "Fishing for Sport in Medieval Europe: New Evidence," *Speculum* 60 (1985): 877–902. Contrast the subsistence activities portrayed in J. McDonnell, *Inland Fisheries in Medieval Yorkshire, 1066–1300* (York, 1981), p. 18; St. Gall's doings on the Bodensee and Steinach in *Vita Galli* 1: 6–12 (*MGH, Scriptores rerum Merovingicarum*, vol. 4; also ed. and trans. Maud Joynt, *The Life of St. Gall* [London, 1927], pp. 72–82); and the peasant fishing on the Orb and Vernazobres reported in Emmanuel Le Roy Ladurie, *The Peasants of Languedoc*, trans. John Day (Urbana, 1976), p. 18.

[9]Johann N. Kisslinger, "Das Abstinenzgebot und sein Einfluss auf die Wirtschaft des Klosters Tegernsee," *Germania: Wissenschaftliche Beilage. Blätter für Litteratur, Wissenschaft und Kunst*, no. 23 (7 June 1906): 177–79.

[10]*Aelfric's Colloquy*, ed. G. N. Garmonsway, 3rd ed. rev. (Exeter, 1978), pp. 26–30, with the fisher's commercial attitude remarked by James Hurt, *Aelfric* (New York, 1972), pp. 113–19, notably p. 118; Richard C. Hoffmann, *Land, Liberties, and Lordship in a Late Medieval Countryside: Agrarian Structures and Change in the Duchy of Wrocław* (Philadelphia, 1989), pp. 255–56; J. Ambrose Raftis, *Early Tudor Godmanchester: Survivals and New Arrivals* (Toronto, 1990), p. 66.

Tegernsee offers a richly documented and culturally important opportunity to explore the social context for professional fishing in the medieval rural economy. This essay delineates the general employment status, duties, and remuneration of the late medieval abbey fishers and then examines the careers of the men who fished between 1443 and 1527. Two extraordinary sources permit closer study of particular cohorts of fishers. Their households and family connections are seen against a servile census (*Leibzinsbuch*) made of the entire Tegernseer Winkel in 1498. A different view of fishers' households and wealth comes from accounts of the "Turk tax" (*Türkensteuer*) they and their neighbors paid in 1526. Results from these first systematic probes into the Tegernsee records will help guide further research there and elsewhere into relations between medieval societies and aquatic ecosystems.

Some knowledge of the Tegernsee fishers' job and its rewards should inform study of its subject. The abbey organized its fishers into two and later three teams, of a master and one or two hands (*knechten*), with designated areas of work.[11] Ordinarily the three-man teams were assigned to deep-water work and the two-man team to the shallows. A 1506 agreement between the abbey and the fishers obliged them to fish each morning and afternoon and always to keep close watch on all runs of fish, catches, and spawning. A seasonal rhythm was set by human demand—the greater consumption of fish from Lent to Pentecost and again in Advent—and by the natural

[11]KL Teg 185 1/2 and 185 1/4 are successive late-fifteenth- and early sixteenth-century collections of internal administrative memoranda from the cellarer's office, with much detail on the fishery. I more fully discuss the aquatic ecosystem and fishing methods at Tegernsee in Richard C. Hoffmann, "The Craft of Fishing Alpine Lakes, *ca.* A.D. 1500," in Dirk Heinrich, ed., *Fish in Archaeology and Quarternary Biology: Proceedings of the 6th Meeting of the Fish Remains Working Group, International Congress of Archaeozoology, Schleswig* (Kiel, 1995).

environment. In the Tegernsee, a deep and cold mountain lake, plankton-eating whitefish were the principal converters of plant material into animal flesh and were themselves the food for large lake trout, catfish, pike, and other predators, which also ate the warm-water cyprinids that lived along shallow shores. The cellarer's procedural manuals of the early 1500s identify when various fish varieties spawn and thus concentrate in certain places, for easier capture. Trout migrating up the Weissach drew the fishers in pursuit between St. Bartholomew (24 August) and Martinmas (11 November), and then the whitefish spawning near the surface over deep water in December and January took them into the open lake. Natural feeding behavior also made fish more accessible at certain times, as when the lake trout came up to eat emerging insects around Pentecost.

Guided by the location and habits of anticipated quarry, Tegernsee's fishers chose techniques from a traditional arsenal. Some situations called for setting large or small fixed devices in order to trap moving schools or individual fish. The abbey maintained an inventory of pound nets, gill nets, and pot gear made of wicker or netting, to be set out with bait. Crews actively chased other fishes with several sorts of seines and trawls designed to surround them near the surface, or with a 40-fathom net (the *schopffen*) that they deployed vertically to strain the fish from great depths, or with framed lift or dip nets for use in rivers. On other occasions the fishers set hooks (*angeln*) dressed with natural or prepared food baits or with feathered lures in gangs on long lines or in ones or twos on shorter lines that they manipulated with a rod. The abbey provided the equipment, but success called for an artisan's physical skills and deft application of local environmental knowledge.

The Tegernsee fishers formed a hierarchical team with titles and pay differentiated among masters, men, and occasional young apprentices or helpers. They counted among the abbey's household servants (*hofgesinde*) and received wages in cash and kind.[12] Money payments were semiannual in the mid-fifteenth century, quarterly later on. The oldest surviving accounts of the 1440s give each of the two master fishers 12 schillings (ß) pfennig (i.e., 360 pfennig) a year and the four ordinary men, nine. After 1450 these rates doubled to 3*£b* and 18ß, respectively, and the agreement of 1506 set them at 4*£b* and 3*£b* 30δ. Around the year 1540 this standard *sold* rested at 4fl and 3fl 1ß, paid in pfennig, but then the masters also got 45δ and the men 32δ *opfergelt* (an annual "gift") and respectively 15δ and 10δ *hartzgeld* ("pitch" for their boats?). In addition, in most years between 1457 and 1505 a seventh man, commonly one relatively new to the fishing team and called "knecht" for a named master, received only 12ß. Jacob, Ull Dornacher's son, contracted in 1470 for four years' service with Hansel Leeperger and would get 4*£b* on successful completion of the term; in 1474 he began to receive his annual 18ß.[13] The men could earn more by making equipment for the abbey. Hansel Michel picked up another 4ß as "cordage pay" (*stricklon*) in 1445, and the cellarer offered two kreuzer each for crayfish traps in the 1530s.[14]

Provisions in kind may have matched the money component of the fishers' compensation. The men were normally fed at a table in the lower chamber of the abbey every morning, noon, and evening, with loaves of particular breads, weights of meat or fish, and bowls of soup designated for the masters and the ordinary hands. Extra rations came for treks up the rivers after

---

[12]*Stiftsbücher* accounts confirm and concretize general practices laid out in the fishers' agreement of 1506 (KL Teg 102, fol. 105v) and the procedural manuals (KL Teg 185 1/2 and 185 1/4).

[13]KL Teg 99, fol. 363v.

[14]KL Teg 97, fol. 91v; KL Teg 185 1/4, fol. 32v.

migratory fish or working at night. On Christmas, Carnival, Easter, and Whitsunday each man got a measure of wine and a two-pound cut of meat to take home. That must also have been the destination of the dozens of cheeses each fisher in the 1440s was receiving by assignment from one of the abbey's pastoral tenants. For clothing, each was given a pair of boots and an overshirt every year and a shirt or hose in alternate years.[15] Through their labor for the abbey, then, fishers acquired goods they themselves could not produce because they lacked the time (dairy products from the high mountain pastures), skill (leather and textiles), or resources (grain or wine from lowland arable).

To advance from general description to social analysis of the Tegernsee fishers is possible because beginning in 1443 a special section of every annual *Stiftsbuch* named the fishers whom the abbey employed that year. The six (to 1455), seven (1456–68), and then eight yearly names form meaningful individual sequences and refer to men who also appear in other abbey records. Through nominal linkage the separate mentions become individual and then collective biographies of a form resembling that of Martin Vörchel.

Forty-one men fished for Tegernsee Abbey between 1443 and 1527.[16] Their dossiers are summarized in the Appendix below

---

[15]A mid-sixteenth century passage in a cellarer's manual (KL Teg 185 1/4, fol. 34r) further reserved nine "fishers' houses" (*Vischerheuser*) in Egern (and a tenth "formerly" at Sternlehen am Leeperg) for households from which one member fished for the abbey. We see below that this is no accurate portrayal of earlier conditions.

[16]No women fished for Tegernsee, but I cannot yet determine how much this reflects monastic misogyny and how much a real difference in gender roles. Some ethnographic evidence reports women active in central European peasant subsistence fisheries (Bela Gunda, "Fish Poisoning in the Carpathian Area and in the Balkan Peninsula," in Gunda, ed., *The Fishing Culture of the World: Studies in Ethnology, Cultural Ecology, and Folklore*, vol. 1 [Budapest, 1984], pp. 186–88; Laszlo Mákkai, "Economic Landscapes: Historical Hungary from the Fourteenth to the Seventeenth Century," in Antoni Mączak et al., eds., *East-Central Europe in Transition: From the Fourteenth to the Seventeenth Century* [Cambridge, 1985],

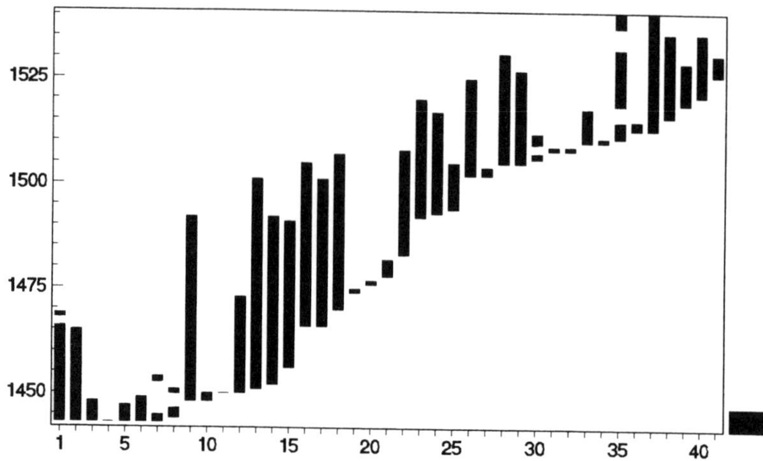

Figure 2. Careers of 41 fishers for Tegernsee Abbey, 1443–1527

(where numbers are assigned); their documented fishing careers are displayed in Figure 2.[17] Because men fishing in 1443 could have begun work earlier, their careers cannot be treated as complete. Hence the data now extant cover 34 *complete careers*, from Haintzl Krapf (no. 8, fishing 1444–51 but not 1448–50) to Liendel Dorndel (no. 41, fishing 1526–31) and some of Liendel's more senior colleagues who continued to fish as late as 1541. What follows here looks collectively at the timing and length of the fishers' working lives and the roles of familial succession, tenure, residence, and other variables in them.

---

p. 30), but none is known from the more specialized or commercial sectors. Widows of Tegernsee fishers retained the tenures of their deceased husbands, but they themselves did not fish.

[17]The year 1527 is the second and last year of the same fishing crew whose moveable goods were inventoried for the 1526 *Türkensteuer*; it is also late enough to detect reverberations (if any) from the 1525 Peasant War. Further checks on the work force employed up to 1530 revealed no informative changes, so the careers of the 1527 cohort are the latest here traced to their ends. The Appendix also tabulates the two men who entered the work force between 1527 and 1530, but their later careers were not traced and they are omitted from all statistics and figures.

The average late-medieval fisher worked 18.47 years for the abbey, but few real fishers resembled "the average." Complete careers begun before 1480 averaged 23.5 years, and those after 1490 only 14.4 years. A bimodal distribution of short and long careers was normal throughout the observed period. Men fished for a few years or for a lifetime: 40 per cent stayed fewer than 10 years; 60 per cent before 1480 and 40 per cent after 1490 lasted for over 20 years. So the markedly longer average career of a mid-fifteenth-century cohort came entirely from the extended service of its veterans. Some men probably born in the 1420s or '30s were remarkably long-lived. Hans Hanig fished from 1448 to 1492 and then kept his tenement to 1501; Hans Rapfnvogel von Weyssach, after fishing from 1451 to 1501, survived in residence at Asch in Egern for four years more.[18]

Familial succession by birth or marriage marked the group of fishers. Four families each gave the abbey three generations of these workers. Hansel Michel was already a master fisher for the abbey in 1443 and continued in that position until his (probable) death in 1465. An unnamed son joined him briefly in 1450 and his son Liendel succeeded him in 1466. Liendel fished for 40 years, the last 32 as a master, before giving way in 1505 to his own son, Thoman Vischer am Asch, who then worked for 23 years. Likewise, an elder Hansel Leeperger, who fished off and on up to 1455, was followed by his son Hansel 2 (fishing 1456–91) and grandson Jorg (1492–1520). Ull Dornacher fished for 41 years (1452–92) and two sons nearly matched his record of longevity, Jacob Dorndel working from 1470 to 1507 and the younger Hans Dorndel Lerer from 1493 until 1517. They were briefly followed by two younger kinsmen, Lorentz and Liendel

[18]Hanig is named consistently the same and recurs in the same place in all records. Rapfnvogel went by several different names, but each of them, at one time or another, is explicitly equated with another of the set. Note as well the two 40-year men, Ull Dornacher and Liendel Michel.

Dorndel, whose precise connections are obscure, and by Jacob's two sons-in-law, Jorg Staudacher Dorndel and Hans Toltzer, who fished into the 1540s while putting in about a quarter-century each. Also, the intermarried group called Ferg and Heys provided fishers in the 1440s (Hansel Ferg), around the turn of the century (Liendel Heys), and during the 1520s and '30s (Andre and Michel Heys). Two generations each fished from patrilines called Ruedel, Hanig, and von Weyssach, and in the sequence of Lang Michel Vischer and his two sons, Peter Vischer and Hans Spitzer. In all, known family ties joined about 25 of the fishers.

Common residential patterns were also shared by the abbey fishers. From the mid-fifteenth through the first third of the sixteenth century representatives of six tenures (farms) were regularly found among them. Five were in Egern, the settlement in the middle of the peninsular delta at the southern head of the lake. From the 1440s into the 1530s a holding called Asch supported fishers from the Michel family and then the (unrelated) Michel Heys. The nearby location eventually named Spitz housed first Hans Hanig and after 1466 the Vischer-Spitzer lineage, while Hanig and his son moved to a site called Vischerlehen. From Caspar Hanig that farm passed in 1506 to one Cristof Vischer (fished 1508–09), to Cristof's widow, and to Hans Vischer Suess (fished 1513–15). Hinderlehen belonged to the Ruedel and then to Jacob Dorndel and his sons-in-law, so between 1443 and 1543 it lacked a working fisher only in 1510. In every year but 1518, from the 1450s into the 1530s someone fished from Kashutten, as that tenure passed from Ull Dornacher and his son Hans Dorndel Lerer to Lorentz Teybler, who acquired it from a Dorndel who did not fish.[19] The sixth

[19]Without equal regularity but still often, a worker came to the fishery from another tenure am Asch (belonging to the von Weyssach) and/or from the Palerslehen farm of the Heys family. Both sites are in Egern.

regular residence of a fisher lay across the southeastern cove from Egern, where Sternlehen am Leeperg supported the three generations of Leepergers who fished steadily from 1453 to 1520. So the variation remained limited: the abbey hired fishers only from the small group of settlements along the south end of the lake, and not from the west-shore hamlets or the more populous parish of Gmund at the north end. Unlike other abbey craftsmen, no fishers lived in the cluster of houses around the abbey itself.

Exceptional individuals and residential mobility among the Tegernsee fishers and their kin make plain that at the end of the Middle Ages neither familial inheritance nor designated landholdings automatically made a man a fisher. The longest-serving master fisher among those working in 1443, Hans Antlocher, lived until 1452 at Geygerslehen in Rottach (and for the next dozen years at an unknown site). That hamlet at the head of the southeastern cove also housed a much later counterpart, Liendel Ungerl Sneider am Puhel. At least five times in such incidents as Hans Hanig's 1465 cession of Spitz to Lang Michel Vischer or Thoman Vischer's 1527 transfer of Asch to Michel Heys, what might be thought "fishing tenures" were alienated outside the close and recorded kin group. Michel Heys thereby moved from Palerslehen to Asch, a change of familial tenure of the sort also recorded for Jacob Dorndel (from Kashutten to Hinderlehen in 1477) and others.

Parallel indicators are tenures that passed to men who did not fish and fishers' sons who left the paternal craft. No one remotely connected with the Vischerlehen can be found among the fishers after that farm (once the Hanigs') passed in 1516 from Hans Vischer Suess to a Paul Öttl and his heirs, who still had it in the 1540s. The Sternlehen am Leeperg gave no fishers to the abbey after Jorg Leeperger retired in 1520 and left it in 1525 to his maternal kin Paul Kuening. Hans Dorndel Lerer's son Peter Dorndel did not fish, nor did Hans Rapfnvogel's son Jung Hans.[20] Even within customary patterns, some element of conscious choice helped match the abbey cellarer's need for skilled fishers and the lakeside peasants' need for work.

The collective longitudinal view represented by Figure 2 further reveals alternating stability and change in the abbey's fishing personnel. The earliest records suggest considerable flux; with eight changes before 1456, a new man was joining the team about every other year. Only two men working in 1443 still did so a dozen years later. But a later fifteenth-century cohort formed an effectively stable team from the 1460s to the early 1490s, during which time seven of the eight members were unchanged. Indeed, consistency of make-up really lasted until 1500. Liendel Heys, the only new recruit between 1476 and 1492, spent a decade helping two successive Leepergers before attaining regular status. Every new fisher in the 1490s, Jorg Leeperger, Hans Dorndel Lerer, and Caspar Hanig, followed a father who had fished for more than 30 years. Even with that generational succession, a new man joined the work crew only once every four years between 1470 and 1501.[21] In 1491 a total of 239 years of fishing experience sat at the fishers' table beneath the abbey.

An inexorable cost of long stability in a group of people is eventual wholesale replacement, and the slow generational change of the Tegernsee abbey fishers in the 1490s accelerated into rapid turnover in the first two decades of the new century—a new member every 1.6 years between 1502 and

[20]Note that the present research strategy of pursuing Tegernsee's fishers through all available documentation is not intended to keep track of *non*-fishers, so these few cases are to be seen as exemplary, not representative or exhaustive.

[21]Three of the other changes were successive *knechten* whom Hansel 2 Leeperger took on in the 1470s.

1530, over twice as fast as in the previous period. Even with an extra crewman in 1514, the nine then at the fishers' table had among them but 85 years of experience.

For the new situation of the early sixteenth century we may find, if not cogent explanations, then tantalizing covariants. Were pressures rising against the fisheries resource and abbey budgets? Abbey and fishers renegotiated their relationship in 1506. Their agreement affirmed a *third* position as master fisher, for Jorg Leeperger, who was instructed to set out more traps than the recent norm.[22] As had been customary since 1469, the agreement spoke still of eight fishers, but the number climbed to nine in the years 1510–11 and 1513–14. At about this same time the abbey went outside its usual local labor pool and the customary path from helper to crewman to master for two successive master fishers. Neither Cristof Vischer nor Hans Vischer Suess was known around Egern before each took the Vischerlehen tenure and the post of Vischermeister. Cristof lasted two years (1508–09) and died; Hans Suess lasted three years (1513–15), yielded the tenure to a non-fisher, and departed from the annual *Stiftsbücher*. This novelty was not repeated, but in 1505 and again some years later the cellarer was consulting with a master fisher from Schliersee about the design and cost of seines and other gear.[23]

Increasing numbers of fishers and the replacement of old with young correspond with the many local children reported in 1498 (see below), and ultimately with the expansive demographic and economic trend in south Germany during the reign

---

[22]KL Teg 102, fol. 175v, and KL Teg 185 1/4, fols. 29v–34v. Leeperger was certainly receiving a crewman's wage as late as 1501, and only two annual masters are recorded as late as 1504. His occupancy of a third master's post is confirmed in annual listings from 1506.

[23]KL Teg 102, fol. 236v; KL Teg 185 1/4, fol. 33v.

of Emperor Maximilian (1490–1519).[24] It is tempting to see in the Tegernsee fishers of the early sixteenth century a microcosm of how growing demand, rising human numbers, and a more mobile population were shifting the cultural setting for resource use and environmental awareness.

Most individual details fade in the long perspective offered by the serial data of the annual *Stiftsbücher*. Against the sweep of long-term stability and change in group membership, two different sources can now set single microscopic views of the Tegernsee fishers in their socioeconomic surroundings. One narrow but deep and nuanced insight into their familial situations at the cusp of social change comes from information in the *Leibzinsbuch* that the abbey prepared in 1498, and another, into their economic resources on the eve of the German Peasant War, from returns for the 1526 *Türkensteuer*. The first of these glimpses reveals the fishers sharing family household structures, reproductive success, and much movement of people with all of upland society. The second identifies employment in the fishery as a survival strategy for members of a resource-poor mountain community.

Tegernsee's fishers and their neighbors not only were employees and tenants of the abbey but they also were abbey serfs, *Leibeigene*. From the thirteenth century in Bavaria the servile obligation to work on the lord's farm was replaced with

---

[24]Francis Rapp, *Les origines médiévales de l'Allemagne moderne: de Charles IV à Charles Quint (1346–1519)* (Paris, 1989), pp. 299–392, comes at the issues from the Middle Ages. For research probing this period for origins of the German Peasant War of 1525, see John C. Stalnaker, "Auf dem Weg zu einer sozialgeschichtlichen Interpretation des Deutschen Bauernkriegs 1525–6," pp. 38–60 in H.-U. Wehler, ed., *Der Deutsche Bauernkrieg 1524–1526, Geschichte und Gesellschaft*, Sonderheft 1 (Göttingen, 1975), abridged as "Towards a Social Interpretation of the German Peasant War," in Robert W. Scribner and Gerhard Benecke, eds., *The German Peasant War of 1525: New Viewpoints* (London, 1979), pp. 23–38. The Peasant War did not spread to Bavaria.

a small annual payment in recognition of servile status and of freedom from labor service. At Tegernsee as elsewhere, custom called for a pfennig a year from each adult, regardless of marital condition or residence. Where peasant status was not in doubt, as in the entire Tegernseer Winkel under the abbey's sole lordship, servile dues were not actually collected after some time around 1400. Three remaining issues then vexed lords and serfs alike: intermarriage, tenancy, and emigration. Marriage between serfs of different lords was commonly permitted by the 1300s, but lords tried to keep track of the offspring, who were customarily held to follow the status and lordship of their mothers. Serfs could and did hold land from third parties but were still deemed liable for service or dues to their own lords—if the lords could recall their identities. Unless serfs who moved to a privileged town or market were claimed by their lords within a year and a day, they became free. By the fifteenth century Bavaria's dukes had released their own emigrant serfs and showed little will to enforce the claims of other lords. Others, notably the monasteries, were loath to surrender this right.[25]

The legal and social situation at the end of the fifteenth century caused Tegernsee Abbey to survey the status and familial connections of all who inhabited its lordships. The resultant inventory, or *Leibzinsbuch* of 1498, describes each resident household in a reasonably standard way, naming the head (usually male) and spouse, counting their children, and reporting the names and present residence of any other kin. Nonresident or married children are commonly also named and any marriage connections and offspring identified, as are resident serfs

---

[25]Adolf Sandberger, "Entwicklungsstufen des Leibeigenschaft in Altbayern seit dem 13. Jahrhundert," *Zeitschrift für bayerischen Landesgeschichte* 25 (1962): 71–91, treats the customs of Tegernsee as generally representative of the region.

of other lords.[26] Through this record the households and families of the abbey fishers from 1498 can be seen against the norms of their local and regional community.

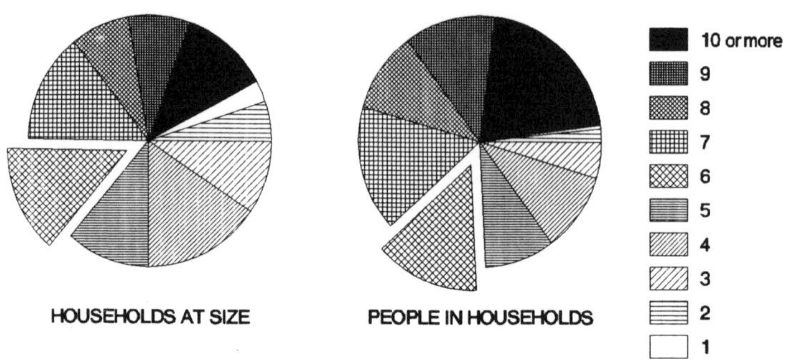

Figure 3. Tegernseer Winkel household size, 1498: 329 peasant households totaling 1,987 people (average, 6.04 per household)

The 1498 survey lists 366 households in the three parishes (Gmund, Tegernsee, and Egern) of the Tegernseer Winkel. It fully specifies the composition of 329 households; their 1,987 people work out to an average household size of 6.04 people. Figure 3 displays the household sizes and distribution of people among them. More than half the valley's peasants lived in households of seven or more—up to 14—persons. Another 108 people are named in 37 more incompletely documented households, so the valley then held more than 2,095 people. This was

[26]KL Teg 21 "Leibzinsbuch de ao 1498" is the original, and KL Teg 22 "Leyb zinss puech Anno dni. 1498," a closely contemporary copy with a bare handful of corrections. The three parishes of the Tegernseer Winkel are fols. 2r–22r and 8r–24r, respectively, and each book then goes on to the outer *Ämter* and serfs living off the abbey lordships. Because the precise spelling of personal and farm names, the sequence of farms, and the allocation of farms to settlement groupings differ somewhat from contemporary *Stiftsbücher*, and because the formats, hands, and provenance of the manuscripts suggest a different part of the abbey archive, I suspect the survey was prepared by an independent enquiry, not by the cellarer.

a young population in 1498. The *Leibzinsbuch* credits to 332 families a total of 1,419 living children—not necessarily then resident or of the current marriage—and thus the impressive rate of 4.27 offspring per married couple.[27] Plainly, the society was more than reproducing itself, but much of that reproduction flowed out of the Winkel to surrounding regions. One in three (119) households reported offspring or parental siblings living abroad, whether in nearby valleys such as at the village of Schliersee or the Wessobrunn abbey or in more distant Munich, Regensburg, Ulm, and various Tirolian and Styrian mining towns. Residents from outside the nuclear family group did not make up for the outflow, for they joined but one in six (64) households and were chiefly parents, siblings, or more distant relatives of the conjugal pair. Stem or other forms of extended family households were thus common stages in regional life cycles. Only six households reported lodgers or other persons not described as kin.[28]

In all known respects the eight men who fished for the abbey in 1498 fit well into their craft and their community.[29] They manifest the social and occupational continuity already seen as normal among late-fifteenth-century fishers and they shared in the demographic upsurge that required adaptive

---

[27]Large household and family sizes must surely reflect a rapidly expanding population so far little checked by resource shortages. For analytical and institutional contexts and comparisons see Michael Mitterauer and Reinhard Sieder, *The European Family*, trans. Karla Oosterveen and Manfred Hörzinger (Chicago, 1982), pp. 27–34, and David Herlihy, *Medieval Households* (Cambridge, Mass., 1985), pp. 131–56.

[28]Note, however, that the 1498 survey was interested in kinship, not co-residence, so it omits the servants found by the tax assessors of 1526 (see below) in 36 per cent of households. In 1498 the fishers' village, Egern, fell close to the regional average on all variables reported: mean household size, 6.03; 4.17 children reported per family; 37 per cent of households with kin resident abroad; 16 per cent with non-nuclear co-residents.

[29]Particulars in what follows come esp. from KL Teg 21, fols. 4v, 8r–9r, 20v; KL Teg 22, fols. 11v, 14r–v, 22r; KL Teg 101, fols. 221v, 227r–230r, 247v.

responses from country people. Figure 4 sets the survey year against the span of the fishers' careers. This team, then, had long previous experience—22.25 years on average, including four men who had already fished for 30 or more years—and deep local roots—six were sons of earlier fishers. Seven of them lived along the Egern shoreline and the eighth, Jorg Leeperger, just across the channel.

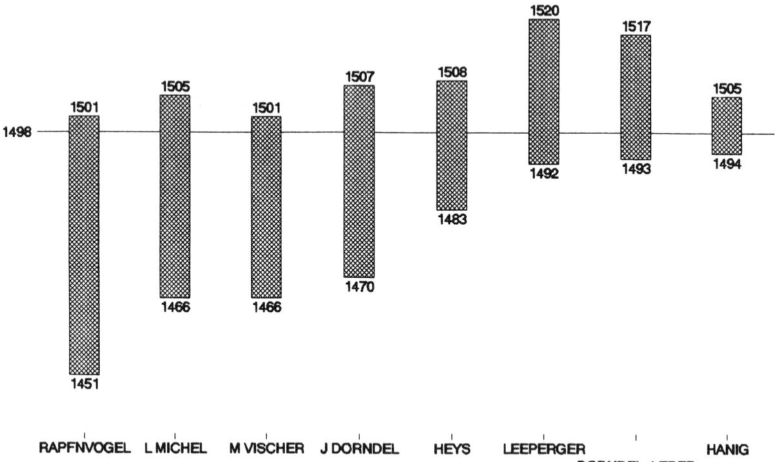

Figure 4. Tegernsee Abbey fishers, 1498

The two master fishers, Liendel Michel and Jacob Dorndel, were sons of fishers and among the most experienced men. Ironically and for no known reason, the more senior Michel is not detectable in the *Leibzinsbuch*, although the year's *Stiftsbuch* lists him at the Asch Vischerlehen, as it had since 1466. The *Leibzinsbuch* finds Dorndel living with his wife, Margred, and six children at the Hinderlehen tenure he had acquired in 1477.

The other two senior men in years of service, Hans Rapfnvogel von Weyssach and Lang Michel Vischer, never went beyond ordinary 18ß hands. Rapfnvogel was at home at Asch from 1465 or 1466 and, perhaps fitting for a man tough enough to fish for 48 years, with his second wife, Kathrein, and seven children. His first wife must have been a serf of the duke, not the abbey, for that was the status reported for Hans's son "Young Hans" Rapfnvogel, a shareholder tenant at the mill tenure on the Staudach creek in 1498. Until two years before, Young Hans had lived with his father. Lang Michel Vischer lived at the farm called Spitz, also his since 1466, with his wife, Anna, and four children. His two maturing sons, Hans and Peter, were about ready to take up their father's craft.

The 16 years of service Liendel Heys had done by 1498 made him the odd man in the fishing crew, much younger than the grizzled veterans and years ahead of the new successors. From 1495 he held a formal half share with his father, Heys Ferg, in the family tenure at Palerslehen. Liendel and his wife, Barbara, had five children by 1498, including unmarried daughters Anna and Elspet and three more unspecified. If the latter already included sons Andre and Michel, they were very young, for it would be 20 years before they joined the fishers.

The three junior members of the abbey's fishing team also had more youthful property and household situations and smaller families. Hans Dorndel, also called Lerer, younger brother of Jacob, had been fishing for only six years and still lived at Kashutten with their father, Ull Dornacher, the father's wife, and two unmarried siblings. Hans and his own wife, Barbara, had an unmarried daughter and also reported on two kinswomen (Barbara's?) who lived at Schwaz, a Tirolian mining camp on the Inn River. Jorg Leeperger, son and grandson of fishers, had just taken possession of the family's Sternlehen am Leeperg from his step- or marriage kin, the Kuening. Jorg and his wife lacked children and shared the household with his four unmarried siblings. Another sister and brother were off to Munich and "the mountains," respectively. The newest member of the group, Caspar Hanig, was still receiving only 12ß and was described as "knecht" to Jorg Leeperger, though he, too, came from a fishing lineage. Caspar's father, Hans, had retired from fishing but remained at the Egern Vischerlehen, where Caspar's little family (wife and child) still lived in his household. Two married sisters had moved away from the area.

To summarize, the *Leibzinsbuch* reports critical details on the social situation of seven fishers from 1498. All were married and six had children, totaling at least 24 then living. Their average of 3.4 children per reporting conjugal pair is just slightly below the district average, but the greater frequency of small young families who held this number down itself manifests the incipient generational replacement of an aged cohort of senior fishers. Indeed, with sizes of from three to nine persons and an average of 6.28, the households in which the fishers lived closely approximate regional norms. The four youngest fishers, Liendel Heys, Hans Dorndel Lerer, Jorg Leeperger, and Caspar Hanig, belonged to households with stem family forms including parental nuclei or unmarried adult siblings. This makes non-nuclear co-residents more common than in the general population. But reports of outmigrant kin in three of the seven households correspond to the rest of the Tegernsee data. The abbey fishers of 1498, therefore, comprised a cross-section of adult males in valley society, men at different life stages in normal careers and household units.

The social view from 1498 contrasts with variables of household economy documented through the 1526 *Türkensteuer* on moveable wealth. Whereas the *Leibzinsbuch* derived from the abbey's effort to master indigenous social change, the tax account that supports this second deeper probe was a response to external events. Ottoman successes in Hungary and a new offensive in 1526 spread concern across Austria and southern Germany. The Imperial Diet called for war taxes assessed against moveable wealth, and later that year they were collected in some cities and ecclesiastical lordships, including Tegernsee. The cellarer's office did the work in the Winkel. Precisely copying the route and sequence of farms in contemporary *Stiftsbücher*, clerks inventoried and evaluated the livestock, other productive equipment, domestic luxuries, and servants in each household and marked in the margin the tax paid by each. Different conventions used in the booklets for the Gmund parish and for the Egern and Tegernsee parishes obscure evaluations and rates of tax, but the plainly-given inventories and total payments adequately represent the productive resources and relative worth of the abbey's subjects, including the fishers.[30]

By 1526 the fishing crew (Fig. 5) had entirely changed from 1498; thus its composition resulted from newer trends. The men's experience averaged only 12 years and spread along a smooth curve from Hans Spitzer and Thoman Vischer (with 20 years' service) down to the total neophyte Liendel Dorndel. Thoman had been a master fisher for 14 years, Hans Toltzer and Andre Heys for only five. All the men now lived in Egern, where their local and occupational roots went, if anything, deeper than had their predecessors'. Three of the team belonged

---

[30]KL Teg 105 1/2 has a binding dated 1527 around two pamphlets entitled "Hilfsgelder wider die Türken. 1526," "Gmunderpfarr" (fols. 01–011) and "Anno dni 1526 Turcken Steuer" (not numbered; fols. 1–33 by our reckoning) covering the Tegernsee and Egern parishes. Both sections correspond precisely to the sequence, identification, and holders of tenures listed in the 1526 *Stiftsbuch* in KL Teg 105 (also unfoliated). The tax in question was legislated at the imperial Diet of Speyer in summer 1526 and implemented in Bavaria as fixed sums from lordships (e.g., Tegernsee Abbey) and, from peasants, 3.33 per cent of assessed wealth or 5 per cent of wages. Ludwig Hoffmann, *Geschichte der direkten Steuern in Baiern vom Ende des XIII. bis zum Beginn des XIX. Jahrhunderts* (Leipzig, 1883), pp. 52–54; Walter Friedensburg, *Der Reichstag zu Speier 1526, im Zusammenhang der politischen und Kirchlichen Entwicklung Deutschlands im Reformationzeitalter* (Berlin, 1887), pp. 431–33; Winfried Schulze, *Reich und Türkengefahr im späten 16. Jahrhundert: Studien zu den politischen und gesellschaftlichen Auswirkungen einer äusseren Bedrohung* (München, 1978).

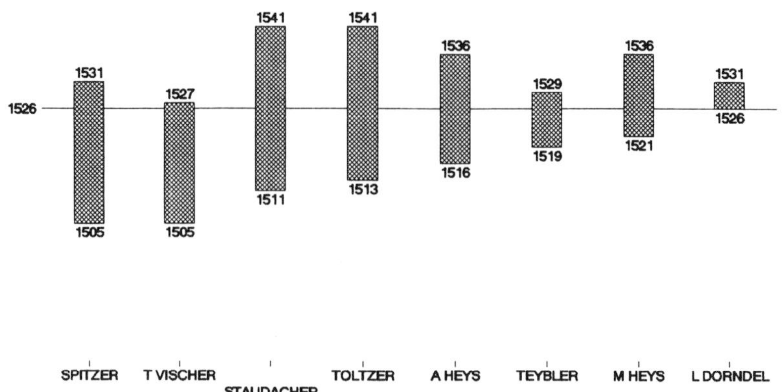

Figure 5. Tegernsee Abbey fishers, 1526

to the Dorndel family: Jorg Staudacher and Hans Toltzer had both married daughters of Jacob Dorndel, occasionally used the Dorndel name, and since 1515 had divided possession of Jacob's old tenure at Hinderlehen; no particular links for Liendel Dorndel have so far appeared. The brothers Heys (Andre and Michel) lived together at Palerslehen, their landed inheritance from their father, Liendel. Hans Spitzer and Thoman Vischer were sons and successors—on the water and the land—of Lang Michel Vischer and Liendel Michel, respectively.[31] Only Lorentz Teybler, who came from Rottach and acquired the Kashutten tenure in Egern from the heirs of Hans Dorndel Lerer when he began to fish in 1519, lacked background in the fishery. Generational turnover had narrowed recruitment to men with family connections. Some tenures were housing more than one family household. What, then, of the fishers' economic condition?

The tax accounts depict men who were distinctly fisher-peasants or fisher-pastoralists.[32] Seven of the eight paid taxes

[31]Both also had brothers who earlier appeared in tenurial records, and Spitzer's brother Peter had briefly fished.

[32]KL Teg 105 1/2, fols. 15r–16v, contains the men the *Stiftsbuch* knew as fishers.

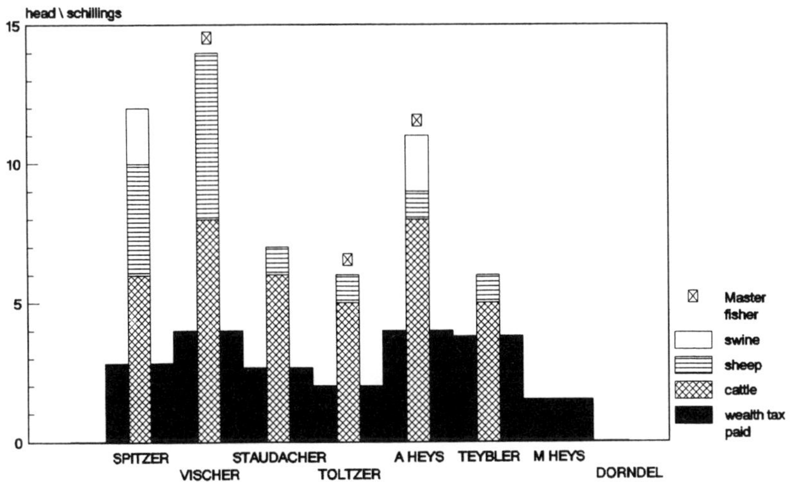

Figure 6. Wealth of Tegernsee Abbey fishers, 1526

from six households on five tenures: Young Liendel Dorndel escaped fiscal notice; Michel Heys was taxed individually in the household of his brother; Jorg Staudacher and Hans Toltzer had separate households assessed under the same heading of Hinderlehen. The summary data in Figure 6 show herds of six to 14 head, chiefly cattle and secondarily sheep. Two of the master fishers ranked among the more endowed but Hans Toltzer ranked among the less endowed.[33] Other taxable resources here were limited to an extra bed (*Gastped*) in the house of Thoman Vischer, a lodger with Lorentz Teybler, and servant children at the homes of Hans Spitzer and Hans Toltzer. The distribution of taxes paid by the fishers—between 1.5ß and 4ß (mean 2.77ß) individually, and between 2.83ß and 5.5ß (mean 4ß) for their household assessment units[34]—reasonably repli-

[33]Note, however, that recombination of the two herds at Hinderlehen (Toltzer and Staudacher) would raise it to second place.

[34]The latter includes payments shown as allotted to subordinate individuals within a household assessment unit, like, e.g., Michel Heys or a servant.

cates that of the herds. The three lowest taxpayers (Michel Heys, Jorg Staudacher, and Hans Toltzer) were subordinates or shareholders in divided tenures.

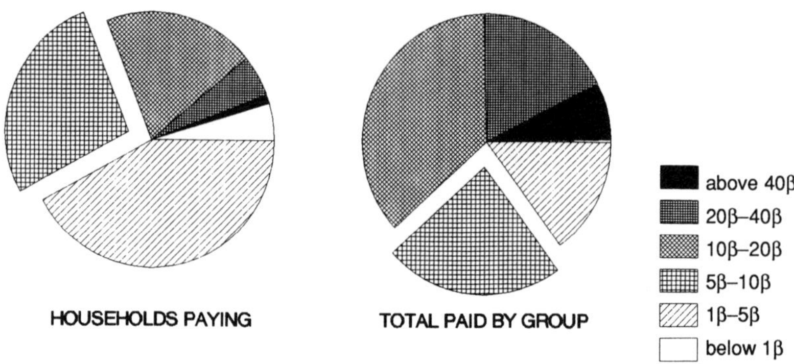

Figure 7. Tegernseer Winkel *Türkensteuer*, 1526: 361 peasant households paid 2,813ß; average payment, 7.79ß.

As a group and without real exception, by the standards of all 361 farms taxed in the whole Tegernseer Winkel in 1526 (Fig. 7);[35] the abbey fishers were poor. Their average household paid half of the mean district tax, and five of six fell into the bottom 40 per cent paying under 5ß. Only the joint household of Andre and Michel Heys, who together paid 5.5ß, belonged to the quarter of all farms clustered about the mean. Like poverty is evident in productive and capital resources. Where the average farm in the Winkel had almost 15 animals, including two horses to help work arable land, the fishers' herds averaged eight animals and included no horses (Fig. 8). Nor did any fisher possess one of the district's 280 declared beehives, 15 specialist tool kits, or 31 silver cups and chains.

The relative poverty of the fishers had roots less occupational than residential, for these men ranked among the middle

[35]For consistency's sake, the figures and following discussion omit the 19 (of 380) households for which KL Teg 105 1/5 reports neither possession nor taxes paid.

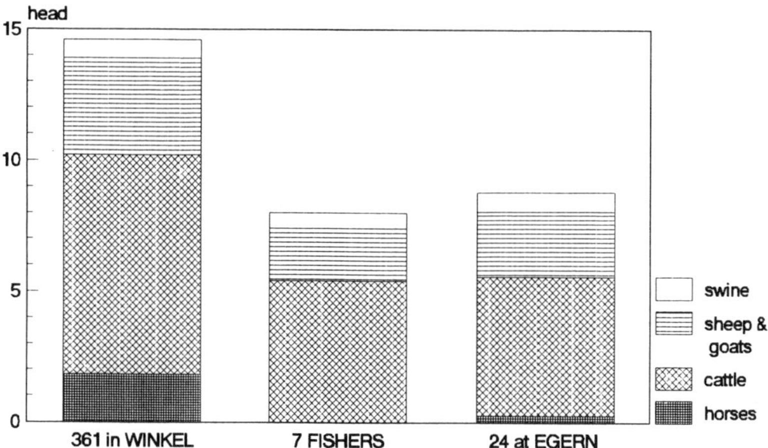

Figure 8. Peasant herds around Tegernsee, 1526. Average holdings.

group in their own village. Only three of the 24 farms taxed in Egern had horses. The average herd stood less than one animal above those of the fishers.[36] The average Egern taxpayer paid only 3.83ß tax and a solid majority of them, less than 5ß (Fig. 9). In contrast to resource-poor Egern, the 95 farms in the Gmund parish, where there were no abbey fishers, averaged 12.6ß tax. Paying work as an abbey fisher thus offered a way to survive in a mountain environment much poorer than even that at the other end of the fishers' own lake. Other kin and neighbors worked for the abbey in other capacities—masons, sawyers, etc.—or, as was plain in 1498, looked for a livelihood outside the valley.[37]

Findings from the one longitudinal and two synchronic studies reported here call for concluding observations in two

---

[36]Omitting the horses, all herds had similar ratios of cattle, ovicaprids, and swine, but the lake-head villages may have held more young animals.

[37]In 1498 only 17 per cent of households in the Gmund parish reported emigrant kin; the Egern rate was 37 per cent and the whole Winkel, 33 per cent.

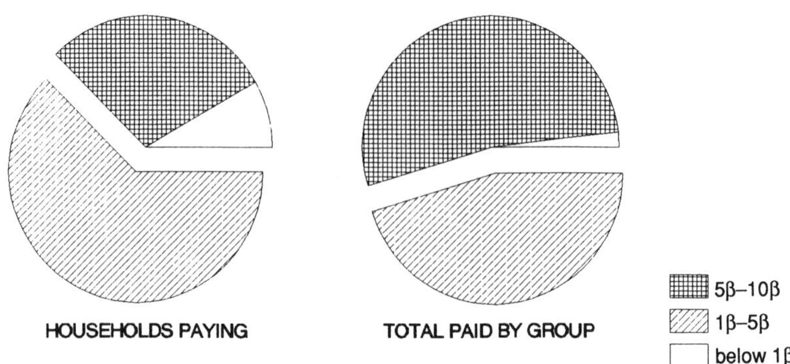

Figure 9. Egern *Türkensteuer*, 1526: 24 households paid 91.94ß; average payment, 3.83ß.

contexts, namely, south German peasant society at the end of the Middle Ages and freshwater fishing as an occupation in medieval Europe.

In the generations around 1500 the rural community grouped about the Tegernsee and dependent upon the abbey showed many symptoms of population growth. As well, the fiscal records especially reveal much economic inequality among the few hundred peasant family households. The reconstructed situations and life cycles of individual fishers, and indeed the very creation of the *Leibzinsbuch*, have further evidenced the pressures these developments were exerting against a social system of families, lineages, lordship, and clearly identifiable tenurial units. Institutional and personal responses differentiated further between definable social groups—rich and poor, heirs and dispossessed, landholders and workers. Although this essay lacked occasion to explore issues of access to common resources in mountain meadows and forests (the fishery was not commons here), of wage rates paid in abbey expenditure accounts, and of conflict and violence in the lakeside villages, Tegernsee recalls David Sabean's now classic study of social tensions in southern

Upper Swabia before the German Peasant War.[38]

There was, however, no Peasant War at Tegernsee or in Bavaria. Hence this first systematic venture into the rich social record from Tegernsee supports the thesis of Rainhard Riepertinger, who would explain Bavaria's exceptionalism on dual grounds of more stringent monitoring and suppression of unrest and of greater socioeconomic flexibility and opportunity. The latter included less obnoxious servile customs, official help with real peasant grievances, and a broad range of rural economic options[39]—as here exemplified in the fishery. So results from even this preliminary exploration do bear usefully on some traditional scholarly issues and encourage continued digging into these relatively late records from Tegernsee. Further extension of proven research methods back to older but less obviously tractable materials from Tegernsee and elsewhere in German-speaking Europe may cast light on rural life in the early fifteenth and the fourteenth centuries.

This essay has focused on the fishers for their relevance to a wider and less traditional historical enquiry into medieval freshwater fisheries, a little-investigated area of contact between humans and their environment. Seen here from the social side, the Tegernsee evidence depicts a largely self-perpetuating group of artisans. The abbey fishers were not socially marginal but a stable component of a local community, and

[38]Sabean's original English-language dissertation (Univ. of Wisconsin, 1969) appeared complete in German as *Landbesitz und Gesellschaft am Vorabend des Bauernkriegs. Eine Studie der sozialen Verhältnisse im südlichen Oberschwaben in den Jahren vor 1525* (Stuttgart, 1972), and then often in abridged English summaries or adaptations (e.g., *Peasant Studies Newsletter* [1974]; Janos M. Bak, ed., *The German Peasant War of 1525* [London, 1976], pp. 76–88; Scribner and Benecke, *German Peasant War*, pp. 174–89). As Stalnaker demonstrates, Sabean's painstaking regional research has achieved the ironic apotheosis of more frequent praise and citation than emulation.

[39]"Typologie der Unruhen im Herzogtum Bayern 1525," *Zeitschrift für bayerische Landesgeschichte* 51 (1988): 329–86.

integrated into the regional social structure as one of the poorer occupational elements. What role, then, had the fishery for participating households and for the whole community? As so far seen, the Tegernsee fishery provided neither subsistence nor by-employment for the many but full-time work for particular individuals. These men constructed a strategy for survival by pairing fishing with marginal livestock resources. The few families of poor mountain people who held most of these jobs sustained their otherwise inadequate economic position. By this means—and even though fish from the Tegernsee were meeting the demand of the monks and not of the peasants—the fishery increased the economic opportunities (resource niches) available to support human communities in what was, by normal pre-industrial standards, a resource-poor area.

The recognizable social group of abbey fishers necessarily supported an occupational subculture that included precise knowledge of the local environment and of skills to exploit it. Shared daily and seasonal routine, kinship, and neighborhood enabled the fishers to perpetuate this culture both by the spoken word and by example. They also had ample opportunity for face-to-face interaction with other neighbors of similar condition and overlapping interests, such as Martin Vörchel.[40]

The ideas sketched here from a preliminary quantitative social study of the Tegernsee fishers need testing and further articulation. At Tegernsee the cellarer's income and expenditure accounts and the district court books will illuminate relation-

---

[40]In 1526 Martin's son Oswald had five cows worth 10fl, three wethers worth 2fl, an extra bed for guests worth 3fl, mason's tools, and unvalued financial reserves of a silver cup and two chains (KL Teg 105 1/2, fol. 17r). On all measures except herd size he ranked among the wealthier men in Egern, but his 5ß tax left him well below many big farmers from Gmund and even some on the meadows along the Weissach and Rottach rivers. By implication, Martin also probably stood a bare financial step above his fisher neighbors and was well placed to maintain close relations with them.

ships among abbey fishers, the monks, competitive users of the fishery, and others in the regional community. Comparable investigation of well-documented fisheries in more prosperous and economically integrated regions of medieval Europe is surely a co-requisite. These case studies should include other alpine lake fisheries serving more commercial ends than did Tegernsee and some fisheries exploiting (with whatever economic orientation) other kinds of aquatic ecosystems. How much did the features found in the Tegernsee fishery vary elsewhere?

APPENDIX

FISHERS FOR TEGERNSEE ABBEY, 1443–1530

(Individuals listed under *Piscatores* or *Vischer* in annual *Stiftsbücher* [KL Teg 97, 99, 100, 101, 102, 104, and 105] with results of cross-references to tenurial records in the same volumes and elsewhere.)

	NAME[a]	Years of Work First	Last	Total[c]	Identified at Tenure[b] (R = Rottach, E = Egern)
1	ANTLOCHER Hans	1443	1469	24[d]	R Geygerslehen 1443–52
2	MICHEL Hansel Vischer	1443	1465	23	E am Asch 1443–65
3	RUEDEL Chuntz	1443	1448	6	E Hinderlehen 1443–75
4	SCHNEIDER Liendel	1443	1443	1	R Linthin 1443

[a]SURNAME followed by personal name, both standardized to a commonly used but distinctive form. Of course, like other pragmatic German texts from the end of the Middle Ages, the Tegernsee account books themselves have no standard for handling personal names, either as regards form (spelling; use of full, abbreviated, or diminutive forms) or sequence (family name, personal name, patronymic, nickname, residence, etc.). For instance, Liendel MICHEL (16) is at various times also called Liendel Hansel Michel, Liendel Hansel, Liendel Hansel's son, and Liendel von Asch; his own son, Thoman VISCHER am Asch (29), was commonly given only as Thoman.

[b]Names of farms have been standardized. Tenures have not been systematically followed beyond 1530.

[c]Years of work are totaled to take account of a few individuals (also identified below) who did not fish continuously. Note that the first and last years are both inclusive, and that the total is a count of annual records, not the arithmetical difference between the first and last (e.g., Hansel NASCHEL [20] fished in each of the two years 1476 and 1477, etc.).

[d]Hans did not fish during 1466–68.

APPENDIX—*Continued*

	NAME[a]	Years of Work First	Last	Total[c]	Identified at Tenure[b] (R = Rottach, E = Egern)
5	FERG Hansel	1443	1447	5	E Urfar or Palerslehen[e]
6	UNGERL Chuntz	1443	1449	7	E Straucherslehen 1443–80+
7	LEEPERGER Hansel 1 Vischer	1443	1454	30[f]	Leeperg Sternlehen 1443–55[g]
8	KRAPF Haintzl	1444	1451	5[h]	E am Schorn 1443–47
9	HANIG Hans	1448	1492	45	E Schorn 1446–65[i] E Vischerlehen 1466–1501
10	HELCHINGER Hans	1448	1450	3	E bei dem Kirchen 1449–51
11	MICHEL "Hansel's Son"	1450	1450	1	E am Asch[j]
12	RUEDEL Caspar	1450	1473	24	E Hinderlehen[k]
13	RAPFNVOGEL von WEYSSACH Hans	1451	1501	51	E am Asch 1466–1505
14	DORNACHER Ull	1452	1492	41	E Kashutten 1452–1501

[e]Hansel probably lived on the farm, which the *Stiftsbücher* do not then clearly name, held during 1443–50 by "Haincz" Ferg.

[f]Hansel fished only in 1443 and 1453–54.

[g]And then followed there by his widow in 1456–70.

[h]Haintzl did not fish during 1448–50.

[i]This part of the tenure at "Schorn" would later be called "Spitz."

[j]See Hansel MICHEL above.

[k]See Chuntz RUEDEL above.

APPENDIX—*Continued*

	NAME[a]	Years of Work First	Last	Total[c]	Identified at Tenure[b] (R = Rottach, E = Egern)
15	LEEPERGER Hansel 2	1456	1491	36	Leeperg Sternlehen 1468–90[l]
16	MICHEL Liendel	1466	1505	40	E Asch Vischerlehen 1466–1505
17	VISCHER Lang Michel	1466	1501	36	E Spitz 1466–1501
18	DORNDEL Jacob	1470	1507	38	E Hinderlehen 1477–1514
19	LUIA Chrisogonus	1474	1475	2	(see note [m])
20	NASCHEL Hansel	1476	1477	2	(see note [m])
21	TAUBENSCHLAG Liendel	1478	1482	5	(see note [m])
22	HEYS Liendel	1483	1508	26	E Palerslehen 1495–1524[n]
23	LEEPERGER Jorg Vischer	1492	1520	29	Leeperg Sternlehen 1497–1525
24	DORNDEL LERER Hans	1493	1517	25	E Kashutten 1502–14
25	HANIG Caspar	1494	1505	12	E Vischerlehen 1501–07

[l]With his widowed mother, 1468–70.

[m]Three successive short-serving helpers to Hansel 2 Leeperger seemingly held no tenures during their fishing.

[n]His father, Heys Ferg, had it from 1459 to 1500.

APPENDIX—*Continued*

	NAME[a]	Years of Work First	Last	Total[c]	Identified at Tenure[b] (R = Rottach, E = Egern)
26	SNEIDER Liendel Ungerl	1502	1525	24	R Puhel 1511–28+[o]
27	VISCHER Peter	1502	1504	3	E Spitz[p]
28	SPITZER Hans	1505	1531	27	E Spitz 1505–28+
29	VISCHER am Asch Thoman	1505	1527	23	E Asch Vischerlehen 1505–27
30	VISCHER am Puhel Jacob	1506	1512	6[q]	E Puhel ?
31	DORNDEL Lorentz	1508	1509	2	(see note [r])
32	VISCHER Cristof	1508	1509	2	E Vischerlehen 1507–09[s]
33	von WEYSSACH am Asch Liendel	1510	1518	9	E am Asch 1505–28+
34	WITIBER Cuentzel	1510	1511	2	E Witiberlehen[t]
35	STAUDACHER DORNDEL Jorg	1511	1541	23[u]	E vodern Schorn 1481–1524 E Hinderlehen 1514–28+

[o]Following Ungerl Sneider, who had been there from the 1480s until 1511.

[p]With his mother, widow of Lang Michel VISCHER, in legal possession 1502–04.

[q]Jacob did not fish in 1508.

[r]Not in evidence at either Kashutten or Hinderlehen, the two tenures at Egern then associated with the Dorndel and their close kin.

[s]Followed by his widow to 1513/14.

[t]Cuentzel is described as "der Witib knecht"; Hans Witiber Smid possessed Witiberlehen from 1498 into the 1530s.

[u]Jorg did not fish during 1515–17 and 1533–37.

APPENDIX—*Continued*

	NAME[a]	Years of Work First	Last	Total[c]	Identified at Tenure[b] (R = Rottach, E = Egern)
36	SUESS Hans Vischer	1513	1515	3	E Vischerlehen 1514–16
37	TOLTZER Hans	1513	1541	29	E Hinderlehen 1516–28+
38	HEYS Andre	1516	1536	21	E Palerslehen 1524–28+
39	TEYBLER Lorentz	1519	1529	11	R unnamed tenure 1517–18 E Kashutten 1518–28+
40	HEYS Michel	1521	1536	16	E Palerslehen 1524–27 E Asch Vischerlehen 1527–36+
41	DORNDEL Liendel	1526	1531	6	(see note [r])
42	FERG Partel	1528	1530+[v]	3+	E Verglehen am Urfar ?
43	RANHART Gastel	1529	1530+[v]	2+	E Kashutten in the 1530s

[v]Fishers who began after 1527 were not traced past 1530, so the eventual length of their careers remains undetermined.

"FAMILIES HAVE THEIR FATE AND PERIODS": VARIETIES OF FAMILY EXPERIENCE IN THE PRE-INDUSTRIAL VILLAGE

Sherri Olson

"The family of the Downtons is soe antient in this towne," wrote Richard Gough in his history of his native parish, Myddle, Shropshire, in 1700,

> . . . and such a numerouse offspring hath branched out of this family, that there was three familyes of the Downtons at one time in this towne . . . but now all these famylyes are extinct, soe that there is not one of that name now in this parish, except one widow; soe that it appears that familyes have their fate and periods as well as particular persons—and noe marvell, since famylyes are made up of particulars.[1]

Gough's reflections on the Downtons embody a view of family dynamics that bears striking resemblance to an approach enjoying some currency among historians of the family, that of the "life course," described as encompassing "individual and family development in relation to each other" and concerned with capturing "the complexity of interaction between individual transitions and collective family goals, as both change over the individual's and the family's life."[2] The present paper attempts

---

[1]*The History of Myddle*, ed. David Hey (Harmondsworth, 1981), p. 214.

[2]Tamara K. Hareven, "Family History at the Crossroads," *Journal of Family History* 12/1–3 (1987): xiii.

to apply this conceptual framework to the English village of the thirteenth through fifteenth centuries, a time and place admittedly less well-provided with evidence than others, yet perhaps not plunged as deeply into "informational darkness" for some kinds of family history as has been suggested.[3]

Anthropologists for a long time have recognized the centrality of the family in structuring and stabilizing society and in orienting the individual within his or her community. Studies of the village community of medieval England are finding that the family in this traditional society played a similar role.[4] Local history is perhaps one of the more useful approaches for an inquiry into the interaction between individual and family, because court rolls—the primary documents for medieval village study—lend themselves to the recovery of varieties in family as well as individual experience and the interactions between the two. By definition, local history reconstructs the setting within which families have survived, thrived, and disappeared: the small community. Indeed, some students of the medieval village have developed a working typology of families as *primary* and *secondary*, based on the principle that the evidentiary pre-eminence of specific individuals and families, particularly in the court rolls, is a reflection of a real pre-eminence achieved by these people in village society.[5] Here we shall consider the

---

[3]The term is Peter Laslett's, referring to the period before 1500 in European history. See "The Character of Familial History, Its Limitations and the Conditions for Its Proper Pursuit," *Journal of Family History* 12/1–3 (1987): 217.

[4]A recent anthropological perspective on the value of historical ethnography can be found in Ruth Behar, *Santa Maria del Monte: The Presence of the Past in a Spanish Village* (Princeton, 1986). This question is handled in more detail, with special reference to family historians and anthropologists, by David Kertzer, "Anthropology and Family History," *Journal of Family History* 9/3 (Fall 1984): 201–16. For a general discussion of the family as an agent in promoting social stability in late medieval and early modern England, see Lawrence Stone, *The Family, Sex and Marriage in England, 1500–1800* (New York, 1977), pp. 22–27.

[5]Extra-village records such as subsidy lists, royal inquisitions and charters—the latter conveying sizeable properties wholly or partially within the village of

histories of some of the men and women of Ellington, Huntingdonshire, a village belonging to the estates of Ramsey Abbey.[6] This wealth of evidence emanating from the abbey has fueled several innovative studies of lordship and peasantry, agrarian economy and society, over the past 70 years.[7]

Village society produced many prominent individuals and families, whose recoverability in the evidence is often based largely (though not solely) on the fact of their lengthy residence in the village. This enables the student of the medieval village to use even fragmentary or discontinuous evidence, such as court records. Gaps in the evidence are rarely substantial enough to obscure prominent Ellington men such as Geoffrey Buk, whose record of activity spans the half-century between 1285 and 1333, or John Faukes, whose career covers the 38 years from 1443 to 1481. Families are in an even more favorable position for investigation, whether they be long-lived, as were the Holcote family who appeared in Ellington in 1310 and

---

Ellington—confirm the evidence of the court rolls: many of the same people who were conspicuous in regional and royal affairs were also prominent in strictly village affairs.

[6]The court rolls and account rolls for Ellington are located in the British Library (Additional Rolls) and the Public Record Office (hereafter, PRO), London (Special Collections 2 and 6, respectively). Ancillary documents are in the Cambridge County Record Office (hereafter, CCRO), Huntingdon, and include the parish records as well as approximately 100 wills and administrations dating from the late fifteenth century and continuing through the sixteenth century. Additional records include a collection of records held by Peterhouse College, Cambridge (Ellington Slade documents), covering the period 1313–1598.

[7]See, e.g., Warren O. Ault, *Private Jurisdiction in England* (New Haven, 1923); J. A. Raftis, *Tenure and Mobility: Studies in the Social History of the Mediaeval English Village* (Toronto, 1964); Edwin B. DeWindt, *Land and People in Holywell-cum-Needingworth: Structures of Tenure and Patterns of Social Organization in an East Midlands Village, 1252–1457* (Toronto, 1972); Edward Britton, *The Community of the Vill: A Study in the History of the Family and Village Life in Fourteenth-Century England* (Toronto, 1977). Most recently, Frances and Joseph Gies have published a useful introductory study of a medieval village using the court rolls of the Ramsey village of Elton; see *Life in a Medieval Village* (New York, 1990).

continued into the seventeenth century, or as comparatively short-lived as the Mersch family, whose seven identifiable members appeared between the years 1286 and 1333.[8] Even in a fragmented and unsystematic record collection, some of the life patterns and peculiarities of many families and their individual members emerge.

In the same way that court roll evidence reveals models of typicality and deviance with regard to individuals, so too does it suggest the patterns exhibited by families and how these changed over time. These patterns have been conceptualized rather schematically along the lines of the "developmental" or "family" cycle of the peasant household, which interprets the growth, expansion, and decline of a family's agricultural output, resources, and commitments as expressions of the needs of a growing household, achieving the peak of its activities when the children reach maturity and add their labor to that of their parents. Contraction follows as the grown children leave their natal family.[9] Such a cycle is of course subject to a complex range of factors, including inheritance practices, reproductive failure, birth of females only, migration, and poverty, as well as the more elusive determinants of personal initiative and

---

[8]It should be noted that the dates given for Ellington individuals and families throughout this study are merely the termini formed by the first and last surviving references to these people; hence the dates represent absolute minima.

[9]This model has been explicitly employed by Lutz K. Berkner in "The Stem Family and the Developmental Cycle of the Peasant Household: An Eighteenth-Century Austrian Example," *American Historical Review* 77 (1972): 398–418. See also Richard M. Smith, ed., *Land, Kinship, and Life-Cycle* (Cambridge, 1984). For a discussion of the peasant land market following such a model see Christopher Dyer, *Lords and Peasants in a Changing Society: The Estates of the Bishopric of Worcester, 680–1540* (Cambridge, 1980), pp. 298–315. In addition, the working concept of a developmental cycle is apparent in several other recent works, e.g., Ralph A. Houlbrooke, *The English Family, 1450–1700* (New York, 1984); Cicely Howell, *Land, Family, and Inheritance in Transition: Kibworth Harcourt, 1280–1700* (Cambridge, 1983).

decision-making, competence, and ambition. Recognition of this fact has led some family historians to adopt the more dynamic approach of the "life course," which investigates not simply the stages of family development from the point of view of the parents but rather the "interaction between individuals and the family unit over time, and under changing historical conditions."[10] Thus, involvement in local government, participation in the land market, local industrial production, practice of a trade or craft, marriage, extra-village ties, economic ventures, and working as wage labor all constituted avenues of activity open in varying degrees to each new generation, with consequences for the stability and success (real and evidentiary) of the family, as well as the prosperity of individual men and women. All these factors influenced the level and quality of a family's profile in the surviving evidence.

The actual range and type of factors that made up a family's documentary profile also varied considerably over time. Each family, given its own set of preconditions and circumstances as well as its own changing "personnel," might combine and recombine the foci of its activities in an ever-shifting pattern, suggestive of changes in the "collective goals" of the family, the aspirations of individual family members, and the pathways of reciprocal influence as well as tension that were created between the two. Court roll data do not allow us fully to recover the "timing" of life transitions of individuals or their families in all their complexity. Nor do the data provide the same type of systematic detail found in Richard Gough's parish history, narrated with all his sensitivity to the ebb and flow of family fortunes and their underlying causes. If court roll data are not precisely similar to other sources, they do have a kind

---

[10]Hareven, "Family History," p. xiii.

of utility all their own for the study of the family. The following discussion attempts to illustrate the diversity of interactions between family and individual and to sketch out how these changed over time, through reconstructing the case histories of some dozen Ellington families from the late thirteenth into the sixteenth centuries.

The Mokke Family (1321?–1543) and the Burgeys Family (1280–1566). Perhaps the most striking familial type is that which combines lengthy duration of the family in the village with a high and varied documentary profile. Some 40 Ellington families over the period from 1280 (the date of the first surviving court roll) through the sixteenth century conform to this type. The Mokke family is one of the largest of these, with 28 known members.[11] The earliest secure reference to a member of this family occurs in 1327, when "Ricardus filius Moke" (already a second generation) paid 11*d.q.* in the subsidy of that year. More than 200 years later another Richard Moke paid 2*s.* in the subsidy of 1542/43.[12]

Only four other families (Bate, Buk, Burgeys, and Henson) outdistance the Mokkes in the number of identifiable members (29, 33, 31, and 44, respectively); only the Holcotes and Burgeys surpass them in longevity.[13] The Mokkes constituted a prominent village family in every regard, providing jurors, ale

[11]Ellington's data are not sufficient for estimating population beyond a crude measurement of the total number of surnames over some well-defined period: some 300 different surnames occur in Ellington's records from the late thirteenth century through the sixteenth century, numbering very roughly 1,800 individuals.

[12]See *Early Huntingdonshire Lay Subsidy Rolls*, ed. J. A. Raftis and M. Patricia Hogan (Toronto, 1976), p. 165, for the 1327 subsidy. For the 1542/43 subsidy see PRO E179/122/122.

[13]The Henson and Buk families have been discussed at greater length by the present author, "Family Linkages and the Structure of the Local Elite in the Medieval and Early Modern Village," *Medieval Prosopography* 13/2 (Autumn 1992).

tasters, beadles, and collectors of court fines in every generation for over 200 years and participating in the local brewing industry in the fifteenth and sixteenth centuries. The quality of entries for the family reflects high levels of involvement in village and regional affairs, from hue and cry presentments, trespasses, impleading fellow villagers outside the lord's jurisdiction and contentious behavior in court to being outside the fee without license, marrying without license, poverty, and failure to repair tenements.

The history of the Mokke family displays many of the features that are observable in other families of long duration and high visibility in the village, such as the near-continuous residence of at least one prominent male in each generation, especially in the thirteenth and fourteenth centuries, and multiple officeholding in the fifteenth century. Other typical features include the migration of men and women from the 1370s, as well as a somewhat higher profile for the women of the family in comparison with less prominent families.

These phenomena constitute some of the generic "signs of success" for village families of long-term resident status who were fully integrated into the community. In addition, the Mokkes also exhibit some peculiar features, providing rare glimpses of familial "co-operation" both within and outside of the village.[14] For example, in 1429 Robert Mokke impleaded Joan Mokke for trespass. These individuals undoubtedly came from

[14]While we might expect such co-operation to have been the rule rather than the exception, evidence of such associations is rare in the court rolls. Presumably, agreements made between relatives might not require a public act, and any disputes that arose would normally be settled out of court. Clear exceptions to this rule, however, are the maintenance agreements between the elderly and younger associates or children that appear in the court rolls usually because they were violated, but also sometimes because the parties wished to have the agreement and its terms set forth in the public record of the court. For examples see Raftis, *Tenure and Mobility*, pp. 42–46.

two separate households and perhaps two different generations: Robert first appears in the court roll of 1407 for trespass with animals, while Joan's second husband, John Ilger, in 1452 paid for her daughter to marry. Another case in 1429 involved an exchange of land between Richard and Thomas Mokke, one receiving a cottage with garden, the other one rod of arable—an exchange that suggests the differing needs of their households. In a more unusual instance of family co-operation, Richard, Robert, and Thomas Mokke were cited in court in 1428 for disruptive behavior and speaking against the steward and the court's clerk.[15] These few examples are only the merest surface reflection of what may have been pervasive working relationships among some of the members of this family.

We may see an extension of this type of association in references to members of the family illegally staying with each other outside the fee. Between 1405 and 1454 four men were recorded as doing so, and in one case in 1432 Richard Mokke drew his son John outside the village, to stay with him in nearby Brampton ("elongavit filium suum usque Brampton"). This same John was reported in 1449, 1450, 1451, and 1454 as staying with a Robert Mokke at Stukeley.[16] Like other long-lived, successful Ellington families such as the Bates, Buks, Burgeyses, Coupers, and Hicsons, numerous members of the Mokke family left the village permanently in the late fourteenth and the fifteenth centuries. Most stayed in other villages within the Ramsey Abbey estates, while a few went as far as Norfolk and Essex, and a Thomas Mokke was reported to be overseas between 1426

---

[15]For the court rolls of 1407, 1428, and 1429, respectively, see PRO SC2/179/51, BL Add. Roll 34370, PRO SC2/179/59. For the 1452 marriage license see *The Liber Gersumarum of Ramsey Abbey: A Calendar and Index of B. L. Harley MS 445*, ed. Edwin B. DeWindt (Toronto, 1976), p. 355, no. 4190 (hereafter, *Liber Gersumarum*).

[16]For the court roll of 1432 see PRO SC2/179/61. For the account rolls of 1449, 1450, 1451, and 1454 see, respectively, PRO SC6/876/2, SC6/876/3, SC6/876/4, and SC6/876/6.

and 1443. All in all, 12 Mokke men and women left the village between 1373 and 1473, the largest number of emigrants from any single Ellington family found in over 250 years of village history.[17] In what is now recognized to be part of a natural response to the challenge of reproductive success, the sons and daughters of large families left their native villages to seek employment and marital opportunity elsewhere when the family resources of their native villages were not adequate for maintaining such numbers or, perhaps, for meeting changing individual expectations. It is likely, for example, that post-plague notions about the desirable size of the patrimony would have been quite different from those commonly entertained earlier.

The mobility of men and women of the Mokke family intensified in the 1440s, when a record number of eight people were outside the village at various times. In that decade the evidence also bears witness to difficulties at home: in 1444, Robert Mokke's total rent arrears of 27*s*.6*d*. was allocated to the current reeve from the terms of two previous reeves, "quia nullo modo possunt levari causa paupertatis."[18] In 1446 both he and Richard Mokke, two of the three continuously resident representatives of the family, were cited for having dilapidated tenements.[19] It was also in the 1440s that five other men of the family were fined for holding land *ingersumata*. In the *Liber Gersumarum* there are subsequent references to "land once his" for two of these five individuals, and in the later 1440s, '50s, and '60s they and one other male relative had left

[17]The considerable distance covered by migrants from this family confirms Anne Reiber DeWindt's findings that the extent of a family's territorial "region" varied, depending on its socioeconomic status; those with more resources tended to travel farther (see "Redefining the Peasant Community in Medieval England: The Regional Perspective," *Journal of British Studies* 26/2 [Apr. 1987]: 191).

[18]PRO SC6/876/1.

[19]See BL Add. Roll 39876. See also Raftis, *Tenure and Mobility*, pp. 190–98, for discussion of the meaning of dilapidation of tenements in the late medieval village.

the village forever.[20] The history of the Mokke family, and particularly its evident difficulties in sustaining family fortunes during the fifteenth century, serves as a reminder that (independent of the larger socioeconomic context) success in one generation could be followed by hardship in the next. As has been observed recently in the family histories of a modern agricultural community, because wealthy villagers have larger families than those who are less prosperous they are often hard-pressed to provide adequately for all their offspring: hence, "the children of the rich are poor."[21]

The Burgeys family exemplifies the long-lived, high-profile family whose history, like that of the Mokkes, mirrors rather closely that of the village itself and also provides rare data on familial links over an extended period of time. Among the approximately 19 individuals appearing between ca. 1360 and 1513, fully 15 are noted as relatives of other Burgeyses.[22] For the period before the 1360s the evidence yields the names of some 10 individuals in Ellington with the surname Burgeys. In the years between ca. 1280 and 1366 the eight men recovered from the sources served as jurors (nine occasions), special inquisition jurors (twice), ale tasters (three times), and pledges (13 times).[23]

---

[20]DeWindt, *Liber Gersumarum*, p. 351, no. 4145, and p. 365, no. 4292.

[21]Behar, *Santa Maria del Monte*, p. 115.

[22]There is additional evidence of family relationships over this period between these family members of the later fourteenth and early fifteenth centuries and the last individual so named appearing in the records. Thomas Burgesse, priest of the parish of Easton, which adjoins Ellington, was recorded in a deed of 6 May 1566, enfeoffing 10 Ellington men with a holding of arable and meadow in Ellington. He was described as heir of Robert Burgesse, once of Ellington, now deceased, whose property had originally been granted to another Robert Burgesse by John Swyfte in a deed dated 5 Jan. 1399. Both deeds are in the collection of Ellington parish records in the County Record Office, Huntingdon; see List 6.

[23]The heading for the court record here styled as "1360/66" is partly missing. The court was held on a Tuesday on the vigil of the feast of Simon and Jude in the reign of Edward III, hence it had to be either 1360 or 1366.

Their principals included members of some of the more important Ellington families of the later thirteenth and early fourteenth centuries (e.g., Bate, Elington, and Godman). A trace of reciprocal pledging—itself rather rare—between members of the Burgeys and Hunte families also suggests the kind of relationships that could develop among more or less stable family groups in pre-plague Ellington. For example, in 1299 John Burgeys pledged for the brewer Beatrix le Hunte, while William le Hunte pledged for Walter Burgeys and another unnamed Burgeys male in 1311 and 1332/33 in cases involving a land purchase and leaving the village with license, respectively.[24]

Burgeys involvement in the land market is also evidenced by the rather spectacular case that burst upon the village ca. 1310 concerning a full virgate of land claimed by Richard in Estrate and Nicholas Burgeys.[25] The inquisition jurors, who awarded seisin to Nicholas, also learned in the course of their fact-finding investigation that Nicholas had been the previous tenant of this same virgate, for which he now paid the high *gersuma* of 40*s*. Other entries indicating the landed interests of the family include purchases of land in ca. 1310 and 1311, Dionysia Burgeys's receiving offenses (1332/33) and misplaced dungheaps (1321), and trespass with animals by two Burgeys men (1321). References to defaulting on a joint debt (1325), brewing (1321), and paying to be outside the fee (1332/33) are other typical indications of the character, though not the level, of family integration into the village economy and society. The subsidy payments of Dionysia and Nicholas Burgeys in 1327 are

---

[24]See PRO SC2/179/10, SC2/179/16, and SC2/179/26.

[25]See BL Add. Roll 34320. The dating for this court roll is approximate. Prof. Raftis gives the year 1335 as a possible date (see *Tenure and Mobility*, p. 291), but internal evidence would place it somewhat earlier. For example, Bartholomew in Lynlond, discussed below, is described as "mortuus" in the court roll of 1311, and he appears in this court. Other evidence suggests a date after 1306; hence, I have dated the roll ca. 1310.

also evidence of separate Burgeys households.[26] In short, the involvement of this family in pre-plague Ellington prepares us for its long-lived, if modest, success in the post-plague village, although the character of that involvement changed greatly over time.

The single most important index of success in the fifteenth-century village was reproductive success, and here the Burgeys households truly distinguished themselves. Nine of the 19 known family members appearing in the records between 1360 and 1513 were women, an unusually high profile for the females of the family since, as will be seen below, a substantial decline in the representation of women characterizes the histories of even prominent families in the fifteenth century. Most of these references come from the *Liber gersumarum* and are notices of payments of marriage fines for five daughters of at least two Burgeys households in the 1420s and 1430s; other references include one in which the groom paid the fine;[27] another (1434), when two sisters, Agnes and Alice, daughters of Thomas Burgeys, paid 3*s*.4*d*. to marry whomever they wished.[28] These two may be same Agnes and Alice who were active in a modest way in the brewing of ale in the 1420s, '30s, and '40s. Other female activity, on the same marginal scale, concerned Margaret Burgeys, who married without license at Kimbolton, a parish about one mile southwest of Ellington.[29]

The same level of steady though modest activity is also evident for the men of the family in the area of officeholding.

---

[26]For the court rolls of 1311, 1321, 1325, and 1332/33 see, respectively, PRO SC2/179/16, SC2/179/19, SC2/179/22, and SC2/179/26. For the subsidy of 1327 see Raftis and Hogan, *Early Hunts. Lay Subsidy Rolls*, p. 166.

[27]DeWindt, *Liber Gersumarum*, p. 214, no. 2575.

[28]DeWindt, *Liber Gersumarum*, p. 238, no. 2916.

[29]This notice appeared in five different courts: 1400, 1402, 1405 (two courts), and 1407. See PRO SC2/179/45, SC2/179/47, and SC2/179/49–51.

While other families and individuals were virtually defined by frequent and sometimes multiple officeholding in the fifteenth-century village, the Burgeys men did not follow this pattern. They served as jurors in every known court between 1360 and 1429, even serving simultaneously on occasion.[30] Yet only Thomas Burgeys (1400–39) approached something like the level of officeholding so typical of other men of long-lived fifteenth-century families. In 1400 he was elected constable; he served as affeeror in 1406 and 1429, as reeve in 1407 and 1415, taster in 1407, and beadle in 1407 and 1429.[31] In addition, he served as juror in seven of the 10 courts from which records survive between 1400 and 1429. Some five other men—Robert, another Thomas, John, and two William Burgeys—who span the period 1400–1513 never appeared as officeholders. Still another William Burgeys, who may have served as a juror in 1400 and 1402, was less active as an officeholder than as a trespasser; he was presented for that offense five times between 1400 and 1432. One of the non-officeholding men left the village altogether: the *Liber gersumarum* records in 1439 that land once belonging to William Burgeys had passed to another tenant, and that he paid 2*s*. to marry his daughter Alice to John Jemesson of Hamerton, a parish about five miles north of Ellington.[32] From 1440 to 1473 the court presented that this William was outside the fee without license at Hamerton. It may have been a son of his, also named William, who was still reported as living at Hamerton as late as the autumn court of 1513.[33] Altogether,

---

[30]Walter and William Burgeys served on the jury in 1391 (PRO SC2/179/43); William and Thomas Burgeys served in 1400 (PRO SC2/179/45); John and Thomas Burgeys, in both courts of 1405 (PRO SC2/179/49 and 50).

[31]See PRO SC6/875/24 and 26, SC2/179/45, 50, 51, 59, and 60.

[32]DeWindt, *Liber Gersumarum*, p. 260, no. 3180.

[33]The rather bewildering number of men named William Burgeys is easier to unravel than is sometimes the case with villagers' names. The three Williams of the

one woman and three men of this family are noted in the fifteenth century as being outside the fee for some length of time.

Families as long-lived and relatively stable as the Burgeys and Mokke families constituted a significant proportion of the known families in medieval and early modern Ellington; they must have had an important impact on the character of life in the village. Equally instructive, though less easy to trace in some regards, are the case histories of families whose careers were more discontinuous and variable than theirs.

The Godman Family, 1280–1340. The Godman family illustrates the decline and eventual disappearance of a once prominent family that, in view of its landholding, officeholding, pledging, and brewing activities and reproduction of male heirs, might have been expected to survive beyond two generations. Six members of this family have been identified, beginning with Beatrix, wife of Thomas Godman, first recorded for a brewing infraction in 1280. This marked the commencement of her long history of ale production, which lasted until 1311. Thomas, who held a full virgate in this period of land scarcity, first appeared in 1292 as a juror and a pledge; he went on to serve as a juror again in 1308, served on two special inquisition juries in ca. 1310, and was pledge for his wife, son, and several others a total of 12 times. In 1311 his two pledges were amerced when he failed to pay back a debt of grain and money to Petronilla le Bere, a prominent village creditor for over 20 years. Evidence of defaulting on debts indicates that Thomas was of sufficient stature to require and command local lines of credit, not that he

later fourteenth and fifteenth centuries are easily distinguished by their chronological spread as well as by their children's names as given in the *Liber gersumarum*. For the court roll of 1513 see BL Add. Roll 34310.

was financially bankrupt.[34] The family's wealth is also indicated by the large brewing fines (12*d.* and 18*d.*) that Beatrix paid over the last two decades of her brewing career.

Yet within a few years this once prosperous family apparently had fallen upon hard times. The first indication of this lies in the omission of the Godmans from the subsidy roll of 1327. Thomas Godman the elder was dead by 1322, as suggested by a reference in that year to the virgate "once his" and now held by two other men evidently unrelated to the Godmans. Thomas Godman the younger had left the village as early as 1308, paying the high sum of 2*s.* and two capons for license to leave.[35] By 1311 he had permanently established himself in the adjoining village of Brampton, where, as noted in the court roll of that year, he had married ("manet uxoratus apud Brampton") and was still outside the fee *licite*. A decade later his pledges were amerced when he did not pay the one capon owed for license to be absent.[36]

The remaining three family members, whose specific relationships to the earlier three are not known, show the family in its final phases before extinction. An Alice Godman brewed once in 1325 and may have been a subtenant on what was once Thomas Godman's virgate, since her pledge, John Beaumeys, was one of the two men receiving that land and holding it in

---

[34]See Elaine Clark's study of credit and debt relationships in Writtle, Essex, in *Pathways to Medieval Peasants*, ed. J. A. Raftis (Toronto, 1981), esp. pp. 264–65, 267. For the courts of 1280, 1292, 1308, ca. 1310 and 1311, see PRO SC2/179/4, BL Add. Roll 34336(1), PRO SC2/179/15, BL Add. Roll 34320, and PRO SC2/179/16, respectively.

[35]An entry in the court roll of ca. 1310 may indicate that Thomas jr. was involved in a case of assault, his father serving as pledge. The roll is damaged, so positive identification is not possible. For the courts of 1308 and 1322 see PRO SC2/179/15 and 21.

[36]See PRO SC2/179/16. An entry in the roll for 1332/33 that Thomas pay one capon as long as he is outside the fee has been canceled; see PRO SC2/179/26.

1322.[37] John Beaumeys also served as pledge at least once, possibly three times, for Walter Godman, the last male representative of the family, presented for being outside the village in 1332/33 and 1340, who disappears from the records after that date.[38] In the latter year Milicent Godman the younger was amerced with eight other women for gleaning badly; the impoverishment of the Godman family, or at least some members of it, is indicated, since permission to glean was a concession usually extended to the village poor.

The members of the second generation of Godmans were unable to capitalize on the secure position created by the labors of the first generation or even to maintain that position. Whether or not they were adversely affected by the famine years of the second decade of the century cannot be determined; however, most of the families established in the village before the famines managed to survive. We must look to other factors to explain the evident susceptibility to decline of families once so secure as the Godmans. In their case, the decision of the son to migrate long before the death of his father seems to have been the most significant, discernible cause, since it may have affected the family's ability to retain control of the family tenement.[39] Walter, the last male, was recorded only three

---

[37]The possibility that Alice Godman may have been a subtenant on her family's ancestral virgate is suggested by the fact that masters often pledged for their dependant servants (see Raftis, "The Concentration of Responsibility in Five Villages," *Mediaeval Studies* 28 [1967]: 116–17). In Ellington, Hugh Prencost pledged for his servant Joan, who brewed in 1321 (PRO SC2/179/19). Some such explanation may lie behind the frequency of villagers having amercements excused at the instance (*ad instanciam*) of men who otherwise seem to have enjoyed no special status in the village; see, e.g., the brewing amercement of Beatrice Thatcher excused in 1311 by Hugh Hirne (PRO SC2/179/16).

[38]For the courts of 1332/33 and 1340 see PRO SC2/179/26 and 30. Whatever Beaumeys' pledging for two Godmans may mean, it was most likely related to the passage of that virgate out of Godman control and into his own control.

[39]In the court of 1322, Richard le Woodeward acknowledged his debt to Beatrix Godman, now widowed, for five bushels of corn and was amerced for unjust deten-

times in the surviving documents; each instance deals with his absence from the village in the 1330s and 1340s. Apparently he had no reason for remaining. Why he did not take up the family virgate before it was received by Richard le Woodward and John Beaumeys ca. 1322 is unknown.[40] While the records do not allow us to recover the fleeting circumstances that might surround personal decisions, such as the one not to take up land, they do signal to us that such circumstances did exist and could be as potent in determining individual and family histories as other factors more readily recovered from the records. The life course of the Godmans, only partly culled from court rolls, offers suggestive clues to the forces that shaped individual and family in the pre-plague village.

The Lynlond/Brymbel/Underhill Families, 1290–1325/1454. The history of the Godman family is also useful for reminding us that the "disappearance" of a family does not necessarily represent its extinction. Thomas Godman junior moved to Brampton and married there. The Lynlond family provides an exceptionally clear case of a family whose name disappeared but who continued in the female line for 130 years after the original surname vanished from the records. Unlike the data for Godman family history, the court rolls are more informative regarding some of the personal, indeed emotional, circumstances surrounding the events of this family's transitions in the early fourteenth century.

---

tion. This was the same year in which Woodward received Thomas's old virgate in joint tenure with John Beaumeys. The debt of grain may have been some form of payment to the widow as part of the purchase price of the holding, as part of a maintenance agreement, or perhaps as part of a subletting arrangement. See PRO SC2/179/21.

[40]Professor Raftis has completed a study dealing in part with capital resources of village families; it may cast further light on situations such as this.

The Lynlonds were an important village family primarily because of the prominence of the first-generation male, Bartholomew, who served as juror twice, inquisition juror twice, and pledged nine times between 1290 and 1310. He had also acquired sufficient capital resources in the last four or five years of his life to purchase one messuage, one croft, and three acres of land for his daughter Alice, who came of age in 1309–10. At around the time of his death (1310) his estate was sound enough to sustain a 40*s.* payment for license to permit Alice to marry Geoffrey Underhill, a freeman.[41] In the court roll of that year (1311) she is noted as being seised of one messuage, 10 acres, one rod "and more" of free land.[42] Clearly, Alice had benefited from the ambition and industry of her father.

In the court of ca. 1310 Bartholomew's wife, Alice, paid the large sum of 2*s.* for a brewing infraction, which indicates that she was a major village brewer. But in that year she was also presented before the bishop for "losing the lord's chattels" on a charge of adultery with John Warde "et aliis diversis." Sometime between then and the court of 1311 Bartholomew died, and in 1311 the whole vill was fined 40*s.* because the reeve and customary tenants had permitted an outsider, John Brymbel (alias Warde?), to enter into Bartholomew's half virgate "ad relictam Bartholomei" without the lord's license and for a *gersuma* agreed upon among themselves ("per gersumam inter eos factam"). Revelation of these proceedings may have been brought to the attention of the court through Bartholomew's daughter Alice, the heiress, who raised the hue and cry justly on John Brymbel in that same year for an unspecified cause. That the older Alice—now Alice Brymbel—suffered no decline in her

---

[41]See PRO SC6/876/26. It is also recorded in the court roll of 1311 that the payment appears in the *rotulum gersumarum*.

[42]See PRO SC2/179/16.

economic position is suggested by her subsidy payment of 12*d.* in 1327.[43] Indeed, the account roll of 1312 records the receipt of 20*s.* from John Brymbel for a *gersuma* of one-half virgate.

John Brymbel was never fully integrated into the community and certainly never achieved the stature of Alice's first husband. Over the period 1311–25 he served as pledge only once (1312) and never held any office. His other references include four cases of the hue and cry raised upon him justly (1311, twice in 1321, 1325), trespass by misplaced ditches and appropriation of common (1311, twice in 1325), committing housebreaking (*hamsoken*) on his stepson Basil (1321), rescue (1321), and unjust detention (1325).[44]

The surnames Lynlond and Brymbel did not endure beyond the events of these years, since the two dominant personalities—the mother and daughter—both married and changed their surnames in the same year, while the Underhills, a Lynlond affine, survived until 1454. Like the Godmans, the continuity and fortunes of the Lynlonds were adversely affected in the course of the transmission of the family tenement between generations. The court roll entries concerning the raising of the hue and cry against Brymbel by the younger Alice in 1311 and Brymbel's aggression against Basil Lynlond in 1321 are tantalizing fragments of evidence of the emotional turmoil within the Lynlond family even a full decade after the death of Bartholomew. The subsequent fate of Bartholomew's two sons is unknown, except that Richard Lynlond in 1325 entered into one rod of land formerly held by his brother Basil.[45] Another daughter, known only as "Basilia in Lynlond" from a single

[43]See Raftis and Hogan, *Early Hunts. Lay Subsidy Rolls*, p. 165.

[44]See PRO SC2/179/16, 18, 19, and 22.

[45]That Richard and Basil were sons of Alice and Bartholomew is inferred from their being noted as the "sons of Bartholomew." Bartholomew Lynlond is the only person with that Christian name in all of Ellington's records.

court roll entry, brewed twice in 1322. It is indeed significant that the entries for Richard, Basil, and Basilia Lynlond are confined to the 1320s: this suggests that they may have been too young to hold the family half-virgate ca. 1310 when Bartholomew died. (Their sister, Alice, evidently the oldest, came of age ca. 1310.) This allowed their mother to remarry, and, although it should not have done so according to our current understanding of the descent of property within the family, this somehow altered the ultimate disposition of the tenement.[46] The entries concerning all three children—housebreaking against Basil (which proves he was a householder), the receiving of land, and brewing—suggest that at one time, at least, their commitment to the village was not marginal. Evidently, bearing sons and seeing them successfully reach maturity were not enough to ensure continuity of the family name in the village.

Geoffrey Underhill (1307?–49), who had married the younger Alice Lynlond in 1311 and whose entry into the ranks of Ellington's landholding families was not attended by the kind of controversy that surrounded John Brymbel, achieved greater integration into the community than did the latter. He served as juror in 1316 and taster in 1329 and 1332/33, and he pledged three times in the 1320s. His official service is especially interesting in view of his status as a freeman holding free land through marriage to an unfree woman. He served with William Walkelyn—the head of an important Ellington family—on a panel of inquiry into the value of all churches in Leightonstone Hundred in the early fourteenth century, and he stood witness to a land transfer in 1349.[47] His descendants, Thomas

[46]See Raftis, *Tenure and Mobility*, pp. 48–62; he adds that "inexplicable applications" of what seem to be principles of rights in land "only serve to underline the gaps in our knowledge" (ibid., pp. 61–62).

[47]For the inquest with William Walkelyn see BL Add. Roll 39591. For the land transfer see Peterhouse College, Ellington Slade doc. A.3.

(1349–1402) and Richard (1446–54), although they were not Geoffrey's equals in terms of service activities, were fairly substantial men in the very different climate of later medieval Ellington. Thomas served as a juror on two occasions but otherwise is noted only for beating a fellow villager in 1375, defaulting on a debt to a Joan Tebbe in 1400, and failing to clean his ditch near the king's highway, a charge also made against Richard Underhill in 1446 and 1447.[48]

The Foot Family, ca. 1280–1460. The record of events of the year 1310–11 in the Lynlond family demonstrates the value of court rolls in occasionally revealing the spectacular, the aberration that suggests how the complex of norms may have functioned. This was not the case because Brymbel, an outsider, entered the village and married a prosperous widow but rather because of what may have been his own truculent personality. As a body of evidence, however, studies based on court roll series have favored a longitudinal perspective, reconstructing the main lines of gradual, cumulative change over fairly extensive periods of time. This fact is particularly apparent with respect to families such as the Foots, who typify another variety of familial experience in the medieval village, that of the long-lived, fairly low-profile family that was less prominent in office-holding, pledging, and brewing, the very activities that distinguished men and women of the Mokke, Burgeys, Godman, and other families at different moments in their life courses.

The 19 members of the Foot family were notable neither for the number or the variety of their entry types. More than two-thirds of all entries are notices that someone was outside the fee, usually without license. For example, Nicholas Foot was

[48]See PRO SC2/179/40, 45, and 65 for the courts of 1375, 1400, and 1447, respectively. For 1446 see BL Add. Roll 39867.

cited 21 times between 1373 and 1454 as outside the fee, while John Foot was reported 28 times between 1434 and 1460 for the same. Only one instance of pledging is recorded, and two of brewing; only one individual—Stephen Foot—is known to have served in an official capacity, as one of eight jurors in an inquest into the dues and services of virgaters in Ellington before 1280.[49] This Stephen Foot may be the same man who abjured the realm as a thief, as reported in the Huntingdonshire eyre of 1286. The eyre roll also notes that a William Foot (*Fot*) was hanged as a thief, the Crown receiving one-half mark from his chattels.[50]

Yet if the success of a family is defined in part by its ability to endure, then the Foots, who extended over some seven or eight generations in the village, may be termed successful, despite their rather low profile in local society. Their history demonstrates clearly that for all their density and richness, court rolls are relatively weak for recovering the long-term history of the unexceptional.

In every generation up to the fourth the Foots, like the Mokkes, maintained at least one continuously resident male in the village; there are rare fragments of evidence pointing to the existence of separate households as well as intrafamilial associations. In a very unusual case—although it is evidently something of a pattern for this family—two women, Alice and Agnes Foot, were prohibited the vill in the famine year of 1316 as

---

[49]See *Cartularium monasterii de Rameseia*, ed. W. H. Hart and Ponsonby A. Lyons, 3 vols., Rolls Ser., no. 79 (London, 1884–93), 2: 23–25. The inquest is not dated but probably belongs to the third or final quarter of the thirteenth century since several jurors, including Stephen Foot, appeared in the earliest court rolls, some as late as 1311.

[50]See *Royal Justice and the Medieval English Countryside: The Huntingdonshire Eyre of 1286, the Ramsey Abbey Banlieu Court of 1287, and the Assizes of 1287–88*, ed. Anne Reiber DeWindt and Edwin B. DeWindt, 2 vols. (Toronto, 1981), 1: 444, no. 703 (xcv), and p. 364, no. 541.

malefactors against their neighbors, possibly for theft of food; and in the early 1360s William Foot unjustly detained chattels valued at 8*s.*3*d.* from Nicholas Foot.[51]

The Foots in the later fourteenth and the fifteenth centuries were somewhat more obstreperous than other families discussed thus far, yet their history is very much of a piece with the atmosphere of dislocation in the years after the plague. William Foot (1356–91) was presented for seven acts of trespass, Thomas Foot (1360/66–75) for four acts of trespass and one each of housebreaking, rescue, and unjust detention of money. The last resident male—Thomas Foot (1380–1415)—was charged with two acts of trespass, one act of withholding land unjustly, and with his wife, Elena, was ordered by the lord in 1391 to "get along" with Agnes Reynold ("bene se habeant versus alteram"). Finally, in 1444 and 1449 the account rolls state that the chevage due from John, who was outside the village at Alconbury, is put in respect because the reeve "doesn't dare" restrain him ("non audet ipsum distringere").[52] Had it not been for activities such as trespass, absenteeism, and unjust detention, the evidence would have yielded only a handful of references to the 11 identifiable members of this family between 1350 and 1460. Yet the nature of their entries, and the family's survival over nearly 200 years, suggest a very high level of integration into village life. Although their engagement did not take the form of pledging before 1350 or officeholding in the fifteenth century, they were neither negligible nor marginal in the village.

The danger of losing sight of, and hence underestimating, nonofficial families intensifies in the fifteenth-century records,

---

[51]For the court roll of 1316 see PRO SC2/179/18. The entry states that Alice and Agnes were "malefactores gallinis vicinorum."

[52]See PRO SC2/179/43 and SC6/876/1 and 2.

when the documentary profile of women declines sharply in comparison with earlier periods, and even the variety of entries for the most prominent people is reduced as the rolls increasingly emphasize notices of officeholding. Had the members of the Foot family been less mobile and less prolific, as well as less recalcitrant, their profile in the records would have been even more lackluster. Many of those families who appear to be uninfluential or nondescript may simply have been smaller in size, more continuously resident, and more orderly. Uncovering their histories and evaluating their roles in shaping events in the village present virtually insoluble problems for a holistic reconstruction of village society and culture.

The Caus Family, 1356–1473/1528?, and the Muriell Family, 1290–1391. We have seen that the documentary profile of families alters, depending upon record survival and quality as well as the level and quality of their activities, and the timing of such activities in relation to larger social and economic change. For example, the Foots appeared in the records of the late fourteenth century primarily because of their unruliness, clearly a village preoccupation since throughout most of the period 1350–1425 families with members exhibiting "nonconformist" behavior tended to overshadow those engaged in other, less explosive activities. To a lesser extent, this trend continues in the later fifteenth-century records, with the exception that officials—by means of their election notices and their arrears—become more prominent. This permits us to explore another variant of the phenomenon already discussed with regard to the Godman family, the influence of individuals on the changing fortunes of families.

The Caus family illustrates the fluctuations that arose not only from a changing economy and society but also from the specific responses of family members to those conditions. Like many others, the Causes reaped substantial benefits from the depopulation of post-plague Ellington, in the new tenurial and officeholding opportunities that emerged. In the first generation, John Caus served as juror in 1356 and was one of five jurors in that year who belonged to families that had apparently never before provided officials.[53] The remaining entries for him and one Alice Caus occur in the 1360/66 court roll (a period when the court roll series is particularly weak) and are representative of the entries for most individuals appearing in the court that year: John was presented for two acts of trespass, as victim of a similar act, and for justly raising the hue and cry on Robert Beaumeys, possibly in connection with Alice Caus's attack upon the latter. As for Alice herself, a certain Agnes Aldith had committed housebreaking against her and attacked her, for which Alice had raised the hue and cry. In the second generation, Thomas Caus (1391–1405), who served as constable in 1391, had a similar career: two acts of trespass, victim of three acts of trespass and of housebreaking, unjust detention, default of court attendance in 1400 and 1402, and a final entry in 1405, that he had a ruinous tenement and had not found the required pledge.

In the third generation, the character of entries for this family changes significantly with another Thomas Caus (1428–73) and his wife, Matilda (1438/39–47). Alongside the usual entries of misplaced dungheaps, cutting underwood, receiving land, arrears of amercements in the 1440s and 1450s, and witnessing deeds on three occasions in the 1450s,[54]

---

[53]R. H. Britnell has described the same phenomenon of post-plague opportunities in the government of the town of Colchester, in *Growth and Decline in Colchester, 1300–1525* (Cambridge, 1986), p. 110. See also J. Ambrose Raftis, "Changes in an English Village after the Black Death," *Mediaeval Studies* 29 (1967): 158–77.

[54]See DeWindt, *Liber Gersumarum*, p. 260, no. 3181; Peterhouse College, Ellington Slade doc. A.19 and A.20; and the Ellington parish records in the CCRO, Huntingdon, for the year 1457.

Thomas's record is distinguished by 31 entries referring to offices held, including notices of elections and arrears. The records show that he held office some 27 times, serving as a juror, taster, collector of court fines, affeeror, beadle, bailiff, and constable. Even this impressive record seriously underrepresents his level of activity, since court and account rolls survive for only 22 of the 45 years spanned by his career.[55] Also noteworthy is the absence of presentments for acts of aggression or violence that frequently characterized the profiles of other prominent men in the same period. As for his wife, Matilda, she was recorded as a brewer in three of the four surviving court rolls of the 1440s, which reminds us of a pattern more commonly seen earlier, when officeholding and brewing families tended to be the same.

The high profile achieved by this couple was not sustained after them. John Caus, of unknown relationship, was noted only twice in the 1440s, for holding land *ingersumata* and for serving as collector of rents and fines (1447).[56] Since the court and account rolls are relatively numerous for some 30 years after his first appearance in 1440, his low profile cannot be attributed to poor record survival. Nor does it seem likely that the family was in the process of "disappearing" with John and Thomas. If a William "Calte" who witnessed a will in 1528 was a descendant, then the family continued well into the sixteenth century.[57] Rather, the Causes fade from view because their integration into

---

[55]Thomas Caus and John Faukes (1443–81) hold the record for the highest number of times an individual held office, followed by John Tousland (25 times) and Thomas Isbell (22)—the latter two, also fifteenth-century men.

[56]See PRO SC2/179/63 and 65.

[57]The surname Calte resembles some of the fifteenth-century variant spellings of the surname Caus—e.g., Caws (1405), Cawte (1432), and Caux (1465). For the will of 1528 see the testament of John Holcote in the "Wills and Administrations for the Archdeaconry of Huntingdon," vol. 3, fols. 42–43, located in the CCRO, Huntingdon.

village society changed, particularly in terms of officeholding. John, who seems to have been a younger contemporary of Thomas and Matilda, does not appear to have taken advantage of the possibilities for official service in the late fifteenth century.

Beginning in an earlier period, the Muriell family's history parallels many of the features noted for the Caus family. Indeed, it provides even clearer examples of a pattern that has been noted and described elsewhere: that within a single generation one man tended to dominate the affairs of the family, as well as to represent it officially. This phenomenon has not been sufficiently appreciated, even by historians most interested in village individualism.[58]

Adam, Thomas, and William Muriell were men of the second generation, but Adam alone makes any substantial appearance in the records, serving as a juror in 1325, 1329, and 1332/33—the only surviving court rolls for the late 1320s and the 1330s. In the subsidy of 1327 he paid 13*d.*, and between 1321 and 1340 he stood pledge nine times, in each case for a nonrelative.[59] By contrast, Thomas Muriell was essoined from the view by his son John in 1329, while William Muriell was involved in a debt plea in the same year—the only references to these two individuals.

In the fourth generation, again three males have been recovered from the records; only one, Robert Muriell, held office,

---

[58]For a discussion of this phenomenon see Raftis and Hogan, *Early Hunts. Lay Subsidy Rolls*, pp. 23–24. Alan Macfarlane in *The Origins of English Individualism: The Family, Property and Social Transition* (New York, 1978) was surprisingly little concerned with *real* individual villagers, although these abound in the records.

[59]The importance of the sex of the pledgee and his or her relationship to the pledge is discussed briefly by the present author in "Jurors of the Village Court: Local Leadership Before and After the Plague in Ellington, Huntingdonshire," *Journal of British Studies* 30 (July 1991), esp. pp. 246–47. For the court rolls of 1325, 1329, 1332/33, and 1340 see PRO SC2/179/22, 26, and 30 and BL Add. Roll 39468. For the subsidy of 1327 see Raftis and Hogan, *Early Hunts. Lay Subsidy Rolls*, p. 166.

serving as a juror in the three courts whose rolls survive for the 1370s and 1390s. In this period, when court roll entries show an increasing preoccupation with trespass, violence, and general unrest, he had no further entries, while John Muriell had a hue and cry justly raised upon him in 1356 and was violently assaulted (the 1360/66 roll). Thomas Muriell assaulted another villager and was amerced for unjustly raising the hue and cry upon the rector of Ellington and his servants in 1375. As is argued elsewhere, the very different careers of juror and non-juror males of the same family (and frequently of the same generation) indicate the capacity of the village community to differentiate among individuals, in selecting men to hold local office.[60] Indeed, such evidence suggests that the village conceived of people first as individuals and only secondarily as members of a particular family.

The Pilcok Family, 1280–1373. The possibilities of prosopographical research opened up by court roll evidence have scarcely been fully appreciated. This is particularly the case for those village families who are more notable for the activities of their womenfolk than of their menfolk.[61] From the thirteenth through the fifteenth centuries women were cited most frequently as participants in the local brewing industry. So prominent a place did this industrial activity assume in the ranks of several Ellington families that the women easily overshadowed the men. For example, of the eight known members of the Plouwright family appearing in the records between 1290 and 1375,

[60]See Olson, "Jurors," esp. pp. 244–52. For the courts of 1356, 1360/66, 1373, 1375, and 1391 see PRO SC2/179/36, 39, 40, and 43 and BL Add. Roll 39738.

[61]Judith M. Bennett, *Women in the Medieval English Countryside: Gender and Household in Brigstock before the Plague* (New York, 1987), is the fullest and most recent study of medieval English countrywomen.

two of the four men are known only for having pledged for their wives, who brewed ale (the husbands of Matilda [1290–1315] and Alice [1316–40]). Between them, the four women of the family maintained a brewing tradition that spanned a period of some 85 years. Of the 13 members of the Pilcok family, the most frequently mentioned among the eight men were Thomas and John, the husbands of Joan and Margery, whose chief activity was pledging for wife or sister-in-law, either for brewing infractions or disruptions of the peace.

The Pilcok women were the steadiest of all brewers in Ellington. Four of the five women brewed and did so over an extended period: Joan, for 32 years (1290–1322); Margery, for 27 years (1306–33); Matilda, for 29 years (1311–40); and a second Margery, for at least 14 years (1340–54), before the court roll series is interrupted. The average length of brewing career of the first three women was more than 29 years. That these three women also brewed concurrently between ca. 1311 and 1322 suggests that there were at least three separate Pilcok households in early fourteenth-century Ellington, but the collective brewing tradition of all four Pilcok women extended over the period 1290–1356.

These women were also involved in acts of violence among themselves, as well as raising the hue and cry and selling land. In a rather complicated sequence of events in 1321, Joan justly raised the hue and cry upon Margery, who bit her ("dentibus suis morsit Johannam"). Joan also committed housebreaking against Margery, and the latter's husband, John, was assigned the undoubtedly difficult task of pledging for both women.

By comparison the Pilcok men were an undistinguished lot. In the total of 23 separate activities for which the men were noted in the court rolls, 10 of these involved pledging for a female Pilcok who brewed. The last two men, John in the 1360s and William in 1373, were presented for violent behavior. In short, for families such as these the only thread of continuity in their recoverable histories is the tradition of family brewing, sustained by the activity of individual women.

The Fifteenth-Century Village Family. The occasional phenomenon of families who are prominent by virtue of their women is one that disappears altogether in the records of post-plague Ellington. Throughout the full body of the village records there is a dramatic lowering of the profile of women after 1350, which intensifies in the fifteenth century and is redressed somewhat after the 1480s only by the survival of village wills, wherein women figure prominently as legatees. The traditional scope of female activity contracted in the fifteenth century, in comparison with earlier periods. This can be demonstrated by examining the timing of recoverable activity of women belonging to prominent families who first appeared in the village in the later fourteenth and fifteenth centuries. This decisively indicates that newcomers to the village in the years ca. 1400 faced a very different set of circumstances from those faced by new or emerging families in the period before 1350.

Among the successful and highly engaged families who appeared in Ellington from the later fourteenth century on, some of the most prominent were the Bateman, Gate, Gymber, Hicson, Henson, and Penyell families.[62] In each of these families not only is the ratio of female to male representatives extremely low[63] but also women do not appear in the records until long after the apparent establishment of the family in the

[62]The dates for these families: Bateman, 1399–1618; Gate, 1453–1633; Gymber, 1373–1567; Henson, 1454–1637; Hicson, 1391–1513; Penyell, 1396–1618.

[63]For the entire village population of Ellington 1425–85, the ratio of notices concerning women to those concerning men is ca. 1:11. For the period from 1280 to the Black Death the figure is a quite different 1:4.

village. On average, the first female members of these six families appeared some 57 years after the first known reference to the family. The first 113 years of the Gymber family history, for example, produced no references to women. The earliest women of the Henson family to appear in the records do so only after 41 years, as legatees in 1495.[64] The only mention of a Henson woman outside of a testamentary bequest concerns Isabelle, who was presented as a brewer in the courts of 1520 and 1527 and as a baker in 1527.[65] Similarly, the first Gate women mentioned outside of wills are found in 1527, 74 years after the first appearance of the surname, when Alice Gate was amerced as a brewer and baker and Margaret Gate received land with her husband. An extreme example of the underrepresentation of women is found in the Penyell family, where only two women are noted in over 200 years of family history.[66]

Such a marginalization of women contrasts forcibly with the histories of families of earlier origin in the village. A similar analysis of six families present in Ellington in 1280 and surviving into the fifteenth century elicits very different results. The first reference to women of the Buk, Hirne, Leonard, Peverel, Walkelyn, and Wyne families occurred on average about 19 years after the earliest surviving mention of the family.[67]

---

[64]See the testament of Richard Henson (d. 1495), in the "Wills and Administrations of the Archdeaconry of Huntingdon," CCRO, Huntingdon, vol. 1, fol. 149. The bequests were to his daughters, Helen and Agnes.

[65]See PRO SC2/179/85 and 86.

[66]Margaret Penyell (*Peinell*), whose marriage license was paid for in 1454 (DeWindt, *Liber Gersumarum*, p. 357, no. 4202); Alice Penyell (*Pannell*), who left a will dated 1618. (See "Original Wills in Bundles, 1615–1652," Bundle 91, vol. 21, fol. 93, CCRO, Huntingdon.)

[67]Buk, 1280–1459; Hirne, 1280–1407; Leonard, 1280–1416; Peverel, 1280–1416; Walkelyn, 1280–1405; Wyne, 1280–1453.

The Hicson Family, 1391–1513, and the Brydder Family, 1429–1529. We may consider these phenomena in more detail by looking at two families who were of later origin in Ellington, the Hicsons and the Brydders. Both were prosperous in terms of their participation in, and level of commitment to, the village. John Hicson first appears in the court roll of 1391, presented for three acts of trespass—one against an individual, one with animals in the open fields, and one in the lord's park. In 1402 and 1405 he was cited for default of court attendance, trespass in the lord's wood, and purchasing two acres of land from Adam Buk. In 1391 and 1405 he also served as a juror, an office he held in almost every extant court from 1405 to 1429. His other offices included those of constable (elected 1407) and beadle (elected 1429). In terms of officeholding, involvement in the land market, and acts of aggression against the community, the lord, and other individuals, he foreshadows the essential career of every resident Hicson male over the course of the fifteenth century and into the sixteenth century.

Although reconstruction of the career of each Hicson male is difficult, given their concentration, numbers, and the family's fondness for the Christian name John, this first John Hicson also exemplifies the reproductive success and longevity that characterized prominent families in the period after the Black Death: his great-grandson John was sworn into tithing in 1460, while he himself was still living! It was undoubtedly a John of the following generation who received a major tenement jointly with 11 other Ellington men (1496).[68] Some 10 adult male Hicsons were alive in Ellington in the mid-fifteenth century,

[68]For the deed of 1496 see the Ellington Parish records in the CCRO, Huntingdon. Also, the court roll of 1446 (BL Add. Roll 39867) notes the swearing into tithing of "John son of John son of John Hicson," the only such triple generational citation in all of Ellington's records. These were long-lived people, another factor that may explain their prominence in fifteenth-century Ellington.

which explains why at least eight of them were outside the village for varying lengths of time between 1434 and 1500.[69]

Despite these numbers, only two women of the Hicson family appear in the records—although such a multitude of men certainly suggests the existence of several Hicson women. Joan Hicson was a brewer, with small amercements of 1*d.*, 2*d.*, and 3*d.*, who was active between 1429 and 1460. Agnes Hicson's father, Thomas, paid 6*s.*8*d.* for license to marry her in 1410, and her *gersuma* of 6*s.*8*d.* was described as being allocated to the reeve in 1411.[70]

In contrast to these modest female "careers," that of John the son of the first known John Hicson fairly bristles with activity, confrontation, and economic engagement. Between 1438 and 1454 he served as collector of court fines, juror, taster, and beadle, holding office at least 11 times. He received 1.5 virgates of land in 1416/17, and he unjustly detained one rod of land from Alice Mokke in 1426. His tenurial status is further indirectly suggested by his failure to make closes as ordered in 1443 and 1446, failure to clean ditches in 1455 and 1465, and various pleas of trespass involving cutting and carrying wood (1428, 1443, 1454) and trespasses with animals (1452, twice). He was also presented in at least one instance of an unjust plaint in 1446, and he impleaded another villager in a charge of trespass

[69]These configurations in the life course of the Hicsons resemble those of the Davies family of Myddle, described by Richard Gough, who claimed that some have "reckoned up" their numbers to be "noe less than sixty." He goes on to note that "many familyes in this parish have been extinct, but this has gott soe many branches that it is more likely to overspread it" (*History of Myddle*, p. 243). For the Hicsons, in the 1440s and 1450s alone, John son of John, John son of William, Thomas son of John, William son of William, John son of John son of John, and William son of John are noted as being outside the village, usually without license, at, respectively, Eton; London; Leighton; London; Ramsey and Higham Ferrers; Houghton, Ramsey and Biggin; Ramsey; and Higham Ferrers and Longstowe.

[70]See DeWindt, *Liber Gersumarum*, p. 93, no. 920, and PRO SC6/875/25.

in 1453.[71] In short, his career mirrors that of his father. Indeed, apart from his officeholding, the recoverable career of this second-generation John Hicson differs little from that of nonresident regional landholder or even a newcomer in the village. Earlier we examined the case of John Brymbel, who was a type of "newcomer" in early fourteenth-century Ellington, and contrasted his activities with those of more established families and individuals. Such a contrast was less apparent between old resident families and new arrivals in the fifteenth century.

This phenomenon of a lessening of the difference between newcomers and older established residents in the later medieval village is more clearly seen by comparing the careers of the Hicsons of the mid-fifteenth century with that of the Brydders of Grafham, a parish just south of Ellington. The Brydders's growing contacts with Ellington can be traced in some detail, going back to at least the middle of the fourteenth century, when a John and Margery Brydder (*Bridder*) appear in the court rolls. John was presented with 15 other men—many described as outsiders—in 1340 for trespass in the lord's wood, while in 1356 Margery was attacked by the aggressive Margaret Pilcok, upon whom she raised the hue and cry. These isolated entries suggest that the Brydders may not have been resident in Ellington. In the early fifteenth-century records their probable native village is disclosed with the appearance of a John Brydder "of Grafham."[72] John, along with two other men with the same surname, is first mentioned in the court roll of 1429, when each was fined 2*d.* for trespass with mares and foals "in bladis et herbis." He continues to appear between 1440

[71]See PRO SC2/179/58, 66, 67 and BL Add. Rolls 34370, 34825, 39867, and 34322. For the land acquisition see DeWindt, *Liber Gersumarum*, p. 131, no. 1457.

[72]The surname Brydder is also spelled "Birder" and "Byrder" in court rolls of the 1440s and 1450s.

and 1455 in entries concerning default, trespass in the common, penalties for not cleaning his ditch, and notices that his fines could not be collected because the reeve was unable to distrain him "infra dominium"—an indication that he had no chattels in Ellington. In short, his identification with the village was limited, in spite of his tenure of land. Interestingly enough, apart from not holding village offices his career is quite similar to that of John Hicson, a second-generation Hicson whose family had settled in Ellington at least 40 years before this John Brydder first appeared.

The Brydders's primary link with Grafham is further indicated in the careers of Roger, Robert, and Henry Brydder, all described as "of Grafham," who were active as trespassers with animals in Ellington in 1405, 1425, and 1429. They were contemporaries of John Brydder, as was a William Brydder "de Greffham,"[73] of unknown relationship to John, who did fealty in 1454 for a messuage and some free land in Ellington once belonging to Richard Underhill. Subsequent entries for him—a citation for default in 1465 and notice of his being essoined in 1486—indicate nonresidence. His son, Thomas, left a will dated 13 January 1529 that reveals more clearly how an important landholder in Ellington, whose family had first held land in the village some 70 years earlier, could yet maintain significant ties with other villages through landholding, past family history, present family ties, and sentiment.[74]

Thomas asked to be buried in the churchyard of All Hallows in Ellington and left a ewe to the sepulcher light there, as well as 2*s.* for the torches and bells. To his eldest son, William, he

[73]PRO SC2/179/70.

[74]For Thomas's will see "Wills and Administrations of the Archdeaconry of Huntingdon," vol. 3, fol. 115. For the courts of 1405, 1425, 1429, 1454, 1465, and 1486 see PRO SC2/179/50, 57, 60, 70, 73 and BL Add. Roll 34322.

bequeathed his ancestral estate, "late William Birdare my father's," which consisted of a house in Grafham and "arable land, pasture and meadow" in Buckden, a parish east of Grafham, and in Grafham and Sibthorpe, a hamlet within Ellington. His daughter, Agnes Rede, received a "mease" with a close in Buckden, which Thomas had received from his sister, Agnes Lyne, "late of Bugden," on condition that his daughter "shall every year during her life" keep an obit in the parish church there in memory of her aunt. His son William was to keep an obit for Thomas's soul and those of Thomas's parents in the parish church of Grafham and also was to give the church 2*s.* yearly "at the said obit," provisions suggesting that the Grafham church was perceived by the family as its ancestral church. William was also charged with two separate legacies, to Buckden and Grafham churches, of 3*s.*4*d.* each.

The evidence suggests that Thomas and his family were resident in Ellington: his wife, Agnes, was both a brewer and baker in the village in 1527, and he himself chose to be buried there. Yet his area of personal identification was obviously based on a region comprising three villages, not a single village, and was founded not simply on landholding but on a remembered and evidently important family history, extending back possibly to the fourteenth century. Ties of sentiment and belonging bound individuals to a region as well as a village, largely through family tradition and connections.[75] Such ties were built upon a long history of openness in the village. Historians have tended to see the growing presence and importance of the regional landholder in the village as necessarily militating against the community of interests so often described as characteristic of the medieval village. The fragments of

[75]Anne DeWindt amply demonstrates this in "Redefining the Peasant Community."

evidence available for the life and personal identification of Thomas Brydder suggest the existence of other more complicated possibilities.[76]

The Late Medieval "Isolate"? Another type of fifteenth-century village figure that seems to have fewer historical antecedents than either the Brydders or even the Hicsons is paradoxically found in the case histories of men who were fully engaged in the village, men such as John Tousland (1428–60) and John Swasethe (1426–53), both of whom were extremely active as officeholders and landholders. Tousland held some six different offices (juror, constable, collector of rents, reeve, affeeror, and bailiff) at least 23 times over a period of 28 years. Indeed, his performance was so exemplary that in the account roll of 1450 he is forgiven 10*s.* of his arrears as reeve "per auditores ex gratia causa boni sui servicii."[77] John Swasethe held four different offices (juror, constable, taster, and affeeror) at least 20 times over a period of 27 years and had the added distinction of being chosen as "arbiter" for the defendant in two separate cases before the court in 1452.[78] These individuals also demonstrate the now familiar pattern of high levels of activity in various types of trespass, as well as general failure (from the lord's point of view) to maintain their tenements properly.[79]

---

[76]For some remarks on "gentrification" and its effects on the solidarity of the village community see Dyer, *Lords and Peasants*, pp. 372–76.

[77]PRO SC6/876/3.

[78]PRO SC2/179/66.

[79]The landed holdings of Tousland and Swasethe are reasonably well documented. According to the *Liber Gersumarum* (DeWindt, p. 351, no. 4144), Swasethe surrendered one messuage, one virgate, and one quarter of land in 1453. Tousland received an ancient freehold property of some 120 acres in 1453, to be held jointly with eight other men (see Peterhouse College, Ellington Slade A.19). He also held jointly with six others a wood in Ellington known as Eyryswood, as evidenced by a charter of 1459 in which he and his co-tenants gave the holding to three other men (BL Add. Ch. 33255).

Where a departure from the past seems to be most striking is that both men are almost completely isolated individuals. Apart from one reference to a John Tousland (possibly a son) who was sworn into tithing in 1446[80] and one reference to Swasethe's servant, these men apparently conducted extensive village careers over a period of some 30 years isolated from the activity of any other family or household member.

This is a profound contrast to the family histories of the Mokkes, Burgeys, Lynlonds, and other families considered above. It is inconceivable that the prominent men of the Swasethe and Tousland families could have had distinguished careers in the village over periods of two and three decades without most members of their families also finding their way into court on their own initiative, or being drawn into court as a necessary consequence of their participation in the everyday life of the village. Women as well as men of secondary stature appeared as integral actors in the careers of the dominant men in their families in the earlier period.

The "individualism" of major fifteenth-century landholders finds its most complete expression in the cases of men such as Tousland and Swasethe; so, too, does the lowering (indeed, the complete effacing) of the profile of women. These are the products of a degree of change in village society that cannot be fully explained by our sources but seem to point to something more than a contraction in the jurisdiction of the village court or changes in scribal practice in the fifteenth century, significant as these were. The careers of Tousland and Swasethe suggest that intense participation could be achieved with few or no

[80]The account roll of 1443 refers to a "Thomas" Tousland as collector of rents two years earlier, but this is surely a case of scribal error. No other references to a Thomas Tousland occur elsewhere, and the same account roll refers to John Tousland as collector of rents two years earlier. (See PRO SC6/875/28.) He served as collector of rents at least eight times after 1443.

familial antecedents or contemporaries. The same was also true for the earliest Hicsons, but their prominent men were not isolated; instead, they were the central actors in a dense web of family relationships. Was the result of such extreme "individualism" a diminution of community integration? Or was there a new social climate, more difficult to describe, in which individual and family—and village—interacted in ways that a thirteenth-century villager would certainly have recognized, though perhaps with some difficulty? Thomas Brydder's history suggests ways in which a long-standing tradition of mobility, broadly defined, and a land market increasingly shorn of seigniorial control could alter the personal, territorial identification of individuals. Here, in short, are both continuity and discontinuity.

The important influence of the individual, not simply the group, in determining family fortunes; the difficulty of passing on status and position from one generation to the next; the limitations on the scope of public female activity; the importance of officeholding to personal stature—all were constants over the thirteenth through the fifteenth and sixteenth centuries. Regional landholding, if not as pervasive and fluid in the thirteenth century as it was later to become, would still have been eminently familiar to the villager of the pre-plague era. Collective action was also a fundamental part of village life in both periods, despite some changes in character: in the later period group trespass (an interesting and unexplored instance of personal alignment in the village) has replaced pledging or community policing as the most ubiquitous instance of recoverable group activity, other than officeholding, in the village.

The numerous households of the same family and the continuously resident males of the early fourteenth century are not such typical features in the life course patterns of successful families in the fifteenth century. Frequent and varied forms of trespass (against individual neighbors, the lord's lands, the *communitas ville*) seem to be part of the normal career profile of men like John Hicson, John Tousland, and John Swasethe. The pattern of several men "representing" the family in the village, for good or ill, so typical of the prominent families of earlier years, was gradually superseded. It became increasingly rare for a family to produce more than one male in each generation who survived into adulthood, remained in the village, and promoted long-term familial interests in that village alone.

A considerable amount of work remains to be done before the students of the late medieval village will begin to understand the chronology and etiology of family and individual success and disappearance as well as Richard Gough understood that of the families of Myddle in the seventeenth century. In the conclusion to his path-breaking study of the Ramsey Abbey villages published nearly 30 years ago, J. A. Raftis remarked that "the individuality of the villager escapes easy historical formulation."[81] We may add that the same thing continues to be true for the village family, and for the ways in which family and individual interacted and shaped each other over the high and later Middle Ages.

[81]*Tenure and Mobility*, p. 211.

THE HISTORIOGRAPHIC UNCONSCIOUS AND THE RETURN OF ROBIN HOOD

Kathleen A. Biddick[1]

Critical studies of medieval and early-modern popular culture have taught historians not to oppose high and low, literate and illiterate, textual and visual, aristocratic and peasant. The work of scholars such as M. M. Bakhtin, Michael Camille, Aron Gurevich, and Peter Stallybrass have shown the complicated ways in which different medieval thought-worlds intersected and constructed each other.[2] The "academic" history written in our universities and "popular" history represented by the media today are no less subject to such interplay. The lessons learned from the study of medieval popular culture

---

[1]For their encouragement and critical readings I am grateful to Dana Benelli, Madonna Hettinger, Sandra Joshel, Bill Krier, Robert Rosenstone. I am indebted to Ambrose Raftis, who emphasized in an introductory graduate seminar a sentence from *The Historian's Craft* by Marc Bloch (New York, 1953) that transformed history for me: "How can I know what I am about to say?" (p. 71).

[2]Bakhtin, *Rabelais and His World*, trans. Hélène Iswolsky (Bloomington, 1984); Camille, "Seeing and Reading: Some Visual Implications of Medieval Literacy and Illiteracy," *Art History* 6/1 (1985): 26–49; idem, "The *Très Riches Heures*: An Illuminated Manuscript in the Age of Mechanical Reproduction," *Critical Inquiry* 17/1 (1990): 72–107; Gurevich, *Medieval Popular Culture: Problems of Belief and Perception*, trans. János M. Bak and Paul A. Hollingsworth (New York, 1988); Stallybrass and Allon White, *The Politics and Poetics of Transgression* (Ithaca, N.Y., 1986). The scholars of the above school have their opposition. For a vision of clerical and peasant culture in opposition see Jean Claude Schmitt, *The Holy Greyhound: Guinefort, Healer of Children since the Thirteenth Century*, trans. Martin Thom (Cambridge, 1983).

inspire this study of remembering and forgetting as both the academy and popular film and television produce medieval histories.[3] Historiographical and cinematic representations of the legend of Robin Hood offer rich examples of such interruptions. Historians and film-makers of the twentieth century keep returning to the forest in search of Robin Hood. His return, I will argue, is about the return of the pastoral in academic and popular history. The pastoral, from the time of Virgil, has offered an imaginary site at which historical contests over "authentication" and "truth" in public culture can be waged.[4]

Neither an exhaustive study of the filmography of Robin Hood—a frequent subject of the earliest silent films, later sound films, color films, television, and cartoons—nor a systematic analysis of the extensive historiography of this legend, instead this essay discusses two powerful, popular representations of the legend, *The Adventures of Robin Hood* (Warner Bros., 1938) and *Robin Hood: Prince of Thieves* (Morgan Creek Productions, 1991), in conjunction with post-war historiography of Robin Hood appearing in such journals as *Past and Present*.[5] These films and the historiography interrupt each other at crucial

---

[3]For discussions of history and film see Robert A. Rosenstone, "What You Think about When You Think about Writing a Book on History and Film," *Public Culture* 3/1 (1990): 50–66; idem, "Revisioning History: Contemporary Filmmakers and the Construction of the Past: A Review Article," *Comparative Studies in Society and History* 32/4 (1990): 822–37; Natalie Zemon Davis and Daniel J. Walkowitz, "The Rights and Responsibilities of Historians in Regard to Historical Films and Video," *Perspectives* 30/6 (1992): 15–17.

[4]For an illuminating meditation on forests see Robert Pogue Harrison, *Forests: The Shadow of Civilization* (Chicago, 1992). For important critical discussion of the pastoral see Annabel M. Patterson, *Pastoral and Ideology: Virgil to Valéry* (Berkeley, 1987). References to the historiographical framing of English peasant historiography may be found below, n. 8.

[5]For a list of Robin Hood films and films on other medieval subjects 1898–1988 see David Williams, "Medieval Movies," *Yearbook of English Studies* 20 (1990): 1–32; R. B. Dobson and John Taylor, *Rymes of Robyn Hood: An Introduction to the English Outlaw* (Pittsburgh, 1976), p. 61 and relevant notes.

moments in their efforts to use history as a resource in the production of the pastoral as a cultural space. A study of the return of Robin Hood helps an understanding of how the pastoral marks historically shifting borders of nature, gender, family, community, national and supranational identities, even history itself. There is, therefore, much to be learned about historical representation from these interruptions.

The Return of Robin Hood in History Today. The return of Robin Hood to a recent issue of *History Today* offers an ideal place to begin this study. In October 1991 the editors reprinted an article entitled "Robin Hood: A Peasant Hero," which had first appeared in an issue in 1958.[6] The opening caption to the 1991 reprint states that the essay reflects an approach that "he [the author, Maurice Keen] now cheerily admits to having moved on from." Readers who had followed Keen's work would know that he had abandoned his 1950s quest for a peasant hero. In 1976 Keen had appended to an article, "Robin Hood—Peasant or Gentleman?" (reprinted from 1961) a note in which he retracted his hero thesis: "I do not believe that my attempts to relate the Robin Hood story to the social pressures of the period of the Peasants' Revolt will stand up to scrutiny."

Readers of the 1991 reprint could nevertheless begin to guess that the romance of the peasant origins of Robin Hood was in question, without knowing anything about the history of Keen's work. The editors of *History Today* left clues to this

[6]Maurice Keen, *History Today* 8 (Oct. 1958): 684–89, repr., ibid. 41 (Oct. 1991): 20–24; idem, "Robin Hood—Peasant or Gentleman?" *Past and Present* 19 (Apr. 1961), repr. in *Peasants, Knights, and Heretics: Studies in Medieval English Social History*, ed. R. H. Hilton (New York, 1976), pp. 258–66; his retraction there appears at the end. It is noteworthy than in the collection of 15 essays selected from *Past and Present* (1958–73) five are devoted to Robin Hood. For other guides to the historiography of the Robin Hood legend see J. C. Holt, *Robin Hood* (New York, 1982); John G. Bellamy, *Robin Hood: An Historical Enquiry* (Bloomington, 1985).

effect through their manipulation of the illustrations of the reprint. It would be clear to readers when they turned to the end of the article and saw the promotional shot of Kevin Costner, star of *Robin Hood: Prince of Thieves*, a Hollywood film released in England in July 1991, that the editors had changed the illustrations when they reprinted the 1958 essay. A comparison of the two versions indeed shows that the editors retained only two of the original seven illustrations from the earlier piece. They opened the reprinted article with a quarter-page copy of a wood engraving taken from an important antiquarian collection of Robin Hood ballads published by Joseph Ritson in 1795, in which Robin Hood stands dressed in the fashion of an eighteenth-century aristocrat, with his bow drawn and aimed at 15 foresters. Small and elegant wood engravings like this one head each of the 33 ballads of the Ritson edition. By Ritson's time Robin Hood had already acquired a noble pedigree, and Ritson reproduced in his edition the genealogy drawn up by none other than the antiquarian William Stukeley. The wood engravings of the Ritson edition consistently depict Robin Hood as an eighteenth-century aristocrat.

The editors set this wood engraving of an aristocratic Robin Hood sporting a plumed hat over an inch-high title: "Robin Hood: A Peasant Hero." The editors played on the contradiction between the desire of historians in the 1950s to fashion a peasant identity for Robin Hood and the evidence of a tradition of illustration to this legend going back to the first printed editions of the legend in the early sixteenth century, which depicted him according to changing aristocratic fashion. Other illustrations in the article offer some sense of this fashion. They include a woodcut of Robin Hood as a well-dressed yeoman-like figure flanked by a lord and a lady from the incunabula of Wynkyn de Worde's "A lyttle geste of Robyn Hode," published ca. 1510, and an illustration from *Robin Hood's Garland* (dating to

1686) in which Robin Hood is dressed up as a cavalier. As readers leaf through the 1991 article they realize that no illustrations dating from the sixteenth to the eighteenth centuries depicted Robin Hood as a peasant. To illustrate Robin Hood in the nineteenth century, the editors selected a picture from a Victorian children's book. The trappings of Victorian medievalism further obscure the class identity of Robin Hood. Readers of *History Today* who had seen *Robin Hood: Prince of Thieves* would know that Hollywood also represented Robin Hood as a nobleman and adapted the Stukeley genealogy, which identifies Robin Hood as Robin of Locksley.[7] The 1991 reprint thus opens and closes with representations separated by two centuries of Robin Hood as an aristocrat.

The original article and the reprint also include reproductions of medieval illuminations of laboring peasants taken from the Luttrell Psalter, a source heavily mined for peasant images by designers of textbooks and book covers in medieval social history. In a study of the ideology of the Luttrell Psalter, Michael Camille has shown how problematic the unexamined use of such images as simple representations of peasants can be: "we can see that our ploughman is no more 'real' than his modern brother in a Soviet revolutionary poster."[8] Both

---

[7]For a concise introduction to the textual tradition of the Robin Hood ballads see Dobson and Taylor, *Rymes*; Joseph Ritson, *Robin Hood: A Collection of All the Ancient Poems, Songs and Ballads, Now Extant, Relative to That Celebrated Outlaw*, 2 vols. (London, 1795). Ritson made available reliable texts of the major works of the Robin Hood canon. Dobson and Taylor claim that the collection "remains an indispensable handbook to the outlaw legend even today" (p. 54).

[8]Camille recovers the complex manuscript tradition and social context of these "disembodied" peasant illustrations in "Labouring for the Lord: The Ploughman and the Social Order in the Luttrell Psalter," *Art History* 10/4 (1987): 423–54, citation from p. 448. The 1991 *History Today* article thus plays on these contradictions. The captions precisely attribute the source and date of the Robin Hood illustrations for the early modern and modern periods. The captions of the medieval illustrations in the 1991 reprint show a contrast to this precision. They cast doubt on the medieval depictions (the caption under the illumination from the

versions of the article also include an illustration from a Flemish manuscript of Froissart's *Chronicles* showing the beheading of the archbishop of Canterbury during the Peasants' Revolt (1381). The Flemish illuminators have drawn Wat Tyler's men as helmeted, partly armored, beswordeded footmen, more reminiscent of an urban militia than a peasant company. The medieval images of peasants, examples of highly problematic and ambivalent representations by dominant classes, further make ironic the romantic desires of historians who wish to use these images as a template for their own myths of Robin Hood.

Readers could conclude, on the basis of this editorial relationship of text and image in the 1991 reprint, that historical readers of Robin Hood never received visual cues that would enable them to read this legendary figure as a "peasant." What the 1991 version does not address with its artful rearrangement and recaptioning of illustrations is the strong desire of British historians in the 1950s and early 1960s, who wrote at great length about Robin Hood, to do just that, to read him as a peasant hero. The desire of these English historians writing in the wake of World War II and decolonization, especially the imperial loss of the Raj, marks a desire, I argue, for the pastoral. Where there is desire, there is loss. The loss of a rural past, a past not located in England but in India, an imaginary past that decolonization amputated from the historiographic unconscious of English academic history, produced such desire. To understand the desire of these medieval historians for a peasant hero in the 1950s, we need to understand better the history of the loss a rural past experienced in the loss of the Raj.

Luttrell Psalter reads "downtrodden peasant?"), and attributions of date and source available in the 1958 version are inexplicably left out from some of the captions to the medieval pictures in the reprint.

Medieval English Peasants and the Historiographical Order. It is perhaps not too much to claim that the medieval English peasant village was invented in imperial India.[9] We know the broad outlines of the story. To write a progressive history of national freedom, English scholars appropriated German scholarship on the Teutonic village community as a guide for imagining Saxon villages as the workshop for the English parliamentary system. British scholars in the India Service, who grappled with framing tenurial policies for Indian village communities, then extended the concept of the Teutonic village community to the *Aryan* community. Publications such as *Village Communities in the East and West* (1871) by Sir Henry Maine, a classicist, jurist, and Legal Member of the Viceroy's Council in India (1862–69), helped to produce India as the rural past of England and England as the constitutional future of its colony. In a paradoxical way the medieval English village was invented by the India Service. Back in industrializing England, unencumbered as it was by contemporary survivals of peasant villages, this imperially-informed notion of the village community and its peasants could lend itself as a Romantic emblem attractive to both liberal and conservatives in parliamentary debates over colonial land settlements in the mid-nineteenth century.

---

[9]For a historical perspective on the disciplinary formation of problems of English medieval peasants and their village communities see Clive Dewey, "Images of the Village Community: A Study in Anglo-Indian Ideology," *Modern Asian Studies* 6/3 (1972): 291–328; J. W. Burrow, " 'The Village Community' and the Uses of History in Late Nineteenth-Century England," in Neil McKendrick, ed., *Historical Perspectives: Studies in English Thought and Society in Honour of J. H. Plumb* (London, 1974), pp. 255–84; Peter Gatrell, "Historians and Peasants: Studies of Medieval English Society in Russian Context," *Past and Present* 96 (1982): 22–50; Kathleen Biddick, "Decolonizing the English Past: Readings in Medieval Archaeology and History," *Journal of British Studies* (Jan. 1993). For an excellent study of the invention of the canon of English studies and its relation to imperialism, a study that has served as an inspiration for my own analysis, see Gauri Viswanathan, *Masks of Conquest: Literary Study and British Rule in India* (New York, 1989).

The romantic aura of the village community began to fade, however, as English politicians and scholars attempted to reconcile theories of private property, a symbol of English freedom, with common and joint property relations purported to be the ancient custom of village community. Scholars dealt with such contradictions between property and commons in different ways. Some scholars disengaged the romantic notion of the village community from politically charged debates over property relations by claiming that collective property was a recent aberration forged in villages as a response to taxation and conscription. Frederick W. Maitland argued elegantly for a hybrid solution. He claimed that communal rights on the commons were based on individual shares in the arable. His colleague the Russian émigré Paul Vinogradoff used the family holding as a wedge between individual and community. Indivisible units of arable land constituted family holdings in the village: "Everything goes by heredity and settled rules of family property."[10]

Emphasis on the individual and the family went a long way toward short-circuiting the commons of the village community as a concept easily appropriated by radical critique in England at the end of the nineteenth century. Unmoored from ongoing political debate by the close of the nineteenth century, discussion of the village community subsequently devolved upon historians, anthropologists, and sociologists in the twentieth century. Study of peasant life flourished at the University of Birmingham, which became a haven for Marxist-inspired history after World War II. The founding of the journal *Past and*

---

[10]H. S. Maine, *Village Communities in the East and West: Six Lectures Delivered at Oxford* (London, 1871); Maitland, *Domesday Book and Beyond: Three Essays in the Early History of England* (Cambridge, 1907); Vinogradoff, *Villainage in England: Essays in English Mediaeval History* (Oxford, 1892), p. 403. Dewey, "Images" brilliantly works through the politics of these shifting positions on village community and property.

Present, a sign of post-war scholarly vitality and Marxist intellectual activity, became a showcase for social history.[11] Important works appearing just after the war, such as Rodney Hilton's *The Economic Development of Some Leicestershire Estates* (Oxford, 1947), announced an integrated interest in issues of lordship, economy, and peasant cultivators. The pioneering work in medieval peasant archaeology that began at the deserted medieval village site of Wharram Percy in 1952 also inspired great interest in peasant life.[12] The next two decades saw the florescence of systematic family and village reconstruction by Ambrose Raftis and his students.[13] Robin Hood became a charged emblem of this historiography as his historical reality and class identity became the subject of a series of articles published in *Past and Present* in the late 1950s and beyond.

---

[11]The first issue appeared in Feb. 1952. The editor subtitled the journal "a journal of scientific inquiry." In the editorial introduction to the new journal (pp. i–iv), Polybius is cited: "but we share the belief of Polybius in the value of history for the present, and in particular for his conception of historical discipline as an instrument enabling us 'to face coming events with confidence'." The first editor and assistant editor were John Morris and E. J. Hobsbawm. For subsequent reflections on the early years of *Past and Present* see Christopher Hill, R. H. Hilton, and E. J. Hobsbawm, "*Past and Present*: Origins and Early Years," *Past and Present* 100 (Aug. 1983): 3–13.

[12]Maurice Beresford and John G. Hurst, pioneers of medieval English village archaeology, struck up their interdisciplinary partnership at excavations at Wharram Percy, Yorks., in 1952 and in that same year founded the Deserted Medieval Village Research Group. Enthusiasm for the Wharram Percy project provided an important impetus for founding the Society for Medieval Archaeology, the first professional group for medieval archaeology in Europe. The society's journal, *Medieval Archaeology*, also a pioneering effort, published its first issue in 1957. A survey and gazetteer of village work appear in *Deserted Medieval Villages: Studies* (London, 1971), ed. Beresford and Hurst.

[13]J. A. Raftis, *Tenure and Mobility: Studies in the Social History of the Mediaeval English Village* (Toronto, 1964); idem, *Warboys: Two Hundred Years in the Life of an English Village* (Toronto, 1974); Edwin B. DeWindt, *Land and People in Holywell-cum-Needingworth: Structures of Tenure and Patterns of Social Organization in an East Midlands Village, 1252–1457* (Toronto, 1972).

The loss of the Raj cut English culture off from one of the peasant pasts it had imagined for itself. Medieval English peasant studies once again but for different reasons became, as it had been in the mid-nineteenth century, a contested cultural site. English historians and those colonial subjects trained in its historiographic practices labored to recover the medieval English village and in so doing to work out the problems of continuity and change in post-imperial public culture. These labors bore directly on a work of public culture to mourn the loss of empire, to refigure the imperial site at which nineteenth-century peasant history was produced. The historiography that emerged in the post-war period provides historians with an opportunity for a specific understanding of what Michel de Certeau has described more generally:

> to take seriously the site of historiography is still not tantamount to expounding history. Nothing of what is produced in it is yet said about it. But taking the place seriously is the condition that allows something to be stated that is neither legendary (or "edifying") nor atopical (lacking relevance). Denial of the specificity of the place being the very principle of ideology, all theory is excluded. Even more, by moving discourse into a non-place, ideology forbids history from speaking of society and of death—in other words, from being history.[14]

This intersection of peasant history with the recasting of issues of continuity and change in post-imperial English historiography is vividly epitomized in the introduction to *The Midland Peasant* by W. G. Hoskins.[15] There he describes spending an April afternoon in the mid-1950s in the bottom of a newly dug grave in the modern cemetery of Wigston, Leicestershire. This cemetery lies over a large Anglo-Saxon burial ground: "on emerging from the grave into the bright sunshine once more, I

---

[14]*The Writing of History*, trans. Tom Conley (New York, 1988), p. 69.

[15]*The Midland Peasant: The Economic and Social History of a Leicestershire Village* (London, 1957).

saw all around the visible evidence of the continuity of life in this community whose history I was trying to unravel" (p. xix). After an elegiac-like description of this continuity, Hoskins changes tone: "in spite, however, of the apparent continuity of life in this village, which is reflected in a multitude of ways wherever one walks in the streets or fields, there has in fact been an almost complete break with the past" (p. xxxi). I would argue that we students of peasant studies need to think more carefully of how this elegiac trope of continuity and change characteristic of peasant history of the immediate post-war period can also be read as a trope for the cultural problems of managing continuity and change in post-imperial, cold-war England. The staging of Robin Hood in popular culture straddles this historiography and contemporary contests.

It is interesting to note that television also interrupted the historical study of Robin Hood in the 1950s. In the mid-1950s the BBC began to air the first of over 150 half-hour programs on the adventures of Robin Hood. Mordechai Richler has described how Hollywood exiles from McCarthyism then resident in England wrote scripts and helped to produce the television series. At the same time, Warner Bros. sold its 1938 swashbuckler *The Adventures of Robin Hood* to British television. This film, which had been one of the most popular films to be screened among the armed forces during the war, now had its popularity promoted again through television broadcasts. It is tempting to relate the marked interest of English historians in Robin Hood in the 1950s not only to their political commitments to social history, to the unconscious project of restoring the pastoral that inspired this social history, but also to the popularity of the Robin Hood television series and recirculation of *The Adventures of Robin Hood*.[16]

---

[16]For an excellent introduction to the film history of Robin Hood, as well as the screenplay of the 1938 Warner Bros. film, see Rudy Behlmer, ed., *The Adventures*

Robin Hood returned to popular and academic history in the 1950s and figured in the unconscious historiographical project of reconstructing the rural village, now lost with the loss of the Raj, in realistic detail on English soil. Historians read Robin Hood as a peasant as part of a post-imperial project of re-imagining rurality in Britain—a project that has provided us with painstakingly constructed histories of medieval villages and their inhabitants. Debates over change and tradition, once figured as the difference between imperial metropolitan development (England) and traditional economies (India), could now be refigured as the difference within English peasant communities.[17] In such refiguration, the nineteenth-century terms of peasant historiography have embedded the study of peasants and village communities in essentialisms. Essentialist concepts of the peasantry focus on socioeconomic forms of landholding organized around family labor. These concepts have become a shell that encapsulates and homogenizes heterogeneous histories of gender, work, social and economic hybridity to which much contemporary research has pointed.[18] Such fossilization has

---

of Robin Hood (Madison, 1979); information about the film's popularity among the armed forces, p. 38. The 1991 Robin Hood was produced by Morgan Creek Productions, Hollywood, distributed by Warner Bros. I am planning a study of the BBC television series for a longer study of the medieval and the pastoral in post-war popular culture.

[17]The debate over the Toronto School is in need of deconstruction for its implicit working notions of peasant essentialism on both sides. For statement of the debate see Zvi Razi, "The Toronto School's Reconstitution of Medieval Peasant Society: A Critical View," *Past and Present* 85 (1979): 141–57; Judith M. Bennett has made clear how unexamined aspects of peasant essentialism left out the analysis of gender in "Medieval Peasant Marriage: An Examination of Marriage License Fines in the *Liber Gersumarum*," in J. A. Raftis, ed., *Pathways to Medieval Peasants* (Toronto, 1981), and her book *Women in the Medieval English Countryside: Gender and Household in Brigstock before the Plague* (New York, 1987); see also Gyan Prakash, "Postcolonial Criticism and Indian Historiography," *Social Text* 31/32 (1992): 8–19.

[18]For a critical review of the heterogeneity of medieval English regional economies see Kathleen A. Biddick, "Malthus in a Straitjacket? Analyzing Agrarian Change

also short-circuited heterogeneous spatial histories and reduced them to dichotomies of rural/urban, arable/pastoral, local/regional. This kind of encapsulation and containment of peasant histories has succeeded in representing peasants and villages as natural and organically linked, such that they must persist or disappear together. Such essentialism necessarily precludes analysis of its own founding categories as well as critical study of the political and ideological effects of retaining such categories among both radical and conservative scholars.[19]

Hollywood / Sherwood. In the space between the invention of the medieval village in the nineteenth century and its re-invention in post-war historiography lies another site of historical production—Hollywood. Could English historians so busy at work in the 1950s on the Robin Hood legend have learned anything from one of the defining popular versions of this legend, produced by Warner Bros. in 1938—*The Adventures of Robin Hood*? To answer this question, I would like to begin with a cartoon that for me depicts some of the historical tensions with which I wish to deal in this section of the essay. The cartoon appeared

in Medieval England," *Journal of Interdisciplinary History* 20/4 (1990): 623–35; and more recently Bruce M. S. Campbell, James A. Galloway, Derek Keene, and Margaret Murphy, *A Medieval Capital and Its Grain Supply: Agrarian Production and Distribution in the London Region c.1300*, Historical Geography Research Ser., no. 30 (London, 1993).

[19]Louise Olga Fradenburg incisively critiques such essentialism from an urban perspective in her brilliant study *City, Marriage, Tournament: Arts of Rule in Late Medieval Scotland* (Madison, Wisc., 1991): "if the city functions as an ontological problem in historical narrative, then we need to understand why this is so" (p. 8). For studies bearing on the problem of essentialist concepts of the peasantry from diverse historiographic perspectives see: Tom Brass, "Peasant Essentialism and the Agrarian Question in the Columbian Andes," *Journal of Peasant Studies* 17/3 (1990): 444–56; Biddick, "Decolonizing the English Past"; Gyan Prakash, "Can the Subaltern Ride? A Reply to O'Hanlon and Washbrook," *Comparative Studies in Society and History* 34/1 (1992): 168–84; T. V. Sathyamurthy, "Indian Peasant Historiography: A Critical Perspective on Ranajit Guha's Work," *Journal of Peasant Studies* 18 (Oct. 1991): 90–144.

in the London *Times* (6 July 1991), just as *Robin Hood: Prince of Thieves* opened in London cinemas. The cartoonist used the well-known Hollywood logo, transposed as SHERWOOD, to make the connection between Holly*wood* and Sher*wood* and inspired the reader to pause and ask, in what space does public culture invent the dream of pastoral in the twentieth century, and how has that space changed in the half-century elapsed between the distribution of *The Adventures of Robin Hood* and *Robin Hood: Prince of Thieves*?[20]

The return of Robin Hood in technicolor in 1938 historically frames the post-war historiography of Robin Hood and it also frames the most recent cinematic version of the legend, *Robin Hood: Prince of Thieves* distributed by Warner Bros. in 1991. Warner Bros. filmed the 1938 Robin Hood in Bidwell Park, located some 350 miles north of Los Angeles. For the 1991 Robin Hood, Morgan Creek (the production company) went to England and France for filming. It shot at Shepperton Studios and used New Forest in Hampshire and Burnham Beeches in Berkshire for Sherwood scenes and the walls of Carcassone in southern France for exterior shots of the town of Nottingham. Sherwood came to Hollywood in 1938; Hollywood used the countryside of England as its Sherwood in 1991.[21] Ironically,

---

[20]For the undesirability of closely defining the pastoral as a generic category see Patterson, *Pastoral and Ideology*: "It is not what pastoral *is* that should matter to us. On that, agreement is impossible, and its discussion inevitably leads to the narrowing strictures of normative criticism, statements of what constitutes the 'genuine' or the 'true' to the exclusion of exemplars that the critics regard as 'perverse.' What can be described and, at least in terms of coverage, with some neutrality, is what pastoral since Virgil can do and has always done; or rather, to put the agency back where it belongs—how writers, artists, and intellectuals have *used* the pastoral for a range of functions and intentions that the *Eclogues* first articulated" (p. 7). The pastoral props up cultural authentication of the state, intellectuals, and other powerful privileged groups in society by appeal to "nature," in the shade of the greenwood tree.

[21]Behlmer, *The Adventures*; John Calhoun, "*Robin Hood: Prince of Thieves*: Designing a Postmodern Middle Ages," *Theatre Crafts* 25 (Aug./Sept. 1991): 48–53; 86–87.

the village sets erected at Shepperton Studios for *Robin Hood: Prince of Thieves* have now been moved to Sherwood Forest, to help to develop green tourism in the county.[22] Both films locate the legend by means of an appeal to history. In representing history, each re-presents the pastoral. A study that locates itself at the gap between history and the pastoral can help to explore the unconscious of peasant historiography. The remembering and forgetting between film and historiography occur in this gap in the Robin Hood films.

History as Logo. To "seal," as it were, its 1938 Robin Hood film as a historical instrument, a kind of visual charter, Warner Bros. designed a special logo. The characteristic graphic "WB" was drawn with metallic solidity, so that it looked like the visor of a knight's helmet. Heraldic-like devices curl out of this graphic. The logo announces the reign of Warner Bros. over a chivalric past. The title, *The Adventures of Robin Hood*, handwritten in an imitation "Gothic" script, is set within quotation marks. The punctuation refers the reader to the authority of a prior text. Then follow two texts written in the same Gothic script. They inform viewers of the historic setting of the adventure they are about to watch. A model of history as document prevails.

The politics of establishing the historical setting are of interest. The two brief introductory texts never mention the country of England or the English. They focus only on King Richard the Lion-Heart, his regent, Longchamp, his brother King John, and Norman barons and Saxons. The nation is carefully occluded and the moral and immoral individuals as perceived through ethnic identity receive foregrounding. The

---

[22]A report heard on NPR, Sunday, 6 Sept. 1992.

film relies on the old myth of the "Norman Yoke," which featured prominently in nineteenth-century romantic medievalism and in peasant historiographical debates. The mobilization of the myth by Warner Bros. in the late 1930s may be read as a gesture of anglophilic alliance as the threat of fascism grew in Europe. Warner Bros. pursued an antifascist stance, and as it finished work on the *The Adventures of Robin Hood* it began production of *Confessions of a Nazi Spy* (1939), for which, and among other things, it was called to Washington in 1941 by isolationist factions to answer for "moving picture propaganda."[23]

The first scene after the titles brings the viewer to a public space, the town square of Nottingham, where a cryer announces the news of Richard's capture near Vienna. The constitutional problems of the plot are then developed in ensuing scenes that introduce King John (Claude Rains) and Sir Guy of Guisborne (Basil Rathbone). It is not until they reveal their plots against Richard that the camera shifts to shots of local town life in Nottingham, where John's tax-collectors oppress the townspeople. Only after the camera has set up state and urban spaces does the scene move to Sherwood Forest.

In Sherwood Forest the film constructs its emblem of the pastoral by framing and holding a shot of a solitary deer feeding in a glade. Only after Much-the-Miller's Son (Herbert Mundin) shoots the deer and is caught by the retinue of Guy of

---

[23]For some transcripts of a statement by Harry M. Warner, president of Warner Bros., before a hearing of a subcommittee of the committee on interstate commerce of the US Senate regarding moving picture propaganda (25 Sept. 1941), see Rudy Behlmer, ed., *Inside Warner Bros. (1935–1941)* (New York, 1985), pp. 188–91. For other works on the studio upon which this essay relies see Douglas Gomery, *The Hollywood Studio System* (New York, 1986); Nick Roddick, *A New Deal in Entertainment: Warner Brothers in the 1930s* (London, 1983); Thomas Schatz, *The Genius of the System: Hollywood Film-making in the Studio Era* (New York, 1988). An excellent discussion of the myth of the Norman Yoke appears in Christopher Hill, "The Norman Yoke," in his *Puritanism and Revolution: Studies in the Interpretation of the English Revolution of the 17th Century* (London, 1958), pp. 50–122.

Guisborne does the viewer finally see Robin Hood (Errol Flynn) and his companion, Will Scarlet (Patric Knowles), at the border of Sherwood Forest. The film thus travels through a space of history established by the opening authorizing texts, through "state" and "urban" spaces. It then cuts to the forest as a place of passage between urban centers, Nottingham and London. The pastoral then punctuates the film with the frame of the lone deer in the glade. The character of Robin Hood is first introduced to the viewer on the edge of the forest, as a border figure in between these heterogeneous spaces.

When Robin Hood rides into the forest and encounters the scene between Much-the-Miller's Son and Guy of Guisborne, he claims to have killed the deer himself. He later brings that slain deer to the banquet of barons at Nottingham Castle. In a celebrated scene he crosses the threshold of the banquet hall with the dead buck draped around his shoulders. He flings the carcass onto the table before King John, and in so doing he challenges the space of illegitimate state (the plot has already carefully constructed John as a traitor) with the sign of the pastoral. The staging of this famous scene was only finalized days before shooting began in late September 1937. The earlier version of the script had Robin riding into the banquet hall with a dead peasant slung across his saddle.[24] The substitution of the deer, the sign of the pastoral, for a peasant, the sign of historical material relations, is an interesting one that suggests the need for an allegorical reading of this pastoral space imagined by Hollywood in the late 1930s. I would like to argue that the vacillation about how to stage this scene can help us to understand a crisis of the pastoral and a crisis of history to which the film gestures. To understand this crisis we

---

[24]Behlmer, *The Adventures*, p. 26.

need to ask what is haunting this scene. To answer, I think, we need to turn to the question of dead animals, the totemic, in popular culture of the late 1930s.

The deer can be read as a totem, an object that stands in for the death of the pastoral. But how can an imaginative space be slain in a culture, cease to be constructed as an active site where on-going struggles about authority and identity can be staged, not simply repeated nostalgically? We can begin to find the answer in another totem seen in newsreels and popular picture magazines, such as *Life*, during the 1930s. The dead creature of the newsreels and photo-essays is an eagle, the Imperial Eagle of the Nazis. Readers of *Life* magazine in the late 1930s, at the time that Warner Bros. put its Robin Hood film into production, could have seen the Imperial Eagle in the spreads like those on Hermann Goering, "heir apparent of Hitler," in the issue of 8 February 1937.[25] The stone image of this eagle had also served as the opening shot of *Triumph of the Will* in 1935, a film written and directed by Leni Riefenstahl, distribution of which was banned in the United States and several European countries.[26] This eagle, a sign of fascism, marks in its totemic deadness the achievement of the Nazis "to

---

[25]A survey of *Life* for its representations of Nazism in the late 1930s is illuminating. Noteworthy are the 1937 photo-essay on Goering; an essay on Austria "between Habsburg Kings and Nazi rulers" (22 Mar. 1937), and I note here that this essay appeared just short of one year before the Nazi invasion of Austria; an essay on what American tourists think of Germany and Italy (13 Sept. 1937); Mussolini visits Hitler in Berlin (18 Oct. 1937)—a photo-essay that appeared as Warner Bros. shot *The Adventures of Robin Hood*. Most important, *Life* featured *The Adventures of Robin Hood* as its weekly film in its issue of 23 May 1938; Errol Flynn made the cover as a "glamor boy" at the same time *Life* covered the visit of Hitler to Rome on May Day.

[26]For an interesting insight into reception of *Triumph of the Will* in the USA see the account of Frank Capra, who saw the film as he began work for the US government at the opening of World War II, to prepare for his *Why We Fight* films (Capra, *The Name above the Title: An Autobiography* [New York, 1971], pp. 328–32).

organize the resurrection of dead life in the masses."[27]

The Depression and the rise of Nazism and Fascism in Europe bracket the making of *The Adventures of Robin Hood*.[28] Warner Bros. was not immune from either. It struggled to keep its studios open at a time when many of its competitors declared bankruptcy.[29] In 1935 a Warner Bros. agent in Berlin, Joseph Kaufmann, a Jew, was beaten to death by a Nazi mob. The uncanny frame of Nazism is perhaps most strongly marked in the *Life* promotional of *The Adventures of Robin Hood* in its issue of 23 May 1938. The magazine featured Errol Flynn, "Glamor Boy," on its cover and celebrated his physical and sexual prowess in a photographic essay. The same magazine also featured stills and text on its film of the week, *The Adventures of Robin Hood*, which had just opened in movie theaters. In the same issue *Life* included a photo-essay, "Two Little Men in Rome: Mussolini Shows Off for Hitler," which covered May Day celebrations in Rome attended by the two dictators. They are shot at a distance, unlike the close work of the camera on Errol Flynn's body. The magazine actually cites the height of the two dictators, as if to contrast them to the tall Hollywood hero celebrated in the same issue. I have concentrated on the unconscious and threatening intersections of the threat of Nazism in *The Adventures of Robin Hood*, because Nazism itself can be viewed as a state form of the pastoral that imploded into the pastoral to authenticate itself.

---

[27]For critical discussion of *Triumph of the Will* see Klaus Theweleit, *Male Fantasies*, 2: *Male Bodies, Psychoanalyzing the White Terror* (Minneapolis, 1989), pp. 408–16, and his comments on dead life and resurrection in fascism, p. 189; Brian Winston, "Reconsidering *Triumph of the Will*: Was Hitler Really There?" *Sight and Sound* 30/2 (1980–81): 102–07.

[28]For the New Deal politics of Warner Bros. see Ina Rae Hark, "The Visual Politics of *The Adventures of Robin Hood*," *Journal of Popular Film* 5/1 (1976): 3–17.

[29]See Gomery, *Hollywood Studio System*, for discussion of comparative Depression finances of the big-five studios, p. 110.

Audiences in the United States still flocked to the movies during the Depression, as rural space transformed in America through large-scale public works projects and a migration of subsistence farmers from rural areas in a move that for many was to prove irreversible. The dead deer can be read as a sign of the historical brackets of the rural transformation by the Depression and the political transformation by fascism that frame the production of the film. Both transformations radically compromised, in different ways, the capacity of the pastoral to serve as a space or image to represent authentication. The effects of Nazism by the late 1930s (the fall of Vienna in March 1938 and the confiscation of his property by the Nazis supposedly forced the reluctant Austrian composer Erich Wolfgang Korngold to write the award-winning music for *The Adventures of Robin Hood*), and a few years later in the Holocaust, would profoundly challenge history itself and radically taint the pastoral as a Euro-American space of authentication.[30]

History as Palimpsest. When Robin Hood returns again in *Robin Hood: Prince of Thieves* the viewer encounters a different model of history framing the film. The 1991 version does not rely on a "document" but on a historical artifact of another sort, a tapestry (Bayeux Tapestry, eleventh century) that reads like a comic book. The camera tracks horizontally over segments of the tapestry as the credits roll vertically over the embroidered scenes.[31] Occasionally the camera emphasizes a detail of the tapestry, such as a horse and rider, with a kind of stereoscopic close-up. The techniques anticipate for the viewer the camera

---

[30]Extracts from the Korngold correspondence may be found in Behlmer, *Inside Warner Bros.*, pp. 52–53.

[31]See Shirley Ann Brown, *The Bayeux Tapestry: History and Bibliography* (Woodbridge, Suff., 1988); bibliography on the tapestry 1729–1988.

work characteristic of the narrative sequences of the film. The titles and credits function like a palimpsest. The credits, written over the graphic and visual text of the tapestry, appear as running graffiti on the tapestry.

After the opening credits, the film informs the viewer of the details of the historical setting by means of a caption. Unlike the 1938 version, the lettering of the caption in *Robin Hood: Prince of Thieves* makes no appeal to some antiquarian pretense. In crisp, contemporary-looking white letters on a black background the caption states that 800 years ago Richard the Lion-Heart set out on the Third Crusade to claim the Holy Land from the Turks. We learn further that most of the young English nobles who flocked to the crusade never returned. In contrast to the 1938 film, this latter *Robin Hood* constructs a historical context that foregrounds things "English" and focuses on the young nobility rather than constitutional crises occurring in the absence of the monarch. The film producers make no claim to reign over history as did Warners in 1938, nor do the opening credits and introductory captions aim at any kind of historical verisimilitude. History is already fractured. Ironically, when choosing the Bayeux Tapestry for the background of the opening credits, the producers chose a visual narrative of the conquest of England by the Normans. The choice of the tapestry figures, perhaps unconsciously, what might be construed as a cinematic conquest of the English countryside in 1991 by Hollywood. The opening appeal to history thus inverts, ironically, the myth of the Norman Yoke invoked for anglophilic identification in the *The Adventures of Robin Hood.*

No obvious, emblematic scene of the pastoral akin to the lone deer standing in the glade in the 1938 version is as apparent in the 1991 film. The latter film constructs a very different spatial trajectory. The opening scene locates the viewer in what is usually the "unrepresentable," or the "elsewhere" of the Robin Hood legend—the crusade in the East. After the space of historical graffiti the film cuts to an aerial view of Jerusalem and cuts again to a "Moorish" prison in which English crusaders are being held captive. This strong "eastern" frame signals that the film will attempt to grapple with orientalism, the co-construction of fantastic notions of the East and West.[32] As my argument unfolds in this section, I will show how the "orientalism" of the Persian Gulf War, a war being waged as the film was in production, interrupts the film in various ways. The central issue of the film, established in its first efforts to represent what is usually unrepresented in the legend, returns to the crisis staged by the totem of the dead deer in 1938, the crisis of producing a sign for the pastoral in a post-pastoral world.

The first clues to the construction of an orientalism in this film, an orientalism linked to contemporary politics at the time of its shooting in England, come with depictions of "bad" Moorish prison guards and the "good" Moorish prisoner, Azeem (Morgan Freeman), whose life Robin (Kevin Costner) saves. The film's representation of the East is, significantly, interrupted by a return to the "West," when the scene shifts from Jerusalem to Locksley Castle, England, where the lord of the castle, Robin's father (Brian Blessed), writes a letter to inquire about his crusader son's welfare.

---

[32]This is not the place to discuss the epistemological and ontological challenges of a post-orientalist history. For selected references that set out, revise, and criticize the pioneering work of Edward W. Said see: Said, "Representing the Colonized: Anthropology's Interlocutors," *Critical Inquiry* 15 (Winter 1989): 205–25; James Clifford, "On *Orientalism*," in idem, *The Predicament of Culture: Twentieth-Century Ethnography, Literature, and Art* (Cambridge, Mass., 1988), pp. 255–76; Timothy Mitchell, *Colonising Egypt* (Cambridge, 1988); Robert Young, *White Mythologies: Writing History and the West* (New York, 1990); Gyan Prakash, "Writing Post-Orientalist Histories of the Third World: Perspectives from Indian Historiography," *Comparative Studies in Society and History* 32/2 (1990): 383–408.

The film is very slow to construct the space of the forest and the way in which it finally does suggests a real change in the representation of the pastoral between the 1938 and the 1991 versions. At first the viewer sees no forest and no acts of poaching. The first reference to the forest occurs when Robin and Azeem (now returned to England) encounter men of the sheriff of Nottingham on Locksley land hunting human quarry—a young boy, Wulf (Daniel Newman)—for poaching deer in the forest. Robin does not enter the forest himself until he, too, is pursued by the sheriff's men. Once the camera finally brings the viewer into the forest, it is a forest strangely devoid of animal life. Any sign of the pastoral is absent. The audience never sees one live deer in *Robin Hood: Prince of Thieves*, nor does it ever see Robin Hood feasting on forest game, a carnival feature of the pastoral that the 1938 version delighted in staging.[33] The only visual reference to game appears for a moment at the edge of one of the frames, where an attentive viewer can catch a glimpse of skinned deer carcasses suspended from the wagon of Friar Tuck (Michael McShane). The sign of the pastoral has changed from a sublime shot of a buck grazing alone in a forest glade, which animal is then shot and brought into the urban and state space of the castle at Nottingham, to a fleeting glimpse of carcasses of dead skinned deer suspended at the edge of one of the frames.[34] Should we interpret this split-

[33]For a discussion of carnival and the Robin Hood legend see Peter Stallybrass, " 'Drunk with the Cup of Liberty': Robin Hood, the Carnivalesque, and the Rhetoric of Violence in Early Modern England," in Nancy Armstrong and Leonard Tennenhouse, eds., *The Violence of Representation: Literature and the History of Violence* (New York, 1989), pp. 45–76.

[34]To think of this "sublime" shot of the deer, it is helpful to recall the words of Edmund Burke: "I know nothing sublime, which is not some modification of power," in his *A Philosophical Enquiry into the Origin of Our Ideas of the Sublime and Beautiful*, ed. Adam Phillips (New York, 1990), p. 59. For the intersection of Burke with the intimacy of colonial terror see Sara Sulen, *The Rhetoric of English India* (Chicago, 1992), pp. 24–48.

second glimpse of deer carcasses as the sign of the pastoral, or rather do these abject, almost-unrepresentable carcasses offer a clue that the film has relocated the pastoral and we must look elsewhere in the film for its sign?

I argue that *Robin Hood: Prince of Thieves* locates the sign of the pastoral not in a deer or its totem but divides it across two bodies, the richly robed body of Azeem, the black-skinned, tattooed Moor who accompanies Robin Hood back from the crusade, and the naked body of Robin Hood, whom viewers see with Lady Marian (Mary Elizabeth Mastrantonio) as he bathes in a forest glade. Through the character of the "other," Azeem, who conducts a running commentary of "truth" on English society, the film constructs a "concessionary narrative" for itself, meaning a narrative that "goes some way towards recognizing a native point of view and offering a critique of European behavior, but can only do this by not addressing the central issue."[35] If we think of the pastoral as a place of the "primitive" within Europe constructed in relation to the "primitive" that Europe constructed elsewhere through its anthropology and ethnography, then it seems fitting (according to a neocolonial logic) that the native informant return and give life to a deeply endangered pastoral within England.[36] The return of

---

[35]For discussions of concessionary narratives and their function in colonial literature see Mary Louise Pratt, *Imperial Eyes: Travel Writing and Transculturation* (New York, 1992), p. 100. Pratt takes her inspiration from Peter Hulme, *Colonial Encounters: Europe and the Native Caribbean 1492–1797* (London, 1986).

[36]The following references offer evocative but by no means exhaustive examples of a history of the European construction of the primitive and some neocolonial efforts to relocate the primitive in idealizing and essentializing use of voices from former colonized societies: *Representations* 37 (Winter 1992), special issue on Imperial Fantasies and Postcolonial Histories; Said, "Representing the Colonized," pp. 205–25; Michael T. Taussig, *Shamanism, Colonialism, and the Wild Man: A Study in Terror and Healing* (Chicago, 1987); Clifford, *Predicament of Culture*; Anna Maria Alonso, "The Effects of Truth: Re-presentation of the Past and the Imagining of Community," *Journal of Historical Sociology* 1/1 (1988): 33–57; see

the "other" to England enables the rebirth of the pastoral space signified in the naked body of Robin Hood. The film highlights the fact that rebirth of the pastoral is at stake by staging an obstetrical crisis. Fanny (Soo Druet), wife of Little John (Nick Brimble), encounters grave difficulty in giving birth in the forest camp. Azeem, significantly, saves her and the infant by using "ethnographic" knowledge gained from birthing mares to deliver their infant son.

The viewer can read the intersection of the concessionary narrative of Azeem with the rebirth of the pastoral at the naked body of Robin Hood through the historical events of the Persian Gulf War that bracketed production of the film. The shooting of *Robin Hood: Prince of Thieves* began in England in early September 1990, approximately one month after the invasion of Kuwait by Iraq and the arrival of the first United States ground forces in the Middle East, on 8 August 1990. The film was released in the United States on 14 June 1991, just a few months after the so-called victory of Desert Storm. Thus the shooting and editing of the film spanned this war in which Britain joined the United States as part of the Desert Storm alliance.

The military images of the Gulf War invaded the film. The war has been described as the first cybernetic war, a "vision war" replete with digitized photography, infra-red and radar imaging. These cybernetic images "promote a new high-tech version of Orientalism, dehumanising the Arab population, who

also *Inscriptions*, the journal published by the Group for the Critical Study of Colonial Discourse, Univ. of California, Santa Cruz, vol. 1 (Dec. 1985)—to the current time, esp. 3 and 4, devoted to Feminism and the Critique of Colonial Discourse; Young, *White Mythologies*; the books of Michel de Certeau: *The Practice of Everyday Life* (Berkeley, 1984); *Heterologies: Discourse on the Other* (Minneapolis, 1986); *The Writing of History*; and most recently Judith Butler and Biddy Martin, eds., *Critical Crossings*, a special issue of *Diacritics*, 24/2–3 (1994).

become 'collateral damage' deserving of destruction because they hide from the West's enlightened vision."[37] The missile-nose view of targets that became familiar to a television audience watching the trajectories of Scud missiles translated into the signature special-effect of *Robin Hood: Prince of Thieves*—arrow-nose views of "medieval" Scud-archery. The images of this Scud-archery appeared prominently in the promotional trailers for the film. The editors of the music-video, "Worth Dying For" (by Bryan Adams), over which the closing credits of the film roll, also used the "Scud" arrow scenes for special effects. Thus, audiences who did not actually get to see the film but watched the trailers and music-video shown on MTV got to see Robin Hood's cybernetic arrows.

Within the brackets of this cybernetic war the presence of Azeem in the film can be read in a variety of ways. He is the "good" ally, like Syria or Kuwait, who represents the best of orientalism. He can also enact nostalgically a proximity and embodiment that the video-image targets of cybernetic bombing uncannily distanced for the television viewers of the war. Others would read Azeem as the sign of new orientalism governed by a new imperialism that will pit "progressive" Arabs against Islamic fundamentalists. Within a larger technological frame cybernetics is a technology of simulation with no referent. It does not rely on any traditional, foundational notions of nature to use as a resource to authorize its images. As a technology it profoundly questions traditional Western notions of

---

[37]Les Levidow and Keving Robins, "Vision Wars," *Race and Class* 32/4 (1991). Related to reception of the Gulf War in Europe is also the 1992 inauguration of the united European Community structures. For an analysis of the relations of the "Arab nation" to the "European nation" see Etienne Balibar, "*Es Gibt Keinen Staat in Europa*: Racism and Politics in Europe Today," *New Left Review* 186 (Mar./Apr. 1991): 5–19: "the two complexes making up the 'Arab nation' and the 'European nation'—neither of them securely fixed, for different historical reasons—are closely bound up with the other and cannot evolve independently" (p. 9).

nature. Cybernetic technologies help to empty out the "pastoral," which relies on a vision of nature as its guarantee. It is not surprising, then, that within such a historical frame *Robin Hood: Prince of Thieves* very precariously stages the pastoral and relies on a very old anthropological move, the introduction of the Other, to guarantee this fragile imaginary space.

Lady Marian as Go-Between: Gender, Family, State. The 1938 film, as we have seen, foregrounds issues of the state. It opens with news of King Richard and focuses on the constitutional plots against him, and it closes by undoing these plots at a coronation scene. The restored King Richard (Ian Hunter) grants Lady Marian to Robin Hood in marriage, but the film does not displace the restoration of Richard with a wedding. In contrast, the 1991 version contains no reference to the state. The comically villainous sheriff of Nottingham (Alan Rickman) parodies the state. The viewer never sees the barons in assembly, nor does the film bother with any spectacular scenes of public feudal pageantry. It closes with the forest wedding of Robin Hood and Lady Marian. The 1991 film thus ends in the pastoral space, where the 1938 film ends in the space of the state and church, the medieval cathedral. The 1938 film with its New Deal politics brings the pastoral virtues of the good leader to the state. The pastoral becomes the state in the restoration of King Richard and Robin Hood. The 1991 film never brings the state to the pastoral, because there is no state. Even the intervention of Richard (Sean Connery) at the forest wedding, which has begun without him, occurs seemingly as an inter-textual afterthought (Connery having acted as Robin Hood in the film *Robin and Marian* [Columbia Pictures, 1976]). The state becomes located in the individual in the 1991 version but cannot continue or reproduce itself without the family.

The different location of the state in the two films can help us to understand the significance of gender and its use as a resource to construct the pastoral. Here the character of Lady Marian is crucial as the figure of the Robin Hood legend who moves back and forth among the spaces of the state, the town, and the forest.[38] The ways in which Marian negotiates these spaces can help us to understand the changing use of gender in constructing the pastoral. Historically, Lady Marian became attached to the Robin Hood legend as a transvestite carnival character of sixteenth-century May Games in England. Ironically, the transvestite nature of Lady Marian has been inverted in the twentieth century—Lady Marian dresses up like a man, sometimes. Her cross-dressing or lack of it becomes a sign of how the space of state, forest, and family will be negotiated.

Lady Marian twice tricks Robin Hood about her identity in *Robin Hood: Prince of Thieves*. First, her lady-in-waiting, Sarah (Imogen Bain), a Brünhilde-like character, claims to be Lady Marian. Robin Hood is then attacked at Lady Marian's castle by an armed knight; a swashbuckling swordfight ensues. It is only when Robin Hood holds the hand of his opponent over a candle that the knight speaks and the audience learns her gender. Robin Hood pulls off her visor to unmask Lady Marian. In contrast, the Lady Marian (Olivia de Havilland) of the 1938 version of Robin Hood does not cross-dress. Difference in the 1938 film is strongly defined as the difference between Saxon and Norman. The film constructs no family history for Robin; the viewer

---

[38]See Dobson and Taylor, *Rymes*, for a history of the association of Lady Marian with the Robin Hood legend. She is not part of the medieval tradition. Their joining occurred in Tudor May Day celebrations and morris dances: "Here Marian, played by a boy, developed into a by-word for sexual impropriety. . . . The consequent liason between Robin Hood and his Maid Marian gradually introduced a more romantically sexual element into the greenwood myth, an element completely absent in medieval tradition but absolutely essential for the later elaboration and survival of the legend" (p. 42). For cross-dressing, unruly women, and the carnival aspect of Lady Marian in the early modern period see Stallybrass, " 'Drunk with the Cup of Liberty'." In the film *Son of Robin Hood* (Twentieth-Century Fox, 1959), Robin Hood's son is really a daughter cross-dressed.

never encounters his father as the 1991 audience does, nor are there any tales of his mother. Ethnicity, not family history, counts in 1938. Sir Robin of Locksley is a Saxon; Lady Marian is Norman. As a Norman, she becomes part of the carnival feasting in Sherwood when the Norman party of the sheriff is waylaid by Robin Hood's men. In this sequence the men of Sherwood disrobe the sheriff of Nottingham and Sir Guy of Guisborne and in true carnival spirit make them wear their Saxon rags as the outlaws don the clothes and regalia of the Normans. There is no carnival exchange of clothes with Lady Marian (there are no women among the merry men), but she does participate in the carnival feast. Eventually persuaded of Robin's cause, Lady Marian begins to serve as a go-between between Sherwood and Nottingham, between Saxon freemen and the Norman court.

Robin Hood, in another crucial scene in the 1938 version, begs Marian to join him in Sherwood. She opts for the cause of the state over romantic love:

> You taught me then that England is bigger than just Normans and Saxons fighting, hating each other! It belongs to all of us, to live peacefully together . . . loyal only to Richard and England! . . . I could help more by watching for treachery here and leaving you free to protect Richard's people, till he returns. Now do you see why you have to go back to your men—alone?[39]

At its close the film parodies this alignment of personal relations on the state when Robin cries out after Richard has awarded him Lady Marian in marriage: "May I obey all your Majesty's commands with equal pleasure!"[40]

The definition of difference is cast not in terms of ethnicity but in terms of a family romance in 1991. As the plot of *Robin*

---

[39]Behlmer, *The Adventures*, p. 172.

[40]Behlmer, *The Adventures*, p. 212.

Hood: Prince of Thieves unfolds, viewers learn that when Robin was 12 years old his father, a widower, took up a peasant concubine. This story accounts for the unresolved quarrel between father and son. The film emplots Robin's fight against the sheriff of Nottingham as a family feud. Robin seeks revenge against the sheriff, who trumped up witchcraft charges against Robin's father, in order to have him killed and to confiscate his lands. Later it is also revealed that Will Scarlett (Christian Slater), a bitter rival of Robin Hood, is his bastard half-brother. The film makes no space for the state and instead constructs an elaborate family space that is divided between absent mothers (aristocratic and peasant) and their offspring, noble and bastard.

Within the family space, the film roots allegiance and action in individualism. In an important scene—which can be read as the counterpart to the scene in the 1938 film in which Robin invites Lady Marian to join him—Robin asks Marian to use her influence as ward of the king, to get word to Richard of the treachery against him. Marian replies: "I could lose all I have." Robin then asks her if she would do it for the king. She replies: "No, I will do it for you," a reply that echoes in the lyrics of the music-video distributed in conjunction with the film. The "state" as such no longer motivates action in 1991. Only romantic alliance does. Where does this leave gender?

We can try to answer this question by thinking again of the contemporary brackets of the film. All advanced states, American and European, as national-social states, rely on family policy (both by intervention and neglect) as the core of their state power. The ambiguities encountered by these states over the last five years, with events in Eastern Europe, the merging of the European community, the new cybernetic imperialism of the Persian Gulf War, render ambiguous family policy at the same time the state seeks to use family policy to defend itself against ambiguity. Within this context Marian's cross-dressing in *Robin Hood: Prince of Thieves* can be read in an interesting way. Her cross-dressing brings the ambiguities of family policy out of the closet. As the state collapses into family policy, women as the chief bearers of the policy become the state but in so doing blur the neat sexual divisions based on stereotypes of heterosexuality. This struggle is perhaps nowhere more acute than in the United States.

This allegory of the state and family policy can be read in the sequence of Lady Marian's dress in *Robin Hood: Prince of Thieves*. The viewer first encounters Marian cross-dressed. As the only living, responsible actor for the state in the absence of Richard, her kinsman, Marian is the state. Her mother is at court, but Marian has chosen to execute her aristocratic responsibilities alone on her landed properties around Nottingham, in spite of the abuses of its treacherous sheriff. As the embodiment of the absent state, Marian's encounter with Robin bathing naked in the forest pool is a crucial one for the pastoral. Her gaze at his naked body figures the alignment of the pastoral, in the body of Robin, with the state in the person of Marian.

The staging of carnival scenes in the 1991 film supports this strong reading. It will be recalled that the film never depicts Robin Hood and Lady Marian feasting together at this celebration; the carnival world of food with its suggestions of digestion and elimination are neatly absent. Instead, a birth becomes the central focus of the scene of merriment. Fanny, the wife of Little John, is in an agonizing labor. Friar Tuck and religion cannot help her. Finally Azeem feels her belly and offers to try to deliver the child. From his experience with birthing horses he knows how to turn the baby in the womb, to ease the breech birth. The "infidel" does this successfully, and there is great celebration for a baby boy. Robin and Marian both attend the birth, and Robin is the first to display the baby to his merry men.

Here the pastoral embraces not only Azeem but also the infant. The native informant and the family simultaneously occupy the space of the pastoral and restore good order. This space is not, however, invulnerable. It can be threatened by "minority" cultures within. The sheriff of Nottingham calls up the Celts at the command of the witch Mortianna (Geraldine McEwan): "Recruit the beasts that share our God." They invade the forest and attack, and it is only with great peril that Fanny and her newborn are saved in the attack. This scene is important because it also echoes contemporary problems within advanced states. Their family policy is always mobilized within forms of neoracism in which "biological" stereotypes pass into "cultural" stereotypes "corresponding to the search for 'little differences' between equally impoverished proletarians."[41]

The History of a Legend and the Legend of History. My reading of the staging and restaging of the Robin Hood legend by Hollywood in 1938 and 1991 has tried to trace a history of the cultural status of the pastoral. The 1938 film depicts the pastoral in a crisis that only the state can save, by subsuming the pastoral under the state. That is the happy ending of the film, but one belied by the dark days of Nazi history to follow, which already haunt the film in the prefigurement of the state imploding into the pastoral. By 1991 the pastoral has disappeared and so has the state from the Robin Hood legend. The film itself seeks to reconstruct the pastoral. The pastoral is located in the native informant, a Moor, who comes to England to revitalize this space by a commentary of truth. To guarantee the continuance of space, the native informant delivers an infant, restores

---

[41]Balibar, "*Es Gibt Keinen Staat*," p. 15.

the family. The film ends with a wedding in the forest, the film subsumes the family under the pastoral. This happy ending is also one that current events belie. Just as the state today in Europe is "neither national nor supranational," the family is no longer nuclear or private. The pastoral thus bears the burden of inscribing the family nostalgically in *Robin Hood: Prince of Thieves* as the last sign of life in the forest.[42]

I would now like to return to the passionate historiographic debates over the class identity of Robin Hood waged in the late 1950s and continuing today.[43] My reading of contemporary visual images of Robin Hood available in the movie theater and on television, produced as historians engaged in this debate, helps to put this historic debate in a broader cultural perspective. My reading asks of the historiography, to what extent is it also an aspect of the construction of the pastoral as an imaginary space in English public culture? As we have seen, the detailed reconstructions of peasant villages that began in earnest in the post-war, post-colonial period helped to reconnect public culture to an agrarian past that England had imaginatively located in India and then lost. Perhaps it is a historic irony that a country that experienced the earliest capitalist transformation of the countryside and pioneered enclosure has so assiduously produced cultural artifacts of the pastoral in its poetry, in its popular legends, and in its historiography. One is tempted to make a pun that the pastoral is *essential* to England

---

[42]As another component of this project I plan to show how a counter-pastoral is under construction by British film-makers and can be seen in such films as the *Passion of Remembrance* (England, Sankofa Film/Video Collective, 1986) and *The Last of England* (Anglo-International Films, 1987), by Derek Jarman.

[43]The collection edited by Hilton, *Peasants, Knights, and Heretics*, gathers together important papers in the controversy up to 1961. For more recent restatements see Holt, *Robin Hood*; P. R. Coss, "Aspects of Cultural Diffusion in Medieval England," *Past and Present* 108 (Aug. 1985): 35–79.

and that its intersections with a historiography of the peasantry that has had difficulty in *not* essentializing them as a historic category are not surprising.

These readings of Hollywood films may also provide us with clues to rethinking the pastoral. *Robin Hood: Prince of Thieves* offers perhaps the strongest clue. The arrival of Azeem on the shores of southern England echoes in a parodic way the arrival of Gibreel Farishta on the beach below Battle Hill as told by Salman Rushdie in his *Satanic Verses*.[44] William the Conqueror had landed on this same beach in 1066. Up on Battle Hill, Rosa Diamond, 88 years old, prays as Gibreel washes ashore, "and closed, for a moment, her sleepless eyes, to pray for the past's return. Come on, you Norman ships, she begged: Let's have you, Willie-the-Conk." In *Satanic Verses*, Rushdie suggests that it is only through the "dissemi*Nation*," the joining of new meanings, times, peoples, cultural boundaries, that "the radical alterity of national culture will create new forms of living and writing."[45] *Robin Hood: Prince of Thieves* fails to create new forms of pastoral and relies on an old colonial trope of the native informant and the concessionary narrative. But in its historiographic unconscious, the staging of the Arab in England, it does show symptomatically the crisis of the pastoral. Historians of the peasantry can learn from the historiographic unconscious of Robin Hood films.

Epilogue. After I posted this essay to the editor, a colleague passed on to me an article that had appeared in the *Sun*, a

---

[44]*The Satanic Verses* (New York, 1988); the citation is from p. 129.

[45]For an inspiring meditation on the historical aspects of Rushdie's cultural project see Homi K. Bhabha, "DissemiNation: Time, Narrative, and the Margins of the Modern Nation," in *Nation and Narration*, ed. Bhabha (London, 1990), pp. 291–322.

tabloid that attracts browsing at supermarket checkouts.[46] The cover of the *Sun* acclaimed: "Robin Hood's Body Found in Sherwood Forest." Inside, the reader found the headline reproduced in a pseudo-Gothic script, under which the editors had situated a promotional photograph of Kevin Costner as Robin Hood. According to the two-page article, hikers had found the five-foot-seven-inch corpse dressed in green homespun, a green Hessian jerkin, and leather boots. Expert testimony from Bernard Forsythe, an archaeologist, and Nigel Hays, a Cambridge historian, punctuated the text.

On the body, excavators had discovered a gold medallion inscribed "to Robert of Locksley for invaluable services to the king and country—1172." The *Sun* did not picture the medallion, but it did provide a photograph of the body, "covered with a lacquer-like film, a rare embalming solution used in the Middle East." So here again we find the "East" distributed on the body of Robin Hood, as a preservative, just as we found Azeem distributed on the pastoral site founded by the body of Robin Hood in the film *Robin Hood: Prince of Thieves*. The pastoral has collapsed into the body, and the body of Robin Hood provides a fantastic guarantee of the pastoral at a post-pastoral historical moment.

---

[46]I am grateful to my colleague Teresea Krier for bringing this article to my attention (*Sun* 10/46 [17 Nov. 1992]: 4–5).

THE SOCIAL, ECONOMIC, AND INTELLECTUAL LIFE OF RICHARD DEPYNG, VICAR OF FILLONGLEY (1487–1529)

Denis Brearley

In 1967, P. A. Bill published a short monograph, *The Warwickshire Parish Clergy in the Later Middle Ages*,[1] in which he pointed out the relative scarcity of serious study of the parish clergy of the later Middle Ages when compared to research undertaken on the papacy, episcopate, or regular clergy. Drawing upon the records of the parish of Fillongley,[2]

---

[1]Dugdale Society Occasional Papers, no. 17 (1967).

[2]For a general history of the parish of Fillongley see *The Victoria History of the Counties of England: Warwick*, vol. 4 (London, 1947), pp. 69–75 (hereafter, *VCH Warw.*). My interest in the late medieval history of this parish (northern Warwicks.) began as a genealogical project to identify my paternal ancestors. Names of family members had been recorded in various documents concerned with the parish of Fillongley and nearby Maxstoke Priory (Warwicks.) from as early as 1432. My ancestors moved to the nearby parish of Shustoke during the eighteenth century and stayed there until my great-great-grandfather Joseph moved to Inkberrow (Worcs.) in the nineteenth century and his son Henry emigrated to Canada in the 1870s. It soon became clear that to solve some rather complicated problems concerning the identification of certain relationships before the 1570s, it would be necessary to reconstruct the genealogies of several families in the parish and study the local history of the parish and surrounding areas. In adopting a suitable methodology to pursue this work, I was drawn to the works and methods of Prof. J. Ambrose Raftis, his colleagues, and his students. While I was investigating the earliest wills left by members of the parish of Fillongley, a number of interesting facts emerged that began to put a recognizably human face on the prosopographical skeleton of the village of Fillongley during the late fifteenth and early

located some six miles northwest of Coventry in Warwickshire, I offer data and commentary on the life of one parish priest who was certainly one of the most influential and important figures in his village in the period just before the Reformation.

The single most important document for investigating the clergy of pre-Reformation Fillongley is the will of Richard Depyng, who held the post of vicar of the parish from 1487 to 1529.[3] Depyng's will, in conjunction with other extant records, both fiscal and demographical,[4] gives considerably more information about this one man than is available for any other contemporary figure of the parish. Using these records, I attempt first to reconstruct an outline of Depyng's life and career. Second, I have provided a *catalogue raisonné* of all bequests made in Depyng's will, including the names of all legatees and other names cited. In addition to discussing the vicar's intellectual interests as reflected in his will, I have also appended a number

---

sixteenth centuries, until I reached the point where it seemed feasible to attempt to reconstruct an outline of some of the economic, social, cultural, and educational aspects of the life of one of the last pre-Reformation parish priests of Fillongley. It also became clear how closely related are the concerns and methods of contemporary genealogists and economic, social, and other local historians.

[3]For a brief treatment on the typology and bibliography of wills as sources for the social historian see W. B. Stephens, *Sources for English Local History*, rev. and expanded ed. (Cambridge, 1983), pp. 63–65.

[4]The principal *manorial* documents for the study of fifteenth- and sixteenth-century Fillongley are located in record offices at Warwick, Stratford, London, and Birmingham. The lay subsidy rolls and the minister's accounts are at the Public Record Office (PRO), London. The parish register, which begins in 1538, is now at the Warwick County Record Office (WCRO) in Warwick, along with some other sixteenth-century materials, including a number of early deeds that have not yet been fully catalogued. Except for a very few wills proved at the Prerogative Court of Canterbury (PCC), most of the surviving wills of parish members have been preserved at the Lichfield Joint Record Office (LJRO) at Lichfield, along with the bishops' registers. Other records are at Oxford University (where there is an important manuscript containing the records of Maxstoke Priory) and Coventry. I have been able to consult most of the surviving classes of documents, with the exception of the 2,000 or so plea rolls in the PRO, which may contain scattered information on the activities of clergymen and the unclassified or still only summarily classified deeds and bills of sale to be found at the WCRO.

of prosopographical and other notes designed to give more detailed information about the acquaintances of this parish priest, as well as the role or status of the individual or group in the contemporary village society. The Appendix contains a near-diplomatic transcription of the will of Richard Depyng from the surviving probate copy in the Public Record Office, London.

The earliest extant will that survives from the parish of Fillongley was made and dated by Richard Depyng on 9 April 1529. He was the vicar of the parish from 1487 until his death in 1529.[5] This will was proved on 4 May 1529 by the Prerogative Court of Canterbury. A probate copy has been preserved at the Public Record Office (PRO PROB 11/23, fol. 48r–v)[6] (see Figs. 1 and 2).

From the various bequests that he made to the church of Sutton Coldfield (co. Warw.) and to the chantry attached to that church, it seems likely that Richard Depyng came from a family long established in that parish.[7] A John Depyng, perhaps an older brother or cousin,[8] is named in the Sutton Coldfield lay

---

[5]No other wills are listed in the *Index of Wills Proved in the Prerogative Court of Canterbury,* vols. 1–2: *1383–1558*, comp. J. C. C. Smith (London, 1893). See also Christopher Kitching, "The Prerogative Court of Canterbury from Warham to Whitgift," in Rosemary O'Day and Felicity Heal, eds., *Continuity and Change: Personnel and Administration of the Church in England, 1500–1642* 8 (Leicester, 1976), pp. 191–214. Copies of two other wills, both dated 1531, have survived elsewhere. The first belongs to Thomas Palmer, vicar of Fillongley 1529–31, immediate successor to Richard Depyng; the second, to a Rauff Smythe. Both wills were proved in the diocese of Coventry and Lichfield; copies are to be found in the *Early Register of Copy Wills* at the LJRO (B/C/10). No contemporary copies of original wills for this parish have survived until after 1535 (B/C/11).

[6]The prerogative of the PCC was ill-defined at this period. See Kitching, "Prerogative Court." It would normally suffice to have owned property in two different jurisdictions or to have possessed assets deemed worthy of the attention of the court, perhaps as little as £5.

[7]The Depyng family had property recorded at Sutton Coldfield as early as 1364–65 and still in 1500–01. See Lucy Drucker, ed., *Warwickshire Feet of Fines*, vol. 3 (1345–1509), Dugdale Society, vol. 18 (1943), nos. 2114, 2777 (see also no. 2134).

[8]This is a possible reconstruction; there remains the problem of the identification of the *William* Depynge whose name appears in twenty-eighth place on the 1524

subsidy roll for 1524/25.[9] Members of the Depyng family had also been clerics in the diocese of Coventry and Lichfield during the fourteenth century,[10] and there were Depyngs who graduated from both Oxford[11] and Cambridge[12] universities. The Depyngs regularly gave some of their sons to the service of the church, and so the names of still other Depyngs (John, Edward, etc.) appear on the ordination lists of the diocese of Coventry and Lichfield in the latter part of the fifteenth century. A John Depyng was ordained subdeacon, deacon, and priest in 1471 and 1471/72 for the monastery of St. Mary of Whalley.[13]

The dates of any of Richard Depyng's ordinations are unknown, either because of a possible gap in the bishop's

---

Fillongley lay subsidy roll (PRO E179/192/139) (Fig. 3). William may have been a nephew or cousin of Richard's. While clergymen would not appear to have been subject to the lay subsidy for their clerical livings, they would appear to have been liable for this levy for lands or goods that they held in their own right, i.e., for properties or other monies not part of their clerical livings. For recent work on the typology of lay subsidy rolls see the bibliography in Stephens, *Sources*, pp. 36, 49–50, 170. See also J. C. K. Cornwall, *Wealth and Society in Early Sixteenth Century England* (London, 1988).

[9]There are 66 names for the parish of Sutton on the lay subsidy roll for 1524/25 (dated 17? Jan. 16 Hen. VIII). A John Depyng (perhaps the same as the one referred to in the *Warwicks. Feet of Fines*, no. 2114) was assessed on land valued at 20*s*. for a levy of 12*d*. His name is fifty-sixth on this list in descending order of value of assessment (PRO E179/192/130a).

[10]John Le Neve, *Fasti ecclesiae Anglicanae, 1300–1541*, 10: *Coventry and Lichfield Diocese*, comp. B. Jones (London, 1964), pp. 19, 32: Roger de Depyng, archdeacon of Stafford, 1349, also prebendary of Dernford; pp. 9, 27, 32, 42: John de Depyng, who held various offices, 1329–54.

[11]A. B. Emden, *A Biographical Register of the University of Oxford to A. D. 1500*, vol. 1 (Oxford, 1957), p. 571: John Depyng, friar, Dominican, London Convent, 1494, 1495; Oxford Convent 1497, etc.; Thomas Depyng, monk, Benedictine, Peterborough Abbey, d. 1442.

[12]John Venn and J. A. Venn, comps., *Alumni cantabrigienses: A Biographical List*, pt. 1, vol. 2 (Cambridge, 1922): John Depyng, grad. 1421, canon of Lincoln; Nicholas Depyng, scholar at King's Hall 1388–96.

[13]See Bishop Geoffrey Blythe's register (1503–31), LJRO (B/A/1/141). Whalley Abbey (Lancs.) remained in the diocese of Coventry and Lichfield until 1541.

register[14] or perhaps because for some reason or other these events occurred outside the diocese. We know that Depyng was already a priest when he was appointed vicar of Fillongley for life on 20 May 1487, following the death of John Tayler,[15] the previous vicar. He held this office until his death in 1529. Since he was priest at his appointment, he is not likely to have been younger than 26 years of age, and he probably was older. If Depyng were 26 years old when he was appointed vicar, he would have been born ca. 1461 and been 68 years old at his death. His birthdate is likely to have been sometime between 1450 and 1461.

The bishops' registers at Lichfield for this period regularly list any titles[16] held by incumbents. There is no indication in the brief note recording Depyng's appointment or in any other source that he ever held a university degree. There is no indication of licensed nonresidence.[17] Consequently, it is reasonable to assume that Depyng spent most of his working life in or near his parish, with occasional visits to his family in Sutton Coldfield. It is also clear that at least one other member of the family—William Depyng—moved to Fillongley, and his name appears on the lay subsidy roll (see Fig. 3).

---

[14]See Staffordshire Record Office, *Cumulative Hand List, Pt. 1, Diocesan Probate and Church Commissioners' Records*, LJRO (1978): 3(b).

[15]Bishop John Hale's register (1459–90), LJRO (B/A/1/12, fol. 33v). See also Joel A. Lipkin, *Institutions in the Diocese of Coventry and Lichfield* 1480–1543 (Silver Spring, Md., privately issued, 1979), no. EA0044. A copy of this work is on deposit at the LJRO with the call number B/A/1/12 (part)- 14 iii. n.

[16]Thomas Palmer, Depyng's immediate successor, held the degree *in legibus baccallaureus* (Lichfield B/A/1/14, fol. 14v for the year 1529). Depyng is listed simply as a priest (*presbyter*). Mention is also made at this point in the bishop's register of the right of the priors of Maxstoke to present the candidates for this post.

[17]It appears that only one vicar of a parish in Warwickshire was given permission to be nonresident during the period 1300–1500. See Bill, *Warwicks. Parish Clergy*, p. 6.

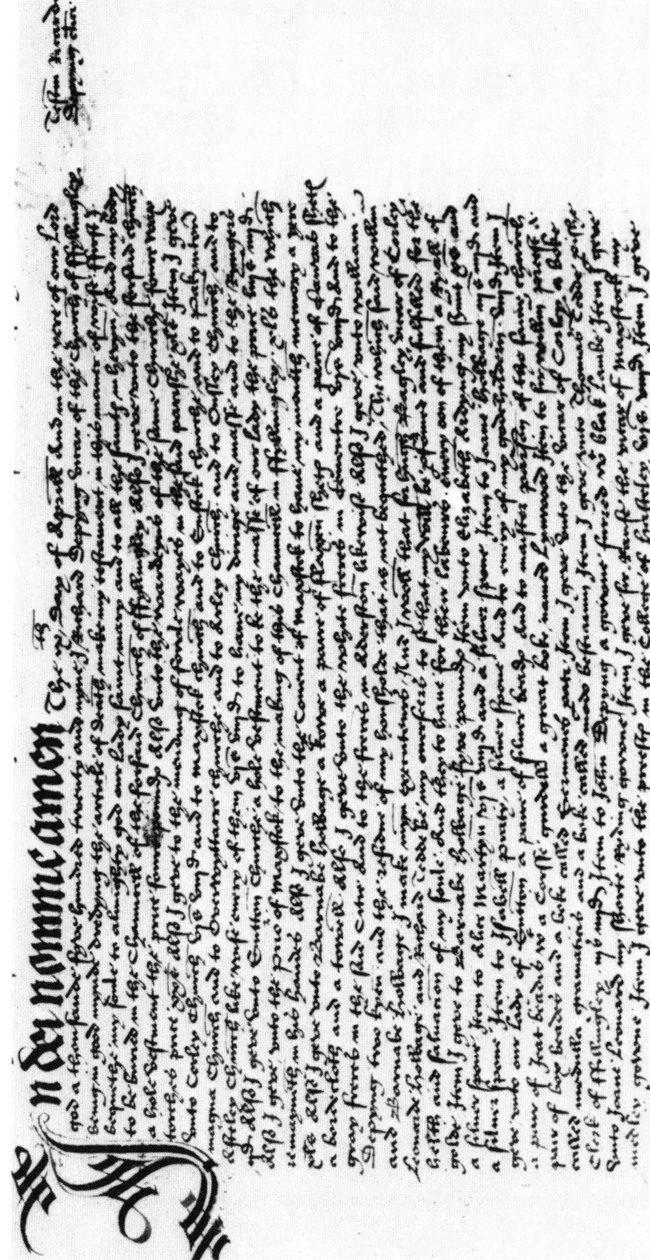

Figure 1. Copy of the will of Richard Depyng (PRO PROB 11/23) (fol. 48r); original in the custody of the Public Record Office, London

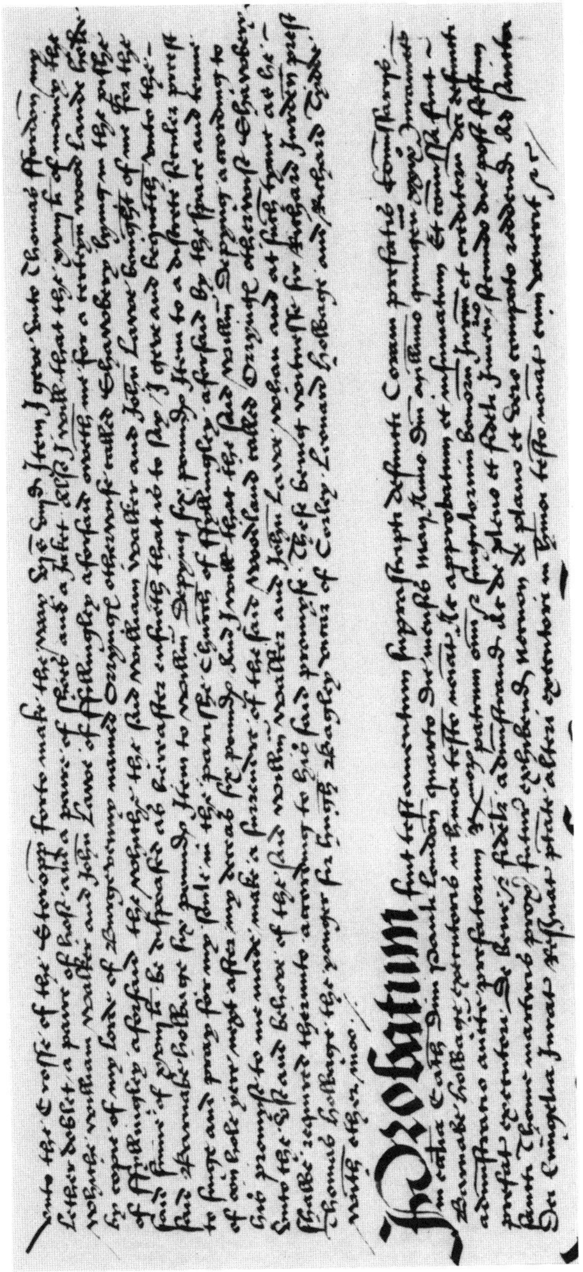

Figure 2. Copy of the will of Richard Depyng (PRO PROB 11/23) (fol. 48v); original in the custody of the Public Record Office, London

Figure 3. (top portion) Lay Subsidy Roll, 1524 (PRO E179/192/139 BC/238); Crown copyright; reproduced with the permission of the Controller of Her Majesty's Stationery Office.

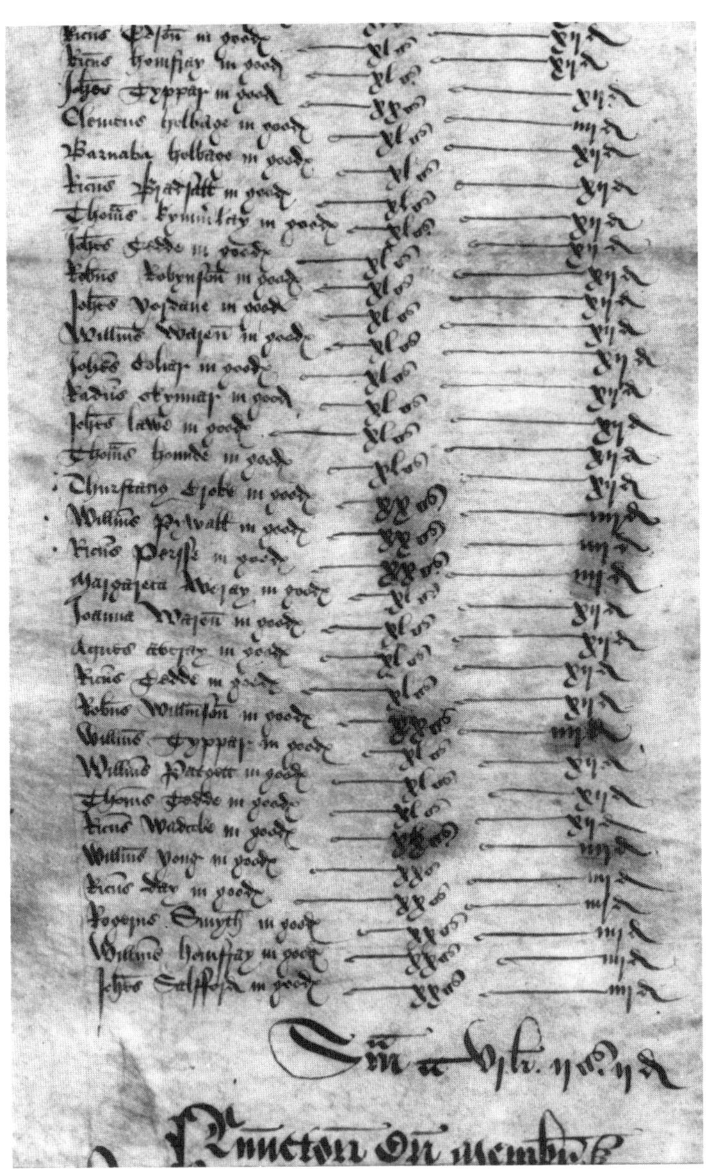

Figure 3. (bottom portion)

In 1512 there is mention of Richard Depyng's membership in the Guild of St. Ann of Knowle, a parish that was some four parishes to the southwest of Fillongley.[18] Richard Depyng died a "natural" death[19] shortly after his will was made on 9 April 1529. His immediate successor, Thomas Palmer, was named vicar only eight days after the date of the will.[20]

That the will was proved by the Prerogative Court of Canterbury may or may not be an indication of Depyng's importance. It may, for example, only indicate that he had property or assets in more than one ecclesiastical jurisdiction or that his assets were considered to have reached a certain level. Some wills from this period were proved for sums amounting to little more than £5. His will, however, is the only will from Fillongley until after the middle of the sixteenth century to have been proved at the Prerogative Court of Canterbury. Even so, to judge from the bequests, there is no reason to presume that this will was written for other than the usual purposes. There was no complicated transfer of property but rather the usual bequests to family, friends, and servants and an honorary mention of important members of the parish. The bequests to the circle of his clerical friends and acquaintances are limited to the immediately surrounding geographical area. The list of parishes mentioned does not extend further than Atherstone and Sutton Coldfield.

Depyng made small bequests to his servant-housekeeper, Elizabeth Harding, and to four other females. Except for this

---

[18] *The Register of the Guild of Knowle in the County of Warwick: 1451–1535*, transcr. and ed. W. B. Bickley (Walsall, 1894), p. 206. The entry for 1512: "tempore Johannis Brerlay de Fynnyngley, Dominus Richardus Depyng vicarius de Fynnyngley."

[19] Part of the notice for the appointment of Thomas Palmer (Lichfield B/A/1/14, fol. 14v for 1529) reads: "per mortem naturalem domini Richardi Depynge. . . ."

[20] Bishop Geoffrey Blythe's register (1503–31), LJRO (B/A/1/141, fol. 14v). See also Lipkin, *Institutions*.

Elizabeth Harding there is no mention of the status of these females, and it is not certain whether they were adult women or girls. While it is possible, even probable, that they may have served him in some regular or occasional capacity, such as cook or housekeeper, the will offers no other details, and it is not yet possible to confirm from any other extant documents even that they were residents of the parish. Indeed, the order of the bequests to three of the four leaves open the possibility that some or all of them may have been his goddaughters.[21]

Depyng's other nonclerical friends and associates whom he made legatees, with the single exception of Thomas Fordon, all appear on the April 1524 and the January 1525 lay subsidy rolls for Fillongley.[22] They would therefore appear to constitute a cross-section of the more prosperous residents of the parish. Almost all of them came from families who had long been established in the parish.

There do not appear to have been any members of the nobility among these legatees, nor were there any members of the nobility then normally resident in the parish. The principal manors in Fillongley were held by the lords Abergavenny and the priory of St. Mary Coventry. The priors of Maxstoke had the

---

[21]While Elizabeth Harding may be the same one whose burial is recorded in the parish register in 1543, the circumstantial placing of the bequests to the other women and the bequests to his godchildren are the main reasons advanced for linking the two groups.

[22]PRO E179/192/139 (Fig. 3), for which the indenture is dated 14 Apr., 15 Hen. VIII (1524), and PRO E179/192/130a, for which the indenture is dated 17? Jan., 16 Hen. VIII (1525 [new style dating]). Since William Holbache (of Fillongley) was one of the collectors of these two subsidies, it is probable that the list is as complete as his personal knowledge permitted. We cannot know if he would have been embarrassed by charges of favoritism, had he omitted any names. There are 68 names on the Apr. 1524 roll, 74 names on the Jan. 1525 list. This figure is near that of the tally of the 86 households taken during the ecclesiastical census of 1563 (BL Harleian MS. 594, fol. 166v), possibly indicating a modest growth in population 1524–63.

right to nominate the vicars of the parish. It is unlikely that the heads of the Averey and Holbech (Holbecke, or Holbage) families had yet been recognized as being members of the gentry. No surviving document speaks of gentlemen or gentry living in the parish before 1570.[23]

From a financial point of view, Richard Depyng appears to have been the richest man living in the parish. He had held at one time a copyhold lease on a woodland called Orrynges (alias Shawbery) that belonged to the lords Abergavenny. He had sold this lease before his death for the sum of £18 and left specific instructions about how the proceeds of this particular sale were to be distributed.[24]

No inventory of this will has survived, nor has it been verified whether or not he had enough assets to cover all the bequests that he made. It seems reasonable to assume that sufficient funds were available, and nothing seems to have impeded the rapid probate of this will shortly after his death.

The simple method of adding together the amounts of the bequests and all other assets should give an approximation of his wealth. That sum was at least £42 6*s.*2*d.* When the values of various items to which no monetary value was given in the

---

[23]In the earliest wills of Fillongley the testators refer to themselves as "husbandmen" or "yeomen," if this fact receives any mention at all. The earliest document referring to gentry living in the parish dates from 1580, when 14 residents in the parish were listed in "A Booke of the Names of ye Gentlemen and Freeholders in ye County of Warwicke" (PRO SP12/137, fol. 130). The first Holbech ancestor listed (certainly retroactively) in Thomas C. May, *The Visitation of the County of Warwick . . . 1682 . . . – . . . 1683*, ed. W. Harry Rylands, Harleian Society, vol. 62 (1911): 77, is Thomas Holbeach (d. 1528).

[24]The woodland name Orrynges (alias Shawbery) is mentioned in a later document, "The Rentall de Fylongley" (Shakespeare Birthplace Trust Office [Stratford] DR 18/30/10/1). This is the only rental document of the manor of Fillongley known to have survived from the sixteenth century. A Richard Grene was in possession of this property at this time and paid a rent of 2*s.* (in both spring and autumn). I believe the rental can now be dated to the period before the death of Nycolas Hardynge recorded in the parish register in 1573.

will (e.g., silver beads, two ryals of gold, two cows, etc.) are added to this theoretical sum, the result could have been three or four times the amount of the highest assessment in the 1524 and 1524/25 lay subsidy rolls (£18). It would thus appear that Depyng was considerably wealthier than any of the yeomen or husbandmen who had the highest assessments during those levies.[25]

It has been a commonplace to criticize the medieval parish clergy for low standards of literacy. This does not seem to have been the case with Richard Depyng, nor, indeed, with the other clerics in his circle of friends and acquaintances. From the intellectual point of view, the most interesting aspect of Depyng's will are four books that he names.[26] These books are identified as *Lynwood*, a textbook of canon law, *Sermones Parati*, a collection of sermons or homilies, *medulla gramaticis*, a Latin-English grammar and vocabulary, and *modo bestiarum*, a bestiary.

The "great book named Lynwood" became the standard text on English canon law soon after it was written. The *Constitutiones Provinciales* of Bishop William Lyndewood was first

---

[25]The highest assessment in this subsidy was on goods of John Breerlay, resulting in a subsidy of 9*s*. Sixty-five of the names on the list for 1525 were assessed in goods from values of £18 to 20*s*.; the remaining nine, on lands, with a descending value from £4 to 20*s*., the minimum assessment. The subsidy granted in 1523 and collected in 1524/25 was levied on goods, lands, or wages worth £1 or more a year and in country districts seems to have applied to almost all householders. If they paid on their goods, this indicated that they did not own land of a greater annual value than the worth of their personal estates. For the sixteenth-century subsidies generally see Cornwall, *Wealth and Society*, passim.

[26]Although the four books in Richard Depyng's library are not numerically impressive and give him no claim to being a scholar or notable collector, the scope of his collection compares favorably with the range of books owned by the canons of Exeter Cathedral during this same period. See Nicholas Orme, "Education and Learning at a Mediaeval English Cathedral: Exeter 1380–1538," *Journal of Ecclesiastical History* 32 (1981): 265–83 and the table on pp. 276–77. See also John West, *Village Records*, 2nd ed. (Chicester, 1982), pp. 117–19. There is no need to suppose that these books were in manuscript form rather than printed books.

printed in 1483 and quickly went through a number of editions.[27] In the will, the use of the term "great book" probably designates one of the quarto or octavo editions published in 1501 or 1504.

The *Sermones Parati* seems to have been a particularly popular work, to judge from the number of early editions that were published.[28] The book contains sermons for all Sundays and major feast days and would have served the busy country vicar, who knew enough Latin, with a good range of homiletic material to draw upon for his sermons.

The third book in Depyng's collection is described by its more popular title as the *Medulla gramaticis*.[29] Also called the *Promptuarium parvulorum clericorum,* it is perhaps the earliest English-Latin dictionary to have been published. The first printed edition appeared in 1499, with editions by Wynadum de Worde in 1510 and again in 1516. While we might suppose that a Latin-English dictionary would have been of more use to Depyng, this book gives only the Latin equivalents for English words.

---

[27]For the first three books see the numerous editions listed in A. W. Pollard and G. R. Redgrave, comps., *A Short-Title Catalogue of Books Printed in England, Scotland, & Ireland and of English Books Printed Abroad, 1475–1640*, and in the *British Museum Catalogue of Printed Books* (London, 1883). The legend "Provincialis Guillermi Lyundewode" is printed in the top margin of the verso of each folio in the 1501 edition and is entitled *Provinciale seu constitutiones anglie*.

[28]The British Library has nine copies of this work printed before 1518 under the author's name, Paratus. The earliest edition appears to be the *Sermones Parati de tempore et de sanctis*, printed in 1480 without pagination in double columns.

[29]In all the editions of this book that I have been able to consult the short title is *medulla gramatice*, with *gra<m>matice* in the genitive singular rather than in the dative or ablative plural *gramaticis*. Possibly either the scribe of the original will or the scribe of the probate copy of the will recorded the title from a handwritten note from the inventory or from some ticket or syllabus that may have been placed above or near the printed title. Then again, the scribe may never have seen the book. The edition that Depyng possessed may well have been *Prompturarium parvulorum clericorum quod apud nos medulla grammatice appellatur* (London, 1510).

The fourth book is the most difficult to identify with precision. If, as is likely, the first word, *modo*, has only adverbial force in the context of the will and was used by the scribe or notary to introduce the next (here the last) item in the list, then the second word, *bestiarum*, is the *incipit* of several versions of the Latin *Physiologus* that were popular during the Middle Ages.[30] One version was ascribed to Hrabanus Maurus[31] and another to Hugh of St. Victor.[32] The more popular version by Theobaldus has a different beginning.[33] In the usual medieval versions of the Christianized bestiary we find a scriptural text that first mentions the animal under discussion. Then there follows what the *Physiologus* has to say about the creature. The discussion then concludes with a spiritual or moral lesson. The object of the book was religious and ascetic. The bestiary would have furnished the country vicar with a wealth of easily understood *exempla* for use in his sermons.[34]

During the time Richard Depyng served as vicar of Fillongley, interest in learning and education seems to have

---

[30]On the subject of bestiaries in the Middle Ages see Florence McCulloch, *Mediaeval Latin and French Bestiaries* (Chapel Hill, 1960). See also *Physiologus*, trans. M. J. Curley (Austin, 1979), which has a good bibliography of early editions. Lynn Thorndyke and Pearl Kibre, *A Catalogue of Incipits of Mediaeval Scientific Writings in Latin* (Cambridge, 1937) mentions (p. 78) the bestiary of BL Royal MS. 12 C/XIX, which begins "Bestiarum vocabulum proprie convenit."

[31]B. Rabani Mauri, *De Universo libri viginti duo (liber 8) Bestiarum vocabulum proprie convenit leonibus, pardis, tigribus, lupis*, in J. P. Migne, ed., *Patrologia latina*, vol. 111, cols. 217ff.

[32]Hugonis de S. V., *De bestiis et aliis rebus libri quattuor liber secundus: Bestiarum vocabulum proprie convenit pardis*, in PL 177, cols. 55–164. On the incorrect ascription of this book to Hugh of St. Victor see H. Silvestre, *Le moyen âge* 55 (Paris, 1949), pp. 247–51.

[33]Theobaldus Episcopus, *Physiologus*, ed. and trans. P. T. Eden (Leiden, 1972).

[34]On the use of animal legends in preaching see G. R. Owst, *Literature and Pulpit in Medieval England: A Neglected Chapter in the History of English Letters & of the English People* (Oxford, 1966), pp. 196–204.

increased considerably in the surrounding region.[35] The monastery closest to Fillongley was located in the next parish, a short distance to the west. There, the Augustinian priory of Maxstoke (which also nominated the vicars of Fillongley) supported a prior, a subprior, six monks, and two novices during the period 1518–22. The records of Bishop Blythe's visitations (1515–25) show no indication that any of the Augustinian houses in the diocese of Coventry and Lichfield were interested in university education.[36] There were complaints at Maxstoke during the visitations of 1521 and 1522 that the teaching of grammar was being neglected in the novices' training, but this fault seems to have been corrected by the time the visitation of 1524 had been concluded.[37] In his will made on 24 April 1525,[38] William Brycland (Bryclonde) of Maxstoke requested that his body be buried "in the monastery of Maxstoke under the newe library."[39] Therefore, although the prior of Maxstoke regularly complained about his financial resources, it seems that there was enough interest and concern on the part of local benefactors to permit the construction of a *new* library.

A few miles and two parishes to the south of Fillongley lay the city and parish of Coventry. From the record of the visitation of Bishop Blythe we know that in 1521 the Black Monks of

---

[35]For a general orientation, esp. for the period before 1500, see Bill, *Warwicks. Parish Clergy*.

[36]Peter Heath, ed., *Bishop Geoffrey Blythe's Visitations, c. 1515–1525*, Staffordshire Record Society, 4th ser., vol. 7 (1973): xxxvii.

[37]Heath, *Blythe's Visitations*, pp. xxxvi, 73, 111, 119–21.

[38]The will of William Brycland was proved at the PCC, 4 July 1526. See PRO PROB 11/32 (9 Porch), fols. 66v–67r.

[39]J. R. Holiday, "Maxstoke Priory," *Transactions of the Birmingham and Midland Inst. (Arch. Section)* (16 Apr. 1874): 56–105, does not specify the location of any library, but it is not unreasonable to suppose that the building he designates as F, which adjoins the nave and is indicated in the plan on p. 67, served this purpose. See also *VCH Warw.* 2: 136.

Coventry had some 20 "inmates" in their monastery, and that they had at least one graduate monk and were supporting three or perhaps four scholars at university.[40] Richard Depyng's immediate successor, Thomas Palmer, who died two years after Depyng, in 1531,[41] had close contacts with the White Monks of Coventry and left them "all such books as be of *sermones* or of divinite." Thus we have several indications from different sources that by the end of the second decade of the sixteenth century two successive vicars of Fillongley, and perhaps the vicar of Corley and the master parson of Sutton (both recipients of a book from Depyng's library) were working in close contact with the priors of Maxstoke, who were the patrons of the church of Fillongley, and with the nearby White Monks of Coventry in a climate favorable to education and learning.

Some 80 extant wills from the parish of Fillongley survive from the sixteenth century. Only a few of these date from the pre-Reformation period. Given the often fragmentary and usually statistical nature of the manorial and other documents, these wills are important for the reconstruction of aspects of the social and economic history of the parish during this period. Of these the will of Richard Depyng is of particular interest and importance, not only because it is the earliest surviving will but also because of the many and varied bequests to individuals or institutions both inside and outside the parish, which, when collated and compared with other records, now make a more comprehensive prosopographical study of the parish a feasible project.

---

[40]Heath, *Blythe's Visitations*, p. xxxvii.

[41]Thomas Palmer's will is dated 31 Mar. 1531 and was proved on 13 May 1531 (LJRO: B/C/10). Palmer also requested that other books in his possession (he does not tell us how many or of what kind), which he borrowed from the library of Peter in Cornehyll, including a book named *Seneca*, were to be returned to the priest there.

The bequests that Richard Depyng made can be divided into seven distinct classes:

1. bequests to churches;
2. bequests to secular and monastic clergy;
3. bequests to presumed relatives;
4. a bequest to his servant-housekeeper;
5. bequests to other females;
6. bequests to laymen;
7. a miscellaneous class of other bequests.

In addition, there are a few laymen named in the will who were not left any bequests and probably expected nothing. These are listed under number 6. All the bequests are listed in the following table.

THE BEQUESTS OF RICHARD DEPYNG

	Name	Nature of Bequest	Value
1. Bequests to churches			
1	Ansley	cash	6*s.* 8*d.*
2	Astley	cash	6*s.* 8*d.*
3	Arley	cash	6*s.* 8*d.*
4	Corley	cash	6*s.* 8*d.*
5	Fillongley	(a) a whole vestment	£4 0*s.* 0*d.*
		(b) four wax torches	20*s.* 0*d.*
6	Great Packington	cash	6*s.* 8*d.*
7	Maxstoke	cash	6*s.* 8*d.*
8	Maxstoke, convent of	annual month memory	40*s.* 0*d.*
9	Over Whitacre	cash	6*s.* 8*d.*
10	Shustoke	cash	6*s.* 8*d.*
11	Sutton	(a) a whole vestment	53*s.* 4*d.*
		(b) a pair of silver beads	?
12	To 7 bell-ringers	cash	14*d.*

Name	Nature of Bequest	Value
2. Bequests to secular and monastic clergy		
13 Atherstone[a] (friars)	cash	6*s.*8*d.*
14 Asteley[b] (priests, the college)	cash	6*s.*8*d.*
15 Bagley, Hugh[c] (vicar of Corley)	(a) a gold ryal	?
	(b) book: *medulla gramaticis*	?
	(c) book: *modo bestiarum*	?
16 White Friars, Coventry[d]	cash	6*s.*8*d.*
17 Grey Friars, Coventry[e]	cash	6*s.*8*d.*
18 Jurden, Richard[f]	[no bequest]	
19 Maxstoke, prior of[g]	for making a chancel	40*s.*0*d.*
20 Maxstoke, vicar of[h]	woolen gown	?
21 Preest, William[i]	a pair of beads and a book called *sermones parati*	?
22 Sutton, master parson at[j]	a pair of beads, with a coarse girdle; the book *Lynwood*	?
23 a discreet secular priest	to sing and pray for a year	£6 0*s.*0*d.*

[a]For further information on the Austin Friars of Atherstone see *VCH Warw.* 2 (1947): 106.

[b]See *VCH Warw.* 2: 117.

[c]Hugh Bagley (Baguley), d. 1543. See William Dugdale, *The Antiquities of Warwickshire Illustrated*, 2nd ed., 2 vols. (London, 1730), 2: 1023.

[d]For the Carmelite Friars of Coventry see *VCH Warw.* 2: 104.

[e]For the Franciscan Friars of Coventry see *VCH Warw.* 2: 103.

[f]Richard Jurden (Jorden) is probably the same person who was appointed incumbent of the parish of Little Packington on 24 May 1537. See Dugdale, *Antiquities* 2: 979.

[g]William Dyson, alias Dicons, alias Symons, was prior of Maxstoke from 1505 to the time of the dissolution (1538). See *VCH Warw.* 2: 91.

[h]Dugdale (*Antiquities* 2: 1000) writes (citing the bishops' registers at Lichfield as his source) that D. Christop. Dugdale was appointed vicar of Maxstoke on the resignation of Rad. Hodde on 8 Mar. 1511. There does not appear to be a record for any other Radulphus (Rauffe) at Maxstoke during the period.

[i]William Preest (Priest) was *custos cantarie* of the chantry of Sutton Coldfield at the time of the *Valor ecclesiasticus* of 1535 and was still receiving a pension of 15 (shillings?) in 1553. See *VCH Warw.* 4 (1947): 244.

[j]A John Burges, Bac. S. Theol., was appointed rector of Sutton Coldfield in 1521 (Dugdale, *Antiquities* 2: 915). Doubtless he had obtained his M.A. by the usual means by the time of Depyng's death.

Name	Nature of Bequest	Value
3. Bequests to presumed relatives		
24 Depyng, William[k]	(a) 2 cows	?
	(b) residue of household	?
	(c) 1/3 of proceeds, sale of Orynnges	£6 0*s.* 0*d.*
25 Depyng, John[l]	furred gown	?
26 each godchild	cash	8*s.* 0*d.*
4. Bequest to his servant-housekeeper		
27 [H]ardyng, Elizabeth[m]	(a) a silver spoon	?
	(b) cash	10*s.* 0*d.*
5. Bequests to other women		
28 Holbage, Joan[n]	(a) a silver spoon	?
	(b) cash	3*s.* 4*d.*
29 Leonard, Joan[o]	a short riding gown	?
30 Martyne, Alice[p]	(a) a silver spoon	?
	(b) cash	6*s.* 8*d.*
31 Praty, Isabell[q]	a silver spoon	?

[k]It is possible that William Depyng, an executor of the estate, was a younger(?) brother, or uncle or cousin, of Richard. He is twenty-eighth on the 1524 lay subsidy roll (PRO E179/192/139), twenty-sixth on the 1525 roll (PRO E179/192/130a), with an assessment of 60*s.* and a levy of 18*d.* in each case.

[l]John Depyng may have been a son of the William Depyng referred to in n. k above. *The Rentall of Fillongley* (Stratford Shakespeare BTRO: DR 18/30/10/1) refers ambiguously to the "heires of depinge."

[m]According to the parish register, an Elizabeth Harding was buried in 1543. See F. W. Willmore, *Transcript of the Old Parish Register of the Parish Church of St Mary and All Saints, Fillongley 1538–1653* (Walsall, 1894).

[n]There is no entry in the parish register for any Joan Holbage (Holbach) for the period before 1600.

[o]The family names Leonard, Martyn, and Praty do not appear in the Fillongley register. It is possible that if they were housekeepers of a certain age, they may have died before entries were made in the first parish register in 1538, or, if widowed, they had remarried; if they were Depyng's godchildren, they might have been resident outside the parish.

[p]See n. o, above.

[q]See n. o, above.

Name	Nature of Bequest	Value
6. Laymen named in the will		
32 Abergavenny,[r] lords	named as owners of woodland named Orrynges alias Shawbery	
33 Fordon, Thomas[s]	(a) a leather doublet	?
	(b) a pair of hose	?
	(c) a pair of shoes	?
	(d) a jacket	?
(The names of the following men (nos. 34–40) appear in order on the 1524 lay subsidy roll (14 Apr. 1524: PRO E179/192/139:[t])		
34 Holbage (Holbach), Barnaby[u]	(a) a cow	?
	(b) a pair of flaxen sheets	?
	(c) a pair of canvas sheets	?
	(d) a bord cloth	?
	(e) a towel	?
	(f) 1/3 proceeds from sale, copyhold lease, Orrynges	£6 0*s.*0*d.*
	(g) <cash>	£5 0*s.*0*d.*
35 Holbage, Leonard[v]	a gold ryal	?

[r]The lords Abergavenny were the owners of the principal manor in the parish, which bore the name the Manor of Fillongley. See *VCH Warw.* 4: 69–75.

[s]As there is no mention of any Thomas Fordon in the parish register of Fillongley or in the lay subsidy rolls, he might have been an indigent person to whom Depyng had left some much-needed clothing, or a resident of another parish. A John Fodon was named rector of Sutton Coldfield in 1563.

[t]For the most part in this particular roll the names are given in descending order of assessment, by rank, name, assessment, and subsidy: 6, Thomas Holbage (in goods) £7, taxed at 3*s.*6*d.*; 7, Thomas Holbage (in goods) £8 (probably the Thomas the Elder, d. 1528), 4*s.*; 11, Richard Tedde (in goods) £7, 3*s.*6*d.*; 14, William Walcar (in goods) £5, 2*s.*6*d.*; 27, Leonard Holbage (in goods) 60*s.*, 18*d.*; 28, William Depping (in goods) 60*s.*, 18*d.*; 37, Barnaby Holbage (in goods) 40*s.*, 12*d.*; 47, John Lawe (in goods) 40*s.*, 12*d.*; 49, Richard Tedde (in goods) 40*s.*, 12*d.*; 55, Thomas Tedde (in goods) 20*s.*, 4*d.*

[u]Barnaby and Leonard Holbach (Holbage, Holbech) appear to be the fourth and third sons of Thomas Holbech of the White House of Fillongley (d. 1528). Since this Thomas Holbech married before 1483, both sons probably were in their thirties at the time of Depyng's death. Barnaby was married on 5 Mar. 1539; the will of Leonard was proved at Lichfield, 20 Apr. 1547. See Burke, *Landed Gentry* (1952), p. 1258: Holbecke of Hillybroom; *The Visitation of Warwickshire 1682–3*, Harleian Society, vol. 62 (1911): 77.

[v]See n. u, above.

	Name	Nature of Bequest	Value
36	Holbage, Thomas[w] the younger	[no bequest]	
37	Lawe, John[x] (one of two purchasers of the copyhold lease on Orrynges)	[no bequest]	
38	Tedde, Richard[y]	a gold ryal	?
39	Tedde, Thomas[z] parish clerk of Fillongley	[cash]	3*s*.4*d*.
40	Walker, William[aa] (one of two purchasers, copy-hold lease, Orynnges)	[no bequest]	

7. Other Bequests

41	To the mending of the foul ways in Fillongley[bb]	40*s*.0*d*.
42	To the Cross of the Storopp[cc]	6*s*.8*d*.

[w]Thomas Holbecke the younger (probably still so-called even after his father's death) is probably the second son of the Thomas Holbecke mentioned above and the one who married Elizabeth Brierley (Brearley) sometime before 1512 and who was buried at Fillongley 12 Sept. 1588. See Burke, *Landed Gentry*, p. 1257, and *Visitation of Warwicks.*, p. 77.

[x]In the Fillongley parish register two entries refer to the baptism of a son of John Lawe (1541) and a daughter (1544) and the burial of another son of John Lawe (1548). After three marriages of women named Lawe in 1555, 1567, and 1578, the last entry made with this family name is of a death of an Alicia Lawe (1588).

[y]The family Tedde (Ted, Tedd, Ted de Dale, Tydde) appears from the large number of entries in the parish register to have been one of the largest in the parish. Records from as early as 1320 contain mention of members of this family. There is an entry for the burial of a Richard Tedd in 1538/39 and again during the plague of 1546.

[z]A Thomas Tedd was married in 1540; a Thomas Tedd was buried during the plague of 1546.

[aa]There are almost as many entries for the Walker family as for the Tedds. A child, William Walker, son of Richard and Dorothea, was buried in 1540; a William Walker *cecus* (blind) was buried in 1563.

[bb]It was normal practice in the wills from this parish to include some provision for repairing the roads. See the will of John Brereley (31 Hen. VIII, 1539, now at LJRO: ". . . I gyff & bequeyth toward the reparasion & mendynge of the fowle way atte ffotte of the hyll in Corley next to the House of Weybus 5s 8d."

[cc]What or where was the Cross of the Storopp remains unknown. There appears to have been no place name at Fillongley or in the other parishes named in the will

Over 40 institutions, individuals, and specific projects are mentioned in the will. This fact in itself suggests that Richard Depyng had a wide range of interests, friends, and acquaintances during his lifetime. It compares favorably with the tally of 68 householders on the 1524/25 lay subsidy roll.

The facts concerning the life and circumstances of Richard Depyng that have emerged from the available information seem to indicate that he was one of the younger sons of a fairly well-to-do family who lived in Sutton Coldfield, near Birmingham, and that he entered the clerical state with sufficient money of his own to purchase a lease on some revenue-producing land. While retaining strong connections with his family and the clergy at Sutton Coldfield, he also cultivated and enjoyed good relations with other members of the clergy in the local area as far as four or five parishes away in each direction. He apparently had many friends and, certainly, numerous acquaintances, especially among the more prosperous members of his parish. Throughout his career he remained perhaps the wealthiest man in Fillongley, and at his death his bequests were sufficient to offer at least some support to some of the less fortunate members of his parish. He appears to have maintained an interest

---

called STOROPP. See J. E. D. Gover, *The Place Names of Warwickshire* (Cambridge, 1970). There appears to be no known market or other type of cross bearing this name. See J. Nelson, "The Medieval Churchyard and Wayside Crosses of Warwickshire," *Transactions of the Birmingham Archaeological Society* 68 (1952): 74–88. The most plausible explanation so far advanced was made to me by M. W. Farr, Warwick County Archivist, who in a letter (6 Aug. 1984) suggested, "it is probably a wayside cross away from habitations, and *to make the way* means to repair the road near it. It does not have to be a shrine with a resident priest or anchorite, because the other gift to *the mending of fowle ways* in Fillongley is not given to anyone in particular: presumably the executors paid for the work to be done in the appropriate spot. The word *Steropp* or *Storopp* is in fact *stirrup* of which both *steropp* and *storopp* are acceptable <16th century> spellings according to the *OED*. Many wayside crosses had heads of the tabernacle type, where a group of figures were enclosed in an architectural frame, usually a crucifixion with the Virgin and St John, as in the Weeping Cross near Stafford. A canopy with a pointed arch might look like a stirrup and so give its name to the cross."

in keeping up his professional qualifications and was fortunate (by the standards of his day) to have acquired at least four printed books, all of which would have been useful to him in carrying out his pastoral duties.

Of the over 4,000 parish clergymen who lived in Warwickshire in the last two centuries before the Reformation and for whom we have at least the names preserved,[42] it is unusual to possess so many details about the career, resources, and associates of a parish vicar, especially for the years immediately preceding the parliamentary acts of 1534 that severed all financial, administrative, and judicial ties with Rome and ultimately heralded in a new age. The composite portrait of Richard Depyng that emerges from the surviving details is of an active and interactive individual who made a considerable and positive contribution to his parish, certainly on the material level. He appears to have been a good example of the active and co-operative type of individual which the late medieval English church was able to recruit. Further research into the careers of his colleagues and contemporaries is needed to determine how typical he was of the Warwickshire parish clergy of the early sixteenth century. As this brief inquiry has attempted to show, sources that have become associated with uncovering the lives of English peasants can be exploited to recover the identities and experiences of the ministers of the pastoral care. If the individual villager has emerged from obscurity through the examination of subsidy rolls, wills, accounts, and village court records, can the parish priest be far behind?

---

[42]See Bill, *Warwicks. Parish Clergy*, p. 13.

Appendix

THE TEXT OF THE WILL OF RICHARD DEPYNG
(PRO PROB 11/23, fol. 48r–v)

IN DEI NOMINE AMEN The ixth day of Aprill And in the yere of our Lord
god a thousande fyve hundred twenty and nyne, I Richard Depyng Vicar of the Church of ffyllingley
being in good mynde dredyng the article of death make my testament in this maner of wise. ffirst I
bequethe my soule to almighty god our lady saint mary and to all the saints in hevyn, And my body
to be buried in the Chauncell of the forsaid Church of ffyllingley. Also I geve unto the forsaid Church
a hole vestment the price foure poundes Also unto the wardeyns of the same churche foure wax
tourches price xx s. Also I geve to the mending of fowle wayes in the said parishe xl s. Item I geve
unto CORLEY Church vi s. viii d and to MAXSTOK Church and to SUSTOK Churche and to PAKYNTON
MAGNA Church and to OVERWYTTACRE Churche and to ARLEY Church and to ONSLEY Church and to
ASTELEY Church likewise every of them vi s viii d to have my dirige and masse and to the Ringers
ii d. Also I geve unto SUTTON Churche a hole vestment to be the masse of our lady the price liii s iiii d
Also I geve unto the PRIOUR OF MAXSTOK to the making of this chauncell in ffyllingley xl s the which
remaynith in his handes. Also I geve unto the convent of Maxstok to have my moneth memory a yere
xl s. Also I geve unto BARNABE HOLBAGE a kowe a paire of flaxen

shets and a paire of canvas shetes
a borde cloth and a towell. Also I geve unto the
WHITE FRERES in Coventre vi s viii d and to the
GRAY FRERES in the said citie. And to the FRERES in ADERSTON
likewise. Also I geve unto William
Depyng two kyen and the residue of my householde that is not
bequethed The which said William
and Barnabe Holbage I make my executours. And I woll that
SIR HUGH BAGLEY Vicar of Corley,
Leonard Holbage and Richard Tedde be my overseers to
se that my will be performed and fulfilled for the
helth and salvacion of my soule. And they to have
for their labours every one of them a Ryall of
golde. Item I geve to Barnaby Holbage fyve pounds. Item
unto Elizabeth <H>ardyng my servant x s and
a silver spone. Item to Alice Martyn vi s viii d and
a silver spone. Item to Joane Holbage iii s iiii d and
a silver spone. Item to Isabell Praty a silver
spone. And to every of my godchildern viii d. Item I
geve unto our Lady of Sutton a paire of silver
beades. And to Maister Parson of the same Church
a pair of Jeat beades with a corsse gurdell a great boke named *Lynwood.*
Item to Sir William Preest a
pair of box beades and a boke called *sermones*
parati. Item I geve Unto the Vicar of Corley a boke
called *medulla gramaticis* and a book called *modo bestiarum.*
Item I geve unto Thomas Tedde parishe
clerk of ffillingley iii s iiii d Item to John
Depyng a gowne furred with blak lambe. Item I geve
Unto Joane Leonard my shorte ryding gowne. Item I
geve Sir Raufe the vicar of Maxstock my
wooley gowne. Item I geve unto the preestes in the college
of [H]asteley vi s viii d Item I geve

Unto the Crosse of the Storopp for to make the way
vi s viii d. Item I geve unto Thomas ffordon my
lether doblet a paire of hose and a paire of shoes
and a Jaket. Also I will that the xviii Li<bri> of money the
whiche William Walker and John Lawe of ffillingley aforsaid
oweth me for a certeyn woodlande hold
by copie of my lorde of Burgevenny named Orrynges otherwise
called Shawbery lying in the parishe
of ffillingley aforsaid the whiche the said William Walker
and John Lawe bought of me for the
said sume of xviii Li<bri> be dispoased as hereafter
ensueth that is to say I geve and bequeth unto the
said Barnabe Holbage six pounds. Item to William Depyng six
pounds. Item to a discrete secular preest
to singe and pray for my soule in the parishe church
of ffyllingley aforsaid by the space and terme
of oon hole yere next after my deceas six pounds
And I will that the said William Depyng according to
his promyse to me made make a surrendre of the said woodland
called Orrynges otherwise Shawbery
Unto the Use and behove of the said William Walker
and John Lawe whan and at such tyme as he
shalbe required thereunto according to his said promyse.
These being witnesse Sir Richard Jurden prest, Thomas
Holbage the yonger Sir Hugh Bagley vicar of Corley, Leonard
Holbage and Richard Tydde
with other moo.

[PROB 11/23 48v (8)]

PROBATUM fuit testamentum suprascripti defuncti coram prefatis commissariis
in ecclesia Cathedrali <Sancti> Domini Pauli London<iensi>- quarto die mensis
Maii Anno Domini millessimo quingentesimo xxix^{0} iuramento
BARNABE HOLBAGE executoris in huiusmodi testamento nominati
Ac approbatum et infirmatum Et commissa fuit
administratio auctoritate prefatorum Reverendissimorum
patrum omnium et singulorum bonorum
Inventorum et creditorum dicti defuncti
prefato executori. De bene et fideliter administrando ac de
pleno et fideli Iuramento secundo die
post festum
sancti Thome marturis proximi futuri exhibendo
necnon de plano et vero compoto reddendo Ad sancta
Dei Evangelio Iurat. Reservata potestate alteri executori
in huiusmodi testamento nominato cum venerit.

RAMSEY ABBEY:

THE LAST DAYS AND AFTER

F. Donald Logan

Ramsey Abbey must be numbered among the most important monastic institutions in medieval England.[1] Founded ca. 969 by St. Oswald, bishop of Worcester, and Ethelwin, ealdorman of East Anglia, Ramsey Abbey stands with such other tenth-century foundations as St. Albans, Westminster, Ely, and Peterborough as part of the great monastic movement of that century. At the time of the Domesday survey it was the fourth wealthiest monastery in England, and at the time of the Henrician survey of 1535 it was the tenth richest Benedictine house and, overall, the eleventh wealthiest religious house in England. In fact, its vast wealth, based on estates in the rich lands of the East Midlands and the fenlands, earned for it the sobriquet "Ramsey the Rich." Despite its national status, precious little is known of the inner life of Ramsey Abbey. It is an irony that more is known about the economic and social life of the Ramsey estates than is known about the life of the monastery itself, whose existence justified the holding of these estates. Ramsey Abbey was established as a school of perfection, as an institution

[1]For Ramsey Abbey see William Dugdale, *Monasticon anglicanum*, new ed., 6 vols. in 8 (London, 1817–30), 2: 546–92; *Victoria County History: Huntingdonshire*, vol. 1 (1926), pp. 377–85.

dedicated to the life of the spirit, as a place where men renounced the cares of this world and sought meaning for life by work and prayer, following the rule of St. Benedict. The successes and failures in living these ideals, as well as the almost inevitable compromises, are mostly unknown to us. It is a further irony that we perhaps know more about the inner life of Ramsey Abbey in its final days than we do about any other time in its 570 years. This paper describes the last days of Ramsey and the fate of the monks at its dissolution.

Bishops of Lincoln, within whose diocese lay Ramsey Abbey, frequently conducted canonical visitations. About a century before the period with which this paper is concerned, Bishop Fleming visited Ramsey in 1420, 1422, and 1427; Bishop Gray, in 1432; and, most significantly, Bishop Alnwick, in 1439. The next records of visitations that survive are for the visitations of 1518 and 1530: they provide us with "snapshots" of what we now know were the final decades in the life of Ramsey Abbey.

On 15 June 1518 William Atwater, bishop of Lincoln (1514–21), sat in the chapter house at Ramsey and there interviewed, one by one, each of the monks of the community. From the records of these interviews a picture of the life of Ramsey Abbey appears.[2] It is the picture of a monastery whose life was far removed from pristine and even reformed Benedictinism. The ideal of a community of men working and praying together did not exist at Ramsey. Most striking is the fact that, of a community of 30 or so, only the prior and one or two other monks attended the daily conventual Mass. Few monks rose at night to pray matins, at most a mere handful comprised of the

---

[2]For the text see A. Hamilton Thompson, ed., *Visitations in the Diocese of Lincoln, 1517–1531*, vol. 3, Lincoln Record Society, vol. 37 (1947): 83–88. For Thompson's remarks see ibid., vol. 1 (LRS, vol. 33 [1940]): lv–lvii.

prior and some young monks. When senior members attended liturgical hours, they attended daytime offices and, even then, they were said to chat while the young monks sang. Moreover, there is not even a suggestion that the abbot was in any way a participant in the liturgical life of the monastery. One would expect cenobitical monks at least to share the same table. Although many complaints were made to Bishop Atwater about the subject of meals—the servants were rude, there was daily uncertainty about where and when to eat—one has the clear impression that only a small fraction of the community actually shared a common table at any one time.[3]

Further, the work of Ramsey monks by 1518 had long been involved in the obedientiary system whereby many of the monks acted as agents for the monastery, managing parts of the monastic estates. Even if the ever-present temptations of fraud and peculation were resisted—and some of the charges in 1518 suggest that temptations occasionally had been yielded to—the managerial demands required monks to be frequently absent from choir and table.[4] While a community of 50 monks was thought to be the customary size at Ramsey, Atwater found only 40 monks—in 1437 there had been 44—and enjoined Abbot John Lawrence to increase the number. Professor A. Hamilton Thompson, noting that in 1518 one monk asserted that there were 30 monks at Ramsey, concluded that the other 10 were living at the Ramsey cell at nearby St. Ives (sometimes called

---

[3]About monastic diet, see Christopher Harper-Bill, "The Labourer Is Worthy of His Hire?—Complaints about Diet in Late Medieval English Monasteries," in *The Church in Pre-Reformation Society: Essays in Honour of F. R. H. Du Boulay*, ed. Caroline M. Barron and C. Harper-Bill (Woodbridge, Suff., 1985), pp. 95–107.

[4]For the dangers to the monastic life inherent in the obedientary system see David Knowles, *The Monastic Order in England: A History of Its Development from the Times of St. Dunstan to the Fourth Lateran Council, 940–1216*, 2nd ed. (Cambridge, 1963), pp. 431–39.

the Priory of St. Ives).[5] The actual Ramsey community at any one time, given the coming and going of obedientiary monks and the presence of aged and infirm monks living in the infirmary, perhaps seldom exceeded 20 or so.

Atwater's interviews show that many of the monks wanted a more cloistered life, in which their privacy was respected. As it was, the monastic gates were not properly closed at night, and the walls and enclosures were not secured. Thus, monks could and did leave the enclosure at night, and lay persons were able to enter the monastery, even the monastic church, from which a gold chalice had been stolen. The prior, often drunk, allowed his lay friends to enter the monks' dormer, where they secretly spied on the young monks. Much of the complaint about the prior centered on his familiarity with laymen, to whom, when drunk, he revealed the secrets of the monastery and even the confessions of the monks. Amidst the laxity of the enclosure and the secular occupations of many of the monks one looks for evidence of intellectual activity, only to be disappointed. Atwater, in what sounds like exasperation, enjoined the abbot yet again to provide for education in basic studies for the novices: "sepius ante hac fuit taliter sibi iniunctum et non curat illam adimplere" ("he has been so enjoined often in the past and has done nothing").

The fabric of the monastery itself was in serious need of repair. The roof of the dormer leaked so that rain fell on the monks at night in their beds. The great monastic church had a roof that allowed rain to fall on the organ and, even, on the high altar. At St. Ives the church and other buildings were said to be in a state of great ruin, and a carpenter, after erecting a scaffold there, stopped his work because he had not been paid.

---

[5]For the cell at St. Ives see *VCH Hunts.* 1: 388–89; for the fullest treatment of the town of St. Ives see Ellen Wedemeyer Moore, *The Fairs of Medieval England: An Introductory Study* (Toronto, 1985), pt. 2.

In addition, the records of the visitation of 1518 contain complaint after complaint from monks concerning the inefficiency of their colleagues who allowed the monastic tenements to fall into ruin, wasted the wood, failed to pay their bills, and left office retaining money acquired while they had been in office. Atwater demanded an open rendering of accounts each year by the abbot, cellarer, sacristan, prior of St. Ives, almoner, and pittancer: it should be rendered to the community in the chapter house and last at least two or three days, and the extent of ruin and waste should be determined and remedied.

On 18 June, Bishop Atwater concluded his visitation and moved on to Peterborough Abbey, having given injunctions to correct the abuses that have been summarized here. He reserved to himself the right to send further injunctions. It is difficult, even at this remove in time, not to detect at Ramsey Abbey in 1518 a monastery suffering from neglect spiritually, intellectually, and even materially. Thirteen years later another bishop of Lincoln was to sit in the chapter house at Ramsey Abbey.

On 30 August 1530 John Longland, bishop of Lincoln (1521–47), personally appeared for the beginning of a two-day visitation.[6] Some echoes of 1518 can be heard, but they are not so insistent or so strident. The difference could be the difference in visitor or, indeed, record-keeper. Now there is no mention of lay infringements of the monastic enclosure, now no indictments of inefficient obedientiaries, now no reference to a generational gap between junior and senior monks. In 1530 Ramsey had 38 professed monks (including the abbot) and, in addition, six novices. The responses of 33 of the professed monks survive. Of these, 14 said simply, "omnia sunt bene." Most of the senior officials were among these: abbot, prior, sacristan, warden of

[6]For this visitation see Thompson, *Visitations* 3: 89–94. Longland's vicar general, Dr. John Rayne, had formally opened the visitation on the previous day.

the chapel of the Virgin, infirmarian, subsacristan, sacristan of the shrine of St. Ives, and precentor.

About the keeping of the liturgical hours no complaint was made, at least about Ramsey itself, but, indeed, about St. Ives, it was reported that only three or four monks attended matins. Although clearly some instruction in learning had been introduced in the years since 1518, five of the monks now urged the need of instruction in grammar: there had been no such instruction since Lent and the (unnamed) instructor was remiss and negligent. The subprior, William Alwyn, was criticized for his harshness in correcting the faults of the monks and for his drunkenness, whereas he, in turn, complained that his efforts to reform the monastery were not supported by the prior, John Dryver alias Ramsey. One presumes that the leaking roofs over dormer and church had been repaired, but now the monk William Swasey said that the monastic buildings were ruinous and subprior Alwyn, more specifically, reported that the refectory needed repair in the buttresses and columns and that the dormer and chapter house needed repair to their foundations. Reports, too, were made about the ruinous conditions of tenements pertaining to specific obedientiaries: in Ramsey, in Redybone, in the farms at Wigan, Broughton, and Berysted.

The reports of the 1530 visitation are difficult to assess. Had reforms taken effect since the last visitation? Was a more regular life being lived at Ramsey? Were the hours of the office being chanted by the well and able? Was the community now more aware of itself as a community? Were the community activities of eating and praying together now playing a more central role in the monastic life at Ramsey? One suspects that, although some changes followed the visitation of 1518, Ramsey continued much as it had done for over a century, not without fervent monks but not with the spiritual feeling and high idealism of some of the reformed monastic institutions of the time, such as the Observant Franciscans, the Bridgettine nuns, and the Carthusians.

The years that immediately preceded the surrender of Ramsey Abbey in November 1539 witnessed the most radical changes in the history of the English church, changes in which Ramsey was both spectator and participant. The personal role of Abbot John Lawrence alias Warboys in these affairs is not always easy to detect, yet he does appear frequently as an actor in the great events of the times. With 25 other Benedictine abbots he was summoned to the parliament which first met in November 1529, which sat until 1536 in seven sessions, and which is called by modern historians the Reformation Parliament. How often he attended is impossible to say: attendance records exist only for the fifth session (15 January–30 March 1534), when Lawrence was represented by proxy.[7] He also was called to sit in the upper house of the convocation of the clergy of the southern province, which met concurrently with Parliament. Again attendance records are unavailable. What is known is that in 1531 he joined other members of the Lords (including Bishop Longland, who had visited Ramsey during the previous year) in a strongly worded letter to the pope in favor of the king's divorce.[8] Lawrence was presumably present in convocation in 1531 when nine bishops (including John Fisher) and 62 abbots and priors acknowledged the king as supreme head of the church in England "quantum per Christi legem licet."[9] His presence on 16 May 1532, when convocation gave

[7]In general, see the invaluable work by Stanford E. Lehmberg, *The Reformation Parliament 1529–1536* (Cambridge, 1970).

[8]See Nicholas Pocock, ed., *Records of the Reformation: The Divorce 1527–1533*, 2 vols. (Oxford, 1870), 1: 429–33.

[9]David Wilkins, ed., *Concilia Magnae Britanniae et Hiberniae*, 4 vols. (London, 1737), 3: 742; Gilbert Burnet, *The History of the Reformation of the Church of England*, ed. Nicholas Pocock, 7 vols. (Oxford, 1865), 1: 191.

up its right to legislate independently, is less certain; Dr. Michael Kelly has demonstrated that the clergy in very large numbers absented themselves on that day and that merely a "rump" voted in favor.[10] Lawrence was clearly not present during the fifth session (15 January–30 March 1534), which *inter alia* enacted the Act of the Submission of the Clergy, the Ecclesiastical Appointments Act, and the Act of Succession, which recognized the royal divorce and the validity of the king's marriage to Anne Boleyn.[11] It seems unlikely that he attended the concomitant convocation, which in March 1534 rejected papal supremacy. In June of that year Henry VIII declared himself Supreme Head of the English church, and in the second half of that year commissioners were busy taking oaths from every religious in England, oaths rejecting papal authority and affirming the royal supremacy. Although only about a hundred certificates of these oaths survive—not, alas, the certificate for Ramsey—there can be little doubt that Abbot Lawrence and the monks of Ramsey sometime in the second half of 1534 under oath accepted the king as head of the church. No saving clauses appear in the oath: the clear and unambiguous rejection of the pope and the just as clear and unambiguous affirmation of the king as *caput ecclesiae*. The refusal of any abbey to take this oath would surely have caused considerable attention and almost certainly would have left some traces in the records. With Professor David Knowles, we must conclude that the religious houses of England affirmed the royal supremacy in 1534.[12]

---

[10]"The Submission of the Clergy," *Transactions of the Royal Historical Society*, 5th ser., 15 (1965): 116–17, where he quotes the sources as identifying the heads of religious houses merely by the words "quidam prelati."

[11]*Journals of the House of Lords*, vol. 1 (London [?1742]), p. 58, where it records that he constituted the abbots of Hyde and Hulme as his proxies; see Lehmberg, *Reformation Parliament*, pp. 258–59.

[12]*The Religious Orders in England*, 3 vols. (Cambridge, 1948–59), 3: 178–79.

There the matter could have remained—an autonomous English church with religious houses. It is quite conceivable that the monasteries of England could have continued; there was no inevitable connection between the royal supremacy and the suppression of the monasteries and other religious houses. Other factors, however, did intervene.[13] In early 1535 commissioners conducted an evaluation of all property of the church, of which the king was acknowledged head. Local commissioners came to Ramsey and quickly accomplished a survey of the property subject to the new tax (a tenth) on ecclesiastical property. The report, contained in the *Valor ecclesiasticus*, shows the net annual value of the taxable wealth of Ramsey was £1,715 12*s*.3*d*.[14] During the latter half of 1535 and the early part of 1536, Cromwell sent visitors to conduct a visitation of the religious houses of England, the purpose of which (it is now commonly agreed) had little to do with spiritual renewal. Thomas Bedyll, archdeacon of London, visited Ramsey Abbey in January 1536, where he seems to have spent at least three days.[15] This ungenerous critic of the monasteries he visited gave an uncharacteristically glowing account of Ramsey:

---

[13]The literature on the dissolution of the monasteries is vast. It is led by a classic of modern historical writing, Knowles, *Religious Orders*, vol. 3. Older, somewhat partisan, yet still useful are Francis A. Gasquet, *Henry VIII and the English Monasteries* (London, 1899), and G. G. Coulton, *Five Centuries of Religion*, 4: *The Last Days of Medieval Monachism* (Cambridge, 1950). Most recent general studies include G. W. O. Woodward, *The Dissolution of the Monasteries* (London, 1966), and Joyce A. Youings, *The Dissolution of the Monasteries* (London, 1971).

[14]*Valor ecclesiasticus temp. Henr. VIII*, ed. John Caley and Joseph Hunter, 6 vols. (London, 1810–34), 4: 271–75. The standard study of the *Valor* is Alexander N. Savine, *English Monasteries on the Eve of the Dissolution* (Oxford, 1909), where the net taxable revenue of Ramsey is given as £1,843 4*s*.10*d*. David Knowles and R. Neville Hadcock, *Medieval Religious Houses, England and Wales*, new ed. (London, 1971), p. 56, give the total as £1,761, possibly a misprint for the total of the *Valor* rounded off to £1,716.

[15]See Thomas Wright, ed., *Three Chapters of Letters Relating to the Suppression of Monasteries*, Camden Society, vol. 26 (1843): 98–100. He was at Ramsey at least from 13 to 15 Jan. The *comperta* for Ramsey Abbey have not survived.

> . . . in mine opinion the abbot and convent be as true and as faithful obedientiaries to the king's grace as any religious folks in this realm and live as uprightly as any other, after the best sort of living that hath been among religious folks this many years, that is to say, more given to ceremonies than is necessary. I pray God I may find other houses in no worse condition, and then I will be right glad that I took this journey.[16]

This appraisal stands in sharp contrast to the situation found at Ramsey by the bishop-visitors in the previous decades. If Bedyll's report was accurate, a remarkable change had occurred since Bishop Atwater's visitation in 1518. It has been suggested that "more material considerations" may have contributed to Bedyll's satisfaction.[17] We shall never know. Two other issues arose from Bedyll's visit to Ramsey. He told Cromwell that Abbot Lawrence had exhibited in the parish church at Ramsey a charter of King Edgar, which Lawrence interpreted as the acceptance by the monastery of the supreme headship of King Edgar over the English church.[18] The other matter concerned two monks who wished to be relieved of their monastic obligations. Bedyll noted that other visitors were granting such requests, but he needed further direction from Cromwell. The two monks undoubtedly were Richard Chickenwell alias Triamell and Thomas Benson alias Burton, who on 13 February 1536 received *capacities* (i.e., dispensations) to abandon their habits and to hold ecclesiastical benefices.[19]

---

[16]Wright, *Three Chapters*, p. 98. Spelling and punctuation have been modernized here and elsewhere in this paper. Knowles describes Bedyll as "one of the least attractive of Cromwell's minions," a man of "coarse texture of mind," whose "letters are almost universally repellant" (*Religious Orders* 3: 274 and n.).

[17]Knowles, *Religious Orders* 3: 284.

[18]Bedyll sent a letter to Cromwell about this charter on 13 Jan. 1536 (*Letters and Papers, Foreign and Domestic, of the Reign of Henry VIII*, ed. J. S. Brewer, James Gairdner, and R. H. Brodie, 22 vols. in 35 [London, 1862–1932], 10: 90).

[19]David S. Chambers, ed., *Faculty Office Registers, 1534–1549: A Calendar of the First Two Registers of the Archbishop of Canterbury's Faculty Office* (Oxford, 1966),

Ramsey no doubt felt secure when in March of that year Parliament enacted the dissolution of the smaller religious houses, that is, those with an annual taxable income of less than £200. It was widely thought (with justification) that this was the extent of the intended suppression. The language of the act gave reassurance: the dispossessed monks would be able to live the monastic life more religiously in "divers and great solemn monasteries of this realm wherein (thanks be to God) religion is right well kept and observed."[20] In January 1536 Abbot Lawrence attended the funeral of Catherine of Aragon at Peterborough Abbey. It is quite probable that no further action against the monasteries was contemplated at the time of the suppression of the lesser houses and that it was the realization of the income from these houses that whetted the king's (and, indeed, Cromwell's) appetite for the major houses. From our vantage point mixed signs are seen. Twice in July 1537 the king refounded religious houses to pray for him and his queen, Jane Seymour, then pregnant with the future Edward VI: the Benedictine abbey at Chertsey, Surrey, was re-established in the former monastery of the Augustinian canons at Bisham, Berkshire—the move was effected in December—and Premonstratensian canonesses replaced the Benedictine nuns at Stixwold, Lincolnshire.[21] While the king was re-establishing these religious houses, rumors of the dissolution of the major monasteries were clearly in the wind: on 11 December 1537, John Hussee wrote to Lord Lisle that Warden Abbey had already been suppressed and that Ramsey, Peterborough, St.

---

p. 45. Benson later appeared in Boulogne (1546) and at Throcking, Herts. (1550) (see G. A. J. Hodgett, "The Unpensioned Ex-Religious in Tudor England," *Journal of Ecclesiastical History* 13 [1962]: 202).

[20]27 Hen. VIII, c. 28 (*The Statutes of the Realm* 3: 575).

[21]See Knowles, *Religious Orders* 3: 350. For more detail see Knowles and Hadcock, *Medieval Religious Houses*, pp. 59–60, 62, 266, 283.

Albans, and Sawtrey would also surrender.[22] In the event, Ramsey did not surrender for almost two years.

Although the actual surrender of Ramsey Abbey did not occur until November 1539, preliminary measures had been under way for over a year. On 15 October 1538, Richard Williams alias Cromwell, nephew of Thomas Cromwell (his sister's son) and a commissioner visiting religious houses in that part of England, wrote to Cromwell from Ramsey: he had already visited Ely Priory and would go next to Peterborough, and at Ramsey he found the abbot "conformable to everything."[23] When Parliament met in 1539, Abbot Lawrence was among the 19 heads of religious houses summoned (for the last time) and was present on the days (May 13, 16, and 19) when the bill for the suppression of the greater monasteries was read.[24] One suspects that Lawrence, having accepted the inevitable, was using his time at Westminster arranging a suitable pension.

Ramsey Abbey surrendered to the Crown on 22 November 1539. It was a voluntary surrender, yet voluntary only in a most circumscribed sense. During 1538 and 1539 intimidation by bullying and threats caused one after another of the greater houses to surrender. The Act for Dissolution of Abbeys (1539) gave statutory right for the estates of these houses to be ceded to the Crown.[25]

Like a row of pins, the greater abbeys began to fall. Many of the Cistercian houses surrendered in 1538: in January, Boxley; in February, Coggeshall; in March, Holmcultram, Stratford,

---

[22]Gairdner, *Letters and Papers* 12 (2): 283.

[23]Wright, *Three Chapters*, pp. 146–47.

[24]For those summoned see Stanford E. Lehmberg, *The Later Parliaments of Henry VIII, 1536–1547* (Cambridge, 1977), pp. 52–53. For attendance see *Journals of the House of Lords* 1: 110.

[25]31 Hen. VIII, c. 13 (*Statutes of the Realm* 3: 733–39).

Revesby; in April, Beaulieu, Robertsbridge; in July, Vale Royal, Combermere, Bordesley; in September, Croxden, Biddlesden, Hutton; in October, Dieulacres; in November, Pipewell; and, in December, Rievaulx.[26] The major Benedictine monasteries were among the last to fall. In November 1539 there began a flood of surrenders that did not ebb until early in the next year.[27] During November alone such great abbeys as Reading, Bury St. Edmunds, St. Mary's, York, Peterborough, Winchester Cathedral Priory, Evesham, and Ramsey among the Benedictines, and Fountains, the wealthiest of the Cistercian houses, all accepted terms of surrender. As is well known, commissioners sent to receive the surrenders made their circuits. Five commissioners comprised the team that came to Ramsey. Philip Parys, who was appointed sheriff of Cambridgeshire and Huntingdonshire while visiting Ramsey, corresponded with Cromwell and appears to have led the commissioners. The actual negotiations were probably left to two experienced canon lawyers, John Tregonwell (who had been involved in the 1535 monastic visitations) and John Hughes (who in 1535 helped to draft the Henrician canons).[28] Two officials of the Court of Augmentations, William Legh and Robert Burgoyne, filled out the team,[29] but it was Parys, Tregonwell, and Hughes who sent the agreement for the approval of Sir Richard Rich, chancellor of the Court of Augmentations.

---

[26]See Knowles and Hadcock, *Medieval Religious Houses*, passim.

[27]Virtually completed by the end of Jan., 1540, the surrenders continued to trickle in until 23 Mar., when the Augustinian abbot and canons of Waltham Abbey surrendered.

[28]For Tregonwell see A. B. Emden, *A Biographical Register of the University of Oxford, A.D. 1501 to 1540* (*BRUO*) (Oxford, 1974), pp. 575–76; for Hughes, ibid., p. 308, and F. Donald Logan, "The Henrician Canons," *Bulletin of the Institute of Historical Research* 47 (1974): 103n.

[29]See Walter C. Richardson, *History of the Court of Augmentations, 1536–1554* (Baton Rouge, 1961), pp. 50, 55.

The commissioners who had been at Ely Priory on 18 November 1539 remained at Ramsey Abbey probably from 22 to 25 November before moving on to Peterborough (29–30 November), Thorney (1–3 December), Crowland (4 December), Spalding (8 December), and Wallingswells (14 December).[30] Writing from Ramsey a letter destined for Cromwell's eyes, Parys said that he found "Dr. Tregonwell and other [John Hughes] very honest men, conformable and diligent."[31] That this whole business was being conducted in a great hurry is eminently clear. In the same letter Parys admitted that mistakes might have been made at Ely in assigning pensions, but their time was short and they worked until ten o'clock every night. It would be a mistake to think that the commissioners came to Ramsey to convince the monks to surrender. The surrender of the abbey was rightly presumed; their task was to arrange the terms of surrender. The deed of surrender, now lost, was signed on 22 November 1539 amidst discussions of pensions.[32] On that day there ceased to exist the religious community that since the mid-tenth century had endeavored, often quite imperfectly, to be a witness to enduring, nonworldly, transcendental spiritual values. The last words were not psalms and antiphons—they were about pounds, shillings, and pence.

Abbot Lawrence and 29 other monks comprised the community of Ramsey Abbey at the dissolution. The monastic site at Ramsey and a large part of the Ramsey estates were granted in March 1540 to Richard Williams alias Cromwell, who had

---

[30]Gairdner and Brodie, *Letters and Papers* 14 (2): 542, 565, 602, 621, 629, 631, 652, 681.

[31]Gairdner and Brodie, *Letters and Papers* 14 (2): 584.

[32]For a surviving surrender see the English translation of the surrender of the Cistercian abbey at Forde, Dorset, in Youings, *Dissolution*, pp. 185–86.

visited "rich Ramsey" in October 1538.[33] This is already well-known. But the story of the monks themselves remains to be told.[34] Soon after the surrender the monks were released from their monastic obligations. In the new order, dispensations from monastic vows—"capacities," as they were called—were given by the Faculty Office (set up in 1534 to replace the papal granting of dispensations in England): each monk of Ramsey on 29 January 1540 was allowed to exchange his habit for the garb of a secular priest and to hold a benefice.[35] It should be emphasized that these capacities did not allow monks in holy orders to marry or to become laymen. One further provision was still needed: pensions, although agreed upon at the time of the surrender in late November, still needed to be formally granted.

[33]Gairdner and Brodie, *Letters and Papers* 15: 436 (20); see *VCH Hunts.* 2: 193.

[34]On the fate of dispossessed monks, a reliable general account awaits writing. Geoffrey Baskerville's "The Dispossessed Religious after the Suppression of the Monasteries," in *Essays in History Presented to Reginald Lane Poole*, ed. H. W. C. Davis (Oxford, 1927), pp. 436–65, is to be preferred to his later *English Monks and the Suppression of the Monasteries* (London, 1937). Among the local studies see W. A. J. Archbold, *The Somerset Religious Houses* (Cambridge, 1892); Hugh Aveling, "The Rievaulx Community after the Dissolution," *Ampleforth Journal* 57 (1952): 101–13; idem, "The Monks of Byland Abbey after the Dissolution," ibid. 60 (1955): 3–15; Geoffrey Baskerville, "Dispossessed Religious of Gloucestershire," *Transactions of the Bristol and Gloucestershire Archaeological Society* 49 (1927): 63–122; J. H. Bettey, *The Suppression of the Monasteries in the West Country* (Gloucester, 1989); R. V. H. Burne, "The Dissolution of St. Werburgh's Abbey," *Journal of the Chester and North Wales Archaeological Society* 37 (1948–49): 5–35; W. G. Clark-Maxwell, "The Monks of Much Wenlock after the Suppression," *Transactions of the Shropshire Archaeological Society*, 4th ser., 9 (1923–24): 169–75; Claire Cross, "A Metamorphosis of Ministry: Former Yorkshire Monks and Friars in the Sixteenth Century," *Journal of the United Reform Church History Society* 4 (1989): 289–304; Christopher Haigh, *The Last Days of the Lancashire Monasteries and the Pilgrimage of Grace*, Chetham Society (1969); Denys Hay, "The Dissolution of the Monasteries in the Diocese of Durham," *Archaeologia Aeliana*, 4th ser., 15 (1938): 101–12; Francis A. Hibbert, *The Dissolution of the Monasteries . . . of Staffordshire* (London, 1910); G. A. J. Hodgett, ed., *The State of the Ex-Religious and Former Chantry Priests in the Diocese of Lincoln, 1547–1574*, Lincoln Record Society, vol. 53 (1959); idem, "The Dissolution of the Monasteries in Lincolnshire," unpub. M.A. thesis (Univ. of London, 1947).

[35]Chambers, *Faculty Office Registers*, p. 207.

The adequacy of pensions given by the Crown to dispossessed religious continues to be the source of debate. In general, friars and women religious fared very badly, receiving much less than what was required for subsistence, and many of these religious received no pensions at all. The Black Monks fared better than the friars and women religious, but even here the generosity of the pension is not always clear. The smallest amount received by a Ramsey monk was £5 per annum, which allowed the monk a bare subsistence.[36] Of course, senior members of the community received more than this. It is clear that the actual amounts were hammered out by the commissioners during their visit to Ramsey in November. Sir Richard Rich's Court of Augmentations must have been working overtime to process the large number of pensions flooding from Augmentations at this time. On 10 February 1540 the abbot and monks of Ramsey were given letters patent that granted them their annual pensions. The amount was to be received annually, in two equal installments at Annunciation Day (25 March) and Michaelmas (29 September), beginning with the Michaelmas just past. If the pensioner received one or more benefice or other promotion paying the amount of the pension or more, the pension would cease. Otherwise, it was for life.[37]

From these letters patent and from two contemporary lists it is possible to reconstruct what provisions were made for the former monks of Ramsey at the time of the dissolution. One of these is a pension list, which in fact was the warrant for the letters patent and which summarized the provisions of the

[36]For the income of beneficed and (particularly) unbeneficed clergy see M. L. Zell, "Economic Problems of the Parochial Clergy in the Sixteenth Century," in Rosemary O'Day and Felicity Heal, eds., *Princes & Paupers in the English Church, 1500–1800* (Leicester, 1981), pp. 1–43.

[37]Copies of the letters patent for Ramsey monks are PRO E315/234/147v–155v. For an example see the Appendix below.

letters patent; the other is a list, undoubtedly drawn up at this time, that lists the offices held, where applicable, and the names and aliases for most of the monks. All three sources list the abbot first, then the prior of St. Ives (a cell of Ramsey), the prior of Ramsey, and, obviously in order of seniority, the remaining 27 monks.[38] The list of pensioners and pensions that follows conflates these three sources:

John Lawrence alias Warboys, abbot
- Bodsey House with its appurtenances
- 100 loads taken in equal measure from local woods
- a mark of swans and the profits thereof
- certain fishing rights in waters and ponds in Ramsey
- a piece of marshland called the "Hylke" (hillock?)
- annual sum of £266 13*s.*4*d.*

Robert Huchyn alias Stamford, prior of cell at St. Ives
- the chapel and chamber on the bridge at St. Ives
- £12

John Dryver alias Ramsey, prior of Ramsey
- £20

John Pakye [senior] alias Ringstead, infirmarian
- £8

John Anyson alias Downham, subcellarer
- £8

John Nycolls alias Glatton, an old man
- £8

Lawrence Bardeney alias Langham, warden of the chapel and land at St. Ives, being aged
- £8

[38]The pension list is PRO E315/245/64r–v, calendared in Gairdner and Brodie, *Letters and Papers* 15: 1032 (p. 548). The other list is in BL Cotton MS. Julius R.IX, fol. 1, which is faded towards the bottom and then torn, thus omitting the last name: George Marshall.

William Sylke alias Sawtry, chamberlain
- £8
William Rogers alias Holywell, prior of the cell at Modney and warden of Hurst
- £8
William Alwyn, cantor
- £9
Stephen Bawdwyn alias Bennett, guestmaster
- £7
Thomas Baker alias Therfield, cellarer
- £10
William Cooke alias Barnwell, warden of Barnwell
- £7
Thomas Powle alias Brancaster
- £6
John Pakye [junior] alias Crowland, treasurer
- £6 13*s.* 4*d.*
John Hodyngsells alias Lilford, bachelor of canon law, secretary to the lord abbot
- £9
John Faunte alias Kingston [i.e., Wistow], bachelor of theology
- £10
John Pawmer alias Holywell, subprior
- £6 13*s.* 4*d.*
Thomas Andrewe alias Eaton, being a sickly person
- £7 6*s.* 4*d.*
William Pricke alias Swavesey, subsacristan
- £5 6*s.* 8*d.*
John Brigeman alias Burwell
- £6
Robert Harrys alias Stanground, subcantor
- £5 6*s.* 8*d.*

Richard Hawling alias Ramsey, scholar of Oxford
- £6 13*s*.4*d*.
Hugh Phillippe alias Broughton, sacristan at St. Ives
- £6
William Ireland alias Earith, scholar of Oxford
- £6 13*s*.4*d*.
Thomas Fylde alias Hemingford
- £5
John Pycarde [alias Warboys]
- £5
John Smyth alias Tichmarsh
- £5
John Whitwell alias Billingborough
- £5 6*s*.8*d*.
George Marshall alias London
- £5 6*s*.8*d*.

This pension list requires comment—first, with respect to what was granted. The award to John Lawrence was very large by any measure. Apart from the use of Bodsey House and the wood and fishing rights and other incidentals, he was to receive an enormous annual payment, more than twice that of the rest of the monks combined. One suspects that this large pension was by way of reward for the accommodation Lawrence showed in securing the surrender. Apart from the priors of Ramsey and St. Ives, the amounts assigned to the other monks varied from £10 to £5 (for three of the junior monks). We shall never know precisely how the amounts were arrived at, but it seems clear that they bore some reference to years in the monastery and offices held at the time of the dissolution. Not counting the cash value of the rights conceded to the former abbot and the value to Robert Huchyn of his room and chapel, the amount to be expended annually out of the Court of Augmentations to the

Ramsey pensioners totaled £489 out of a net annual taxable income from the Ramsey holdings of £1,715 12*s*.3*d*. For how long this sum of £489 was paid is uncertain; all that is certain is that half that amount was paid out almost immediately (i.e., the retroactive payment from the preceding Michaelmas). Lawrence, who had been abbot since 1507, was not to live very long to enjoy his pension: he moved to the Ramsey manor house at Burwell in Cambridgeshire, where he died in 1542 and where, in the parish church, a monumental brass in his honor was placed.[39] At his death he was attended by three of his former monks—John Faunte, John Pawmer, and George Marshall, whom he called his chaplains and who apparently constituted a small community, a sort of miniature Ramsey Abbey. These three chaplains are mentioned in the ex-abbot's will. In addition, Lawrence bequeathed the sum of 6*s*.8*d*. to each of "the prests that were of the house of Ramsey."[40] Others also may not have survived long after the dissolution: in the pension grants John Nycolls was called "an old man," Lawrence Bardeney, "being aged," and Thomas Andrewe, "a sickly person." None of these pensioners appears subsequently in the records. Thus, the actual amount paid out to the Ramsey pensioners from Augmentations was a diminishing expenditure.

How adequate were these pensions? If we put to one side the generous amounts given to the abbot and the two priors, the average is slightly over £7. A national average does not exist,

---

[39]See Mill Stephenson, *A List of Monumental Brasses in the British Isles*, Monumental Brass Society (1964 repr.): 56; also, Muriel Clayton, ed., *Catalogue of Rubbings of Brasses and Incised Slabs*, 2nd ed. (London, 1968 repr.), pp. 10–11, 129, who states that the brass was originally engraved during Lawrence's lifetime (probably ca. 1520), showing the abbot in full pontificals, but was later reversed and a new engraving made, showing him simply in cassock and surplice. See also John Page-Phillips, *Palimpsests: The Backs of Monumental Brasses*, 2 vols. (London, 1980), 1: 84 and 2: 153.

[40]PRO PROB 11/29, q. 11, fols. 86v–87r. The will was witnessed 12 Dec. 1541, probated 7 Nov. 1542.

but Knowles reckoned that it would be about £5 10*s*. In this case, Ramsey would be higher than the average. The older monks fared fairly well, and the younger monks might find other employment. What needs emphasizing in all this is that the amount granted in the letters patent was in fact never received: deducted at source were a twice-yearly fee of 4*d.* on the pound and, for most years, a tenth (i.e., 10 per cent), which, when combined, seriously eroded the pension (by 11.5 per cent).[41]

From this list some progress can be made towards drawing a profile of the religious community at Ramsey at the dissolution. Most significantly, we can see the catchment area from which Ramsey drew its monks at this time. It can be taken as fairly certain that with one exception the *alias* refers to the place of origin of the monk. The exception is Stephen Bawdwyn alias Bennett, which was a common surname in Huntingdonshire villages.[42] For William Alwyn no *alias* is given. For the remaining 28 monks, however, it is possible to identify the places from which they came. From Ramsey itself, in apparent exception to the monastic statutes, came two monks.[43] Seven others came from neighboring villages in the Hurstingstone Hundred: two from Warboys, two from Holywell, and one each from Broughton, Wistow (i.e., Kingston), and Earith. A further four monks came from other parts of Huntingdonshire: Glatton, Sawtry, Stanground, and Hemingford. Thus, 13 of the 28 about whose places of origin we have information came from the local county. The three monks from Lincolnshire derived from

41Knowles, *Religious Orders* 3: 407.

42See, e.g., the village of Warboys in J. A. Raftis, *Warboys: Two Hundred Years in the Life of an English Mediaeval Village* (Toronto, 1974), pp. 71–72.

43For the statute prohibiting the monastery from accepting recruits from Ramsey lest they waste the alms of the monastery on their relatives, see A. Hamilton Thompson, ed., *Visitations of Religious Houses in the Diocese of Lincoln*, Lincoln Record Society, vol. 21 (1929), 3: 309.

villages near the fenland area: Stamford, Crowland, and Billingborough. Two others came from Cambridgeshire villages: Swavesey and Burwell. Four came from Norfolk places (Ringstead, Brancaster, Langham, Downham), in the first two of which places Ramsey held property. Three monks were from places in Northamptonshire: Barnwell, where Ramsey held property, Lilford, and Tichmarsh. Ramsey also held property in Therfield in Hertfordshire, whence one monk came.[44] Two places remain: London (one monk), which is clear enough, and Eaton (one monk), which is not so clear. Of the many Eatons it is difficult to determine the place of origin of Thomas Andrewe; the nearest appears to be Eaton Socon in Bedfordshire. The conclusion is obvious: the majority of the monks of Ramsey came from the immediate area, 75 per cent from Huntingdonshire, Cambridgeshire, Lincolnshire, and Northamptonshire. Despite its national prominence because of its wealth, Ramsey Abbey was essentially a regional monastery, drawing not only most of its wealth from local estates but also most of its recruits from local villages.

One further observation: Five of the 30 Ramsey monks were university-trained: Abbot Lawrence was a doctor of theology; John Hodyngsells, a bachelor of canon law—he had also spent three years studying in the arts faculty; John Faunte, a bachelor of theology; Richard Hawling and William Ireland were both students at Oxford at the time of the suppression.[45]

---

[44]Outside of Hunts., Ramsey also held property at places at Burwell (Cambs.) and Barnwell (Northants.) from which monks came. See *Valor ecclesiasticus* 4: 271ff. for Ramsey holdings.

[45]For Lawrence see Emden, *BRUO*, p. 605, s.v. Warboys: he supplicated for this degree in 1519. For Hodyngsells see ibid., p. 368, s.v. Lylford: he was admitted to this degree in 1532. For Faunte, ibid., p. 335, s.v. Kyngston: he became B.Th. in 1532. For Hawling, ibid., p. 474, s.v. Ramsey: he supplicated for D.Th. in July 1539. For Ireland, ibid., p. 192, s.v. Ereth. Faunte and Ireland had been at Gloucester College and so, no doubt, had the others.

Whatever one's judgment about the state of Ramsey at the dissolution, one must conclude that there can have been few monasteries in England at that time which could compare with Ramsey in terms of the proportion of university-trained monks in their communities.[46]

In addition, we can get at least a partial view of the changing composition of the Ramsey community by comparing the pension list of 1540 with information available from the visitations of 1518 and 1530. The visitor in 1518 did not compile a list of the monks, but from his record of the visitation we can glean the names of eight of the 40 monks at that time.[47] Three of these eight were still at Ramsey in 1539: the abbot, John Lawrence; John Pakye senior, who in 1518 held many offices (about which complaints were made to the visitor), who in 1530 was prior of St. Ives, and who in 1539, probably an elderly man, was infirmarian; and Stephen Bawdwyn, subcellarer in both 1518 and 1530 and guestmaster in 1539. The visitor in 1530 made a list of the community: 38 professed monks and six novices. Two other names appear in the 1530 visitation records, to produce a total of 40 professed monks and six novices.[48] What happened to them? Let us consider the novices first. All became professed, one was later dispensed

---

[46]Westminster Abbey, the wealthiest religious house in England, in 1540 had 11 university-trained monks in a community of fewer than 40: see Hugh Aveling, "Tudor Westminster, 1540–1559," in P. Justin McCann and Columba Cary-Elwes, eds., *Ampleforth and Its Origins: Essays on a Living Tradition* (London, 1952), p. 56. Also for Westminster see Barbara F. Harvey, "The Monks of Westminster and the University of Oxford," in *The Reign of Richard II: Essays in Honour of May McKisack*, ed. F. R. H. Du Boulay and Caroline M. Barron (London, 1971), pp. 108–30. For Norwich monks at the universities see Joan Greatrex, "Monk Students from Norwich Cathedral Priory at Oxford and Cambridge, c. 1300 to 1530," *English Historical Review* 106 (1991): 557–83.

[47]Thompson, *Visitations* 3: 83–89.

[48]Thompson, *Visitations* 3: 89–94.

(1536), and five were pensioned in 1540.[49] In addition to these five, 25 of the 40 monks who had been at Ramsey in 1530 were still there 10 years later. Of the others, one was dispensed and the others apparently had died.[50] The pension lists contain no new names, which may suggest that the 1530s was not a particularly attractive time to enter the monastic life.

What happened to the Ramsey "monks" after the dissolution and the granting of pensions? Four major sources assist us in answering this question: a 1551 list of former Ramsey monks still receiving pensions; a similar list for 1552; the 1554 return, only partially surviving, to the questions raised by Queen Mary about ex-monks; and the full list of pensioners drawn up by Cardinal Pole in 1556. Other sources fill in some details.

Of the 30 monks pensioned in 1540 only 17 were still receiving pensions in 1551, according to the list of pensioners of that year.[51] What had happened to the other 13 former monks of Ramsey during the intervening 11 years? It might prove helpful to list them:

John Lawrence, former abbot
Robert Huchyn, former prior of St. Ives
John Dryver, former prior of Ramsey
John Nycolls
Lawrence Bardeney
William Sylke

---

[49]The six were Thomas Fylde, Thomas Benson, John Pycarde, John Smyth, John Whitwell, and George Marshall. Benson was dispensed in 1536 (see above, p. 522).

[50]Richard Triamell was dispensed in 1536 (see p. 522 above).

[51]John Pakye sr., John Anyson, William Rogers, Thomas Baker, William Cooke, John Pakye jr., John Faunte, William Pricke, John Brigeman, Robert Harrys, Hugh Phillippe, William Ireland, Thomas Fylde, John Pycarde, John Smyth, John Whitwell, and George Marshall (PRO E101/533/4/16, reproduced in Hodgett, *State of the Ex-Religious*, pp. 26–27).

William Alwyn
Stephen Bawdwyn
Thomas Powle
John Hodyngsells
John Pawmer
Thomas Andrewe
Richard Hawling

It will be remembered that pensions were to cease upon death or ecclesiastical preferment bearing a sum equal to or greater than the pension. Only Richard Hawling can clearly be said to have received a benefice during this period.[52] It would be reasonable to presume that many of the older and sickly former monks had died. Abbot Lawrence, as we have seen, had died and was buried at Burwell in 1542.[53] Stephen Bawdwyn had been one of the three monks at the dissolution who had been present at the time of the 1518 visitation. Both John Nycolls and Lawrence Bardeney were so advanced in years in 1540 that the pension list noted the fact, just as it noted that Thomas Andrewe was sickly. A common-sense view would suggest that these four former monks also were no longer living in 1551. We are on thinner ice with respect to the others. William Sylke and William Alwyn were among the more senior monks in 1540 and may have died before 1551. About Thomas Powle and John Pawmer, the present writer has no evidence that they received benefices and would incline to the view that they had not survived. What should be underscored here is that the total amount of the pensions drawn from Augmentations had drastically declined between 1540 and 1551. The death of former

[52]See Emden, *BRUO*, p. 474, where his appointments are listed.

[53]See above, p. 532.

Abbot Lawrence in 1542 reduced that amount by over 54 per cent. By 1551 only about 23 per cent (i.e., £113 6*s*.8*d*.) of the original amount was still being given.

Another list is extant for the following year (1552).[54] It differs from the preceding list only in that, in the interval, William Rogers (pension £8) had died and William Ireland was not living in Huntingdonshire. The other 15 were either residing in Huntingdonshire or able to appear in person before the royal commissioners. The year 1552 is often cited as the nadir of the severe mid-century depression. During the 1540s there had been a continuing rise in the price of agricultural goods (by 100 per cent) and of industrial goods (by about 70 per cent). This inflation obviously had an adverse affect on the real value of the pensions, and what have been judged adequate in 1540 could scarcely sustain that description a dozen years later.[55]

The list generated early in the reign of Queen Mary had a different purpose. In the letter to Lincoln Cathedral directing a survey of surviving pensioners, she wrote,

> We be desirous presently to know the certain number of such the late religious persons men or women, and chantry priests also, as being pensioners do receive at this date any yearly pension within our realm. [Send us] the several names and yearly pensions of every such person or persons as also to signify in the same their dwelling places, whether they be married or not and of what state of life they be and what spiritual promotions and other livings they have besides and to what yearly value they have of each kind.[56]

[54]For the Ramsey monks see PRO E101/76/16, repr. in Hodgett, *State of the Ex-Religious*, pp. 32–34.

[55]For the concern over monastic pensions in 1552 see A. G. Dickens, "The Edwardian Arrears in Augmentations Payments and the Problems of Ex-Religious," *English Historical Review* 55 (1940): 384–418.

[56]Quoted in Hodgett, *State of the Ex-Religious*, pp. 75–76.

Returns for the dioceses of Lincoln and Norwich are extant.[57] Twelve former Ramsey monks are mentioned in these admittedly incomplete records. Four had married: John Smyth, John Pycarde, William Pricke, and John Brigeman. It should be noted that priestly celibacy remained the rule until 1548, when marriage was permitted; this in turn was repealed in 1553 under Queen Mary, who in the following year ordered the removal of married priests from ecclesiastical benefices and promotions.[58] There had been only a five-year window of opportunity. Brigeman, who appears in the Norwich records, was in fact deprived. Smyth, Pycarde, and Pricke held no preferments from which to be deprived. Except for John Smyth ("non habet certam mansionem"),[59] for each of the others specific reference is made to where he was currently living. Even Smyth is known to have been living in the archdeaconry of Bedfordshire in the Lincoln diocese. Only five of these 12 had pastoral employment:[60]

John Pakye senior
Old Hurst, Huntingdonshire
Not married
No preferments

William Cooke
Ramsey, Huntingdonshire
Not married
No preferments

---

[57]For Lincoln diocese see Hodgett, *State of the Ex-Religious*. For Norwich diocese see Geoffrey Baskerville, "Married Clergy and Pensioned Religious in Norwich Diocese," *English Historical Review* 48 (1933): 43–64, 199–228.

[58]2–3 Edw. VI, c. 14 (*Statutes of the Realm* 4: 67) and 1 Mary stat. 2, cap. 2 (ibid., p. 202). For the order to deprive see Henry Gee and William J. Hardy, eds., *Documents Illustrative of English Church History* (London, 1896), p. 381.

[59]Hodgett, *State of the Ex-Religious*, p. 90.

[60]For Faunte see Baskerville, "Married Clergy," p. 222; for Brigeman, ibid., pp. 64, 225. For the others see Hodgett, *State of the Ex-Religious*, pp. 90, 93–95.

John Pakye junior
Wood Hurst, Huntingdonshire
Not married
Curatus of chapel of Wood Hurst (Lincoln diocese)

John Faunte
Not married
Parish priest of Burwell St. Andrews, Cambridgeshire (Norwich diocese)

William Pricke
Wistow, Huntingdonshire
Married
No preferments

John Brigeman
Married
Deprived of chaplaincy of Kennett, Cambridgeshire (Norwich diocese)

Robert Harrys
Bennington, Hertfordshire
Not married
Curate of Bennington (Lincoln diocese)

Hugh Phillippe
Graffham, Huntingdonshire
Not married
Rector of Graffham (Lincoln diocese)[61]

Thomas Fylde
Hemingford, Huntingdonshire
Not married
Curate of Hemingford (Lincoln diocese)

John Pycarde
Clapton, Northamptonshire

---

[61]He had formerly been chantry priest at Fenstanton, Hunts. (see Hodgett, *State of the Ex-Religious*, p. 27).

Married
No ecclesiastical preferments

John Smyth
No fixed dwelling place (in archdeaconry of Bedford, Lincoln diocese)
Married

George Marshall
Cookley, Suffolk
Not married
[Rector of Cookley, Norwich diocese][62]

There is a distinct possibility that those for whom no ecclesiastical preferments are listed were employed as priests. Curates, since they did not hold preferments but were employed by rectors or vicars, seldom appear in the records. An occasional glimpse appears. John Pakye senior, for example, had been a curate at Old Hurst immediately after the dissolution, but by 1554 he was probably of advanced age—he had been at Ramsey in 1518—and perhaps was not active pastorally.[63] Also, according to Baskerville, George Marshall, who was rector of Cookley from 1554 to 1557, had previously served as rector of Long Stanton St. Michael, Cambridgeshire. Thus, including Brigeman, who was deprived because of marriage, at least eight of the 12 whose lives surface in the Marian survey of 1554 had served in the pastoral ministry.

The Marian list gives us, for at least the 12 pensioners for whom records survive, a good indication of where the dispossessed monks went after Ramsey was closed down. One might assume that they returned to the villages from whence they came. This does not appear to have happened frequently,

---

[62]See Baskerville, "Married Clergy," pp. 219–20.

[63]See Hodgett, *State of the Ex-Religious*, p. 93n.

at least in the sense that 14 years later only one former monk was residing in his native village (Thomas Fylde of Hemingford). John Faunte, a native of Wistow in Huntingdonshire, was at Burwell, Cambridgeshire, whereas William Pricke, a native of Swavesey in Cambridgeshire, was living in Wistow. Both John Pakeys (not known to be related) were living in Huntingdonshire, although the elder was from Norfolk and the younger from Lincolnshire. Robert Harrys of Huntingdonshire was in Hertfordshire, John Pycarde of Huntingdonshire was in Northamptonshire, John Smyth of Northamptonshire was in Bedfordshire, George Marshall of London was in Suffolk. William Cooke of Northamptonshire was living in Ramsey itself. Some were living in their native counties: John Brigeman in Cambridgeshire and Hugh Phillippe in Huntingdonshire. What strikes one in all this is that, except for the Londoner George Marshall, all 12 of the ex-monks who appear in the Marian survey were living fairly close to Ramsey, either in the county of Huntingdon itself or in the neighboring counties.

Cardinal Pole's list of 1556 exists in full in two manuscript copies.[64] It contains 16 names but not precisely the same 16 names in the full list of 1552.[65] Added is the name of Richard Hawling, who did not appear on earlier lists because he was beneficed, and deleted is the name of John Anyson, a very senior monk who presumably had died between 1552 and 1556. Thus, 16 years after they left Ramsey Abbey, at least 16 of the men were still living and receiving pensions.

The theologian Richard Hawling had been appointed a royal chaplain in 1546, the same year in which he seems to have been

---

[64]PRO E164/31; BL Add. MS. 8101, fol. 21.

[65]John Pakey sr., Thomas Baker, William Cooke, John Pakey jr., John Faunte, William Pricke, John Brigeman, Robert Harrys, Richard Hawling, Hugh Phillippe, William Ireland, Thomas Fylde, John Pycarde, John Smyth, John Whitwell, and George Marshall.

appointed to two benefices. He may not have been resident, for he appeared in Oxford in June 1548. In that year he was appointed canon and prebendary of Gloucester Cathedral, from which office he was deprived in 1559.[66]

Only traces of other former Ramsey monks appear after 1556. John Faunte, B.Th., was rector of Pickwell, Leicestershire, until 1570.[67] In other cases precise identifications are difficult to make because of possible duplications of names, yet a Robert Harrys was instituted vicar of Norton Disney, Lincolnshire, in 1561 and a William Ireland served as vicar of Tewing, Hertfordshire, until his death in 1571.[68]

Queen Mary reconstituted Westminster Abbey as a monastic institution in 1556.[69] During its short new life of less than three years, Westminster Abbey had certainly two and possibly three former Ramsey monks in its community. Hugh Phillippe became sexton of the abbey and later treasurer; he was involved in the funeral arrangements for Anne of Cleves in 1557 and for Queen Mary in the following year.[70] Also at Westminster was the Londoner George Marshall, a young monk at the time of the suppression.[71] As has been noted, he had previously been rector of Cookley, Suffolk. In addition, there was a Mr. Filde,

---

[66]Emden, *BRUO*, p. 474.

[67]Baskerville, "Married Clergy," p. 222.

[68]For Harrys see Charles W. Foster, "Institutions to Benefices in the Diocese of Lincoln, 1540–1570: Calendar No. I," *Architectural and Archaeological Society of the Counties of Lincoln and Nottingham* 24 (1897–98): 17. For Ireland see idem, *Lincoln Episcopal Records in the Time of Thomas Cooper, S.T.P., Bishop of Lincoln, A.D. 1571 to A.D. 1584*, Lincoln Record Society, vol. 2 (1912), and Canterbury and York Society, vol. 11 (1913): 65.

[69]See Aveling, "Tudor Westminster," pp. 53–78, 271–79, and Ernest H. Pearce, *The Monks of Westminster: Being a Register of the Brethren of the Convent from the Time of the Confessor to the Dissolution* (Cambridge, 1916), pp. 214–17.

[70]See Aveling, "Tudor Westminster," p. 274.

[71]Aveling, "Tudor Westminster," pp. 276–77.

whom one author suggests was Thomas Fylde late of Ramsey Abbey.[72] Thus, two and possibly three of the 16 monks surviving at this time returned to their monastic vocations as Black Monks of Westminster.

While Marshall and Fylde fade from the records, the redoubtable Hugh Phillippe continues to appear. He clearly identified himself with the recusants in London. In 1561 he attempted to flee England with two other Westminster monks, but they were arrested at Canterbury.[73] Phillippe continued to minister to the recusant community at least until 1576, when he was apprehended for celebrating Easter Mass at a private home in Westminster.[74]

With Hugh Phillippe's arrest on Easter in 1576 the last of the Ramsey monks disappears from our view. If there was a Ramsey monk who, like William Lyttleton of Evesham Abbey, lived into the next century, he has escaped our notice.[75] It is with Hugh Phillippe, the last in the procession of black-clad men who had come to this fenland religious house since the tenth century, that Ramsey Abbey passes out of sight.

---

[72]Aveling, "Tudor Westminster," p. 275.

[73]Aveling, "Tudor Westminster," pp. 76–77.

[74]BL Lansdowne MS. 23, fol. 123.

[75]For Lyttleton see Knowles, *Religious Orders* 3: 417n.

APPENDIX

Letters patent granting an annual pension of £5 to George Marshall alias London, former monk of Ramsey Abbey, 10 February 1540 (PRO E315/234/155r–v)

Rex omnibus ad quos etc.
Cum nuper monasterium de Ramsey in comitatu nostro Huntendonie iam dissoluatur, unde quidam Georgius Marshall alias London tempore dissolucionis illius et diu antea monachus ibidem fuit. Nos uolentes racionabilem annualem pensionem siue promocionem condignam eidem Georgio ad uictum, exhibicionem et sustentacionem suam melius sustinendas prouideri, scitatis igitur quod nos, in consideracione premissorum de gracia nostra speciali ac ex certa sciencia et mero motu per aduisamentum et concensum cancellarii et consilii curie augmentacionum reuencionum corone nostre, dedimus et concessimus ac per presentes damus et concedimus eidem Georgio quandam annuitatem siue annualem pensionem quinque librarum sterlingarum habendam, gaudendam et annuatim percipiendam, easdem quinque libras prefato Georgio et assignacionibus suis a festo sancti Michaelis archangeli ultimo preterito ad terminum et pro termino uite ipsius Georgii uel quousque idem Georgius ad unum uel plura beneficia ecclesiastica siue aliam promocionem condignam clari annui ualoris quinque librarum aut ultra per nos promotus fuerit, tam per manus thesaurii reuencionum augmentacionum corone nostre pro tempore existentis de thesauro nostro in manibus suis de reuencionibus predictis remanere contingentibus quam per manus receptoris exituum et reuencionum dicti nuper monasterii de eisdem exitibus et reuencionibus, ad festa anunciacionis beate Marie uirginis et sancti Michaelis archangeli per equales porciones annuatim soluendas. Eo quod etc. In cuius rei etc.
Teste Ricardo Riche milite apud Westmonasterium decimo die Februarii anno regni nostri tricesimo primo.

—per cancellarium et consilium
predictos uirtute warranti
predicti